"I have no prouder boast than to say I am Irish and have been privileged to fight for the Irish people and for Ireland. If I have a duty I will perform it to the full in the unshakeable belief that we are a noble race and that chains and bonds have no part in us."

Francis Hughes
Long Kesh
10 March 1981

"Not only was the situation worsening, the Archbishop reminded Mason, but there were more and more men now on the blanket and dirt protest. All Mason would say was that it was their own fault; they'd started it. He said to Mason that it didn't matter who or what had started it; that if it went on it was going to lead to an awful lot of trouble.

"There would be a hunger strike, or perhaps an epidemic. Somebody would be found dead in his cell; there'd be an uproar about this, and the news would get out that hundreds of men had been kept day in and out, for months and years, locked in cells with no outdoor air, sunlight, exercise; with no clothes, no furnishing or comfort except blanket and mattress: no bed, no table, no chair, nothing to read, nothing to write with, nothing to do . . .

"And it was the British government that would be blamed.

"Mason would admit no responsibility . . ."

What happened was

THE IRISH HUNGER STRIKE

READ ON . . .

THE IRISH HUNGER STRIKE

TOM COLLINS

FOREWORD BY TIM PAT COOGAN

WHITE ISLAND BOOK COMPANY
Dublin and Belfast
1986

First published 1986
by White Island Book Company Ltd
38 Fenian Street
Dublin 2
Ireland

Made and printed in Ireland
ISBN 0 946968 01 2

To

Peggy Reynolds,

Alan, Bill

and the Men of Tyrone

IN MEMORY OF

BOBBY SANDS
FRANCIS HUGHES
RAYMOND McCREESH
PATSY O'HARA
JOE McDONNELL
MARTIN HURSON
KEVIN LYNCH
KIERAN DOHERTY
THOMAS McELWEE
MICKEY DEVINE

D.1981

+

I learned of centuries of strife,
Of cruel laws, injustice rife.
I saw now in my own young life
The fruits of foreign sway.
Protestors threatened, tortured, maimed,
Division nurtured, passions flamed,
Outrage provoked, right's cause defamed—
This is the conqueror's way . . .

Does Britain need a thousand years
Of protest, riot, death and tears?
Or will this past decade of fears
To eighty decades spell
An end to Ireland's agony,
New hope for human dignity,
And will the last obscenity
Be this grim H-Block cell?

> So I'll wear no convict's uniform
> Nor meekly serve my time
> That Britain might brand Ireland's fight
> Eight hundred years of crime.

From Francie Brolly's H-BLOCK SONG

CONTENTS

FOREWORD

THE HUNGER STRIKES which broke out in Long Kesh in 1980 and '81 had a marked effect on contemporary Irish history.

Abroad, they heightened the consciousness of being Irish, particularly in America. The death of Bobby Sands was marked by signs of mourning and respect all around the world. In New Delhi for instance the Parliament stood for one minute's silence on receiving the news.

Back in Ireland the strike had the effect of overthrowing a government, and in the North, of creating a political platform for Sinn Féin from whence it took some 42 percent of the Nationalist vote. The vote has fallen somewhat since but has not completely diminished, nor does it show any sign of so doing.

The hunger strikes thus deserve to be examined in some detail, both for themselves and for the light they shed on a traditional Irish method of bringing pressure to bear on an opponent from a position of weakness.

Just as in days gone by one starved oneself to death outside the home of a patron or landlord who had disappointed one over payment for poetry or services, so in Long Kesh did a number of IRA and INLA Volunteers show that there was an ability to endure as well as inflict within the Republican movement.

This phenomenon deserves to be examined. Not alone are the stories of these hunger strikers dramatic in themselves; they shed light on contemporary Northern Ireland society, on the dilemmas and conditions which give rise to the troubles there, and on the Irish character as such.

As many efforts have been made to downplay the importance

of the hunger strikes as there have been to propagandize them. I believe that neither course is correct. These events occurred and whether we liked them or disliked them they are now part of our history. History has to be looked at squarely if one hopes for any guidance for the future, particularly the future of a troubled and unstable situation such as now exists in the northeastern part of this island, periodically threatening the peace and stability of the Republic and occasionaly that of the United Kingdom, as for instance the Brighton bombings showed.

We should not be asked to condone such happenings but neither should we pretend not to understand. To the degree to which Tom Collins' work contributes to our understanding it is to be commended.

Tim Pat Coogan
Dublin
28 January 1986

Where are they gone that did delight in honour,
Abrupt and absolute, as an epic ends?
What light of the Last Things, like death at morning,
Crowns the true lovers and the tragic friends?

G. K. Chesterton
IN OCTOBER

PREFACE

I BEGAN THIS BOOK because of something Oliver Crilly said to me. He'd been with the Irish Commission for Justice and Peace in its abortive effort at mediation; and though he was a cousin of both Francis Hughes and Thomas McElwee, Father Crilly bore particular witness to Kieran Doherty, whom he had met several times in the prison hospital and whom he flatly said was a saint.

Were they "tragic friends," these men? Were they victims? The image keeps recurring of James Connolly, unable to stand, whom the British shot sitting in a chair. But these men created their own images, too, physical and moral: Patsy dragging himself cheerfully around to the very last; Francis, the ruthless and legendary guerrilla fighter, hobbling about now with his eyepatch and cane; Raymond's warm and persevering loyalty; and of course Bobby's stepping forward first, on behalf of the younger men, on behalf of that whole broken but unyielding brotherhood: one dying for all.

This book is largely the recounting of what members of their families felt and were willing to tell me about the men who died. Bobby Sands of course left his own detailed testimony. But tragedy is not his or their theme.

The world of these men, and of the families who mourn them, is a world of harsh reality, a world where men who saw themselves as fighting for their country were systematically and cruelly degraded by the barbaric, vindictive Thatcher and her torture-ridden prison regime; a world corrupted by the insolence of her government and its institutionalized hypocrisy, by the boring habitual lying of these English colonial rulers, who (aided and abetted by the West British among the Irish) posture as democrats while trampling upon freedom and upon the noblest aspirations of the human spirit—an old, old story.

boring habitual lying of the English, who posture as democrats while trampling upon freedom and upon the noblest aspirations of the human spirit—an old, old story.

It is a sad and depressive world of suffering and slow death.

But it is also a world of men and families who are filled with— at times charged with—hope: Hope for a world in which men could lay down their lives so selflessly. Hope for the fulfilment of the dream of freedom in another world where—"in a flash, at a trumpet crash!"—all things would be made new. Hope even for this world; even for Ireland: even in this generation. *Tiocfaidh ár lá!* Inexorably, their day will come. And surely it will come more quickly because of what they were and did.

They do not stand to history as tragic heroes, then. They stand as reasonable if determined men, brought to the pitch of hunger strike and maintained there by the tyranny of Westminster. They stand as brave men, who suffered and fought as proud soldiers the foulest regime "all the practices of England" (Edmund Campion) could visit upon them. Thatcher, mistress of rack and thumbscrew, will shortly re-emerge ("murder is murder") as the remote-control bomber of the Belgrano.

Not tragic heroes, but heroes all the same? Well, they wrote a new chapter in the annals of the human spirit—the ten of them and their comrades, among them those like big Matt Devlin of Ardboe who nearly died and were brought back; Matty Ban was taken from a terminal coma—against his will, because he had already seen a light beyond the grave, finding there a better resurrection.

Were they men of heroic courage, who endured all these things?—men of whom the world was not worthy. Nor were the poor, blind Irish! for whose cause these men, in their innocence, walked slowly one by one down the road to death, in a joint and serial sacrifice the historian Tomás Ó Fiaich has characterized as "unique in the history of the world."

But the Irish people are no worse than any other, are they, in their passivity? They want the news or music or TV chatter to wash over them without stirring thoughts of painful responsibility. Most people, lulled by the currents, would be frightened to discover any word of challenge or of personal imperative riding in a message atop the flow. The Irish knew that the commitment of these ten men was likely to tear them asunder! So it is no wonder that they found their hunger strike discomfiting.

Yet what the men in their persistent innocence kept half expecting was a new rising of the Irish people.

Tom Collins
Dublin
30 January 1986

Chapter 1

THE CONVEYOR BELT

Where are the lads who stood with me
When history was made?
     O grá mo chroí I long to see
     The boys of the Old Brigade . . .

Pat McGuigan

IT WAS ABOUT FOUR O'CLOCK on a Monday afternoon—2 May, 1977. A tall young man, just turned twenty-one, was hustled into a police van parked in a large yard behind the Crumlin Road prison, opposite the courthouse. There was another young man in the van, named Neil McMonagle, a fellow INLA prisoner. The driver and three armed prison guards settled into the front of the van. Ahead of it a landrover carrying three police guards was parked in the prison drive under an archway; behind the van was a second landrover, also carrying three prison guards. The day was bright and sunny, the sky blue with white cloud.

Tony O'Hara had been prepared for this move the previous day when he had been taken from his cell in the old Crum and frog-marched by three warders down a damp dismal corridor to a barbershop, set up in a cell next to the latrines. The warders held him forcibly while the barber sliced away at his dark brown hair, cutting it very short.

Tony was a big, good-natured, optimistic lad, full of nervous energy, who carried his head bent slightly above his broad shoulders. His enthusiasm was not for war but for music, especially Irish traditional music; his favourite instrument was the bass guitar.

Tony was over six feet tall. He had a way of nodding his head

17

vigorously when he laughed, and he spoke rapidly with traces of a stutter. He was proud of what he'd been able to accomplish, though, fighting alongside his friends as a boy and young man in the streets of his native Derry.*

The van doors closed behind Tony and his companion. The police driver turned his key in the ignition switch and the engine began turning over.

FOR TONY THE WAR that had brought him to this prison van had begun nearly nine years earlier, when he was twelve. On 5 October, 1968, there was a civil rights demonstration in Derry City. The demonstrators wanted the police to let them march across the bridge to a rally in the centre of the city, within the city walls. The march was banned, but the organizers decided to go ahead anyway. They meant this to be peaceful march: provocative, perhaps, but peaceful.

Some of the leaders of the march were expecting a certain measure of violence—were in fact almost inviting it. This was a public act, not a private petition. It was a demonstration. And the point of the demonstration would perhaps best be made if there were trouble from the police. Martin Luther King had invited such trouble, as had Mohandas Gandhi before him . . .

Tony was twelve and didn't know any of this. Nor did he know that this was to be the hour from which the beginning of the war in Northern Ireland would be dated.

Tony, now eight and a half years older, sitting under armed guard in the van, would have preferred to be back as a boy in the streets of Derry. He was being taken to a place where he knew well enough he would face terror, and would have to face it without the freedom of movement he'd known at home. He was worried as the van with its six passengers moved out into the wide Crumlin Road, a good half hour or so before the rush hour traffic would begin. The van and the landrovers turned off the Crumlin Road into Upper Library Street; passed the Unity Flats on the right near the traffic lights at the bottom

*See Note 1, at end of this chapter.

18

of the Shankill and moved straight ahead through the intersection.

Tony stared at the younger prisoner in the seat across from him, his face pale in the dark of the van.

In Derry Tony had had plenty of support from people in his own family. Though his mother, Peggy McCloskey O'Hara, had a tolerant and even sentimental turn of mind, she was nonetheless a woman of the city, sharp and witty, and inclined to call a spade a spade. Tony's father, James O'Hara, had never been afraid of a fight. Tony's older brother Seán Séamus, though only seven stone or so, had as fierce a will as any boy in Derry. A wiry, small, stormy lad, Seán Séamus soon outgrew street rioting and began to operate with a tommy gun. He was interned for three and a half years in Long Kesh. Tony's younger brother Patsy, more like their mother in disposition, had the native intelligence and street sense of both parents.

Tony stood there waiting for the march to begin, holding a placard, nervously excited about what was coming. There were some speeches, and then the crowd began to move towards Craigavon Bridge. Keeping one eye on his brother Patsy, Tony walked on behind the first marchers, the placard lifted high above his head. He noticed television cameras taking pictures of the advancing demonstrators, film that would be broadcast around the world. He and Patsy were three rows from the front when the police moved in, forming a cordon to prevent the march going any further.

The police met the front rows, and there was a lot of scuffling. Everyone started pushing forward. Then a man with a megaphone shouted "Sit down! Sit down!" A woman in the front called out the same thing: "Sit down!" So Tony and Patsy sat down. Then there was a big commotion. People in the crowd suddenly began falling backwards, tripping all over each other. The placard was knocked out of Tony's control. He and Patsy began crawling through people's legs; he could see only legs. As he crawled out of there he kept bumping his head. Eventually he pulled himself up onto the footpath. Dazed, he saw more legs going past, the legs of people walking and then running.

Some of the people were screaming. Tony couldn't tell what was happening. Then the police began running after the demonstrators and batoning them.

Some of the police were coming in his direction, very fast. Afraid of being hit, Tony began to run, but one of his shoes caught in a grating. He wanted to run but couldn't pull his shoe away.

"Me shoe!" he cried out. "Me shoe!"

Finally he managed to get it free. He was bent over, trying to tie his shoelace, when he saw an RUC man coming towards him. He looked to be about twenty feet tall! He hit Tony, but it was only a glancing blow to the side of the head. Tony was trying to get up and run, when suddenly another policeman appeared. This time Tony felt three sharp blows. He fell back to the ground, crying. More cops were running past him, and several took swings at him as they ran by. Tony started crawling away as fast as he could, towards Craigavon Bridge. He reached the bridge and Patsy was there, staring at him.

"You're bleeding!"

"It's okay," he said to Patsy. "I'm okay."

Tony turned around. He saw a monster machine coming at them across the bridge, hosing what was left of the crowd. A water cannon! Tony had never seen a water cannon before in his life. He had to get out of there.

The two brothers began running, as fast as they could. They tore across the bridge and ran down the road. They didn't stop until they reached Bishop Street.

"Look at you. You're all blood!" somebody said to Tony as the boys ran towards their house. They went in, and Tony went to the sink and washed himself off. Then he sat down and had his tea.

Blood? He was so numbed he hardly knew the difference.

Tony never forgot October 5, 1968. Neither did Patsy.

AS THE MONTHS AND YEARS went by, both boys became regulars among the rioters in the Bogside. In his first riot Tony stayed well to the back of the crowd. In the second he was in the middle; he felt more courageous. In the third, he saw that he couldn't hit anything if he stood back in the crowd, so he moved up to the front. When a rubber bullet was fired, everyone ducked his head automatically. It was more healthy to be on the move—darting out, attacking with stones, twisting and catching the rubber bullets bouncing and thudding around him. Tony was never hit by a rubber bullet. Not even once.

One day in the summer of 1969, when the Bogside was a no-go area for the RUC, a small army of boys marched to the Diamond in the centre of the old walled city, looking for a fight with the police. There were about five hundred boys, and Tony was in the front line. But the cops were out in force that day, about as many policemen as marchers. The boys began taunting them: "SS—RUC, SS—RUC!" Next thing Tony knew there were angry cops running towards them—a baton charge.

"Come on, boys," Tony found himself shouting. "We'll charge them!"

He began to run up towards the police with a large stone in his hand. Just before throwing it he looked around.

"Oh, oh!" he said to himself, dropping the stone. Of the five hundred boys in the crowd about five were with him. He and that handful of boys cut towards a line of shops along one side of the Diamond. But on came the RUC and circled the boys. Tony got a fierce working over. He was battered and beaten silly by several cops, using their long, heavy batons.

Next thing he knew, two of his friends were leaning over him. He was looking up at them, cross-eyed.

"Are you all right?" one of them said.

Tony lifted his head. He was coming out of his daze, still dizzy but half aware of what was happening. His friends dragged him to his feet.

He picked up a stone from the pavement and fired it at a cluster of police. Then another stone, and another. He was thirteen, and crazy enough to keep fighting—thirteen and in cuckoo land.

Tony played his part in the fateful events of that summer, whose high point was the Battle of the Bogside, in which the young people of Catholic Derry—with the Hon. Bernadette Devlin,

Member of the British Parliament, aiding and abetting and leading them on—fought off the RUC, the B-Specials and loyalist vigilantes. Tony was still thirteen when the British Army "peacekeepers" came to Derry, and he and his friends retired for awhile from the fray. By mid-1970, however, the British Army had taken on the role of the RUC—to far more devastating effect, especially in Belfast and Derry. They didn't just harass and beat people up. They killed them.

Tony was fourteen now. Again he and his friends took to the streets. Three or four times he was able to climb on top of an armoured ferret car, banging on its turret and roof with a large stone—harmless enough, but it really annoyed the soldiers inside. The drivers of the armoured cars would lurch backwards and forwards, braking hard, trying to shake the boys off. But while they were on top, holding on with one hand, they were safe from the guns. So they'd hang onto the big awkward cars like ticks and keep hammering away at the turrets.

One day Tony and Patsy had a lot of lads in the garden behind their house on Bishop Street, all of them out there sawing and banging, making pipe bombs. That evening Tony and Patsy sent the other boys around to different parts of Derry. And at the dot of nine o'clock all that could be heard around the town was boom, boom, boom! And then police and soliders began running about the city like frightened madmen.

In those days Tony and Patsy and the other boys tried to enlist in the fighting under the banner of either the Officials or the Provos.*

In 1970-71 and into mid-1972 they helped maintain the no-go areas of Free Derry, building and repairing barricades, operating checkpoints, and joining the riots, especially the Saturday afternoon riots local people called "the matinée." The boys helped keep the police and Army at a distance.

In August 1971 the British Army began rounding up older boys and men and hauling them off to internment camps where some of the internees were tortured. Tony was there at the anti-internment rally on Bloody Sunday, 30 January 1972, when British Army paratroops shot and killed thirteen unarmed men

*See Note 2, at end of this chapter.

and boys in cold blood. Several dozen were wounded, and a fourteenth died later. Patsy was on crutches, recuperating from a leg injury, watching from "the Bankin'," as it was called, above the Bogside. Micky Devine was one of the lads in the paratroops' sights, but he was lucky that day. He was running from the paras with two other lads when shots rang out. The soldiers, missing Micky, killed the boys on either side of him.

That massacre of civilians fired the anger already in the hearts of the people of Derry. Tony was often out fighting in the streets during the months of bloody aftermath.

By this time Tony had begun to think about why he was in the streets, to reflect on what he was doing. He was developing a kind of working faith for himself, inspired by his experiences and by what he knew of Irishmen like Wolfe Tone, Fintan Lalor, Padraig Pearse and James Connolly.

The first tenet of this embryonic faith was that Ireland was one nation, trying to fight itself free of the shackles of British imperialism. The second was that the era of peaceful resistance was definitely over. They'd have to fight fire with fire—guns with guns. The Brits had begun an all-out campaign against militant nationalists in Derry. Their homes were continually raided. Their brothers and sisters were beaten; their fathers and brothers interned and tortured. After Bloody Sunday they would take armed action against an armed enemy.

Tony's third tenet was that freeing Ireland meant freeing not patches of land, but a people. "Ireland as distinct from her people is nothing to me," Connolly had said:

> And the man who is bubbling over with love and enthusiasm for "Ireland," and can yet pass unmoved through our streets and witness all the wrong and the suffering, the shame and the degradation brought upon the people of Ireland—aye, brought by Irishmen upon Irishmen, and women—without burning to end it, is in my opinion, a fraud and a liar in his heart, no matter how he loves that combination of chemical elements he is pleased to call "Ireland."

This led to a fourth tenet—that the struggle was to rid Ireland

23

not only of Britain but of the colonial system that was Britain's legacy. All exploitation of the poor had to be ended. There was a socialist principle to be kept in the forefront alongside the Republican one.

And Tony's fifth tenet arose from the third and fourth. The only people who could free Ireland were the working class, the people who had been tyrannized by colonialism. Tony felt he was coming to a degree of maturity when he read and understood what Padraig Pearse had said about war not being evil; about the tyrannies, the lying formulae, the hypocrisies that war stripped naked, being the real evil.

In 1972 Tony joined the Provisional IRA and the following year Patsy joined, having left the Official IRA which was then committed to a cease-fire. Both brothers had moved off the streets to involve themselves directly in military activities. When the Provos declared a truce in the last days of December 1974, the O'Hara boys decided they didn't want to be a party to it: British troops were still on Irish soil. So in early 1975 they joined the newly-formed INLA.

On 28 August 1976 at about six o'clock in the morning soldiers arrived at the house. Tony had fallen asleep reading and had slept all night on the sofa. Awakened by a knock on the door he looked out and saw the troops and the landrovers outside. He knew it was a raiding party. His mother Peggy, hearing the commotion, came downstairs and went to answer the door. Tony thought it was just a routine raid.

The soldiers went through the motions of searching the house. They rummaged through closets, tore up floorboards, did all the usual upsetting and humiliating things.

When they had searched the house top to bottom, one of them came, put his hand on Tony's shoulder, and said he was arresting him under a section of the Emergency Powers Act. This didn't particularly worry Tony. He'd been arrested and taken for questioning many times before. Usually he was held for a few hours and then released. It was nothing new.

"Cheerio!" he called over his shoulder. "Back in a few hours." Tony was taken to Strand Road barracks, a huge, featureless

24

box of a place, its interior walls painted insipid pastel colours. He was taken to the army section where he was photographed and questioned for ten minutes by a plainclothes British intelligence officer. He asked Tony what his work was. Tony explained that he was involved in a co-op, making canoes, but he refused to say who else was working in the co-op. He was required by their law only to give his name.

Tony was not surprised when the Army officer handed him over to the RUC. He was familiar with the routine. They'd hold him for a few hours, harass him and let him go. He knew no reason why it should be different today. Usually he'd be grilled by Special Branchmen, who'd go directly to whatever questions they had for him.

He'd been treated brutally on a number of occasions. Several times when he was taken by soldiers he'd been beaten up and then quickly released. Twice the beatings and abuse had gone on for three days or so before he was let go. Once he'd been threatened by RUC men who produced a petrol can, forced him to put his hand on it and then told him there was gelignite in it. He had his hand on a bomb, they said, and unless he talked they would set him up.

Today he was taken to a cell by the police, an absolutely bare cell with only a board for a bed. Maybe, he thought, it's just that it's early in the morning and they're not ready for me yet.

After a quarter of an hour they came for him, taking him to an upstairs room. It was very plain, just a table and three chairs. He was directed to a chair facing the one window in the place, with the door behind him. The window had venetian blinds; the blinds were pulled shut.

He was left by himself in the room for a few minutes. Then two plainclothes detectives arrived, CID men,* one of them tall and heavy, the other tall and thin. They went through the formalities. Anything Tony said could be taken down and used as evidence against him, and so forth.

*From the Criminal Investigation department of the RUC. These were local detectives, not Special Branch. CID men were often more brutal than those from the Branch.

"I refuse to say anything until I see a solicitor," Tony said. They ignored this. Under the Judges' Rules they were supposed to let him see a solicitor when he asked for one. But in Northern Ireland the rules were a joke. The practice was to keep a suspect for at least three days before they let him talk to a lawyer.

"Do you drive a car?" the heavy one asked.

"No."

"You're lying."

"No! I'm not."

"You're a liar. You've been stopped at checkpoints."

"I've never been stopped at a checkpoint in my life."

It was true. He'd never been stopped at a checkpoint. Probably, though, Patsy had been stopped at different times without a driver's licence, and had given his older brother's—Tony's—name.

"You were driving the car in that post office robbery in March."

"I wasn't. I couldn't have been. I can't drive." He was in fact a terrible driver.

"What's your name?"

"Tony O'Hara."

"You were in the car during the post office robbery. You were the driver . . ."

Tony had no response to this. They kept repeating themselves. This gave him a certain comfort. They might let him go any minute now. The whole thing was just a fishing trip.

But they went on like this for two hours. They'd question him for a period and then they'd start slapping him on the face or on the ear. Both of them. He'd refuse to speak, and everytime they came to the end of a line of unanswered questions they'd give him a few thumps, and pull his hair. After two hours it became a game just to get him to say anything. Finally they opened the door and two uniformed cops came and took him downstairs, back to the cell. He was brought a cup of tea and a bun. He ignored them, afraid they might be drugged. He was left alone for a couple of hours. Then the police guards came again. He was taken upstairs to another room at the top of the building. The same two CID men, a hard one and a soft one.

"This room is used for police training," one of them said. "It's soundproofed. You can shout and scream all you want. Nobody's going to hear you up here."

Tony hadn't been shouting or screaming; they were just trying to frighten him. He'd been through this a couple of times before.

They began their questioning and battering again.

"You were involved in the robbery. We know that."

"No, I wasn't."

The first man, leaning over Tony, began punctuating his questions with a knee to the groin. The soft one was talking. "Go ahead. Tell us. We'll speak up for you in court. We'll tell the judge you're a good guy. We know you're not heavily involved. You're not in the Provos, you're in the INLA . . ."

Tony said nothing and they began beating him again, working over his head and face, twisting his arms, pulling his hair. One would spin around and knee him in the groin. It went on for another two and a half hours. There was a further interrogation that first day. He spent the night in the cell. Next day, two more sessions, one of them accompanied by beating and punching and kicking.

"We'll tell them you're not a bad lad . . ."

Nothing from Tony. But he was getting disoriented at times. Sometimes he'd push back and there'd be a scuffle.

"Look, if you don't own up, there's some guys upstairs are going to question you about certain murders."

"Oh piss off! I didn't murder anybody."

He was punched again—on the back, then in the testicles.

"Do you have any idea how tough these guys can be?" He got a fist in his cheek, drawing blood. "A hell of a lot tougher than us."

"You're going to be charged with the robbery, you know. You did it, didn't you?"

Tony was silent. The heavy one loomed over him, hitting him again and again. Tony's bone was coming through his cheek. He was further disoriented now. His resistance was weakening. It was getting harder to sustain.

"Did you hear him? He was saying 'Aye.' He admitted it—"

"I never said a word. You have nothing on me."

"You heard him say 'Aye,' right?"

"Right."

"Get lost," said Tony. And he was hit hard in the head from behind.

"Get lost," he said again.

That got him another heavy working over. He wished in a way he could be like Patsy. If they tried to put words into Patsy's mouth, Patsy wouldn't say "Get lost." He'd say "Fuck off!" Patsy would get a severe beating for this. Some detectives used to burn Patsy's face with cigarettes. But Patsy always managed to keep silent. They could only knock him unconscious, Patsy used to say.

After three days of this, they wore Tony down.

They prepared a statement for him to sign. He refused. They kept beating him. He had to get them off his back somehow. Suddenly he thought: I can get them to stop. I can give them a vague statement that will be no use to them. He wouldn't sign their prepared statement. He'd only sign what he himself would write out.

> My name is Tony O'Hara, and I live in Bishop Street in Derry, County Derry, Ireland . . .

When he was finished Tony had produced a vague 100-word statement for them, accompanied by a second statement—

t   h   s   s   t   m   n t

—in tiny letters above the line:

t   h s   s   t

My name is Tony O'Hara, and I live in Bishop Street in

m   n   t

Derry, County Derry, Ireland . . .

Completed the tiny letters read, "Ths stmnt mde undr duress."

He was pleased with himself when he saw they had not noticed the tiny letters above the line. They weren't satisfied with the vague statement, but saw that this was all they were going to get.

After he wrote out the statement, Tony was taken up to the court in Coleraine. It was the first day of September.

There were three charges. One was connected with money taken in the robbery on 18 March. One was for driving a car in the robbery. The third was for possession of a firearm: an ornamental shotgun someone had seen being used at the robbery.

Tony was charged on all three counts, and then sent to Crumlin Road jail on remand. He was worried about going to prison. He'd heard about the harassment and beatings in the prisons—the torture.

He would be in prison on remand, till his depositions were completed. This would take a long time. Meanwhile he would be interned. They called it remand, but it was really internment.

Tony's elation when they failed to notice the tiny letters turned to despondency after he was charged. But now, in prison, he felt a new access of spirit. As the memory of the beatings receded, his morale improved.

Soon after Tony came to Crumlin Road, on 2 September, Republican POWs held a military parade to commemorate the death of Tom Williams—a Republican volunteer hanged in 1942 for killing a policeman. In retaliation for the parade the men were locked up for 24 hours a day in their cells.

Along with another INLA prisoner, Fra McMahon from Belfast, Tony began a hunger and thirst strike, demanding an end to the 24-hour lockup.

The days of that hunger and thirst strike were the hardest of Tony's life. On the third day he was very weak, and blinded by his hunger pains. He was beaten that day but was so numbed he didn't feel it. After three days, the 24-hour lockup was ended—their demand met. So they began taking food and liquids again.

From the moment they had word that Ciarán Nugent had gone on the blanket—in mid-September—Tony and other

29

remand prisoners began a series of court protests to highlight the blanket protest. The remand prisoners were determined to show their total nonconformity with the police system. When due in court, Tony would refuse to leave his cell, forcing the police to drag him up to the dock and then back again. In December 1976 Tony and others escalated this by appearing in underpants. He used the weekly remand hearings to show resistance in his own way. He'd laugh at the judge. He'd refuse to walk from the holding cell to the court, so that they'd have to carry him in.

He was on remand for eight months in all. Prison life on remand was normal enough. He wore his own clothes, he had association with other prisoners, he had reading material, and there were weekly visits from relatives and friends. The food was edible, and the abuse from the screws minimal. Apart from lack of freedom and his weekly acts of resistance, life on remand was dominated by boredom. His efforts of resistance continued. One day he was able to dramatize his rejection of their system in a colourful way.

The INLA OC (commanding officer) in the prison approached Tony with an idea for a ploy to attract media attention. The idea was that, while in the dock, one of the remand prisoners would set himself on fire.

Tony decided to try. So for his next remand appearance, he put on four undershirts and two sweaters beneath his shirt, adding two jumpers and a polyester anorak to complete the costume. Armed with a lighter and six tubes of petrol, he let them walk him into the court building. In the holding cell he soaked his anorak in the petrol, slipped his handcuffs and then obediently went into the courtroom, palming the lighter and the last tube of petrol. As he entered the dock, he bit the top off the last tube and in one sweeping motion spread the petrol over his already wet coat and flicked the lighter.

There was a whoosh as he burst into flames. Everyone in the court was stunned. He stood there burning for about seven seconds before the police knocked him to the floor and beat the fire out. Then he tossed his handcuffs at the judge—he missed him. Tony was dragged out and down the stairs. In a cell below he was battered black and blue.

A report next day in the London tabloid *The Sun* got his age wrong. The paper said he was 25 and he was 21. But he was chuffed to find the lads had given him a nickname—"Zip." Others called him "Sunny Jim." These were brands of firelighters.

Despite his demonstration during the remand period, Tony was hopeful about the trial. With the obviously forced confession he'd have no problem getting acquitted. Between the time of the charge and the trial itself there was to be a PE—a preliminary enquiry. It took six and a half months till Tony got his.

They didn't know at this stage about the tiny letters on his statement. He was saving this for the trial. After the PE, he was sent to Long Kesh. They put him in H-Block 1, where some of the recently charged remand prisoners were kept. The Crum was an old damp, dreary prison but it was more open. At Long Kesh the new blocks, with their small cells, kept men isolated. Tony had a feeling there of claustrophobia.

There was endless discussion among remand prisoners in the Crum and the Kesh about what they'd do if convicted. All prisoners convicted of crimes committed after 1 March, 1976 had been denied Special Category status. They were to be treated as common criminals. The symbol of this was the uniform. Some said they would wear the uniform, get through the prison term as painlessly as possible, get remission of half their sentences, and get out. If they refused to wear the criminal uniform, they'd have no choice but to go naked, with only a prison blanket to cover them. Stories were told about the treatment blanket prisoners were getting, how badly they were abused by the warders in charge of the non-conforming block, H-2. And there was no remission of sentence. But for the protesting Republican prisoners there was a principle at stake. They were political prisoners, prisoners of war. Criminalization— just like "normalization"—was an attempt to convince the world that the prisoners were common criminals, not prisoners of war.

If Tony were convicted, he would have to accept the logic

of the protest and join the blanketmen. He would never wear the criminal uniform. Whatever the denial of rights or suffering or abuse—he didn't want to think about it. He was confident, however, that he'd be found innocent of that post office robbery. His complaint about duress would clear him.

The depositions were finally ready and Tony's trial took place on Friday, 29 April 1977. After a month and a half in the Kesh he'd been moved back to Crumlin Road. They took him from his cell and marched him through the tunnel connecting the prison with the courthouse across the street.

He expected the trial, in the High Court, to last two or three days. The judge would be one of *them*: either a Black man—a member of the Royal Black Institution of the Protestant-supremacist Orange Order—or an ordinary Orange lodge member who'd been recruited to help staff the British judiciary in Northern Ireland. Tony's information was that most of these judges were Unionist party political hacks, given a judge's wig and robes as a reward for services rendered. Tony didn't expect much sympathy from a man like that.

Under the Diplock rules introduced in 1973, there would be no jury, just that judge sitting alone to decide the merits of the case and to pass judgment.*

Tony had the opportunity, during the eight months prior to the trial, to ponder his prospects under the Diplock arrangements. In the Crum and the Kesh, among the hundreds of political prisoners, there were plenty of jailhouse lawyers who'd been only too delighted to discuss his chances with him. On the whole, their forecasts had been dismal. Nonetheless, Tony had something besides his own instinctive optimism to fall back upon. He had two aces in his hand: the total lack of evidence against him and his written proof that the statement was made under duress.

True, these Diplock courts almost automatically convicted anyone brought before them. The conviction rate was 94%. The smoothness of the mechanism and its well-trodden sequence (arrest—interrogation—charge—remand—trial—conviction—

*See Note 3, at end of this chapter.

32

sentence—prison—criminalization) led people to call it the conveyor belt.

Of the ninety-four per cent convicted, some eighty-five per cent were convicted on the basis of confessions. Only fifteen per cent were convicted on the basis of evidence, whether strong or flimsy. Well, they had no evidence on him. There could be no witnesses to his presence at the post office robbery; and no firearm was produced to support the charge of possession. His statement contained built-in proof that it wasn't voluntary. There was no case whatever; all they would have is the word of the police who'd beaten him into making the statement. Tony felt absolutely confident that he would be released and would be able to walk the streets again a free man—in two or three days, when the trial would be over.

But the trial finished that afternoon.

The morning session was taken up with Tony's complaints about the ill-treatment he'd suffered in Strand Road barracks. Tony's and his lawyers' reasoning was that, since there was no valid statement and no evidence, the only possible line of approach the prosecution could take was that Tony had made an oral admission to the interrogators at Strand Road barracks. And the depositions by the crown prosecutor suggested as much: that the detectives' statements were going to provide the basis of the case against him.

So Tony began his testimony with complaints about his injuries at the hands of the interrogation team. They'd hit him on the head and beaten him up all over his body. They'd continually pulled his hair and punched his face—his face was so badly injured that when they'd finished his cheekbone came through the skin. He'd been black and blue all over. They'd twisted his arms, he said, and his wrists were red afterwards. Tony was relieved when the examining doctor testified that after the interrogation he'd found marks on Tony's body. The judge asked the doctor whether if a man's arms were twisted, his wrists would become red. The doctor said they wouldn't. (There was very little flesh there to redden.)

The judge spoke of "discrepancies" in the testimony of the

33

accused. During the lunch break Tony sat in a holding cell in Crumlin Road courthouse and ate a lunch sent over from the prison kitchen. He was a little worried now about the verdict. Perhaps his testimony about his wrists being red might be used against him. Still he was hopeful. He knew there was no evidence to link him to the post office robbery.

Tony's lawyer picked up the written confession and pointed out the small letters above the words of the statement—showing that it had been made involuntarily. This was "ingenious," the judge said. In the afternoon, the trial moved away from Tony's complaints about duress and concentrated on the robbery charges. Two of the detectives from the CID gave their testimony.

They both told the same story: the accused repeatedly admitted involvement in the robbery. He'd acknowledged he was the driver of the car. He'd confessed to having a firearm in the car. Tony was stunned to hear them say it in court. He'd heard stories about how the police lied to get convictions. But here they were in front of him, perjuring themselves left and right, in a case where his future and his freedom were at stake. The judge kept referring back to the testimony of the morning. It was apparent, he said, that Tony had been exaggerating the degree of his ill-treatment. The doctor had said not only that Tony's wrists weren't red, but that a man whose arms were twisted wouldn't have red wrists.

Tony wasn't sure now. They may have been red when they were twisted. He couldn't remember for certain. A slight exaggeration? Well, it was now being used against him.

He hadn't been trying to exaggerate. He'd only been trying to explain what had happened to him during the interrogations. But what he'd said in court was more vivid than what he'd put on paper in his complaint at the time. And his writing the tiny letters was "ingenious."

The judge picked up on this. Tony could almost see the wheels going round. The honest policemen were telling the truth: this was proven by the discrepancies in Tony's testimony, and even by the ingenuity of his self-cancelling statement. Clearly, the judge said, the accused had been making ingenious efforts to discredit the police. And those discrepancies! Not only had he been exaggerating about his wrists: he'd been telling lies about the gun, about not driving the car, about the post office robbery and the stolen money.

Tony shook his head. He said he couldn't drive. The judge refused to believe him. Against the police testimony everything had now become an ingenious trick or a discrepancy. The wheels were turning. Since the accused was telling lies about being beaten, then he was lying about being unable to drive. The detective said he'd admitted possession of an ornamental shotgun. No shotgun of any kind was produced! Yet Tony was judged to be lying when he denied possession of the shotgun.

The wheels kept turning. The judge summed up, finding the accused guilty on all charges. On each charge he was given five years: three five-year sentences to run concurrently. The trial was over. Tony felt sick.

Tony learned something that day he hadn't known about the Diplock courts. He learned that he could be convicted, without evidence of any kind, with an involuntary statement. He'd seen the police perjure themselves, and he'd seen the Diplock judge understand and help them along.

Tony had been Diplocked.

They pretended this was justice. But in the end it was police state procedure plus propaganda, the propaganda of "due process of law." Tony wondered: couldn't the Brits themselves realize that any outsider with any respect at all for legal procedure would be disgusted to see what had gone on in this court today?

Now, three days after the trial, Tony's little convoy passed through the centre of Lisburn, and continued in a southwesterly direction. In less than five minutes they turned left into a country road, then right again into a smaller road. There was a place deep in the valley of the Lagan river surrounded by a tall corrugated iron fence topped by thick coils of barbed wire. The van, with its satellite landrovers, front and back, approached a guard tower, and then an opening in the fence. The outer gates, also of corrugated iron, swung hospitably wide to admit the convoy carrying Tony and his fellow Derryman through the entrance to this vast spread of 134 acres or so of walls, fences, huts—and new buildings built in blocks shaped like the letter H.

This was the destination awaiting Tony at the end of the conveyor belt. They called it the Maze; Tony knew it as Long Kesh.

It was four-thirty on the sunny evening of 2 May 1977. Tony, knowing what was ahead of him, was terrified.

NOTE 1: *Irish Catholics in a Protestant State*

"NORTHERN IRELAND" was a state created in 1921 by a gerrymander engineered by the British government. For nearly half a century the unionist government discriminated heavily and even proudly against the Catholic Irish—who were at first only half as numerous as Protestants in the northeastern six counties. The unionists discriminated against Catholics in the matter of votes and housing, and especially in the matter of jobs that might give Catholics independent economic power and thereby encourage them to have more children. The best jobs in government agencies at state and local level were held by Protestants. In most areas west of the river Bann, which separated the eastern third from the western two-thirds of the six-county state, Catholics had a definite or a decisive majority; but no town or city council was run by Catholics. The voting requirements and electoral boundaries laid down by the unionist controllers of Northern Ireland prevented that.

Unionists had an argument for so organizing things that seemed to them to be valid. After the foundation of the six-county state, most Northern Irish Catholics remained Irish nationalists. They wanted to join politically with their cousins in the overwhelmingly Catholic twenty-six county Free State.

Catholics undercut the new arrangements in the North by every possible means, including at times armed violence. The Protestant unionist rulers, who wanted the infant state to survive, felt impelled to reshape electoral boundaries in such a way as to prevent Catholic nationalists from voting whole areas of the six counties into the new Free State. The unionists—so-called because they wanted not an independent Ireland but continued union with Britain—raised a huge force of armed police and armed auxiliary police to deal with the threat from the recalcitrant Catholic Northern Irish: roughly ten policemen for every hundred Catholics. If this was repression, Protestant unionists felt, it was justified by centuries of unhappy history. Since the twelfth century the native Catholic Irish had sporadically tried to unseat colonists sent over from England and Scotland to conquer and control Ireland and secure its loyalty to the English crown.

Since the early seventeenth century—when in the wake of the Elizabethan campaigns against the Irish rebels, a vast and systematic British plantation of Ireland was undertaken—the native Irish had been a constant thorn in the side of the transplanted Britons. For three and a half centuries, in sometimes bloody campaigns, the descendants of the native Irish kept rising up against the British and the settler people and their descendants—whom the British had sponsored, and *kept on* sponsoring, by grinding oppression against the natives' descendants, and constraints on them of every description, backed by armed force and violence. Finally in 1921 the Irish in 26 of the 32 counties succeeded in getting a measure of independence from Britain; and the Protestant settler people reluctantly settled for the largest area of Ireland they could control for the indefinite future: a fifth of a loaf was better than none.

But they didn't want the Irish poisoning the portion which the Lord and the British government had given them. Their only wish was that Catholics in Northern Ireland, and on the island as a whole, would live and let live. But Catholics had proved uncooperative in the past and so various measures were implemented to prevent the destabilizing of the fledgling state: these measures included the police and special auxiliary police;

37

the voting restrictions and electoral arrangements that secured absolute unionist control; the discrimination in favour of Protestants in housing and jobs; and the employment of trustworthy Protestants in the agencies of government itself.

Over the years Catholics in Northern Ireland had come to resent being treated as second-class citizens in their own country. They had grown up with the idea that the land of Ireland belonged to all the Irish people, and had been taught from earliest childhood to resent Protestant unionist domination of their part of the country. Catholics saw discrimination in favour of Protestants as discrimination against them. Yet there had been relatively little violence in Northern Ireland since the inception of the state. Sons and daughters of the Catholic Northern Irish had grudgingly accepted a situation they seemed powerless to change.

The world, however, was changing. In spring and summer 1968 the news on radio and on television had carried stories about the workers' riots in Paris and the battles between police and young people on the streets of Chicago during the Democratic National Convention in the United States. In America, Senator Robert Kennedy, a favourite of many American civil rightists, had been assassinated, as had the black civil rights leader Martin Luther King. It was a time of ferment and a time for civil rights. Under the new education arrangements mandated by the British government over the past decade, third-level colleges in Northern Ireland, notably Queen's University, were beginning to turn out Catholic graduates in their hundreds. From among these there arose a new generation of Catholic leaders. They might think Irish nationalism and republicanism and the idea of a united Ireland old fashioned. But they were nonetheless aware that they were growing up in a world in which they would not enjoy the same rights as their Protestant fellow countrymen. These young, educated Catholics began organizing demonstrations to test the will of the state to grant what they felt were reasonable requests—one man, one vote, equal opportunites in housing and jobs—particularly jobs in the public and civil service. Though some civil rights leaders hankered a little after the dream of a united Ireland, they were primarily concerned with freedom of opportunity within the state as it existed. They had nothing particular against the union with Britain. But they wanted an end to the policies that deliberately kept them in poverty. They wanted jobs. They wanted a stake in the future. They wanted equal voting rights. And they wanted drastic changes in the system—a system that had been set up to repress Irish Catholics. In many cases, their own fathers and uncles had fought alongside the fathers and uncles of Protestant Northern Irishmen in the British armed forces during World War II. Why should they be second-class citizens? It was this sort of thinking that gave rise to the 5 October civil rights demonstration in Derry city.

NOTE 2: *Provos, Sticks and Irps*

AT THE TIME of the 5 October 1968 march, what was left of the Irish Republican Army—the IRA that had persisted through the Irish War of Independence (1918-21), the subsequent Free State civil war, and the battles and skirmishes of the1920s, 30s, 40s and 50s—was largely a non-violent political talking shop.

The last serious sorties had taken place in the late 1950s. In the early 60s the leaders were devoting themselves to the non-violent study and discussion of Marxist revolutionary theory. The physical force men, who believed in removing the British presence from Ireland by armed rebellion, were entirely in eclipse. In the late 60s, under attack from the armed sectarian police and loyalist vigilantes, Irish Catholics in the North stirred to the thought that the IRA, so long in the shadows, would rise now to defend them. But even in a city like Belfast there were almost no guns available to the few fighters left in the IRA. It was all but non-existent as a military force. In Catholic areas contemptuous wall slogans appeared: "IRA—I Ran Away." Even in late 1969, at the annual Dublin convention or Ard Fheis of Sinn Féin (the political wing of the IRA), the more numerous Marxist advocates who had come to leadership in the 60s voted down demands for offensive action. Most of the physical force men and women in the party walked out of the Ard Fheis, and in January 1970 formed their own "Provisional IRA" and "Provisional Sinn Féin." The Marxists began calling themselves

39

the official (later Official) IRA and their political wing official Sinn Féin, to distinguish themselves from the breakaway group. This new group claimed continuity with the IRA that had emerged from the Easter Rising of 1916 and had fought the War of Independence against Britain in 1918-21.

After January 1970 the Official IRA was also militarily active for awhile, then began to wind down. The Marxist enthusiasts of Official Sinn Féin (subsequently called Sinn Féin the Workers' Party in the South and the Republican Clubs in the North, and finally in 1981 renamed The Workers' Party countrywide), turned increasingly to purely political activity. In mid-1972, under a leadership which espoused a very peculiar form of Stalinist communist ideology—but with a sense that the day of proletarian revolution would be long delayed—the Officials declared a unilateral ceasefire. They were nicknamed "Stickies" (and later "Sticks") from the paste-on back of the paper lilies (the Easter flower, symbolic of the 1916 Rising) they sold at Eastertime. The other IRA continued as a frankly physical force group: it fought as the Provisional IRA and its closely aligned political wing—which up to the 1980s continued to be preoccupied with propaganda and support for "the armed struggle"—continued on as Provisional Sinn Féin.

They were called "Provos" and sometimes—affectionately or contemptuously—"Provies." Their fighters also sometimes themselves "the 'RA" (pronounced "Rah").

Meanwhile a great many members of the Official IRA and Official Sinn Féin had become dissatisfied with the Sticks' ceasefire, or with the peculiar brand of Marxism being promoted by their hierarchy. In 1974 these dissidents joined with outside elements in the formation of a second militant offshoot, the Irish Republican Socialist Party (IRSP), under the leadership of the charismatic Séamus Costello and the brave young civil rights veteran Bernadette Devlin McAliskey. (She later dropped out because of policy differences.) In early 1975 the Sticks, their ceasefire notwithstanding, reacted violently to this splitting off of their members. Because of the Officials' armed attacks the IRSP quickly developed its small but strong military wing, using People's Liberation Army (PLA) as a cover name for its counterattacks against the Official IRA; it was soon to emerge openly, and on the offensive, as the INLA or Irish National Liberation Army.

The IRSP's military wing was at first heavily based in the huge and monstrously ugly towers of the Divis Flats housing complex at the bottom of the Falls area in Belfast. By a jokey bit of free association (IRSP—Apes), Divis Flats became known as "the Planet of the IRPS." Outsiders, trying to cope with the complex paramilitary nomenclature of Northern Ireland, tended to overlook the fact that "Irps" had developed as a handy appellation not for the political IRSP—an often quite separate entity—but for the military INLA.

To further confuse the issue INLA prisoners in Long Kesh and other prisons were dumped together with actual or putative IRSP prisoners. This had a double significance: (1) IRSP welfare officers looked after all these men, and so all INLA prisoners became in that sense wards of the IRSP; (2) not all INLA prisoners had admitted to, or been convicted of, membership in the INLA, but all were looked after by the IRSP welfare arm.

NOTE 3: *The Diplock Courts*

THE MAIN ASSUMPTION underlying the Diplock Report of 1972 was that internment—which began on 9 August 1971 with pre-dawn raids throughout Northern Ireland, and was to continue until the end of 1975—created bad publicity for the British government. Virtually every Northern Irish Catholic knew the words of Pat McGuigan's song:

> Through the little streets of Belfast
> In the dark of early morn,
> British soldiers came marauding,
> Wrecking little homes with scorn.
> Heedless of the crying children,
> Dragging fathers from their beds,
> Beating sons while helpless mothers
> Watched the blood pour from their heads . . .

The internment camps where suspects were caged, in crude corrugated Nissen huts behind a series of barbed wire fences, resembled all too obviously the concentration camps familiar from World War II. Thousands of these suspects, many in their teens, were locked up *without trial*—in some cases for years.

Nearly all the internees were Irish Catholics:

> Not for them a judge and jury
> Nor indeed a crime at all.
> Being Irish means they're guilty
> So we're guilty one and all.
> Round the world the truth will echo,
> Cromwell's men are here again.
> England's name again is sullied
> In the eyes of honest men . . .

When he was appointed in 1972 to look into the situation, an English judge named William J. K. Diplock concluded that courts were the answer: Instead of interning suspects (bad publicity for the British) the thing to do was convict them in courts of law (good publicity).

But the existing courts of law didn't suit Diplock's purpose.

In Diplock's view, the heart of the problem was *trial by jury*. Jurors, he argued elaborately, might be subjected to intimidation by the violent Irishmen the British were anxious to put behind bars. Diplock did not, of course, deal with the fact that jurors the world over might be subjected to intimidation by criminal suspects, and that such considerations had not altered the suspect's right, fundamental to common law arrangements throughout the English-speaking world, to a fair trial by a jury of his peers. Diplock's solution was to hold trials before judges rather than juries: single judges, sitting alone. "Trial by jury, with all its inbuilt safeguards, recognized to be the cornerstone of the English judicial system was therefore to be abolished."*

Diplock's second problem was with the constraints imposed by common law and judicial practice on the evidence considered admissible in court. Prisoners' statements or confessions constituted the principal problem area. Any such statements— under the law and rules commonly applied—*had to be voluntary*, made of the suspects's own free will, and had to be very clearly

* Peter Taylor, *Beating the Terrorists* (Harmondsworth: Penguin, 1980 p 31).

so: the slightest promise or threat by an interrogator, to say nothing of the use of physical violence, was sufficient for a statement or confession to be thrown out. Diplock saw these legal requirements as "hampering the course of justice . . . and compelling the authorities . . . to resort to detention [i.e., internment] in a significant number of cases which could otherwise be dealt with both effectively and fairly by a court of law."*

So Diplock invented another rule. The courts would consider voluntary all statements and confessions obtained by *any method other* than "torture, inhuman or degrading treatment." And who would decide whether there had been torture, inhuman or degrading treatment? The Diplock judges would decide. Not only was *the burden of proof no longer on the prosecutor* to show that a suspect's statement or confession had been voluntary—as had been the case before Diplock and continued to be the case under common law in Britain. It was *the single judge* who in his wisdom would decide—a judge who would be ninety per cent certain to belong to the unionist establishment and one hundred per cent certain to be in league with it.

And not only would the lone judge, his bias a foregone conclusion, decide on these questions without benefit of jury; he would be virtually guaranteed the help of police intimidators. Proof of police intimidation—including proof of the use or threat of physical violence short of "torture, inhuman or degrading treatment" as defined by the judge—would be insufficient to render a statement involuntary.

Once Diplock's recommendations had been translated into law (no problem for a distant British parliament with no fear of being answerable to nationalist Catholic voters in Ireland), the police found that they could do more or less as they pleased with suspects, as long as the statements of confessions produced by their sweaty efforts were considered by the right judges to be "voluntary."

The Diplock rules meant that in Northern Ireland a judge had a despot's power over the fate of suspects delivered over

* Report of the Commission to Consider Legal Procedures to Deal with Terrorist Activities in Northern Ireland, Cmnd. 5185, para. 87.

to him by the police: police who routinely threatened and assaulted people they suspected of "terrorist" offences (called "scheduled offences"). But there was more. Not only did Britannia waive the rules—its own common law—in its zeal to jail these suspects. In Alice in Wonderland style it gave itself Humpty Dumpty powers of nomenclature:

> "When I use a word," Humpty Dumpty said in rather a scornful tone, "it means just what I choose it to mean—neither more nor less."

> "The question is," said Alice, "whether you *can* make words mean so many different things."

> "The question is," said Humpty Dumpty, "which is to be master—that's all."

If convicted of any of the listed "terrorist" offences—terrorism having been defined by the British themselves as *political* crime: as "the use of violence for political ends"—a prisoner was to be considered and treated not like a political prisoner but like a *common criminal*. His "political ends" didn't matter. Nor did it matter that armed police and an entire judiciary had been organized in political fashion under a political mandate to get convictions against this kind of offender. None of this had any bearing on the suspect's political status, because by decree of the Westminster government any such political crimes committed in Northern Ireland after 1 March 1976 were to be considered the acts of common criminals; and this despite all the contradictions in law and statute and practice. So, a conviction for a political crime (supposedly) committed on or before 29 February 1976, earned the prisoner "Special Category" status, a British euphemism for political or POW—Prisoner of War—status. The same crime, committed the next day, earned the prisoner the status of common criminal.

Here was a Humpty Dumpty control of names. But the issue really was which was to be master—this British regime or the Irish people. In Northern Ireland after Diplock a police suspect was guilty beyond a doubt unless he could establish his innocence beyond a doubt.

That really tidied things up.

44

Chapter 2

THOSE WHO ENDURED THE MOST

If I forget you, O Jerusalem,
let my good right hand forget its skillfulness.
If I do not remember you,
let my tongue stick to the roof of my mouth—
  if I do not love Jerusalem
    more dearly than my heart's desire . . .

Psalm 137

I salute courage and sacrifice wherever I find it. Whatever the past deeds of the men in the H-Blocks may or may not have been and whatever the justice or injustice of the sentences, one has to admire their courage, fortitude and endurance against impossible odds.

The Athenian prisoners in the stone quarries of Syracuse could not endure their deprivations for two months. The American and British prisoners collapsed in Korea. The men in the H-Blocks, the vast majority of them seventeen to twenty-one years of age, have already created a place for themselves in the records of human endurance. The words of Terence MacSwiney ring true—it is not they who inflict the most but those who endure the most who have the victory.

Raymond Murray
December 1978

CURLING AROUND the top of the outer fence of the prison were S-shaped rolls of heavy wire like those on the fence around the Crum. The men who erected this S-wire had to be specially trained and specially equipped to handle it. Even so, a man working on it all day might go home, shower, put on a white

45

shirt, and then discover that it was all stained with blood from minute cuts on his arms and hands and face.

The fence would entrap and tear away the flesh of anyone who tried to scale it. Tony had seen seagulls at the Crumlin Road jail, ensnared in the wire, being slowly cut to shreds as they struggled bloodily and uselessly to free themselves.

This S-wire was (and is) outlawed by the Geneva Convention. But there it was, eighty thousand feet of it, the outer rampart of this British prison. The prison as a whole took six years to build, using for each of the projected blocks an H structure which Tony understood was of German design, originally engineered for members of the Baader-Meinhoff gang. The H structure made for very tight prison control. It was all part of the "normalization" of the prison regime that accompanied the move towards "criminalization." A former Maze prison warder would say of the H-Blocks: "In attempting to achieve so-called prison normalization, the British administrators have created the most bizarre, dangerous and abnormal prison problem in the history of these islands."

Tony would be a guest here, and a part of the problem.

The place had officially been called Long Kesh until very recently. To Irish prisoners like Tony, "Long Kesh" evoked six years of history and personal memories (Tony's brother Seán Séamus, for example, had spent three and a half years in the cages), and it evoked associations with Vietnam. Some Irish prisoners were brutally mistreated in Long Kesh by the British direct rulers and their warders.

Tony thought of the prison warders as mercenaries. Many of them had served in the British Army in Northern Ireland. On being discharged they had taken the warder jobs because of the money. Tony and other Republican prisoners regarded all the warders as underlings of the British. They saw themselves, proudly, as Irishmen.

The day Tony came, the work of building the prison was more than half-completed. There was a large central administration building. Of the projected eight H-Blocks, four were fully functioning, three were unfinished, one finished but with a broken heating system.

Most of the wire-enclosed "cages" were still standing. Internment without trial had ended in 1975. The prisoners in the cages were all men whose alleged crimes were pre-March 1, 1976, and were on Special Category status (Special Cat).* Prisoners were more or less in charge within the compounds and the wired-off enclosures immediately surrounding them. They still lived in huts, erected for internees, but these had been made more permanent and more comfortable.

Special Category prisoners had the benefit of the status and conditions introduced as the result of a hunger strike in 1972 by a prisoner named Billy McKee, who had been a leader in the Belfast Provisional IRA. Special Category prisoners were entitled to a visit and a food parcel each week. There was no limit on incoming or outgoing mail. They were free to associate with other prisoners and were not required to do any prison work if they didn't want to. They had the right to wear their own clothes at all times.

AS THE VAN was cleared through the outer gates, Tony O'Hara tried to relax. But what was uppermost in his mind was the question of when and under what circumstances he was likely to get his first beating.

For the past month, and especially since that charade of a trial three days ago, he'd been faced with a grim choice. Either he would accept the uniform with the criminal status it conferred, or he would refuse it.

To accept the uniform would mean spending what remained of his sentence in relative comfort. He would have specified prison work to do (for which he'd be paid up to £2.00 a week): work like sewing mailbags or acting as orderly or making furniture, tasks assigned him by warders whom he would be expected to call "Sir." He would be treated like a rapist or wife-murderer or other ODC (a British acronym for "ordinary decent criminal") locked up for a non-political offence.

The benefits that went with the criminal uniform were many. He would have books, newspapers, magazines, writing material,

*See Note 1, at end of this chapter.

47

access to a workshop where he could practice handicrafts. He would have a choice of educational or vocational trades classes. He'd have a bright room, a hospital-style bed with a comfortable mattress, sheets, a pillowcase, as many blankets as he'd need. There'd be television every evening. He'd have a six-foot metal locker for his things; he'd have his bass guitar to play. He'd be treated fairly well by the screws, and his sentence, given reasonably good behaviour, would be cut to half the original five years. Half the sixty months, less eight on remand. In 22 months he'd be free again.

The alternative? It was bitter to contemplate. But Tony had already chosen the alternative.

In the prison reception area Tony was photographed. He was presented with a set of prison clothes—a drab jacket and trousers of light brownish-grey denim. The jacket had no collar; it was a V-necked affair with two buttons on the front. The shapeless trousers had a zipper fly and a button at the waistband. There was cream-coloured underwear, and a shirt with vertical blue stripes. There were brown socks and low black boots.

Tony shook his head.

"This is a criminal's clothing," he said. "As a political prisoner I refuse to wear it."

One of the screws in the reception grinned.

"We'll see," he said.

Tony was taken back to the van and driven to H-Block 4. In the circle, as they called the crossbar at the cente of the H-shaped block, there were four screws. One of them told Tony to strip off all his clothes. Tony protested.

"If you don't take them off, we'll rip them off," one of the screws said. Tony might have let them do that, but he was wearing an expensive borrowed suit. (It belonged to his brother Patsy.) He removed the jacket.

"Where will I put it?" he asked.

"There, on the floor."

He folded the jacket and reluctantly laid it down on the floor.

He took off his shoes and put them beside the jacket. He removed his trousers, his shirt, his socks and finally his underwear. As he stood there naked, the screws began walking past him, staring down at him and making crude remarks. He was kept standing there, with nothing on, for half an hour, until two of the screws finally took him through the heavy gates at the edge of the circle to D-wing.

Tony knew what his cell would be like. It would be eight and a half by nine feet in size, with a grey concrete floor and cement block walls painted white. In the far wall there would be a window; beneath the window two heating pipes; overhead a rectangular plastic light fixture. The room would contain a metal bed, a chipboard bedside locker, a table and a chair. There would be a two-shelf unit affixed to the wall, and in the corner a six-foot high metal locker. Tony remembered all that, as the two screws marched him, stark naked, down the corridor. They wore *their* prison uniform—dark trousers, black boots, white shirts, black caps with visor and badge.

The walls were dark to a point halfway up and light-coloured as they rose towards a ceiling lined with rectangular plastic light fixtures like those in the cells. There were radiators flattened against the walls. Staggered down the length of the wing were two rows of heavy metal cell doors.

They walked Tony to a cell at the end. The cell door was big and heavy, like the door of a safe. In it there was a small rectangular peephole with a metal visor. Two screws stood on either side of the door as a third unlocked it and swung it open. Tony was pushed into the cell, and the door was clanged shut behind him. There was a rasp of metal on metal as the key was turned in the lock.

Tony was alone now. Outdoors the sun was gone. A diffuse pale light came through the slitted window from the courtyard that separated this wing from A-wing across the way. There was the bed, table, chair, the bedside stand, the steel locker. In the stand stood a po, a plastic chamber pot, for use during night lockup—eight-thirty until seven next morning. There was a foam mattress on the bed, sheets, a pillow and three grey striped blankets. A blue towel was hung folded over the bottom of the bed frame.

Tony went over to the bed and picked up a blanket. He shook it out, hanging it around his waist, adjusting it to cover his bare legs. He was a blanketman now. There were other blanketmen—there might be nearly a hundred by now—mostly in H-5.

He spent the evening getting used to the confinement of the cell. A cloying damp closed in on him, made damper by the cement block walls. Soon he heard the trolley bringing food down the wing, the food smells mixing with the odour of the polish on the corridor floor. Sounds eddied into the cell where he stood—the trolley, the muffled voices of the screws, the sharp clicking noise of their steel-tipped boots, the scraping and grating and banging as the heavy cell doors were opened and shut along the wing. There was an occasional loud shout.

He was handed a plate, and a tepid cup of weak tea. He began to eat the indifferent food.

Tony steeled himself everytime he heard footsteps. He never knew when the beatings might begin. As it grew dark, three screws came in.

"Don't be thinking," one of them said, "that because you're in the IRSP you'll be harder to break than the others. We break the best—Provos, INLA, Sinn Féin, IRSP. It won't matter—you'll all be broken."

Tony said nothing and the screws left.

Soon the night patrol came on. Through the long hours he found it impossible to sleep. Every hour he heard heavy clicking footsteps moving down the wing, accompanied by the weird, high-pitched sound of the clock-timer. Each hour, after the timer was reset, there'd be a kick at the door of his end cell. The metal flap would be lifted and slammed shut again. Sometimes he'd hear the jangling of keys before the footsteps retreated.

He knew that the excuse for this harassment was his refusal to wear the uniform.

Even from the British point of view, criminalization and the mandatory criminal's uniform were stupid policies. And their choice of Ciarán Nugent as the first victim of this policy was particularly lame-brained. Tony heard what one journalist had said: if they wanted a headliner for their criminalization policy, they should have chosen a man who'd murdered his granny with an axe. Instead they chose a man against whom the charges were so light that he was sentenced to only three years.

The second task an intelligent government should have set itself in selecting a figurehead for criminalization was to find a man who would be likely to submit to it. Horses for courses. It would be hard to imagine a man less likely to submit than the hard little guy from Leeson Street in Belfast. If ever there was a tough horse for a tough course, Ciarán Nugent was it. In 1973, when Ciarán was first wounded at the age of 15, he took eight submachine gun bullets, probably from a British Army plainclothes execution squad. Ciarán was standing talking to a friend named Bernard McErlean at the corner of Merrion Street and Grosvenor Road when a car drew alongside. One of the occupants asked directions. The others in the car opened fire. McErlean was killed and Ciarán took the eight rounds in his chest, back and arms.

Not only did he live. He had been given every reason to fight. He did fight and was arrested, fought again and was re-arrested. He served five months in Crumlin Road jail and nine months in the cages in Long Kesh.

This was the man that the British government chose as the first criminalization case to test their new policy. He was put through the conveyor process, and imprisoned in one of the new facilities in Long Kesh on 14 September 1976. He refused the prison uniform. Two days later he accepted the uniform for a visit with his mother. He had in mind a little demonstration of his own. While on the visit he began to strip off the uniform. He was not a criminal, he declared, as he stood in his underpants. And if they expected him to wear their criminal uniform, they would have to nail it to his back.

And so Ciarán Nugent became the first blanketman.

On Tuesday morning Tony was ordered to wear prison clothing. He refused. The screws laughed at him. They said he must do prison work. Again he refused. An hour later an assistant governor came into his cell to tell Tony that he would be adjudicated for breaking prison rules. Tony knew what this meant.

It was to be a periodic ceremony, recurring every fortnight. The screws would read out charges about violations of prison rules. The governor would listen, then produce a paper itemizing the infractions, asking Tony to sign it. Tony would refuse. At each adjudication they'd put another bead on his string of punishments. Each fortnight Tony lost fourteen days' remission of sentence, fourteen days earnings from prison work, and fourteen days' privileges, including visits, letters and access to the tuck shop where cigarettes and sweets and other items could be bought with the pittance earned from prison work. He would be denied use of leisure clothing for fourteen days and given three days' cellular confinement, with his bed and bedding removed during the day.

"Can I have exercise?" Tony asked the assistant governor.

"Yes," he said, and left the cell.

When exercise time came, Tony tried to walk out of his cell wearing a blanket. The screws pushed him back into the cell. "You'll go out naked," one of them said, "or you'll wear prison uniform. Or else you won't go out at all."

By Tony's fourth day in the place he'd had plenty of harassment but he'd still not had the beating he'd expected.

That morning, however, a screw came down and told Tony to collect his breakfast in the canteen. The screw wasn't going to allow him out in his blanket. Tony didn't want to go naked, so he refused. The screw stormed off, returning a few minutes later with a tray in his hand: a breakfast of cold tea, cornflakes with no milk and two unbuttered slices of mouldy bread.

The screw literally threw the tray at Tony. The edge of the tray and the teacup struck Tony on the head, covering him in tea. The screw charged in, followed by three others. They hurled Tony against the wall; his head struck the cement a heavy blow, and he fell to his knees. The screw who had thrown the tray kicked him in the face below his left eye. A second screw kicked him in the nose, bursting it. The blood spurted over the screw's boot. He grabbed Tony by the hair and pulled his face down, screaming.

"Lick it off, you bastard!"

Tony refused. The others began kicking and punching him. He became nauseated and vomited all over the floor. This seemed to infuriate them the more; and they beat him again, even more brutally than before, until finally he lost consciousness.

He had no watch in there, and didn't know how long after that it was when he awoke, sore from head to foot, lying in his own blood. He seemed to be bruised everywhere. His mouth tasted of blood and vomit.

The door opened noisily. The screw who had started the beating shouted in to him.

"Are you ready to put the gear on yet?"

"No," Tony said, shaking his head.

The screw laughed and clanged the door shut again.

Next morning, as Tony was standing looking out the window, his head started spinning. He was completely exhausted. With the screws kicking at the door during their hourly checks, he'd had hardly any sleep during the five nights he'd been in there. He'd been awake all day. Tony lay down on the cold floor, hoping to clear his head. He dozed off. When he opened his eyes the same four screws were punching and kicking at him again.

"No one sleeps when we're around!" one of them was shouting.

They took their batons and hit him heavily across the face, arms and legs. This went on for five minutes.

"Stop, before we kill him," one of them said. Then they left.

The screws, with their black uniforms, reminded him of the B-Specials—as though the colour itself had been chosen to touch chords in the hearts of people victimized by them. Beneath the uniform the screws were very much the B-men as Tony remembered them from childhood. They spoke the same way— no statements or requests; just orders harshly put, with all sorts of unnecessary aggression—as if they weren't satisfied unless they were sure they had inflicted pain, as if they took great pleasure in making men cringe at the thought of being hit.

Would he break down? Tony wondered.

He was heartened the next day when three other blanketmen came onto the wing. But when he heard them being beaten, heard the cries of pain, then heard them subside, he wondered if the screws would be coming to beat him again. He was relieved to hear them walking away up the wing.

Thank God, he thought. He didn't know whether he'd be able to stand another beating: next time they might kill him, or somehow break him.

That night he had his first conversation with the newly-arrived blanketmen. One of them, Raymond McCreesh from South Armagh, had been moved to this wing from H-5, the blanket block. Until Tony came, H-4 had been used for ODCs—there were ten or eleven "ordinary prisoners" in D-wing and thirty or so in the other three wings. Now they were beginning to move the ordinary prisoners out and move blanketmen in. The two younger men who had come with Raymond McCreesh were newly sentenced and, like Tony, had been brought here directly when they refused the uniform.

Every night the four of them talked—shouted—through cracks alongside the doors. They described their beatings and injuries and Tony learned that they had been treated as brutally as he. Yet despite their pain and exhaustion they were all in high spirits. Raymond McCreesh said he had decided to refuse his monthly visit rather than wear the criminal uniform, and had refused to send out the monthly letter. He sounded very determined, and Tony took heart from that.

The next day Raymond's cell was raided by four screws, who pretended to find tobacco there and used this as an excuse to give him a beating. As the days passed, and more and more blanketmen came into the wing, the beatings were fewer. But the level of verbal and mental abuse rose—abuse not just from the screws but from the assistant governor and PO (principal officer) as well. Every night the prisoners continued their conversations through the cracks along the doors, and one night they managed a singsong. Then they discovered that they could talk out through the windows to men in adjoining or nearby cells or on the same side of the wing. And by kneeling on the floor they could talk through the spaces in the cement where the heating pipes passed through the cells.

On 29 May all the protesting prisoners on D-wing, H-4 were transferred to D-wing, H-5, and doubled up in the cells with other blanketmen already there. (Another wing in H-5—B-wing—was filling up. It would come to be called the "Yippie wing" because there were so many young prisoners in it—mostly teenagers.) In D-wing it was crowded and uncomfortable: two men cooped up in an eight-and-a-half by nine foot cell crammed with furniture. They were locked up 24 hours a day, except for a shower once or twice a week.

Originally the blanketmen had been able to leave their cells, not only for the weekly shower, but to go to the toilet and shave and wash, wearing their blankets in the corridor. In November 1976, six months before Tony came, the screws said that they could not leave the cells in their blankets. The men solved this by wearing a small towel in the corridor, carrying a second towel for drying themselves. In 1977, before Tony arrived, the screws decided to hand out only one towel. The prisoners had to wear this towel down the corridor. If, after shaving or washing, they took off the towel to dry themselves, there would be two or three screws around jeering at their nakedness. It was degrading even to take it off in front of their fellow prisoners. So when only one towel was provided the prisoners decided not to shave or wash. They would go out for their daily toilet, and some of them took the weekly shower. There were shower cubicles where a man could stand and not be seen except for his head and legs. He wasn't exposed, wasn't standing in the open naked, and it wasn't so degrading. For their daily wash they used the basins provided in the cells.

The regime was less harsh in H-5. Though there were plenty of threats of beatings, the prisoners were not beaten every day. It was different in the Yippie wing, where the screws were trying hard to break the younger blanket prisoners.

But they'd only been in H-5 a short time when rumours began

to fly: the protest had succeeded! The authorities were going to concede political status! Some prisoners coming in from Crumlin Road had a hard date—17 July. This buoyed the men up. "See you on July 17th," they'd be shouting out across the courtyards to men in other wings.

When 17 July came and went, the word was that the date had been changed: the whole thing would be over by August. The delay, it was said, was due to negotiations going on with the British government. "See you in August! " the men shouted across the yards.

The numbers on the blanket protest kept swelling. By August the total was more than one hundred fifty men. But the months passed and nothing happened. Tony and the others realized that all the talk had been wishful thinking. Perhaps there had been a rumour, started off as a joke and kept going in the hope that maybe it might come true. If there had ever been any substance to the rumours, the facts had certainly become distorted as they were passed along. Yet Tony himself was willing to believe that even if there wasn't going to be an August announcement, there would be one sometime soon.

The men had convinced themselves that if their protest and refusal to cooperate was intense and absolute enough, they would force the authorities to bend. And what they were going through was too ridiculous to last. Human consideration would make the British yield; if not that, then public shame. There was a point, a limit beyond which even the British would not go, because no civilized authority could go beyond it: a line that would mark off the acceptable level of degradation, of misery, suffering and pain. Surely the British government had seen by now that the blanket prisoners were not going to break! The men only had to stand firm, prove their ability to endure, keep up their resistance. It seemed as simple as that.

Meanwhile Tony had to find a way to deal with the boredom that was beginning to be his principal problem. He always ended up sleeping.

THEN, LATE ONE AFTERNOON in early November 1977, an intense twenty-three year old Belfastman was shoved into Tony's tiny cubicle—cell 14, D-wing, H-5. This man had spent three years in the cages as a Special Category prisoner after his first arrest in October 1972 on a charge of arms possession. He'd spent those years studying the Irish language and reading heavily in Irish history and revolutionary literature. Released in April 1976, he'd returned to his family in Belfast. There he became involved in various social activities in the community: the Green Cross, a tenants' association—and, naturally enough, Sinn Féin. He'd been active in the IRA too, and had been re-arrested in October 1976. In September 1977 he'd been given a fourteen-year sentence for co-possession of a gun. After the sentencing, which also involved several other men (Joe McDonnell among them) there was a scuffle in the courtroom.

The men were being ushered out by police and screws, when there was some hassle—with relatives calling out, and the judge too—and this man found himself being shoved out of the courtroom quickly, the first to go. He resisted, taking his time.

"Go ahead!" the police and screws shouted angrily. Trying to hurry him, one hit him on the back of the head, and one of the other men turned and slugged the cop who was shoving him. The other prisoners lashed out. There was a free-for-all and, as a result, Tony's new cellmate had spent the first 22 days of his sentence, fifteen of them completely naked, in solitary confinement in Crumlin Road jail.

What Tony saw now was a wreck of a man, pale, thin and drawn—but with a rare fire inside him—a sense of purpose backed by tremendous energy.

His new cellmate's name was Bobby Sands.

Tony soon found out how fluent an Irish speaker Bobby was, and how ardent a political revolutionary. That first day Bobby busied himself learning songs from the other men and memorizing them. He organized a plan for reading the Bible, and another plan for reviewing his Irish. He made a schedule for his exercises. He seemed to have his whole day worked out.

Next morning when Tony woke, Bobby was up doing exercises. Breakfast came at about eight o'clock. Tony got up to have his breakfast, then went back to bed and slept. At midday he got up to have his dinner, then went back to bed again. Bobby sat on a chair looking at him.

"I can't believe it, Tony," he said. "What do you do all day?"

"I sleep," Tony answered.

"It's a waste of your opportunities, isn't it?"

Tony explained to him that it wasn't that he wanted to sleep all day. It was just that there was little else to do. He was bored. He was also escaping.

This went on for five days or so, until one afternoon at about three o'clock Tony got up to go to the toilet and saw Bobby fast asleep on top of the two-decker bed—Tony slept in the bottom bunk. Tony was surprised. That evening Bobby started to needle Tony again about sleeping.

"But everybody sleeps," Tony said.

"Sure, I never sleep."

"I caught you sleeping today," Tony said gleefully.

But Bobby hardly ever did that. He was all business. He spent his first week or so assessing the attitudes of other blanketmen on the wing. Then he began quietly telling Tony what he thought. The Brits, he said, would be quite content to have them lying there, thinking that all they had to do was stick to their protest and the government would be forced to give in. This, Bobby thought, was very foolish. As far as he could see, the authorities were prepared to live with this situation indefinitely. It made no difference to them: they had plenty of blankets. The only way for the men to get political status back, Bobby argued, was to organize themselves and map a campaign to let people outside the prison know what was happening. As it was, the British had not only isolated but silenced them. Any propaganda put forward about this place would be British propaganda, unless they managed somehow to break through the walls and let people outside know what was going on. Bobby felt that the best place to begin was with their own relatives.

Up to then most of the men had been toughing it out on the blanket protest, taking the beatings and abuse, and as far as possible hiding their injuries from their families. The families, of course, knew about the deprivations. But the men felt that there was no need for them to know more, to suffer any more than they were suffering already. Usually only the married men took the statutory monthly visits, because taking them meant wearing the criminal uniform. Bobby, however, felt that direct contact with people outside was necessary, that what they would have to do was to start writing letters, as many as they could manage to produce, and use the visits to smuggle them out.

As a practical matter they would have to have pens or biros. How could they get them? They learned to pickpocket the screws, and the priests at Mass on Sunday. Soon they began to accumulate refills, and the blocks became a hive of industry. They'd sit down with a ballpoint refill in one hand and a thin piece of paper in the other—usually cigarette paper or paper from a toilet roll—with the paper placed on the knee for support. They'd begin printing or writing, in tight, tiny, clear lettering which would enable them to cram a lot into very little space. Whenever they were writing they'd keep an ear cocked for the approach of the screws. (Anyone caught writing a letter would be dragged off and put on the boards—meaning put into solitary confinement for three days.)

Halfway through a letter, Tony's eyes would get strained and very sore. He would close and open them again to try to get rid of some of the strain. But write he did, because Bobby had made a convincing case for some kind of activity. And this was the beginning of a counter-propaganda campaign, with Bobby as one of its prime movers.

Life in the cell was not all work. When they were short of refills or tired of writing letters, the two of them would play chess, using a paper hankie for a chessboard and bits of paper marked K, Q, B, and so on, for chess pieces.

During their first few games Tony was able to learn Bobby's style of play and to devise an approach to counter it. For the first thirty or forty games Tony was able to beat him. But when Bobby, who was a fierce competitor, began to study Tony's style, the tide of play turned. Bobby won the lion's share of the next games. After they'd played more than a hundred—some lasting a few minutes, some hours—they decided to play a sudden death sort of game.

The rule was that the first to get a man up on the other would take the other's chess pieces, man for man, right down the line. They'd play for hours and hours with the opening gambit, each trying to get the advantage. There wasn't much harassment from the screws at the time, and so they were able to really concentrate.

Bobby caught Tony quite a few times. But one day Tony caught Bobby. They'd been playing that day for three or four hours. Bobby made a mistake and Tony took a piece, then lifted Bobby's pieces man for man. Bobby, who'd been working several hours to get the advantage, stood up suddenly. He didn't think this was a fair way to play chess, he said. One by one he watched his pieces go. With each man he lost, Bobby's temper rose.

Tony watched the fire build.

"Hard luck," Tony said, as he took Bobby's queen.

Bobby started in.

"You can't play chess like that, Tony. When you're playing a friendly game with someone, you shouldn't be rubbing salt in the wound. And that's what you're doing!"

Tony laughed. All this excitement because Bobby had made a mistake that cost him a chess game. Bobby hated to lose.

What Tony thought most remarkable about Bobby Sands was his absolute dedication and commitment. Bobby was a revolutionary twenty-four hours a day. He was a great builder of morale. He devised games, quizzes and entertainment for the night-time lockup. He had a good voice and would stand sometimes for hours at his door, singing out into the corridor for the forty-five or so men now on the wing.

There was a command structure organized within the blocks. Each wing and block elected its OC, who in turn picked a deputy. Then the two picked their other staff: an intelligence officer, a quartermaster and a PRO.

Bobby was soon appointed PRO for his block.

The letters went out, their messages printed on both sides of a sheet, the slips rolled or folded up tightly, carried somewhere on the person and transferred by hand, or a kiss, to visitors. The messages were carried out beyond the prison, beyond the S-wire, into the larger community. Gradually they began to make their way along the network of family, relatives, friends. Some of the messages were typed up, or rewritten in large ordinary-sized script, xeroxed and further distributed. Some of them found their way into newspapers, pamphlets and booklets prepared by groups who supported the prisoners.

Bobby Sands was a catalyst in discussions and debates. He was also a pillar of the Irish language effort, and soon became teacher of Irish in D-wing.

To scratch out words in Irish, the men used anything that was at all sharp, the crucifixes on their rosaries, miraculous medals or the metal edges of toothpaste tubes. They would carve the words on a square of cement block in the cell as the man giving the lesson shouted them out. Taking a verb at a time—past, present and future tenses—they painfully assembled a vocabulary and grammar, memorizing it off by heart, bit by bit, day by day. There were of course no tapes or sound equipment. No copybooks, no pencils or erasers, no paper, nor even basic grammar books. Men who had studied Irish in the cages, who had got out and then been re-arrested, became the H-Blocks Irish teachers—Bobby prominent among them. The constant influx of new men enabled them to keep developing and enriching their peculiar Long Kesh Irish, and to correct its mistakes.*

* In the fifteenth chapter of *On the Blanket* Tim Pat Coogan described the prison governor Stanley Hiltditch taking him on a tour of Long Kesh, during which some prisoners were heard talking incomprehensibly. Coogan quoted a warder saying that the prisoners "have an argot of their own."

This, Tony thought, might have been Iggy-Figgy.

It was simple enough. The men would fashion syllables from letters combined with ig (big, cig, dig, fig, and so on) making ig-compounds. Then these compounds would be used to interrupt and refashion words. For example, the word cat would be cig-at. Bowl would be big-owl, cup would become cig-up, po would become pigo, and so on. The men could hold a conversation in that way. For instance, "Migy cigup igis igempigtigy bigut migy pigo igis figull." When they spoke very fast it sounded like gibberish. It was impossible for a screw to understand. Even to the men who hadn't enough practice it would be unintelligible.

Irish was useful not only for morale, but as a private language—a weapon against the system. Usually, whatever they didn't want the screws to understand they would shout down the wing to the other men in Irish. They had a code for their secret messages. As it became clear what the men were doing, the screws grew to hate Irish. They became abusive. They called it a lost language, a thick man's, a dead man's language. They sealed up the cracks along the doors with metal strips. Still the men managed to communicate by shouting along the heating pipes below the windows. Eventually they managed to put small holes into the walls between the cells, holes useful not just for talking, but for passing things along. They put the holes where small hollows, originally used as grips by cranes lifting prefabricated sections of walls into place, had been plugged up. All they had to do was unplug them.

As their internal communications improved, so did their contacts with people outside the prison. Most of the men were taking their monthly visits, even though this required wearing the prison uniform, meaning often tattered, ill-fitting trousers and outsize jackets deliberately given them by the screws to make them look ridiculous.

Accepting Bobby Sands' suggestion, Tony took his first visit since he'd entered the blocks. That day Miriam Daly came to see him along with his brother Patsy. Miriam, then a leading figure in the IRSP, was Belfast organizer for the Relatives' Action committees. The point of the RACs was to alert people outside to what was happening in the prison and raise support for the prisoners' protest. Miriam coordinated activities between the IRSP and the RACs, trying to help build a campaign. Other political groups, including Sinn Féin, more or less ignored the relatives' efforts for a couple of years, till they saw they were gaining momentum, then jumped on the bandwagon. Till then about the only service Sinn Féin provided the blanketmen was to print letters Bobby Sands and other prisoners had sent out in the *Republican News*.

In all, Tony saw Miriam Daly about ten times. Every day she spent several hours visiting prisons. She was a prison welfare agency all by herself. She'd go from the Crumlin Road jail to Long Kesh, from Magilligan to Armagh. Some days she'd manage three or four visits in Long Kesh alone. Miriam had begun as a teacher in the cages—she taught Irish to loyalist prisoners, too—and then expanded her activities to build contacts between the prisoners and the relatives. By now, Tony thought, she must have been the most knowledgeable of all the prisoners' supporters, with the broadest range of contacts and experience.

The IRSP prisoners sent out messages through Miriam. She was a complete humanitarian—she really believed in helping people. When she saw the suffering going on in the blocks, she devoted most of her time and attention to that, yet continued her teaching in the cages. Finally she was banned for giving a speech at a protest meeting in which she criticized the prison governor and characterized the regime as inhumane.

In 1980 she was tragically murdered by loyalist assassins—aided and abetted, it appears, by British intelligence.

It was mainly through Miriam that Tony learned what people outside were doing. In October 1977, four mothers of blanketmen spent two weeks demonstrating in European cities—Paris, Brussels, Antwerp, The Hague, Amsterdam—dressing themselves in blankets and standing barefoot in the streets. The novelty of their demonstration attracted press attention. In France the women received coverage in *Le Monde* and *France Soir*. Various Irish committees throughout Europe gave them support.

By early 1978 Bobby had been moved from Tony's cell. Tony began to feel isolated. It had been a miserable year, 1977, more than half of it spent on the blanket. He'd had no freedom, no books, no radio, no television, no reading matter except for bits of things smuggled in; no method of contact with life outside except through the monthly visit. He was feeling very much alone. He didn't know even small details of what was going on at home: neighbours who might have died, what his friends were doing. Because of the pressure he was under during visits, he might not learn these things even then.

When he was on remand in Crumlin Road, he had books and access to radio and television, and he'd been able to run and exercise and play football. Even then he'd been aware of the lack of freedom. But Long Kesh was far worse. There was something pressing down on him, something pressing in on his heart; holding his chest tight, pressing on and holding his brain. When he'd look around him he could see only barriers. Everything was walls and barbed wire, gates and locks, the clanging of keys—that old symbol. He was a cog in the mechanism of an efficient and grinding machine. When he looked out at it, the sky seemed to close in on him.

Yet he felt a sense of freedom in his heart. He still wanted to resist, still wanted to fight. His spirit was unbroken. Although a prisoner, he was able to continue his struggle somehow, resisting the warders' every attempt to diminish him or weaken his resolve. He knew that suddenly one day there would be no more locks or chains or keys—the day of freedom.

Meanwhile there was always some sort of humiliating or degrading thing to weaken the men's resolve. Sometimes the beatings were isolated. Sometimes there seemed to be a policy of beatings: the screws would mount a kind of campaign in search of forbidden items, and any trivial possession found in a cell would provide them with an excuse for beating its occupants, or for putting them on the boards for three days. The prisoners used to try to win little victories. Already they had devised ingenious ways of getting messages out and smuggling items in. A priest would be sitting hearing a man's confession, and the man would be picking his pockets, letting the priest know of course that he was doing it. "The screws are watching, Father," he'd say, "but don't worry." Whatever the priest would have in his pockets the prisoner would reach for—cigarettes, matches, lighter, pens. He'd be plundered of everything he carried. After a few cells the priest would be picked clean.

In January 1978 the new Catholic Archbishop of Armagh, Tomás Ó Fiaich, visited the cell Tony was sharing with a lad from South Derry—part of which was in Ó Fiaich's archdiocese. Of course the men were supposed to have nothing at all in there except furniture, mattresses and blankets. The Archbishop came into the cell, shook hands and started chatting. Tony found him very down to earth—a very holy man, he thought, and very Irish. And of course the Archbishop spoke the language, and was a

64

Gaelic games enthusiast. Wee Tommy, as they called him, hadn't ever missed an Armagh game.*

"Here," the Archbishop said. "Have a cigarette." He gave Tony four or five. "We might as well smoke one now," he said, and then discovered he had no matches left.

"Don't worry," Tony said, leaning over to the shelf and pulling out a lighter. "Here you are, Father." The Archbishop sat back, a little stunned.

The men tried to maintain an internal communications system in the prison. It didn't always deliver reliable information. They were so isolated that a nuclear war could have started and they wouldn't have known about it. In the earlier years of the protest, information brought in from a visit could become very distorted by the time it was passed around. On one occasion, at about the time of the papal visit to Ireland in 1979, a soldier was shot in a lorry on the Falls Road. By the time the story reached the end of the line, the news was that a soldier had been shot while trying to assassinate the Pope in a lorry up the Falls Road. Word would be passed that Frank Sinatra or some other notable was dead when he wasn't. People who believed this and then found they'd been taken in, disbelieved the news that Bing Crosby, say, was dead. It wasn't until three months afterwards that Tony was ready to believe the news about Elvis Presley's death.

And when a new prisoner would come on the wing the men would stand at the cell doors for hours, picking his brain. After awhile the men got to be fairly good at smuggling in and using miniature radios. But what happened outside the prison during those first few years would ever afterwards seem a kind of dream memory.

Things were going from bad to worse in the blocks.

Whenever the prisoners were out of their cells the screws did

* One Sunday Father Denis Faul, a regular visiting chaplain, announcing that there would be no sermon that day because he had to go to Croke Park for the match, told a story about the previous year:

" . . . And here I was, speeding along the motorway, and I passed a car, and there was wee Tommy himself on his way to the All-Ireland finals."

65

something to abuse them. While the men were gone to the showers the screws searched and messed up their cells. They allowed them no privacy in the use of the toilets. Steadily, as the numbers of blanket prisoners grew, the screws increased their harassment. They began to search the prisoners' bodies.

It was a step by step thing. First they ordered the prisoners to shake the towels they were wearing. The men were willing to do this. After that they ordered them to open out their towels and shake them. The men, wearing only towels, refused to cooperate. Some of them were taken to punishment cells and had tongs inserted into their anuses. The screws followed that up with the bend-over search, in which prisoners were forced to let warders probe their back passages before going to see a medical officer, or before a visit, or before Sunday Mass in the canteen.

Finally, in February 1978, the warders began strip-searching and beating the prisoners whenever they'd leave the cell.

The men resisted. They would be overpowered by the screws, dragged, punched, kicked and sometimes viciously beaten. For most, the internal search meant being thrown on the floor, turned upside down by four screws. It got to the stage where the men actually dreaded going out to the toilet. Finally some of the prisoners began refusing to leave their cells unless their safety was guaranteed. It wasn't. So they were forced to rely entirely on their chamber pots.

It was decided that since the screws were escalating their harassment, the men would escalate the protest. But it was important to act together. The word was passed along. On Monday 20 March 1978 they all stopped going down for the daily wash; and they stopped brushing and mopping out their cells.

A new series of bizarre reprisals and counter-reprisals would now begin.

By this time there were nearly three hundred blanketmen, all of them refusing to wash or shower, or to brush or mop out their cells. They were still taking their chamber pots down to the lavatory, washing them out, filling their water containers, and using the toilet facilities. This was supposed to be a privilege. It was a dubious one. The screws withdrew it whenever they wanted to punish or harass certain men. Because of the no-wash protest the screws picked ten men arbitrarily and put them on the boards. So on Monday, 27 March, the men refused to leave their cells at all.

They let it be known that they would accept a bucket to slop out the full pos and that they would put out their water containers for the orderlies to refill.

After breakfast, on Tuesday 28 March, the prisoners set their water containers alongside their dirty dishes at the door of the cell. The screws began hurling the water containers back in. Some men were injured; some of the water containers burst and soaked the bedding. As additional punishment they were handed only half a sheet of tissue paper for the day's toiletry. Their dinner that day was served cold, and half an hour late. Afterwards the screws took the dishes the men had left out and threw them back in at the prisoners.

More men were hauled away to the punishment block.

The slop buckets were not forthcoming, so their excrement and urine accumulated in the pos. The cells became very dirty. Waste overflowed onto the floor. The screws finally began coming round with the slop buckets to empty the pos of urine and excrement. But they sometimes kicked the pos over or spilled the contents onto the mattresses, the blankets or the prisoners themselves. The men's own bodily waste was now to be used as a weapon against them.

The screws and orderlies regularly came up with new tricks to harass them. They'd put maggots or excreta or urine into the food, making it impossible to eat. Or when they sent orderlies around with food on a big trolley on which the plates were piled high, they'd send slop buckets around at the same time, and on the same trolley: usually at breakfast time. A screw or orderly—they were usually loyalist prisoners or common criminals—dressed in a rubber apron suit with an industrial face mask and surgical gloves, would dish out food with one hand— bread, tea, cornflakes, a little milk—holding out the slop bucket with the other. So nauseating was the stench of the slop bucket that the men found it hard even to go near one. There was no disinfectant used. The screws found great cause for amusement when this made some of the men retch and vomit.

What the orderlies typically did was to set the large open slop bucket inside the tiny cell. They would be deliberately careless in handling it, splashing and spilling the contents onto the floor, mattress and bedclothes. When the po would be emptied into the bucket, and set back down onto a floor still dirty with decaying food and wet with urine, the orderlies would slam the door and the air would stir. The odour in the damp cell would be foul and nauseous, every breath sickening. The odour would go into a man's nostrils and down his throat and convulse his swallowing reflexes, and the strong smell make him want to retch. The orderlies would repeat the procedure in five or six cells before finally emptying the slop bucket.

To prevent their urine being used against them the prisoners began pouring it out below the cell doors each night. But the excrement couldn't be dealt with that way. The prisoners packaged the solid waste by wrapping it up in paper—toilet tissue or Mass leaflets or sheets torn from bibles or religious magazines. They piled up the oozing packages for four or five days—enough time, they thought, to give the screws a chance to come to the cells and remove them. But they were not removed. So the men passed the word back and forth, and decided to dump the solids out the cell windows as had been done in the Crumlin Road jail. In the Crum the men had called them "mystery parcels." The screws didn't know what was in them till they opened them.

In their bucolic retreat at Long Kesh someone—Tony thought it was Joe McDonnell—rechristened the parcels "blue ducks." When the decision was made to put them out the windows, the message was passed. "The blue ducks will fly." On the day it was planned, the word was passed, "The blue ducks are flying tonight!"

So that night they pitched the parcels out the window.

An hour later a regiment of screws and orderlies descended on the yard, wearing gloves and protective clothing, and hurled the parcels back in again. Some of the screws reached their hands through the bars to improve their aim. The stuff, its paper wrappings ripped and torn, usually hit the men. In the small cells they had nowhere to hide. They found themselves fouled with excreta. It was in their hair, on their faces, all over their bodies, on their blankets and mattresses.

It was in April that they figured out another way to deal with the solid waste. They discovered that if they put the gear (as some of them called it) on the walls, it would dry in a short time—after only fifteen minutes or so, leaving far less odour than in its original state. There was general agreement: this was the best, the most hygienic solution in the circumstances. So all the men began smearing the stuff on the walls. They used different methods. Tony used pieces of sponge from his mattress.

Conditions in the place were sickening.

The walls became covered in stucco patterns of dried excrement. Rotten food piled up in the corners, a breeding ground for the ever-present flies. Maggots squirmed and crawled about the floor and up the walls. The worst of it was the urine on the floor near the doors.

The men themselves stank. At Mass on Easter Sunday the air was so bad the screws themselves left the canteen.

The protest became ritualized: a dirt or, in British journalese, "dirty" protest. Bitter as the conditions were, the men's use of the walls diminished, for a time at least, reprisals from the warders, and provided a symbol of the degree of their degradation in this English prison in Northern Ireland. "A fecal protest for a fecal society," is the way the writer Tim Pat Coogan put it.

That month, April 1978, the screws began removing all furniture from the cells. As the men saw this happening, they passed the word from cell to cell and wing to wing. They decided they were not going to simply look on passively. So they began smashing up what furniture they could before it was removed from the cells, and threw the smashed-up furniture out the windows. Acting together gave their morale a terrific boost. Instead of striking out helplessly in isolation they were defiantly asserting themselves as a group. Breaking the furniture gave them a chance, too, to lash out physically against a British regime filthy enough to try to use their bodily waste to break their resistance to criminalization.

The day they began smashing their furniture the screws panicked. Tony heard them pounding around the place, swinging open cell doors and racing in to grab still unbroken pieces. They seemed especially anxious to save the six-foot metal lockers. By the time they got to them, most of the lockers were dented, twisted and bent, the men using remnants of other furniture as hammers.

The prisoners' heroes that day were Paddy O'Hagan and Seán Treacy, two young lads from Tyrone. When the screws came rushing into their cell they found no locker at all, not even a bent and twisted one. In fact there was nothing in the cell except the remnants of the metal bed frame. The screws began frantically searching the tiny room, peering under the bedframe and even behind the pipes, as though somehow bits of the locker might be hidden there. Still nothing. The boys from Tyrone were delighted with themselves. Before the screws arrived, they'd managed to break the riveted locker into little pieces and force the pieces out the window.

After the furniture-breaking episode the men were of course severely beaten. But there was to be further retaliation. One April night, while the prisoners were asleep on the floor on their damp and filthy mattresses, the screws began pumping in large amounts of ammonia-based disinfectant through the peepholes, using high-powered hoses which forced jets of liquid in, choking the men with fumes, completely soaking them, their bedding and their blankets.

By June 1978, after about thirteen weeks on the no-wash, no-slop-out protest, all furniture had been removed from the cells. The men, sleeping on damp, soggy, dirty sponge mattresses, were getting filthier by the day. They were all undernourished and underweight, with pale, scaly, yellowing skin. They were sleeping, living and eating on the floor. Their cells were littered with huge piles of putrefying waste food. It was three months since most of them had had a shower.

When they'd wake in the morning their blankets and mattresses would be covered with white, crawling maggots that bred in the piles of garbage and decay, maggots which got into their hair and all over their bodies. The mattresses were full of lice, the walls covered with excrement and flies. Each morning filthy washbasins were handed into the cells.

The men were hounded by the screws, who continually carried out searches, ransacking the cells, kicking pos full of urine over already filthy bedding. They were repeatedly drenched with high-powered fire hoses pushed through the cell doors and windows, spraying the cells with the strong disinfectant, whose fumes would leave them choked, vomiting and at times blinded.

Because of the degrading internal body searches, during which they were forced to lay across a table while screw put their fingers up their back passages, many of the prisoners were now refusing the precious monthly visit. Nor could they see a solicitor or doctor without submitting to this barbaric anal search and the criminal uniform. And they could be put on the boards anytime a screw might arbitrarily decide—sent to the punishment cells.

A punishment cell was bare, with a wooden board for a bed, a concrete slab jutting from the wall serving as a table, another concrete slab as a chair. There was a starvation diet of tea and dry bread morning and evening with watery soup at midday. In all the cells the electric light was on continuously, affecting a prisoner's eyesight.

The one relieving factor about the punishment block was that it was very quiet after the noise of the normal H-Block wing. There was an intolerable noise level in the blocks: the constant banging and clanging of the heavy steel doors sent sound vibrations and echoes rolling through the whole wing. The heat was often turned up high in hot weather. The food, always rationed, was sometimes deliberately destroyed.

THESE WERE THE CONDITIONS in which Archbishop Tomás Ó Fiaich found the men when he revisited Long Kesh in late July 1978, and issued a statement comparing the prisoners to people he'd seen living in sewer pipes in the slums of Calcutta. The skin on the men's faces and ears was flaking. Many of them were covered with sores. Their eyes had a wild, dazzled look.

71

Most of the time they had nothing to do but stare at the grey floor and the four dirtied walls in their bleak and fetid cells. The view from the window was limited to twenty square yards of corrugated iron and barbed wire.

Through August 1978 the screws continued pumping in the heavy disinfectant. Finally, to get air, the prisoners smashed out the cell windows. Through the following months, with the windows smashed, the men were subject to the power of the elements. The wind would sometimes drive rain into the cells, soaking everything. The prisoners were often battered through the open windows by orderlies using high pressure fire hoses to clean the outside of the blocks. But at least they had fresh air, and could see the sun. Tony used to stand for hours looking out the open window at little birds hopping about the yard and then flying away. But his captivity was to continue for years.

Meanwhile they had only the most limited contact with the world outside. For Tony the visits were ordeals. The one statutory visit a month, which lasted a half hour, became an endurance test. Tony's nerves would begin to go a week before it. On the day itself he'd wake up from a restless night's sleep, feeling a churning in his stomach. Soon after waking, he'd have an acute attack of diarrhoea repeated at half-hourly intervals. Then, at eleven o'clock or twelve o'clock, he'd hear the screws shouting, "O'Hara for a visit!"

His heart would begin thumping as he'd hear them coming down the wing. The door would open and he'd be taken to a cell at the top of the wing where screws would probe his anus. Later they had the men squat over a mirror: what was called the mirror search. Tony would refuse to do this and the screws would drag him forward, forcing him over the mirror. When they'd searched, or pretended to search, his back passage, he'd have to put on the uniform.

He'd be taken to the clean part of the prison to wait for transport to the visiting area. In the prison van his pulse would be pounding so hard that he'd think he was on the verge of a heart attack. He'd be in a state of nervous excitement, as if he were getting ready to run a race. While he was waiting—about a quarter of an hour—to see his people, he'd desperately try to recall questions he wanted to ask, things he wanted to say. His visitors would come in. They'd shake hands or kiss, then sit down across the table. He'd be offered a cigarette. He'd chain-smoke while trying both to listen to what his people were saying and to blurt out the questions in his head. He'd go too fast with the questions, hardly hearing the answers. Everything would become confused. The half hour would fly by and a screw would call time. He'd be removed from the visitors' area and taken back to the block. There he'd be searched again over a mirror. Reaching his cell, he'd collapse on the mattress, utterly drained. Even if his visit brought news, he'd go blank trying to remember it. But he endured these visits to keep some flow of information going, to keep some contact with the people outside, to let them know what was happening. Because only they could help the prisoners.

In November 1978 the glass windows were replaced by hard, tight plastic windows made of perspex. With these windows in, the prisoners found the fumes from the disinfectant overpowering. So one night they smashed the windows. The screws again fire-hosed the cells from outside.

In December the prison doctors began ordering that all blanketmen be forcibly bathed and shaved and have their hair cut. The prisoners resisted this with all their strength. The screws responded brutally, severely injuring a number of prisoners, among them Kieran Doherty.

The haircuts and forced bathing began in H-3. They were proceeding block by block, wing by wing, beating the men, dragging them off by the hair, bouncing them off the walls, kicking and punching them to the top of the wing, throwing them into a bath, scrubbing them with scrubbing brushes and then trailing them back to the cells. Tony and the others decided that when the screws came to H-5 they would fight them. But H-4 was next. So the blanketmen in H-5 got word to H-4, suggesting that the men there fight back.

The screws came to H-4. They opened a cell door. Crack! They were hit. They opened the next door. Crack! again. And so on—crack, crack, crack!—through the first ten cells on the wing. The men were good fighters, and the screws were getting cracked every time they went in. It didn't matter whether a man was eighty pounds or two hundred eighty, six stone or twenty stone, he could still poke a screw in the eyes. After the first ten cells the screws quit for awhile. Later, of course, they beat the men up. Everybody in H-4 got a bad beating. But the forced baths stopped for a time because the screws themselves were getting hurt.

The men in H-3 had also fought back, but they hadn't the advantage of foreknowledge and so hadn't been able to organize themselves. Tony knew of a number of men in H-3 who would have loved to have had the chance to be forewarned of the forced bathing. He thought, for example, of Thomas McElwee, one of the most resolute of all the blanketmen, whose determination was like Kieran Doherty's. Thomas was very quiet and self-possessed. Though serious and religious, he wouldn't give the screws an inch. He was always on the boards. But he wouldn't let them get the better of him. His brother Benedict (in H-4) was the same. Tony first met Benedict when they were on remand in Crumlin Road jail, then met him again after three and a half years in Long Kesh. He would meet him later through the comradeship of the hunger strike.

AN ICY CHILL came from the open window. There was no heating on in the cells. Tony was walking up and down, pretending to himself that he was not cold: one-two-three-four, turn, one-two-three-four, turn. His cellmate was walking up and down, too. There was not enough room to swing a cat but there they were, two men, pacing the floor at the same time.

Tony could only take four short steps—there was no space to stride out. He had to shorten his steps or run the risk of bashing his toes against the wall. His bare feet had hardened so that he could walk around on the floor and not feel the cold. They had become so calloused that he felt as though he were wearing shoes.

At first he had used two of his three blankets to walk on, putting them down so that they joined on the floor and formed a path. But now there was no feeling in his feet, and he needed the blankets for warmth. He had wrapped one blanket around his waist, and draped it like a robe. The towel was around his back, covered by the other two blankets, folded and hanging from his shoulders. He was walking up and down as fast as the smallness of space permitted.

He walked three or four hours every day. It kept his limbs from getting stiff, and gave the dark, stinking, clammy mattress a chance to dry a little. It never dried completely: that would have taken at least a week. But with some of the moisture out, the mattress was a bit more bearable to lie on. Tony's cellmate, a newer arrival, had found it impossible to walk on the floor and was walking on his mattress.

Up and down, up and down. One-two-three-four, turn. Now and again their teeth would chatter as they walked, each lost in his own thoughts. Tony knew that his cellmate, like himself, would have preferred to lie on his sponge and try to doze or sleep—except for the cold. There was no way they could lie in such cold.

One-two-three-four, turn. One-two-three-four, turn . . .

Suddenly they heard someone shouting. Purely out of instinct they dashed to the door. There was no sense in this because there was no crack or opening through which they could see. Still they all went to the door whenever there was any commotion.

"It's a new man!" someone shouted. "Sentenced yesterday."

Tony knew in a flash what was happening. The new arrival, if he were lucky, would be huddled in a corner with a blanket wrapped around him. But he might very well be naked. There'd be five or six screws with drawn batons in the cell with him: threatening him, looming above him. The prison uniform would be lying on the ground in front of him.

"Put it on, you Fenian bastard," a screw would be saying.

Tony remembered what they'd done to him during his first beating. He was clubbed with batons, kicked, pulled around the cell by his hair. With his bare feet he couldn't kick back. They held him down and jumped on his hands and toes.

So each prisoner standing there at the door could see without being able to see. Each of them was aware of what the new prisoner was going through, wishing he were out there and could do something to help. Tony's heart was with the new man. He felt his suffering almost as though it were his own.

Out in the compounds the screws couldn't behave the way they did in here. If they did the men would gang up on them. Here they could be sadists, and many of them were. In Tony's book they were all rotten. Every one of them did the mirror search. Some of them hadn't beaten anybody. But when the prisoners were beaten, even badly beaten, no screw would come forward to testify in defence of the man. Rather they would lie—testifying when a prisoner was up on an assault charge that the prisoner had hit the screw first.

Among the screws there were heavy drinkers, some of them obvious alcoholics. They were all mercenaries. For a long period there was an IRA campaign to kill screws outside the prison in retaliation for what they were doing to the men. So the screws were always pressing for danger money. Then, when the no-wash, no-slop-out protest began, the screws threatened to go on strike, saying that they refused to work in the blocks unless they got extra pay—because of the risk involved, because of the dirt, because they might catch something, might fall and break a leg on the wet floor, might be attacked by the prisoners. And as long as they got something extra, they'd keep on working. They exploited the protest, made money from it.

When the noise of the beating stopped, Tony resumed walking. His arms and legs were numb. His privates were numb. His head was very cold. He'd sneeze and feel his nose running. But he'd say to himself: I'm not cold. I don't want to be cold. If he thought about the cold, he'd freeze to death.

Tony decided to exercise. He jumped up and down. He did press-ups. He tried running in place. And suddenly he felt sweat under his arms—very cold sweat, turning to ice. But, he thought, sweat should be hot. Why was he trying to warm up?

I'm not cold, he told himself. He started walking again, pretending he was in Derry, on the riverside, walking along the bank of the Foyle, the sun shining down, the temperature 75° Fahrenheit. He could feel the heat. He could feel the sun on his skin: unless he put oil on himself he'd get sunburn.

Other times he'd imagine himself in Donegal, lying on a sandy beach near Gweedore in the hot sunshine. Or on a bright day he'd look through the vertical openings in the window wall, see the sun and pretend he could feel its rays burning deep into his body. He heard the familiar jingle of keys. Suppertime. A cup of tea! A cup of hot tea to warm him up. The door opened, the tea was handed in to him. Ah! Nice hot tea. He took a sip. A-a-ah.

But the tea was cold, too.

The food at Long Kesh was terrible. When there was any amount of it, it was heavy with starch and bloated their bodies. Often it was inedible. Once when Tony was on remand he saw a prison menu in a Belfast newspaper. It read like the menu of the dining room in the Europa Hotel. He wondered what journalists would write if they had to eat this food. The Northern Ireland Office told journalists that the temperature in the H-Blocks was kept at an even 65°Fahrenheit. It was, when there were priests or other visitors coming in. The Brits also told journalists that the men were never beaten by the warders.

BY MID-MARCH 1979, a quarter to a third of the sentenced Republican prisoners were on the protest. There were 360 Republicans and twelve Loyalists on the blanket in the H-Blocks, mainly in H-3, H-4, and H-5, but some in H-6. In H-5, Tony's block, there were 140 prisoners, 134 of them blanketmen, the rest orderlies. By 11 March there were 38 women on protest in Armagh jail. The total fluctuated from time to time. Prisoners came off the protest, because they'd gone mad or had had nervous breakdowns, or because of bereavement or other family problems. Some were literally beaten off. Now and then the prisoners could hear the sounds of the stiff, synthetic boots as men who were abandoning the protest walked out of their cells and down the corridor. They called them "squeaky booters." But the men who stayed on the protest did not spend their time thinking ill of the others. They all had their reasons.

The prison authorities began putting in new, more permanent perspex windows, built into a wooden frame structure sitting about a foot outside the outer wall. Inside the frames were reinforced concrete bars. The window was covered in such a way that it was impossible to look up and see anything except the roof of the box. Tony could look down and see the ground; he'd notice shadows, or sometimes birds, or feet walking past. A metal grille was erected on the inside of the window to prevent the men from interfering with the perspex. The grille blurred Tony's vision and made his eyes sore.

After the new windows were up, the men tried for two days to break them out, but had no luck. Then someone suggested burning them away. It took a couple of days to get everyone fixed up with flints and matches. They propped pieces of sponge from the mattresses onto the windows, lit them, and the perspex soon caught fire and melted. The screws put their high-powered hoses through the windows in pretence of putting out the fires, soaking everything. In Tony's cell the water rose several inches before flowing out under the door. The hosings were repeated through that night, and again the next, so that no one was able to sleep. But the men had generally done a good job of burning out the windows, and there was sunlight and fresh air in the cells again. During the next few days the screws vented their anger by beating the prisoners.

BY LATE 1979 the men in Long Kesh, who'd been thinking vaguely about a hunger strike for a couple of years, began thinking very seriously about it. They couldn't just lie there and rot. The prison regime had driven some three dozen men insane. The threat of coffins coming out of Long Kesh might wake the world up to the horror of the place. It was necessary to take the battle to the British in the most dramatic way possible. So far, nothing the prisoners or the Relatives' Action committees or anyone else had done had forced the British to end this degradation.

Cardinal Tomás Ó Fiaich was made aware of the prisoners' intention to go on hunger strike. Tony understood that the Cardinal had sent word in asking the men to hold back while he did what he could in talks with the British government.*

Beginning in February 1980, he held a series of meetings with Humphrey Atkins, then Northern Ireland Secretary of State.

*See Note 3, at end of this chapter.

The prisoners felt they had some grounds for hope. The Cardinal and Bishop Edward Daly of Derry urged Atkins to broaden the definition of prison work, and to let the prisoners wear their own clothes. Yet after six or seven months of intermittent negotiations the British had done nothing in response. So by the autumn of 1980 the men were determined to go ahead. Beginning on a date in late October, a number of them would hunger-strike to the death unless they were granted five demands:

1. The right to wear their own clothes.
2. The right not to do prison work.
3. Free association with fellow prisoners.
4. Full 50 per cent remission of their sentences.
5. Normal visits, parcels, educational and recreational facilities.

Association was important, because it meant that prisoners could thwart efforts by the screws to bully one or two prisoners at a time.

The Cardinal kept trying but nothing at all substantial came of his efforts. Then on 23 October, the Northern Ireland Office announced that the men would no longer be required to wear prison uniform. They could wear civilian clothes instead. That same day, the Cardinal and Bishop Daly met with Atkins and discovered that this meant that the men were going to be given, in place of the hated uniform, prison-issue civilian clothes. The Cardinal and the Bishop were angry. The prisoners, seeing that the British had tried to deceive the Cardinal, felt more than ever compelled to use the hunger strike weapon. It was terrible, Tony felt, that the men had been driven to this extreme. He would always remember the words—he thought they conveyed a sense of dignity and even greatness—in which the hunger strike was announced:

> The birth pangs of a nation are terrible, and we her children must once again bear her suffering. We have come in search of a thirty-two county Irish socialist Republic . . .

On 27 October the strike began. The hunger strikers' leader

was the joint IRA OC in the blocks, Brendan Hughes. Darky Hughes he was called. Tony particularly respected him, and he was always considerate of the feelings of the INLA prisoners. Jogn Nixon decided that as INLA OC he should be the first of their men on hunger strike. Completing the group of seven were Tom McFeeley of Dungiven, the other joint OC of the IRA prisoners; Seán McKenna of Newry, OC of H-5; Leo Green of Lurgan, Co. Armagh, OC of H-4; Tommy McKearney of Moy, Co. Tyrone, OC of H-3; and Raymond McCartney of Tony's own city of Derry, OC of A-wing, H-5.

Tony's old cellmate Bobby Sands was the new OC of the blanketmen.

From the outset of the hunger strike Tony felt a great sense of pride in the men. He knew some of them very well. Tony regarded John Nixon, who came from Armagh City, as a man of many talents: a poet, a playwright, a leader—as well as a trusted friend. Tony was particularly worried about Nixy, as they called him. He'd been shot and badly wounded some years before; Tony felt that he didn't stand much chance of surviving a prolonged hunger strike.

Tony also wondered about Raymond McCartney, who was only a couple of years older than himself. Though Raymond was stocky, he was small.

He was sharp, too. Once in 1979 still photographers had been allowed into Long Kesh. The prisoners were overjoyed, because they thought the publicity would help their cause. The cameramen were allowed to take photographs here and there, but weren't allowed to interview any of the men. The next time there was a photo session was in late 1980—while Raymond McCartney was on hunger strike. This time television cameras were allowed in. The TV crews weren't permitted to speak to any prisoner but were allowed to listen if a prisoner spoke to them. By chance a TV crew went to Raymond's cell. His cellmate was laughing, so the story went, at the ludicrousness of the prisoners being photographed in silence, as though they were animals in a zoo. But Raymond had the presence of mind to seize the opportunity to speak out.

"I'm a political prisoner!" he said into a live microphone.

"And I am on hunger strike—"

It was a rare chance, and he made the most of it.

The visit of the television crews, and the fact that the brief encounter with Raymond was broadcast, gave the men hope. They were taking comfort where they could find it.

Tony knew five of the hunger strikers personally. But it was the seven of them together who occupied his thoughts and prayers through the next days and weeks. Each day he would wait anxiously for news. For more than a month their condition was stable. On 1 December three women from Armagh jail went on hunger strike in solidarity with the men in Long Kesh, and in protest at the brutal conditions they themselves were suffering. The hunger strikers were Mairead Farrell and Mairead Nugent from Andersonstown and Mary Doyle from Greencastle. Mairead Farrell was OC of the Provisional IRA prisoners in Armagh.

The women in Armagh wore their own clothes. But they had been living for nearly eleven months, in hideous conditions, on a protest parallel to that of the men in Long Kesh. It had begun on 7 February 1980 when their cells were invaded by male warders coming to seize the black skirts and berets that the women used in drills as a kind of paramilitary uniform. Some of them were kicked and severely beaten by the male warders.

They tried to fight back and were locked in their cells. They were refused the use of toilet facilities. Then their pos began to overflow with urine and excrement, and the windows of their cells were boarded up to prevent them emptying the pos outside. The conditions forced them to go on a dirt strike, smearing their excreta on the walls. They would line the pos with paper tissues and after defecating would use the tissues to put their solid waste on the walls and finally on the ceilings. During their monthly periods they were given only a few unwrapped sanitary towels. So they smeared their menstrual blood on the walls as well.

After several days they were allowed out for midday exercise but were locked up in their cells the other 23 hours. They refused to wash or brush their teeth, and went for ninety days without a change of clothes or underwear. The women suffered from a variety of illnesses, from cystitis, from headaches (the electric light was on all the time), from period cramps, skin disease and ulcers. There was vomit and diarrhoea in all their cells. They had taken to wearing sanitary towels as masks to help them breathe.

So three of them had joined the hunger strike.

In early December, as the strike in Long Kesh reached its fortieth day, Tony began to feel miserable. The fact that the first seven men were now confined in the prison hospital, segregated from the rest of the prisoners, didn't help. Then, in Long Kesh, thirty more men went on hunger strike—among them INLA prisoners Micky Devine, Kevin Lynch, Liam McCloskey and Tony's brother Patsy O'Hara. There were worrying rumours. Tony wanted to see the men win political status, but he didn't want any of them to die. He prayed and prayed.

On about the forty-eighth day Seán McKenna went blind.

Tony knew something of McKenna's background: how his father had been one of the men—"the Guinea Pigs"—tortured during the 1971 internment interrogations, when the Brits used the hooded tratment and white noise to try to break some of the internees. Seán's father was one of the worst cases brought before the European Commission on Human Rights, which eventually in 1976 declared Britain guilty of torture and inhuman and degrading treatment. In 1975 Seán's father, his personality almost completely changed, died as a result of this treatment, at the age of 42.

The McKenna family moved to Edentubber in County Louth, to a place a mile and a half by car from the border, but across fields about six hundred years. In 1976, during an illegal incursion into the Republic, the SAS smashed into the McKennas' cottage. Seán was alone at the time. They dragged him out, abducted him across the border and took him to Bessbrook barracks in Co. Armagh where he was kept in a dark room and kicked and badly beaten. His frantic family rang hospitals and police barracks south and north searching for him. The RUC denied any knowledge of his whereabouts. Then, on a Monday morning, his mother heard the news that he would be appearing in a crown court.

After what had happened to his father, it was a shame to see a bright young man like Seán McKenna suffering so. Tony heard that Leo Green had weakened, too, and then Tony's friend John Nixon. On 10 December, when news came that an NIO official had come in to talk to the hunger strikers, the prisoners felt a surge of hope. To increase the pressure on the British government, the thirty others began to go without food.

Day followed day and Seán McKenna's condition kept worsening. Still nothing happened. But then, at 8:30 at night on 18 December, Bobby Sands, accompanied by the two prison chaplains, Fathers John Murphy and Tom Toner, came to the wings to announce that the hunger strike was over, that the British government had promised concessions. The seven men, Bobby said, had taken themselves off to save Seán McKenna's life. The thirty hunger strikers who'd gone on en masse in the last week came off as well, as did the three women in Armagh jail.

Since Tony's brother Patsy and his friends were among the second group, Tony was very happy. He hadn't known in fact just how depressed he'd been during the hunger strike until he heard it was over. It was like a heavy cloud lifted from his heart. And Seán McKenna was going to live.

Men on the wing were very excited. "It's all over—we've won," Bobby Sands had said, although he'd said it cautiously. All sorts of questions passed along the wing. When would they get their own clothing? When would they get out for exercise? They began to think about having normal visits, about getting to see television, listening to the radio, eating decent food. The men laughed and joked about the way they planned to dress. Tony never knew people could be so happy as these men were. They even seemed to forget their confinement.

It wasn't long after that, however, that Tony and the other men began to realize that the British—who had got the men to come off hunger strike by indicating changes in prison rules that might amount to a granting of the substance of the five demands—had no real intention of following through. Rather they seemed to be reneging. And this despite the hunger strike, despite the fact that 140 of the 505 blanketmen had been conforming prisoners who, during the hunger strike, had joined the protest to show their solidarity.

Some of the prisoners were angry enough to want to restart the whole business, right away.

"No more hunger strikes," Bobby Sands said.

It sounded final.

NOTE 1: *Long Kesh*

THE NAME came from the prison's site, a long disused World War II airstrip at a townland of that name just south of a larger, spreading townland called Maze, adjacent to the Belfast dormitory town of Lisburn. Nissen huts and concrete, wire and barbed wire enclosures ("the cages") were hurriedly constructed to handle the internees collected in the 1971 British Army swoops ("Operation Demetrius") through Northern Ireland cities and towns and villages and farms.

Local boys had harassed and threatened the English builders originally sent across the water for the construction work on the internment camp. The English builders were forced to leave, and Northern Irish firms were brought in. In this strange circumstance Irishmen once again found in England's difficulty their opportunity.

In the mid-seventies, the British Labour government set out to build a bigger and tighter prison on the site. They placed a sub-minister named Don Concannon in charge of the prison programme. Not only was Concannon in charge of the building of the new concrete H-Blocks, he also seemed to see it as his responsibility to promote, under Roy Mason, a particularly brutal interpretation of the criminalization policy. His performance earned Concannon a permanent place in Irish rebel obloquy, as in Francie Brolly's "H-Block Song":

> Descendant of proud Connaught clan,
> Concannon serves cruel Britain's plan.
> Man's inhumanity to man
> Has spawned a trusty slave.
> No strangers are these bolts and locks,
> No new design these dark H-Blocks.
> Black Cromwell lives while Mason stalks,
> The bully taunts the brave . . .

There was a lot of hocus-pocus going on inside the vast new prison project. Somehow the costs of the construction work escalated to sky-high figures. In 1977, when Tony arrived, building was still in progress. Northern Ireland boys, not all of the Protestants, had done well out of the Maze prison, making free with the British Northern Ireland Office's open chequebook and amassing fortunes for themselves out of its anxiety to get the place built with minimum trouble at maximum speed.

An important factor in raising the cost of the prison was the switch in prison governors every two or three years. Each new man would want changes, often costing huge sums. The original architect's plan for the prison turned out to be just a working sketch. Drawings were done, buildings went up, only to be rejected or demolished at a later stage. Concannon and the other British government officials, in their passion for prison building, seem to have made utter fools of themselves: according to rumours circulating in the town of Maze itself, the building of the prison set the government back one hundred fifty million pounds sterling, and since the completion of the prison in 1980 an on-site construction operation was being maintained at a cost of ten million pounds a year.

Why had Long Kesh been renamed The Maze?

The British, who had made a massive public relations blunder by allowing internment without trial, had Long Kesh as the symbol of that blunder. The world and his mother knew that Irishmen had been arrested en masse, put in cages behind barbed wire—most of them in an asiatic-sounding place called Long Kesh—and kept there for months and years without trial.

What seemed to solve the problem of nomenclature for the British was the larger, spread-out townland nearby, called Maze. Maze wasn't that fortunate a name, because it suggested a labyrinth, a complex and confining network. But to the tin ear of a British Labour government, Maze had a nice technological ring to it. Therefore: Her Majesty's Prison The Maze.

NOTE 2: *Political ("Special Category") Status*

FOR YEARS the internees and Special Category prisoners had had their own commanding officers (OCs), whom the prison staff dealt with as the prisoner's representatives. There was also a tradition of Republican OCs and Loyalist OCs cooperating to lobby the authorities for fairer arrangements and privileges on a wide variety of matters. In the past they had been able to arrange more frequent and liberal granting of compassionate parole; to mediate on behalf of prisoners who had struck warders; and to decide on who and who not to take into a particular hut. Through their OCs, prisoners set their own schedules and times of rising and lights out.

There was a prisoner quartermaster for each compound; individual prisoners could stockpile food and other goods for use or barter; and there were special dining and laundry arrangements. At one point, during a period when improvements in menus were the burning issue, potted herrings had been brought in at the request of Gusty Spence, a UVF man and principal loyalist OC. A television set, radio, record player and cookstove were provided for each hut, along with frying pans, kettles and pots. The prisoners got metal knives and forks, their own individual mugs and two hundred cigarettes a week. They were allowed to keep money in a prison account and could spend it in a tuck shop, which over time was provided with a wide range of goods.

OCs had also secured an extension of sports activity periods, improved sports equipment and all-weather pitches, and arranged that a film be shown every ten days. For privacy, two-man cubicles were provided in the huts and there were special arrangements on room and body searches. Rather than have the warders body-searching eighty prisoners, for example, two or three would be selected each time. There was freedom of movement for OCs throughout the camp. A Provo OC, on a brief period of parole outside the prison, was once given permission to take a handgun with him for self-protection.

But word had begun to circulate about what bold boys these prisoners were. They were making replica guns in their handicrafts shops. They were giving themselves paramilitary training: drilling and practicing, occasionally using the roofs of the huts for assault courses. The cry went up: Long Kesh was a "university of terrorism." Yet the men, whether internees or convicted prisoners, did not have their freedom or their privacy; their access to goods and services was limited. They had no relationships with women. They were cut off from wives, families, friends and the outside world. They were not really their own masters, and didn't have the independence and mobility they would have had outside.

By the late 70s as the blanket protest began to make its impact, many of the perks enjoyed by the prisoners in the cages and later on in the conforming H-Blocks were taken away. But the basic reforms on clothing, visits, parcels, mail, prison work and freedom of association were still in operation. And remission was increased for Special Category and conforming prisoners at the time of sentence, so that Special Category prisoners could now look forward to getting out sooner.

In contrast to the cages, the H-Block arrangements were designed for very close administrative control. In the compounds there had been no direct personal supervision of prisoners. Prison warders had only general functions like guarding and escorting. But in the blocks prisoners were locked up one or two to a cell, twenty-five cells to each wing, four wings to an H, with numerous guards able to deal with one or two men at a time.

Within the compounds the prisoners were responsible for their own daily routine. Within the blocks the warders had complete control over the prisoners, and could subject even conforming prisoners to any sort of petty harassment they wanted. It made the prisoners, already deprived of liberty, dependent on the warders to a humiliating degree. Even conforming prisoners, locked up under tight control and subject to the whims of their warders, grew to deeply hate some of them.

The whole H-Blocks project was regarded by more thoughtful warders as a fiasco. The Maze cost a sheik's ransom to build. Each month a fortune was spent in paying men to staff the blocks. They pointed out that while among alumni of the easy-going compounds the rate of reconviction was well below the sixty per cent rate of conventional prison systems, the blocks could become a cauldron of hostility to the regime and of recommitment to the struggle. There had been an opportunity here, from the British government's point of view, to keep the compound system and expand it, experimenting with ways of phasing out some of the military activity and other perks (as was later done). They could easily have let the prisoners keep their own clothes. Instead they chose to inaugurate what looked like a vindictive and was certainly a lethal criminalization policy.

NOTE 3: *The distress of Humphrey Atkins*

HUMPHREY ATKINS met with other people besides the Cardinal and Bishop Daly, including members of the SDLP. Paddy Duffy of Dungannon, then a leading figure in the SDLP, told a story about this:

> We made a number of attempts to get the prison situation dealt with. From time to time we met relatives of people on the protest. There was a major effort in May 1980. After we'd met with relatives in Bellaghy, Michael Canavan, John Hume and I arranged a meeting with Humphrey Atkins, to which some of the relatives came as well. Along with Atkins there was a whole array of figures from the British Northern Ireland establishment. Atkins introduced them very courteously before we sat down. Some of the relatives proceeded to describe the sort of torture their sons and daughters were enduring in Long

Kesh and Armagh. One of the big issues then was the mirror search procedure.

Atkins was a terribly polite man and these people were busy describing the facts of the protest, how the cells were being messed, the shit on the walls and so forth. Atkins really didn't want to get down to the basics of shit. He in fact let on that he didn't understand the meaning of the word. The situation became terribly funny as Atkins twisted in his chair, trying to take a polite interest in this unfortunate subject. As the relatives continued with their descriptions of the situation—especially the condition of the women in Armagh—Atkins became more and more embarrassed.

There in the room along with Atkins and all his ministers and the rest of the boys from the British establishment, was one particular character, a man named Hugh Corey of Loup in South Derry. Corey, whose son was in Long Kesh, said nothing for awhile. But then, in front of all those people, he began to speak.

"Mr. Atkins, I'm sort of sittin' here and lookin' at ye. And I'm thinkin' now that ye must have children yourself. Now would ye have children?"

"Oh, yes, yes," Atkins said. "I have two boys. One of them is going to a public school . . . "

Hugh jumped in.

"Well, now then, y'see, I just thought ye probably would have young fellows, like my own lad's age."

"What age is your boy, Mr. Corey?" Atkins said.

"Well, my lad's about eighteen," Corey said.

"Well," Atkins said, "my boys are not quite that old yet."

"But now, how would ye like, Mr. Atkins, if your older lad happened to get into a bit of trouble and be in jail, and if before he could see ye on a visit, how would ye like it if they brought him out and made him walk over a mirror and made him squat down and hold his legs astride it, so that they could look up his arse and see if he had anything up there? Now, would ye like that? Would ye?"

"Oh, oh, Mr. Corey, I do hope they don't do that—"

"Oh, begod, they *do* do that! I'm tellin' ye. That is what they do. And I would just like ye to investigate that . . . "

Chapter 3

RIOBÁRD Ó SEACHNASAIGH

There beside the singing river
    that dark mass of men was seen,
Far above the shining weapons
    hung their own beloved green.
"Death to every foe and traitor!
    Forward! Strike the marchin' tune,
And, hurrah, my boys, for freedom!
    'Tis the risin' of the moon."

John Keegan Casey

BOBBY ACCEPTED the fact that the men had made their decision. They were the ones who had been going through the agony and whose lives were at stake. The seven men had the right to decide.

It was Thursday 18 December, 1980. At least Seán Mc-Kenna's life had been saved. When the Northern Ireland Office documents came into the prison, the NIO and the governor had agreed to let Bobby call a meeting of the block OCs at 8:15 the next morning, Friday, to discuss their contents. The documents were a 34-page statement on the prison regime, and an advance copy of a speech to be given by Humphrey Atkins in the House of Commons Friday afternoon.

But if they were to wait for the Friday morning meeting, Seán McKenna, who was in critical condition, might die. So the other six hunger strikers decided to end their protest, to save Seán's life, believing that the British government had made up its mind to seek a settlement.

Whatever about his own doubts, Bobby's job, as OC of the Provisional IRA prisoners in Long Kesh, was to convey the decision to the thirty men who had gone on hunger strike this past week in support of the original seven, and to let the other prisoners know that the protest was officially over. Together with the prison chaplains, Fr. John Murphy and Fr. Tom Toner, he went from block to block and from cell to cell announcing the decision. He could see that most of them were happy, some were overjoyed. There was a feeling of victory in the air. Bobby smiled, but he wasn't so sure. He didn't trust the English.

He had to admit that the authorities had given him recognition during the hunger strike. There was some acknowledgement of their political status simply in that. On 11 December Bobby had been brought in a prison van from H-3 to the prison hospital half a mile away to visit the seven hunger strikers. After that he had been allowed several meetings with Darky Hughes, OC of the hunger strikers. Tonight he had been allowed to meet the seven hunger strikers again, then see the other hunger striking prisoners and confer with the block leaders in H-4, H-5 and H-6.

The next day, Friday, Bobby worked out a statement on behalf of all the protesting prisoners. The position of the seven men, backed by the people at Sinn Féin headquarters in Belfast, had to be decisive, while keeping in view the ever-present likelihood of British treachery:

> We, the Republican protesting prisoners on the blanket in H-Blocks 3, 4, 5 and 6 salute our comrades in Armagh, in the prison hospital, Long Kesh, in Musgrave Park Military hospital and in the above H-Blocks, on having successfully won their hunger strike victory.
>
> Dependent on a sensible and responsible attitude from the British government in implementing their proposals, the blanketmen will make a positive response. We are satisfied that the implementation of these proposals meets the requirements of our five basic demands.

That morning, during a visit, Bobby worked the statement over with Danny Morrison, publicity director for Sinn Féin. They agreed that it was important to make clear to everyone concerned, and especially to the anti-H-Block supporters outside, that the men would not be wearing any form of prison uniform or doing prison work. On the other hand, they had to build on the indications in the document and in Atkins' speech that the British were willing to make concessions, so long as they could seem to be doing so on their own initiative and not under duress.

The hunger strike was over—an end to that very powerful form of duress—and the ball was in the Brits' court. Bobby's statement went on:

> Republican prisoners will not be wearing any form of prison uniform and will not be participating in any form of penal work. The speed at which the phasing out of the blanket protest proceeds is entirely dependent on the sincerity and upon the manner in which the British government implement their proposals.

There were certainly signs of a new attitude in the prison, a lifting of the four-year pall that had hung over the place.

What would the British do?

In his statement Bobby thanked the men and women in the Republican movement and the H-Blocks/Armagh committee. He saluted the hunger-strikers' families, and suggested that those in high places who had refrained from actively supporting the prisoners should move now to ensure that the British stood over their assurances. There was a further reminder to the British: "For our part, we know that the masses who took to the streets are our real guarantors." Bobby concluded with a Christmas greeting and his own signature.

He was in reasonably good spirits. But what would happen was out of their hands now. The end of the hunger strike had really taken away all their bargaining power. The prisoners could cooperate only in a principled way. It was up to the British to make the running. Assuming that the authorities stood by the promises implied in their proposals, there would be a happy Christmas and an even happier New Year. The visit of John Blelloch of the NIO to the hunger strikers, the diplomatically-worded thirty-four page document prepared at the eleventh hour, Atkins' speech and the fact that the prisoners had been given an advance copy of it—all testified to the British being willing to move.

But would the Brits follow up on all this in a positive way? The document was vague. Bobby had often been disappointed by their behaviour in the past. And what hopes he did have were shadowed by harsh and brutal memories, and by feelings of hatred and revenge.

SUCH FEELINGS had not come naturally to Bobby Sands. Born in 1954 in Rathcoole in North Belfast, the eldest of four children, he spent his early childhood in peaceful enough surroundings. His father, a baker and then a post office worker, settled the family in mixed neighbourhoods where Catholics and Protestants lived side by side. The houses in the row where they lived in the Abbot's Cross district of North Belfast were occupied mostly by Protestants. Many of the men were either in the RUC or the part-time auxiliary B-Specials.

The Sandses were not political, and there was no trouble until, in 1961, the family was forced to move out. At the time Bobby was vaguely aware that the move had something to do with the 1956-62 IRA border campaign. The Sandses had nothing to do with the IRA. They were not a Republican-minded family. Bobby's mother was quiet. Given the name Sands, the neighbours thought she was a Protestant.

It was when they discovered that the Sandses were Catholics that the trouble started. One neighbour in particular began mimicking Mrs. Sands' actions. When she put out washing, the woman put out washing; when she cleaned her windows, the woman would clean hers. There was banging and hammering on the walls. The harassment persisted, and Bobby's mother—deeply sensitive to what was going on—became ill and had to go to hospital. The doctor suggested to Bobby's father, John Sands, that he should either take the neighbours to court, or move house. The Sandses' way of solving the problem was to move house. The family moved, as it happened, to another heavily Protestant area not far away, to Doonbeg Drive, Rathcoole, near where Bobby had been born. This was in December 1961. Bobby was seven years old.

The Sandses were comfortable in Doonbeg Drive. Though

they were living again amid loyalist neighbours, there were no problems. But as the troubles began to heat up in the 1960s, the harassment started again.

Bobby was now going through his middle teens and beginning to draw his own conclusions from the violence he saw on television and read about in the newspapers.

He was particularly affected by the attack in January 1969 on civil rights marchers at Burntollet Bridge in Co. Derry. There the police stood looking on, some of them laughing, as hundreds of loyalists attacked the marchers on their way from Belfast to Derry. The loyalists flew down at the marchers from a hillside, driving them with stones, clubs, chains and broken bottles into the River Faughan below the bridge. The marchers struggled on to Derry. Newspaper pictures of this attack imprinted themselves on Bobby's mind like a scar. He was fifteen and for the first time he began to take an active interest in what was going on in the world beyond his quiet home in Rathcoole.

As the year 1969 wore on, the boiler of nationalist grievances began to build steam. With the events of August 1969, Bobby's peaceful adolescence began to disintegrate in the explosion of the world around him. He remembered the figures, faces, uniforms and alien voices of armed British soldiers in the streets: at this stage it was just something to wonder about. But when, after leaving secondary school at 16, Bobby began serving an apprenticeship as a coach builder, the troubles impinged more and more on his life.

In 1971 a 17-year old Bobby watched from behind drawn curtains, his heart pounding, as British soldiers came to the doors of the Sandses' neighbours, dragging off fathers and sons, some of them by the hair of their heads, and flinging them into the backs of armoured cars.

But the Sands family had Protestant friends; they were as close to Protestants as to Catholics in Doonbeg Drive and Rathcoole generally, and Bobby was a popular footballer in a local club.

Then came Bloody Sunday and the bitter days that followed. Bobby worked on at the coach building until one morning he came in and saw his workmates, Protestant loyalists, standing there cleaning guns. One of them pointed to the guns, indicating that if he didn't leave the factory, they would be used on him. Then he found a note in his lunchbox, telling him to get out. So he did, and his two years of apprenticeship was wasted.

Bobby remembered becoming more and more angry. Yet again the Sandses were being harassed—in fact the momentum had been building for the last year and a half.

Once Bobby was coming out the side entry of his house. Two boys asked him for a light; he stopped and one of them stabbed him. He was able to escape across the wall and into the garden, and he got himself patched up without his mother finding out. He didn't want to worry her.

As the pressures mounted he would often get beatings from Protestants. UDA gangs were beginning to march up and down the streets of the neighbourhood like Hitler Youth. Mobs used to hang around outside the doors of Catholic families, shouting "Taigs out, Taigs out!" It came to the point where Bobby would sit up all night on the stairs in the darkness, protecting the house.

One day a neighbour woman, who seemed to be in charge of finding new housing for young Protestant couples, was standing out front pointing at their house. A week later someone hurled a rubbish bin through the sitting room window. In the dark of night stones were thrown and a couple of shots fired at the house.

The next morning Bobby's mother went down to the housing executive and told them what the family had been through. They'd have to get out immediately, she said. They sent her to the Twinbrook office, where she was told to take whatever house she could find free, put some curtains up, get furniture in, then go back to the housing executive and tell them the number.

And so the Sandses moved to Laburnum Way in the Twinbrook estate in Dunmurry. It was open and pleasant—and virtually all Catholic. Here for the first time, Bobby felt they could relax. It was like living in the Free State, Bobby's younger sister Bernadette said. There was a great spirit of camaraderie—

with people, hard pressed themselves, helping other people out. Bobby would never forget that.

When Bobby thought about his experiences—the harassment, the house-moving his people had been forced through, the fact that he'd been intimidated out of the only job he'd ever had, that he'd seen Irish people being viciously assaulted while the police looked on, seen the police themselves beating people up, seen British soldiers shooting people in the streets in cold blood—Bobby came to a conclusion: he'd have to fight this.

In the autumn of 1972—when he was eighteen and a half years old—he joined the Provisional IRA.

In Twinbrook he'd been feeling the fear slipping away. His family was no longer isolated. He found himself in an environment where he didn't have to be defensive anymore, with young men whose feelings of determination matched his own. But it was only a month or so after he'd joined the IRA that four handguns were found in a house where he was staying. He was arrested and charged with possession. He was tried and convicted, and sentenced to three years in the cages at Long Kesh. This was during the days of Special Category status and Bobby used his time well. He devoted himself to the study of Irish, at which he quickly made progress. He embarked on a programme of reading, particularly revolutionary authors. He studied the Irishmen first—James Connolly, Padraig Pearse and Liam Mellowes especially. He also read Che Guevara and Frantz Fanon, Camillo Torres and George Jackson. Bobby took an active part in heated discussions and debates in the cages as the men tried to deepen their understanding of what the struggle meant, of its historical context and the parallels in other countries.

In April 1976, after the three years in Long Kesh, Bobby returned to his family at Twinbrook. He married; the marriage didn't weather the troubles but it would produce his son Gerard.

Back in Twinbrook he became an advocate of organized republican involvement in social problems. He became very active in the local community, helping to set up a branch of Sinn Féin, and a chapter of the Green Cross which looked after dependants of political prisoners. He became involved in a tenants' association. Bus services were poor and he was able to arrange for Belfast black taxis to run to Twinbrook.

People began coming to him to get things done—arranging, for example, to have ramps put down to stop cars from speeding through streets where small children were playing. Bobby organized a weekly social night in a local parish hall, and a cultural night every Sunday.

During his time in Long Kesh he had learned to play the guitar. He taught music to his younger sister Bernadette and his brother Seán. He organized benefits and sing-songs. Bobby took part in these as a singer—he had a good voice—and as master of ceremonies. He published a community paper called *Liberty*, to which he contributed verse as well as articles.

Bobby was otherwise active, too. Soon after he left prison, he became leader of the Twinbrook IRA. To build it up, he was given the help of more experienced men. One of them, Joe McDonnell, was involved with Bobby in the firebombing of the Balmoral Furniture company, not two miles away from where Bobby lived. While trying to make their escape afterwards, Bobby, Joe and several other men were captured. A single revolver was found in their car. There was no hard evidence to link them with the bombing.

But it was October 1976, and at Castlereagh Interrogation Centre they were waiting for him.*

Immediately after they were picked up they were hauled off to Dunmurry police station from where they were taken to Crumlin Road jail. There Bobby was beaten—but far worse was coming. They took him to Castlereagh, where he gave his name, age and address and an account of his movements, refusing to say more than that until he had spoken to his solicitor.

He was interrogated for two two-hour sessions by two pairs of Special Branch men. He was slapped on the ears and punched or kicked in most parts of his body.

*See Note on Castlereagh, at end of this chapter.

98

Then came the third interrogation.

Bobby was seated at a table. One detective sat across from him. Another who had been drinking heavily was standing behind him, at his left. Bobby was in the chair for about five minutes when the man behind grabbed him by the throat with both hands.

"Before you leave here," he said, "you will talk, all right. You will even make up fairy stories."

Bobby was told to stand up. The detective opposite stood up and started asking questions. Bobby kept refusing to answer them. With each question, the detective behind him, who reeked of drink, would slap him heavily on the head, ear or face and say, "Answer him!" Bobby wouldn't answer. After half an hour of this he was spreadeagled, with his fingertips up against the wall and his feet apart and far back. The half-drunk detective began punching him hard in the kidneys, sides, back and neck, punching him all over his body. The other detective, holding him by the hair, was flinging questions into Bobby's face. This continued until Bobby finally stood up straight, saying he was exhausted and would not stand in that position again.

He was told to sit down and was given a cigarette. They threatened to bring his wife in; she would get what he got, he was told, even though she was pregnant. Bobby was cold and in pain, but he felt that he still had will enough to withstand them. Then he was hauled up onto his feet, beaten, forced to take his boots off. Although he tried to resist, he was spreadeagled again, punched in the head and back. He felt dizzy. The detective who smelled of alcohol stood at one side of him and was leaning into Bobby's face, screaming abuse. Then he put his hands around Bobby's neck and pressed two fingers in under Bobby's jaw. This was excruciatingly painful. He repeated the pressure on other parts of Bobby's body.

Bobby was still spreadeagled. The half-drunk detective began swinging his foot between Bobby's legs, kicking him in the genitals five or six times, sickening him and knocking the breath out of him. He fell. They hauled him to his feet. The half-drunk detective began chopping him on the back of the neck, with twenty or thirty heavy and continuous blows. Bobby couldn't be sure of the number because the other detective was punching him in the stomach and yelling questions at the same time.

He didn't remember falling, but he must have, because when he came to he was being hauled off the floor and onto a chair. He was given another cigarette and asked if he was all right.

They said it was early days yet; it would be easier for him if he just put his name to their piece of paper.

This third session ended about one in the morning. He'd been interrogated for seven hours that day, with only a break for the doctor to examine him. He kept asking to see his solicitor. When he was told this time that he was going back to his cell, Bobby asked again for a doctor. They just laughed at him.

"You have some chance! And so has your fucking solicitor."

It took him till two to get to sleep. There was a large bright light shining down into his eyes. In the middle of the night the noise of the ventilation system woke him up. He was freezing. Then the system was turned off, and the cell became very stuffy and warm. The mattress was covered with cellophane, so he had to soak in his own sweat.

All that happened on a Friday night. Next day, Saturday 16 October, Bobby was awakened and given breakfast on a paper plate at about nine in the morning. A little later the door opened and he was brought down the stairs and taken into one of the small rooms. They began with a formal request for his name, age and address. This interrogation lasted two hours. It was followed by another just as long. He was closely questioned, slapped around, punched and threatened. But the interrogators were not as severe as the two at the Friday night session.

He had dinner in the middle of that afternoon and was taken to the last room on the right in the interrogation building. He remembered this very well. He was standing there, not being asked anything, not saying anything, when suddenly he was set upon by two detectives, punched, slapped hard on the head, ears, face and eyes and kicked in the legs. His head was smashed against a wooden wall. He couldn't hear the things they were saying to him while they were beating him. Then, as if nothing had happened, he was calmly told to sit down and was given a cigarette. They told him that he'd only had a taste of what was to come unless he gave the right answers.

The questioning began again. Bobby gave his name, age and address. He repeated what he'd said about his movements and asked for a doctor and a solicitor. He wouldn't answer any other questions until he saw them, he said.

They hauled him out of his seat, spreadeagled him against the wall, and beat him again. When he refused to spreadeagle, he was thrown to the floor and told to do press-ups. He refused and was kicked several times until he started doing the press-ups. Only able to do three or four, he just lay down, exhausted and disoriented. They dragged him up and went to work on his arms, twisting them up his back. The two men worked together, one of them holding his arms together while the other concentrated on hitting him. He was defenceless. When his arms were released he could barely bring them down, and only with considerable pain. They asked him what was wrong with them, which arm hurt him most. He said his left—he had once broken it. They grabbed both his arms, and hammered his head against the wall.

One of the detectives, about to twist Bobby's arm again, suddenly stopped, apparently afraid of breaking it. They spreadeagled him, but he immediately fell because of the terrible pain in his arms.

Yet it went on and on.

They told him to close his eyes and began punching him suddenly in places where he was not expecting to be hit. When he refused to close his eyes, one of the detectives held his hand around his eyes from behind, while the other one beat him.

This session ended at five in the evening. When he got into his cell the bright light was still on. Depressed by the four grey walls, he got off the bed and began walking up and down the cell, four paces each way. Exhausted and demoralized as he was, he knew that if he didn't keep walking up and down and keep his mind going, he might break down and sign his name to something. The harder they tried to break him, the more determined he became not to be broken.

This went on for four more days: a terrible experience, but

one that served to confirm his will to resist, and gave him strength afterwards through the years of suffering, beatings and degradation in the H-Blocks. For Bobby, simply to remain unbroken in spirit despite all they hurled against him was a great victory. The men in black uniforms in the H-Blocks would be animals, too, like those detectives in Castlereagh: monsters at the service of the British imperial monster. It kept playing with him, it humiliated him, tortured him. He was like a mouse in comparison. But whenever he withstood its torture he felt ten feet tall.

He knew that he was what he was, no matter what could be brought down on him. The road would be a hard one, but he kept making up his mind that everything along the way had to be conquered, would be conquered. He kept saying to himself that nothing else mattered except never giving up. No matter how bad or black or painful, no matter how heartbreaking the torment, he would never give up, never despair. He found consolation in the prophet Sirach: "Blessed is he whose heart does not condemn him, and who does not give up his hope." *Tiocfaidh ár lá!* he would say to himself: Our day will come.

After the six-day interrogation, Bobby was charged and held on remand for eleven months. Then he was tried and sentenced. Because of the fight in the courtroom* he spent the first twenty-two days of his sentence in solitary confinement at Crumlin Road jail. He refused the uniform, and for fifteen of those days they kept him entirely naked. In November 1977, Bobby was moved to the H-Blocks at Long Kesh. There he joined the blanket protest.

His first cellmate was Tony O'Hara from Derry. Bobby spent several months with Tony. Then, because they had heard him teaching Irish, he was put in a cell down at the screws' end of the corridor. During the next three years he spent much of his time alone, with several spells in the punishment block. An activist in the prison, he was made PRO of his wing, then PRO of the block. By late 1978 he was PRO for all the protesting prisoners. He spent as much time as he could writing letters to people outside, trying to convey some sense of what the men

*See Chapter 2, above.

were suffering. He began sending articles to *The Republican News*, the Provisional Sinn Féin newspaper, using as a pseudonym his sister's name, Marcella. Bobby was only a year older than Marcella and they'd always been very close.

As the struggle went on he saw himself more and more as a fighter for the people outside the prison. It was for them that he was suffering. He would think of them as the risen people, and visualize them moving onto the streets in their thousands, marching in defiance of the British oppressor—the mass murderer and torturer. How the spirit of freedom rose in every one of them! He wept sometimes, he was so proud of them. For them, as well as for the men in the prison, he could shout it out: *Tiocfaidh ár lá*: Our day will come!

The attempt to criminalize the men in the prison was like the attempt to criminalize the people outside, but the men and women of no property kept rising up. No matter how hard it was for Bobby, lying there on his mattress, pulling his blanket around him, he knew that some day there would come a victory, and that after the victory an Irish man or Irish woman would never again have to rot in an English hellhole.

Bobby was prepared to endure the beatings and humiliation involved in going out for a visit. He would gain the reward not only of seeing the family he loved so dearly, but also the other families whispering together around the tables of the visiting room, smiling and offering words of kindness and encouragement. It moved him to see the mothers' faces lined with sorrow, the fathers speechless or crying, the children weeping as they watched their daddies being bundled away by monsters in black uniforms—the same monsters who hung over their shoulders listening to every word spoken, who kept people queuing for hours on end for a mere 30-minute visit, who treated them like cattle, herding them through gates, and from one degrading search to another.

He knew the screws despised the Irish people as much as they despised the prisoners they were trying to treat as criminals. They insulted the families. They broke their hearts by torturing their sons in Long Kesh, their daughters in Armagh.

So after each visit Bobby would go back to his filthy concrete tomb to fight, not only for his right to be recognized as a prisoner of war, but also for his people, for the men and women of no property. He knew they supported him. He heard them, their voices, when his body was cold and broken and he needed comfort.

From somewhere afar he would hear those voices: "We are with you, son, we are with you! Don't let them beat you down!" The voices drove the devils into retreat. The monster would fall back, angry and frightened, at the sound of those voices. At times Bobby really longed to hear those voices of the Irish people; he knew that if they shouted louder it would frighten the monster away forever, and all the men's suffering would be ended.

In the blocks they were always talking about *scéal*—the news from outside. There was nothing like a good bit of *scéal* to raise morale in the prison. After the 1978 Coalisland/Dungannon march, one of the lads smuggled in information about the number of people there, along with a small photograph. Bobby had been living through his nightmare, without a friendly face in sight. But when his turn came to see the picture, he looked at it and nearly cried. He felt happier than he had ever felt in his life—staring at it, never wanting to let it go. He was amazed and humbled.

He felt proud to be fighting for such people.

HERE HE WAS—on 2 January 1981— still surrounded by miles of tangled gruesome wire. There was barbed wire fencing everywhere, a jungle broken at intervals by looming guardposts in sinister camouflage, manned by armed British soldiers scanning the perimeters of the camp. It reminded Bobby of something he'd seen when he was a small boy, a film clip of a Nazi concentration camp in winter. He remembered his shock at the evil of the camp—a shock cushioned by the fact that he was only a little boy, sitting secure in his chair by the fire, thinking, *knowing*, that that sort of place was a horror of the past, and would never again be tolerated. Surely never in Ireland— and certainly never to be inflicted on him.

And now Bobby was a man, in this concentration camp, and OC of the prisoners here.

Christmas had come and gone, but these malefactors had still not moved on the prisoners' demands. He'd had his doubts about them. His doubts were beginning to harden.

And as they hardened, he began to understand what the consequences for himself might be.

He was working on a statement in the name of the prisoners. Among other things, he asked that people in authority in the Irish Church and the Free State should immediately bring public pressure on the British to act sensibly to ensure the speedy resolution of the protest and the defusion of the crisis, both in the H-Blocks and in Armagh jail, where their women comrades were.

He asked that the prisoners' relatives and supporters remain alert and vigilant, assuring them that the men would not continue indefinitely to accept the present situation. He reminded them that the British government were past masters at deceit and double dealing:

> We were aware of this when we accepted with some qualification their [December] document. We were dubious about the sincerity of their intentions, but were convinced that even they would not be stupid enough to waste another opportunity to settle this issue.

If the British remained intransigent, the prisoners would be forced to fall back upon their own resources. In that case their only guarantors would be the masses of people who had supported them on the recent hunger strike, supporters whom they would once again ask to take to the streets:

> If the British government clings to the forlorn hope that they can yet break the men and women of the H-Blocks and Armagh, they have but to look at their failures during the last four and a half years of our protest.

Bobby was aware, too, of the problems of the INLA prisoners on the protest. They were fighting almost a separate battle, trying to establish their political identity within the prison protest as a whole. The INLA men were a tiny minority—about eight per cent of the protesting prisoners. There were only two or three Irps on a wing. They had never been able to meet together as a group to discuss the outcome of the hunger strike. Their principal outside liaison man had been barred from the six counties.

They were as unhappy about the aftermath of the first hunger strike as Bobby himself. Besides that, they had been kept from contact with their fellow Irps in the prison. This lack of contact was symbolized by the isolation of John Nixon. Throughout the entire hunger strike John had been kept from contact with either the IRA strikers or the people outside. He was allowed very few visits.

Since December, the Irps had been talking about mounting their own hunger strike. Bobby had talked to Patsy O'Hara, the INLA OC in the prison. So far, Patsy had been able to keep the Irps' problem separate and secondary to the overall protest and effort.

Patsy, speaking for the INLA men, made a statement in a 7 January letter—Bobby was given a copy—saying that the success of the campaign for political status rested on maintaining a broad non-sectarian political strategy. Patsy also said:

> If the agreement were implemented it would be a great victory. [But meantime] our position remains that we stay on the blanket. We will wear no uniform and if the protest needs to be escalated, we are prepared to escalate it. Three of our . . . comrades have volunteered for this, aware of the possible consequences to their own lives. We will continue to play our full part in this protest.

The problem for Bobby was that the INLA prisoners were determined to mount a new hunger strike campaign—independently of the IRA prisoners if necessary.

On 9 January there was a new statement from Humphrey Atkins, and Bobby was furious. It was a clawback on the December statement, in which Atkins and the NIO had outlined the sequence of events to follow the ending of the hunger strike.

The sequence was crucially important.

Within a few days, according to Atkins' December statement, "clothes provided by their families" would be given to the prisoners. Only after that would the prison-issue civilian clothing be distributed. And of course the men would refuse to wear it. But they would be off the no-wash, no-slop-out protest— and, with their own clothes, off the blanket protest as well.

Now Atkins' 9 January statement was giving a different sequence of events. First, after moving to clean cells, the prisoners would be "given the new civilian-type clothing" and then, *afterwards*, "be allowed to send for their own leisure clothing." This stupid statement reversed the promised order of events. It was a squalid manoeuvre which would only bring them back to square one.

On Saturday, 10 January, Bobby asked for a meeting with the prison governor, Stanley Hilditch. Hilditch had signed a statement distributed to all the protesting prisoners that morning, in which the authorities said they hoped the prisoners involved in the next wing shift would not damage cell furniture or continue with the no-wash protest. The statement went on:

> This will be a first step only and, if [it is] accepted by those prisoners, our intention is to supply others with furnished cells, and also to offer to supply the new prison-issue civilian clothing to prisoners prepared to wear it.

This clearly contradicted the promise of the December statement, in line with Humphrey Atkins' clawback of 9 January. The prison governor was obviously worried about the repercussions. So he agreed to meet with Bobby at nine o'clock on Sunday morning, 11 January.

Then on Sunday afternoon the OCs of H-Blocks 4, 5 and 6 were brought to H-3 for a meeting with Bobby. Bobby was of course happy with the continuing recognition of the command structure that this meeting implied. But on the issue of prison change he and his fellow OCs were angry. The new plan ran directly contrary to their efforts to organize principled cooperation with the prison authorities. In a statement issued on Sunday night through Sinn Féin Press Centre in Belfast, the prisoners said:

> We view the proposed move with acute cycnicism, given the treacherous manner in which the British government has handled the protest, especially since the ending of the

hunger strike. However, as a gesture of our sincerity, and wishing to end the protest in a principled fashion, we have agreed that all the prisoners affected by the proposed move [the wing shift] will not soil their cells for such a period of time as will facilitate the process which has been outlined to us.

On Monday morning forty-eight blanketmen in H-5 were moved to clean cells, many of which were furnished. They began to slop out—meaning to carry their pos down to the washroom at the end of the wing. This had been agreed with the prison governor. They were willing to abandon the no-slop-out protest on a pilot basis, as a test of the regime's willingness to take the next step which, as far as the prisoners were concerned, meant letting the men send out to relatives for their own clothes. The OCs had agreed that the prisoners in H-3, where Bobby was block OC, would be involved in the next wing shift, to take place later in the week. They would abandon the no-wash, no-slop-out protest, and of course the soiling of cells which had been going on for the past three years.

The wing shifts worked well, and ten men from each of the two blocks (H-5 and H-3) were expecting to claim their own clothes on Friday 16 January. These twenty men would wash and shave and have their hair cut, and then collect their own clothes for the weekend. At a meeting with Hilditch on Thursday 15 January, Bobby had asked him to confirm this timetable. Hilditch asked him for a week's grace.

To show the prisoners' sincerity, Bobby acceded to Hilditch's request. So the twenty men waited until Friday 23 January to request the wash and shave.

By eleven that Friday morning, clothes had been delivered to the jail by the twenty prisoners' relatives, but the men were still waiting to be let out for their wash and shave. Then Bobby contacted the governor and told him that the prisoners wanted to end the no-wash and blanket protest and requested washing facilities and their own clothes.

Hilditch hesitated and said he would respond later.

Finally at two-thirty that afternoon, six and a half hours after the first request for washing facilities, the governor returned and said that the men could wash and shave. But he also said that they would not get their own clothes until there was strict comformity.

The prisoners, despite their growing skepticism, went ahead with their washing and shaving.

The weekend began technically at four o'clock on Friday, because after that hour, apart from orderlies, there was no prison work to be carried out. Conforming prisoners were normally allowed to wear their own clothes throughout the weekend, so none of the men would be breaking the standing prison rules. Once again, then, the men requested their own clothes. But throughout the weekend they were repeatedly refused. Not only that, but the twenty men were threatened with transfer to conforming blocks.

Bobby issued a statement on Saturday 24 January in which he attacked the new British position, and showed how it contradicted their December one:

> The intransigent position of the British is in violation of a whole spirit of cooperation which followed the ending of the hunger strike, and which included talks between myself and the prison governor, and the recognition of our command structure by the prison administration [in their] allowing H-Blocks OCs to meet and discuss the settlement.

The prisoners had felt morally bound, Bobby said,

> to explore all avenues that might have solved the H-Block crisis. [We have] made genuine attempts to resolve the prison protest but have been exasperated and frustrated by the British administration . . .

Bobby ended his statement with a ringing reminder of the prisoners' resolve:

> We have endured four and a half years of the blanket protest, and were forced to escalate it when all else failed. *We will not crawl now.*

He could hardly believe the stupidity of the British in exacerbating a crisis they could so easily have resolved. It made no sense.

The screws, who had been reasonably well-behaved for more than a month, were again shouting insults and obscenities at prisoners. During an ordinary wing shift in H-4, five men, forced into a mirror search, were physically assaulted by two of the screws.

It had seemed possible for them to end their protest. All the authorities had to do was to give them their own clothes. They could have distributed piles of prison-issue civilian clothes later. For the British—and this was obviously important to them—appearances would have been saved. But now the British authorities seemed to have made a decision to reinflict the whole barbaric regime.

For several weeks, despite his efforts to end the protest and despite moments of hopefulness, Bobby had been thinking very seriously about their next move.

On Tuesday, 27 January, Bobby circulated a letter to the OC of H-5 to all men on the protest. For Bobby himself it meant a crossing of the Rubicon:

Comrades,

As you are fully aware, following four and a half years of torturous protest and inhumanity, we prisoners here in the H-Blocks were, in the face of continual British intransigence, forced to embark upon a hunger strike on 27 October last . . . [in] a drastic attempt to force the British government to move. But unfortunately, as the circumstances unfolded, we had nothing to bind them to their commitments and what was mistaken by us as good will . . . was soon to prove British treachery.

In a further attempt to show our flexibility and good will to end this protest, we sought to bring the no-wash, no-slop-out protest to an end, while hoping to encourage the British government to avail themselves of that opportunity to end this crisis in a quiet and unembarrassing manner.

There were signs and indications of [their] unwillingness in the governor's statement of 10 and 14 January—

particularly in the terminology of a "step by step process to end the protest." In the spirit of this document we acted in a cautious and more than reasonable manner. Ninety-six men stopped fouling their cells and moved to clean and furnished cells . . .

Yet once again, Bobby went on, the prisoners' flexibility had been to no avail. The NIO, "wearing their true face of vindictiveness," clearly refused to permit the prisoners their own clothing—something promised by Atkins in his December speech. This refusal was also in contrast to the spirit of cooperation clearly displayed by the prison authorities at the end of the hunger strike. They'd made an effort to entice the men to end their protest, but then in their arrogant fashion they'd begun to demand strict conformity:

> They went so far as even to try and humiliate us, probably under the misconception that we were weak. But we are not weak and will conform to no one! Thus we have yet again been left in a situation where, having tried every means and avenue available to us, we have been unable to find an end to this continuous atrocity . . .
>
> At every corner we have been confronted and defied by a vindictively intransigent British government and once again we have been left with but one terrible weapon to fight back with—hunger strike. To fully understand what has happened here in the H-Blocks, comrades, we must recognize the importance of what is no longer a simple matter of a jail struggle or a protracted jail dispute.
>
> H-Block has for some time now, because of its vital importance to the British government policy of criminalization and the resistance [to it] . . . become a rallying point of the Irish struggle.

So vitally important was the symbol of the H-Blocks to everyone concerned that the British government would let men die in the blocks before even thinking of capitulating. This, Bobby said, called into question their commitment at the end of the first hunger strike.

To Bobby, being imprisoned was in itself bad enough! In a

favourite poem of his, Oscar Wilde's "Ballad of Reading Gaol,"
were the lines:

> This too I know—and wise it were
> If each could know the same—
> That every prison that men build
> Is built with bricks of shame,
> And bound with bars lest Christ should see
> How men their brothers maim.
> With bars they blur the gracious moon
> And blind the goodly sun;
> And they do well to hide their Hell,
> For in it things are done
> That Son of God nor son of Man
> Ever should look upon!

But the even worse spectre of the H-Blocks, of merciless
beatings, of filth and degradation, of torture piled on torture,
had come to symbolize and represent the Irish people suffering under British repression. It was for them, Bobby reflected,
that the prisoners had been locked away naked in Long Kesh,
had been beaten and degraded and tortured—for the right of
Irish men and Irish women to a country of their own, where
they could live with dignity.

Bobby was aware that the prisoners could not do it alone,
but he knew that what happened in the prison was crucially
important. There were those who had conformed. Some were
in terrible health, or had gone mad, or had problems at home,
and had conformed with the blessing of the prisoners and their
own prison command. The purpose of the protest, however,
was to weigh the scales in favour of the cause of the people
of Ireland. In their attempt to criminalize the protesters, the
British had been attempting to criminalize the Irish people.

> For our part we must realize that another hunger strike,
> should it collapse, [would] present the movement. . . with
> disastrous consequences. Therefore [a second] hunger
> strike cannot and will not end in defeat because . . . as
> I have said before, when the balance of conformity
> outweighs that of resistance, then criminalization is in-
> deed winning.

It is also worth remembering that when the spirit of a freedom fighter is crushed and tamed, then the spirit of the risen people, whom he represents, becomes demoralized. Therefore, comrades, that spirit must fight back and fight back it will . . . It has resisted through four and a half years of torture and eleven years of war.

He had presented the prisoners with a hunger strike as an urgent consideration. He had given his reasons for it. Now he would become more specific. Bobby was going to put more than a theory on the line:

So, comrades, once again under the duress of British barbarity and in the ugly face of further British intransigence, we are forced to embark upon a hunger strike in the coming weeks. The announcement of this should be made public, along with the date, on Friday 30 January. The number of hunger strikers shall be small, myself and three others, among them of course . . . a representative of the IRSP . . .

I accept now that men will sacrifice their lives on this hunger strike. But you all must cast aside everything for total unity within these blocks—unity and steadfastness. You should, when a comrade dies, remain steadfast. Because, comrades, at the end of the day men will die and the responsibility of ending this protest for once and for all will not lie with dead comrades, but with you. Because only your unflinching resistance and steadfastness will force an end to this protest.

He was asking, he realized, that they support him personally:

Therefore, stand together and give your fullest support to the OC of these blocks. And in one way or another, comrades, victory will be ours, because we have the will to win. And we will win!

Fir pluid Abú—Marcella
OC Blocanna
27.1.81

Bobby's appeal for unity was not just rhetorical. The prisoners had been sharply split after the ending of the first hunger strike. It was the old British trick: to isolate and divide people struggling for their freedom. Now, Bobby hoped, they would unite behind him, so that the Brits could see once and for all that they could not criminalize the men, rob them of their identity, depoliticize them, and churn them out as institutionalized, law-abiding robots. The British must never be allowed to label the Irish struggle as criminal.

Even after all the torture and barbarity, Bobby was amazed at British logic. Never in eight centuries had they succeeded in breaking the spirit of a single man who refused to be broken. They had not dispirited, demoralized or conquered the Irish people, nor would they ever.

Bobby had decided, therefore, that he would lead a hunger strike; that he would die, if necessary. He would die not just to try to end the barbarity of the H-Blocks, or to help the men gain their rightful recognition as political prisoners. The reason he would die was that if they continued to suffer this brutal oppression, what would be lost in the fight against criminalization would be lost for the Republican movement, and for the wretched oppressed people he loved. How could eight hundred years of struggle be branded as criminal? He would take his stand on the right of the Irish people to sovereign independence, and the right of any Irish man or Irish woman to assert that right in arms, as Padraig Pearse had written in 1916.

BOBBY HAD OFTEN THOUGHT of the lark as his symbol of freedom. To what sort of freedom he was flying, he couldn't be certain. But one way or another he'd be free in the end.

During the summer months the finches were abundant around the prison, and the lark provided both a symphony of sound and the continual reminder of the possibilities of a life that was, above all, free. Whenever he was able, Bobby would stand watching the birds and listening to the song of the lark, trying to find out where it was in the immense blue ocean of sky. He longed for the freedom of the lark.

When the screws blocked up the cell windows, cutting off even this limited view of the world outside—torturing men already tortured—they were blocking out nature, the very essence of life. He recognized that this was symbolic: that the torturers had begun long ago, and were still trying, to block up the windows of their minds.

But even with the windows closed he could sometimes hear the lark, whose beautiful song would tear at his heart and make him think of his childhood. It was his grandfather who told him once that to imprison a lark was the cruellest of crimes, because the lark was one of the great symbols of happiness and freedom. His grandfather had known a man who imprisoned a lark in a small cage. The lark, no longer happy, stopped singing. The man who had committed this atrocity—that was his grandfather's word for it—demanded that the lark sing. The lark refused to sing and the man became violently angry. He tried to force it to sing, but it would not. So the man covered the cage with a black cloth, taking the sunlight away from the lark. He refused to feed it and left it to rot in the dirt in its cage. Deprived of freedom, deprived even of sunlight, the bird died.

The lark died underlining its refusal to conform.

Bobby remembered the Psalm about the exiles hanging their harps on willow trees, and their captors asking them for a song: "Sing us a song of Sion!" How could they sing the song of the Lord, the song of freedom, in this alien place? A political prisoner was very like the caged lark. He hadn't fought for his freedom in captivity only; he'd fought on the outside, too. He would not sing or change his tune to suit the whims of his jailers. Stripped of his clothes and locked in a dirty, empty cell, beaten and tortured, he might actually have been put to death like the lark. But he was alive; he had the unquenchable spirit of freedom. And like the caged lark, he could soar with longing.

These people who held the prisoners captive were like the seagull, who ruled the little twenty-yard patch Bobby could see from his window. The seagull had to have it all. Its appetite seemed insatiable; it would go to any lengths to gorge itself. Bobby wondered why the blue starlings were always squabbling among themselves and didn't direct their attention towards this predator instead. He found it very difficult to grasp the mentality of the screws—so savage, always vindictive, always full of hate. Most people outside never understood this. They liked to

115

imagine a kind of balance, with brutish screws matched against the "gunmen" they held captive. Bobby wished people outside could see the faces of his companions at Mass, could see the effect the black monsters had on them.

They were young men, his fellow prisoners; but they had old mens' faces, with sunken hollow cheeks and eyesockets, with glazed or piercing eyes. Bobby sometimes wondered whether the telltale signs of the rigours of torture would ever leave their faces, or ever be erased from their minds. He could see—knowing in himself a hatred so intense that it frightened him—the hatred on the faces of his comrades at Mass, the hatred in their eyes. One day these young men would be fathers and their bitterness would be passed on to their children.

This was the harvest Britain had sown in Ireland. Who among the so-called humanitarians outside the prison could put a name to the treatment given Irishmen in this place, where human beings were forced by brutal treatment and extreme torture to embark on a dirt strike—to highlight the inhumanity, the barbarity, the humiliation, hatred, the nightmare suffering inflicted on these prisoners? With their bodies naked and unwashed and racked with pain, squatting amid piles of putrefying food—with the white, wriggling, crawling maggots squirming in their thousands in these dens of disease—and forced to defecate on the ground where their excrement would lie and the smell mingle with the sickening evil stench of urine and waste and decay?

Let the humanitarians who had kept their silence on the H-Blocks, but who pretended to understand what had happened at Belsen and Auschwitz and Buchenwald: let the silent humanitarians find a name to put on this nightmare.

ON THE EVENING of Tuesday 27 January—the day Bobby sent his letter around—the ninety-six prisoners who had been involved in the wing shifts in H-3 and H-5, angered by the authorities' refusal to give the twenty men on the pilot scheme their own clothes, began smashing up the furniture and the windows in the clean cells.

The response of the screws was swift and brutal. There were

116

sudden wing shifts, during which more than eighty prisoners in all were assaulted, some of them severely. The prisoners were moved to unfurnished cells, the men in H-3 and H-5 to cells in wings which had only recently been vacated by blanketmen still on the no-wash protest, so that walls of the cells they were moved into were covered in excreta. On the floors were pools of water, food waste and urine. The men were forced to remain in these cells throughout the night, without water, blankets or mattresses, and without any toilet facilities.

But the smashing up of the furniture had given the men a chance to assert again their independence of this machine, their longing to be free of it. They had found new inspiration in the group effort, taking the battle back to this vicious regime in the only way available to them.

Bobby managed one great thing before embarking on his hunger strike—to get the worst sufferings of his fellow prisoners ended. On 2 March, the day after Bobby began refusing food, the other men would officially end their no-wash, no-slop-out protest: he and the other men going forward on hunger strike would represent the prison protest as a whole. The men would continue on the blanket protest, but the dirt protest would be formally at an end.

Bobby had been careful in preparing and vetting the statement announcing the beginning of the new hunger strike:

> We, the Republican POWs in the H-Blocks of Long Kesh, and our comrades in Armagh prison, are entitled to and hereby demand political status, and we reject today as we have consistently rejected every day since September 14, 1976, when the blanket protest began, the British government's attempted criminalization of ourselves and our struggle.

The British government, the statement went on, had set 1 March 1976, as the key date in their criminalization policy. Five years later, the prisoners were still able to declare that through their suffering and resistance this policy had failed.

> If a British government experienced such a long and persistent resistance to a domestic policy in England, then

117

that policy would almost certainly be changed. But not so in Ireland, where its traditional racist attitude blinds its judgment to reason and persuasion.

Only the loud voice of the Irish people and world opinion can bring them to their senses; and only a hunger-strike, where lives are laid down as proof of the strength of our political convictions, can rally such opinion and present the British with the problem that, far from criminalizing the cause of Ireland, their intransigence is actually bringing popular attention to that cause.

The silent humanitarians, Bobby knew, liked to make distinctions between the five demands, some of which they considered reasonable, and the demand for political status, which they thought unreasonable. Bobby saw to it that the announcement of the hunger strike laid the issue directly on the line. He and the other men were there not as criminals, but as fighters for the cause of Ireland:

> We have asserted that we are political prisoners and everything about our country, our arrests, interrogation, trials and prison conditions, shows that we are politically motivated and not motivated by selfish reasons or for selfish ends. As further demonstration of our selflessness and the justness of our cause, a number of our comrades, beginning today with Bobby Sands, will hunger-strike to the death unless the British government abandons its criminalization policy and meets our demand for political status.

THE NIGHT BEFORE he went on hunger strike, Bobby got the statutory weekly piece of fruit. Symbolically enough it was an orange. Ironically it was a bitter one.

The die was cast . . . On Sunday morning, 1 March, Bobby refused breakfast.

At every meal the food was left inside the door; there were much larger portions than usual, piled up on the plate. After Mass that morning, he wrote at the beginning of his hunger-strike diary: "I am standing on the threshhold of another trembling world. May God have mercy on my soul . . ."

118

He was proud. He was also sad, knowing the heartbreak he was causing his mother. The family would be hardest hit: his mother, his little son Gerard, his sisters Marcella and Bernadette, his brother Seán, and his father.

Bobby's meditations, during those first days of his fast, often focused on the people he represented, on his friends in the movement and the women suffering in Armagh jail. He thought of the Irish people, the risen people of the present—and of the past.

His twenty-seventh birthday came on 9 March, a Sunday. He remembered James Connolly that day; and Liam Mellowes, who fought in the War of Independence and was shot afterwards by order of the Cosgrave government, the first government of the Free State. "Men will get into positions," Mellowes had said, "Men will hold power, and men who get into positions and hold power will desire to remain undisturbed, and will not be moved; nor will they take a step that will mean removal in case of failure."

But Bobby was not all alone, dealing with the British government and the men of power. He had the risen people of Ireland behind him, their voices echoing his father's voice: "Take heart, son. Take heart." He had the support of the Republican movement. All through his years in this prison he'd been thinking of how the British had taken the life of Thomas Ashe, the lives of Terence MacSwiney, Michael Gaughan, Frank Stagg and Hugh Coney. Now it was more than likely that he'd join them in the sacrifice of his own life.

Dear God, he thought, they have taken so many! Another one means nothing to them.

But he had hope nonetheless. He knew that he must have hope and never lose heart. His hope, like the hope of those dead heroes, was centered on the prospect of ultimate victory for the people of Ireland. He could not allow himself to be crushed and tamed, because then the spirit of the risen people would be crushed. He thought of the parasites, the political magpies and opportunists, who slept on the people's wounds, on their sweat and their toil. Equality and fraternity among the Irish people would never be achieved while these parasites ruled the nation. Only the great mass of the people could ensure the achievement of a socialist Republic, and then only by hard work and sacrifice. All Bobby could do, as he lay there with his hunger, was to fight the battle against his old friend depression. He had only his mind to fight with. But while his mind remained free, victory was assured.

On 11 March, the National H-Blocks committee raised the prison issue with the UN Commission on Human Rights at Geneva. Bobby appreciated this effort, but he couldn't place much hope in it. But he did take great encouragement when on 15 March, the great soldier from Bellaghy, Francis Hughes, joined the hunger strike.

On 14 March Bobby was moved to a cell on his own. This was standard procedure with the British, wasn't it, to isolate men as far as possible from their comrades? He had asked to remain in the blocks, to die among his fellow prisoners. Perhaps they would let him, perhaps not.

By 18 March Bobby had lost sixteen pounds. The screws were harassing him in different ways. On 23 March, the day after Raymond McCreesh and Patsy O'Hara joined the hunger strike, Bobby was moved from H-3 to the prison hospital. It was an obvious effort to isolate him.

Before he left he saw that the screws, who were staging a go-slow protest, were making life as difficult as they could for the men. Since the prisoners had come off their no-wash protest, the screws were complaining of having to do more work for less money. They were losing the bonuses they'd been paid for working in the dirty conditions, so they began to create difficulties. Some men had to wait three or four days before being allowed to the end of the wing to wash their hands and faces. It was as though the screws were trying to force them back on the no-wash protest. One advantage, though, of the screws' work-to-rule was that most of them had stopped carrying out the mirror search, complaining that they were not getting paid well enough, or that they needed more warders to do this nasty chore. Bobby knew that the men wouldn't miss the mirror search.

The prison hospital contained eleven cells, six on one side of a polished corridor and five on the other. The cell doors were wooden and the place was very clean. Bobby could read newspapers; he had a radio and was able to watch television. He was comfortable enough, apart from the fact that he had nothing to eat. His morale was high. He was proud when he heard he'd been nominated as nationalist candidate for the Fermanagh/South Tyrone seat at Westminster vacated by the death of Frank Maguire.

The day he was nominated he saw Jim Gibney of Sinn Féin. Jim had come with Bobby's mother and his sister Marcella. Bobby was sitting on top of the bed in a coloured dressing gown, with his hair cut short and his face clean-shaven. Jim had evidently been expecting to see someone a bit more desperate looking. They discussed the election. Jim was very good at assessing the feelings of the people, especially country people, and seemed confident that Bobby might be elected. Jim talked about the people coming out in support. Bobby told him that he wasn't expecting massive support just yet, not until his condition worsened. He wanted to show Jim, and thus get word out to the movement, that he was on top of the situation—that he had heart for the fight.

The next day was Tuesday 31 March. Since he'd gone on hunger strike a month earlier—weighing just under ten stone—Bobby had lost twenty-three pounds. He was feeling weak. But he was able to see Owen Carron that day—his newly appointed election agent. Owen helped Bobby prepare his election statement:

> There is but a single issue at stake, the right of human dignity for Irish men and women who are imprisoned for taking part in this period of the historic struggle for Irish independence.

It was important to point out that they were not setting themselves above ordinary prisoners when they refused the criminal identification:

> We are not elitists, we do not seek a different status to that afforded the ordinary prisoner . . .
>
> Our protest in this hunger strike is to secure from the British government an end to its policy labelling us as criminals. This can be done by them conceding to us the

121

same status that several hundred men in the cages of Long Kesh and the women in Armagh prison have.

People would respond to his campaign, Bobby knew, on the humanitarian principle: by voting for him they could help save his life. But the principle behind the humanitarian issue in the election was the rejection of Britain's right to rule in Ireland. There were humanitarians who had been heard from. There were also the silent humanitarians, who thought that the hunger strike was being manipulated from outside the prison. What they didn't understand was that there was a war on.

As OC—he had relinquished that now to Brendan (Bic) McFarlane—Bobby felt that he had been exercising leadership on behalf of the people outside, who would be freed one day from repression and degradation, and this partly because of the sacrifice he was making. It was his job to lead the men in the prison. It was the responsibility of the Republican movement outside to supply him with whatever support he might need to keep up his end of the fight. The leadership of the movement outside had paid insufficient attention in the past to the plight of the prisoners—and that included the people in the present leadership. But now they were there, providing logistical as well as propaganda support. And there were the marvellous people in the H-Blocks/Armagh committee. Leaders in both the movement and the committee had been concerned that they might not be able to raise the support needed for a second hunger strike. But Bobby knew it was coming.

People were saying that Bobby was under orders from Gerry Adams and others in the leadership outside. But they'd never ordered him to go on hunger strike. In fact, they'd been completely and outspokenly against it. It was Bobby's own decision; it was the prisoners' own decision. They couldn't endure the regime—the beatings and degradation and torture—any longer. And the only way that Bobby and the others could see to break it was to put their lives on the line.

What most people failed to understand was that the desire for freedom, when it became internalized, was not dependent on orders from outside, on orders from anywhere. It was the men and women in the prisons who were giving the lead now, were in fact in the forefront of the struggle, not the men and women outside. Bobby had long since accepted the likelihood that men would sacrifice their lives on this hunger strike. People wanted to blame him for it—many people, probably. But he had tried everything possible to avert it, short of surrender. The price of freedom was a terrible price, and of all the prisoners he would be the first to pay it.

OVER THE MONTHS AND YEARS the H-Blocks had become a battlefield on which the Irish Republican spirit of resistance had fought a savage struggle against a barbarian British prison regime. It had taken a long time for the lid of silence on the H-Blocks to lift even a little. They had been on the blanket protest nearly two years when the new Archbishop of Armagh, Tomás Ó Fiaich, spoke out after a visit to the prison in his "sewer pipes of Calcutta" statement. It was just after the beginning of the no-wash protest. Since then the situation had worsened. Their cells had turned into disease-infested tombs. The screws kept up with their incessant torture, hosing the men down, spraying them with disinfectant, ransacking the filthy cells, forcibly bathing and torturing the men to the brink of insanity.

The worst of it had been the punishment block.

One day Bobby was dragged off , for no reason at all that he could fathom. There had been no verbal abuse either way. The screws hadn't even been threatening him. But before he knew what was happening they had burst into his cell and dragged him by the hair and down the wing. Then they trailed him out into bitterly cold weather, trailed him on his back, his head bouncing, across a stretch of concrete rubble to the gate of the punishment block. There they shouted to the screw in charge to open the gate.

Bobby lay at their feet, dazed, out of breath, his heart pounding. His body felt as if it were on fire. His skin was shredded where it had been cut by the hard rubble. His face was warm and wet from blood spurting from a gash in his head. He lay absolutely still, hoping they'd think he was unconscious. Then he heard a screw jangling keys. Their gloved hands gripped his arms and feet, lifting his body off the ground and swinging him backwards in the same movement. They hurled the full weight of his body forward, smashing his head against the corrugated iron along the gate, and then dropped him to the ground. It was like the sky falling in on him. They picked him up and dropped him again. Stars exploded in front of his eyes before he sank into black unconsciousness.

When he came to he was lying on the floor of a cell in the punishment block. Bobby opened his eyes. The bright light spiralling down from the ceiling blinded him. He was afraid to move. The pain in his head and body was crippling. He felt the taste of blood on his swollen lips, as he lay on the ground in a trance.

Where was he? What had happened since? It was terribly cold on the concrete floor. He knew he'd have to get up; otherwise— he had a chest problem—he could easily get pneumonia.

He rose slowly to his knees. The walls came hurtling towards him. After a long time he tried again to stand up. He made it as far as his knees. His skin was burning; some of the raw flesh from the scrapes and cuts he had suffered clung to the cold floor.

When he made it to his feet he nearly fell again. Using the wall to lean on, staggering towards the concrete block that served as a stool, he slumped down on it. He was so distracted by shock that he didn't know what to do. He couldn't think. He felt as if he were actually dying. The slightest movement and he would shudder and gasp in an agony of pain.

The cell door opened and a white-coated orderly stepped in—a glorified screw, pretending to be a doctor. He started fiddling about Bobby's body, poking and probing, imitating a doctor's movements, trying to impress the screws standing behind him at the entrance to the cell. Then he left off his mock doctoring and arrogantly announced that if Bobby wanted medical treatment he would first have to bathe.

Bobby stared in disbelief at the creature, who repeated what he'd said, this time in a threatening voice. He knew that Bobby was hurt and in need of immediate treatment; but he was holding him to ransom. If Bobby didn't accept the bath he wouldn't get the treatment. Bobby was so sore he could hardly move.

124

But he had no intention of voluntarily taking a bath. He'd die before he'd give in.

The screw spoke a third time. Bobby was going to have to take that bath, he said.

"Drop dead!" said Bobby.

Then the screws moved in and lifted his body like a bundle of rags. They carried him out to a tub already filled with water, dropping him into it like a bar of soap. The water was icy cold. And the shock, as it engulfed his tattered body, almost stopped his breath. The strong disinfectant in the freezing water stung Bobby's raw and naked flesh.

He tried to get up, a brave attempt, but his body was no use to him, and the screws held him down while one of them attacked his battered back with a heavy scrubbing brush. The pain was shattering. He struggled to get free. The more he fought the harder they held him. His eyes flooded with tears. He wanted to scream but had no breath for it.

They persisted in scrubbing every part of his body, throwing fresh buckets of ice-cold water and stinging disinfectant over him. One sadist grabbed his testicles and, using the hand brush, scrubbed away maddeningly at his private parts, until finally Bobby passed out.

He vaguely remembered being lifted out of the water and hauled to the prison hospital in a large fawn-coloured blanket. A doctor examined him and patched him up, putting seven stitches in his head. Then they returned him to the punishment cell. He sat there shivering, wrapped in a single filthy blanket reeking of stale smoke and urine.

Left alone for a time, Bobby regained some of his composure. But he was still disoriented. He couldn't summon help. There was no one to do anything for him. He was alone, completely vulnerable, entirely at their mercy. The worst thing now was the freezing, shrivelling cold, and the fact that he couldn't get up to walk and exercise and get warm.

Later in the day, the screws returned and dragged him out of the cell again to stand before a prison governor, for a trial in one of their farcical courts. He was naked, embarrassed, humiliated, his head bursting with pain from his beatings. They charged him with "disobeying an order," meaning that he'd refused to cooperate with the screw in the white coat who wanted to probe and search his anus. Yes, he had refused absolutely to allow this. The whole object had been to degrade and humiliate him. Then he was charged with assaulting the screws who had brutalized and nearly murdered him that morning, and further charged with self-inflicted wounds. He was found guilty in this sham court, and sentenced to three days in the punishment block, where he would be fed on what was euphemistically called the No. 1 diet, a starvation diet of cold tea and stale bread, with watery soup once a day. He also lost one month's remission. Then they let him know, in no uncertain terms, that if he dared make a formal complaint he would be charged with making false allegations against prison officers.

As they dragged him back to the punishment cell he had to keep himself from vomiting.

The bare cell was freezing cold and it was lonely. He'd been there before and knew how terribly isolated it was. A board on the concrete floor served as a bed, a concrete slab as a table and a concrete block as a stool. There was a Bible, a po and a water container. During his three days there, he was beaten up twice more, but not as severely as the first time. When the filth in the po needed emptying, they tried to hold him to ransom again, telling him he'd have to put on prison clothes to empty it. He refused. So it spilled over onto the cell floor and the contents lay there.

He became weaker with the starvation diet, and on the third day he collapsed on the cold stone floor. He lay there for a long time, perhaps hours, before he came to.

Back in the block after that ordeal, he felt physically and mentally shattered. Even the screws were shocked at his deathly appearance. His recollection of the starvation, the beatings, the forced baths, the isolation, the terrrible cold, left him with feelings of hatred and thoughts of revenge.

Then, only two weeks later, he began a *fifteen-day* stretch in the punishment block—the same hideous experience, but five times as long. During those two weeks he lived like a maddened animal, eating with his hands, except during alternate three-day periods, when they gave him no food at all and let him starve. He kept plodding through the filth, exercising to keep warm. He took the beatings. He prayed. He cried in his sleep. He kept fighting the urge to give in to them, to surrender. Instead he endured and became more determined than ever.

AND HERE HE WAS, fighting the British system with his hunger strike, while other people out there fought a campaign to get him elected to the British parliament. The situation was richly ironic.

Bobby hoped and prayed that the result of the Fermanagh/South Tyrone election would reflect the Republican and nationalist majority in that part of the country. Should he win, and should he somehow be freed, he would proudly represent the people of Fermanagh/South Tyrone: not in the parliament of the oppressor, but by doing all he could to remove that parliament from their lives. Should he live, even if he remained in prison, he could be their spokesman in the parliament of the world, as he had been spokesman for the protesting prisoners in the H-Blocks of Long Kesh.

The people of the world would be watching to see what happened on polling day. He hoped that at least he might get a good vote—not for his own sake but for the sake of the people who had given him this new political forum.

He had his doubts. There was so much against his actually winning the election. He saw the newspapers. The cards were stacked against him. Not only the unionists, but the silent humanitarians in the SDLP and many among the Catholic clergy were against his candidacy. People canvassing for him were told—and there was a lot of truth in it—that votes for him amounted to votes for the IRA. Still, there were larger issues at stake, ultimately the issue of British rule in Ireland. Bobby hoped that people who might reject the IRA yet who hated British rule would vote for him as their standard bearer.

Then on Thursday, 9 April, came the astonishing news. More than thirty thousand people had voted for him. He had won political status from voters in Northern Ireland! He had actually won the seat. He was now Bobby Sands, MP. Were he not so weak, he could really have enjoyed the irony of this: The Honourable Bobby Sands, MP! By opening their hearts to him and the cause he represented, by going in their tens of thousands to the ballot box, the people had given him a vote of support that brought tears to his eyes.

Happy as Bobby was about the victory, he could not take it as a good omen. He realized that it was highly unlikely that it would save his life. The day the result was announced he told Owen Carron that in his position he couldn't afford to be optimistic. The British would need their pound of flesh. Almost certainly he would have to die.

It was necessary that one man die for the risen people. And he was that man.

He had dropped nearly two stone—twenty-seven pounds— in weight. There were pains in his eyes, headaches, and dizzy spells; he was conscious of a slurring in his speech and he was having difficulty keeping water down.

On 10 April, Francis Hughes, who after four weeks on hunger strike was having serious problems with his bad left leg, was moved to the prison hospital. Bobby, weak as he was, was happy to see him. Francis was a big man. But he had lost a lot of weight in the prison and had begun his hunger strike at only about 157 pounds. He was now down to 144.

Because of the election Bobby was receiving floods of telegrams and messages from all over the world. But now there was an effort being made, by those Bobby smilingly thought of as his fellow MPs, to unseat him from their parliament. This tawdry effort was worth a statement:

> No matter what moves are made, Ireland and the rest of the world will continue to recognize the democratic decision of the people—even if the British parliament cannot abide by the very tenets which it professes to uphold.

> A decision to unseat me will have grave implications for the British people and their democratic process and will represent a further whittling away of civil liberties spilling over from the war in Ireland.

> It is not Republican hunger striker Bobby Sands, MP, that

is the problem, but it is Britain's failed policy of attempting to brand Irish political prisoners as criminals which has your government scurrying for legal procedures to unseat a dying man—which, if you allow it, will shame you in the eyes of the world.

Enough MPs agreed with him that the international repercussions of a move to expel him would be enormous. Even unionist MPs from Northern Ireland were not pressing the issue. The Tories knew that they were not going to get all-party agreement for such a move, so in the end they decided not to push for his expulsion. It was a significant if small victory.

But Bobby was moving nearer and nearer to the abyss, and in the circumstances he couldn't see any value for him in this victory. What did give him encouragement was meeting Raymond McCreesh and Patsy O'Hara, when they were moved into the hospital. Four comrades together, they could stengthen one another for the final fight that seemed increasingly inevitable.

Bobby was bedridden now. He knew that the doctors were trying to talk his mother and Marcella into taking him off his fast, telling them in great detail about the effects of the hunger strike on the body, telling them that his life was daily more and more in jeopardy.

He could still speak well enough. He warned Marcella and his mother about the doctors. He knew they would try to get at him through his family. He told his mother and sister that if he were to lapse into a coma he didn't want them to try to save his life. And sure, he agreed with them that the election victory had been a great boost to the cause, and that he was grateful for it. But he wanted them to know that he didn't feel it would be enough to move Mrs. Thatcher.

It was painful for him to see his mother sitting here, her heart breaking, as it was difficult to convey his own sense of realism to her. As a mother she had to hold tight to her hopes.

Bobby was slipping badly now. He was in bed all the time. They'd put a sheepskin rug under him to keep his bones from piercing his skin. To ease his bedsores they gave him an oil rubdown several times a day. He blacked out occasionally and had spells of confusion. His sight and his hearing were going. He was down to 103 pounds.

On Easter Monday, 20 April, there was a horrific killing of two Derry boys, Jimmy Browne and Garry English, by British soldiers who rammed a landrover into a crowd of demonstrators at a speed of some sixty miles an hour. The RUC was calling it a traffic accident.

That same day three Irish members of the European parliament came into the prison to talk to Bobby—Neil Blaney, Síle de Valera and Dr. John O'Connell. They were also representatives in Dáil Éireann. They stayed for nearly an hour and told him that they would try to intervene directly with Margaret Thatcher.

Bobby was not surprised when he heard news of her reply shortly afterwards: "It is not my habit or custom to meet MPs from a foreign country about a citizen of the United Kingdom, resident in the United Kingdom." It was as unfeeling and arrogant a response as she could have made. Bobby was cheered when told what O'Connell had said about him: "He was very determined . . . I saw in this man more determination than I have ever seen in any person before."

On Saturday 25 April three Euro commissioners (from the European Commission on Human Rights) were trotted into the prison. Bobby had agreed to talk to them, on condition that Bic McFarlane, the prisoners' OC, and Gerry Adams and Danny Morrison of Sinn Féin be present. The authorities refused, and so Bobby declined to see the commissioners. In his severely weakened condition, he didn't want to negotiate with strangers. Nor did he want to be a party to a conversation which would raise hopes while offering little or no prospect of securing the five demands. The ECHR had had its chances—in 1978, 1979 and 1980—to do something about the treatment of the men in Long Kesh. Instead, in June 1980, they had declared that the "almost sub-human" degradation of the protesting prisoners was "self-inflicted," and "designed to create maximum sympathy . . . for their political aims."

In August 1978 the prisoners had appealed to the ECHR on the basis of their *physical mistreatment* in the prison, a horrifying reality. But the commissioners—who had never bothered to interview any of the four appealing prisoners—had added to their negative verdict a gratuitous *political judgment*: "The Commission must observe that the applicants are seeking to achieve a status of political prisoner to which they are not entitled under international law or the European Convention." With this insulting opinion, uncalled for in terms of the appeal case, and a judgment *outside the Commission's competence* to render, the ECHR had made great propaganda for the British.

The Commission's long-delayed verdict on the 1978 appeal had been worse than useless to the prisoners. Besides, their bureaucratic wheels ground slowly. Bobby didn't have much time left. Why should he expect them to suddenly help him now? The prospect of an intervention by the ECHR commissioners was only being used by the British to take pressure off themselves. If they wanted a settlement, why had they denied him the presence of McFarlane and Adams and Morrison, his nominees?

The commissioners' dramatic arrival meant that attention was diverted from the issues for which Bobby was starving to death, and focused on theatrics.

Bobby had other reasons to be wary. Two days earlier the British had refused permission to Ramsey Clarke, former United States Attorney General, and the American civil rights advocate Father Daniel Berrigan SJ, to visit him. If the British thought they could determine who could and could not see him, Bobby could at least exercise his veto on the people they were inviting in.

On Saturday evening, he lapsed into a sleep, a kind of coma. They told him afterwards that at eight that night he had nearly died. He was lying on a water bed now. Through Sunday and most of Monday he suffered almost continuous nausea. On Monday evening he sank into unconsciousness, but managed to pull out of it.

He'd been receiving Holy Communion every morning during the past week. On Monday he received the last sacraments.

On Tuesday 28 April he saw the Papal envoy, Father John Magee. Father Magee spent an hour with him and indicated he was going to see Humphrey Atkins the next day to try to get something moving. Bobby appreciated this visit. He didn't feel that Father Magee was trying to pressure him at all. The priest gave him a gold crucifix from the Pope. On Wednesday, Father Magee saw Atkins. Nothing came of it, of course. But the priest did see the other three men there in the hospital, and gave each of them a papal crucifix.

That same day Jim Gibney came in, while Bobby's father and mother were there with Marcella. Bobby was wearing the gold crucifix. His mother seemed proud that the Pope had honoured him with the gift. Bobby was blind now and couldn't see any of them, but he recognized Jim's voice and stretched out his hand to welcome him. Jim asked him how he felt. Bobby said that he was very weak, that he was blind, but that Jim should tell the lads to keep their chins up and not be down-hearted. He'd see the thing through.

On 1 May Bobby received a visit from Don Concannon, who had been NIO minister in charge of prisons for several years, and had supervised the building of the H-Blocks and the implementation of the criminalization policy. Bobby felt disgust— why had such a man been admitted to his hospital cell? Had he been asked whether he'd see Concannon he'd have flatly refused.

And what was Concannon there to say? That Michael Foot and the British Labour party leadership supported Thatcher's policy! "My struggle," Bobby told Concannon, "is a *political struggle*." Concannon had to admit this. But he said he couldn't support the prisoners' five demands, because to support them would mean *political status*. Concannon had contradicted himself, and, pighead though he was, he knew it.

That same day Bobby saw Owen Carron and told him about Concannon's visit. Owen, who was Bobby's constituency agent now, was allowed only fifteen minutes. He'd been kept away from the prison during the diversions of the past several days.

Bobby was in tremendous pain now. While he was talking he had to sit up. He must have looked like a skeleton, his chest all folded in on him, his teeth and gums protruding, one eye swollen shut, the other eye unseeing. He told Owen how Concannon had contradicted himself on the issue of political status. Haughey—Bobby wondered whether there was any news from Charlie Haughey. Had he spoken up yet? Owen said he hadn't. He urged Owen to try to get Haughey to speak out in support of the five demands.

Bobby asked Owen to do what he could to comfort his mother, and to pass the word along that the people outside should keep their hearts up, that they should accept his death. The other boys were sound; the hunger strike would go on without him. Francis Hughes wouldn't have an election victory to work with. But the support that had brought the people out into the streets was there, and Bobby felt sure it was growing. When Owen was ready to go, Bobby tried to lift his hand and wave. He told Owen to tell everyone that he'd see them somewhere, sometime.

Two days later—he'd had five heart attacks in the course of his hunger strike—he went into a terminal coma.

On Tuesday 5 May, at 1:15 in the morning, Bobby Sands died in the prison hospital at Long Kesh.

ON THURSDAY 7 MAY 1981, more than ninety thousand people attended his funeral in West Belfast. The piper played:

> The Minstrel fell! but the foeman's chain
> Could not bring his proud soul under;
> The harp he lov'd ne'er spoke again,
> For he tore its chords asunder;
> And said, "No chains shall sully thee,
> Thou soul of love and bravery!
> Thy songs were made for the pure and free,
> They shall never sound in slavery."

There were messages of condolence in the 9 May issue of the *Republican News* from Raymond McCreesh and Patsy O'Hara; and one from Francis Hughes, which read:

SANDS: To the family, friends and comrades of my gallant comrade Vol. Bobby Sands, *Óglaigh na Éireann* [Irish Republican Volunteers] who died on the sixty-sixth day of his hunger strike for political status, I extend my most deep sympathy. *Thug sé a shaol go mbeimid saor.* [He gave his life that we might be free.] From his comrade Francis Hughes, prison hospital, the H-Blocks, Long Kesh.

The last message of all in that issue of the paper was from the women in Armagh Prison, who quoted Terence MacSwiney:

> SANDS: The Irish Republican Prisoners of War in Armagh jail express their deepest sympathy to the family of our comrade Bobby Sands. "It is not they who can inflict the most but those who can endure the most who will ultimately triumph."

In Poland, Lech Walesa said that Bobby Sands was "a great man who sacrificed his life for his struggle."

Father Daniel Berrigan, the Jesuit priest poet and civil rights activist who had come to Ireland to help save Bobby's life, said that in dying Bobby had won himself a crown of glory.

In an article in the August issue of the British Medical Association's *News Review*, Dr. Michael Thomas, chairman of the Association's Ethics committee and a serving lieutenant-colonel in the British Army medical corps, described Bobby as "like the piper walking in front of a highland battalion, the bloke who was prepared to be shot down first." It was a kind of military salute, a tribute from a soldier on the other side of this war. Dr. Thomas added a final volley, as though for the particular benefit of that amateur moral theologian, the English Catholic Cardinal Basil Hume:

> Is it suicide for a soldier to charge a machine-gun nest, knowing that he was almost certain to get killed? Isn't it what we describe as laying down one's life for a brother? That's what Bobby Sands was doing . . .

POSTSCRIPT

IN MARCH 1982, the year after he died, Bobby Sands was posthumously voted Honorary Grand Marshal of the St. Patrick's Day Parade in New York. In an ad in a New York paper, *The Irish Echo*, an Irish-born businessman saluted the choice of Bobby Sands as Grand Marshal.

This businessman did a regular trade with the Irish consulate in New York. When the ad appeared, he got a phone call implying that he had insulted the Irish government by honouring Bobby Sands. They were cancelling their business, he was told.

A friend of the businessman, hoping to intercede, spoke to Sean Donlon, the then Irish Ambassador to the United States. What could the businessman do to get back in the good graces of the people at the consulate? Donlon was asked.

"He can crawl," said the Irish Ambassador.

NOTE: *Castlereagh*

THE USE OF OUTRIGHT TORTURE to get confessions was practiced at other police barracks like Omagh in Country Tyrone. But Castlereagh Interrogation Centre in Belfast, which got underway in 1976, turned out to be the worst place. Its twenty-one interrogation rooms became notorious as headquarters for the new Northern Ireland Secretary Roy Mason's decision, carried out by Chief Constable Kenneth Newman and his RUC, to bring every sort of interrogatory violence to bear in an effort to defeat the IRA and INLA.

Some of the defence lawyers representing the men remembered lines from the poet Shelley characterizing Robert Stewart, Viscount Castlereagh and Marquis of Londonderry—the man after whom the place had been named—the man who had corrupted and destroyed the Grattan parliament, and who had pioneered the exporting of repression from Ireland to England:

> I met Murder on the way—
> He had a mask like Castlereagh . . .

In Castlereagh, complaints of assaults during interviews dramatically increased through the last months of 1976 and the early months of 1977.

Mason had come to Northern Ireland on 10 September, and

had set to work to fill the prisons. In January 1977, he would write:

> With the increasingly important role of the RUC . . .
> The forces of law and order are now effectively put-
> ting behind bars many of the murderers and terrorists
> . . . The RUC will gradually tighten the net around
> these gangsters. It is this that we must encourage.

Spurred on by Mason, Kenneth Newman's interrogators at Castlereagh produced the most vicious beatings of prisoners examining doctors had ever seen.

They banged men against walls, choked them, kicked them in the genitals, beat them savagely with cudgels, ruptured their eardrums, burned their bodies with cigarettes and threatened to kill them. Some detectives admitted privately that what went on in the interrogation rooms was "indescribable." Suspects, including some who were utterly innocent of any involvement in paramilitary activities, were savagely beaten, then threatened with further beatings and with thirty-five year sentences if they did not sign false confessions prepared by the police.

At Castlereagh in October 1976 Bobby Sands got the full force of the Mason/Newman treatment.

Tony O'Hara (left) during Battle of Bogside in 1969.
Graffito on wall probably reads "Armed Intimidation"
(Photo courtesy of Clive Limpkin)

Tony O'Hara in Dublin in 1986 *(Photo: Derek Speirs/Report)*

Army observation posts at gates of Long Kesh prison at Maze near Lisburn.
The photo was taken in December 1980, at the end of the first hunger strike
(Photo by Pacemaker)

Letter from Tony O'Hara intended for
newspapers—printed on toilet paper and
smuggled out of Long Kesh in February
1981—asking support for the men about to
begin the second hunger strike *(Photo courtesy of
the O'Hara family)*

Cell in Long Kesh during the no-wash, no-
slop-out ("dirt") protest *(Photo by Pacemaker)*

Bobby's mother Rosaleen, with supporters from the Falls and Andersonstown, after a demonstration on 1 March, 1981, the day Bobby began his hunger strike *(Photo by Pacemaker)*

Bobby Sands, during his time in "the cages" at Long Kesh *(Pacemaker photo)*

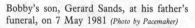

Bobby's son, Gerard Sands, at his father's funeral, on 7 May 1981 *(Photo by Pacemaker)*

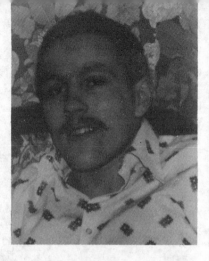

Police photo of Francis Hughes. The photo used during the hunger strike was taken from Francis's driving license *(Photo courtesy of Kevin Agnew)*

Police photo of Francis Hughes at Fallylea the day after his shootout with the SAS
(Pacemaker photo)

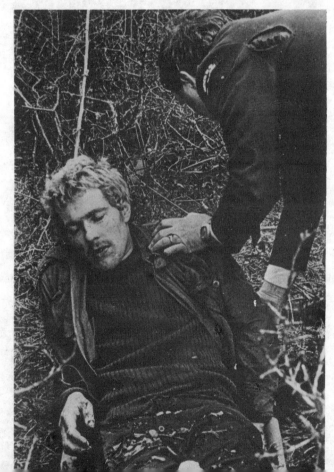

The McCreesh family at Fr. Brian McCreesh's ordination on 17 June 1973. From left to right: Raymond, Teresa, Patsy, Susan, Brian, James, Michael, Marie, Malachy and Bridie *(Photos courtesy of the McCreesh family)*

James, Fr. Brian and Susan McCreesh in June 1985

Chapter 4

THE LIFE AND DEATH OF FRANCIS HUGHES

Moving round the countryside
   he often made the news
But they could never lay their hands
   on my brave Francis Hughes.
Finally they wounded him
   and captured him at last.
From the countryside he loved,
   they took him to Belfast.

On from Musgrave Park to Crumlin Road
   and then to an H-block cell,
He went straight on the blanket then,
   on hunger strike as well.
His will to win they could never break,
   no matter what they tried.
He fought them every day he lived
   and he fought them as he died.

As I walked through the Glenshane Pass
   I heard a young girl mourn.
"The boy from Tamlaghtduff," she cried,
   "is two years dead and gone.
Oh my heart is torn apart.
   this brave man to lose.
I'll never see the likes again
   of my brave Francis Hughes."

Christy Moore
THE BOY FROM TAMLAGHTDUFF

IN THE MOONLESS DARK of the cold, clear night of 16 March, 1978, at a quarter past nine, Francis and a fellow IRA man were walking through a field near Ranaghan Road in Fallylea townland, two miles northwest of Maghera. A two-man SAS patrol had set up a surveillance (what they called in their jargon a SFOP: a Security Forces Observer Point) near a manure pile in the same field. The field belonged to Barney Cassidy, a 62-year old farmer. The SAS had set up shop directly across Ranaghan Road, opposite the driveway in front of Cassidy's house.

Francis and his companion were dressed in a form of military uniform: in Francis's case a black beret, a well-worn pair of faded olive green army trousers (underneath them beige trousers over red longjohns, against the cold), a green shirt and army pullover beneath a green army combat jacket, on the arm of which was a shield carrying the word "Ireland." He also wore woolen socks and black Dr. Martin boots. In his jacket and his pockets he carried two St. Joseph prayer cards, a pack of cigarettes, a lighter, a tube of Blisteze, some toffees, a handkerchief and tissues, a comb, an English pound note and 62 pence in change. Also in his pockets he had a flashlight, a roll of insulating tape and a pair of gloves; a plastic bag containing thirty-six rounds of .38mm bullets and two spare 20-round magazines—each two thirds full of 7.62mm rifle shells.

On a leather belt buckled outside his jacket he carried a rough-hewn holster and in it a short-barrelled .38 Special Smith and Wesson revolver loaded with six bullets. At his right shoulder he carried an M-14 Garand rifle with a nearly full magazine. He held the M-14 in the military "alert" position—the butt of the rifle against his shoulder.

Francis and his similarly dressed and armed companion— his rifle was an armalite—came to within 12 feet of the two SAS men, who took them to be British military like themselves, though probably from the UDR. The SAS men announced in low voices that they were soldiers and awaited a reply. Francis and his companion cocked their rifles, stepped back a pace and began firing. Francis squeezed off ten rounds of automatic fire, while his companion got off six rounds from his rifle.

The shots tore into the first SAS man, a Corporal David Jones, knocking an SLR out of his hand and fatally wounding him in the stomach, lung and liver. The second SAS man was hit in the stomach, and the Browning automatic at his hip was hit, too, and rendered useless. He was knocked on his back. As Francis and his companion stood there shooting, with Corporal Jones screaming, the second SAS man struggled onto his knees and just managed to get his submachine gun cocked. He fired a long automatic burst, fired wildly, but got off 26 rounds. Francis's companion was injured and Francis's left thigh torn open. Francis dropped his M-14 and, with his companion supporting him, moved quickly away from the scene.

When they'd moved about fifty yards west, down to the end of the field, Francis dropped his belt, his leather gloves, his .38 Special and the plastic bag of bullets into some bushes. The thing now was to get away. He lightened his pockets further by dropping the two spare rifle magazines into a depression in the roadway. He ordered the other man, less seriously injured, to leave him there and make his getaway. Francis slipped through the gate. Moving across Ranaghan Road, he struggled over some barbed wire and fell painfully four feet into a ditch in a marshy field on the northwest side. His left thigh was so badly injured that his leg came up over his shoulder and head, and it took him half an hour to work it down. He crawled across the field—its patches of water iced over—and made his way agonizingly through more barbed wire and into a potato field.

Meanwhile, the second soldier had radioed other SAS men down the line, who alerted police and the Gloucestershires, members of a QRF (Quick Reaction Force) based at Kilrea. Soon the area of the shooting, now three fields away from Francis and across Ranaghan Road, was covered with soldiers and police.

In the distance Francis could hear the sirens and see the flickering lights of an ambulance. The Cassidy house was quickly surrounded, as was another house nearby belonging to a family named Doherty. Francis somehow made his way across an opening at the bottom of the potato field, and crawled along to a gorse thicket in another field belonging to an old woman named Maggie Otterson. Francis made his way up along the thicket of gorse on his right, till he found a sort of culvert with a tiny clearing in it, the place half-shielded by whitethorn and blackthorn bushes and whin. He worked himself painfully through the brambles and into the culvert, and slowly covered himself as best he could with bushes and brambles and fog— the local moss.

Through the night Francis lay there beneath the frost. Stabs of pain from his shattered thigh alternated with thoughts of imminent death. He was bleeding heavily from his open wound. He might die from that, or be discovered and murdered. He thought that if any of the SAS patrols in the area should find him there that night, they would very likely kill him on sight. But as the night wore on, the movement down near the road subsided. Nobody came towards his hide. His companion would be safely away by now, far across the fields . . .

It was terribly cold; he had torn open both pairs of trousers to ease the pressure on his thigh wound; his head was splitting with his pain and anxiety, and he had to keep muffling a cough. He snatched what sleep he could through the long moonless starry night.

In the morning he was exhausted, hungry, and shivering with cold and pain from his shattered and still bleeding thigh. He heard the sound, advancing and then retreating, of soldiers and a barking dog. They were looking for him now in earnest.

It was the morning of St. Patrick's Day.

The dog lost the trail it was following, but Francis could still hear them coming and going. About noon he heard footsteps behind and above him. He had no weapon to defend himself. The footsteps nearest him stopped and suddenly one of the soldiers in the potato field behind his cover of whin and thorn bushes was speaking to another soldier.

"There's someone in there," he was saying. It was a relief in a way. Ordinary soldiers, probably, and not SAS. Less likely to kill him on sight. Maybe he could get to the hospital and have his leg attended to.

"Who are you?" called one of the soldiers.

Would they shoot him as he sat there, his legs straight out in front of him? He said nothing.

"Who are you in there?"

He heard the two of them cock their rifles.

"Don't shoot," he said quickly. "You've got me."

"Christ, mate," one of them said. "We've got the bastard."

The other ran around to the other side of the gorse bushes, and pointed his gun at Francis.

Someone else was coming up now. The dog, too. They were radioing for more.

"What's your name, in there?"

"Eamonn Laverty." It was the name of a young IRA man from Derry City who'd been killed by the British—had half his head shot off—during the post-internment fighting in August 1971.

"Have you got any weapons in there?" the soldier facing him said.

"No. You can come in and search me."

They didn't seem all that eager to come in.

"You were lucky those other patrols missed you."

"Yes, I was."

Another soldier—an officer by the sound of him—came up behind Francis. Was this one going to arrange to have him shot?

"I'm unarmed," Francis called out. The officer crawled in and began searching around. He went into his pockets and found the toffees and a blood-stained handkerchief. He put them back and wiped his hands.

Francis got a look at him. A major—a hard bastard. Probably SAS.

"How many are you?"

"No one else."

"Who was with you?"

"I'll tell you everything once I get medical treatment."

An RUC detective arrived. The same line of questions as the two soldiers.

"Your name?"

"Eamonn Laverty," Francis repeated. He couldn't risk giving them his own name till he was safe in hospital. The police hated him. They'd kill him if they knew who he was.

"Where do you live?"

Francis was seized with a fit of coughing.

142

"Letterkenny. County Donegal."

"That isn't your proper name. I think you're Francis Hughes."

"If I was Frank Hughes, I would tell you. I only met him the once. He is an ignorant—"

"Then what happened to you?"

"I was walking up the field and somebody fired a burst of shots at me."

"Where are you hit?"

"The ould leg—"

"Who was with you?"

"I'm saying nothing until I get medical treatment. I'll tell you when I get into hospital."

A police sergeant was standing opposite him, out in front of the bushes, covering Francis with an M-1 rifle.

"You're Hughes," the detective said.

"I'm saying nothing more until I get treatment."

Another policeman came. The same questions repeated—

"I told you before, and I'm not telling you again." Were they going to let him lie there and bleed to death?

Again the questions.

"I am Laverty. Eamonn Laverty . . . Letterkenny. Look, you have a gun there. Why don't you shoot me? I'm not afraid to die."

The detective went off. An ambulance was on the way. Good. His thigh was very painful now. The detective came back with what sounded like his boss—a detective inspector. The usual about his name and where he lived.

"All right, where in Letterkenny?"

"Why don't you ask the gardai? You are fucking friendly enough with them!"

"You *are* Hughes."

"If I was Hughes, I would say I was. Fuck off."

"You are not in a position to dictate to me what I should do."

"Why don't you put a bullet through my head, and finish me right?"

The ambulance came, and was parked two fields above the thicket. The pain tore through him as they bound his legs together and lifted him onto the stretcher. They carried him up to the ambulance.

As he was about to be lifted in, Francis raised himself up on the stretcher so that all the soldiers and police could hear him.

"Up the Provos!" he shouted.

MEAGHER (MICK) HUGHES was the oldest of Francis's three brothers. Mick knew that the family name went back a long way. There was an Irish name Hughes which was cognate with Hayes and Ó hAodha. But their father, Joe Hughes, thought the family name was Welsh and had originated with people who came to Ireland centuries ago, long before the Reformation, planter people who had quickly become assimilated into the dominant Gaelic culture. There was supposed to be a Scandinavian strain in there somewhere. Like so many Irish Andersons and Johnsons they'd originally come to Britain in Norse longboats; eventually they'd been transported ("Britain didn't want them, either," Joe used to say) and planted in Ireland by the English in the twelfth century. Joe Hughes and his brother Peter used to wander around local graveyards, putting bits of their family history together. The father and the uncle would talk for hours about history and ancestors and the historical meaning of things, gathering all sorts of information: "none of it true," someone had joked.

Francis's father, Joe, who was seventy-three, was an outspoken Irish Republican. He was fiercely proud of Francis, whom he thought of as keeping the British at bay. Their mother, Margaret McElwee Hughes—a sister of Jim McElwee, father of Thomas and Benedict McElwee—was not so politically minded, but she found that in marrying their father she'd married into a strong Republican tradition. Yet she didn't know Francis was involved until he had to go on the run.

There were ten of them in the family and Francis was the

youngest—the baby brother. That's why his absence, and the danger he was in, was especially hard on their mother.

In the family there were the three oldest sisters—Philomena, Josephine and Veronica. Then Mick, followed by Noreen, a senior nurse at the Royal hospital in Belfast, and Oliver, who lived next door to the family home and who had become involved in the IIP—the Irish Independence Party. Next came Roger, a carpenter, who lived and worked in England.

After that there was Maria, who lived in Scotland; Dolores, who lived in Magherafelt; and finally Francis, born 28 February 1956 and now twenty-five. Three of the sisters had married Protestants, two of whom became Catholics. Their mother and father were strongly religious and much of this rubbed off on Francis.

Mick was born in 1944, the first son and fourth child in this small farmer's family. The Hugheses had about twenty-five acres. Only by making the pigs work for them did their father and their mother manage to scrape out a living from the little bit of land. They had very little in tillage: potatoes and oats— which went mainly to feed the chickens. There were two or three hundred hens, fourteen cattle and a yard full of pigs. They kept from a hundred fifty to three hundred pigs at a time, which was a lot in those days, although modern farms could keep five or six thousand pigs in the same space.

Mick attended only primary school. Then he helped on the farm for awhile. But on the small holding there wasn't enough work for all the boys and girls coming up, so after a couple of years on the farm Mick began to learn carpentry. He spent a year with one firm, a year with another, and at eighteen went on to a third. Those were quiet times, and it never occurred to him to involve himself in IRA activities. It was 1962 and the IRA border campaign had already wound down. (Had it come to it, Mick often thought afterwards, he'd have done his own wee share.)

On his third job he'd left home and gone to live on his own, working for Evans, a Protestant firm which was building a big housing estate in the town of Antrim. Things went well enough the first year, but when 12 July came around a Union Jack was raised at the main site office. The Catholic workers—eighty out of a hundred in the company—passed no remarks. The second year when the Twelfth season arrived, the Union Jack was again raised at the site office. Again the Catholic workers said nothing. Then the loyalists decided to put a Union Jack over the canteen that all the workers used. This meant that every time the Catholic employees went into the canteen they had to walk under it. The flag extended six inches below the top of the door, so that the men had to stoop on their way into and out of the canteen to avoid touching their heads against it.

The Catholics were of course nationalists. A few of them went to the foreman and asked him to remove the flag. Otherwise, they told him, they'd go out on strike. It was a Friday evening and the flag was removed. But on Monday morning it was back up over the canteen door. Again the Catholic workers objected. This time the foreman said that if any of them didn't like the flag they could quit.

In Northern Ireland, then as now, Catholics did most of the manual work. The Protestants got the government and clerical jobs—the white collar work. The foreman didn't really expect Catholic workers to walk out and leave their jobs. But they banded together and decided that they would leave until the flag was removed. The Evans people refused. So every Catholic on the job asked for his cards.

It took the Evans people a long time to get replacements. The word was out, and Catholics wouldn't work for them. They couldn't easily get Protestants because of the kind of work involved. Finally the Evans company fell behind on its contract, and had to indemnify Antrim Council because of its failure to finish the job.

Meanwhile the Catholic boys went out and looked elsewhere for work. At the time there were few Catholic contractors. If the men went to a Protestant firm they'd be told, "You worked for Evans," and there'd be no job. They lost a lot of money, but they had stood their ground. In the end there was one consolation. The Evans firm went bankrupt.

Over the years, more and larger Catholic contractors began to appear, and it got to the point where sixty per cent of the builders in the North were Catholic. Meanwhile Mick had decided to chuck it in and go up to Dublin. He started there doing carpentry and joinery for houses, and was content to keep it small. Within a short time he was doing well and had all the work he needed to make a living.

By the later 70s Mick was thinking of going back to the North. But he knew that because he was a Hughes he'd be harassed by the police. He'd be picked up every week until they got sick of picking him up, and it would be a year before they'd start leaving him alone. People at home seemed not to mind the harassment; they got used to it after awhile. But Mick had got used to the peaceful life around Dublin. From that point of view, compared to the North, the South really was a Free State.

At home in the North there'd usually be no problem during the day. The sun would be shining, the fields green, the cattle grazing. But a farmer or a workman out for a stroll late at night would find an entirely different scene. Coming up to a UDR checkpoint, he would have had to suffer insults ("Papist Bastard," "Fenian Scum!" "IRA Bastard") and perhaps a beating. A man could be utterly blameless yet still be subjected to this sort of carry-on. On a back road at night, when there were no people or cars about, he could be in for a real hiding. By day the countryside was quiet, but at night it was no different than the toughest area in Belfast. In the country it was subtler, though. It meant someone he knew—a neighbour, another farm boy, another carpenter—turning up at the checkpoint and demanding to know Mick's name.

THE HUGHESES, like the McElwees, were often big, strong men. Mick knew that seventy or eighty years ago their grandfather, Mexican Jim McElwee,* and their great uncles on the Hughes side were tall and powerfully built. Francis was like that. He was six feet one inch or more, the biggest of the lot of them, built like their father. There wasn't much fat on him. He was tall and strong, with blue eyes and brown hair, and he walked with his shoulders back and his head up.

Mick remembered that, when Francis was a little fellow, he would come tearing at him with two fists, and Mick, then

*See Chapter 12 below.

147

a teenager, would hold him at bay to get him going. Francis was quite a fighter and would just keep tearing into Mick. If he got a bit of a slap he didn't care—he'd still keep going. Francis was the greatest in the world—always spirited.

Honest to God, Mick used to think, the way brothers got on together! They would often get fed up looking at one another's faces. Mick and Oliver had many a row, though they were always friends at the end of the day. But it was impossible, even for a brother, to fall out with Francis. Mick didn't feel about him as he would about a brother. He admired him. Francis was twelve years younger, yet Mick's instinct was to treat him as he would a highly respected stranger.

As a man, Francis was absolutely dedicated. Nothing was too big for him to tackle, no risk too great for him to take. He didn't smoke or drink much. He was always full of energy. He had great warmth and a sense of humour to match. But he could also switch off and become very serious. Francis was far brainier than Mick ever pretended to be. He had a keen grasp of the subtleties of political issues.

When Francis was at home, before he got deeply involved in the fighting, he worked as a painter/decorator. He left school at sixteen, and there was no work at that time for a young lad. For most of them it was either the dole queue or a brother-in-law. Their sister Vera's husband, Frank Donnelly, gave Francis a start in painting and decorating, enabling him to make good money.

But he wasn't selfish about it. He gave his mother every penny he earned. He so arranged his life that he needed very little money. At night he'd go running about with the lads on old bicycles and acting the monkey. Once a week or once a fortnight he'd ask their mother for a few bob to get into a dance, and for the price of a bottle of mineral and ten cigarettes: a pound would have covered it. The rest of the forty or fifty pounds a week he was earning went to their mother.

The H-Blocks poster picture was a good likeness in some ways. Francis had grown his hair a bit long at the time the picture was taken. But he had a far livelier look than that. He smiled a lot. He was a singer, or thought he was. When he stayed in homes around South Derry and Tyrone he sang for the old people in the house. They didn't always know a good singer from a bad one, so it didn't matter to them. They liked him as a person. Francis was inventive, full of tricks, and he was always playing the comic. He could be talking to somebody, a fellow or a girl, out in the hall; and people would be in the sitting room or the kitchen listening to him, and they'd be laughing and shaking their heads at one another. Or he'd come into the room and sit down and tell some old fool story—no sense in it at all—and people would howl. He could have made a living as a comedian.

He was mad for a joke. When he was out on building sites he'd have done just about anything. Once he was painting for Frank Donnelly, who had subcontracted a job doing a row of terraced houses on the outskirts of Belfast. Some of the lads used to come to work on bicycles. One day Francis carried a bicycle up to the ridge of a roof on a ladder, and began riding along the ridge. Though the roof wasn't too steeply pitched, Frank Donnelly's heart stopped. If Francis were hurt, what would Vera say? And Frank was liable to get into trouble with the main contractor because of this idiot riding a bike up on the roof.

FRANCIS BECAME INTERESTED in the war in the North when he was a boy and joined the Fianna—the Republican youth organization. But he found in an incident that occurred when he was seventeen, driving back from a dance at Ardboe, a powerful motive for deeper involvement. Ardboe was no more than a dozen miles from Bellaghy. British soldiers stopped Francis and another Bellaghy boy, named McCloy, whose brother was wanted by the RUC. The soldiers asked where his brother was. McCloy said he didn't know, but that people at home had letters saying he was in America. The soldiers didn't believe this. They started asking whether he was up in Dublin, and whether he came back home often. The McCloy lad kept insisting that his brother was in America, and that that was all he knew. The soldiers took them out of the car and got very nasty. They gave the two boys a terrible beating.

Mick happened to ring home soon afterwards and their mother

told him vaguely that Francis had gotten a bit of a hiding. She didn't make a long story of it on the phone, because she didn't want Mick rushing home just for that. Everything was all right, she said; just that Francis would be taking it easy for a couple of days. But the next time Mick came home their father pointed to a radio covered in black plastic, and said that Francis had been beaten as black as that radio. He'd had to spend several days in bed.

Francis himself wasn't a boy to complain. He said it was nothing, just a bit of a beating, and that he would get his own back on the people who did it, and their friends.

As far as Mick knew, Francis hadn't been active before that. He was a boy for doing his work and going to dances, and liked nothing better at night than to play a game of cards with the lads. But after the incident on the road from Ardboe he was suddenly into the thick of it full time.

Francis's earliest active sympathies were with the Sticks, the Official IRA, who after the split were the more influential paramilitary group in his part of the country. The Sticks declared a ceasefire in 1972. And so—soon after Francis was beaten up— he formed his own independent unit, called the "Unrepentants." In 1974 Francis's unit was incorporated into the Provisional IRA. He liked to think of his unit as an IRA flying column. He admired Tom Barry and Dan Breen. Francis was calm, unexcitable, and unafraid. He was willing to take risks. He combined the guerrilla talents of a Barry or a Breen with the antic fearlessness of a Michael Collins.

It was not so long after the dance at Ardboe that the regiment responsible for beating Francis up lost a sergeant and another soldier in a booby-trap bomb. The soldiers had opened a gate in a field and been blown to kingdom come. Francis never told Mick about it in so many words. But Mick gathered that Francis and someone else had been waiting with a trip-wire. Had a farmer come through the gate, they would not have set off the charge. But when they saw the soldiers coming they detonated the bomb. What made Mick sure that Francis had done it was Francis's going on the run for the first time the Christmas after that. Mick could always tell later when Francis was on the run—

the countryside around the house would be covered with soldiers whenever he drove up. That first Christmas Francis came in, had his dinner, and was away.

For a short time he was OC of the South Derry brigade, commanding overall about a hundred volunteers. But there came a point when he was on the run when he had to give up the command. The OC had to be able to move around freely, seeing people in all sectors of the area, and Francis no longer could.

Francis had a great deal of bravado. He developed a habit of ringing up the RUC from telephone kiosks, and telling them where he was. It wasn't a death wish—quite the contrary. He used to get fed up waiting for members of the security forces to come looking for him. He'd wait for them for hours, sometimes for days, so that he could shoot them.

They had an uncle named Barney, an easygoing man, nearly old enough to be a pensioner. He cycled into the village every evening for a drink. One time he was riding along to the village on his bicycle. Francis had been waiting most of the day for the RUC or the army to appear. It was getting dark, and Francis and his unit had just about decided to pull out. Then Barney cycled past on the road just opposite them. Francis, a crack shot, fired off a round and winged the bike in the back wheel. Barney leapt off the bike and ran into a neighbour's house. "The loyalists are trying to assassinate me!" he shouted. For three months Barney never went out on that road at night. And then when he found out it was Francis he was very hurt. People who knew would tease Barney about what for him had been a very painful practical joke. But it showed what Francis had in mind for the security forces when he phoned to get them to come looking for him.

When he was on the run, and had the time, Francis used to help people fix up their houses. But Mick was never sure how much Francis liked being a decorator. There was a story about a butcher shop in Bellaghy, and a butcher who was a decent enough man but a brother of Bob Overend—"Black Bob," a unionist councillor very unpopular with nationalists in the area. Francis was doing some painting in the shop, and the man came along when Francis was finished. This was just before Francis went on the run.

"Hey," said the butcher. "There's a bit up there in the corner that you missed."

"Ah," Francis said. "Don't worry. That'll be all right in the morning. In the morning there'll not be a word said about it."

The butcher shrugged his shoulders. He didn't understand what Francis was saying. But the boys were planning to hit certain commercial targets in Bellaghy that night, and the butcher shop was one of those that got "touched up," as the locals put it.

Mick had heard all the standard stories about Francis—the story, for example, of the time Francis was transporting a load of explosives on a trailer hooked up to a tractor, the explosives hidden under some bales of hay. He came around a corner and there was a British Army checkpoint. Francis looked out, saw some cattle in a field, and pulled up alongside a hedge. He lifted off a bale of hay, walked to the side of the road and threw it over the hedge. He walked on a bit, through a gap in the hedge, and went back and collected the bale. Then he took it over to the cattle and began feeding them. As the soldiers watched, he went round examining the cattle, looking them up and down. Then he meandered back to his tractor, turned it around, waved at the soldiers and drove off.

Once, according to another story, Francis was crossing a field with his unit. They walked out onto the road just when it was starting to get dark, and noticed four or five soldiers sitting alongside the hedge. When a car would come they'd get up and form a checkpoint to stop it. Though Francis was with his unit, and probably carrying a revolver, he didn't panic when he saw the soldiers.

"What are you walking through the fields for?" he was asked.

"Bloody Provos on the road," Francis said. "You can't take the roads these evenings. They were stopping cars up there last night."

The soldiers didn't know what to make of it, but let the boys walk on. Then suddenly Francis turned, walked back and asked one of the soldiers for a cigarette and a light. They lit a cigarette for him and he walked away again.

There was the story about Francis and another lad sleeping in a loft in a big hay barn. It was raining heavily outside. Francis heard noise and woke. He looked down. The place was crawling with British Army. There'd been a checkpoint up the road and the soldiers had come in to dry off. The barn had no exit other than the big main door. Francis gently nudged the other man to wake him, hoping he wouldn't speak out. The other man copped on right away; he didn't make a sound. Francis told Mick that he would have sprayed the whole lot of them, except that he knew there were more troops in landrovers outside, and that he and his friend would never have got out of there alive. So they'd let the soldiers alone.

There was the story about the time on Good Friday, in April 1977, when Francis and two others were in a car being followed by RUC men, who overtook them and flagged them down. The man driving the Hughes car swung sharply around in an effort to make a U-turn, jamming the accelerator to the floor, and the car went into a ditch at the side of the road. Three RUC men moved towards them. Jumping from the car, Francis and his friends opened fire on the RUC men, killing two of them and wounding a third. Then they leapt back into the car and drove off. A few hundred yards further along the road was another RUC unit. After an exchange of gunfire, Francis and the other two made their escape.

It was after that that the RUC issued the wanted poster of Francis, Dominic McGlinchey and Ian Milne, describing Francis—whom they called Seán Hughes—and the others as the "most wanted men" in Northern Ireland. That brought on increased harassment at the Hughes home. In the middle of the night, when he was staying there, Mick would hear them rumbling up in their landrovers, turning around, and driving away again. Police kept coming in and searching the house— they must have searched it fifty times—looking for Francis.

Their father Joe often came across soldiers lying about in fields. There were hundreds of places where they could hide. One night a neighbour's cattle were out in one of the Hughes' fields. Joe, on his way to put the cattle back in the owner's field, stumbled across three SAS men in a ditch. He turned around and began to walk away, but they jumped up and assaulted him.

153

Their father didn't mention it at the time, in case Mick and Oliver should decide to try to take some action on their own.

Other farmers out looking over their cattle or collecting wood often came across soldiers. They'd be lifted in and out of the fields by helicopter—dropped off at night and collected at daybreak. They hated being discovered, but it wasn't difficult to spot them. They were all over the place at the time.

Francis was involved in the shooting at the RUC station in Ahoghill, an Orange town up towards Ballymena. He was out in a car with two other IRA men.

They pulled up outside the police barracks, and two of them walked in while the third remained at the wheel of the car. There were three or four police inside and the two men started riddling the place. When they had almost emptied their weapons, they ran out into the street. By this time, with all the commotion, bystanders were down on the ground, flat on their bellies. The boys fired a couple of shots in the air.

"This is the Bellaghy gang!" Francis shouted. They hopped into the car and away they went. The RUC made some effort of pursuit, but Francis and his friends were long gone before the police got going. Francis told Mick afterwards what had happened. Lough Neagh was nearby, and the boys had driven down to an open boat. They abandoned the car, jumped into the boat and were across the lake and into Tyrone before anyone spotted the car.

There was something about Francis most people didn't know— his policy and his criteria for a target.

Francis hit commercial targets on orders—like the bombing in Bellaghy. But he didn't think much of the commercial campaign. What he liked were military targets—soldiers, police, and UDR, whom he saw as armed enemies. He preferred them to be on active duty, but they had to be at least on active service. To Francis the war meant getting the British so frightened that they would leave Northern Ireland; and that meant killing as many of their soldiers and their police as possible. To him it seemed the only way.

There were all sorts of stories about Francis going around the district. One UDR man told a journalist about eight or nine killings that he said Francis Hughes had been responsible for. Some of the UDR called him "the baby-killer," from the time when a member of the security forces was blown up by a bomb planted in his car, and his young daughter was killed. They held Francis's unit responsible. They also held it against Francis that some of the security men he'd shot had been known to him since he was a kid. The UDR men complained about his routine attacks on security forces. These were "cowardly," they said.

Francis and his men were feared because they were always on the lookout not only for armed men in uniform, but also for off-duty police and soldiers, on their way home after a night's drinking in a pub or whatever. Word had got around that Francis was an accomplished bomber as well as marksman—it was unusual to have to deal with a man who was both. Operating alone or in combination with other people, Francis was responsible for a lot of deaths: twenty-five or thirty maybe—Mick simply didn't know. The Maghera UDR barracks alone lost five men during the time Francis was active. It was the highest casualty figure for any barracks in Northern Ireland.

Francis told Mick about a time he went to shoot one UDR man. The man was alone at home. Francis came bursting in the door and the man couldn't do a thing. Francis told him to say a few prayers, that he was there to get him, and the man went down on his knees. But he wasn't praying; he was swearing. "I swear I'm not in the UDR—I've left it. I swear I've left it." He gave Francis the name of a man who could establish the truth of this. Francis doubted the story, but it was his policy not to shoot civilians. So he gave the man the benefit of the doubt. "I walked away," Francis said to Mick "I was ready to believe him." Then it turned out that the man actually had left the UDR, as he'd said.

"Thank God for that," Francis said to Mick.

There was a terrible intensity of feeling in that part of the country. Catholics knew all too well the old history of confiscation of land and landlordism, where Protestants got the best land. That had something to do, too, with the feeling the local UDR men and RUC had about Francis. He was a Taig who always got the better of them, and they hated him for it.

Mick didn't think Francis hated any of them. But he was ruthless towards men he regarded as enemy soldiers. Francis was a gentleman, but he stopped being a gentleman when he had soldiers, or UDR, or armed RUC in his sights.

And yet he felt particularly sorry for the English soldiers.

"They're just kids," he once said to Mick. "For God's sake, I don't want to be shooting them. I want them to bloody go home in the morning. But what other way do I have to protest, can you tell me?

"Do you know," Francis said, "that I hate what I'm doing? I really hate it. But I'm going to keep doing it—that's the funny thing about it. Tomorrow night I might blow up ten of them. I hope I do. But, Jesus, I hate doing it. It's just that I don't know any other way."

Shooting soldiers was one thing, but shooting local police—mostly Protestants—quite another, people said. But Mick knew that, for Francis, shooting RUC men was soldiering. The men he killed were paid by the British government to carry guns in support of a British occupation of part of Ireland.

Francis certainly had no hatred for Protestants as such. Their father had taught them not to be bigoted. He used to tell them about a Protestant shopkeeper in the middle of Bellaghy he knew as a boy. Whenever the B-Specials or loyalists started annoying Catholics kids standing outside the shop, the shopkeeper would come out and tell them to leave the Catholic boys alone.

At home, around Tamlaghtduff townland, the people were all Catholic. But it wasn't necessary to go far to find Protestant neighbours, and by and large the Hugheses got on well with them. They knew that some of them might have been reporting to the police or the UDR, or might even have been under an arrangement to watch the Hugheses' house. The family could never know. But none of their Protestant neighbours was ever disturbed.

Their father had great respect for certain Protestants. He trusted them. If any of the family started running down Protestants as a group, their father would object. Certain

Protestants, okay; but they had to be taken individually. Francis was like their father in that.

Francis, when he was younger, would go to a Protestant house to do some painting. In the morning he'd walk in as a Catholic. They'd look down on him or be suspicious of him. Once he'd spent time there and eaten at their table, they'd have come to know and like him, and in the end they'd have had great respect for him.

It was probably his charm. Francis could overwhelm people with his charm. Everyone liked him. The colour of people, or their religion, didn't matter to Francis. He'd laugh and joke, and maybe take the mickey out of them, and they'd love it. Francis's feeling was that, apart from freeing Ireland of the British, the whole object was for people to live together and get on together.

And so later when he was on the run he sometimes slept in Protestant homes. If he was really stuck he'd call into them. Not to local places, but to the homes of people not too far away whom he'd worked for in the past and who'd got to know him well. And there he'd be, Mick thought, in the safest houses in the country, with Protestant friends who were protecting him from the Protestant police and the Protestant UDR.

Some Protestants who'd known Francis would even call in to see their father. They'd get him to promise to tell Francis that if he were around their area, and needed a bed to sleep in, they wouldn't see him stuck: there'd always be a welcome there for him.

Mick himself felt that Protestants and Catholics should be brought up and schooled together. Bellaghy was a sad case of the opposite practice. There was one school for Catholics and one for Protestants. When they shared a canteen, the Catholic kids went out at 12:30 for their lunch. They finished at one o'clock, as the Protestants kids were going out for theirs.

They were segregated in every way possible. Housing was a prime example. They'd built some two hundred houses in Bellaghy in recent years. A hundred of them went to Catholics and a hundred to Protestants, with a dividing line between. From Mick's point of view it was ridiculous. The border didn't only run below South Down or South Armagh and above Dundalk and Monaghan: there was a border in every second village in the North. People up at home didn't realize how cut off they were. Mick, living in the South, getting away from the North and then coming back to visit, could see the stupid mistakes the Brits and unionists made in the way they organized things—and the mistakes the Catholic Church made in insisting on separate education. Mick felt that if he'd gone to school with young Protestant lads and if they'd seen that he was a human being and he'd seen them as human beings, and if they'd all seen that they were able to get on with one another, then they wouldn't be strangers or enemies anymore.

One of the reasons Francis got on so well with Protestants was that he was a countryman through and through. He understood how a countryman thinks. Mick used to be amused at the socialism that was so much talked about in Republican circles in Derry and Belfast. Francis wasn't a bit socialist in his politics. He was a country Republican, very much a chip off the old block, a son of their father.

Despite living in Dublin, Mick knew more about some aspects of Francis's career than the father himself knew. When Mick visited home, people would come up to him who had sheltered Francis and knew something about the military activities Francis had been involved in. They might not want to worry the parents, but they knew that they could tell Mick anything, and that he'd listen and share their pride in Francis's exploits.

Periodically Francis would go down to the Free State, often with his friend Dominic, to get away from the war and the hassle for awhile. But there were times when it seemed that the Garda Siochána were waiting for them at every crossroad.

"We don't come here looking for trouble," Francis used to say. "But trouble sure follows us."

It became almost a routine. They'd be driving along and the gardai would stop them. For fear that they'd radio the armed Special Branch, Francis and Dominic would order them at gunpoint into the boot, take the car and drive off. On occasion they'd go back to the border driving a garda car, with the boys who'd stopped them locked up behind.

158

Through the years, Mick had seen Francis every few months—in Dublin, never at home. Francis would ring someone; they'd get in touch with Mick and Mick would meet him somewhere. Francis never stayed at Mick's place; it wouldn't have been a safe house for him.

The British authorities used to make a great deal of Francis's disguises to cover up their own inability to capture him. Sometimes he wore disguises, but Mick never saw him in one. When he was down in Dublin he was always immaculately dressed. He'd have a collar and tie on, and a bit of after-shave; his hair would be well-groomed.

Mick used to wonder sometimes whether Francis wasn't, in a sense, reporting in to him as his oldest brother. He knew, anyway, that Francis was aware how happy Mick was to see him. The longest space between visits was six months. Often Mick saw him at two month intervals. Whenever he came, Mick brought him out for a good meal. Francis didn't drink much. When he was out for a night with Mick he might have three or four bottles of lager, five at the most. No spirits. Mick never saw him drinking a short. In fact, he never drank at all until the last three years of his life. He probably began then because of the families he stayed with. Places he'd go, people would offer him a drink and he'd take something to be sociable.

Whenever Francis turned up, Mick would give him a few pounds. Mick's work was fairly steady, and he'd offer Francis thirty or forty quid. But Francis would only take five, or maybe a tenner. He might be going off for a drink with some girls and would want to be able to pay his way. As long as he had enough money to buy his round, he was okay.

In Dublin he used to give money to the tinkers when they came around to a pub. Mick tried to explain that tinkers in Dublin were different from the ones at home. Francis was used to the McGuires, who had their caravan at the corner of Scribe and Tamlaghtduff roads, and who were fine, responsible people. He couldn't understand why Mick wouldn't readily give the Dublin tinkers money. Mick would tell him to cop on, but he wouldn't take Mick's point.

Even when Francis was relaxing in Dublin, he was working too—collecting the gear he needed. He never told Mick about this, but Mick could put two and two together. One of the reasons for his personal trips was that he liked to be sure he was getting the right stuff. Mick gathered that he was carrying it back home himself, and he didn't like that. He thought Francis was taking too many risks.

Mick never tried to talk him into quitting the fighting, chiefly because he admired what Francis was doing. He was very proud of his young brother. But he told Francis that if he ever thought of packing it in, that he would set him up as a painting contractor—he'd give him all the money and help he needed. But Francis refused even to consider it.

In late 1977, when Francis had been on the run for four years, Mick used to ask him whenever they got together if Francis would like to take a holiday for awhile. But he always wanted to get back into action. Later Mick stopped mentioning the idea, hoping that at some point Francis would volunteer to come for a few months and let Mick spend a little money on him.

Once, near the end, he saw him two weeks running. From the conversation he gathered that Francis was now continually on the go, spending all his nights in haysheds or lying out in fields and ditches. Mick had the impression that he was getting only one good night's sleep out of two or three. He was undernourished and thin and pale. So this time Mick really pressed him to take a rest. He said he'd just have to take three or four months off and then go back.

"No," Francis said. "I'm with the boys down home."

Mick didn't regard Francis as a man of violence or a terrorist. He could hardly be a terrorist, fighting mercenaries working for a foreign government which was in armed control of his country. What Francis was trying to do was to drive out the terrorists. Francis was a soldier and did things a soldier does in war. He did them extraordinarily well, especially considering the circumstances of this war. Somebody had told Mick that in the entire conflict the only man whose reputation as a fighter could compare to Francis's was Big Joe McCann, the famous Belfast Official IRA man who was killed in 1972.

Apart from Francis's soldiering, one unusual thing about him was his religiousness. He wasn't gone in the head about praying, but there'd be ten minutes or so of prayer every night and maybe a few minutes in the morning. Up in Derry—Mick heard the same story from several people—Francis would be staying with a family during the time he was on the run. The people of the house, at the fire down in the kitchen or the sitting room, would suddenly turn and ask one another "Where's Francis?" They'd go look for him and someone would find him up in the box room, on his knees, praying. Mick wasn't all that great a Catholic himself, and didn't pray much at all. But he'd never pass any remarks on Francis's praying. It was just something Francis did.

The same people that told stories about Francis praying would tell stories about where he slept out. People would say, "Mick, come up some time and I'll show you where Francis used to lie in wait for the British Army"—maybe for three or four days running. Some day, Mick promised himself, he'd go around and see all those hides. One farmer told him about the day when he was out with his dog, walking down a potato field. Suddenly the dog became nervous and started barking. It was about midday, and the farmer wondered what the dog was barking at. Then he saw what he thought was a jacket. The dog wouldn't go any further. So the farmer went down and there was Francis lying asleep between two drills of potatoes. He'd been out all night on some operation. When it started getting light he couldn't go tramping across fields or he'd be spotted, so he just got in under the potato plants and fell asleep exhausted.

As far as their mother was concerned, Francis spent most of his time in the South. She didn't know that for a given period he might be spending weeks within a couple of miles of the house. She used to worry a lot—he was her youngest—and since he was on the run so long she had to face her anxiety about him every day for four years. Francis, who knew what she was going through, would see her as often as he could. He'd get a note to her to meet him someplace. He'd make sure he looked his best for her. If he had to borrow clothes for one of these secret meetings, he'd do it. They had a ritual between them. He'd give her a few bob, to let her know he wasn't broke—even though he was. And she'd give the money back to him.

He'd let on sometimes that he'd been away from it all, living in Donegal, for example. But many a night he'd be sleeping rough in fields not two hundred yards from home.

In the early days on the run he did stop at the house the odd time. But only in the beginning. Later on it became too risky. The whole of South Derry was crawling with soldiers—and with SAS—who were determined to get Francis.

Mick used to quote the old adage to him. "Long runs the fox, but caught at last." Wanted posters and all, it still took them four years.

KEVIN AGNEW was a 67-year-old solicitor in Maghera. A civil rights activist in the late 1960s, he had been, throughout his life, a rock of local Irish Republicanism. Yet with his voice of soft granite and his direct Ulsterman's manner he was respected by many Protestants of the legal profession and the Northern Ireland judiciary.

It would have been no secret to any of them where Kevin Agnew stood politically. He could be found outside the Catholic chapel in Maghera every Sunday, selling the Provisional Sinn Féin paper, the *Republican News*. His office on the Main Street, Maghera, had been destroyed early in the troubles, and he now worked from his house on Hall Street.

Early in the afternoon of 17 March 1978 Kevin received a number of phone calls about a volunteer named Francis Hughes of Bellaghy, who'd been badly injured in a gun battle in Maghera. Several of the calls had come from Oliver Hughes, Francis's brother. The family wanted Kevin to act as Francis's lawyer. Kevin began making notes. He always kept a detailed chronology on his cases. By that night Kevin had assembled a sketchy picture:

> This man involved in a shooting incident at Fallylea on Thursday night 16/3/78, and was badly wounded. He was unable to move far from the scene of the shooting and was found on the forenoon of 17th by soldiers, lying in a ditch near Barney Cassidy's home at Fallylea. He was left lying for two or three hours before being taken away by ambulance to Magherafelt hospital. He was kept there

a very short time, and was then taken by helicopter to Musgrave Park hospital, Belfast.

He apparently was not cooperative with the police or soldiers, and would not tell them anything about himself, and he appears to have given them the name "Laverty."

I got several messages about Hughes around dinner time on 17th.

During the afternoon I phoned Magherafelt police. They said they had no one by the name of Hughes in custody. I did not make much progress.

Tonight (17th) phone calls from Oliver Hughes and Fr. Donnelly, Bellaghy.

Also, tonight, I phoned Dr. Sayee, [Dr. Hugh] Glancy's assistant, Magherafelt, and spoke to the doctor and also spoke to Oliver Hughes who was with him.

On Saturday morning, 18 March, Kevin Agnew had a positive report on Francis's condition. He talked to Dr. Sayee, who had seen Francis at Musgrave Park; Francis was reasonably well and though badly wounded in the left leg was receiving the best of medical attention. Kevin made no headway in his efforts to arrange a meeting with Francis. By Saturday night, however, the doors had been opened, probably through the good offices of Bishop Edward Daly of Derry. A Sergeant Arlow phoned from Magherafelt saying that Kevin and Francis's parents would be allowed in on Sunday afternoon at three.

Francis was in Ward 18, the top security ward at the military hospital. There were two guards on duty in the ward itself at all times, and all access corridors were heavily covered by police and closed-circuit television. Later there was talk of a huge and expensive buildup of security after Francis arrived. But to Kevin this was nonsense: Ward 18 was already a fortress. Nothing moved in that place without it being seen. In Kevin's opinion security was so tight you couldn't get a fly into Musgrave.

In his diary Kevin noted the following about the visit:

Sunday morning, 19th, I phoned Oliver. Told him I would meet him and parents at the entrance to Musgrave Park hospital, at 2:50 . . .

Met up with Oliver and his father, and also Peter Hughes, Oliver's uncle. We got into the military hospital without any difficulty. The father and Peter were allowed to see Francis for ten or fifteen minutes. Two police sergeants were present during both talks, one of whom made notes from time to time during my visit.

I found him in good enough form. He is a strong young man. He has a very bad leg wound. Thinks the main bone in his left thigh has been badly shattered. His leg was obviously in splints and plaster, and he said he expected to be in the hospital for a month or two.

He said a detective had been in with him during the forenoon and had asked for a cutting from his hair. He refused and told the "visitor" to leave.

I told Francis that he was not obliged to answer any questions, other than to give them his proper name and address, and to leave it at that. He knows his position well enough and will not be doing any talking.

JUST AFTER TWO in the afternoon, on Wednesday 24 January 1979, more than ten months after he'd been taken in the thicket at Fallylea, Francis was arrested in Musgrave Park hospital by an RUC sergeant named Richard Nixon Arlow.

Francis was standing at the reception desk at Musgrave when he overheard two uniformed policemen behind him.

"If he doesn't talk one way," one was saying, "he'll talk the other. We'll dope the fucking bastard's food."

Then Arlow and several other RUC men took Francis across Belfast to Castlereagh Interrogation Centre. Francis was fortunate that the high tide of beating and torture at the place under NI Secretary of State Roy Mason and Chief Constable Kenneth Newman had receded, because of the Amnesty Report and the complaints of examining doctors (the Bennett Report was in preparation at the time). The interrogating officers were generally far more careful now in their treatment of suspects.

Fortunately too, Francis was still under medical supervision because of his leg. After the surgery performed to deal with the gunshot damage to his shattered thigh and broken femur

164

bone, he'd ended up with his left leg an inch and a half shorter than his right. He had a built-up shoe for walking, and an elbow crutch. When sitting he liked to keep his left leg propped up.

When Francis overheard the two policemen talk about doping his food to get him to talk, he resolved that he would neither eat nor drink anything during the period of interrogation.

Among his early questioners at Castlereagh was Detective Inspector (later Chief Inspector) Francis Dempsey, who came to him during the first session just after four o'clock that day.

"We're holding you under section 12 of the Temporary Provisions Act, and we're going to interview you about certain offences." Section 12 meant that they could interrogate him for 48 hours and then get an order to continue the interrogation for another five days.

"I can't see," Francis said, "why I couldn't have stayed where I was—in Musgrave Park hospital."

Dempsey gave the standard caution to the effect that Francis was not obliged to say anything unless he wished to do so, but that anything he said could be taken down in writing and given in evidence against him at his trial.

"How's your health? Anything you need?"

"Jesus, you know I should still be in Musgrave Park. That's all I'm saying."

"We're going to ask you some questions. We believe you've been involved in terrorist offences—"

"Oh, is that right? You're talking a lot of balls to me, boy— because I know nothing of what you're talking about."

Dempsey left him with the other detective.

"Now, will you give me your full name?"

"I don't feel like telling you boys my name. You know so much about me—surely you know that."

The detective complained about Francis tapping the legs of the table with his foot. He kept on tapping. Dempsey came back.

"Are you going to talk to us?"

"I don't talk to strangers."

"Well, you can thank the police for saving your life—"
Boys, oh boys!"

"Are you prepared to sit there and say nothing to allegations which will be put to you?" the other detective asked.

"That's my business."

"Is your father alive? Your mother?" asked Dempsey.

"Jesus, you don't know that, either? You're a smart outfit!"

"Do you deny that you are or were a terrorist?"

"I'm an innocent man, you boy, you!"

"What is your name?"

"Jesus, it's a poor outfit if you don't know that."

They wanted his fingerprints. Well, he wasn't going to give them his fingerprints. They'd tried that in the hospital, too.

"Can you recall your fingerprints ever being taken before?"

"That's my business."

The session lasted an hour and a half. The grilling he got later that night lasted two and three-quarter hours. Two detectives: a sergeant and a constable.

"What's your name?"

"Well, you are some boys if you don't know my name!"

"We know you're Hughes. Wouldn't it just be good manners to give us your full name?"

"I'm saying this now: I'm not saying anything until I see my solicitor."

"All we're asking is your name. And you're throwing your solicitor up to us."

"I don't talk to strangers."

They soon started questioning him about the shooting in Fallylea in which the SAS corporal named Jones was killed. He told them in answer to almost all their questions that he was saying nothing until he saw his solicitor. He yawned elaborately.

"Were you on the road or in the field when you were shot?"

He smiled at them. "You said that." He kept yawning, and

reminding them that he had asked to see his solicitor.

"Who is your solicitor?"

"Kevin Agnew."

"Where can he be reached?"

"You are some boys if you don't know that . . . I'm answering no questions till I see my solicitor."

"Will you answer our questions after you've seen your solicitor?"

"Most likely I won't, but I want to see him just the same."

"Why?"

"It's none of your fucking business. I just want to see him, that's all."

"What type of clothing were you wearing the night of 16 March 1978?"

"That's my business."

"We're making enquiries into the murder of Corporal Jones, so it's our business."

When they asked him more questions, he just sat there, giving his voice a rest.

"Why are you not answering at all?"

"I'm a very quiet fellow—don't speak too much, you know."

"What school did you go to?"

"Boy, you are some smart outfit—"

"What school did you go to?"

"The high school," he said, "high on the hill," and laughed at his own joke.

They tried another tack.

"Did you watch TV in the hospital?"

"It's none of your business." He smiled. "But I didn't watch much."

They asked him about the colour of his hair the night of the shooting, and he told them it was none of their business. They said the judge wouldn't think well of his answers and his general attitude. He told them that he didn't give a damn what the judge thought; and that, besides, it was nonsense to tell the same story twice—to the police and to the court.

"Isn't it nonsense to tell the police nothing when they put a series of questions about an incident?"

"It's none of your fucking business, because I'm an innocent man."

One of them gave Francis a hard belt on the side of his head with his open hand.

"We have facts that link you to the scene of the shooting and yet you say it's none of our business—"

"Boys, you have got it now!"

One of them was pointing a pen at him along the table.

"It would be different if we were ramming facts down your throat about an incident you weren't involved in—"

Francis sat forward and thrust out his jaw.

"Go ahead! Ram that *pen* down my throat."

They asked him if he'd been living at home, who his mates were, and so on, and again he told them it was none of their business.

"Milne and McGlinchey are your friends, aren't they?"

"You are the smart boys—"

"Smart in intelligence? Or the way we dress? Or insolent, like you?"

Francis laughed and studied the ceiling of the interrogation room.

Next morning, Thursday 25 January, one of the previous night's interrogators and a new one started in on him at 10:30. Francis had had nothing to eat or drink since lunch in the hospital twenty-one hours earlier. He was feeling a little giddy.

"Our information is—and the facts prove it—that you were involved in the shooting of Corporal Jones. How did you get into that thicket where you were caught?"

"I'm saying nothing till I see my solicitor. I'm innocent, and I'm quite entitled to sit here and say nothing."

They told him he could be charged with murder.

"I'm an innocent man, and if I'm charged with that it will be on your conscience."

They went on and on. They wanted to know what he thought of the Army, the RUC, the UDR, and the IRA. He told them it was none of their business what he thought about them.

After two hours the interrogation was over.

In the afternoon he had a couple of shorter sessions. They asked him where he was immediately before he was found injured on 17 March 1978.

"It's none of your business, and that's the way I'm leaving it."

"We have reason to believe that, on 16th March 1978, you, together with another person, were engaged in a shooting incident with members of the security forces; that you exchanged shots with soldiers and as a result of this incident one soldier died and another was injured. Can you deny that fact?"

"Innocent."

"When you say you are innocent, are you denying that you were present at the shooting incident?"

Francis smiled to himself.

"I'm saying nothing until I see my solicitor."

"Is it true to say you were present at the scene which I have just described at Ranaghan Road, and prior to your encounter with the security forces you were carrying a firearm—?"

"I want to see my solicitor."

"—And that when the soldiers approached on that occasion, both you and another fired aimed shots at them?"

"I don't know what you're on about. I haven't the foggiest."

And so on.

"Are you or were you a member of the PIRA?"

"Innocent."

"I have asked you this question. Your answer would suggest that I have accused you of being a member. What do you mean when you say you are innocent?"

"I am not prepared to say. I will tell when the court time comes if they ask. I have said I am innocent. Is that not enough?"

169

"I am going to ask you again about the 16th of March, 1978. Can you recall that date?"

"I've told you that's my business, you stupid old fucker."

"I must remind you again: that night a soldier lost his life, and we are making enquiries into that."

"I'm telling you again I want to see my solicitor."

The next interrogation was shorter.

"What have you been up to the past few years?"

"I'll be seeing my solicitor before I say anything. Look, I'm an innocent man."

"Could you tell us how you came to be shot?"

"I'll see my solicitor about that."

"If you're innocent, why did you not report the matter and cooperate with the police?"

"It's near time you bundle of whores started to think that I'm innocent."

They asked him whether he was prepared to talk in a general way about his political views.

"I'll see my solicitor first."

"You are quite entitled to your own views and opinions, and by these views we are not suggesting you're breaking the law, provided you go about them in the proper way."

"My views are my business."

"Why not cooperate, if you're so innocent?"

"That's my business. I want to see my solicitor."

That night they went at him hammer and tongs. They knew he hadn't eaten anything or taken liquids for 28 hours. He hummed to himself as they asked him the opening questions.

"Your name?"

"Frank Hughes is all I'm called."

"Are you comfortable?" They knew he couldn't have been very comfortable.

"You'd need to ask the doctor about that."

"Why could you not answer?"

Francis smiled.

"Away and fuck yourselves."

"Do you think that's the right attitude to adopt?"

"I'll adopt whatever attitude I fucking want."

"What about your tea? Did you get any?"

"Find out for yourselves."

"Why will you not eat in here?"

"Go to the doctor and he'll tell you."

"Do you want a cigarette?"

"Not from you boys."

"Why not?"

"I'm not answering you whores."

"Your attitude is not the attitude of an innocent man . . . Why did you kill a soldier that night?"

"I deny all knowledge."

"Why do you think you were shot?"

"I would need to see my solicitor about that."

"If he tells you to tell the truth, would you?"

"I would have to make up my own mind, then."

"If he advised you to tell the truth, would you?"

"I'd have to consider that."

"What were you wearing on 16 March 1978?"

"I'm prepared to answer no more questions about that."

"Have you any remorse for what you did?"

"I would need to see my solicitor."

"Would he know if you were remorseful?"

"You'd need to ask him about that."

This interrogation went on for nearly two and a half hours, during which the pangs in his stomach were bothering him. At one point he farted.

"Do you have a bad stomach?"

"Ask the doctor."

"Why did you give the name Eamonn Laverty when you were arrested?"

"I'd need to see my solicitor about that."

"Did you shout 'Up the Provos' when you were lifted?"

"I'd need to see my solicitor about that."

"How long were you lying in the thicket?"

"I'd need to see my solicitor about that."

"Are you in the Provos—that is, the Provisional IRA?"

"I'd need to see my solicitor about that."

"Would your solicitor know you were in the Provisional IRA?"

"You better ask him that yourself."

"Were you with someone when you were shot?"

"I'd need to see my solicitor."

"Did you have a rifle that night?"

"I'd need to see my solicitor about that."

They seemed to be upset because he kept laughing and smiling. Between questions he sang to himself—little snatches of tunes.

"What have you got to be happy about?"

"That's nothing to do with you."

The second interrogation that night came right after the first without a break. It was more than thirty hours since he'd had anything to eat or drink. He stretched his bad leg out on a chair, settled back and waited. They'd sent down two new boys. Francis was the experienced man in the room now. He'd have to be careful. But so far he hadn't given them any satisfaction.

"What were you doing when you were caught in the gorse bushes?"

"I'll have to see my solicitor about that."

"Why had you your hair dyed?"

"Was it dyed? I'd have to see my solicitor before I'd tell you boys."

"Have you no feelings for the relatives of Lance Corporal Jones?"

"I'd have to see my solicitor before I'd answer that."

172

They talked a long time about his family, the circumstances at home and so forth. They talked. He didn't.

After about forty-five minutes of this, Francis asked if he could stand up. He'd been sitting there for over three hours, and his leg felt stiff.

"Would you like to walk up and down the corridor outside the interview room?"

"I would."

They walked him along the corridor for a few minutes. Then back to the interrogation cell.

"How does your leg feel?" Very friendly.

"I suggest you see the doctor about that."

"Tell us about the shooting . . ."

Francis smiled.

"I'd have to see my solicitor before I'd tell you . . ."

"What's the name of your solicitor?"

"That's my business."

"It's not in your interest to adopt such an attitude."

Francis looked around the room and smiled. It was nearly 11 o'clock.

"Can I stand up? My leg feels stiff."

"Would you want to walk up and down the corridor again?"

"I would." They led him to the toilet. He threw water over his face. The water here would be safe enough. He took a quick drink of it.

They went back to the interrogation room. They asked him about the shooting and about whether he was in the IRA. Francis laughed and smiled. But he let them know he was answering none of their questions.

The next day was Friday, 26 January. No breakfast. Francis had already had his bellyful of interrogations, but there wasn't much he could do. First in the morning came Inspector Dempsey and a detective sergeant. Francis was worn out.

"Have you eaten yet?"

"Ask the fuckin' doctor."

"How are you feeling?"

Francis gave the same answer.

Dempsey said it was a bit disappointing—his adopting that kind of attitude.

"Could you not face up to the fact that it's all over for you? Hasn't the time come to tell us what you know?"

"You're fuckin' sayin' that, not me. I want to see my solicitor."

There was a knock on the door and another peeler came in and said that the extension beyond forty-eight hours had been granted. They'd had him there for about forty-four hours at this point. His trouble here was by no means over.

Francis felt irritable. They must have known by now that he'd die of hunger and thirst if he had to before he'd give them any satisfaction. Dempsey's pal left, and Dempsey kept up the grilling. Then, about an hour after the boy had come in to announce the extension, in came another one.

"Stand up, please," Dempsey said.

Francis stood up.

"He's going to take your picture."

Francis sat down again.

"Please stand up."

"You'll have to fuckin' paste me against the wall to get me to stand!"

The other peeler photographed him where he sat.

"You fucker, you," Francis said to him. "Away and fuck yourself!"

"This is the normal name sheet for photographs," Dempsey said, handing him a paper.

Francis screwed up the paper and threw it across the room.

"Fuck off," he said. He was tired of their little tricks.

The next interrogation was after lunch that day—for those having lunch. Francis wouldn't risk it. They kept trying to link him up with other incidents. This interview was followed by a two-hour one. There was a detective sergeant and a detective constable and an RUC woman detective. He kept refusing to

174

answer. He could tell from their lack of hard evidence that they knew they weren't getting anywhere.

They went at him again that night for nearly four hours. The detective who had hit him on the head and the one who was there when he did it, began interrogating Francis at about seven o'clock. By Francis's calculation he had gone 54 hours without food and only one drink of water. He tried to relax and smile down their questions.

"Have you thought further about your situation?"

"I would have to ask my solicitor before I could answer that."

"Why was your hair dyed the day you were arrested?"

"Why were you hiding in the thicket that day—17 March 1978?"

He kept telling them he would have to see his solicitor before answering.

After a couple of hours of this they turned him over to two other detectives. They opened with the exercise gambit.

"Would you like to walk in the corridor for a bit?"

"No."

"Are you comfortable enough?"

"I would need to see my solicitor before I could answer that."

"Maybe you do want some exercise, you bastard!" one of them said. He caught Francis by the arm and the other one caught him by the shoulders, and they lifted him off the chair and trailed him, his legs bumping along the floor, out into the corridor. They trailed him to the lower end and then swung him around and trailed him straight back up the corridor again.

"Maybe you want a wash? Or to go to the toilet—"

"I'm all right—"

They dropped him where he was, and one of them went into the washroom and filled a sink with water.

They picked him up and pulled him over to the basin. He turned his head aside. They threw water into his face. Finally they dragged him off and trailed him back to the interrogation room.

They asked him whether he was a member of the IRA, or

whether he'd been approached to join the IRA. How had he gotten injured? What was he wearing when they found him? They asked him whether he was injured, and where he went after he was injured. What did he have to say to that? he was asked.

"I've nothing to say until my solicitor comes."

And so it went. They produced some exhibits—his two pairs of trousers, his pullover, his combat jacket, his "docs" (boots); his M-14 rifle, a 7.62 magazine, his .38 and a lot of .38 ammo, some black tape, a tube of Blisteze, two gloves, a black beret, his leather belt and holster. Taking them one by one they asked him had he ever had possession of these things, and he said that he'd have to ask his solicitor before answering. What did he mean by shouting "Up the Provos"? Hadn't he said that the only good peeler was a dead one? Where had he lived at the time—March 1978—and was he working prior to that time, or drawing the dole?

To all their questions he replied by saying he would have to see his solicitor—

"Aren't you getting a bit bored always saying you have to see your solicitor before answering questions?"

"I would have to see my solicitor before I could answer that."

They took Francis back to his cell just before eleven o'clock, and he wondered when they were going to let him see Kevin Agnew. He had a right, even under their Act, to see his solicitor after 48 hours' detention. He was sure that Agnew would have asked to see him. Probably they would have given him the old line that Francis was in there "helping the police with their enquiries," and told him that Francis had not asked to see a solicitor.

On Saturday morning, 27 January, they started in on him again at ten o'clock. They were not too happy. It occurred to Francis that they were running out of steam, and wondering what the hell to do with him. He'd have felt good about the way he'd handled them, except that he was weak from not having eaten for three days, and with only the one drink of water. At times he felt a fierce hunger and thirst. He wanted to eat, but he decided he could not risk it. They'd have more reason now to dope his food and drink than before, because he'd given them nothing.

If they doped his water he wouldn't be able to tell the difference until he woke up on the other side of a confession. Confessing was something he was not going to do, even if he died refusing food and water. How long could he last? He'd heard that people on hunger and thirst strike lasted ten or twelve days.

What he'd told the peeler at the gorse thicket was true. He was not afraid to die.

The line in the first interrogation that morning was routine by now. The second interview began with a question about whether he'd had breakfast that morning.

"I'd have to see my solicitor before I'd answer that question."

They offered him sweets. They asked about his leg, and about his teeth, which they said seemed to be bothering him. And they kept asking him about the Fallylea shooting. They said he'd left a trail of blood that showed his progress across several fields to where he was caught. They wanted to know how he felt about Corporal Jones' family.

Francis kept smiling and telling them he wanted to see his solicitor.

In the afternoon they started again, after three, but they had a fresh subject for a change—an explosion at Coagh, Co. Tyrone, in January 1977, when a Constable Montgomery's back door was blown by a booby-trap bomb. They claimed they had a fingerprint of his on a length of adhesive tape used in making the bomb.

There was a break in the session after half an hour, during which Francis was taken out to the doctor. He complained about being pulled and dragged up and down the corridor the night before.

When he was taken back into the interrogation cell, they went into detail about the Coagh bomb—which had exploded without injury, other than shock, to anyone. But they wanted to hang a charge of attempted murder on him. To all their questions he replied that he would have to see his solicitor before answering.

At about six that night the two boys who had trailed him in the corridor were on again.

"I see you're making complaints against us," one of them said.

Francis had his left leg propped on a bar underneath the table. The detective kicked his leg hard, knocking it off the bar.

"That will give you something to complain about, you fucker!"

Francis said nothing.

At about 7:30 that night two others started in on him. He'd gone three and a half days without food or drink. He was ravenously hungry, and quite tired of their questions. He told them nothing. At the end of this interrogation he was quite surprised when they told him that Kevin Agnew was outside in the visiting room, and that he'd be taken out to see him right away.

KEVIN AGNEW had phoned the police several times that week. He'd learned on Wednesday that Francis had been arrested in the hospital and taken to Castlereagh. Under the Temporary Provisions Act Francis had a right to see his solicitor after 48 hours' detention. When Kevin had phoned earlier in the week they'd kept fobbing him off. But on Saturday evening he'd been at a special court at Magherafelt when he got a message through the Magherafelt police that he could see Francis.

He wondered whether he should leave it until the morning. It was a cold evening, and got dark very early that time of year. There was snow, and ice too, on the roads. The black ice was treacherous. And at 67, Kevin was not as agile a driver as he used to be.

He reached his home in Maghera at a quarter to six and decided to give Oliver Hughes a ring, to let him know he'd been notified. Kevin mentioned the roads.

"Kevin," Oliver said, "If you'll go to Castlereagh, I'll drive you."

"That's all right, then" Kevin said.

So Oliver came at half past six and drove him to Belfast. On the way Kevin dropped into McKenna's shop in Toomebridge, and bought some cigarettes along with a big block of Cadbury's chocolate. He often brought chocolate and apples to his prisoner clients, and only once did a warder object. They let him pass them cigarettes, too, and the boys could smoke while their solicitor was with them. On an impulse Kevin bought a second block of chocolate for Francis. Later he was very glad he had.

Kevin was concerned about Francis's reaction to all that interrogation. He'd cautioned him several times at Musgrave Park. "You're liable to be shipped to Castlereagh at any time, Francis. And you'll be there a few days, and maybe not see me. I don't have to keep telling you: don't answer any questions. Don't have any discussion with them at all." He knew that Francis understood even without him saying it. Nonetheless, Kevin was concerned. Castlereagh was, after all, Castlereagh.

When Kevin arrived there at about ten to eight, he quickly learned that it was not anything Francis had said but his health that was the problem.

The officer in charge—Detective Inspector Francis Dempsey—took Kevin aside.

"Mr. Agnew," he said, "we've had many tough men here. But Hughes beats them all." Kevin was pleased, but not at all surprised.

"Look," Dempsey said, "his food and liquids just would not be tampered with. It's in his own interest to eat . . . If you can persuade him to eat, we will take him to the kitchen, and he can watch his food being prepared—or he can prepare it himself if he likes."

Kevin went into the visiting room at 8:30. The visit was supervised by a constable. The first thing Kevin did was produce the chocolate. From Francis' point of view, it was safe food. Kevin never saw two blocks of chocolate disappear so fast.

They talked for the best part of an hour. Clearly, there was little need to counsel Francis on how to answer the charges. There was a soldier dead, another seriously wounded, and Francis was found a few fields away, his upper leg badly shot up. It was very hard for a lawyer to work his client out of that kind of situation. What Kevin *could* do was try to persuade Francis to eat.

Kevin asked him if he had any complaints. Francis had none, except for one or two long interrogation sessions. Francis told him he hadn't make any statements. It was clear he hadn't indulged in any conversation with the police—none at all. Kevin was under the impression that Francis had been a bit rough with them—told them quite a few times to eff off and so on. Kevin didn't approve of that sort of language. Otherwise he was very pleased.

They spent some time on the matter of food and liquids. He told Francis what the inspector had said. Francis wanted to know what Kevin thought. By the time they were finished their meeting, at 9:20, Kevin had succeeded in persuading Francis.

"Okay," Francis said. "If you recommend that I go to the kitchen and take food, I'll do that."

"Well, that's what I'm telling you I hope you'll do."
Kevin heard later that Francis had in fact gone down to the kitchen next morning and supervised the cooking, assuring himself that there were no drugs or anything being put into his food.

FRANCIS WAS HEARTENED by Kevin Agnew's visit. He'd been handling the questions just the right way. He'd had the chocolate. And in these circumstances he could safely try taking food and drink.

They brought him back to the interrogation room, and began with the explosion at the Montgomery house.

"Were you responsible for placing the explosive device at the home of the Police Constable at Rusty Road, Coagh?"

Francis smiled to himself. No point in talking now about seeing his solicitor.

"I'm not prepared to answer that question," he said.

"Did you make or provide the device or supply any of the component parts?"

"I'm not prepared to answer that question."

180

They tried to get him into a general discussion; but he let them know he wasn't interested.

Next morning Francis was taken under guard down to the kitchen. He hadn't enjoyed a breakfast so much in a long time. There was a long interrogation afterwards.

"Did you have your breakfast this morning?"

"I'm not prepared to answer that question."

"Would you like a cigarette?"

"I'm not prepared to answer that question."

"Would you be prepared to box me then?" one of them said, twisting Francis's hands. "Would you be fit for it, you bastard?" he said as he slapped him on the face. "Would you?" He hit him on the chin with his fist.

Then they went into the SAS shooting, except they didn't call it that. They talked about Lance Corporal Jones. Francis sat there and smiled. He pulled a few faces on them. He was not going to be intimidated.   After an hour Inspector Dempsey came in.

"You are already aware of who I am?" he asked Francis.

"I'm not prepared to answer that question."

Dempsey left after half an hour of trying. Then another one announced himself. "I'm Detective Chief Superintendent William J. Mooney—"

Francis smiled. This was their top man—

"Boys, oh boys!" he said.

"Have you been well treated in Castlereagh?" Mooney asked.

"I'm not prepared to answer that question."

"We have evidence to connect you with serious offences. You should search your conscience about your part in these."

Francis burped—a report from the breakfast—and laughed.

"Do you reckon?"

"All your laughing and bad manners are only a facade. Beneath it you are aware of your serious predicament. At some time in the future you will have to face up to your responsibilities. You will not be laughing and mocking then."

"Do you reckon?" Francis laughed.

Mooney changed tack.

"Do you want a cigarette?"

"I'm not prepared to answer that question."

"Well, you should tell the truth, if only to ease your own conscience."

"Do you reckon?"

"I'm asking you to think about things and ponder your position."

"Is that a question?"

"No, it isn't. But it is good advice."

"Do you reckon?"

It was his fifth day of interrogation.

Early in the afternoon they brought in a couple of new boys to grill him for awhile. They had no luck with him either. Then he had nearly two hours with men he'd seen four or five times before since Wednesday. They talked about his health, asked him about people he knew. In response he grinned and grunted and sucked on his teeth. This seemed to annoy them.

"Did seeing your solicitor change your attitude in any way?"

"I am not prepared," Francis said, "to answer that question."

There was a further interrogation by new boys that night, asking him about what they called "terrorist crimes" in South Derry.

"Boys, oh boys!" Francis said, when at the end of this session Inspector Dempsey joined them. "I'm not prepared to answer any questions."

"Have you given the Jones murder any more thought?"

"I'm not prepared to answer that question."

"Is this on the advice of your solicitor? Surely you're aware of all the evidence we have against you in the Jones murder and the attempted murder of Constable Montgomery?"

They were working with very little, after all, weren't they? "I'm not prepared to give any answer to that," Francis said, smiling.

"Why not?"

"I'm not prepared to answer that, either."

Next day was Monday, 29 January, his sixth day at Castlereagh. They seemed to be just going through the motions now.

They wanted him to give all the questions some serious thought, they said.

"Is that a question?"

"No. It's stating a fact."

"Oh, I see, boys."

Would he be willing to give them a sample of his hair? Francis smiled and shook his head.

They tried again in the afternoon. There was a final session that night, for twenty minutes, with Arlow and Dempsey.

They asked him about the booby-trap bomb at Constable Montgomery's house in Coagh. Of the dozens of incidents they would have liked to stick him with, all they could come up with, apart from the SAS shooting, was this bomb in Coagh.

"I'm not answering any questions." Francis said.

"Can you offer any explanation why you are so closely linked to a number of serious crimes?"

"I'm not prepared to answer that question."

"There is evidence that you were involved in the outrages I have mentioned."

"Do you reckon?"

The interrogation ended at nine that night.

Francis was taken to the police office at Townhall Street, and the magistrate's court at Chichester Street, and charged with the shooting of the SAS man and the bomb at Coagh. On each charge he was asked how he pleaded.

"Not guilty on any trumped-up charge," he said.

He was remanded in custody next day, Tuesday, and taken to Crumlin Road prison.

KEVIN AGNEW had seen Francis frequently at Musgrave Park hospital. He'd seen him that one night at Castlereagh. During the year Francis was on remand, waiting for his trail, Kevin saw him virtually every week for his remand hearing in a private interview room in Crumlin Road prison. The one-judge no-jury Diplock trial was held in Belfast Crown Court before Mr. Justice Murray during an eight day period in February 1980.

"Trail of Blood Evidence in Murder Trial Court" was the way the trial was played in one loyalist newspaper. The barristers Kevin had chosen for the trial—Michael Nicholson was senior counsel and John McCrudden the junior—made a great case for nearly a fortnight out of nothing. What could be said, after all, to defend a man who had brazenly walked up a field with an automatic rifle and then shot two soldiers from twelve feet away?

During the trial Kevin winced a little when he heard the police witnesses repeating some of Francis's strong language. Yet, he thought, they must have found him interesting—the way he steadfastly resisted all their questioning.

Kevin reflected on this man he'd talked to some seventy times during the two years since he'd first seen him at Musgrave Park. This was an ordinary man, Hughes, but he was a real man. He was so young! He'd enlisted just after leaving school, and had served as an absolutely dedicated volunteer, carving himself such an IRA career over a few short years that he became probably the greatest soldier of them all. Francis was not a man of education; he hadn't gone much beyond the primary school level. And such was his dedication that he couldn't have had much chance to live a normal life and enjoy the years of his youth, from the time he was a young boy until they took him away in that ambulance to Magherafelt hospital.

Was Francis a hard man? He was ruthless, surely. He was a born Republican and a highly motivated soldier. He was a man prepared to give his life and equally prepared to take life. He would not have had any compunction at all about shooting a British soldier he saw as an enemy. It was a question either of shooting him first or getting shot. Was he out looking for people to shoot? Obviously. He was on active service.

Kevin had a warm professional relationship with him: and

they had the bond of their shared Republicanism. But there was an age gap between them. Kevin couldn't imagine that, had Francis been at large, he would have been a pal.

And yet in the trial there were lines of testimony in which Kevin took personal pleasure:

> "It was put to him that we only wanted his name. Yet he was throwing his solicitor up to us . . . "
>
> "I don't talk to strangers . . ."
>
> And when they'd asked him why he refused to answer, he'd said, "I'm a very quiet fellow. Don't speak too much, you know."

Hardly the perfect case to defend; but Francis was, in the way he had handled police questioning, the perfect lawyer's client.

In summing up, the judge said: "I want to record the fact that in reaching my decisions on the various charges I have entirely disregarded the various interviews of the accused at Castlereagh Police Office save to note that during these interviews the accused maintained throughout his innocence of the charges."

Francis was given a life sentence for killing the SAS man, and a total of eighty-three years on five other counts.

Kevin saw Francis a few times afterwards in Long Kesh* in

---

*Tony O'Hara had some contact with Francis Hughes in the H-Blocks and knew the legend of the great guerrilla leader and fighter. Yet when Francis came to Long Kesh in February 1980 the officers had all been appointed and the chain of command had been well established. Francis didn't hold a position in the command structure, but because of his quality as a natural leader, and his reputation, there was an aura round him. With his wit and his easygoing way he was great for the morale of the men in Long Kesh. He took his full part in the protest. He immediately went on the blanket and on the no-wash no-slop-out protest.

His family called him Francis, but he was "Big Frank" to the men in Long Kesh. He was also called "Pixie Hughes." The story as Tony heard it was that Francis went to sleep one night in the cell he shared with Raymond McCreesh from Camlough. He had special boots

connection with a complaint about his treatment at Castlereagh, connection with an effort to get an appeal on the Murray verdict. Francis eventually abandoned the appeal.

MICK HUGHES looked at his young brother as he lay in his hospital bed. Francis had suffered through more than a year on the blanket and the no-wash protest in Long Kesh. He was run down generally. And there was his leg, which was bothering him all the time. He should have been in a convalescent home, not on hunger strike. It might have been a long time till the amnesty, when Francis would walk through the door of the new bungalow at the farm in Bellaghy, but Mick thought it would have been well worth the wait.

During that first prison hospital visit, Mick asked him whether he really wanted to go through with it.

"Francis, I'm not saying what you should do. But if you want to call this thing off, you've one man here who'll back you."

Francis smiled and shook his head.

Mick had known, of course, how determined Francis was to go through with it. But he did think he might be saved—that the Irish and British governments could work out a compromise that the prisoners could agree to. Mick even thought that Bob-

---

because one leg was shorter than the other as a result of his gun battle with the SAS. The two big boots were left near the wall overnight and in the morning when he was putting them on he found excreta in one of them.

Had Raymond put it in his boot as a practical joke? Raymond denied it, saying that it must have fallen off the wall, or maybe the pixies came in the night and put it there. So the story went the rounds and Francis became "Pixie Hughes."

There were people who said to Tony afterwards that Francis had retired from the war when he came to Long Kesh. But to Tony there was nothing easy or passive about the prison protest—it was a continuation of the fight against the British. And Francis's determination to continue the struggle was proved by the enthusiasm with which he offered himself in December 1980 for the first hunger strike, joining with the 29 other men in support of the seven original hunger strikers. Now, in the second one, he was second in line.

by Sands' life would be saved. He didn't know at that point just what sort of person Margaret Thatcher would turn out to be.

He asked Francis about the screws in the hospital. How had they been treating him? There was one orderly named Billy from Armagh. During his visit with Francis, Billy kept coming in and going out. Mick asked Francis what he was like.

"Billy's one of ours," Francis said.

"What do you mean, Francis? Is he a Catholic?"

"No," Francis said. "But Billy has looked after me a hundred per cent. Be sure and look after Billy when I'm gone."

Francis could see that Mick didn't quite understand.

"You don't have to provide for him or anything. Just shake his hand and say, 'Thanks very much, Billy, for everything you've done for my brother.'"

So on the day a couple of weeks later, when Mick left the hospital for the last time, he made a special point of going over to Billy and thanking him for all that he'd done for Francis.

He was a small, dark-haired boy—a very nice character. As a Dub is a Dublin man, Billy was an Armagh City man.

"Don't thank me," Billy said. "I only did my best. I never tried to change his mind, or anything like that. Francis was just a very good friend of mine."

It was not surprising that Francis had great affection for him. And that was Francis's way, too—to return loyalty.

Francis had shown this loyalty to the people at home. Mick recalled that before Francis went on hunger strike he wrote a letter that showed not only his clarity of mind about the issues involved, but a sense of what the prisoners' supporters outside were going through:

> To the People of South Derry and Surrounding Areas:
>
> A Chairde,
>
> By the time this letter is read to you I shall have joined my comrade Bobby Sands, already on hunger strike. I need not go into any great detail in explaining to you the reasons for this present hunger strike, as you have all followed

events closely and seen openly for yourselves the end result of the dishonourable fashion and deceitful way in which the British government abandoned her commitments and assurances after December the 18th.

These commitments and assurances were not won lightly, but were the result of fifty-three torturous days of pain and suffering to obtain them. They were not won lightly and they shall not be given up lightly either.

You must realize the importance of what is happening here. This prolonged protest has become more than a minor prison issue for the British government. Its very roots lie in the eleven years of struggle waged around you and its outcome will have great bearing on whether the British stay or go. For this sole reason and no other we have been confronted and opposed at every turn in our attempts to find an acceptable solution which would end the four and a half years of conflict.

The British know that any solution other than outright victory would be a defeat for them. It was in this frame of mind that they masterminded events leading into the new year, and when they foolishly thought they had won the day through their treachery they asked us for a white flag. Our action alone answers their hypocritical request and as before the message is loud and clear. There is no white flag and there shall be no surrender.

I know many of you people personally and I know too that if you were in our position you would not compromise your principles, but you too would fight; and it is in this knowledge that we embark upon this great trial, in full confidence of victory. There is one demand and this lies in our interpretation of what we believe constitutes political status. This demand was met on December the 18th, 1980. It was met after you had marched and tramped for eight full weeks in a relentless campaign which finally broke the British. They know we broke them and we know we can break them again. What you must do is close the ranks and remain steadfast in your determination.

As you march and rally, refuse to be intimidated by the harassment of the much hated RUC and those who cower beside them. Your sufferings and your hardship are well known to us. We salute you for the courage and perserverance you have shown in the face of everything. You serve as a great example to us all, and in the coming weeks we shall draw much strength and encouragement as we remember you in our prayers and hold you in our thoughts.

I have no prouder boast than to say I am Irish and have been privileged to fight for the Irish people and for Ireland. If I have a duty I will perform it to the full in the unshakeable belief that we are a noble race and that chains and bonds have no part in us.

Slán,
Francis Hughes
Republican POW
Long Kesh 10-3-81

It was five days after that that he began his fast.

Mick knew that Francis wasn't suffering now from pangs of hunger as such. But he could see that he was in great pain. It was said that with men on hunger strike, the first six days or so were the worst. After that they'd go into a sort of dreamland as far as food was concerned. Some days they'd feel terrible pain from other causes, but hunger didn't much bother them.

The thing was that Francis had gone through this hunger strike experience before. When he'd been taken to Castlereagh after recovering from his operation, he'd refused food and even drink for several days for fear they were going to drug him. In December 1980 he'd spent the best part of a week on hunger strike. And beginning in March 1981 he'd started going through the whole experience again.

On the earliest of his visits, Mick found Francis still in good spirits. Mick only wished that he himself had more to say. Later he saw Francis becoming very weak—suffering from the constant pain in his leg, from dizziness and rapidly fading vision. He was finding it hard to hold down water. He often vomited. He'd already lost the sight of one eye—temporarily, Mick hoped—and wore a patch over it except at night. During a visit at the end of the first week in May, he'd found Francis unable to talk. Mick had spent a long time in silence, thinking about his brother and the family.

But now Bobby Sands had died. Mick couldn't have the same hope for Francis's life that he'd had just a week earlier. Francis was visibly more emaciated each day. He was fading, and on Thursday 30 April he received the last sacraments. For much of his hunger strike his mother hadn't come to visit because she couldn't stand to see him wasting away. She came, finally—and then took several visits. Once during his last days she threw her arms around his neck.

"I'm the proudest mother in the world," she said. "The family are all proud of you, Francis."

"I always like to see you happy," he said, tenderly kissing the cross that she held out to him—the cross the Pope had sent him.

Watching him towards the last, Mick thought to himself that Francis was tougher than shoe leather. He never cried out or complained. With Bobby Sands gone, Francis seemed to have lost all fear of death.

THE DAY BEFORE FRANCIS DIED Mick came into the hospital at three o'clock. Only two members of the family were allowed to stay overnight with him and Mick was joined by his sister Dolores. Francis was beginning to sink. But he was still lucid enough to ask to be allowed to see Raymond McCreesh and Patsy O'Hara. The doctor agreed and had Patsy O'Hara brought in in a wheelchair. He and Francis talked for awhile and then they took Patsy away. They couldn't bring in Raymond, Francis's old cellmate, because Raymond was only semi-conscious; he'd had a bad spell and was very weak. But Patsy somehow managed to be in great form for Francis. A fine lad, Mick thought. And he seemed to give Francis heart.

Afterwards, there was a lot of silence in the room. An empty cell had been set aside for them, and when it was late Mick suggested that Dolores go and lie down. After a couple of hours he woke her, as she'd asked him to.

Meantime he'd been talking with Francis. Francis was still able to talk intermittently, and during those hours of broken conversation, he kept telling jokes, any silly old jokes that came into his head. He brought up things that had happened in the past, reliving part of his life again, reminiscing about things that had occurred when he was a young boy and Mick was still at home. His voice was breaking up, but Mick understood him well enough. Then, at about two o'clock, his voice gave out.

Mick tended him until morning. Water came out of Francis's mouth and Mick kept drying it off. Francis slept for a couple of hours, waking up about seven in the morning. He coughed a lot. Mick kept talking into his ear, telling Francis that he was still with him. Francis would give him the thumbs up sign.

"Aye, thumbs up, Francis," Mick would say. "I see you're okay there." And that would bring a bit of a smile to his face.

At one point a lot of phlegm came up out of his chest, choking him. Mick quickly ran for help. Billy was still on duty and got the doctor in with a suction machine. Francis didn't know what was happening, with the doctor pushing a tube down past his teeth. He resisted. Mick shouted in Francis's ear: "Francis, it's me, Mick. They're not trying to force-feed you, Francis. They're only trying to get that ould stuff out of your mouth." Then he opened his mouth and they cleared his throat. The phlegm kept coming up for another couple of hours. Then finally it cleared entirely.

It was about two or three o'clock in the afternoon that their mother and father and others in the family came. They wouldn't let all of them stay. So Mick and Dolores had to leave. Their mother was in a bad way. Francis was nearly gone, and they wanted to take their mother away, because she was terribly upset. Finally she agreed to leave. "Francis, I'm going now," she said, taking his hand. "I've got to go away. I'll see you in Heaven."

Francis clasped her hand tightly.

That was the last time Mick saw Francis alive. He drove to

Bellaghy and went straight to bed. When he woke up later that night, his brother Francis was dead. He'd died that evening at 5:43 p.m., after fifty-nine days on hunger strike. Noreen and Marie were with him, and Oliver was nearby.

ONE PERSON who did not see Francis during his hunger strike was his solicitor Kevin Agnew. Kevin knew there had been many family members and others eager to visit Francis in the hospital. But it was a matter of great sorrow to Kevin that Francis was on hunger strike for fifty-nine days and yet apparently had not asked to see him. Had he not known of Kevin's emotional commitment beneath the gruff Ulsterman's exterior? Perhaps Kevin had been too professional, with too much respect for the proprieties. Maybe he should have asked to see Francis rather than waiting for the young man to ask to see him. He'd have gladly gone to see Francis. It was not just that Kevin felt they'd had a good working relationship as lawyer and client; it was not just his admiration for Francis and for his final willingness to sacrifice his life: apart from the professional and political bonds between them, there was something Kevin had wanted to do for Francis, and now couldn't do.

He'd wanted to help him prepare a Last Will and Testament.

"Francis, before you go to the next world I would like to have a talk with you . . ." That's how it would have begun. Francis would have discussed his reasons for doing what he did, and Kevin would have put them down as a lasting memorial.

The idea of a testament probably never occurred to Francis. James Connolly and other people left testaments in their time. But new generations arise, and what was written in a condemned cell in 1916 might not be of equal relevance seventy years later.

Bobby Sands' writings and testament would live on as long as the nation lived. Francis's Last Will and Testament—properly authenticated and with his signature on it—would have been a historical record. It could have been printed. Kevin thought about the other men. Apart from Bobby, what would survive? There would be the *in memoriam* cards—with photographs and maybe a poem on them. But it would have been valuable to have testaments from the men themselves, in their own language.

192

Francis could have spoken about his faith in Ireland and his belief in the right of the Irish to be free. If the sacrifice of his life would help bring that about, it would not have been in vain . . .

The day Francis died, Tony Benn, a leading figure in the British Labour Party, said in a radio interview on BBC: "The partition of Ireland was a crime against the Irish people . . . The legitimate objective of this country is to bring about conditions where the Irish people can solve the problem for themselves . . ."

THE McCUSKER BROTHERS of Magherafelt, whom the Hughes family had engaged as undertakers, had never had any difficulty with the RUC until that day: 13 May 1981—the day after Francis died.

It was about five in the evening when Thomas and Danny McCusker moved Francis's coffin from the mortuary at the Forster Green hospital in Belfast to a waiting hearse. Mick's father and mother drove behind the hearse in Noreen's grey Volkswagen beetle. The arrangement had been that the funeral cortege was to follow police landrovers through West Belfast, where thousands of people had been waiting in the streets for hours, then onto the M-2, out to Toomebridge and on up to the Hughes home outside Bellaghy.

The fact that the body had been taken to Forster Green hospital meant that the cortege had to start off through the Pro-testant Belvoir estate. As it moved out, there began a series of confrontations during which loyalist crowds, carrying anti-IRA banners, waving their fists and shouting slogans, threw bottles and stones at the hearse. Then, on the Newtownbreda dual car-riageway, armed police—who had changed the route to bypass the sympathetic crowds in West Belfast—stopped the hearse and ordered the McCuskers out. They were taking over, the police said.

"Not bloody likely," said Thomas McCusker, who was in the passenger seat. He went to lock the door of the hearse. His brother Danny also refused, saying that they were in charge of the hearse. The police yanked the door open, grabbed Thomas McCusker by the legs and body and pulled him out of the hearse onto the road, tearing his clothes while doing it. Other police hit members of the family and friends. Danny McCusker tried to put the keys of the hearse into his mouth, but policemen knocked them away. He grabbed the steering wheel and put his shoulder at the corner of the door to stop them forcing him out. The police yanked at his shirt and tie, pulling at his hair and ears.

Then they tried to take the coffin from the hearse. When Francis's ageing father Joe Hughes moved up to prevent them, they pushed and struck the old man. Jimmy Drumm of Sinn Féin and Owen Carron, Bobby Sands' constituency agent, were both hit. Noreen was crying and their mother was terribly distressed and upset, yet the police kept trying to take over the hearse.

This continued for about twenty minutes until suddenly an American TV crew arrived on the scene and began filming. The RUC quickly backed off. But they insisted on dictating a new route for the cortege. Under duress the family agreed, on condition that they be given custody of the body at Toomebridge. Owen Carron got into the hearse, and stayed there for the rest of the journey. Again the cortege was led by RUC men into a loyalist housing estate and stoned by a crowd there; the police made no effort to protect either the hearse or the family. Finally they got out onto the M-2.

After that, the trip was uneventful until they reached the Randalstown slipway a few miles short of Toome. Here the RUC again stopped the hearse and created another confrontation. The police ordered the relatives to go to Bellaghy through Toomebridge while they themselves escorted the hearse the long way around, through Randalstown and Portglenone. So the hearse was separated from the family and taken under heavy police escort on a detour through Randalstown, while the Hugheses and their friends were harassed and threatened by stationary and mobile police patrols at every junction on their way home through Toome. All the side roads were blocked and they had to run the gauntlet of sectarian insults on the way, their fears intensified by rumours that the RUC wanted to dump Francis's body into the River Bann.

At the Hughes home several of Francis's sisters were waiting, one of them convinced that her brother's body would never reach the house. They'd been waiting three hours for the cortege to reach Bellaghy. Scores of cars were parked along Scribe Road and hundreds of people were gathered, in pouring rain, when finally at 7:25 the hearse arrived at the long laneway leading up to the house. Then the coffin, draped in the Tricolour, was carried up the lane.

Late into the night the people of South Derry and friends from far away filed past the coffin with its masked honour guard of IRA volunteers. People who had never known members of the present-day Republican movement or any IRA men other than Francis, met them at his wake that night and the next day and night.

There was great community sympathy with the Hughes family because of the cruelty of the police that day. And a new bond was forged among Catholics of the surrounding area. As a priest said afterwards to Francis's brother Mick: "The police could desecrate a hunger striker's dead body; they could interfere with and dishonour a cortege. Army helicopters could try to drown out the speakers at a burial. They had control of the roads. But the wakes were in our homes, beyond their reach. The wakes belonged to the Catholics alone . . . "

People who hated or disliked or had been estranged from the IRA angrily decided they'd turn out for the funeral, along with IRA supporters and neighbours and friends of the Hugheses. They came in huge numbers, striding up the roads and laneways and flowing through the fields. The police added what insult they could by diverting the funeral procession so that it could not pass through the Hugheses' own town of Bellaghy. This, Mick thought, had probably been on the orders of the leading bigot in the area, the Paisleyite councillor "Black Bob" Overend. Nevertheless the people marched in swelling numbers to pay tribute to a Francis who even in death had so frightened the RUC that they had felt it necessary to hijack the body from the family. "They feared him more dead than alive," one young woman said. And that became part of Francis's legend, too:

They feared you then, they fear you yet—
For Hughes lives on forever . . .

Among the tens of thousands who turned out for the funeral were a large number of young people, who years earlier had been children in homes where Francis Hughes had been shielded and looked after while on the run. They were older now, and a man said to Mick after the funeral that he had never seen so many crying teenagers in his life. Mick noticed that a great many Protestants, who didn't dare appear at Francis's wake or funeral, sent Mass cards or messages. They were determined to let the family know that they remembered Francis.

Many of the messages reduced themselves to simple acknowledgements. Some said, "There was a man: he could fight and kill for what he believed in; but he could also suffer and die . . ."

Mick noticed that along with the other relatives several members of the McCreesh family—whose brother Raymond was likely to be the next to go—were at the funeral. Among them were Father Brian and Malachy McCreesh. And at the funeral Eamonn Mallie, the Downtown Radio reporter, asked Malachy a curious question. Was there truth in the rumour that Raymond was about to abandon his hunger strike?

Chapter 5

A PROUD YOUNG IRISHMAN

I am a proud young Irishman.
In Ulster's hills my life began.
A happy boy through green fields ran
And kept God's and man's laws.
But when my age was barely ten
My country's wrongs were told again
By tens of thousands marching men
And my heart stirred to the cause.

> So I'll wear no convict's uniform
> Nor meekly serve my time
> That Britain might brand Ireland's fight
> Eight hundred years of crime.

Francie Brolly
H-BLOCK SONG

THE CROSS ON THE WALL of the sacristy where Father Brian McCreesh was vesting for Mass was a small object of highly polished dark wood, probably ash. Originally it had been a memento of a journey to Lough Derg, an Irish place of pilgrimage. This cross dated back more than two and a quarter centuries to the height of penal times in Ireland, when being an Irish Catholic meant being deprived of the right to own property, the right to hold any public office, the right to an education, the right to have bishops or priests, the right to freely practice the Catholic religion. The cross was an authentic relic of those days. Carved into its back was the year 1752.

The young priest was well aware on that Saturday morning, 16 May 1981, of the ravages of time. His brother, Raymond McCreesh—at the age of 24 seven years younger than Brian—was on the fifty-sixth day of his hunger strike in the prison at

Long Kesh, in protest at the practices of yet another British regime in Ireland.

Father Brian had been a curate in this parish in Coalisland, County Tyrone, for two and a half years. Coalisland was one of the few Irish towns to have been marked by the English industrial revolution. That was long ago. The collieries were closed now, the mills shut down. There had been plenty of work in Coalisland until the current phase of the conflict began; but now Coalisland showed the blight of Margaret Thatcher's recession, alongside the blight inherited from the industrial years, the legacy of the exploiters. A friend of Brian's had described Coalisland as a place where everything had been taken out—gravel, coal, sand, clay—and nothing put back in.

The sacristy where Brian was vesting was a low-ceilinged, white-walled room, one of many rooms along one side and under the tapered roof of the large modernistic chapel building. Out in the church itself there was a high ceiling and a feeling of airiness and light. The altar slab at the front was surrounded on three sides by pews, where the people could be close to their priests.

Seen from outside, the chapel, called the Church of the Holy Family, was a rounded polygon, fashioned of red-brown Coalisland brick—from a works that had been moved down the road to Dungannon. The big chapel was set in the side of a hill, in handsome contrast to the bleak and spiky RUC barracks that crouched down the road near the bottom of the hill, the cameras on its rickety steel towers floating high above it like crab's eyes. Above the church was a large plain parish house, shared by Brian and the other curate, Father Dan Treanor, an amiable, rawboned Irish missionary veteran who had served thirty-two years in Burma.

The figure of the crucified Christ that emerged in relief from the native Irish wood of the penal cross was not just bonded to the cross. It was of one natural substance with it, fashioned out of the same single small block of wood. The arms of the Crucified were shortened, so that the cross might be quickly hidden away in a pocket or the folds of a sleeve. Irish and of Irish material, it symbolized the systematic persecution of the people, and their religion, for the sake of English power.

Below the Christ figure were two charming little images incised into the block of wood. The lower figure was of a rounded cooking pot; the upper figure, between the Christ and the pot, was of a cock crowing. There were various explanations. The one Brian liked best lay in an old Irish legend of the Resurrection. The story was that on Easter Sunday morning the soldiers guarding the tomb grew hungry. So they heated a pot of water and, when they'd brought it to the boil, killed a cock and plunged it into the pot to make themselves a stew. While the stew was cooking away, they slept. But when Christ rose from the tomb, the cock rose too, springing alive from the pot, celebrating its escape from the power of its enemies, crowing at their foolishness, trumpeting its freedom and triumph over death.

It was a month into Eastertide, which in the liturgical calendar was supposed to be a time of muted Alleluia, a quiet summery time alive with the diffused light of the risen Christ. But this part of Ireland was still in the throes of a painful foreign occupation. And Brian's younger brother Raymond, a Provisional IRA prisoner, was suffering a terrible personal passion, an agony of starvation that would likely soon end in the young man's death.

Brian never liked the IRA. Did he hate it? Hate would be too strong a word. He had seen in Coalisland and elsewhere in the North the damage and suffering members of the IRA caused their own Irish people and their own families. Brian understood why his young brother Raymond had fought as an IRA man. He understood the impulse to become a soldier and go out and do battle against the British. But Brian himself was, if anything, a pacifist. He would have dissuaded Raymond, if he could have, from involvement in the IRA.

Raymond was well along in his hunger strike before Brian had thought the whole thing through to the point where he, a priest, felt he could and ought to offer himself as a speaker on the H-Blocks circuit. He'd been thinking of Raymond when he made his first speech at a rally. He could hear his own voice at the microphone, the speakers echoing it back: "What I want to state and what I want the British government to hear is this:

that my brother Raymond is not a criminal." The voice was quiet but it was clear: "He is in prison as a direct result of the civil unrest and political turmoil brought about in this community by the denial of basic civil rights. He would never have seen the inside of a prison were it not for these political circumstances . . ."

Brian wondered at the time what effect his witness would have. He'd visited Raymond the next day and taken the speech out of his pocket to show to his brother. But by then, some forty-four days on in his hunger strike, Raymond was unable to read Brian's typescript. He had begun to go blind.

BRIAN HAD BEEN ORDAINED in 1973, after seven years study at St. Patrick's College in Maynooth, in County Kildare.

A week before his ordination he went to Newry to attend the ordination of one of his classmates. Returning to Maynooth afterwards, where he was making his own ordination retreat, he was stopped with several other classmates, all wearing clerical collars, at a British Army checkpoint near the border. They were told to get out of the car and forced to spread eagle themselves against it, their backs to the soldiers, their legs apart.

Then they were interrogated. Brian himself was questioned by a black soldier, who asked him his name and where he was coming from and where he was going. To Brian this was a paradigm. Here Brian was, on his own ground and in his own country, in South Armagh where he belonged, and here on Irish ground was a black man, one of the sons or grandsons of people over whose native soil the British had once seized control. Here was a black man working for the oppressor, interrogating Brian with a gun in his hand. A stranger, putting Brian up against it, on his own Irish soil. "You're far from home," another black soldier had said to a friend of Brian's who was stopped on another occasion by a patrol in east County Derry, not far from Derry city. The friend, who was from Antrim town, fifty or sixty miles away, looked at the soldier. "You're not so near home yourself," he said.

Northern Irish Catholics felt strongly about the land. It was their land. The Irish had thousands of years of history here. There was a long-established bond with the country. It was entirely right and natural that they should be in Ireland. Yet they were confronted and challenged by people who had no right whatever in this country, questioning the right of Irishmen to move about in their own land. Experiences like that would surely have worked on Raymond. And Raymond would have reacted more angrily than Brian to the hostile questioning, the challenges, from men who had no right to challenge or question him.

It wasn't just the wrongness of British soldiers being there, and the hostility of their questions that would have bothered Raymond. There were the local Protestant B-men, too, the B-Special police, who were still around when Raymond was a boy of eleven and twelve.

The same story had been told and repeated in slight variations all over the North, retold hundreds and thousands of times with only the names changed. Somebody would be out at night, walking or driving along, and would be stopped by a patrol of B-men (or, after 1970, by a patrol of UDR men—more or less the same personnel, but now in army rather than police get up). Among the B-Specials would be one of the neighbours, or a workmate. And the B-man would pretend not to know the person, and would ask: "What's your name? Where do you live? Where are you coming from? Where are you going?"

Why was it that this always hurt so much? And why was the same experience recounted everywhere? People felt: "He's my neighbour. He knows me very well. Yet he is out on this road with a gun, demanding to know my name. He damn well knows my name!" That sort of thing bit deep. The British authorities and the police were always talking about normal community relations. How could there be normal community relations in those circumstances, when local people would appear armed on the road, in the dark of night, and ask their neighbours who they were?

Who were they? Who were the McCreeshes? Just one among thousands of families with deep roots in the soil of Ireland. The McCreeshes could trace without effort seven generations of forebears in their ancestral homestead in Dorsey, South Armagh.

The surname McCreesh was an anglicized form of an old

Irish name which had developed locally from Mag Aonghusa or Mag Aonghuis (anglicized Maginnis or MacGuinness or McGuinness). Indeed, in the often crude anglicization of their Gaelic family and place names the Irish could feel keenly and painfully their very identity being degraded or denied. Mag Aonghusa meant son of Aengus. The wandering Aengus was a figure of Irish legend and mythology, celebrated by among others the poet William Butler Yeats.

The McCreesh sept was of very local provenance, limited to a few parishes in South Armagh. In Dorsey there was a McCreesh family who had changed their name to Maginnis to claim a legacy left them in America under that name. Locally they were still known as McCreesh. In South Armagh it was widely known that McCreesh and McGuinness (in its variant spellings) were the same name.

It was a small part, the evolution of their name, of the local history the McCreeshes knew instinctively: a history that gave them an integral sense of their identity and rights as Irish people, and a sense of injustice, of deprivation of their rights, and therefore a sense of loss. The McCreeshes—there were three other brothers and three sisters, eight of them in all—grew up with that awareness of keenly felt loss. Not the least of it was the loss of their own Irish language, which was intertwined with their history, their culture, their music and their way of looking at the world. Raymond had learned Irish at secondary school, and had become fluent during his four years in Long Kesh. (The Long Kesh Irish was a dialect—really Donegal Irish with variations, and with a lot of fresh coinages worked up to meet the prisoners' circumstances.) The first wedding Brian ever officiated at was celebrated in Irish, in Camlough. Several Camlough families had strong traditions of using the language.

Irish had been proscribed throughout Ireland by earlier generations of British direct rulers, because the language gave the people a natural defence, a place to hide their thoughts in. It was a code of their own, and an instrument of rebellious counsel inaccessible to their English-speaking overlords. Only in a few places, mostly along the reaches of distant coasts, far from Dublin and the English Pale, did the original language survive. The local South Armagh dialect had only recently died away. Now all the native Irish speakers in that part of Ireland were gone, like so much else that was Irish there.

THE IRISH IN ARMAGH had lost nearly everything. The *bacall Íosa*, for example, revered by the Irish of Armagh through a thousand years of tradition as the staff of Jesus himself, inherited by St. Patrick—it was the wondrous bishop's staff Patrick was supposed to have carried when he travelled on his journeys up and down and back and forth across the island of Ireland.

This wooden staff of Jesus was maintained in the church of Armagh together with the Book of Armagh and other treasures. When the Normans came in the twelfth century they plundered Armagh, the city and the church, and carried off the *bacall Íosa*. It was taken to Dublin and kept there for four centuries. Then, in the early days of the Reformation, a Protestant archbishop of Dublin came into control of the *bacall Íosa*, the staff of Jesus, Patrick's staff, and decided it was a superstitious relic. He ordered it burned.

Brian knew that there were people who thought it stupid or intolerant to be bothered, to feel injured, by a thing like that. But the injury was there. For someone from Armagh diocese, with a sense of his history, his Irishness, and even his Catholicism, to hear that story for the first time really hurt, because it meant that his own people had been trampled on. Something of value to them, and to him, had been wantonly destroyed.

There were other examples.

In East Tyrone, just up the road from Coalisland, lay the townland of Tullyhogue, very near present-day Stewartstown. Tullyhogue had once been the seat of the O'Neills, kings of that part of Ireland. The O'Neills had originally come from Inishowen, in what was now eastern Donegal. They were a self-aggrandizing tribe, who raided other people's territories and took possession of them by force. They were, in a sense, imperialists. But they were Irish, and Ulster Irish. They were part of the native culture. As they moved east, the O'Neills set up their headquarters at Tullyhogue in the eleventh or twelfth century before moving in and taking control of Dungannon, where they ruled till the first years of the seventeenth century.

There was a stone inaugural chair at Tullyhogue; it was there for centuries, symbolizing the seat of the O'Neills and their power. Each successive O'Neill went to the hill of Tullyhogue and sat in this chair while being inaugurated as chief of the clan. But while on a campaign against the O'Neills, the English deputy Mountjoy crossed the Blackwater, destroyed Dungannon Castle, then went to Tullyhogue and had the chair of the O'Neills smashed to pieces. For the Irish of the North, the most Gaelic part of Ireland up to that time, the breaking up of the chair would ever afterwards be symbolic: "There, that's the English, vandalizing and smashing up everything belonging to the Irish and of significance and value to them."

Then the Irish under Hugh O'Neill were defeated, with their Spanish allies, at the disastrous battle of Kinsale. As the English encroached more and more on their authority and property, O'Neill and Rory O'Donnell, Irish chieftains who had already been downgraded by being made English earls, took flight and found refuge in continental Europe.

It wasn't just the material symbols and the language that had been taken from the Irish. It was the whole structure of images and traditions and usages that had come to codify Irish arrangements and Irish culture. The Brehon laws, for example, were an indigenous institution, worked out to suit native and instinctive Irish styles of thinking and acting. It took the English centuries to undo the Brehon system, which worked on assumptions of freedom of movement and freedom to rearrange things. (It also made extraordinary provision for the rights of women in and outside of marriage.) The English were bewildered—Brian had seen this in plantation documents—by the informality and fluidity of Irish ways. And what bewildered the English, the English destroyed: violently imposing their rigidity and stiff formality on the relaxed and natural procedures the Irish had slowly codified into a stable indigenous system. As a result, Irishmen who understood something of their own cultural style and saw the unnaturalness of the English impositions, came to feel, as Brian himself did, that they didn't really belong to this whole setup at all. They were hedged in by it; they couldn't express themselves through it. They felt stifled and smothered by this cold system against which their own natural way of life had been wrecked.

Together with destruction came oppression. The foreigner who had vandalized Irish artifacts and objects and customs, and even the Irish language, now sat as ruler and judge and warden in Ireland.

The latest symbol was Long Kesh. Brian had known Long Kesh long before Raymond joined the IRA, years before Raymond became a prisoner there. Brian had first gone to the place during the days of the compounds. The first confessions he'd ever heard, after his ordination in 1973, were those of men imprisoned in Long Kesh. It had been bad enough then, but to Brian today Long Kesh was a burning symbol and the exemplar of the oppressed condition of the Irish in Northern Ireland. All Irishmen in the North were prisoners. All who felt and knew themselves to be Irish, who were proud of their Irish identity, saw Northern Ireland as a place where they were demeaned and ground down. It was in this hostile physical and psychological environment that they lived out their lives. Long Kesh represented that in an intensified form . . .

Brian knew that before the Elizabethan period, and before the plantations, the Irish had always been strong enough to absorb outside influences and even incursions of new settlers from beyond the sea. They absorbed the Vikings and the Normans, as they had absorbed over the centuries and millennia a stream of other racial strains. Despite English legislation against early English settlers going native, they had become enchanted with the Irish, had identified with them—becoming, as the saying had it, more Irish than the Irish themselves. It was only in the aftermath of Kinsale, with the systematic plantations *designed* by the English to displace and even blot them out, that the Irish lost their capacity to absorb. In the North they became prisoners in their own land. His people, Brian felt, were a dispossessed race, dispossessed at every level. A very sore people, and full of anger as well as pain.

Anger was the stuff of which rebellion was made. And the results were evident in the revolutionary struggles of the seventeenth through nineteenth centuries, in the Easter rising of 1916 and the War of Independence that followed. The situation of the people in the South changed after 1921. The political system changed. But in the North the realities didn't change: Northern Ireland was still the Ulster plantation. The Irish there couldn't always articulate their deep anger at this. But they could be angry—and they had every right to be angry.

Yet when Brian first became aware of Raymond's involvement in the Provisional IRA, he was very unhappy about it. Though he felt very close to his brother in many ways, he didn't feel close enough to agree with him about the IRA. Brian had many arguments with Raymond—long before he'd ever suspected that Raymond was involved—about the Provos and the damage done by violence. Yet Brian always felt that the two of them were very much alike. Had he grown up when Raymond did, he might have felt what Raymond felt. Oddly, in 1968-69 Brian had actually been approached and asked to join the IRA. It was during his first years in the seminary. He refused. Brian, with his pacifist temperament, couldn't involve himself in killing or destruction.

Not that Raymond did. Raymond wasn't aggressive, or inclined to pick fights. Raymond was fiery, though, and quick to react. He was deeply interested in Irish history. And he was an idealist. This idealism showed itself in different ways. He drank little, if at all. He had high standards for himself, and was disappointed when other people didn't live up to those same standards. Once he'd mentioned to Brian that an IRA man he knew was using his position to make money for himself. Raymond was very unhappy about that, deeply disappointed. Perhaps it was naiveté. In any case, it was the way Raymond saw the world.

RAYMOND WAS BORN on 25 February 1957, the fourth son and seventh of eight children, at the small McCreesh home in St. Malachy's Park in Camlough.

His father James worked as a truck driver for Newry Council, and had been active all his life in Republican politics. After finishing Camlough primary school, Raymond had gone to St.

206

Colman's College in Newry, three miles away. He played Gaelic football with Carrickcruppen and, at the youth club, pool and snooker and basketball. When he was fourteen he helped on a milk round in the mornings, on a route in the local border area. At sixteen, in 1973, he secretly joined the Provisional Republican youth group, *na Fianna Éireann*; towards the end of the same year he joined the 1st Battalion of the South Armagh IRA.

When he'd finished at St. Colman's, Raymond spent a year at a youth training centre in Newry, studying fabrication engineering; this led to an apprenticeship at a steel company in Lisburn. Daily he travelled in a car through heavily loyalist areas with several other Catholic lads from the Newry area. It was a time when a car full of Catholics might be stopped and its occupants killed by loyalists anxious to avenge Lisburn Protestants who, coming from a greyhound meeting, had been shot at the border between Newry and Dundalk. So Raymond soon quit the Lisburn factory. He got a job with a milkman near home, which made him a familiar figure in the area. Doing the milk round he could watch British troops in the area and chart their movements. Raymond was very discreet, and was able to operate as an IRA man for nearly two years without arousing any suspicion. He almost never attended demonstrations, although at one Republican funeral he appeared, in battledress but masked, as part of the colour party. He was not arrested. Neither he nor the family was harassed; their home was never raided.

In 1975 Brian was serving as a curate in Lordship parish, at Jenkinstown near Dundalk, in a portion of the Armagh diocese that lay across the border in the Irish Republic. At two o'clock one morning Brian heard a knock at the door. It was Raymond. Brian wondered what he'd been doing in Dundalk at that hour. Raymond had no girlfriend there as far as Brian knew.

Raymond told Brian that he'd been arrested on suspicion by the Garda Siochána, the Irish police, and taken in for two hours' questioning. The gardai had said they were going to tip off the RUC and the British Army across the border, and they'd be waiting for him. Raymond told the guards he had a priest

207

brother living out in Jenkinstown. One guard said he didn't care whether his brother was "the fuckin' Pope."

For the first time it occurred to Brian that Raymond might actually be involved. He asked the question point-blank.

"Is there anything to it? Are you in the IRA?"

"No," Raymond answered. But he looked away when he said it.

Raymond got up to leave. Brian wanted him to stay. It would be safer for Raymond to drive back home in the early morning. But Raymond didn't want Brian asking any more questions. So he got up and left for home.

Brian followed him, at a distance, in his own car. He was worried that there might be patrols out, and that they'd pick Raymond up. He couldn't keep up and lost him, but took the route he thought Raymond would be taking. Brian drove to Camlough, then checked to see that Raymond's car was at the house. It was, so he turned around and drove back to Jenkinstown.

From his earlier conversations with Raymond he'd learned how strongly Raymond felt. Raymond had picked up that feeling at home, hadn't he, of Irishness, of the rights of the Irish in Ireland? Brian was worried now. The IRA—he'd always thought that one of the worst things about them was that they put so many young lives at risk, ruined these young men. He didn't like the way they set themselves up as guardians of the community, and the way they administered their justice: the knee-cappings, for example. They planted bombs. They killed and assassinated. Brian never trusted the IRA. He had no faith in them. He saw them as a negative thing, of dubious advantage to the community.

The British were an armed and wrongful presence in Ireland. To Brian the IRA's mistake was in choosing to fight the British on the same ground. Yet Brian saw the IRA as an Irish nationalist reaction, perhaps inevitable, to the British armed presence. The British had created the IRA, and it was British arrogance that filled their ranks. Every British soldier was a walking recruiting poster for the IRA.

Less than a year after that night in Dundalk Raymond was

arrested. Nine months after that he was locked away in Long Kesh.

Brian remembered the night of Raymond's arrest. It was a Friday—25 June, 1976. Brian was in bed asleep when the phone rang. It was a quarter to twelve. On the phone was his brother Malachy.

"Someone's been caught." Malachy didn't say it was Raymond but Brian was nearly certain.

"Maybe I ought to go home first—"

"No. I'll meet you. Go to the parish priest's house in Bessbrook."

So Brian went to the priest's house. Malachy was there. He told Brian that Raymond had been taken to Bessbrook barracks.

RAYMOND'S ARREST had followed a shootout with British soldiers. There were various versions of the incident. In one, the rough details went as follows.

Raymond, then nineteen, and three other IRA men, armed, masked and in uniform, had hijacked a car and, at about 9:25 that June night, had driven to a farmyard at Sturgan, a mile or so from Camlough. It was the time of year in Ireland when the sky is bright late into the night, and dusk falls only just before eleven o'clock. The mission that the four men had set themselves was to attack a secret British Army paratroop observation post, hidden opposite the Mountain House Inn, a half mile from the farmyard, on the broad Newry to Newtownhamilton road. As a distraction, one of the men began moving the car down the road toward the observation post, while Raymond and the other two, Paddy Quinn and Danny Maginness, began working their way along the hedge in the same direction.

Unknown to the four, however, there was another paratroop observation post hidden away up a hillside nearby. The soldiers in the second post could see the IRA men below them, and they radioed for helicopter reinforcements. The first of Raymond's friends was returning to rejoin the others when he saw the paratroops from the second post advancing on the others; he had a Sten gun, and fired warning shots to alert Raymond and his two companions. Then the soldiers opened fire with their SLRs and light machine guns, firing off dozens of rounds. They hit, and seem to have killed, a cow grazing nearby. Raymond and the two others ran zig-zag across the fields, avoiding the bullets. Danny Maginness got separated; Raymond and Paddy Quinn took cover in a house where they hoped to find a car. The car wasn't there. So they rang up two priests—and the police! Down the road the first man had been hit by three bullets but managed to crawl away; he hid himself that night, and got away next morning.

Meanwhile the paratroops began firing on the house where Raymond and Paddy had taken cover. A priest from the parish came up to the house and the two prepared to surrender. They came out the front door, hands in the air. But the paratroops opened fire, and so the two of them hurried back into the house. Another priest came, and a little later the police, and Raymond and Paddy Quinn were able to surrender. Danny Maginness had been caught, and they were all taken to Bessbrook barracks, where for three days they were interrogated and abused. Finally they were taken to court in Newry and charged. From there they were taken to Crumlin Road jail and later to Long Kesh, to await trial. The remand period lasted nine months. During that time Raymond was allowed three visits a week and Brian saw him often. In March 1977 the trial was finally held. Raymond refused to recognize the jurisdiction of the British court.

Brian attended the trial. What he remembered most vividly afterwards was the spectacle of British soldiers going into the witness box to testify about an exchange of shots—in the townland of Sturgan, in South Armagh, a mile from Camlough—between themselves and three young Irishmen, natives of the district. The families of these young men had been there for hundreds of years. They were on trial for carrying guns in their own country, and in their own fields. And soldiers from a foreign country, carrying far more efficient and powerful guns, had been moving freely through those same fields. And now here were the foreign soldiers giving evidence, in pronounced English accents, against the native Irish. And the foreign soldiers walked out of the courthouse free, and Raymond and his friends, who had been born and reared in that countryside, were given fourteen-year prison sentences. For Brian, the trial was a microcosm of the wrongs of Irish history.

Raymond was convicted on charges of membership of the IRA, possession of a rifle and a quantity of ammunition, and attempting to kill British soldiers. He was taken to Long Kesh where he refused the criminal uniform and joined the blanket protest which by then, March 1977, had been in progress for several months. Immediately after the trial Raymond saw his mother and father and Brian. But afterwards, for nearly four years, this quiet son of gentle parents refused to take his monthly visits from them because to do so he would have to put on the uniform: a convict's clothing, meant to identify him as a criminal instead of an Irish soldier.

It was not until Sunday, 15 February 1981, that Raymond emerged, pale and thin, his hair cropped very short, wearing those convict's clothes, to take a visit with his parents. He had to wear them, so that he could tell them face to face why he had decided to embark, the following month, on a hunger strike to the death.

BRIAN FIRST WENT TO LONG KESH the year of his ordination. During the two years (1973-75) he was assigned to St. Colman's College in Newry, he went to the prison to say Mass every Sunday he could get free. He kept going there. He had seen the changeover from the more open compounds to the dark H-Blocks.

Brian went whenever he could during those years, and occasionally in the years after 1975. He'd say Mass for the prisoners in the canteen between two of the wings, and then go across and say Mass for the boys in the other two wings. It was a strange sight at Mass: the men wearing nothing but prison-issue trousers, their faces pale and drawn, their hair long, the smell of urine— and Brian feeling so strongly that they shouldn't be there at all. Although they were dedicated to what they called Republicanism and approved of killing, and as a priest he felt he couldn't identify with that, he could and did identify with them as brothers, as neighbours, as oppressed human beings, as fellow Irishmen.

But over the years, though he kept coming, he always hated

211

the place. He found it overwhelmingly oppressive, with the cement walls and barbed wire, the questioning and searching, the armed guards, the system of photographing and passes, the checkpoints, but particularly the hostility. Brian felt that it was the most sectarian place in Northern Ireland, anti-Irish and anti-Catholic.

When Raymond was imprisoned in Long Kesh, Brian's distaste became very personal: Raymond was there, and vulnerable; he was away from the family, and at the mercy of men who hated him. Raymond's vulnerability made Brian feel vulnerable too, and helpless.

Brian saw very little of Raymond in the four years. He said Mass once in Raymond's block. After that he was forbidden to say Mass there—because, the prison authorities said, he was Raymond's brother, and therefore a *security risk*.

Brian learned later that he might have said his Masses in another block, and then asked permission on the spot for a visit with Raymond. Brian felt a deep regret at the missed opportunities. He'd had one when Raymond first came to Long Kesh. Brian had said Mass, then asked permission after Mass to see some of the boys privately in their cells, boys from his own diocese of Armagh. He was given permission, and began to visit boys in the other wings, saving Raymond for last, hoping that by then he could have a leisurely talk. But the other visits took time, and suddenly it was the hour for the midday meal, and the authorities refused to let him into the wing where Raymond was.

Finally, the misery of going to Long Kesh and not being able to see Raymond made him stop going. For more than a year Brian did not visit the place at all.

When Raymond decided to go on hunger strike, before he told their parents, Brian went to see him. He listened as his brother told him of his decision and gave the reasons for it. He began probing, questioning Raymond's reasoning, pursuing his explanations, trying to persuade him not to do it. Finally he fell back from this line of talk, because what Raymond was saying reassured him.

Not that Raymond and the others would succeed. Brian

couldn't think that, not after what he'd experienced himself of the prison system there, its oppression and its implacable antipathy to everything his brother stood for. What reassured him was the way Raymond was looking at what he was about to do. Brian knew well what effect the prison system, and life in Long Kesh, could have on young men: how their thinking could become distorted, their sensitivity dulled, their perspective and their sense of proportion altered. That's why he had tried to talk him out of it. He'd been afraid that Raymond was not in a fit state of mind to make a decision of that magnitude. But listening to Raymond, and watching him, seeing his determination and his clear and lucid way of answering questions, Brian was entirely reassured. Raymond was not at all confused. He knew exactly what he was doing.

Raymond told Brian that he still had *The Imitation of Christ* Brian had given him when he was on remand in Crumlin Road jail. Raymond managed to hold onto the little book, and Brian's only wish afterwards was that he might have given Raymond the *Imitation* in Irish, which Raymond would have liked enormously. Later he was to learn that he could have found a way of getting such things in to Raymond. And here now was Raymond speaking fluent Irish. He was witty, good-humoured, almost bantering. But beneath it was his clarity of mind, his composed determination.

As they spoke, and again as he was leaving, it suddenly occurred to Brian that the time now was very short. He felt terrible, right then; he felt a sense of doom.

Every week after that Brian went to visit his brother. Raymond was peaceful and resigned. He had made a decision; his steadfastness was obvious, as was his strong conviction of the justice of his cause. It was Brian who felt tension and distress, and was sometimes confused. He kept wondering, as day followed day, whether Raymond would come out of the place alive. But through successive weeks Raymond's composure never changed. He kept telling Brian and the family not to build their hopes. He had no illusions about the likely outcome. And he never complained, never even admitted that he was suffering in any way. He smiled and laughed and told jokes.

During those visits it was Brian and the rest of the family who were receiving strength from Raymond. The visits with him lessened their fear and their distress. They all talked about this, about how calm he was. Underneath the calm was Raymond's clear and absolute determination to continue with his fast until the prisoners' demands were granted, or until the end if they were not.

Early on, the others in the family accepted implicitly that Raymond had made his own decision conscientiously and with full knowledge of what he was doing. All they could do now was support him. When Raymond was moved from the cell block to the prison hospital, the family were asked by the medical staff whether they wanted to intervene. They told the doctors that they respected his decision—and had no intention of intervening.

As he drove to the hospital that Saturday afternoon in May, on the 56th day of Raymond's hunger strike, Brian had no suspicion that the medical staff would be taking matters into their own hands.

WHEN HE FINALLY got into the hospital, at about 3:30 that afternoon, Brian passed the rooms where Bobby Sands and Francis Hughes had died. He saw Patsy O'Hara, the tall boy from Derry. Still strong enough to sit up in a chair, Patsy was with his family in the room across from Raymond's.

With Brian were his sister Teresa and brother Malachy. When they walked into Raymond's room Brian saw immediately that Raymond was very weak. Though he spoke distinctly, his voice was weak, too.

They began to talk about the crowds at Francis Hughes' funeral on Friday, about the sheer numbers of people and the tremendous support the families were getting. Brian was not surprised to see that Raymond had been deeply affected by Francis Hughes' death. He'd shared a cell with him for fourteen months. As they recounted the details of Francis's funeral, Raymond was moved with emotion. There had been that tremendous surge in support for Francis's family from the people in South Derry and the area roundabout. Brian started to tell Raymond about the pride people had now, how they were no

214

longer intimidated at the idea of being seen as Irish, no longer afraid to come out and be counted.

Raymond's eyes, open but not focused—he was now almost completely blind—cast about the room and slowly filled with tears as they talked about Francis. Brian told him that people were beginning to feel a new sense of their Irish identity because of the hunger strike. The deaths of Bobby and Francis had not been in vain, someone said.

"It's a very high price to pay," Raymond said, his voice a whisper.

Raymond and Francis had been similar in many ways—the big man from Bellaghy and the small man from Camlough, both country lads, both idealists. Good-humoured, witty, the pair of them. Full of remarks. Francis the fighter, who took lives—

"He proved he could also give," Raymond said.

"You know, Raymie," Malachy began, "Eamonn Mallie—Downtown Radio—was at Francis's funeral. He asked me if it was true that you were thinking of giving up the hunger strike—"

Brian hadn't heard that before.

Raymond threw back his head in a gesture of dismissal.

"Not a chance," he said. "We've gone too far now to be turning back."

There was no doubt, either, about the look in Raymond's face. He hadn't changed. Brian wondered about the rumours. Where had they come from? Some wishful thinking on the part of people in the NIO? Weren't these men to be allowed to die in peace?

They began talking about the five demands and the prisoners' rights, and what they were entitled to.

"God knows what we're entitled to," Raymond said in his weak voice. "But it's not the physical conditions that matter to the men; it's the spiritual things."

Thinking again about the hostile and hateful atmosphere of the prison, Brian understood. Even as they talked, there were two warders standing there in the little room.

They were told at four that their visiting time was up. They left Raymond and went back to Camlough to see their parents. As Brian was driving south along the A-1, toward Newry, he felt his tension ease a little. The road rose and he could see around him the green checkerboard fields of May.

Brian had been happy to see Raymond in good heart. Weeks ago, when he'd become absolutely sure that Raymond was clear about what he was doing, Brian had told him that he wouldn't ask him to come off his fast. As Raymond had grown weaker, Brian would at times become unsettled, and the question would form itself in his mind: was he right not to interfere? Maybe, if you really loved someone, you had to take a decision like that out of his hands. But today, seeing Raymond's calm and his cheerfulness and resolve, Brian felt reassured. Only two or three times during the visit had Raymond's concentration seemed to lapse. Weakened, almost totally blind, Raymond had nonetheless reacted intelligently and incisively to their remarks about Francis Hughes' funeral and the impact the hunger strikers were making on the people at large. Brian recalled the defiant way Raymond had thrown back his head, rejecting the suggestion that he might be giving up his fast. *"We've gone too far now to be turning back"* . . .

But Brian's equilibrium would soon be sharply disturbed.

Once into Newry, Brian would be nearly home. Ten minutes or so through the one-way system, allowing for the Saturday shoppers, and he'd be moving west on the Newtownhamilton road. In no time at all he'd be in Camlough.

He recalled Raymond's thin and emaciated figure on the bed and was suddenly aware again of how helpless Raymond was—a symbol of all their helplessness. Brian himself had spoken out— in the H-Blocks speech he'd wanted to show Raymond, but couldn't, because Raymond was going blind:

> There is a second reality which is clear and plain to us, and which we demand that the British government also recognize: namely, that Raymond was charged under special laws; he was convicted and sentenced in a special court; he has therefore the right in justice to be treated as a special prisoner . . .

Seeing Raymond, it had occurred to Brian that what he ought

to do was go raise a crowd large enough to march on that hideous prison camp and destroy the place once and for all—level it to the ground!

Then Brian had come back to himself, even more aware of his helplessness. The Irish had an anger in them, and here was an absolutely crucial issue they had every right to be angry about. And yet they were totally helpless.

ONE OF THE THINGS Brian was learning from the hunger strike was how completely dependent the people were on their leaders. He'd never realized before the measure of this dependence. There was all that resentment and anger at being ground down—here was Raymond being done to *death*—under the British system, an alien system. Never had this resentment and anger been given strong expression by leaders in the Irish community. If the bishops or the leadership of the SDLP or the Dublin government had been in touch with the gut feelings of the people, and had expressed these feelings in a strong, clear and articulate way, they might have defused the anger. But they hadn't spoken out, and the anger eventually emerged in the form of bullets and bombs. Throughout the years of conflict the bishops had said virtually nothing that gave voice to these innermost feelings of their people.

Almost always the bishops seemed to be—however unintentionally—overbalanced on the side of the British interest. One proud exception was when Tomás Ó Fiaich emerged from Long Kesh during the early days of the dirt protest and made his "sewer pipes in the slums of Calcutta" statement about conditions in the H-Blocks. He must have been let know very quickly by some of his fellow bishops (and by plenty of other people too) that this statement embarrassed them. The bishops didn't want so outspoken an Irish voice.

What developed instead was a strange kind of rhetoric marked by a hysterical imbalance: the bishops could be hysterical when it came to Provo and INLA violence, but utterly silent when it came to the central moral issue of British injustice toward the Irish, and of the British being in Ireland at all.

It could be said in the bishops' favour that, though they tried desperately to remain politically neutral, they took a strong stand on peace and life. They were very consistent in preaching peace, and preaching the value of human life. Though they failed to face up to other matters of deep moral concern like the issue of the rights of an ancient people oppressed by a foreign power, the bishops' stand on peace, and on the sanctity of human life, was a good and valid stand. But without equal emphasis on the justice of the Irish cause, as something deeply felt by so many of their people, the bishops' stand for peace and human life was bound to suffer a loss of force and credibility.

When the hunger strikes came, there was concern among the bishops for the men's lives, concern for the effects of their deaths on the people, concern that the deaths would increase polarization and hatred and violence. But it was an imbalanced concern. There wasn't much concern about the cause for which the men had gone on hunger strike.

There were many issues; the immediate one was the right of these men, who had been charged under special laws and in special courts, to special status. Brian had never heard any bishop say, specifically and publicly: these men are special prisoners; they have a case for special treatment.

Brian had written to all the bishops in the North, asking them to clarify their position on that issue. *None* said a word, publicly. There was strong feeling among many of the priests about the hunger strike, in favour of concessions, in favour of movement by the British government. Some bishops did make representations in their own way. But they did not take a stand. They did not speak.

By deploring violence, and leaving it at that, the bishops were in fact contributing to the violence. They contributed by their failure to stand with their people, to feel with them, to speak out on their behalf. The Church was absolutely terrified of being identified with the IRA. The bishops were very touchy and sensitive about that. *There* was the hysteria. They would go to any extreme to make sure that no action they took, no statement they made, could possibly be interpreted as giving support to the IRA.

This was the measure of the effectiveness of British pressure.

218

For in these circumstances, while Irish Catholic leaders were failing to articulate the feelings of their people, the British were using their own position of public authority, their "legitimacy," their "security forces," their media—including that gutter press of theirs—to make a very effective case for themselves.

So effective were the British that *they were able to silence the Irish Catholic Church*. They even used Catholics in England, notably the English Cardinal Basil Hume, Archbishop of Westminster, to press their case against Irish Catholic boys dying in a British prison. Basil Hume had come to Derry, for an ordination; he had been the guest of Bishop Edward Daly there. He had then gone back to London and immediately sent Bishop Daly an open letter, saying that the hunger strike was "a form of violence." Cardinal Hume insisted in later statements that Bobby Sands and the other hunger strikers were morally wrong in what they were doing: that what they were doing was committing suicide. This was an arbitrary, partisan pronouncement! And coming from the leader of the English Catholic Church at such a time, it seemed to Brian *an insult to Irish Catholics*. Yet neither Bishop Daly nor any other Catholic bishop in Ireland called Cardinal Hume publicly to task over this outrage.

The British had the Irish bishops in a corner. Because of the failure of the bishops to speak out and because of Irish violence, the British felt no need to look at their own uniquely British forms of violence and terrorism, nor at the gross evil of their armed presence in Ireland. The English Cardinal apparently felt quite free to join the fray, using his public position to put a point of view calculated to please the British political establishment. And yet the Irish bishops, on an Irish issue, were cowed into silence.

In such a church, Brian himself was in an anomalous position: he was a priest with a brother on hunger strike. Many priests were strongly supportive of Brian personally, as was Cardinal Ó Fiaich, who had invited Brian to have lunch at his residence next day. But many priests mimicked their bishops' sheeplike performance. It actually came to the point where such priests, at the time of the hunger strikers' deaths, would submit to newspaper and television interviews during which they would disgrace themselves by *explaining* why they were giving

Catholic men a Catholic burial. They were pressured into that position, certainly. But the fact that they felt it necessary to in effect apologize for giving these men Christian burial was in itself a measure of the failure of the Irish bishops, and of the success of British propaganda in Ireland.

So the British government kept reminding the Irish hierarchy what was expected of them, while British television and newspaper commentators highlighted things in such a way as to make the Irish bishops cautious and afraid, throttling their voices. This had been going on for years. But the hunger strike highlighted in a very vivid way the Catholic Church's utter failure to come to terms with the Irishness of its own people. The bishops had let themselves be bullied and intimidated by the British into taking an extremely weak line on the rights of the Irish in Ireland. Brian had never found anything in the Gospel about being so anemic, about not being angry and forthright in the face of injustice and oppression. The Irish bishops had invented and propagated a whole new Gospel—a gospel of cowardice, perhaps.

THE McCREESH FAMILY had their evening meal together, and Brian, Malachy and Teresa gave the others their impressions of the visit with Raymond. How soon, they wondered, would Raymond's condition be considered serious enough for the family to be allowed to stay with him around the clock? As they were talking, the phone rang. It was a Dr. Emerson, from the prison hospital, and he asked to speak to Brian. It was 7:45 p.m.

"Can you come to the hospital immediately?"

"Yes, I suppose—"

"No. It's not what you think."

Emerson then asked him how long it would take. Brian calculated the traffic. It would be light enough at this time on a Saturday night.

"About three quarters of an hour," Brian said.

"Could you come as fast as you can?"

Brian told Emerson he'd like to take someone from the family along.

Emerson hesitated.

"One parent, if you like."

They talked among themselves and decided it would be best if others came as well. Brian set out immediately, with his mother, his brother Malachy, and Bridie, the sister who lived in Australia but had come back to be with the family during the hunger strike.

On the road they wondered what was happening. Had Raymond's condition suddenly deteriorated? Why did Dr. Emerson in the prison hospital initially ask only for Brian? What were they going to hear?

There were some delays getting in, though by the usual standards at Long Kesh they were rushed through. At the prison hospital (it was now nine o'clock) they were met by Emerson and a medical officer or nurse introduced to them as Mr. Nolan. They were shown into Emerson's office. As they sat down, Nolan asked them whether they wanted tea or coffee. He seemed anxious to please.

Emerson said that there was no cause for alarm. Malachy asked to see Raymond. Nolan stepped in and said it wasn't necessary. They should have their tea first, he said.

There was something odd, Brian thought, about this little duet. And if the matter was so urgent ("Come as fast as you can") why weren't they taken in to Raymond immediately? Why were they sitting there, with Nolan taking orders for tea?

The tea arrived. Emerson had seated himself behind his desk. Nolan was leaning against the wall to his left. Finally Emerson asked Nolan to begin telling what had happened that evening.

Nolan smiled, and began by saying that Raymond hadn't taken any water that day, and that this was causing concern. Then he said something very strange. He said that Father Toner—Father Tom Toner, one of the two prison chaplains—had given Raymond what Nolan called, "Extreme Unction," curiously using the old name for what was now called, and had been for some fifteen years, the Anointing of the Sick. Nolan then said that the conferring of this sacrament had left Raymond in a condition of distress, had left him "shocked" and "frightened." Then Nolan, who declared straightaway that he was not a Catholic himself, smiled again and began to give the McCreeshes

221

a little lecture on the significance of Extreme Unction, in which he underlined how much of a last sacrament it was supposed to be, how it was the final sacrament just before death. Nolan said he had explained this significance to Raymond, and had asked Raymond whether he understood what Extreme Unction meant.

Brian had been schooled in sacramental theology and had been administering the Sacrament of the Sick to many people in different conditions and circumstances over a period of nearly eight years. He managed nonetheless to listen without comment to Nolan's lecture. Whether Brian did so out of regard for Nolan's awkward pretence of concern or out of fascination at the shallowness of Nolan's understanding of the sacrament, he could not be sure afterwards.

He did not see, as he later would, just what was happening. But he was finding it very difficult to believe Nolan's tale. In all the anointings he had administered, Brian had never seen anyone react with shock, distress or fear. Invariably the reaction had been peaceful acceptance. How could Raymond, with his deep faith and his courage, with his habit of prayer, have responded in the way described? Father Toner, who would have been a witness to this extraordinary reaction, was away now. Had they waited till he'd left before cooking all this up? Or, if what Nolan was saying was true, how was it that Emerson, and not Father Toner, had been on the telephone to Brian after the anointing? Father Toner would surely have been astonished at such a personality change in Raymond, who was well known—inside Long Kesh as well as out—as one of the more religious among the prisoners. Raymond had regularly read the Lessons at Mass. He had continued doing the scripture readings during his early weeks on hunger strike

Brian focused his mind on what Nolan was saying now. Raymond had been having difficulty drinking water. Nolan (who kept portraying himself as Raymond's good angel) tried repeatedly to help him drink some water, but with no success. He had then asked Raymond whether he'd like some milk. Raymond had answered: "I don't know. I'm confused." Nolan said he had gone straight out of the room to report this, and to ring Emerson, who was duty doctor at the prison that night. It was 6:45.

Emerson then took up the narrative.

He said that as if by telepathy he had phoned the prison at 6:45, just as Nolan was trying to contact him. What Nolan told him made him decide to come straight over to the hospital to see Raymond. When Emerson arrived he went directly to Raymond's bedside. He asked Raymond, he said, whether he understood the significance of Extreme Unction. It meant, Emerson said, that his condition was very serious; it meant that his life was in danger.

"Do you want to save your life?" he said he asked Raymond. Raymond's answer to this, Emerson said, seemed to be positive. So he asked the same question twice again, this time in front of witnesses. Again, he said, Raymond's answer seemed to be positive.

In the normal way, Emerson went on, he would have taken the decision there and then to send Raymond off to an intensive care unit in an outside hospital. But his professional instincts, he said, suggested that in these circumstances he should contact the family.

Emerson spread out his hands, palms upward.

"That is why you are here. The decision will be yours."

His superiors, he said, were awaiting the family's decision. Everything was mobilized, and Raymond could be in the intensive care unit of an outside hospital within seven minutes.

The McCreeshes were thinking about Raymond's near blindness and his emaciated condition when they asked Emerson what Raymond's future would hold if he were put into intensive care right away. What could be expected as a result of treatment? Emerson said that Raymond was in better condition than Seán McKenna had been in December during the last days of the first hunger strike. And McKenna, Emerson said, was doing very well out of his treatment.

Brian expressed surprise that Raymond's attitude should have changed so dramatically since four o'clock, when he and Teresa and Malachy had left a Raymond who was clear and even

223

adamant about his intention to continue the hunger strike until the prisoners' five demands were met. Malachy described the circumstances of the conversation with Raymond, and how he'd raised Eamonn Mallie's question about rumours that Raymond was going to end his hunger strike. Malachy pointed out that Raymond had completely dismissed this idea: They had gone too far now to be turning back.

Emerson protested that he was only doing his duty as a doctor. When someone indicated that he wanted a doctor to save his life, a doctor could not ignore the request, no matter what the circumstances.

But Raymond was in a confused state. So the final decision would have to be made by the family.

Brian asked a question of Nolan, asked him gently. (Brian hadn't yet put the pieces together, didn't yet realize the enormity of what was going on . . .)

Why had Nolan asked Raymond if he would like some milk? Surely Nolan knew that Raymond had been refusing to take anything except water and salt for 56 days. Why suggest milk? Nolan shook his head, shrugged his shoulders, and leaned back against the wall.

"No reason," he said, and smiled ingratiatingly.

Malachy asked if they could go in and see Raymond. Nolan said that they should first have a talk among themselves. Emerson said his office was at their disposal. "Don't worry, it's not bugged," Nolan said, with what was meant to be a smile of reassurance. While they were having their talk, Nolan said, there would be time to arrange chairs for them at Raymond's bedside.

Brian, Malachy, Bridie and their mother talked together. They wondered whether, if they took Raymond off now because of his confusion, then when he'd come to, he'd only go right back on hunger strike. But the situation was strange, to say the least.

Ten days ago Raymond had given Brian very detailed instructions about what he wanted for his funeral. The conversation had distressed and shaken Brian. But Raymond himself had been quite cool about it, and matter-of-fact. He wanted to be buried in the Carrickcruppen graveyard above Camlough, right beside their home in St. Malachy's Park, and not in Cullyhanna, where their forebears had been buried. Perhaps in the Sands family plot at Carrickcruppen—the Bessbrook Sandses were related to the McCreeshes. Raymond never mentioned burial in the Republican plot. He said, too, that he wanted the family to pay for his funeral.

Raymond had been making these calm preparations in his own mind: how would he react if he came to his senses and suddenly discovered that his family, because of his momentary confusion, had snatched him from death?—from the death he had been embracing, as a soldier, as an Irishman, as a protester against the attempt at criminalization, against the dehumanizing treatment he and his fellow prisoners had suffered in this British prison? *What would Raymond then say to them?*

The McCreeshes agreed that they were deeply suspicious of Emerson and Nolan. Hadn't other families had bad experiences with the prison hospital staff? Nolan, especially, seemed false. "Too sweet to be wholesome," their mother said.

But they decided that if they found in talking to Raymond himself that what Emerson and Nolan said was true, that Raymond had had a genuine change of heart, then the family would ask for medical intervention. But if they found Raymond confused to the point that he didn't know what he was saying, or what was going on, then they would have to respect the decision Raymond had made while in his full senses, a decision he had abided by so determinedly through nearly two months of a wasting and painful hunger strike. They wanted desperately to see Raymond live. But they would not act to save Raymond's life if their doing so meant betraying him.

As they were waiting to be let through, Emerson and Nolan approached, coming from the ward, with another man whom they introduced as Dr. Bill. Emerson told them that their visit with Raymond would be completely private, with no guards in the room. They could, he said, take as long as they liked.

It did not occur to any of them that they could be walking into a trap.

THEY GATHERED IN THE ROOM with Raymond. Brian wanted

to deal directly with what Emerson said about Raymond's confusion.

"Raymond, do you know where you are?"

"In Scotland," Raymond said.

He said he was in a small hospital, and that the small hospital was within a bigger hospital.

"They're going to take me to the bigger hospital," he said. Raymond's speech, after fifty-six days of hunger strike, was extremely slow.

He spoke deliberately. His sentences were long drawn out.

"How do you know you're in Scotland?"

"The doctors told me. They tell me I'm not eating. They say I've been refusing food. Is that right?"

"Raymond," Brian said, "you are not in Scotland. You are in a hospital. Where?"

"In bed."

"Where is the bed?"

"Under the window. No, under the light."

"Raymond, you are in Long Kesh," Brian said. "Do you know what Long Kesh is?"

Raymond smiled.

"A concentration camp!" he said, slowly and in a strong voice.

The family laughed at this. Brian wondered whether Raymond was beginning to emerge from his confusion and realize where he was.

"Good man, Raymond," their mother said. "Good man!"

"Raymond," Brian said, "do you know that you're on hunger strike?"

Raymond seemed confused again. He didn't seem to know what Brian was talking about.

He seemed puzzled, as if none of it made any sense.

He asked whether there was anyone else on hunger strike with him, and Malachy mentioned that Patsy O'Hara was, and that he was in a room just across the corridor. He mentioned Joe McDonnell. No sign at all of recognition.

"Bobby—" Brian said. "What about Bobby?" There was the

same puzzled blankness in his look.

"Raymond, do you know who Bobby Sands is?" No sign at all of recognition.

"Raymond, do you know who Francis Hughes is?"

"Where is Francis Hughes?"

"He's dead," Malachy said.

"Is Francis dead?" Tears came into Raymond's eyes. "Who killed him?"

Malachy told him not to worry about Francis. Francis, Malachy said, was in heaven with Bobby, and Francis wouldn't want Raymond to die. The Hughes family, Malachy said, wanted Raymond to live, and wouldn't want him to give up his fight for life, worrying about Francis.

Brian wanted to mirror Raymond's decision back to him; he wanted to try to break through that wall of confusion.

"Raymond," Brian said. "You've been on hunger strike for fifty-six days. Do you know why?"

"No," Raymond replied.

"For the five demands," Brian said to him.

There was a pause. Brian waited for the words to sink in. "Why are you on hunger strike?"

They waited.

They kept waiting. Still Raymond didn't say anything. Brian willed him to remember. At last, Raymond spoke:

"For the five demands."

Brian was encouraged. Was Raymond coming round?

"You are only taking water and salt," Brian said. "If the doctors ask you what you want, ask for water."

Raymond seemed to slip back again.

Brian watched him.

"Will you tell them you want water?"

Again Brian waited, watching Raymond's face and hoping for some further sign of lucidity.

"If they ask you," Brian said, "What will you tell them you want?"

Raymond's face began to brighten. He saw what Brian was getting at.

"To get home!" he said with a broad grin.

"Please God, Raymond," their mother said, "you *will* be home."

Seeing the opening in the clouds, the McCreeshes sought to widen it further.

They mentioned the names of close friends, people Raymond should immediately have recognized. Raymond didn't recognize them.

They mentioned friends from home, including Paddy Quinn and Danny Maginness, the two boys who had been arrested with Raymond, who were both now on the blanket. He recognized Paddy Quinn's name, and asked about him. Raymond volunteered another name, and asked if the man were dead. He seemed to have two different men's names mixed up.

"Raymond," Brian said. "I think you are a wee bit confused."

"Yes," he said, with another grin. "A *big* wee bit!"

Malachy talked at one point about Francis Hughes, and said that Raymond had sent Francis's family a Mass card.

"Yes," Raymond said. "I think that was today."

"No—" Malachy began.

Brian gently nudged Malachy, afraid Raymond would be further confused.

"I saw you nudging him," Raymond said, delighted with himself. (He was almost completely blind.) "It must have been yesterday."

"Yes," Malachy said. "It was yesterday."

As they reminded him about his hunger strike and about the five demands, Brian and Malachy kept trying to help him by building on his closeness to Francis Hughes, with whom he had shared a cell for more than a year. They wanted Raymond to live, they said, and repeated the point made earlier that Francis Hughes, and Francis's family, would want him to live, and not give up his fight for life. There was the possibility, Malachy said, of fresh negotiations through the European Commission. The prisoners might get their five demands,

Malachy added, and the family wanted Raymond to be alive when the five demands were met.

They turned the conversation to the story about Raymond's anointing.

"Was Father Toner in?" Brian asked.

"I don't know," Raymond said.

"Did he give you Holy Communion?"

"Don't know—"

"Did he anoint you?"

"Not sure."

Suddenly the warders came in to tell them that the visit—which Emerson had said was to have no time limit—was over. Brian said some prayers in Irish, and they began to say goodbye. Then Raymond raised his hand.

Beidh an bua againn go fóill, he said: "We will win yet!"

Brian was determined to find out from Father Toner what he knew about Raymond's condition, and what had happened in the prison hospital. But he was not to see Tom Toner until Sunday night. And not until Monday would Brian fully understand what the prison staff had been trying to do.

For the present, Brian knew that some sort of confrontation with Emerson and Nolan would be necessary to protect Raymond.

When they left Raymond's room they went back to Emerson's office. Emerson was sitting at his desk. Nolan was standing, as was the man introduced as Dr. Bill. Brian spoke for the family through most of what ensued.

They had found Raymond very confused, Brian said. Raymond thought he was in a hospital in Scotland. But he had never been to Scotland. Nor did the family have any Scottish connections. When asked how he knew he was in Scotland, Raymond answered that the doctors had told him so. At this, Dr. Bill excused himself and hurried out of the room.

Brian asked Emerson whether Raymond had directly volunteered any request for a doctor to save his life. Emerson said that in all honesty he had to admit that what Raymond had said was only in response to questions. Emerson said that the only concern of the medical staff was the welfare of the patients under their care. The hunger strike, he said, had put them in a very difficult position, had caused them distress. Brian thanked him for the care and attention given Raymond and the other hunger strikers. He assured Emerson that the situation was no less distressing for the family.

Brian explained that the family's position was that having seen Raymond and talked to him they had absolutely no reason to believe he had changed his mind. Before leaving, Brian asked that Raymond be given water, as he was no longer able to take it for himself. That would be done anyway, Emerson said.

ON SUNDAY MORNING when they were visiting Raymond, their mother noticed a sticking plaster on Raymond's right arm, and saw what looked like an injection mark in Raymond's left arm. That morning Raymond was even more confused. He didn't recognize any of them. The family got permission to stay with Raymond from Sunday night on.

That morning Brian sent off a telegram to Margaret Thatcher, saying that his brother had gone fifty-seven days without food, and without clothes and washing for four and a half years. All he had left, Brian said, was his pride as an Irishman and his loyalty to his fellow prisoners living and dead. He asked her to respect Raymond's dignity and move to save his life.

Then Brian saw that day's edition of the *Sunday Times*, in which a piece on the hunger strike concluded with the curious assertion that Raymond had been the least determined of the hunger strikers, and was not expected to continue his fast to the end.

Brian had lunch at Cardinal Ó Fiaich's residence with the Cardinal, to whom he recounted the events of the previous afternoon and evening, and the astonishing change in Raymond's condition that had taken place, according to Emerson's account, between four o'clock and about six-thirty. He told the Cardinal about Nolan's bizarre tale of Raymond being shocked at receiving "Extreme Unction," and how Raymond had said he was in Scotland. Brian said that he was convinced beyond any doubt that the staff at the hospital had deliberately confused Raymond, perhaps by hypnosis or by giving him some form of drug.

Later, when he had thought about the *Sunday Times* piece—written by a reporter known to be an apologist for the British—Brian came to feel that there had been collusion between the prison staff and the British Northern Ireland Office. The drugging, or whatever had been done to Raymond, and Emerson's attempt to get the family to take Raymond off, were moves that nicely suited the political purposes of the British government. The floating of stories about Raymond wanting to end his fast now seemed to Brian to be a clear attempt to break the hunger strike. Brian was told afterwards that the prison staff had been convinced that Brian would take Raymond off.

Had the British got the idea—perhaps from the way the Irish bishops bobbed and weaved—that because Brian was a priest he would put Raymond's life above faithfulness to Raymond himself? Did they think that the McCreeshes, because they were religious, would be a soft touch? Well, they hadn't reckoned with the family's Irishness, or with their respect for Raymond's right to live, or to die, as an Irishman.

What Brian had been anxious to ask Father Tom Toner when he met him on Sunday night was for the priest's description of the anointing and Raymond's response to it. Toner said that naturally he had explained to Raymond what he was doing; Raymond understood, and his responses to the prayers were deliberate and devout. Raymond had been, as he always was, prayerful and attentive. Had Raymond been at all confused or shocked or frightened? No, Father Toner said. He'd been anything but frightened. He'd been composed, and very clear about what was going on.

Brian spent Sunday night in the prison hospital with Raymond. Raymond had slipped into a coma.

On Monday morning a British Army patrol went to the McCreesh home in Camlough, and a soldier asked Brian's sister Bridie what arrangements the family wanted for the funeral of

Raymond—*who was still alive*. Did they want a private or a Republican burial? And what route would the funeral procession be taking?

This insult to the family was quickly followed by another.

Since Friday the British government had been giving out the line that Raymond was expected to go off hunger strike. Now they began floating fresh rumours to the effect that Raymond had wanted to end his hunger strike but was prevented from doing so by his family. Raymond, the rumours said, had asked for nourishment; his family was sent for; and after a visit with his family he changed his mind. The British, who had floated these rumours, were "confirming" through their Northern Ireland Office that the rumours were a true account of Saturday's events.

This whole charade began while Brian was still in the hospital with Raymond. When he heard of it, Brian was angry. It was the old English technique, wasn't it, of *getting in first with their lie*, on the grounds that if they got in first, the lie would stand? No matter that the truth might come after it, no matter what denials, or proof that they had lied: *the lie would be there*.

The McCreeshes were determined to do the best they could. At Camlough a family statement was prepared, giving details of their Saturday meetings with Raymond. The statement concluded:

> We believe our son before anyone else, and are respecting his wishes not to be revived should he again lapse into a coma. None of us have witnessed him asking for food and he is clearly determined to continue with his hunger strike.

Their statement was issued, naturally, through the Sinn Féin office in Belfast. In this sort of crisis situation, how else would people not accustomed to issuing statements, not familiar with the procedures, get their message out? Later that night the family prepared a second written statement, which Brian delivered orally to the hospital authorities, demanding the removal of "certain persons" from the medical staff at the hospital: meaning

Nolan and Emerson. Early next morning the British issued a statement:

> The Northern Ireland Office is satisfied that in spite of the allegations from Provisional Sinn Féin in relation to a prisoner, McCreesh, the medical and other staff at the Maze have behaved with complete and utter propriety.

Their newest lie was to defend their two malefactors, not against the McCreesh family, who had demanded their removal, but as though the demand had come from the Provos. Meanwhile, on Monday night, the British attacked Brian personally on the BBC radio news at ten, when a newsreader referred to a report that the "Roman Catholic" priest-brother had been instrumental in persuading his brother to continue with his hunger strike. Brian, who was sitting up with Raymond in the prison hospital during the night, only heard of this next day.

FROM THEN ON the attack on Brian and the family began to build: the British version circulating in the English press and along the airwaves. The British had lost Raymond now, the man they had cast in the role of breaker of the hunger strike. They had lost the religious family. They had lost Brian, whom they had cast in the role of the priest-brother who would do the weak thing and take his brother off. But they seemed to be brutally intent on lashing together the collapsed framework of their expectations, no matter what the pain to the family.

The power of words, even in telling a lie, was a magical power. Words had that ability to conjure, casting up images, vague, flittering and ephemeral—struggling for attention and recognition among the detritus of other messages laid across a listener's or reader's mind. The English wanted perhaps to conjure up a picture in the minds of their audiences of a shrunken, thin-faced young man, stretched out helpless and dying in a prison hospital, and at the last minute, in a piteous voice, begging the doctors for food and succour. Enter the "Roman Catholic" priest-brother, perhaps a sallow, stern, thin-lipped creature; he begins arguing with the dying young man, threatening him in low whispered tones. In whatever hazy shapes, the impression the liar wants to create is evoked.

By Tuesday night, the British government and media (*Get the lie in first*) had got it firmly implanted in the public mind that Brian had been at the bedside, denying his brother's right to live, and insisting that his brother continue on a hunger strike the helpless lad really wanted to end.

In a *Sunday Telegraph* article (31 May) an English Benedictine priest, Alberic Stacpoole—a former British Army paratroop officer—would combine together his Lord Archbishop Basil Hume's partisan gospel of hunger strike as suicide and the false accounts given out in the British media, and whip up a venomous English-policy-serving concoction full of disgust at "relatives stiffening strikers' resolve to die when they begin to waver." In a libellous and lunatic piece in *The Spectator* of 30 May, Auberon Waugh, yet another malicious and ill-informed English Catholic Tory, attacked Cardinal Ó Fiaich, saying he was condoning suicide and murder, adding that Brian should be arrested and charged with murdering his brother or at least with aiding and abetting Raymond's "suicide."*

BEIDH AN BUA AGAINN GO FÓILL, Raymond had said. Now he was in a coma. They had captured only his body. His spirit was beyond the reach of their machinations.

But for Brian and the family the battle was still going on. On Tuesday the family issued three statements—a general statement repudiating in the strongest possible terms the BBC report of Monday night, and demanding again the dismissal of Emerson and Nolan; another, from Brian, threatening defamation proceedings against the BBC; and a third statement demanding an independent legal and medical inquiry into the treatment of Raymond on Saturday evening, and into the context within which all this had occurred: "We must ask whether this whole

*It could all be traced back to the English Cardinal's idiosyncratic theory that the Irish hunger strikers were suicides, a theory tailor-made to provide English Catholic justification for Margaret Thatcher's arrogant, racist and fanatic obduracy towards these Irishmen dying in a British prison in Ireland. See Note at end of Chapter 7.

affair was deliberately contrived to meet political expectations."

Against those expectations, Raymond's and the family's religiousness had turned out to mean not weakness but strength.

On Tuesday and Wednesday Brian said Mass in Raymond's room. He stayed with Raymond for the four nights from Sunday. Brian would of course have loved to take him off, even then, had he been able in conscience to do so. But he had to watch his brother lying there dying—gaunt, shrunken, comatose, and so small and boyish.

To Brian, Raymond had always been a boy. When he left for the seminary, Raymond was only nine. When Brian was ordained, Raymond, the youngest of his brothers, was there—a small lad of sixteen. And yet (and the thought pierced him now) it was a man who had told Brian and his parents, in mid-February, that he was going on hunger strike. Although it had been terribly hard on their mother, somehow she'd understood. And Raymond's composure, his astonishing composure, a great deal of which he'd got from her, sustained him, without bitterness, through the fifty-ninth and sixtieth days of his hunger strike.

It was past Wednesday midnight, in the small hours of Thursday morning. Brian was there with Teresa and Michael, Raymond's taller brother, who had been sitting up with Brian most nights. Raymond was still unconscious. They watched him, Brian watched him, as he breathed his long, slow, heavy breaths, sometimes with a deep sigh.

At 2:11 on Thursday morning, 21 May 1981, Raymond was dead.

THE EVENTS of the next days—the procession, the wake, the funeral and burial, were clouded for Brian and the family by the riddle of the events of Saturday evening, by the British government's manipulations and their vicious black propaganda campaign.

The day Raymond died, Tomás Ó Fiaich, Cardinal Archbishop of Armagh and himself a native of South Armagh—of Annaghmare-Crossmaglen, not far from the hamlet of Cullyhanna and the townland of Dorsey from which the

McCreeshes had come—issued a statement in which he condemned violence and killing, but also condemned British rigidity on the prisoners' demands.

Raymond's death, the Cardinal said, exemplified the cruel dilemma of Northern Catholics: Raymond had been born into a community that always openly proclaimed that it was Irish and not British. He would never have seen the inside of a jail had it not been for the abnormal political situation . . .

That same Thursday Raymond's body was taken from the mortuary in Daisyhill hospital in Newry and his coffin, draped in the Irish Tricolour, began a three-mile procession to Camlough, a solitary piper leading the way, playing Irish laments. Offices and shops in Newry emptied, and thousands of people watched Raymond's passage home. Every hundred yards four men dropped back from the head of the procession to take their turn carrying the coffin.

During the wake thousands of people made their way to the McCreeshes' small home in St. Malachy's Park. On Saturday, along with their father James, Brian and the three other living McCreesh brothers carried Raymond's coffin out from the house to the road.

As the long funeral procession wound its way to St. Malachy's chapel above the cemetery at Carrickcruppen, the mountain above them, Slieve Gullion, was darkened in shadow, and huge crowds gathered around the small chapel in the misty rain. Fifty yards from the church gates, the procession halted and an IRA firing party saluted Raymond with three volleys.

Inside the chapel Brian was the principal celebrant of the Mass for the Dead, said in Irish. An assistant pastor at Camlough, Father Thomas Woolsey, echoed in a homily the words of the Pope at Drogheda in 1979 when he spoke against violence and against powerful politicians who failed to remedy injustice, so that people felt compelled to remedy injustice by other means. At the graveside Ruairí Ó Brádaigh, president of Sinn Féin, spoke eloquently of the lament the piper had played again today, *Ur chill an Chreagain* ("The Churchyard of Creggan"):

> The poet Art McCooey had a dream and a vision of a wonderful country and a promised land . . . It was the

country where the English didn't rule yet . . . The English government never had any right in Ireland, never any scintilla of right, other than that of the robber with superior force . . .

Generations of McCreesh ancestors were buried in that churchyard at Creggan, and Brian loved McCooey's song, which was a kind of anthem of Gaelic South Armagh. A British Army helicopter circled overhead, bent on drowning out the voices of the speakers at the ceremony. But Ó Brádaigh went on, recalling words of the hunger striker Terence MacSwiney:

"Not all the armies of all the empires on earth can crush the spirit of one true man, and that man will prevail." The strength of Raymond's spirit has conquered over all material considerations . . .

That night there came a phone call to the house in Camlough that sickened Brian more than anything else had that whole week. A stringer from the *Sunday Times* rang to ask Brian whether he was aware of tape recordings of conversations in the prison that the newspaper was going to publish next day. Needless to say, the alleged tape-recordings purported to prove that the accusations made against Brian and the family were true. Was there to be no end to this lying persecution?

The family had gone through all the psychological brutality of the previous week—trying to support Raymond in his last days, while seeking at the same time to defend him from all the slander that had been heaped on him, and them, by the British government, the NIO, the English newspapers, the BBC, ITV—and by RTE, the supposedly Irish broadcasting station with its slave mentality, which picked up whatever line was being sold by English officialdom.

Brian remembered how, at the wake, a young woman reporter from London, from *The Times*, on seeing the crowds of sorrowing people—Irish people—thronging to the house, had come up to one of Brian's priest friends and said spontaneously: "My God, what have we done to you?"

Now they had just buried Raymond, and the British government and the English media were still at it, still coming at them, starting up all over again.

They wouldn't let Raymond live in peace, die in peace, or be buried in peace. Now they wouldn't let him rest in peace nor allow his family to mourn him in peace.

Beidh an bua againn go fóill, Raymond had said: "We will win yet" . . .

Chapter 6

PATRICK O'HARA

Some day of strength, when ploughs are out in March,
The dogs of Fionn will slip their iron chains,
And, heedless of torn wounds and failing wind,
Will run the old grey wolf to death at last.

Joseph Campbell

ON MONDAY 18 MAY, Tony O'Hara saw his brother Patsy for the third time since the start of Patsy's fast. Tony was wearing prison-issue clothing; he had to, to see Patsy. Now the two warders standing there in the prison hospital room were warning them against talking in Irish. Speaking their own language, like wearing their own clothes, was against the rules of this place.

In mid-January it had become clear to Tony that things were moving inexorably towards a second hunger strike. What especially worried him was that his brother Patsy—who had become OC of the INLA prisoners after John Nixon embarked on the first hunger strike—had told Bobby Sands that, if the IRA men were giving up that form of protest just because the December strike had failed, the INLA prisoners were prepared to go it alone and mount a hunger strike that would *succeed*.

During that first hunger strike Patsy had been one of the thirty prisoners to join in the last week. Tony knew that Patsy was certain to be the first man representing the Irps in the second hunger strike. As OC, Patsy would never consider letting anyone do something he wasn't prepared to do himself.

Although not in the same wing, Tony and Patsy had been in the same block, and able to see each other every third Sunday at Mass. To Tony, Patsy was a young lad of twenty-three who'd been forced to become a man before his time; he'd spent a lot of his life behind prison bars, beginning with his internment at eighteen. When Tony had learned in 1979 of Patsy's arrest he'd been shattered. He knew that Patsy had found a girl he loved, and they were planning a lavish wedding on Tony's release in August 1981.

The second hunger strike, like the first, was planned and initiated entirely from within the prison. Those outside didn't want the hunger strike. They thought it was a bad idea. It was the men inside who said: we've had enough. We've got to break this prison regime.

Tony knew that the Provos and IRSP outside understood something of what the men were suffering. But they didn't, and couldn't, understand it in the same depth, because they weren't actually living through it. For the Provos outside it was a matter of realism. They were absolutely sure that the men weren't going to win. When the hunger strike did begin, and the Provos and the IRSP realized the men were determined to go through with it, they supported it. They had no choice at that point but to support the decision taken by the men inside.

The date for the beginning of the new hunger strike was postponed several times. But when 1 March was decided upon, the men in the prison knew that Bobby Sands would be the first hunger striker. Francis Hughes was to follow two weeks later and then, a week or so after that, Patsy and Raymond McCreesh. As soon as it was announced, Tony and the other men started sending out letters written on toilet or cigarette paper, appealing to people all over Ireland and the world to support the hunger strikers. In April, Tony wrote a poem in honour of Mother Ireland, the woman, once young and beautiful, now old and bent under the weight of her long suffering:

> So arise, poor old woman
> and accept the gift they bring.
> For of it every voice will whisper
> and every bird will sing,
> And your wrinkled skin will fade and die,
> to be replaced by youth again;
> And as a noble mother, you'll take your throne
> at the gathering of the clan . . .

Now it was May. Just a week ago, Monday the eleventh, when Tony had his second visit with Patsy, he'd been sitting up in a wheelchair. They'd talked about Bobby and Francis. The last time Patsy had seen Bobby, he was in bed. Bobby had reached out to shake Patsy's hand. *Beannacht leat, a chomrád* , Bobby had said: "All the best, comrade." Tony had told Patsy how it was back in the blocks. They'd been getting reports that Bobby was in pain, that he'd had a series of heart attacks.

Then a few days later one of the prisoners, who had a matchbox-size radio, passed the word along the wing. "*Fuair Riobárd báis*": Bobby has died.

When the word reached him, Tony was shattered. "Jesus Christ!" was all he could say. There was complete silence on the wing for two or three hours, apart from brief, very quiet conversations. Tony had never felt so depressed in all his life. He kept recalling that he'd been Bobby's first cellmate in Long Kesh, and remembered the way Bobby had roused them to the letter-writing effort, leading the fight for survival. And now Bobby Sands was dead.

Patsy had told Tony about Francis Hughes, whom he'd seen that morning just before Tony's visit—Patsy sitting in his wheelchair at Francis's bedside. They'd spent only ten minutes together when the screws came in and said their time was up. Francis had reached out and clasped Patsy's hand, saying: "Well, Patsy, comrade, all the best. He who dies for Ireland lives!" Francis died next day. In the blocks men began to cry when they heard of his death. Tony himself cried.

Today, Monday 18 May, Patsy was lying in the bed, no longer up and about as he liked to be, no longer even sitting in his wheelchair. He was lying in the bed, with a cage over his feet to keep the light bedclothes from rubbing the skin off. Patsy was disoriented at first.

"Are Bobby and Francis dead?"

"Aye," Tony said.

Patsy said he knew they were. It was just that he was confused because of the dreams he was having, even during the day. Tony talked to Patsy about when they were younger, about the co-op they'd started—to build canoes to sell to groups and youth clubs throughout the country. They'd even had a picture in the *Derry Journal* about the canoe project, funded by a government-sponsored program set up so that the unemployed could go into business for themselves. They'd been given money for material and had made two canoes before Tony was lifted. Fibreglass canoes—Patsy had been keen on fibreglass, and knew a lot about it. Patsy had the drive; he was the entrepreneur who could make the co-op work. When he, too, got arrested, the canoe project died.

They talked about their parents, about the house in Ardfoyle, about Seán Séamus who was four years older than Tony and five years older than Patsy, about their younger sister Elizabeth, whom they called Liz and sometimes "The Witch," who was now 22. Tony tried to talk about the old times, though it was hard to talk when he knew Patsy was going to die. He tried, too, to talk about the future. The truth about the future lay unspoken between them.

Since the hunger strike began in March, things in the blocks had been better. They were still on the blanket of course, but they'd ended the dirt protest. There were no more mirror searches and the screws were far less obnoxious. The prisoners could shave and they had half an hour a day for a wash. They could take showers twice a week and had soap, toothbrushes, toothpaste and the like. There was some reading material, and they received unlimited mail. They were still locked up all the time with no exercise. But what the protest had not achieved the hunger strike had already achieved, to this degree.

Tony looked at his younger brother Patsy. He was in terrible shape—very, very bad. But he'd held on for the rest of them: for Raymond McCreesh, who was dying too; for Bobby and Francis; for the prisoners out in the blocks; for the fight for Irish freedom. It was the solidarity that mattered to Patsy. He was here, not for himself, but for them. And there were more blanketmen behind him now. Initially there had been 370 or so. Now there were about 425 men on the blanket, some of whom had come on in response to Patsy's appeal to the conforming prisoners.

Patsy had sent his message around on 8 February, three weeks before the start of the second hunger strike:

Comrades,

As no doubt you are all aware we here in the blanket blocks have been forced once again to embark on the hunger strike . . . a hunger strike to the death or to victory, whichever may come first. What I can assure you is that the coming months will bring both. The attitude of the British government shows clearly that death is not only possible in the hunger strike but that it is assured.

In the face of this terrible prospect I, as OC of the INLA volunteers in these H-Blocks, ask you to show your solidarity with us during the coming months. Hopefully you will do this by returning to this [blanket] protest or at least by . . . refusing to work for the duration of the hunger strike. What I ask will, I know, be scorned by those whose selfishness and conformity now outweigh the principles that resulted in their imprisonment. It is a sad fact that some men value the petty privileges available in the working blocks more highly than the commitment they once had to the Republican cause. But surely your conscience must tell you that you cannot stand by and accept the tag of criminal when a hundred yards away men will be dying to break that same British brand of criminalization.

I can guarantee that any man who does return will be treated like all other men. No questions will be asked and no one will question his motives for returning. But I must stress that any man who does return must be prepared to remain until the protest ends. A few months matched against the lives of those on the hunger strike is indeed a very small sacrifice. Certainly life in the blanket blocks is hard, and not everyone has the ability to endure it for a long and indefinite period. But there will be nothing long or indefinite about this hunger strike.

I know that many men here are confused by the ending of the last hunger strike. Some see it as an anti-climax. This time there will be no anti-climax. Men will die and only we standing together against the enemy can save them.

Even in the event of death, only we can consolidate the victory their deaths will have won. But one thing is clear: there are no victories to be won as criminals. I know that all the words in the world are in vain if the spirit of resistance does not still burn within, but I believe that it does burn in every one of you. So the choice is simple: stand with us or turn your back.

But sometime in the future when the question is asked, "Where were you when your comrades were dying?" will you answer by saying that you were conforming to the system that drove them to their death? There is not only life at stake but the success or failure of these long years of struggle. So think long and hard on what I have said. If your decision is a positive one, then you should encourage as many of your comrades as you can to do likewise. Our strength lies in each other and everyone has a part to play, providing you are prepared once and for all to stand by the principles that other men have in the past and will shortly once again give their lives for.

OC INLA
H-Blocks

Tony was told it was time for him to leave. The armed guards who would bring him back to the blocks were waiting outside the door. He knew it might be the last time he could speak to Patsy. Tears welled up in his eyes. He felt like running off, or just breaking down right where he was. But the screws were staring at him, and the thought formed in his mind that if he cried he would be letting Patsy down.

SEÁN SÉAMUS O'HARA hated coming to Long Kesh. He himself had been interned here, in the compounds, for three and a half years, in the days before criminalization. The compounds had not been a tenth as bad as the blocks for suffering and degradation. Still, Seán had learned years ago to hate the sight of the place.

Yet lately he'd been coming here every day to see Patsy in the prison hospital. All the family had been coming, taking turns at Patsy's bedside. The O'Haras' friend Jim Daly, a university lecturer in philosophy, was putting them up at his house in

244

Belfast and driving them back and forth to the prison. Jim's wife Miriam had been murdered in their front hallway by loyalist assassins the previous year, because she'd been an IRSP activist and prominent in the H-Blocks campaign. Jim told Seán that he used to think of the loyalists as fellow Irishmen; whereas Miriam always thought of them as colonizers, like the French *pieds noirs* in Algeria. Eventually Jim had come to agree with her. His home in Belfast was just twenty minutes or so away from the prison, and his hospitality and kindness saved the O'Haras from a four-hour return journey to Derry each day.

It was Wednesday, 20 May, and Seán Séamus was shocked to see how badly deteriorated Patsy was this morning. He had completely lost his voice. His tongue was twice its normal size, and he was coughing up clots of blood. His eyes were sunken into his head; his hearing was almost completely gone.

A photo of Patsy had been published in this morning's issue of *The Irish Press*, one of several photos Seán had seen taken last Thursday when Patsy was still able to sit up in his wheel-chair. The photos were fuzzy but distinct enough to show Patsy's extreme boniness. They showed him sitting slouched in striped pyjamas; in one of them he leaned to one side, support-ing his head in his left hand. The photos had an eerie concrete-ness nothing else had. None of the fierce publicity, none of the media coverage, could show the public what the hunger strik-ers' parents and relatives saw every day—the hideous physical effects of two months fasting. All that the public saw were the familar H-Blocks campaign head shots: in Patsy's case of a dark, smiling, Mephistophelean imp. Most people who didn't know Patsy imagined him from that head shot to be small-boned and short. But in the new photos, taken when he was fifty-four days on hunger strike, Patsy could be seen for the tall man he was, big and broad-shouldered like their brother Tony, but obviously ravaged by the starvation, the vomiting, the dizziness, and with his eyesight ruined. Seán saw Patsy's pain in these photos, taken with a tiny miniature camera, and though in one Patsy tried to wear a smile on his swollen lips above the beard, there was a tightness in his features and a knot in his eyebrows: the whole impression being of a smile willed down on top of terrible agony.

The first time he had seen Patsy in the hospital, after he'd been four weeks in the blocks without food, Seán had noticed from a side angle, when Patsy was talking to someone on the other side of the bed, how gaunt his brother's face was, how clearly his cheekbones stood out under his skin. It occurred to Seán, even back then, that he was looking at Patsy's death mask. Yet Patsy had been sitting cracking jokes that day, as cheerful as though he were on top of the world. He told Seán how happy he was to be out of the blocks; he was doing exercises and taking a shower every day. He'd walk about or go into the recreation room and watch TV—things undreamt of in the blocks. He commented to Seán on proposals and statements being made about the hunger strike. Seán thought at the time that Patsy was insane to be using up all that energy. Bobby was beginning to get very bad then, in late April, and Francis Hughes and Raymond McCreesh were in bed most of the time. Yet Patsy would be joking with Francis and Raymond and coaxing them to get up and go to the recreation room with him, which was the only place the hunger strikers could be together. Others in the family, too, were alarmed at Patsy expending all his strength, burning himself out. But Patsy said he had to have a happy medium between rest and physical movement; otherwise he'd get bedsores and become lethargic. Seán thought that he was probably also trying to prove that an INLA man could be as good as any Provo. He knew that back in the blocks Patsy and Tony had taken a lot of stick, not all of it just joking, about whether the Irps, the INLA men, could stay the course. Patsy wasn't really trying to be macho. Rather he was proving himself to himself, proving that he was worthy to stand as the first of the INLA men, and be counted as good as the best the IRA had to offer. Patsy had a fantastic commitment to the IRSP and the INLA, and he could never have been the first Irp to go on this hunger strike and then the first to come off.

Seán had always known that once Patsy went on, he would be on till the end; and that if any of them died Patsy would die as well.

Seán remembered a visit with Patsy after that middle period, about two weeks later. He'd had an opportunity to talk to Patsy directly, as oldest to youngest brother.

It was on the day of Bobby Sands' funeral. Someone rushed

up to him with a message from the prison hospital, saying that Patsy had taken a bad turn and that Seán ought to go see him. So Seán left the funeral procession, and because of the crowds he had to run for miles to get to a car. When he got to the prison hospital, he could see that Patsy had indeed worsened. Seán supposed that Patsy had passed that crest all of them seemed to go through, when they'd come up a bit after the first slow and steady decline and get a sort of second wind, before the final deterioration began. Seán had seen Patsy up; and now he was down, worse than Seán had ever seen him.

There were just the two of them in the room apart from the screw standing at the door. Seán was telling Patsy the news about Bobby and the worldwide attention Bobby's death had been getting, that there'd been a hundred thousand people at the funeral, all those people out in support of Bobby, Francis, Raymond and Patsy himself—

Then Seán looked at the screw, who was far enough away, and he said to Patsy: "Listen, there's only the two of us here, you and I, none of the family. Now I'm not asking you to stay on or come off, Patsy. I'm just asking you for the sake of clarification: how are the rest of you feeling since Bobby died? Has there been any change in their attitude, or in their morale?"

"The Brits haven't given in," Patsy said. "And so we can't give in."

Seán asked Patsy what he thought was going to happen.

Patsy was confused. He said he didn't know, that the last thing he remembered was that he'd gone into the recreation room to watch TV, and six screws came in. That's all he remembered. According to the doctor, he'd had a heart attack. Seán asked Patsy whether he knew what cell he was in now. Patsy said he was back in his own cell. With his eyes and ears failing him, and with his general disorientation, Patsy didn't even realize he was facing in a different direction.

At least one of the photographs of Patsy had been published in America, in the morning papers. A camera and tape recorder had been smuggled in days earlier and Patsy had probably gone to Raymond McCreesh and taken picures of Raymond and got Raymond to take pictures of him. After the photographs were published the screws came in and found the camera and a tiny tape recorder on which the fellows had hoped perhaps to make speeches to be broadcast at H-Block rallies. Whatever happened, Patsy was worse after that. Seán would always wonder whether the six screws had beaten Patsy after finding the camera and tape recorder.

Seán had seen all four hunger strikers. He wasn't supposed to, but he had seen them: Bobby, whose face in his last days was a shiny waxy yellow colour, his teeth protruding from what looked to Seán like a mask; Francis Hughes, who had suffered horribly, and had an eyepatch over one eye accentuating the death that was in his face; Raymond McCreesh, less ravaged but sunk now into a coma of sleep, and slipping away; and Patsy: if outsiders could see what the families saw it might help a great deal.

Today Patsy looked terrible. The O'Haras had been hopeful last night after word came from Liz in Dublin. Liz was meeting the Taoiseach, the Irish Prime Minister, Charles Haughey; but looking at Patsy they were afraid—Seán was anyway—that nothing anyone could do would help him now. Although the hospitals had refined their techniques, and seemed able, almost, to bring men back from the dead, Seán couldn't see any realistic hope. Their mother was distraught. Last night, after talking to Liz, her hopes were way up. But she'd be frantic if something didn't happen very quickly.

THEIR SISTER LIZ, with her dark small-boned beauty, her eyes full of sincerity, her complete dedication to Patsy and his cause, had thrown herself into a frenzy of effort to save his life. She was like their mother in her absolute refusal to accept the idea that Patsy would die. She'd met Haughey twice the previous week, with Teresa and Malachy McCreesh, trying to get him to act. "What can I do?" she'd described Haughey as asking. She told him he should publicly declare his support for the five demands. On Thursday night, after pleading with Haughey, she'd flown off to Paris—like a shooting star for Patsy—to meet French H-Blocks supporters and, she hoped, to meet President-elect Mitterand, who before he was elected had spoken so strongly on behalf of the Irish prisoners. She hadn't been able to see Mitterand.

When Liz O'Hara first met Haughey, last week, he said he didn't see what good it would do to publicly ask Thatcher to implement the demands. He didn't want to become embroiled, he said, in a propaganda battle. When asked point blank whether he believed that the prisoners' five demands were justified, he replied that he wasn't willing to answer that question just then.*

Liz and the others had left that meeting last week disappointed and disheartened. Yet she was back on Haughey's doorstep again this week. Seán had to admire his little sister. She kept at it. Last night he'd heard of her escapade in front of Haughey's office at Government Buildings on Merrion Street in Dublin.

Earlier in the day Liz had gone with some H-Blocks leaders to deliver seven boxes containing two hundred fifty thousand signed petitions, and she'd requested a meeting with Haughey at three o'clock. The hour passed without word from Haughey, so they brought a caravan around, covered with hunger strike posters, parked it in front of Haughey's office and sat in it to wait. Still no word. Shortly after four some gardai came, attached the caravan to a tow truck and hauled it off, with the people inside it, to a nearby garda station. But they weren't detained or charged. Then word came that Haughey would be available to meet them at five o'clock. Haughey seemed to think there might be some immediate movement from the European Commission on Human Rights; he had summoned his Attorney General and told him to contact the two barristers working on a plea to the Commission. The Attorney General rushed out, and Haughey said, "Elizabeth, I can't do anything at this point in time, but could you give me a telephone number where I can contact you within twenty-four hours? And make sure you stay by the phone." She'd phoned last night with this news, and she was euphoric, reminding the family that at an earlier meeting Haughey had said to her, in front of Teresa and

* In early September, Haughey, by now no doubt thoroughly fed up with Thatcher, would say that the hunger strike should be settled "on the basis of the five demands."

249

Malachy McCreesh, "Elizabeth, I promise you that Raymond McCreesh and your brother will not die."

When their mother had heard from Liz she was over the moon. That was last night. This morning they'd seen Patsy. Even their mother must have been aware, Seán thought, that he was beyond being saved by anyone.

At midnight, one of Haughey's secretaries phoned Liz, saying that they were working on the matter very urgently and would get back to her if anything happened. At seven in the morning Liz got a phone call asking her to meet Haughey again, at noontime. She'd gone, taking Joe McDonnell's sister Eilish Reilly with her. They were ushered into a conference room. Haughey looked at Liz the moment she came in the door, rose to shake hands and said, "Did you sleep well last night?"

"I did," Liz said, "for the first time in weeks. Because I had hope!"

Haughey shook his head, and turned to Eilish Reilly.

"Now, I'm not talking directly to you, Eilish. I'm talking to Liz because at this particular moment her brother is the one that's critical."

Liz sensed then that something was seriously wrong.

Haughey never looked at Liz after that. He sat with a typewritten statement in front of him and said, "I'm asking you, Elizabeth, at this point in time, to ask Patsy to suspend his hunger strike forthwith, and to put a formal complaint to the Human Rights Commission."

Liz herself had raised the matter of the Commission with Haughey on Tuesday. That week in the press there had been a lot of speculation that the European Commission on Human Rights would be arriving in Ireland to arrange a friendly settlement with Britain on two outstanding issues from the prisoners' complaints. The idea seemed to be that the Commission could move in and, on the basis of dealing with the two complaints, raise its umbrella over other urgent issues like the five demands, and arrange a friendly settlement on those, too.

But what Haughey was proposing sounded a lot like what

he had proposed to her friend Marcella Sands—a petition to the Commission whose only outcome had been to get Haughey off the hook, and take the pressure off the British government. Marcella's brother Bobby had died. Haughey was asking Liz personally to put in a complaint, after getting Patsy to come off his hunger strike—

"Mr. Haughey, stop a minute!"

He looked up at her.

She told him that it was the fourth meeting she'd had with him, that she'd had hope and faith in him the night before, but that now he was asking her to get her brother and Raymond McCreesh to give up their hunger strike after they'd suffered for sixty days and were on the point of dying. She and Eilish stood up to leave. But before they left Liz said to Haughey that she'd never thought an Irish Taoiseach would try like that to take away another Irishman's pride. She told him she hoped that the next time she shook hands with an Irish Taoiseach it would be someone other than him. She said she would never forget his dashing of her hopes and the heartbreak he'd caused.

When their mother heard Liz's report that afternoon, she became frantic with distress. Before that she'd seized on any glimmer of hope, convinced that somehow Patsy would live.

BY THE TIME they left the prison hospital, at about five-thirty, Seán O'Hara was nearly sick. Jim Daly drove them back to his house in Belfast. There were only the three of them there: Jim Daly, Seán and their mother. She had just put on some coffee when the phone rang. It was Father John Murphy, the prison chaplain, and he was very upset. He told Seán that they should come to the prison quickly, that Patsy had got very bad, and was dying. The priest said he'd come in to give Patsy communion, and Patsy had taken what the priest thought was a heart attack. There was no doctor there . . .

When they returned to the hospital, there was still no doctor. Patsy was visibly worse, his eyes shut and one of his ears totally deaf. There were three chairs, all on the side of his bad ear, and Seán was in the chair near the foot of the bed where he couldn't be heard, and where his view of Patsy's face was obstructed by the cage. The reason for the cage over the bottom of Patsy's bed—-which kept the blanket from touching him and the skin from peeling off his feet—was that any touch of the blanket would cause him pain. Seán moved his chair around to the other side of the bed, near the ear that still had some hearing left in it.

He shouted to Patsy that they were there, asking him whether he knew who they were. Then the screw in the room came up and said Seán had to take the chair back around to the other side of the bed. Seán asked the screw whether he realized that his brother was dying, that he was blind, that he was completely deaf in one ear and half deaf in the other and that the only way he could hear anything would be if they shouted in the other ear; and that he couldn't shout, or even see Patsy from the bottom of the bed. Seán had his hands on the bed, in full view, so what was the problem?

The screw became abusive and said to Seán that the doctor had ordered this arrangement, and if he didn't move the chair back he'd be thrown out. Seán asked the screw whether he expected them to play leapfrog to get to the top chair to talk to Patsy and then, from that side, have to roar at Patsy to make themselves heard.

The doctor came in, and denied that he'd ordered the chair arrangement. Seán asked him what had happened to Patsy. The doctor said nothing had happened, there'd been no change. Seán said that Father Murphy had seen Patsy turn blue, with some sort of seizure the priest thought was a heart attack, and yet the doctor was saying there'd been no change. Then Seán shouted, asking Patsy how he felt. Patsy said he felt bad. Seán asked him what he meant, and Patsy talked about pains in his head, his eyes, his ears, pains everywhere. Patsy collapsed then, and lay there for ten minutes or so before he could say anything further. Then he said a few words, about being unable to hold water down at all, about even the smell of water making him sick. Seán shook his head. Patsy was ebbing fast. His stomach was raw, and a rasping sound would come from him with every breath. The sight of him was shaking Seán now.

Had Seán Séamus been responsible for Patsy's being mixed up

in the war? He didn't think so. In fact he was always chasing Tony and Patsy *away* from trouble whenever he found them mixed up in it. But the two lads kept coming back, and as they got older they got involved. Seán himself had become involved with the Fianna, the IRA youth wing, when he was only thirteen.

Seán was half a decade older than Patsy. Born in June 1952, he was nearly twenty-nine now. Tony was born in April 1956, so he was four years younger: aged twelve when the troubles began. Patsy, born in July 1957, was five years younger than Seán, and just eleven when it all started in October 1968. Elizabeth was born in March 1959, so she was twenty months younger than Patsy, and much closer to Patsy and Tony than Seán was. She'd been a girl of nine when the troubles started.

Seán remembered being involved in civil rights activity before 1968. The big issue then was the city boundary. Unionists in control of Derry City Council were making almost no provision for new public housing for the city's poorer people, most of whom were Catholic. In 1967 only six council houses were built in the entire city. Many Catholics lived in densely crowded, desperately substandard homes, packed into the Bogside, the Creggan and the Brandywell. The Unionist-dominated council insisted that there was no more ground in the city on which to build housing. So there was a Catholic movement to extend the city boundary. The Unionist councilmen didn't want to do this because it would cost the ratepayers large sums of money; worse, it would create whole new Catholic areas, endangering the carefully contrived gerrymander that kept Unionist Protestants in control.

There were demonstrations every Saturday at the Guildhall, demanding a boundary extension. It was a new experience for Derry: until then it was assumed that the Catholics simply accepted their lot, accepted whatever happened. Demonstrations, with people carrying placards and demanding houses, were considered totally abnormal. Seán became involved in the demonstrations, and in the housing action groups that were formed. They were always being harassed by the police when they demonstrated, just for walking around the Guildhall with their placards.

In March 1968 there was a grand opening of the lower level of the two-tiered Craigavon Bridge spanning the Foyle. It was an expensive luxury when housing was so badly needed. Seán, then fifteen, was standing with a placard under his shirt in a crowd waiting for the Mayor of Derry to open the new span. The officials were gathered on the city side of the bridge. While the speeches were being made, Seán stood there, right beside the Orange Mayor and the principal dignitaries. The police were there. The press was there, the photographers with their cameras ready for the cutting of the tape.

The Mayor finished telling everyone what a wonderful bridge this was going to be. There was applause, and someone came along with a red velvet cushion on which a pair of gold scissors lay. The Orange Mayor said a few words in tribute to the Orange company that made the scissors. There was more applause.

"I will now officially open this bridge!" the Mayor said. He lifted the scissors, but before he could reach out to cut the tape, Seán streaked over and broke it, and then ran to a spot about twenty yards into the bridge and sat down right in front of the Mayor and the crowd, his placard lifted in front of him: Extend the Boundaries Now—Build More Houses! Another six or seven kids, who'd been hiding in pipes that ran along one side of the bridge, jumped up and joined Seán. The onlookers were outraged. This boy had denied them the grand finale to their dignified bridge-opening ceremony. The police came, and ordered Seán and the others to move. They refused, and the police dragged them across to the side of the bridge. People from the crowd began shouting, "Throw them in the river!" Then Finbar Doherty, a Derry character who'd been at the centre of the protests at the Guildhall, emerged from the crowd with half a dozen women, and they all began singing "We Shall Overcome." Finbar was arrested for disorderly behaviour, and Seán and the others were arrested for obstructing a public thoroughfare—which had not yet been opened to the public.

Since Seán was under sixteen, his case was heard in a juvenile court. At his trial Seán gave a speech, saying that the housing

254

and unemployment situation was terrible, and that instead of him being in the dock the city councilmen should be there, councilmen who should be providing housing and jobs so that people like himself wouldn't have to go about protesting the lack of these things. It was quite a speech and lasted about half an hour. He was given a conditional discharge, and went home; but the funny part was the news at one o'clock: *Fifteen Year Old Youth Gets Up in Court and Accuses City Council.*

But Seán still had to reckon with his mother, Peggy O'Hara.

She had been born a McCloskey, and the McCloskeys were considered solid, upright, law-abiding people. There were police, magistrates, and a tax inspector in the family. Her uncle, who owned a pub and shop he left to her and her husband Jim, was a justice of the peace. Her father had served prominently in the British Army, had fought in France and been wounded— he had open wounds that wouldn't heal. But during the pogroms after the war he involved himself in the IRA in defence of the Catholic Irish, and he became so angry at the results of the 1921 Treaty settlement that he burned his Army pension book. He ended up washing cars in the car park outside Derry jail for eleven shillings a week, far less than his pension would have given him. The mentality among Catholics in Derry had been for years, "Don't take British money." (The attitude these days was: "Take it—it's only taking your own money back.")

When his mother heard that Seán was involved in Finbar Doherty's housing action group, she thought at first that he was helping people find houses. Then one day someone came to the shop and said that Seán was down at the Guildhall marching up and down with a placard. Peggy rushed down to the hall to straighten Seán out. When she saw him among the other teenagers she ran over and grabbed his placard.

"Who gave you that?" she demanded to know.

"Finbar," he said.

So she marched over to Finbar with Seán's placard, broke it around his head, and gave him a few whacks with her umbrella for good measure.

His mother didn't support protest at that stage. Afterwards

she began going to demonstrations, thinking to protect Seán. This embarrassed him, because he was involved in the Fianna and the Irish language movement. But after the troubles started she began to take an interest of her own.

Seán had been involved in Irish language activities from his early teens. When he was thirteen, he thought the family name—Ó hEaghra in Irish—should be pronounced O'Harja (as if it were Japanese!). He'd been baptized John James, but he soon changed that to Seán Séamus, and later got his identity cards made out in Irish. By then he was fluent in Irish, and was teaching the language to some three hundred Fianna scouts every week.

When the soldiers came, in 1969 and 1970, he'd meet one and give him a polite greeting in Irish. Then he'd add the glosses: "Shut your face, you dirty louser; you rotten fink; up yours; go to hell"—all in Irish. And then the really Irish curses like "May your children be born blind, and bump into each other!" He'd grin as he put the curses together and reeled them off.

But he ran into an odd problem once or twice. Bilingual soldiers, who were Irish but in the British Army, were brought into Derry at that period—they were trying to appease Irish nationalists. It was early 1970 and members of the RUC—Catholics if possible—were accompanied by Irish-speaking Army MPs on joint patrols.

In one incident, he, a boy named Séamus Keenan and a couple of others were down in an area called the Wells, just below the Derry walls. There was a woman of ill-repute there in those days—who must have been a little crazy, too—known as Susie of the Wells. Séamus Keenan had on a long coat, like a German officer's. And suddenly Susie of the Wells came streaking down the street, completely naked. Séamus, who was gentlemanly, took off his coat, put it around her, and asked her where she lived. An MP came along just then, with a Catholic RUC man. They wanted to know what was going on. So Séamus Keenan, a fluent Irish speaker, began telling the whole story in Irish. And there, to Seán's astonishment, was the British Army MP writing it all down. The RUC man didn't know what to make of this. He would have given them trouble, but instead he got a lecture from the MP, who said he should be ashamed of himself, not even knowing his own language.

Seán was around when the first civil rights group was formed in Derry before the 5 October 1968 demonstration, at which Seán was a steward, and he was up front during the fracas that ensued. He knew there was going to be trouble from the RUC so he took the precaution of wearing his glasses that day—for the first time in public. Seán particularly admired one of the stewards, a man named Gerry Doherty, who was about sixty. He was called Gerry the Bird because of his famous prison escapes over the years. He'd escaped from Derry jail, from the Crum, and from the Curragh in the Free State. Before leaving jail he used to scrawl on the wall "The Bird has flown."

Seán remembered the police giving them dirty looks before the march was to begin. The demonstrators got rough treatment that day. In the days after the march a Citizens' Action committee was formed, and Seán was again involved. As time wore on his involvement became more military than political, and as a result he was interned for some three and a half years.

Patsy also got mixed up in it while he was still very young. He was shot in the leg when he was fourteen, and had to be hospitalized. That probably had a lot to do with Patsy's serious involvement, which began soon afterwards. He was a kid then, wildly confident. Later he slowed down and became very effective, more effective probably than Seán himself realized. When Patsy was seventeen, he was interned for six months, and after that was sent to jail on charges. He was out of jail two weeks before Seán was released from his long spell as an internee.

Seán remembered how fond Patsy was of cars. Their father and mother kept buying him secondhand cars. At first he had an old Vauxhall 101. And then their mother heard about a Rover, a bank manager's car, in perfect condition. The man wanted six hundred pounds for the car, but Jim and Peggy had only three hundred pounds to spare. So Seán arranged a bank loan to get Patsy the other three hundred, and suddenly Patsy was out running around in an immaculate blue Rover 2000 cc. He was always getting stopped by police. They kept the car under close surveillance.

Patsy liked to go over to Buncrana, in Donegal, which was only half an hour away. He used to take their parents down to the seaside where the family had a couple of caravans. Their father didn't drive, but he was as proud as Patsy was of the Rover. Most of his driving was across the border into Donegal. Patsy used back roads a lot, and got to know them very well: roads on which he'd almost never be stopped. This was doubly important because he was driving without a full licence at that stage.

One day Patsy was coming back across the border with some of his friends, and they were stopped at an improvised Army checkpoint at the border east of Letterkenny. The soldiers ordered everyone out of the car, and held the boys there while they searched it. They searched it a second time, finding nothing. They searched it a third time, taking the panels out, checking inside the tyres. The search took about four hours. Then they checked it a fourth time, and one of the soldiers reached under the front seat and produced a stick of gelignite. "What's this?" he said. Of course the soldier had planted it there. It was beneath the seat, where they couldn't have missed it earlier.

Patsy was well known then, and they'd been looking for an excuse to pick him up. When he was charged, and asked for bail, the police were adamant: Patsy was a dedicated terrorist, they said, and they were not going to see him released on bail. So he spent ten months in prison on remand. It became a celebrated case, because there were two trials. In the first the judge ordered a retrial because of conflicting evidence from the police and the Army. After the retrial Patsy was released—it couldn't be proved that he was in possession of the gelignite.

And here was Patsy, after the years of street fighting, of urban guerrilla warfare, of being on the run. This was the Patsy who had been up in Dublin as right hand man to Séamus Costello, charismatic founder of the IRSP and INLA; Patsy had been an INLA leader there and a political deputy to Costello. This was the Patsy who'd shown such promise in the business of manufacturing, with his and Tony's canoe-building

258

co-op and with a spoiler factory which he'd set up, and which failed only because Patsy was in prison and no longer around to run it. Here was Patsy, lying on that bed, waiting to die.

Seán was shaken by Patsy's deterioration that night; he didn't want to stay around if he didn't have to. And so when his mother said that she and their father would be staying with him, Seán said, right, he'd be there with Liz first thing in the morning to relieve them. Jim Daly had already gone down to meet the train from Derry and drive their father to the prison, so that the father would be sure to get in before closing time and join their mother at Patsy's bedside. His mother said she'd be all right till their father came. So Seán left.

JIM O'HARA had been to Derry on urgent business that afternoon. Then he'd heard that Patsy had suffered a heart attack. There was just time to get the train. But then he was offered a lift to Long Kesh by John McMonagle so he decided to take it, to avoid the long rail journey, and to save Jim Daly the trouble of coming down and meeting him at the station in Belfast. But they were a little late in getting away from Derry, and there was a traffic tie-up, so Jim and John McMonagle reached the prison at ten past ten. Jim was refused admittance, the screws at the gate telling him that the prison closed at ten. Jim was furious with the bastards; his son was there dying, yet they wouldn't let him in.

He sat in the car outside the gate of the prison for two hours after that, thinking he might see a chaplain or someone who could help get him in. He and McMonagle didn't talk much. As the night wore on and the darkness came he was angered to see women coming up to the gates, women who were let in to see the screws; their whores, he thought. They let them in. But they would not let the father of a dying prisoner in because he'd arrived a few mintues after ten. The screws' women kept coming, right up to twelve midnight, and they were all admitted.

Jim wondered whether his wife Peggy would be all alone in there. Probably so, because he'd been expected, and they only allowed two family members to stay the night. Yes, she would almost certainly be alone. And it was a terrifying experience, just sitting there watching Patsy, even when there were several of them there—the most terrifying experience in all Jim's life. Patsy never screamed. There was sort of a moaning sound from him, though, that went on for hours. Jim would be sitting there listening to it; there was nothing he could do. He'd even find himself, after he'd been there a long time, shouting to Patsy to get up. He would get to the point where he didn't know what he was saying to his son.

He'd never agreed with Patsy's reasoning in going on hunger strike. When Patsy was fit to talk, Jim used to say to him that he was needed outside. "We can't afford to lose boys like you," Jim said. And Patsy would say that Jim was missing the point, that he couldn't expect anyone else to go through with it if he himself wasn't willing to. He was the OC, and had to give leadership. Jim grumbled, but he had to admit that Patsy showed good sense about what he was doing, showed he was thinking things through. Patsy had got the Last Rites nearly a week ago, convinced he was going to die, even though Jim and the rest of the family were thinking differently, thinking that something might break. Their daughter Liz nearly ran herself into the ground trying to save him. She would have gone to the moon to do that. She and Patsy, the two youngest, were very close.

Jim was sick about what was happening to Patsy there those last days. It was heartbreaking as well as terrifying. Yet he knew that there was nothing to be done about it. He knew Patsy, and when Patsy said he was going to do something, that was that. If he had woken and found a doctor bringing him round, Patsy would have strangled the fellow.

WHAT JIM DIDN'T KNOW, as he sat there in the car, was that his wife Peggy had made up her mind to intervene to save Patsy's life. She'd had her mind made up about this from the time he first went on hunger strike.

Peggy was there, now, the only one of the family with Patsy in the prison, wondering what had happened to her husband Jim. She was standing beside Patsy's bed, moistening his lips and tongue with wet cotton wool. Patsy couldn't take water anymore. His eyes were open but he couldn't see.

Peggy knew she was in for a long night. She thought at first that she might be able to go in and talk to the McCreeshes, who were there in the prison while poor Raymond was dying. She thought it would be good to go out and talk to them, while having a cigarette and a cup of tea. She couldn't smoke in Patsy's room because it would make him sick.

She tried to go to the McCreeshes but the warders wouldn't let her. Why? What harm would it do if she sat for a few minutes between times with the McCreeshes? But they said no. It was then she knew that she would be sitting up all night on her own. This afternoon Peggy learned that Liz's efforts with Haughey had failed. Elizabeth had gone to Dublin, then to Paris, then back to Dublin, trying to get someone in power to act to save Patsy's life. Mr. Haughey had raised Liz's hopes last evening, but today those hopes had been dashed. Everything looked black.

So Peggy decided that the time had come for her to intervene. She knew who the leaders of the movement outside the prison were, and had managed to talk to them. She'd intended to sign for medication to save Patsy's life, but felt she should tell them first. Peggy found them very sympathetic. They said she had the right to make that decision if she wanted to; and just as they'd stood by Patsy when he decided to go on hunger strike, so they'd stand by her in her decision to take Patsy off. "We won't desert you," they said.

When she'd next seen Patsy after that, he looked terrible. They were alone together for a brief time. She felt heartsick and more than ever determined that she would not let him die. She was distraught, and put her arms around him saying, "Patsy, at this moment I don't care about Ireland, or anything else in the whole world. You are all that matters to me. Everything else has failed, and now I'm the only one who can save you. And I'm going to do it." Then she rushed out of the room, for fear he would say no.

And now she was alone with him again, and he was failing

badly. Her grief overwhelmed her. She was torn by thoughts of what her decision might mean.

OUT IN THE CAR Jim was thinking about the time when Patsy was only fourteen, when he was shot at by British soldiers in the Bogside while handing out leaflets about a sale at a local shop. He'd had a close call. Some soldiers were raiding a house at the top of Westland Street. Patsy was standing watching from a laneway, when some IRA men appeared and began firing up the street at the soldiers. A boy, Robert Canning, standing next to Patsy, was hit in the stomach by the soldiers' return fire; the boy was lucky to be alive. Two months later, when Patsy was on vigilante patrol, he was shot in the leg. Patsy ended up in the same ward as Robert Canning, in Altnagelvin hospital.

The Altnagelvin wasn't a place Derry Catholics liked. It was full of the other crowd, and the RUC were around the place all the time. Loyalists could have gone in anytime and bumped someone off.

But Jim went over to visit Patsy there, and the visit turned out to be a great joke. They had a big dog called Shep. It was Patsy and Tony who had brought the dog into the house when it was a stray, wandering around half dead. Shep had a golden coat—he was half collie and half labrador—and he could read your mind.

That day Jim set off on the visit to Patsy, walking at a good pace, sailing down and over the bridge and up through the Waterside. No such thing as buses available in those days; and there were barricades everywhere because of the No-Go areas. As he trotted on out to the hospital, Jim didn't notice the dog following him.

Jim found the ward Patsy was in, on the sixth floor. The place was even worse than he'd expected: armed Brits were roaming the corridors. Jim walked in and sat down to talk with Patsy. Then suddenly the dog flew into the ward and jumped up onto Patsy's bed.

Men pretending to be male nurses quickly appeared.

"Get that dog out of here," they said. Jim knew from their

look and attitude that they were no more male nurses than he was: they were RUC with white coats on.

"Why?" Jim asked.

They said that they couldn't allow dogs in there. Jim asked them what *they* were doing in there. They asked him what he meant. And Jim said to them that they were dirtier dogs than Shep was. Who did they think they were bluffing? he asked. If they were men at all, they should put on their uniforms. They sure weren't going to play that old white-coat game with him.

Jim made damned sure that a whole lot of people heard him, too. He knew they'd hate that.

"Right," one of them said. "We'll get the matron in here." And she came in and said that Jim had to get the dog out.

"No way," Jim said. If they wanted the dog out they would have to get it out themselves. He knew well they wouldn't be able to. So the heroes came over, and the dog jumped down and went under a bed. They got down on all fours to pull him out, and the shouting could be heard all over the hospital. They didn't get near Shep. If they had, he would have chewed their hands off.

Jim was enjoying the crack. And he thought it was great the way the incident perked up Patsy and the other boy. They were delighted with it all, and were egging the dog on. Later Patsy told Jim that all that night the white-coated boys would be shouting into the room, "Ye wee Fenian bastards!" and saying how they were going to cut the lads' throats and string them up.

They ordered Jim out of the hospital, but he only went to the door at the corridor. He told them that this was as far as he was going. He was entitled to his visit, he said. He didn't have to sit on the bed. He could speak to Patsy from the corridor.

"We're not like you," Jim said loudly. "We have nothing to hide. Anything we do will be done openly. That's the type of us. And if you want to know the name, it's O'Hara. Have a good look at me. Take my photo, if you haven't already. You'll meet me again anyway."

Someone came over to Jim and said, "There's a couple of gentlemen here who want to see you." They were

263

plainclothesmen, CID, and they asked him whether he would be making a charge against the British Army for accidentally shooting his son.

"Accidentally shooting him?" Jim said. "They tried to murder him!"

"Ah, that's not what we were told—"

"I don't give two damns what you were told," Jim said, starting to shout at them. "Those dirty bastards jumped up, and for no reason at all opened fire on those young fellows. And then they told a pack of lies as well. I can prove they were lying. I knew where my son was, where he was coming from. He was shot only a few yards from the house he was in. Don't try that ould crap with me—"

"We'll let the courts decide—"

"I don't give a damn about you and your courts—"

"What do you mean? You're not making a claim?"

"That's right, I'm not. Stick your blood money up your arse—we can do without it!"

Jim knew that if he'd make a claim they'd twist it around, and young Patsy would be locked up. Or they'd make out that he shot himself . . .

The dog stayed there, under the bed, till Jim left the door of the ward to go; then it followed after him.

Jim had grown up in the Waterside, a mainly Protestant area of Derry. He remembered a friend, a tall, thin man named Seán Dolan, who would teach them Irish songs and how to play Gaelic football and hurling. He and Dolan were very close, and sometimes Dolan would say to Jim that he wanted him to do a few jobs for him, and that Jim didn't have to tell anybody. So he'd give him boxes of Republican papers to take around and put into people's doors. Jim was so young that he didn't realize he was putting them into Protestant houses, too, where they weren't supposed to go.

Somebody told Jim's father about this. The father kicked Jim around the house like a football, and afterwards wouldn't let him out for a week. Jim's father was terrified of getting mixed up in anything like that. But Jim himself was proud of what his sons did—John and Patsy, and Tony, who was a quieter sort, and didn't have the experience Patsy had. Tony had played his part, though, and had spent all those years on the blanket, and was still on it.

If the boys were physical force men and fighters, it was no wonder, for Jim had been a fighter before them. Patsy was more like his mother Peggy in temperament, but he certainly had Jim's neck. There were times when Jim's heart swelled with pride: whatever happened to him, he was in fact Patsy O'Hara's father.

World War II was on when Jim was growing up in Derry, a city which in Jim's view was one big whorehouse for the American troops stationed there. He had seen some really good fights, though, when the British boys would pick a scrap with American soldiers and the American boys would beat hell out of them.

Jim had grown up in something better than the worst poverty. His father had a fairly good job, as a foreman at the docks, but even good jobs paid a pittance in those days. Thirty-four shillings a week was the best money his father was ever paid.

At first they lived in a house in a place called Eglinton Terrace, close to the police barracks. The police were all-powerful in Derry at that time. And one day they came along and threw the O'Haras out of the house and gave it to a policeman.

When Jim's family were forced out of Eglinton Terrace they got a house in Tyrconnell Street. There were fourteen in Jim's family, and his father had to pay nine shillings a week rent, and pay for coal and electricity and all the rest, out of his income. Living on thirty-four shillings was hard going, especially with all those kids.

Then somebody passed the word along that there was a house going over in the Waterside. It was a heavily Protestant area, but the house would cost only three shillings a week. So the O'Hara family had a look and finally moved over there. They were all healthy in Jim's family, but within one year of moving into that house there were five of his family laid up, none of whom had ever been ill in their lives. An older brother of

Jim's died, and then a sister. Soon there were three of them dead. What nobody among the neighbours had told them was that the reason for the low rent was that the family who had lived in the house before them had been wiped out—the entire family—by tuberculosis. They had moved into a deathtrap. So they had the house fumigated, and the rest of the family survived.

Jim's mother was a Martin. She was a very quiet woman but she had brothers who weren't. They had been in the British Army, and had once, sometime in 1931, been asked to do guard duty so that some officers could get away. The brothers, Jim's uncles, decided to do the opposite. They took the car meant for the officers and just drove off and never came back. The police were always on the doorstep looking for the Martin boys. But they never found them.

Jim went to St. Columb's college for a time, on scholarship. He was good at school. Then he left St. Columb's because he felt suffocated by the clergy and the clerical types who ran the place. Besides, by this time, living as he did over in the Waterside, most of Jim's friends were Protestants, and he could see no point in continuing at St. Columb's where there was so much talk of what family you came from and all that. He went to Strand Technical college for awhile after that, also on scholarship.

Though he had plenty of friends among his Protestant neighbours, most of them became enemies once a year. On eleventh night, before the annual Twelfth of July celebration of King Billy and Protestant supremacy, their masters would get them all drunk and drummed up, and they would come marching down the street, egged on by the girls—the girls were far worse than the lads—and they'd start spitting in Jim's face. Some of them would gang up on him and beat him. After the Twelfth was over, it was supposed to be all pals again. But Jim's way of getting even was to search them out individually— the ones who had ganged up on him—and to beat up each one. He went looking until he found all of them. After awhile the harassment stopped, because those Protestant lads came to learn that he wouldn't stand for any nonsense. And some of them became Jim's best friends.

Jim returned to thoughts of Patsy, and to Seán Séamus, who'd given the younger lads their lead.

It was after the shooting incident up in the Creggan that Patsy began to look for ways to get seriously involved. Bloody Sunday, too, affected Patsy. It was the same thing—innocent people being shot by British soldiers—and fourteen of them killed. Patsy, Jim realized, would tackle an elephant. He had a heart like a lion. At first all he could do, he and the other youngsters, was to join in the rioting and throw petrol bombs and such. There was nobody available to teach them to use arms—to teach them anything at all. But Patsy began to learn by example.

Jim thought he must have picked up a good deal from Seán Séamus, whom Jim called John, and who was also called Scatter. The legend was that John was a tommy-gun man, that he had a gun held together with blue tape and everytime he wanted to fire the thing he had to bang it against the wall to make it work for him; and that when he was out with his tommy-gun, and Brits were around, he would shout to the crowd, "Scatter!" He was very smart, John was. He knew the fighting game. But to Jim the extraordinary thing about John was his love of reading. When he'd come home from school he didn't go out and play. He stayed in the house and read, and read. They all called him The Professor at that stage.

John was on the streets, though, when the fighting began—almost never in the house. He was one of the first lads to take over the top of the High Flats during the Battle of the Bogside. He and the others—one of them was young Willie Best, who later became a British soldier, with the Royal Irish Rangers, and was killed by the Official IRA while home on leave—were up there for four or five days. Jim and the family used to send them up food, and supplies of bottles and petrol, using the lifts at first, but then, when the lifts were put out of order, finding other ways to supply them. John and the other lads did a brilliant bit of fighting up there.

Once, when they were still living above the bar and the shop in Bishop Street, John came to him and said there was an Army unit outside.

"Come here. Do you see them?"

Jim saw right away that the soldiers were there, and were coming in their direction. After the Army had been in action a few times, it was easy to see exactly where they were heading—they were so stupid about it.

"Right, John," Jim said. "Out!"

John couldn't get out the front way, because they were lying there pointing their guns at the windows. John ran out, climbed up the back wall and jumped down into another yard—a thirty-two foot drop, a miracle he survived it. Jim thought he might have been killed, but couldn't look because the soldiers had come bolting through the door and were running up the stairs. But John knew what he was doing. Jim learned later that he had done a kind of trapeze act. John was very agile, and there were several clotheslines strung in the yard. He'd jumped over to the lines, swung himself down, and he was away.

John had joined the Republican movement at the end of the 1960s. But what was supposed to be the leadership had gone so completely political that they didn't want to fight. The RUC were running through the streets, shooting Catholics, and were threatening to bring in B-Men with rifles and shoot down on them in the Bogside. Yet the people had nothing to defend themselves with.

The original IRA was supposed to have arms, but when forced to cough up, they had nothing at all—they'd sold the arms years ago. So the fighters, those who wanted to have a go, to shoot back at the RUC, split off from them and formed their own Provisional IRA and Provisional Sinn Féin. The Provos got themselves organized and armed. Early on in the real fighting there were just a few lads, John among them. There were six or seven at first, and it grew from that.

The young lads used to patrol the streets of Derry, wearing hoods and carrying their guns, and people would look out and see these hooded boys, with guns, walking up and down the street, and couldn't understand what was going on. They were few, and they stayed out all night, lying out in the fields or in hiding places. At first, hardly any of them were ever lifted or shot. It was only when a lot of others jumped on the bandwagon that things began to go sour.

268

In October 1971, about two months after internment began, John was arrested and interned. When he came out, in early 1976, he didn't want anything to do with any truce with the British. So John began working with the IRSP, which Patsy and then Tony had joined while John was in prison. But John worked by himself, in a low key. He didn't want anyone knowing his business.

John was small and wiry, while Tony and Patsy grew into big men. Before he went to Long Kesh Patsy was a big strapping boy, 6′ 1″ or 6′ 2″, very well built, with no fat on him. Even from an early age they all classed Patsy as a leader. There was an air about him, something that came right out of him. It made you feel that if you were on the wrong side of him he could make you fear him. There was a certain quality of menace there, and if people took him up the wrong way, he could cut them with two words. Patsy had a strong sense of command, and he later became a great organizer for the INLA, travelling about the country setting up units, teaching them what to do and how to do it, and telling them how to go about getting the materiel they needed. Jim's impression was that Patsy was very good at that sort of thing.

Jim used to wonder why the INLA concentrated on shotguns so much—shotguns with the barrels sawn short. He learned later that it was because they had no funds for anything better.

Patsy would come to ask him for money for other things he needed, too—like the blue Rover. It was a real flying machine, that Rover. He used to go solo on many of his missions, spinning around in the car until he saw a patrol of Army or police, and then he'd let fly at them with his gun. He'd drive up to the Creggan, and the first patrol he spotted he would go have a crack at them. They would spin around in their cars trying to pin him down, but they could never catch him; he was like will-o'-the-wisp. And after chasing him, and not catching him, they'd come down to the house—they came there all the time. The blue Rover would be sitting at the door but Patsy would never be there. They'd ask Jim who'd been driving the car. And Jim would say he'd been driving it himself. They'd ask where he'd been, and Jim would say that that was his business. They would threaten to take it apart. And he'd say, "Go ahead. But you'll have to pay for it."

Sometimes Jim or Peggy would say to Patsy that they wanted him to take them out for a run somewhere, and off they'd go. He took them to parts of Ireland they'd never heard of. They travelled all over Donegal and the South. Patsy knew so many unapproved border roads that he was able to get across nearly all the time without passing a checkpoint. He took them to the Bloody Foreland several times, out on the northwest coast.

Patsy would take his friends off in the car, too, but not for drinking and joyriding. Patsy drank very little. He had learned his lesson one night when he was younger, when one of his mates got a keg, and they all sat up in a field drinking beer. They came down to the house afterwards, all roaring. The Army came down the street, and the boys lay down in the road and shouted, "Come on, you British bastards, show us what you're made of!" The Army unit drove down and stopped, and their captain said, "Remove those people." Whatever kind of soldiers they were, they were afraid for their lives, and wouldn't go down to move them. And the officer said, "Run over the bastards!" As they bore down on them, the boys jumped clear of the road and leapt on top of the wagons. It was all very comical. But when Jim and the family told Patsy next day what he'd been doing, that finished him with the drink. After that, when he'd go into a bar with his friends, he would drink only lemonade. And he'd say to the others, "How the hell can you fight a war if you're full of drink?"

Patsy was very much like John in keeping his own counsel. He might come along one day and gather a couple of boys together and say, "Let's go!" But he never said anything in the house. Neither Jim nor Peggy ever knew where he was going or what he was going to do. And Patsy was very serious. Jim would ask him what was up, and Patsy would lay a finger alongside his nose as if to say, "Don't ask." Jim would see him smiling at cops and at the Brits and know that behind the smile Patsy was making his plans for them. He was involved in the political side, the IRSP, in Derry and in Dublin, but he was always active as a military leader behind the scenes.

Patsy trained younger lads in techniques of handling interrogation. Jim would be at nome reading, and in the other room he'd hear a roar or two and know that Patsy and one of the other older boys were in there cross-examining the young lads. Patsy would throw a question and a lad would answer, with his name, say, and Patsy would say, "You shouldn't have told me," and the other older lad would hit the boy a crack. Patsy was a big tough lad, and Jim used to complain about these interrogations. He thought it was all wrong and he'd go into the room and tell Patsy so. And Patsy would turn to the younger lads and say, "Am I bullying you?" and every one of them would say no. This was the way Patsy trained them to face the Army and police interrogators.

During the period of the 1975 truce Patsy was on the run not only from the Army and RUC but also from the Provos, who were trying to trap him and stop him, since his activities were interfering with their truce. As soon as the truce was announced Patsy had gone over to the INLA. And after that experience of having everyone chasing after them—the police, the Army and their own people—Jim thought it was no wonder the INLA had become so extreme. They really suffered in those days. Yet even Provos would go out to help Patsy on occasion. That didn't suit their leadership. But their young fellows knew he was a fighter, and fearless.

One night, Jim remembered, Patsy came along a back lane with a crippled friend, and suddenly a gang of Provos cornered him in the lane. Their idea was to give him such a beating he would retire from fighting—it was during the truce, and his persistence in keeping the war going embarrassed the Provos.

Patsy backed up against a wall, and when the first few came up to have a go at him, he laughed and said, "I'm not even going to lift my hand to you. If that's all you can do, if I were you I would just chuck it." They just stood and looked at him, and then they moved off. They were saying, in effect: what the hell can you do with a boy like this, who just stands and laughs at you?

During the truce period, the Provos would be rolling around in their green Cortinas—all new, fast, good cars. They were policing Catholic areas because the RUC weren't allowed in, and were always trying to catch Patsy. They admired him, and they knew how well thought of he was around the country. When he went on hunger strike they pointed out that he'd once been a Provo—wanting to claim him for one of their own.

Jim remembered Micky Devine, who became INLA OC in the prison when Patsy went on hunger strike. Micky was another Derry lad, and a friend of Patsy's. Micky was not a boy for sitting down and planning things. But he was very good at starting a bit of a war in the street. He was gutsy. He might be walking along the street and shout up into the houses, "Well, Ma, how's your daughter? Get her out here till I have a good look at her!" He'd know there were Brits or cops around, and that they'd be listening in, and would drive over to find out what was up. And as soon as they'd passed him he'd pull a petrol bomb out of his pocket, and whirl around and toss it at them. A little stroke like that could get a riot going. Micky Devine could start a battle out of nothing.

PEGGY, ALONE in the prison cell with Patsy, had finally been told that her husband Jim had arrived just after ten o'clock and had been refused admittance. "Dear God," she said to herself, "must I bear the burden of this night alone?" She asked again if she could sit with the McCreeshes for a little while, but the warder said no. So she stayed there, wetting Patsy's lips with the moist cotton wool and holding his hand. She had resolved to intervene, but had to wait until she was sure Patsy was unconscious before she could do it. Then, just as if he were reading her mind, he suddenly turned his head towards her and spoke in a firm and lucid way, forcing up the words: "Mammy," he said, "I'm sorry we didn't win. But please let the fight go on."
The words took hold of her heart. And then it hit her for the first time: *Patsy was really going to die.* He did not want her to save him. She'd known that, but she hadn't fully faced up up to it until now. Mary, she thought, must have felt as helpless when Jesus said to her, "Did you not know that I must be about my Father's business?" If she signed for medication he would only go back on his fast as soon as he became conscious again: in trying to save him, she would be prolonging his suffering and agony. Then she returned to the decision she thought she'd

272

made, and said to herself that she didn't care, she had to save his life, even if Patsy would hate her for the rest of his days. She wanted him to live. She wanted to cry out the words then and there: "I want to save my son!" But what he'd said had gripped her, and had frozen the speech in her mouth. *"Mammy, please let the fight go on."*

The night went by, the hours like years, and in the morning Elizabeth came in with Jim. They urged Peggy to leave and to get some rest, and finally she did go, and slept for awhile at Jim Daly's house.

SEÁN O'HARA came in a little later. He'd heard, the evening before, the first sounds of what he took to be a death rattle. Now it was more pronounced. The noise, that horrible noise, would come again and again and again. Nobody who'd not heard it could imagine what the noise was like. Patsy had taken no water for two days, and his insides were completely raw. He was so dehydrated that everytime he breathed his insides would rub and scrape against each other. He was in terrible, unbelievable pain. They'd shout out to him, asking him whether he knew they were there, and whether he knew who they were. And sometimes he'd say "Aye," barely forcing the word out. Elizabeth keep wetting a bit of cotton wool and trying to put it to his lips, which were just black blood at this stage. But whenever she'd put the moistened wool to his lips, he'd clench his teeth. Seán thought that Patsy must have felt that someone was trying to revive or force-feed him. Patsy locked his teeth tight, and never opened them again.

That day the warders brought in a cabbage dinner and let it sit there. Even the smell of water made Patsy retch, and now there was this smell of cabbage all day long. The smell of it in that overheated room was even making Seán sick, never mind poor Patsy.

Priests had been in regularly to see Patsy, all through the hunger strike. He seemed to like Father John Murphy, one of the prison chaplains. Father Murphy was close to him. Patsy, Seán knew, was not a man for organized religion. When he was outside he didn't go to Mass. But here he got the sacraments

273

regularly. And Seán knew that it was real, that Patsy would never have become religious to please anyone.

All day long the family continued their vigil, two and sometimes three at a time. And there were three screws in there as well. They didn't need the three screws, who were crowding the room and keeping out family members waiting in the other room until their turn came to be with Patsy.

Tony had repeatedly asked permission to see Patsy. And they kept saying no. Late that morning Patsy went into a coma, in which he didn't recognize anyone. Then Tony was finally allowed in. Before Tony arrived, the rest of the family had to leave. The screws said that the family had not been given permission for a visit with Tony, and that therefore they had to clear the room before he would be allowed in.

Seán imagined how it must have been for Tony, brought over from the blocks under guard, walking in to see the brother he had last seen on Monday when he was more or less lucid, walking in alone and finding Patsy in a coma. Then, after a quarter of an hour, Tony was taken away, under guard, and marched back to the blocks without being able to talk to his family.

Tony was allowed another quarter-hour visit that night, but all he could do was look at his brother dying. Liz told Seán afterwards about Patsy's last hour. Sometime between ten and ten-thirty Thursday night, a priest who'd been in with Patsy came out and told them that Patsy was dead. They rushed in, their father, Jim Daly and Liz, and found him still alive. Probably his heart had stopped for a moment. But he was breathing now, very laboured breaths. Their father called out "Patsy!" and Patsy seemed to try to move his head just one last time. They waited with him, and as he slipped towards death Liz saw him change, and saw a very definite smile crossing his face.

"You're free, Patsy," Liz said. "You've won your fight, and you're free!" Then Patsy stiffened and was cold.

It was at 11:29 that night, Thursday 21 May, that Patsy was pronounced dead. Liz and their father were there, and Jim Daly was with them. Seán had left at 7:30 to begin making the funeral arrangements. Earlier that night, Seán had heard on the

274

radio Charlie Haughey's announcement of an 11 June general election in the 26 counties. Seán thought about this. No other hunger striker would be near death on 11 June. They'd slipped their election in after the first wave of hunger strike deaths. Seán found it ironic that Haughey, who had promised Liz that Patsy and Raymond McCreesh would not die, had made his announcement between the time of Raymond's death and the time of Patsy's.

After Patsy died, everyone went back to Jim Daly's house, where Seán and their mother were waiting. Seán suggested that his mother should stay in Belfast for another day. He would go to Derry ahead of her, he said, get the coffin brought home and get the house tidied up for visitors. He promised her he'd have everything right by the time she came down.

Seán tried to find out where they were taking Patsy's body, but the prison wouldn't tell him. He imagined it would be taken to Belfast. The family didn't know it had been taken to Omagh until they got a call from Bradley's, the undertakers.

At 4:40 in the morning there was another phone call, from friends in Derry, who'd received a message from the RUC, saying: "If you want to collect this thing, you'd better collect it before daylight—otherwise it's going to be dropped at the O'Haras' front door." There was another message, more explicit, from the RUC to the H-Blocks office in Derry. The police had phoned there and said: "Where do you want this fucking body? If somebody doesn't collect it, we're going to drop it from a helicopter on O'Hara's doorstep."

The undertakers collected the coffin from Omagh at six in the morning, and took it to their place in Chamberlain Street, where friends and neighbours, allowed to file by and view the body, saw what Seán was about to see.

Seán had gone down to Derry ahead of his parents and Liz, and prepared the house. He had the undertakers bring Patsy's remains to the house. But when the coffin was opened the first thing he noticed was the condition of Patsy's face. Seán hadn't been there during the last hours, when Patsy died. But when, later on, the family arrived and looked at Patsy there in the coffin, they all asked Seán what had happened.

Seán knew then that something had been done to Patsy's body, that he hadn't been imagining things. Their father and Liz agreed there hadn't been a mark on his face when he died. Only the black blood around his mouth. But there he was in the coffin with marks on him, especially that big mark across his nose; it stood out because it was heavily caked with blood. Someone gently touched the nose and found that it was broken in two places.

Seán thought that it must have happened just after he died; to congeal, the blood would have had to have been warm. Then there were the marks near his left eye—four cigarette burns; and cigarette burn marks on his upper body, and bruises. Patsy's body had been in police custody the whole time. Seán suspected that the broken nose was due to the body having been thrown into a plastic bag and then trailed out to a landrover. Who'd been responsible for the cigarette burns? Seán wasn't too sure, but at some point the County Derry police might have been involved in transporting the body to Omagh; or RUC men had done it—whichever of them had the body in their charge. As Tony was to say to Seán later, at the funeral, it was an example of the British attitude towards the Irish in general, that horrifying and disgusting desecration of a dead body.

IN LONG KESH prison the day after Patsy died, a screw came down the wing at 10:30 in the morning, calling out, "O'Hara for the governor."

Tony's door was opened and he walked out under guard—up between the grilles, out to the circle and into the assistant governor's office. The governor sat there in a three-piece suit, neatly pressed, with shirt and tie. He looked stiffly official and spoke formally in a clipped British accent.

"Prisoner O'Hara, I regret to inform you, as part of Her Majesty's service, that your brother Patrick O'Hara died at half past eleven last night. You are advised to apply for parole, as parole is usually granted in these circumstances."

He gave a nod as if to dismiss Tony.

Tony asked how to get a form for this.

"A parole form," the governor said, "will be left down to your cell."

Tony asked about clothes to wear while on parole.

"Clothes will also be arranged."

Tony turned and walked out. Going back down the wing he held his head high, feeling the eyes of the screws burning into his back. When he reached his cell he slumped onto the bed.

The evening before his parole day Tony was taken down to the punishment block where they kept him till the next morning. He couldn't sleep that night. He was still numbed by his brother's death. He had mixed feelings about getting the parole. Its only benefit would be the chance to comfort his family. He would get out in the morning about half-past six. But after stopping in Belfast, the long journey to Derry and the funeral itself, the twelve hour parole would mean probably only three hours or so with his family.

In the morning Tony was given the clothes he'd been wearing in 1976, which had been kept for nearly five years wrapped in a bag. Patsy's suit—the trousers didn't fit him, and the coat was wrinkled and scraggly.

When he got out to the car park he was suddenly struck by the light in the sky, by the fresh air, the sunshine, the green all around. It was dazzling.

"Over here, Tony!"

It was his friend Brian shouting from a waiting car. Brian opened the door for him and he sat in. As they turned out of the car park Tony noticed TV cameras and microphones moving in towards them. His friends told him that they were an American TV crew and had asked if there was any possibility of an interview. Tony had undertaken, when he'd signed for the parole, that he wouldn't make any public statement or speech. He didn't want to jeopardize another prisoner's chances of getting parole for the death of a relative.

"Better tell them 'No comment,'" he said.

They drove to Turf Lodge in Belfast. Tony was to have a rest, a cup of tea and wait for the car that was to take him to Derry. They were bringing him decent clothes: a suit, shirt and black tie. But in Belfast he was told that the car had been hijacked, and the clothes in the back burned. He'd have to wear what he had on, and wait for a lift to Derry. He sat trying to make small talk, trying to think, trying to laugh, to joke, to show he wasn't sad. Inside he had no feeling at all. All he wanted was to be alone.

Another car was found. By 9:15 they were on their way west.

It was strange, on the road to Derry, seeing cows, sheep, goats; barns, houses and green fields. The blue sky above seemed strange, the sun shining down, the fresh air. He smoked cigarettes. He chatted. But he couldn't feel or even look normal, as he sat there, his face pale and bloated. In the past five or six days he'd had one or two hours' sleep a night.

The Mass was beginning at 10 o'clock. They were speeding down the motorway, but would be lucky to catch even the end of it.

In Derry they crossed the bridge, drove up the hill, and arrived outside the Long Tower church. Huge crowds of people were milling about. Suddenly all the TV cameras, the pressmen and photographers began to turn their attention to him. He noticed Terry Robson, a man he knew from the Derry IRSP, his back turned to Tony, unaware of his arrival.

"Terry!" Tony called. Terry turned around, saw Tony, and spontaneously hugged him: the man was near to tears. He led Tony through the mass of photographers and reporters and cameramen, down a short path and in through the door of the church.

As Tony walked in, the congregation—some 1500 people—seemed to turn around all at once and stare at him. He could almost hear people saying: "There's his brother, the poor fellow. He's come from Long Kesh, from the H-Blocks." Tony didn't care. He didn't know and didn't want to know. In the aisle he saw the coffin.

Tony was led to the seat they held for him. There were nods from his family, and from friends. He could see sympathy in their looks, and pity. There was relief in his mother's eyes that he'd come. His brother Seán moved over to the seat beside him and whispered a question: what had happened to make him late? Tony whispered to him about the hijacked car.

He wanted to concentrate on the Mass, to pay his last respects to Patsy. Kneeling down, he began to join in the responses. They had changed slightly from 1976. When he didn't know the responses he said his own prayers.

He tried to imagine himself alone with Patsy . . .

Suddenly the Mass was over and everybody was milling around him. People were trying to shake his hand, telling him how sorry they were. He was ushered to a small corner of the church where he could wait until the crowd left. Seán took him to Patsy's coffin. Patsy was lying there almost as Tony had seen him a few days earlier—except that now his nose was broken and his face had burn marks on it. His body was covered but Seán told Tony that there were other bruises around the pelvis, legs and arms. Tony didn't want to look further. The desecration, he said to Seán, typified the British attitude towards the Irish people.

Outside once again he passed through the pressmen before climbing into the car to be driven back home to the house in Ardfoyle. Hundreds of local people thronged around. Tony was introduced to scores of them and to members of the National H-Blocks/Armagh committee. He wanted to say to Bernadette McAliskey how sorry he was that she had been shot and how glad he was that she had survived, but he couldn't find words, and could only mumble something to her. He did an interview for the *Republican News* , and realized only at the end that during it he had almost broken down. In a next-door neighbour's house he met the McCreesh family. He noticed the resemblance to Raymond in some of the brothers and uncles: the same quiet sincerity and Christian belief; the same bright fire in their eyes.

Nobody knew what to say. Yet they wanted to make Tony feel at home. He was very uncomfortable sitting there, trying to force conversation. So he said he would like to go out for some air.

He went wandering down around the Brandywell. Everything had changed. People passed him on the streets. Some avoided his look, some nodded their heads. A friend of Tony's, coming out a door, saw Tony and ran back in. Tony understood why. Too much embarrassment, too much call on the emotions. Tony walked on to another friend's house. He went in, and they tried to cheer him up. He was smiling and cracking jokes, but it all seemed unreal.

At about two o'clock it started to rain. Tony went out into it from pure instinct. He hadn't felt the rain on his head for four years. He walked about, getting soaked. Then he realized that his hair and clothes would be ruined for the burial service. He had to go home and get dry.

Back at the house, there were still the throngs of people. He managed to get in and get his hair and jacket dried out. By then it was time for the burial. Tony was driven the short distance to the church. When he got out of the car, his brother Seán said that he should put the flags—the Tricolour and the Starry Plough—on Patsy's coffin: Tony's last chance to pay tribute to his younger brother and fellow blanketman. Seán had been working on a press release about the hijacking of Tony's car. It had been hijacked at gunpoint in the middle of Turf Lodge by men with English accents. Seán was sure it was the SAS.

Tony helped carry the coffin down to the hearse. They moved off slowly, an INLA colour party flanking the hearse while the family walked behind. There were crowds everywhere. Tony stared at them: faces he recognized, faces he didn't. The ones he recognized he barely recognized: only half remembering who they were.

His relatives were behind him, his mother and father, his sister and brother. Beside him was his brother-in-law with some friends. It was a long walk: down through the Brandywell, into the Bogside, up around the Moore, all the way up the Creggan, down into the cemetery. There were tens of thousands of people, their faces strained in the pale sunlight, a seething, bobbing, compacted mass, the piper and the drummer making themselves heard despite the noise of two helicopters buzzing overhead.

Tony's mind was numb, unable to properly register the tumult of impressions. All he wanted now was to get back to his prison cell.

Up in the cemetery the people gathered around the graveside.

Tony and the family carried the coffin the last distance, and then lowered it beside the grave.

SEÁN, standing with Tony and the family, saw only a scattering of priests, and no bishop. At the graveside, at the top of the city cemetery, six of the honour guard of thirty masked INLA volunteers stepped forward and fired three volleys each in salute to Patsy. The coffin was lowered into the ground. Seán saw Father Brian McCreesh among the handful of priests who offered final prayers. Jim Daly, who had stood by them so loyally, was chairman of the graveside ceremonies, and Seán himself spoke: about Charlie Haughey, and the decisive impact of the death of the four hunger strikers, and the true colour of the British: "scarlet red with the blood of many Irish men and women." As he spoke, Seán could see around him what looked like the whole Catholic population of Derry, and with them the Sandses, and the Hugheses, and the McCreeshes who had given their sons and brothers too. Gerry Roche spoke, for the IRSP Ard Comhairle. Then came the final speaker, Bernadette Devlin McAliskey, who had fought alongside them all in the Battle of the Bogside:

> As the cortege left the Long Tower church this morning, personally I could not help but cast my mind back to a time in 1969 when there was no ambiguity on the part of the Catholic hierarchy as to the position of young men like Patsy O'Hara, when I stood in this city and young men like Patsy O'Hara were sent for because the Long Tower church was under attack and so was St. Eugene's cathedral.

> And it is tragic, at this time in our history, that the Irish people, who for centuries have defended their church and their religion, should be, by and large, so sadly abandoned by it in their hour of greatest need.

> So we must go out, not in a spirit of dependency; we must go out, not in the spirit of demoralisation, but knowing—and taking heart from the courage of those who have shown us the way—that unity is our strength . . .

> Let us never forget, but let us leave here knowing that

as we are brothers and sisters in a common fight, so in the death of our prisoners has every mother taken each of the four of them as her own son, has every young man and woman taken each of the four of them as their own brother . . . Let us go forward in unity, in dignity, and in the knowledge that we will win.

We have paid the price, we will not be diverted. And no matter how great the price may become, it can never be more than the families of our four prisoners have been asked to pay. And we will continue, and see that the price was not paid in vain . . .

TONY REALIZED that he'd soon have to go. There would be a short stop back at the house. Raymond McCreesh's brother Malachy clasped Tony's hand, bringing him comfort. He saw girls bursting into tears. *Why can I not cry* ? he asked himself. *Is there something wrong with me?* Why didn't he feel sorrow or pride? It was only later that Tony realized that he was in the throes of a deep depression that would last several months.

Abruptly, Tony found himself back at the house in Ardfoyle. He barely had time for a quick meal. Before leaving he went over and hugged and kissed his mother. "I'll see you next week," he said. He would have a visit with her then.

His mother was heartbroken. His father too, and Seán and his sister Liz. They were all heartsick, and he could feel it. But he could also feel that they were proud.

Tony was whisked into the car. They drove down the hill, crossed the Foyle at Craigavon Bridge, climbed through the Waterside and turned right onto the Belfast road.

When they came to Long Kesh Tony said goodbye to his friends. He went in through the gates, wanting only to get locked into his cell, so that he could get into bed and pull the blankets up over his head.

Séamus Costello, founder of the IRSP and the INLA, speaking at an Official Sinn Féin Ard Fheis in the early 1970s
(Photos courtesy of the O'Hara family)

Seán Séamus and Patsy O'Hara in late 1974 when both were at a funeral in Derry on 24-hour parole from internment in Long Kesh. Seán was 22, Patsy 17

Patsy O'Hara (centre, in black) leading INLA march in Derry, Easter 1978, a year before the organization was banned. Uniformed figure at rear right may be Micky Devine

Liz and Peggy O'Hara

Jim, Peggy and Seán Séamus O'Hara with (second from left) Ramsey Clark, former US Attorney General

"Why can't the British show some Christian charity to some one carrying a cross?"

This is the cartoon by Cummings that appeared in the *Sunday Express* (London) on 31 May 1981: see page 285

Roy Mason, Secretary of State for Northern Ireland from September 1976 to May 1979, pictured with his prisons minister Don Concannon. *(Photo by Pacemaker)*

Tomás Cardinal Ó Fiaich *(Irish Press photo)*

Humphrey Atkins, Margaret Thatcher's Secretary of State for Northern Ireland during the two hunger strikes. In September 1981 he was replaced by James Prior *(Photo: Derek Speirs/Report)*

Joe McDonnell at his first Communion, in 1959, at eight years of age *(Photos at top courtesy of the McDonnell family)*

Joe McDonnell as a young man

At the graveside in Belfast the McDonnell family watches as Joe is buried. From left to right in background: Joe's sister Maura, brother Frankie, Goretti's niece; brother Paul, Margaret (Paul's wife), brother Robert. In the foreground are Goretti McDonnell, Bernadette (it was her birthday) and Joseph Og *(Photo: Derek Speirs/Report)*

Jean O'Brien, at left looking away, in the photo taken on 8 July—the day Joe McDonnell died: see page 391 *(Photo courtesy of The Irish Times)*

Martin Hurson in England, 1973
(Photos courtesy of the Hurson family)

Brendan and Sheila Hurson at time of their daughter Mairead's christening in March 1984

Francie and Sally Hughes Hurson and their family

Francie Hurson—photo taken a few weeks before he died of a brain hemorrhage at age 35, in December 1984, while working in the garage behind the Hursons' home near Carrickmore.

Views of Kevin Lynch as a boy and young man
(Photos courtesy of the Lynch family)

INLA firing party releasing volley of shots over Kevin Lynch's coffin at entrance to Dungiven churchyard as members of Kevin's family stand at attention: at left, above the coffin: Hall, Bridie; above the first star: Paddy Lynch.
(Photo by Pacemaker)

Chapter 7

THE CARDINAL ARCHBISHOP

"The Pope is well. I think many attempts are daily made to get him to take up the English views against Ireland but he is always the same. I trust that he will live many years to defeat English intrigue."

Paul (later Cardinal) Cullen to Archbishop John MacHale, March 1844

"The attacks on the Irish clergy still continue. A gentleman told me a few days ago that the accusations against our clergy occupy all the conversations of the English here in Rome."

Cullen to MacHale, January 1848

"I believe it to be the bounden duty of every ecclesiastic in this country to stand by and sustain her people in all their legitimate efforts for the amelioration of their social condition, as well as the recovery of their national rights."

Archbishop Thomas Croke of Cashel, 1884

"I am getting a dreadful mauling in the English papers."

Croke to Archbishop William Walsh, February 1887

"If the enemies of Ireland imagine that by slander or calumny they can prevent the clergy, priests and bishops, from standing up as one man, shoulder to shoulder with their brave people in demanding justice on lines at once moderate and peaceful, they are entirely mistaken."

Bishop (later Cardinal) Patrick O'Donnell in Letterkenny, January 1900

> "I think there should be a strong protest against the
> insolent attempt of the Council of the English
> Catholic Union to use the Pope as an instrument for
> the coercion of the Irish bishops."
>
> Cardinal Michael Logue to Archbishop Walsh,
> May 1918

THE CARTOON in the newspaper lying on the table displayed in the foreground an overstuffed bishop in full regalia, with buttoned cassock and trimmed cape, a chain reaching around his martinet's shoulders and lying askew across his failed chest, with a Roman collar around his neck and a biretta perched on his head. In the background were four madly marching figures, the first three, in inquisitorial hood-masks, goose-stepping ahead of the fourth, smug in cassock and mask, a lit bomb sitting atop his biretta. Behind him a gun dangled from a cord tied beneath the back of his clerical collar. The lead figure held aloft a processional crucifix formed by two rifles lashed together. The second raised joined hands above a placard reading "Let Us Prey!" The third gripped another placard demanding "A Square Deal for the I.R.A.!"

The Cardinal looked again at the distorted face of the bishop, unmistakably a caricature of himself. Lest the identification be missed, the sash around the cartoon bishop's waist was labelled "Cardinal O'Fiaich, Primate of Ireland." And lest the point be missed, the cartoon cardinal's index finger was shown jabbing in the direction of the crossed rifles, while its inky mouth was twisted open to ask "Why can't the British show some Christian charity to someone carrying a cross?"

All day long the Cardinal's phone had been ringing. Was he aware of the smear campaign against him in the English press?

It was 31 May 1981, and this cartoon was the crudest but not the most bitter deliverance of the day's newspapers. The most bitter had to be the *Sunday Telegraph* piece by Alberic Stacpoole, a Benedictine priest and ex-British Army paratrooper, attacking the Cardinal for daring to question the view that the

Irish hunger strikers were suicides, and for permitting burial ceremonies in which

> Starvation-suicide murderers are accorded paramilitary "show" funerals, with the tricolour draped on the coffin that is shouldered by armed, "uniformed," masked, evanescent thugs, who shoot salute volleys with killer weapons taken from hides—all this in the United Kingdom . . . Priests wash their hands of it; while the Cardinal Primate publicly (not privately and wisely) exhorts the Prime Minister—not once but five times since Sands died; and under threat of "the wrath of the whole nationalist population"—to capitulate, to pay Danegeld.

Cardinal Ó Fiaich had never thought of the deaths as suicide. There had been a great deal of controversy, some of it in church journals, surrounding the hunger strike deaths that occurred during the 1918-21 Irish War of Independence. Catholic theologians had expressed views one way and the other; the issue was a matter of dispute, but had never been settled, particularly not against hunger strikers. A hunger strike like this was, as far as Cardinal Ó Fiaich was concerned, an act with two effects: as long as the good effect (calling attention to the injustice) does not proceed as a result of the bad effect (death) then the act (the hunger strike) is good. During the 1918-21 debate Fr. Paddy Cleary, a famous Irish missionary to China and later a bishop there, had defended very strenuously the right of a man to go on a hunger strike to the death; he saw no suicide in this. And there was the gospel: was it suicide to lay down your life for your friends, as these men clearly thought they were doing? Yet here was this British priest insisting that what they were doing was committing suicide.

Nastier still than Stacpoole's screed was the Auberon Waugh article the day before in the British Tory magazine *The Spectator*, in which Waugh accused the Cardinal and Father Brian McCreesh of conniving in the hunger-strike death of Father McCreesh's brother Raymond: "The wretched Cardinal Fee," Waugh called him.

Yes, the Cardinal had seen the papers. In the same issue of the *Sunday Express* that carried the cartoon, the editor characterized him as "Chaplain in Chief of the IRA." In the *Sunday Telegraph* he was accused of failing to meet Margaret Thatcher last Thursday in Belfast; the implication being that she wanted to give him a lecture on the attitude the Irish Catholic Church should take to paramilitary funerals.

TOMÁS CARDINAL Ó FIAICH was Archbishop of Armagh and, as the one hundred twelfth successor to St. Patrick in the see of Armagh, Primate of All Ireland. He *had* avoided meeting Margaret Thatcher the other day in Belfast, but on grounds very different from those suggested by the *Sunday Telegraph*.

Three things were on his mind at the moment: an invitation to come see Thatcher in London; astonishment at the intensity of the media campaign against him—which some of his friends thought must have been orchestrated by Thatcher's own government in London; and the problem that had been preoccupying him for fourteen months and more: how to settle the desperate situation in the prison at Long Kesh.

The prison situation had brought on the hunger strike, in which four men had already died and around which three dozen other deaths had clustered. There was also, as a direct result, a new antipathy between the Catholic and Protestant communities in Northern Ireland.

The Cardinal had appealed to both the hunger strikers and the British government to give way, but so far there was no break at all in the will of either side. The Cardinal was used to criticism, but he felt it was grossly unjust of the British newspapers, the super-British Stacpoole, the venomous Waugh and those other English Catholics to condemn him. Did any of them have any idea how much he'd done to avert what was happening now? He couldn't get terribly upset about the English gutter press, as it was called, although he was disgusted by the Cummings cartoon in the *Sunday Express*. But why this campaign against him? *

The other problem the Cardinal had to deal with this Sunday

*See Note, at end of this chapter.

287

afternoon was Margaret Thatcher's letter. There was a curious story behind the invitation.

On Wednesday 27 May, the Cardinal had received a call from the Northern Ireland Office, from a secretary in the office of Humphrey Atkins, the Northern Ireland Secretary of State. The message was that Atkins wanted to meet all the church leaders next afternoon in Belfast. The Cardinal begged off, saying he'd already arranged several appointments in Dublin that day—which was, after all, Ascension Thursday, a holy day of obligation on the Catholic Church calendar. Soon there was another call from Atkins' Northern Ireland Office. The Cardinal's secretary, Father Jim Clyne, explained that tomorrow was Ascension Thursday, and that the Cardinal had commitments in Dublin. There were several further phone calls, including one from the Chief Constable of the RUC, Jack Hermon, saying that the Atkins meeting was very important and asking that the Cardinal come. That was a strange one, the Cardinal thought: why was the Chief Constable of the RUC so interested? Late that afternoon another Atkins assistant phoned the Cardinal's secretary. Father Clyne repeated that the Cardinal had several important commitments, some of them of long standing, and that these included appointments in Dublin. Father Clyne was asked whether it would help if Humphrey Atkins phoned and asked the Cardinal personally, and Clyne said he didn't know. He knew that the Cardinal would be going out at 9:30 that night, and so any call would have to be before that hour. At 9:25 Humphrey Atkins rang the Cardinal, asking him to come.

"You're probably aware," he said to Atkins, "that I'm due in Dublin tomorrow for two appointments. I could probably change one of them. But the other involves someone from abroad who is leaving Ireland tomorrow night. I don't think that can be changed."

At that stage, with his time tight, the Cardinal asked Atkins some straight questions.

"Why is it that this meeting must be held tomorrow?" Was there going to be anyone at all at the meeting besides Atkins and the other church leaders?

"Oh, no, no, no," Atkins said. The Cardinal could sense that he was flustered. So the Cardinal repeated what he'd said before, and that seemed to be the end of it.

But he'd been wondering, as those phone calls piled up earlier in the day, and he'd rung a Presbyterian church leader to find out why this meeting, called so suddenly, was now so urgent. Was, say, Thatcher going to be there? The man didn't know, but said that the same question had occurred to him. The following morning John Blelloch rang from the NIO.

"We've decided to take you into our confidence," he said, "and to let you know that the PM is coming to Belfast today. And that's why we were so anxious to have the meeting."

"John," the Cardinal said, "you know what my problems are. You know about my appointments in Dublin. Well, I think I have to honour them, but I'll ring back in half an hour and give you a definite answer."

Half an hour later the Cardinal was ready, but more determined than ever. "Jim," he said to his secretary, "you can ring the NIO now. Tell them I had to go to Dublin."

The Cardinal hadn't liked the NIO's subterfuge—which had been used, he learned later, on the two other principal Northern Catholic bishops as well. It was ridiculous of Atkins' people not to have spelled out yesterday why they were so anxious to have him attend the meeting. Certainly bishops, and the Cardinal, could be trusted to keep such a confidence. Well, he wasn't going to their meeting. And neither, as it happened, were the other two Catholic bishops.

The Cardinal had no wish, anyway, to see Mrs. Thatcher at that particular juncture. Hunger strikers had begun to die. In a month or so others would be in danger. The Cardinal felt that she would love to manipulate him into a situation—and the Belfast meeting was just such a situation—where she could publicize a meeting with, among others, the Irish Catholic Cardinal, and perhaps get a photograph taken of herself shaking hands with the Cardinal: a photograph that would be plastered all over the papers next day, and be published abroad: a picture saying—here is Mrs. Thatcher, at the end of a month in which four Irish boys died on hunger strike, having a cosy chat with the Irish Cardinal. He was going to be absolutely sure that that didn't happen. So he couldn't imagine that he would have gone to the Belfast meeting anyway, even if they'd told him straight out and hadn't played games. Had it not been for her inflexibility the four boys would not have died, nor others been killed as a result.

The Cardinal went off that Ascension Thursday to meet his Dublin appointments. He heard on the radio something about her having made a hardline speech at Stormont that evening.

When he returned home that night, he found a letter from Margaret Thatcher waiting for him. It was on headed British government notepaper, with the British emblem, lion gardant and unicorn rampant, with its legend *Dieu et mon droit*: "God and my entitlement." She'd dictated it at the Northern Ireland Office at Stormont Castle before leaving to go back to London.

She'd come to Northern Ireland, she wrote, and had spoken to people, including Catholic clergymen, who were trying to keep normal life going, because she shared the Cardinal's concern to bring peace and reconciliation to everyone in the community. She was sorry, she said, that the Cardinal's commitments had kept him from coming to see her at such short notice, but she would welcome the chance of a talk with the Cardinal in London if he would find that helpful.

He thought it a bit rich: Mrs. Thatcher's professed interest in keeping normal life going, and her classifying herself as a bringer of peace and reconciliation. He thought of the year and more he'd spent trying to get her government to budge on issues that could have easily resolved the prison dispute. She'd mentioned Catholic clergy who'd been at the meeting. He wondered who. He knew that Bishops Edward Daly and William Philbin had not gone.

The Cardinal had met Margaret Thatcher, briefly, months earlier. He'd sent several telegrams to her, the last of them nearly three weeks ago: the day after Francis Hughes died, when Raymond McCreesh and Patsy O'Hara were beginning their rapid final decline. "In God's name," he'd pleaded, "don't allow another death." Then two more men had died, ten days ago. The second last, just before O'Hara, had been McCreesh, a young man with an innocent face like his priest-brother, fairer but with the same smile. Raymond was religious, too—and had a fine sense of humour: a wonderful lad, whom the Cardinal had met and found thoughtful and considerate.

In the statement he issued that day, 22 May, while on his annual retreat, he'd said:

> In near desperation I appeal to both sides for the fifth time for a compromise which would bring the hunger strike to an end. If the hunger strikers continue with their "all or nothing" policy it will shortly lead to the death of a fourth young man. If the Government continues its rigid stance on prison dress and work it will ultimately be faced with the wrath of the whole nationalist population. Already Government policy has provided the IRA with its greatest influx of recruits since Bloody Sunday and has left some sections of our youth so alienated that they no longer pay much attention to the denunciations of violence . . .

There was no response to this from Margaret Thatcher, except the triumphant hardline response given in her speech and interviews at Stormont Castle on Ascension Thursday, the day he'd declined to meet her. She'd said things that could not be credited as truth, in which the reality lay hidden under a wash of subterfuge: "No one in any responsible position in any religion has urged me to give political status or anything by stages which would amount to special category status," she'd said, using the terminology of political and special category status to cover her refusal to relax her inflexibly rigid stance in any way. To compromise on the prisoners' demands was exactly what the Cardinal had repeatedly asked her to do! And she'd specifically denied the Cardinal's charge, for which there was massive evidence, that her policy was hardening Catholic attitudes in the North.

He'd asked her, in the 13 May telegram, to move immediately "by making prison dress and work optional for all prisoners in Northern Ireland." Instead at Stormont she'd declaimed against the hunger strikers:

> Faced with the failure of their discredited cause, the men of violence have chosen in recent months to play what may

well be their last card. They have turned their violence against themselves through the prison hunger strike to death. They seek to work on the most basic of human emotions—pity—as a means of creating tension and stoking the fires of bitterness and hatred . . .

What point would there be in meeting her, here or in London? She was so determined not to give way, to play her Iron Maiden role to whatever bitter end. She'd try to twist and bulldoze everything to suit her preconceptions. If he could bring himself to hope that a conversation with her could yield any result, he'd be over to London on the next plane. But a meeting now, especially a publicized meeting, would only be represented by her, her propaganda apparatus and the British media, as some sort of cave-in to her hardline view. She'd make any criticism of the IRA, any condemnation of violence, look like support for her stonewalling.

They were great experts, the British, at stonewalling, and at twisting events to suit themselves. They'd managed, for example, to misrepresent the mission of Father John Magee, the Pope's envoy, as a mission to one side of the argument only. Father Magee, the Cardinal knew, had come hoping to mediate, hoping to get something substantial from the British government, which he could take to Bobby Sands and the others in the prison, so that he could get movement from the prisoners in return. The British government* had blocked this, and had seen to it that the NIO gave Father Magee nothing. The British had aborted his mission, and then they and their media tried to pretend he hadn't sought any movement from their government at all.

Then Stacpoole, rowing in, had gone beyond even that and described Magee's gift of a papal gold crucifix to BobbySands (the Pope's gift) as "collusion."

Tomás Ó Fiaich didn't want to have a conversation with Thatcher, and then have it misrepresented as Magee's mission had been misrepresented. One thing he was certain of. Now, after

*Aided and abetted by that bizarre Swiss-German, Archbishop Bruno Heim, the papal delegate to Britain, a man more vociferously and jingoistically British than most of the British establishment. (TC)

that arrogant performance of hers at Stormont, would be no time for him to see her.

He thought about it that Sunday night, and again on Monday. He'd be in London on 1 July. Well, he thought, he'd take the ball on the hop, and try. On Tuesday he drafted a letter, picking up her advertised themes of peace and reconciliation. She'd meet him if he thought it would be helpful, she'd said. Well, he'd meet her, he'd say, if she thought it would be helpful. Yet he wondered whether it would be a good idea to meet her on the occasion of the centenary of a predecessor of his, who had been hung, drawn and quartered at Tyburn by a predecessor of hers. He put it somewhat differently, of course:

> I will be in London on 30th June-1st July but I should point out that the reason for my visit is an invitation from the Parish Priest of Balham to commemorate with his parishioners the third centenary of the execution of a former Archbishop of Armagh, St. Oliver Plunkett. The execution took place on 1st July 1681. You might not consider this the most auspicious occasion for a meeting.
>
> In addition, having read your speech at Stormont last week and being aware that two events will be pending— the death of more hunger strikers unless something happens to persuade them to end their strike, and the marches leading up to the "Twelfth of July" celebrations—I wonder at the wisdom of having a meeting at that time which will undoubtedly become public. We both have a common concern to keep normal life going and to work unceasingly for peace and reconciliation.

But if she thought "that a meeting at that time would be helpful," he'd be free to meet her, he said, the day before or the evening of the Oliver Plunkett commemoration.

Perhaps the thought of those ill omens was persuasive, or perhaps the date was too distant. In any case there was no word from her for a long time. Then suddenly in late June the phones began to ring away, and the appointment was agreed. He asked that the meeting be kept private until after it was over. He didn't want it overshadowing the centenary of St. Oliver Plunkett, who had been canonized only six years earlier. A number of fine people had invested a lot of faith and energy in the centenary preparations, and he didn't want this to become a sideshow to a press circus over his meeting with Thatcher.

Finally it was arranged that the meeting would take place after the centenary celebrations, on the night of 1 July. The Cardinal's friend and auxiliary bishop Dr. James Lennon, would accompany him and take notes. Mrs. Thatcher would bring Humphrey Atkins.

Although the meeting was certain to focus on the prisoners in Long Kesh, the Cardinal felt doubtful about it achieving anything. For years he'd been appealing to the British government to change their policy on this issue. And for years they'd refused to budge.

IT WAS A STRANGE TRAIL that had led the Cardinal from South Armagh, where he was born on 3 November 1923, to the impasse in which he now found himself. His grandfather had been John Fee, born in a famine year, 1848, a propertyless labourer from County Louth; and his father, Patrick Fee, a schoolteacher. They were strongly nationalist but got on very well with their Catholic and Protestant neighbours, particularly a Presbyterian family named Nelson. The Cardinal remembered no tradition of militant or violent nationalism from his years as a boy growing up in those hills, nor could he recall any feeling of religious bigotry.

Finishing Cregganduff Elementary school, he went on scholarship to secondary school at St. Patrick's college in Armagh. There, during his last year, he applied for the Catholic seminary at St. Patrick's college, Maynooth. Though he began there in 1940—he took a BA degree in Celtic Studies with first class honours in 1943—it was not till 1944, when he suffered an attack of pleurisy aggravated by pneumonia, that he finally made up his mind to proceed to holy orders. He remembered the infirmary, and the French Sisters of Charity in their big butterfly hats tiptoeing around what everyone seemed to think was his deathbed. Meanwhile he'd lost a year at Maynooth, so he continued his studies at St. Peter's college in Wexford.

He was ordained there in June 1948, and worked that summer at Clonfeacle parish, which served County Armagh and

County Tyrone Catholics in the Moy, Benburb and Blackwatertown area.

He completed a program in early and medieval Irish history at University College Dublin, taking an MA degree with first class honours. He was sent to Louvain in Belgium for further history studies, and in 1952 received a licentiate with highest honours from the Catholic university there. During the years he was based at Louvain he began to travel, and visited many of the places where Irish monks had gone in the centuries of the great Irish missionary effort in Europe.

After a pastoral year in Clonfeacle parish, he returned to Maynooth as a lecturer in modern history. He became professor there in 1959 and while teaching became involved in administration. In 1974 he became President of St. Patrick's college—where he had begun his studies for the priesthood thirty-four years earlier. During his years at Maynooth he wrote eight books (four of them in Irish) on Irish language, historical and biographical themes; published several hundred articles and reviews in historical and literary periodicals; and edited *Seanchas Ard Mhacha,* the Armagh diocesan historical journal which he had helped found in 1953.

WHEN CARDINAL CONWAY DIED in April 1977, the see of Armagh had become vacant. One day in August, Monsignor Ó Fiaich (as he then was) was called to Dublin to see Archbishop Gaetano Alibrandi, the Papal Nuncio to Ireland. In the shift that was to take place, there was some likelihood that he might be made bishop; he'd been on various lists for a dozen years but had been regularly passed over, partly because of his Maynooth commitments, and partly because of controversy surrounding the Irish language movement in which he'd played a public role. He met with Dr. Alibrandi, and the Nuncio chatted with him for a few minutes. Then, referring to Pope Paul VI, Dr. Alibrandi said, "The Holy Father has appointed you Archbishop of Armagh."

The announcement nearly knocked him over. He'd known that the priests of the diocese of Armagh itself were promoting him for the post. Sometime, eventually, he might be considered for Armagh . . . But he wasn't even a bishop yet! And here was Dr. Alibrandi telling him he had succeeded to the see of Patrick, and would be Primate of All Ireland.

So he left Maynooth and in October 1977 was consecrated Archbishop of Armagh. It was a cross-border diocese, reaching up to South Derry and down to the County Dublin border. It ran southeast to the seacoast towns of County Louth, south to County Meath, and west to the middle of County Tyrone. For all the honour associated with it, it was only a middle-range Irish diocese in numbers of people: 167,000 Catholics (58 parishes, 200 schools) among a population of some 261,000. The largest archdiocese, Dublin, had nearly six times as many Catholics in it.

Because of Armagh's size, however, he felt freer to emphasize the pastoral side of his duties. In the archdiocese into which he had been born, among the 171 priests who had so enthusiastically supported him for this office, he was confident of being able to help break down divisions between Catholics and Protestants. Though he had become known as a scholar in Irish language, literature, history and culture, he could be an active ecumenist here, investing his work with the force of his feeling about the oneness of Christians in Christ.

The motto he set for his episcopate, taken from a Latin translation of Psalm 133, was *Fratres in Unum*: Brothers in Unity. "Brotherly love, peace, harmony, reconciliation, mutual forgiveness," he'd said at his ordination as bishop, "an end to past dissensions and a new beginning in the practice of justice and charity towards all: these will be the objectives of all my work in Armagh, whether it lasts for a year or a day."

Immediately after the announcement of his appointment there was a press conference, at which the political dilemma he faced was posed in a reporter's question about his position on the Irish national issue. His answer was that he looked forward to the day when Ireland would be a united country, though it might not happen in his lifetime. He emphasized, however, that this was a personal view, and that he had no intention of forcing his nationalism on anyone. It would be unthinkable, he said, for him to use his position as Archbishop of Armagh to promote any political creed. But because he was from a townland near Crossmaglen, which was no longer the non-militant and non-violent place of his boyhood, it was assumed that he would be more or less militantly nationalist *as bishop*, and his answer was misconstrued to convey this assumption.

The Cardinal had thought a lot about the problem. He was Irish of the Irish, and had always seen himself that way. But he recognized that some of his people did not feel as he did, and he had to be pastor for them as well.

He'd been reflecting on the dilemma for years. The Church as an organization had no position at all towards Ireland as a nation. Its attitude was indifferent, except in so far as one set of political circumstances might be considered more favourable to its mission than another. And a situation where its people were comfortable in their freedom was not necessarily better for the Church than a situation where they were forced to live under a hostile regime. The Italian church, for example, lacked the vitality of the Polish church. Some felt that the Catholics of Dublin, who lived under Irish rule, were more prone to materialism than the poorer Catholics of Belfast, who lived under British rule. Anyway, the Church as such was neutral in political matters, even though Irish Catholics would in general be attached to the idea of unification; most Catholic Irish, though not all of them, wanted the British out of the six counties.

So while the Church had a neutral view, individual Irish churchmen might have strong nationalist views, and certainly he did. The troubles would be most satisfactorily and lastingly resolved, he felt, by some form of all-Ireland unity. A churchman might want this, and want it deeply. But the Church itself was there for another purpose—for the sanctification of its members, and the salvation of all mankind.

Here lay the heart of the dilemma for a bishop who was a nationalist, as for most Northern Catholics. The unfinished business of nationalism, so to call it, involved two things, and there was great difficulty in combining them: the first was ending the British regime in Ireland—an essentially destructive enterprise; the second was the constructive building up of the

1798 ideal—the Protestant Wolfe Tone's ideal—of fellowship between Catholic, Protestant and Dissenter. At bottom, the problem was that the more decisively a man or woman acted to rid Ireland of the British presence, the nearer he or she would come to the clear advocacy of forceful measures, including hard bargaining and bold constitutional demands; and the more dedicated one became to that side of the effort, the more danger there was of alienating others, the Protestants and the Dissenters, and weakening the ties with them.

These ties could be built up in various ways. There was a strong common heritage, nowhere more than in Armagh. From a religious point of view everything that happened before the sixteenth century Reformation could be considered a common heritage. The Protestants took pride in the early Irish Church and—most of them—took pride in St. Patrick as well, and in the Irish missionary effort in Europe. Protestants in Bangor in northeast County Down were just as proud of the Abbey of Bangor as Catholics were. Music was also a useful bridge. Protestants on the whole were fond of Irish traditional music, with its close affinity to Scottish traditional; and they loved their pipe bands as Catholics did theirs. Often the pipers' tunes were the same, and sometimes even the words. There were whole areas of cultural inheritance common to both, and the land of Ireland was shared too, the green hills and fertile valleys, and the Northern speech patterns with their inflections and idiomatic low-keyed wit, warm and caustic, itself a product of the meeting of cultures. There was a great deal to build on in the direction of fellowship.

The other side of the problem was that this building and rein-forcing of ties led inevitably to the question of what degree of recognition could be given to the *de facto* state. Being non-political about this meant being political in the other direction. He'd come up against some practical questions here, as soon as he became Archbishop. There was the question of recognition of the Union Jack, the British anthem, the British Army, the RUC. He found he had to mix his loyalty to the Irish nation and Irish heritage with a selective pragmatism. For an Irish bishop official functions were the most persistent problem. For example, he'd had to decide (in late '80 or early '81) whether to attend a dinner in Belfast at which Margaret Thatcher was to speak. He'd received some high-level political advice about her speech, suggesting that there would be nothing objectionable in it, and so went to the dinner. His informant turned out to be wrong. It was a dreadful speech, and he wished he hadn't gone.

It had been his rule as Archbishop of Armagh—and it had worked well enough for three and a half years—not to attend British government receptions of any kind. There was (he smiled to think of it) an annual invitation to a garden party at Buckingham palace: he wouldn't dream of going to that. And he never went to any of the receptions held by the Northern Ireland Secretary of State. When he met the Secretary of State he went alone or with other church leaders to discuss matters of common concern.

But he did attend some social functions held on neutral terrain. There was an annual celebration at the French Consulate on Bastille Day, 14 July—he was happy to meet unionists under the aegis of the French celebration of the Fall of the Bastille! He went because of the friendliness of the French consul the first year he was Archbishop; and the fellow used to call in at Armagh a couple of times a year to sound him out on various issues. He liked the American consul too. And ever since David Cook had become Mayor of Belfast he'd gone regularly to the Lord Mayor's reception. He welcomed occasions where he could meet Protestants individually or in groups—especially in mixed Protestant/Catholic get-togethers at his residence, Ara Coeli, where there was often marvellous camaraderie. He'd kept trying to meet Ian Paisley but Dr. Paisley had always managed to avoid him. It would be a long while, he supposed, before he and Paisley would be *fratres in unum*.

As far as anthems and toasts and that sort of thing were concerned, he remembered Douglas Hyde who, as founder of the Gaelic League, was invited to various official functions. Whenever the toast to the King came he'd always manage to let a pencil or something fall under the table at the appropriate moment, and by the time he'd bent down to collect the pencil the toast was finished, the moment of peril passed. Others had their own ways of dealing with this sort of situation. He recalled something he'd heard about working-class loyalists who had their reservations about the British crown. When the British anthem came, they'd sing their own song—with words like "God save the UDA . . ."

In any case, one of the advantages of being Archbishop in a remote city like Armagh was that very little of his time was taken up with occasions. As soon as he took office he began mapping out his pastoral itinerary. One of the first things he did was to visit the institutions in Armagh City itself: the hospitals, the special care units, the geriatric homes—and Armagh jail. Before Christmas that year he went up to Magilligan prison. At Christmas he returned to Armagh jail, with the chaplain, Father Raymond Murray, to attend a Christmas party there. The atmosphere was fairly good at the time: the relationship between the authorities and the women prisoners had not yet gone sour. The presence of the women, the women social workers and even some of the women warders, softened the place a good bit.

Long Kesh was another story. He'd heard, before he first went to Long Kesh in January 1978, that the atmosphere was terrible: that relationships between the warders and the prisoners were poisonous. It was the time of the blanket protest, a few weeks before the dirt protest began. He said Mass in two of the compounds and one of the H-Blocks there that day, then went around and visited some of the prisoners. When he came out he made no public statement, because he still thought at that stage that he might be more effective working quietly behind the scenes. That was before his experience of trying to help Henry Heaney, the old prisoner from Lurgan.

Shortly after he became Archbishop he was told of Heaney's plight. The man was a quarter of a century older than the next oldest prisoner. Heaney had been arrested because of arms found on his property; it was pretty clear, apparently, that someone else in the family was responsible. Henry Heaney's sons were arrested with him; Heaney could have avoided conviction, but he refused to recognize the court. He was convicted, sentenced and locked up in Long Kesh. When the Archbishop went to the prison, he'd sought Heaney out and found a sad, lonely man of 62. At home the family situation was bad; in prison Heaney couldn't take part in the sports, and had no enthusiasm for other activities in which the younger men involved themselves. He was always by himself.

When the Archbishop left the prison after his January visit he immediately began to make representations about Heaney's case to Roy Mason, the Northern Ireland Secretary at the time. More than that, he'd got the support of Bishop Francis Brooks of the diocese of Dromore (Lurgan was in Bishop Brooks' jurisdiction) for his appeal that the old man be released. To no avail: Mason refused to release Henry Heaney.

Then in May poor Heaney, ill with pneumonia, was transferred to Musgrave Park hospital, and died.

The Archbishop remembered Roy Mason as a dark, unyielding little man who was very self-righteous about the tough line he was taking on security and prison policy. In mid-July the Archbishop met with Mason and pointed out that the prison situation was getting steadily worse. By then the blanket prisoners were three and a half months into their dirt protest, the culmination of a protracted battle with the warders. Not only was the situation worsening, he reminded Mason, but there were more and more men now on the blanket and dirt protest. All Mason would say was that it was their own fault; they'd started it. He said to Mason that it didn't matter who or what had started it; that if it went on it was going to lead to an awful lot of trouble. There would be a hunger strike, or perhaps an epidemic. Somebody would be found dead in his cell; there'd be an uproar, and the news would get out that men had been kept, day in and day out, for months and years, locked in cells with no outdoor air, sunlight, or exercise; with no clothes, no furnishings, no comfort except blanket and mattress: no bed, no table, no chair, nothing to read, nothing to write with, nothing to do. It was going to be the British government and Mason's regime that would be blamed.

But Mason would admit no responsibility.

Since he'd got nothing from Mason on Henry Heaney, and no change at all out of that July meeting, Tomás Ó Fiaich decided that after his next visit to Long Kesh, later that month, he'd make a strong statement. He was encouraged by what Bishop Edward Daly of Derry had said in a June interview about conditions of "indescribable filth" in the prison; Bishop Daly had been particularly shocked by seeing one prisoner with unkempt hair who sat naked all day in a foul-smelling cell, its walls covered with faeces, and who'd built a little wall of excreta across the floor to catch a pool of urine. And Dr. Donnell Deeny, a member of the board of prison visitors, had made a statement on 9 July saying that the prison rules were unreasonable, that the prisoners in the protest blocks were ill-treated, and that the conditions in Long Kesh were desperate.

ON SUNDAY 29 JULY 1978 the prison gates swung open to admit the Archbishop for his second visit.

He'd found it necessary to test the ground before going in, because in early July a postman he'd known from Crossmaglen had been murdered by the IRA as an informer, and the Archbishop had gone to the funeral to make an outspoken and angry statement condemning the killing, a statement he knew would be resented in Republican circles:

> Who will be next? Will there be a next? Already threats have been issued to other people in the area. This is an intolerable and frightening situation . . . It poisons the whole atmosphere, destroys normal friendships and breeds fear and terror in a people . . .
>
> Let no one try to suggest that this crime has anything to do with patriotism. No cause is advanced by murder and no Irish cause can receive anything but dishonour from the slaughter of a brother Irishman, Protestant or Catholic. If those responsible . . . will not listen to me then let them listen to the words of the leaders whose cause they sometimes claim to serve but . . . have foully dishonoured: "We place the cause of the Irish Republic under the protection of the most high God . . . and we pray that no one who serves that cause will dishonour it by cowardice, inhumanity or rapine."

So the Archbishop felt that before going into Long Kesh he should ask someone to test the atmosphere in the prison and find out whether the men might reject him for what he said at Crossmaglen, might boycott him, making his visit useless. But he learned that, despite his strong statement at Crossmaglen, the men in the prison wanted his visit. So in he went.

He said Mass that Sunday both in the compounds and in the H-Blocks. He saw as many prisoners in the protesting blocks as he could. On his visit six months earlier there'd been the blanket protest. Now the dirt protest had been on for nearly four months. Though he'd been aware of it, and had talked to Mason about it, the impact on his senses then and there gave him a terrible jolt, triggering his worst memories of human degradation, memories from a trip he'd made years ago, accompanying his predecessor Cardinal Conway to India. But what he'd seen in Calcutta was *not as bad* as this. In the first cell he entered, he was at first unable to speak because of the stench and filth around him. He came home sickened and exhausted that Sunday night. And on Monday he began working on a statement he hoped would bring the conditions in the prison, which Mason had blithely refused responsibility for, to the attention of people in Ireland, in Britain, in Europe, the United States and the world. He managed to provoke the British government and British media. They responded with anger and contempt. But the message had the impact he wanted. For the first time since the blanket protest began, conditions in Long Kesh made news throughout the world.

> There are nearly three thousand prisoners in Northern Ireland today. This must be a cause of grave anxiety to any spiritual leader. Nearly two hundred from the Archdiocese of Armagh are among a total of almost eighteen hundred prisoners in the Maze Prison at Long Kesh. This is the equivalent of all the young men of similar age groups in a typical parish of this diocese.

> Last Sunday I met as many as possible of these Armagh prisoners, as the bishop appointed to minister to themselves and their families, conscious of Christ's exhortation about visiting those in prison. I am grateful for the facilities afforded me by the authorities.

> On this, my second visit as Archbishop to Long Kesh,

I was also aware of the grave concern of the Holy See at the situation which has arisen in the prison, and I wanted to be able to provide the Holy See with a factual account of the present position of all prisoners there, something which I shall do without delay.*

Having spent the whole of Sunday in the prison I was shocked by the inhuman conditions prevailing in H-Blocks 3, 4 and 5, where over three hundred prisoners are incarcerated. One would hardly allow an animal to remain in such conditions, let alone a human being. The nearest approach to it that I have seen was the spectacle of hundreds of homeless people living in sewer pipes in the slums of Calcutta. The stench and filth in some of the cells, with the remains of rotten food and human excreta scattered around the walls, was almost unbearable. In two of them I was unable to speak for fear of vomiting.

The prisoners' cells are without beds, chairs or tables. They sleep on mattresses on the floor and in some cases I noticed that these were quite wet. They have no covering except a towel or blanket, no books, newspapers or reading material except the Bible (even religious magazines have been banned since my last visit), no pens or writing material, no TV or radio, no hobbies or handicrafts, no exercise or recreation. They are locked in their cells for almost the whole of every day and some of them have been in this condition for more than a year and a half.

The fact that a man refuses to wear prison uniform or do prison work should not entail the loss of physical exercise, association with his fellow-prisoners or contact with the world outside. These are basic human needs for physical and mental health, not privileges to be granted

*By the following weekend he had his report on the Long Kesh situation prepared. On Sunday evening he was to meet the Papal Nuncio in Drogheda, to hand over the document for transmission to Rome. Before the Nuncio got back to his Nunciature in Dublin, the news came to Tomás Ó Fiaich in Drogheda that the Pope who had appointed him Archbishop, Paul VI, was dead.

or withheld as rewards or punishments. To deprive anyone of them over a long period—irrespective of what led to the deprivation in the first place—is surely a grave injustice and cannot be justified in any circumstances. The human dignity of every prisoner must be respected, regardless of his creed, colour or political viewpoint, and regardless of what crimes he has been charged with. I would make the same plea on behalf of loyalist prisoners, but since I was not permitted to speak to any of them, despite a request to do so, I cannot say for certain what their present condition is.

Several prisoners complained to me of beatings, of verbal abuse, of additional punishments (in cold cells without even a mattress) for making complaints, and of degrading searches carried out on the most intimate parts of their naked bodies. Of course I have no way of verifying these allegations, but they were numerous.

In the circumstances I was surprised that the morale of the prisoners was high. From talking to them it is evident that they intend to continue their protest indefinitely and it seems they would prefer to face death rather than submit to being classed as criminals. Anyone with the least knowledge of Irish history knows how deeply rooted this attitude is in our country's past. In isolation and perpetual boredom they maintain their sanity by studying Irish. It was an indication of the triumph of the human spirit over adverse material surroundings to notice Irish words, phrases and songs being shouted from cell to cell and then written on each cell wall with the remnants of toothpaste tubes.

The authorities refuse to admit that these prisoners are in a different category from the ordinary, yet everything about their trials and family background indicates that they are different. They were sentenced by special courts without juries. The vast majority were convicted on allegedly voluntary confessions obtained in circumstances which are now placed under grave suspicion by the recent report of Amnesty International. Many are very youthful and come from families which had never been in trouble with the law, though they lived in areas which suffered discrimination in housing and jobs. How can one explain the jump in the prison population of Northern Ireland from five hundred to three thousand unless a new type of prisoner has emerged?

The problem of these prisoners is one of the great obstacles to peace in our community. As long as it continues it will be a potent cause of resentment in the prisoners themselves, breeding frustration among their relatives and friends and leading to bitterness between the prisoners and the prison staff. It is only sowing the seeds of future conflict.

Pending the full resolution of the deadlock, I feel it is essential to urge that everything required by the normal man to maintain his physical and mental health and to live a life which is tolerably human should be restored to these prisoners without delay.

There was plenty of reaction, as the Archbishop had expected. One of the most perceptive comments, he felt, came from the Shankill-born Protestant journalist David McKittrick, Northern editor of *The Irish Times*, in his column the following Saturday, 5 August 1978:

In the eyes of Roy Mason and his men, the Archbishop's crime (or, if you will, political offence) was not that he objected to conditions in the H-Blocks, or even [that he said so]: the crime was to say it to the whole world through a big megaphone—telexing a lengthy statement to newspapers, calling a press conference, then making himself available for interviews with whoever wanted to talk to him.

The whole NIO idea is to keep quiet about this place. There's nothing they can do about the Belfast or Dublin media, but their target is to keep Northern Ireland out of the British and world papers and especially off the television screens. Hence Mason's objections to the most innocuous TV programme: it's not the content the NIO doesn't like, it's the fact that it's on the box at all.

It's a moot point whether Dr. Ó Fiaich's call for government flexibility will have greater or less chance of success for being made so publicly: he appears to have concluded that private approaches he made in the past have been ineffective . . .

The Archbishop received a huge correspondence after that—hundreds of letters—about half pro and half con. There was a great controversy in the press, which raged on through August and into September and then dropped off a bit, to be picked up again in early 1979. In his correspondence the more virulent letters came not from Northern Protestants, whom he knew would tend to say, as the anti-Catholic editor of the *Church of Ireland Gazette* had said, that his statement left them in "little doubt about where his loyalties lay." The nastier letters came from England, and the nastiest of all from prominent English Catholics, some of whom, when it came time to consider a new consistory for cardinals, would try to block his appointment.

But he had learned early on in his public life not to let criticism disturb him overmuch. He'd kept, in this statement at least, the promise made in the ritual of his ordination as bishop: "Are you resolved to show kindness and compassion in the name of the Lord to the poor and to strangers and to all who are in need?"

He'd promised to do that. And he'd been ordered, in the same ritual, to proclaim the message whether it be welcome or unwelcome.

He'd made and would make mistakes, but the August 1978 statement hadn't been one of them.

THROUGH TV AND RADIO INTERVIEWS during the months that followed, he kept peppering the hard little Northern Secretary, Roy Mason, with appeals on behalf of the prisoners—to no avail. Mason actually appeared to enjoy the role of scourge of the men in Long Kesh, just as outside the prison he seemed to rejoice in the smooth running of his lock-them-up-at-any-cost strategy against the paramilitaries, which involved beatings of suspects during interrogation, perjured testimony by police witnesses, suspension of *habeas corpus* and single judge non-jury trials.

Mason continued packing them into the prisons. And in those

307

prisons, in Long Kesh particularly, the situation kept worsening. The interrogations, the perjury, the dishonesty of the Diplock trials masquerading as "due process of law," and the sufferings of the men in the prison were doing tremendous damage. The community in Northern Ireland, particularly the Catholic community, knew what was going on; and Mason's incarcerations were sowing dragon's teeth for the Provos and the INLA, sowing new recruits among brothers and relatives and friends of the prisoners, and among young Catholics generally.

The IRA and Sinn Féin didn't seem to care very much. To them, it seemed, the prison protest was an embarrassment and a distraction. And so they weren't really organizing any protest. The Archbishop kept meeting parents and relatives of prisoners—once or twice with people from the Relatives' Action committees. But they knew that he could do nothing to move Mason.

In the interrogation centres, though, there were stirrings from some of the examining doctors who were beginning to complain of evidence of severe police beatings of suspects. In the jails, while there had been no epidemic, the prisoners were hardening towards the regime. Some dozen or so had quietly gone mad and had been encouraged by their fellows to leave the protest and conform. There was intermittent talk of a final dramatic stroke by the prisoners—of a hunger strike to the death.

In May the Conservatives were victorious in the British general election, which meant the end of Roy Mason as British government supremo in Northern Ireland. A consistory of cardinals was held by the new Pope, John Paul II, in Rome. At the end of June 1979, despite the efforts of some English Catholics, the Church of Armagh was honoured, in the Archbishop's person, with a red hat.

The new Cardinal was asked, when he returned to Ireland in early July, whether he'd met Humphrey Atkins, the new government's Northern Secretary. He hadn't. But along with leaders of other churches in Northern Ireland he met him later that month. He saw that Atkins was courteous and gentlemanly, and wondered whether he would be able to understand Northern Ireland. It was certainly a relief to have Mason gone. Atkins seemed willing to listen.

That summer the Cardinal was caught up in the planning and arrangements for the Pope's visit to Ireland, a history-making event. It was clear that he was not only coming to Ireland but would come to Armagh City itself, to the See of Patrick, and it was in late August that the new Cardinal, just before setting out for Rome, got word that an appearance at Armagh was definitely scheduled, along with appearances at Dublin, Maynooth, the Marian shrine at Knock, and at a youth rally in Galway. As leader of the Irish delegation that went to Rome to make the arrangements, the Cardinal was very happy when he got the news about Armagh.

But it was only hours later that word came of the killing of Lord Mountbatten in Sligo and of eighteen British soldiers at Warrenpoint. It was the wrong climate, he realized, for the announcement of a papal visit to the North. A week before they could have made the Armagh announcement and stuck by it; or ten days later, when the impact of the killings had lessened. But not now. There had always been some danger, of course, in an Armagh visit. (Ian Paisley had been very noisy about a Northern Ireland appearance: "No Pope here," he'd cried.) And in the superheated atmosphere of that week, to announce an itinerary that included Armagh might have been thought inconsiderate of the feelings of the British people, and of those Protestants in the North who regarded themselves as British. The Armagh stop was quietly transferred to Drogheda, which was on the southern side of the border, but within the Cardinal's diocese, so that something was saved of the symbolism—the Pope would stop within the Armagh diocese. Catholics would be provided with a venue readily accessible from the northeast. And no offence would be given Northern Protestants.

Catholics in Ireland, the Cardinal remembered thinking ruefully at the time, were always going out of their way not to give offence . . .

The visit itself went off beautifully. The Pope received an enormous Irish welcome. A million and a quarter people, meaning a quarter of the population of the island of Ireland, turned out to greet the Pope in Phoenix Park in Dublin the day of his arrival, and the Protestant editor of the *Irish Times* headlined a descriptive piece next day: "Joy Cometh in the Morning." The Cardinal was deeply involved, travelling with the Pope throughout the three-day visit, riding with him in what journalists called the Popemobile, shepherding the Chief Shepherd through the Cardinal's old haunts at Maynooth where James Galway—a Northern Protestant and perhaps the finest flautist in the world—had been piping away for the young seminarians as they waited for the Pope.

More than a quarter of the population of the island of Ireland—a million two hundred fifty thousand people—had flocked out to the Phoenix Park for the first and greatest rally. The visit was a triumph of Irish hospitality, historic for the Irish Church: the Pope was the first successor of St. Peter ever to set foot on St. Patrick's island. At Drogheda he appealed dramatically and directly to the Catholic paramilitaries ("On my knees I beg you to turn from the paths of violence . . . Violence only delays the day of justice"). In a passage intended to be of equal weight the Pope spoke of the heavy responsibility that lay on governments to remove the injustices that caused violence.

But the struggle raged on through the autumn, with off-duty prison warders now the special focus of IRA attacks.

For the Cardinal, there was a period of decompression after the Pope's visit. Earlier, during the summer, he had gone to Long Kesh again for brief unpublicized meetings with prisoners from his own diocese. During the autumn he kept getting letters from the prison, and it was clear from these that the situation was worsening, as he'd told Mason it would. There was increasing pressure from the prisoners—on the Republican movement and on other people outside. They wanted support for their stand against criminalization and against the brutal treatment they were getting from the warders.

One letter, which the Cardinal received on 7 December 1979, was printed neatly on tissue paper in the Irish language, and came from a Belfast prisoner whose name the Cardinal couldn't place at the time. Though it was folded and refolded, and somewhat smeared, the Cardinal could translate just about all the words:

Dear Father,

How are you? I'm sure you recognize immediately that this letter comes from the H-Blocks. I wrote you a letter some months ago in which I told you about the evil conditions in which the men here are living. I hope you received it.* But if you didn't it's not worth anything now because it's [out of date]. I would like to give you the latest news from here.

Certainly you know that things have got worse since you visited us a year ago . . . It is no lie to say that many of us are beaten up day after day. There are a hundred blanketmen who have been beaten up during the past week—two of them especially, whom the warders beat with batons, one of them on his way back from Mass, and who are now in the punishment cells.

The warders now give us chairs. The other day without any hesitation we used them to break the [heavy plastic] windows. A chair is no use to anyone in a cell. Where were those chairs during the past year and a half? Besides, the windows have been put up as a further pressure on us, to give us more misery and hardship. A window is no use when you cannot see the sky through it, when you cannot breathe fresh air through it, when you cannot see the world outside. So that's why I say that these windows were built to be a further pressure on us.

Our cells are even more terrible than they were. It's impossible to describe them, but if there is a hell in this world it is surely in the H-Blocks. I find it hard to believe I am still alive when I look at the walls and the dirt around me. We are still lying on the ground. The dampness is very bad. Our blankets are very worn and are as thin as paper. A lot of the boys are ill now. Fifteen of them in the other wing here have diarrhoea and are vomiting. There was

*He hadn't, in fact. Not all the letters got through.

something bad last week, and there will be something bad next week. And it will continue like that so long as people are willing to allow it to continue.

The Irish language is going ahead rapidly. I think it is true to say that this place is now the largest Gaeltacht in the North. If the English continue to fill this camp, it won't be long till the whole country is fluent again.

At any rate the boys are very disappointed that you did not return here again. It's been a long time now since you were in. Some of them think you have forgotten this place entirely. I know that is not so. But you must understand that it is much worse than it was a year ago, and it gets worse and worse every day.

Someone said that evil things happen because good people allow them to happen—I think that's true. I hope this realization doesn't occur to the people of Ireland when it is too late—meaning when one of us has died.

I must go now. But I hope we will see you here soon again. Until then, God bless you, Father, and may you live long.

Yours,

Riobárd Ó Seachnasaigh, LK 3

By the way, happy Christmas to you.

It was not until sixteen months later that the Cardinal learned who it was who had written him that letter. Riobárd Ó Seachnasaigh was Bobby Sands.

The sad and moving letters kept coming, and later that month the Cardinal was asked by Fathers Alex Reid and Des Wilson, two politically concerned priests from Belfast, whether he'd be willing to meet with some leaders of Provisional Sinn Féin. He remembered the Feakle conference in 1974, when leaders of the Irish Council of Churches had sat down with the Provos. Why shouldn't he meet with Sinn Féin? The meetings were kept private at the time, because it served no one's interest to create a press sensation.

In December the Cardinal sat down with the two priests and two of the Sinn Féin leaders. He was anxious to talk about the Pope's message at Drogheda. The Sinn Féiners were polite, but said they found it difficult to swallow the unbalanced message. The more memorable passage, which got all the media attention, focused on the Pope's plea to the paramilitaries to give over their violence; the less memorable passage, which failed to mention British violence, merely called for unspecified government action to remove the injustice that caused the violence.

The Republicans freely admitted that their people had committed atrocities, and they recognized the need for Protestant-Catholic reconciliation. But they felt, they said, that the Catholic Church was letting its people down. Practically speaking, they were concerned with two things. They wanted to know whether the Church might use its good offices to reduce the level of Army and police harassment in Catholic areas, particularly the urban ghettoes. Their principal concern, though, was with the prison situation, particularly in Long Kesh. They wondered whether the Church could do anything to resolve the impasse there.

The meeting was resumed on 1 February 1980—and again the two priests were there. The Sinn Féin leaders spoke of the anger of Belfast Catholics at a parish priest's handling of the Delaney funeral. Kevin Delaney, an IRA man, had been carrying a bomb on the Belfast to Lisburn train on 17 January when it exploded prematurely, killing Delaney and two other people, and badly injuring two more. The parish priest at St. John's church on the Falls Road, upset by the circumstances of Delaney's death, refused to hold a funeral Mass in the church, so that Delaney's body had to be taken directly from his home to the cemetery. One of the priests at the meeting, Father Wilson, said that nothing in the twelve years of the conflict had done more damage to relations between the Church and the working-class people of Ballymurphy than the parish priest's refusal to bury this man.

But the conversation again centred chiefly on Long Kesh, and the urgency to do something about the plight of the prisoners. So far, despite written appeals from the Cardinal and others, Humphrey Atkins and the NIO had done nothing. The men from Sinn Féin said that during the past months there had been great pressure from within the prison for a hunger strike,

313

and that while the leaders in the movement had dissuaded the prisoners from taking this course, the men in the prison were getting fed up and were now determined to make their own decisions without outside advice.

Only recently had a hunger strike been narrowly averted, they said, and help was needed. The two priests asked the Cardinal to let Atkins know that Sinn Féin was prepared to discuss ways and means of resolving the situation, and to ask what the British government was prepared to do. .

Clearly the situation was ripe for action. The Cardinal was due to have a meeting with Atkins, who was coming to Armagh on 26 February. He now knew that the Republican leadership was positively interested in seeing the protest, particularly the dirt strike, ended. If the British government would compromise, the situation could be resolved.

It was time, the Cardinal felt, to get cracking.

When Atkins came to the residence, accompanied by his private secretary, the Cardinal served refreshments and then got down to business.

First he had a bone to pick with Atkins about the treatment of young men and women in the interrogation centres. He showed Atkins two lists of questions and remarks from RUC interrogators in which the Cardinal himself was mentioned. The first list was from interrogations at Gough barracks in Armagh:

> What chapel do you go to? How often?
>
> Do you miss Mass often?
>
> What is the name of your priest?
>
> Re confession—Do you believe in that stuff? You're an intelligent person . . . Surely you don't believe in that rubbish?
>
> When the British leave we'll take over. We've all the guns. We'll sort out the Catholics. We'll get rid of the top boys.
>
> When we take over we don't want to roll Catholics, but when your lawn is full of rats, you don't need to shoot them all.
>
> We need to shoot only a few leaders . . . [We] have links

with the UVF and would pass on information to the UVF.

The second list was from questions asked at Castlereagh Interrogation centre in Belfast:

Who is your local parish priest?

Who says Mass every Sunday?

Who do you go to confession to—i.e., what specific priest?

Who would you go to confession to if you had a serious offence to confess?

Would you confess to a sin such as murder, shootings . . . ?

If you had a serious offence to confess to, would you go to one special priest and if so who would he be?

The time you committed the . . . offence, did you go to confession and confess the sin, and if so what priest did you go to?

Did you feel that you would have a clear conscience if you went to confession and confessed serious offences, and that if you went to confession you would not have to owe anything to the State?

Did you ever talk to Cardinal Ó Fiaich?

Do you think Cardinal Ó Fiaich would have republican views on any matters?

Do you believe Cardinal Ó Fiaich would discuss any republican ideas or ideals with you if he had any republican views?

What do you think of Father X as a priest? If you had a serious offence to confess, is it to him you would go to confession?

These revelations knocked Atkins off balance a bit, as the Cardinal had been aware they might. The Cardinal then mentioned Long Kesh and said he was thinking of visiting it soon. He talked about the prison problem and the dirt protest, which had now spread to thirty women prisoners in Armagh. Atkins seemed more flexible than he had expected.

Was there a way to end the protest? Atkins asked. He was

clearly in a cooperative mood. The Cardinal asked whether Atkins would be prepared to discuss the situation, through some trusted member of his staff, with Provisional Sinn Féin or with intermediaries. The Cardinal was trying to get some kind of indirect communication going, and it seemed that both sides were anxious for a solution.

Atkins seemed quite willing, and the meeting ended there, with Atkins promising to get back to the Cardinal with what, from the tenor of the conversation, the Cardinal thought would be a move towards mediation. But Atkins wrote back within a couple of days to say no, that negotiation, even indirect negotiation, was not on: he must have felt, or been told, that he'd gone too far. The Cardinal thought that Atkins personally was a decent fellow who would have wished as far as possible to avoid trouble, and who would have gone much further than he was allowed to go. There would be another meeting soon, after the Cardinal's visit to the prison. He'd gotten too much of a positive impression out of that first one-to-one meeting to be willing to let things just slide.

On Monday 3 March the Cardinal visited Long Kesh for the fourth time. It was to be a long visit, lasting nearly eleven hours. Bishop Edward Daly of Derry was with him this time.

The prison governor, Stanley Hilditch, was eager to talk about his wonderful new facilities, available of course only to special category and conforming H-Block prisoners. Hilditch went on about the all-weather football pitches and other recreational arrangements, enthusiastically illustrating his lecture from maps and plans on the wall. The Cardinal and Bishop Daly were itching to get around to the men in the cells, particularly the men in Hilditch's sewer-like protest blocks. But Hilditch began talking about the great ecumenical contacts that were taking place in the prison, Protestant and Catholic prisoners together in adjacent cells, and together at meals in certain wings, and how they were out playing football together.

Before one of his earlier visits, in July 1978, word had come to the Cardinal that Gusty Spence, leader of the Protestant UVF prisoners, would like to see him. When he'd come to visit that time, he'd asked to see Spence. Hilditch, who spoke with an

English accent, had said that that would be out of order, unless Mr. Spence were thinking of becoming a Roman Catholic. For the Cardinal to see Spence, Hilditch said, would be like Ian Paisley seeing a Catholic prisoner. All Spence would want to do, Hilditch was sure, would be to make political capital out of a visit from the Cardinal.

The Cardinal said to Hilditch that in his book if a prisoner wanted to see a clergyman of whatever faith, and the clergyman was willing to see him, then—in the Cardinal's opinion, for what it was worth—the prisoner was entitled to see the clergyman. And while he wasn't going to make a big issue of it just now, since the governor had kindly allowed him to see the other prisoners, he would raise it again on another occasion.

Today, with all Hilditch's talk of Protestant-Catholic ecumenism in the wonderful environment of his prison, the Cardinal decided to bring up the Gusty Spence visit again. Didn't Hilditch think, he asked, that his visiting Gusty Spence might have the same sort of ecumenical and healing effect the Governor was talking about? Hilditch suddenly saw that he had baited his own trap. Well, he said, if the Cardinal insisted—and the Cardinal said, okay, that on this occasion he would insist. Right, Hilditch said, they'd make arrangements, and the Cardinal could see Spence later, in the evening.

He and Bishop Daly had a busy day of it, going from cell to cell in the protest blocks, between them visiting all the blocks and all the compounds. The Cardinal made certain that day to see all the Armagh prisoners, and that meant seeing men from other parts of Northern Ireland as well, because the prisoners were often doubled up in the cells, and an Armagh man might have a Belfast or Derry man as cellmate. It was then, while visiting an Armagh prisoner, that he met Bobby Sands again, for the second time. The Cardinal always made a note of the names of the men he was seeing and often jotted down an impression or two. When he consulted his diary long afterwards he found he hadn't made any note on Bobby Sands, whom he didn't yet know as Riobárd Ó Seachnasaigh, and who would have been glad to see the Cardinal, judging from the letter, but who clearly made no special effort to impress him. Bobby Sands

317

was not yet generally known outside as a leader among the prisoners. The Cardinal also saw Patsy O'Hara, and his brother Tony—Tony for the second time.

He and Bishop Daly had lunch in a canteen, in the middle of the day, with someone from the prison staff. The Cardinal had never eaten a meal he enjoyed less. They'd been in one of the dirt protest blocks all morning and by then the smell was in his clothes. Wherever he went he couldn't shake this terrible smell. Even in the canteen he carried it with him.

After lunch they visited the other two protest blocks. They finished these in the late afternoon and had just met one another when it suddenly occurred to the Cardinal that he hadn't seen Raymond McCreesh. He didn't dare go back to Armagh and meet Father Brian McCreesh and have to say that he'd missed seeing Raymond, whom Brian himself hadn't seen for a long time. So he went back to see Raymond, and in seeing him saw his cellmate Francis Hughes. Raymond was very pale and drawn, and far thinner than the last time he'd visited him, eight months ago, in the summer of 1979.

At just five that evening they had tea and sandwiches, and spoke to two NIO men who had been brought in to meet them. One of them sounded very hardline; the Cardinal didn't warm to him at all. He and Bishop Daly made a lot of points about prison clothes and work, the level of punishment, and the prisoners' accounts of beatings. At about a quarter to six they began visiting the other H-Blocks, the conforming ones—in which men wore the prison uniform. This went quickly. In each the prisoners were brought to a recreation room at the end of the wing. The two bishops didn't have to visit the men cell by cell, call for a warder each time they wanted to go to another cell, and wait while one cell was closed and another opened: a terribly slow process.

In each of the conforming blocks the Cardinal and Bishop Daly were able to say a few words, shake hands and talk to each man, and say a prayer with all of them together before leaving and going on to the next. The last two conforming blocks, H-1 and H-2, they did individually. By the time they were finished, it was nearly eight. After eight they did the compounds, forty men at a time, taking most of the compounds together but the last two individually, on the same basis that they'd taken the conforming blocks. The Cardinal drew the Official IRA prisoners as his last compound and, after his meeting and prayer with them, went over to the UVF compound at about ten minutes to nine. Gusty Spence was there, and obviously happy to see him.

"A hundred thousand welcomes!" he said.

"You should say *Céad míle fáilte!*" the Cardinal said. "Aren't you attending Irish classes?"

Gusty Spence said that he had attended some, just a few, but hadn't picked up much. He only went when he did to encourage the younger men. Quite a number of the Protestant prisoners were taking Irish, he said, and six or seven of them were up to the level of the *fáinne*, the ring awarded fluent Irish speakers. They had asked for the president of the Gaelic League to be allowed in to make the award, but the prison authorities had refused.

The loyalist prisoners were proud, Spence said, of the books on Irish history in their library. They'd done the language classes, and the history study, to get some of what they'd lost growing up. They'd come gradually to realize that the Irish language was part of their tradition. Most of the place names in the North were in Irish, many of their own surnames were Gaelic, and there were many close bonds between Irish and Scottish Gaelic culture.

They had quite a chat. The Cardinal explained his difficulty getting to see Spence earlier; Spence's only complaint was that a leading Presbyterian clergyman had refused that year to come visit them in the compounds.

Why had Gusty Spence been so eager to see the Cardinal? Probably partly out of that spirit of friendliness—or ecumenism, as Hilditch liked to call it. There were often these strange, or not so strange, manifestations of fellow feeling across the religious divide, especially among people aware that the divide had been artificially created. Spence was probably also hoping that at some stage the Cardinal might recommend him for parole, or for early release, which he would have done in any case, but particularly if Gusty Spence's release could be played off against the release of someone like Marian Price. He often brought this sort of thing up with Atkins; Catholics would accept Spence's release if some other prisoner would be released in return.

The Cardinal had checked up, put out feelers around Belfast to discover what the reaction might be if Spence were released. Would there be people there who would resent his release, people whose relatives had been killed by men associated with Spence in 1966? Was there any long-standing grievance? The response the Cardinal got was that people felt that after sixteen years in prison Gusty had more than paid his debt to society. He had also come around to an understanding of the Republican side of things. He'd written a few years earlier to the wife of Joe McCann, the famous Official IRA man who'd been killed: he'd written McCann's wife a sympathetic and moving letter. Spence's image among Catholics in general—it was known he'd been doing a bit of Irish study in the prison—was pretty good. So the Cardinal had been glad of the chance to talk with him, and would be helping him along as the occasion arose.

When they left Long Kesh that evening, Bishop Daly followed the Cardinal's car to Armagh and stayed at the residence overnight. They prepared a short statement to be issued next day through the Catholic press office. In it they said that they wanted to have a fresh meeting with Atkins about the prison situation. Atkins arranged the meeting immediately. The quick response was a good omen, but the Cardinal wasn't going into the meeting under any illusions: not after his great disappointment a week earlier.

They met Atkins this time at Stormont Castle, and quickly got down to the nitty-gritty. The two key issues, now as later, were the question of prison clothes and prison work. On clothing, couldn't the NIO simply change the rule so that all prisoners in Northern Ireland were allowed to wear their own clothes? That would get the prisoners what they wanted—no criminal uniform—and would get the Northern Ireland Office off the hook. And work: why couldn't work be interpreted in a very broad sense: anything that promised self-improvement and rehabilitation? Look, the Cardinal said, if a fellow was good at playing the tin whistle, toss him in a tin whistle, let him play it from morning to night and he might come out a James Galway.

But Atkins had his constitutional conference on his mind, a conference which was to go nowhere, but which was judged necessary by the British government as a ploy to forestall Senator Ted Kennedy talking about British political failure in Northern Ireland during the 1980 American presidential primaries. While the Cardinal and others were trying to get movement in the prison to forestall the threat of a hunger strike—with all its potential for disaster—Humphrey Atkins was trying to hold this charade of a conference together, busying himself with preparing and delivering such statements as

> There's no reason for anyone to leave the conference table—we're not going to be voting about this proposal or that; we're going to seek agreement and if we can't find agreement then never mind, we'll leave that point and go on to something else . . .

So all Atkins had time for that morning was an hour and a quarter of conversation about the seething prison protest. The Cardinal suggested forming a liaison group to mediate between the government and the prisoners and make recommendations that might be acceptable to both sides: a group to consist, for example, of a prison chaplain, a parent, a social worker, a doctor and a solicitor. Atkins indicated that he was interested; but his toytown constitutional conference was what seemed to be really on his mind.

On 24 March the Cardinal, anxious to move things forward, got his secretary to phone the NIO to get an appointment with Atkins for the following week. The appointment was set for 1 April. Atkins was to make a statement on the H-Blocks in the House of Commons sometime during the next couple of days, and many people wondered what the implications might be for the men on the protest. Then Atkins got up in the House of Commons on 26 March and offered minor changes in the prison regime: the prisoners could exercise in sports clothing, could receive a letter a week rather than one a month, and could receive two visits a month.

At the 1 April meeting Atkins was unhappy, and strongly attacked Fathers Denis Faul and Raymond Murray because not only had the prisoners rejected the derisory concessions of 26 March, but Father Faul said they were derisory. The Cardinal defended the priests just as strongly, and asked what Atkins' response was to the idea of a liaison group. Atkins said that the sort of group he was proposing existed already—the board of prison visitors. Would the Cardinal be prepared to meet them? The Cardinal agreed. If the board of visitors were unwilling or unable to act, they could re-propose the liaison group. Some hope at least could be placed in the board of visitors, especially because for the first time in the history of Northern Ireland, the chairmen of the two boards, the one for Long Kesh and the one for Armagh, were both Catholics.

At the end of April there was a hopeful sign, when the official then in charge of Northern Ireland prisons, a man named James Hannigan, informed the Cardinal that Marian Price was to be released from Armagh jail. Miss Price had been in terrible health and the Cardinal and others had appealed to the Pope and to the Dublin government to request her release. The Cardinal went to Armagh prison with Hannigan and she was released that evening. But then a meeting with Atkins, scheduled for 12 May, was postponed to 30 June by the NIO—postponed for a month and a half!—while the men lay suffering in prison.

At least the IRA had called off its murder campaign against prison warders pending the outcome of talks between the Cardinal and the NIO. And during the interval the Cardinal met with the chairmen of the boards of visitors, who were not only willing to support the Cardinal and Bishop Daly on prison clothes and prison work but were there at the 30 June meeting to say so. The Cardinal told Atkins that if the British government made substantial concessions then he and Bishop Daly would do their best to ensure that the prisoners accepted them.

Another meeting held with Atkins at the end of July was friendly enough. Atkins seemed prepared to concede to all prisoners the right to wear their own clothes, and seemed willing to make some changes in the rules about prison work. The Cardinal felt good about the meeting, and an agreed statement was issued afterwards saying that progress had been made. The Cardinal offered to send suggestions about changes in prison work. Atkins was going off on a long holiday, so he sent them to Hannigan:

[The Cardinal and Bishop Daly propose] that all prisoners be given the option of engaging in one or other of the following activities in lieu of prison work:

1. Educational courses. These could be in languages, commerce, environmental studies, etc. They could be courses in the Open University for the better students. For many students, however, the most useful courses would be basic ones in writing, grammar, public speaking, etc.

2. Handicrafts, the making of souvenirs.

3. Prisoners with talent in music, drawing and painting, etc., to be given ample opportunity to develop these talents and hours spent thus could be counted as hours of work.

4. Horticulture, vegetable growing; growing of plants, fruit and vegetables under glass, etc.

5. Training in the various types of work available in the workshops—bricklaying, carpentry, motor maintenance, etc.

6. The building of a small oratory or room to be used as a chapel or prayer room either for the Roman Catholic prisoners or on an interdenominational basis.

7. The cleaning of cells, corridors and wings, painting and decoration of same, maintenance of recreation rooms and facilities, cooking and serving of meals as required.

One could think of other suggestions within the general area of "work" but the above listing is sufficient to indicate what activities we have in mind.

The Cardinal still felt, he said, that it was only through substantial change in the entire approach to prison dress and prison work that any hope could be found of ending the protest.

There was a great deal of correspondence between meetings, but the Cardinal did not get to see Atkins again until 18 September. Atkins asked whether he could give him something to show "his colleagues," meaning Thatcher and her cabinet, to indicate that the sorts of changes discussed would be accepted by the prisoners, and bring the protest to an end. It made a curious change from Mason, Atkins and this talk of "colleagues." Mason could make bad decisions, but he made his own, whereas Atkins would have to talk to Margaret Thatcher before he could approve even an extra visit a month.

The Cardinal had to go to Rome for a synod of bishops; but before leaving he took time out to hold a series of consultations and then write a long and, he hoped, convincing letter to Atkins.

The letter was dated 23 September 1980.

He expressed himself as extremely disappointed at the lack of progress on prison dress and prison work through all their meetings. Only a substantial change in these areas would end the blanket and dirt protest, he wrote. What he and Bishop Daly had been strongly urging was that mandatory wearing of prison garb should be abolished for all prisoners, and that *all* prisoners be given a choice of useful and self-improving activities in lieu of prison work.

He had, moreover, the support of the chairmen of the Boards of Visitors of the Maze and Armagh prisons for these proposals. Furthermore, he'd spent many hours over the weekend putting these proposals to relatives and friends of the prisoners, with the following results:

> 1. They all without exception assure me that if the two proposals mentioned above are implemented the prisoners will end their protest; and they themselves will use all their influence to persuade the waverers.

> 2. There has been a growing restiveness among the protesters in recent weeks and an increasing demand for a hunger strike to death. Many of them are now convinced that the authorities have no strong motivation to seek a solution of the present dreadful situation, and that only after a number of hunger strikers die will the government be forced by the outcry of public opinion to search for

a compromise. They have already given up hope of any substantial change coming out of our talks but they decided to let our meeting after the holidays (announced at the beginning of August) take place so that they would not seem to be "jumping the gun." But personnel have already been chosen for a hunger strike, and as it becomes known that I have gone abroad and will not be back for some weeks, they will conclude that we have had a fruitless meeting and a hunger strike seems inevitable in the near future. Already some of the media have been ringing Armagh seeking to establish if a meeting has taken place.

3. Thus if a peaceful solution is to be found, it must be found as a matter of extreme urgency. To allow the conviction to spread among the prisoners that our talks have failed and to provide time for preparations for a hunger strike would be fatal and would set a train of events in motion which it would be impossible to halt or reverse. It would also be tragic if it came on the eve of what might have been the big breakthrough. I must implore you therefore to have the questions of prison dress and prison work examined with all possible speed and decisions taken on these two issues.

Humphrey Atkins had been asking for assurance that the two changes would in fact end the protest. What the Cardinal said in Point 1 was tantamount to giving Atkins categorical assurance of this.

He was satisfied that his efforts that weekend would persuade Mrs. Thatcher and her cabinet, if they were at all reasonable, to make the two changes and thereby avert the hunger strike. But the months of mediation had taught him *not* to expect reasonableness from that quarter. So the same day, before leaving for Rome, the Cardinal, along with Bishop Daly, issued a public statement—an interim report on the status of negotiations—in which his hopes were measured against the realities of the situation: after six months of talks the British government had still not done anything substantial:

During the past six months the Bishop of Derry and I have made strenuous efforts to resolve the terrible situation which exists in the Maze Prison at Long Kesh and in the Women's Prison at Armagh. The "blanket protest" of about 350 prisoners in the former is now entering its fifth year and since March 1978 it has escalated into a "dirt protest' as well. In Armagh the "dirt protest" of about thirty women prisoners has gone on since last February. In view of the loss of life of several members of prison staff as well as the human suffering which the present situation in the prison entails for prisoners, prison staff, and the relatives of both (many thousands in all) we make no apology for doing our utmost to obtain a solution. If we have so far failed to solve the problem, our failure is, we believe, less reprehensible than not to have made the attempt.

In this interim report on our efforts so far we wish to record that apart from visits to both prisons we have had five meetings with the Secretary of State, three other meetings with officials of the Northern Ireland Office, discussions with the prison governors and with the chairmen of the Boards of Visitors and numerous meetings with parents and other relatives of prisoners on protest. All of these meetings have involved a considerable amount of time and travel on the part of everyone concerned.

The overall conviction which has been borne in on us in the course of these meetings is that the H-Block impasse could be solved in the context of a general prison reform in Northern Ireland regarding prison dress and prison work. We have therefore made certain concrete proposals to the Secretary of State under these two heads . . . We have failed so far to secure any substantial changes on these two central issues but our proposals have not been rejected. We shall therefore continue to press for a decision on the part of government to make these changes and a willingness on the part of the protesting prisoners to end their protest if these changes are made.

We are convinced that the vast majority of people in Northern Ireland, irrespective of religious and political loyalties, and especially the thousands of people in our community who are suffering intense anguish because of the present situation, would breathe an instant sigh of relief if this impasse became a thing of the past. We believe a solution would be welcomed by prisoners and prison officers alike, by the relatives and friends of both groups, by the state authorities in charge of the prisons and the organizations to which many of the prisoners belong, by the Irish and British peoples and their governments, by the Churches and by all those who have lost a loved one in the violence of the past decade. Far too many lives have already been lost and we are fearful that if this problem remains unresolved it will inevitably lead to further tragedy.

> Tomás Ó Fiaich, Cardinal Archbishop of Armagh
> Edward Daly, Bishop of Derry

The following day, as the Cardinal was on his way to Rome, Atkins and the NIO responded. They would not discuss or negotiate the principle of political or special category status, they said in a statement. "Murder is murder wherever it is committed."

It was a wretched response.

The Cardinal had been trying to talk about clothing and work in ways that would avoid confrontation on the political status issue, and to keep the discussion above this sort of emotion. What Atkins' statement meant was that the Cardinal's mediation effort was now in ruins.

And so the prisoners at Long Kesh replied on 10 October with the formal announcement that a number of them would embark soon on a hunger strike to the death for political status.

On 16 October the Cardinal issued a joint statement with Bishop Daly, asking Atkins to think again about ways of avoiding the hunger strike.

As the day for the start of the strike drew nearer, the Cardinal, still in Rome, asked his secretary, Father Clyne, to arrange a meeting with Atkins, telling Atkins he was willing to take time out from the bishops' synod to fly to London or Belfast for the meeting. It was arranged for London in the late afternoon of 23 October, four days before the 27 October date set by the prisoners for the start of their hunger strike.

23 October was a Thursday, and the Cardinal flew out from Rome in the morning and met Bishop Daly, who had flown over from Ireland, at Heathrow airport, where they were given a lift into the city by a priest who'd been a student of the Cardinal's at Maynooth. They went to Cardinal Hume's residence—he was still in Rome, at the synod—and had lunch there.

At a quarter past one a note came in from priests next door saying that there'd been an announcement on a news broadcast: in Northern Ireland prison dress was being abolished! They quickly switched on the radio. There were various bulletins. The gist was this: to defuse the threat of the hunger strike, prisoners were to be allowed to wear their own clothes.

The Cardinal and Bishop Daly were elated. They immediately got to work on a statement they planned to issue once they were certain of the change. They felt particularly good because it sounded as though the concession had been worked out by the cabinet that morning with a view to Atkins' afternoon meeting with them. The Cardinal and Bishop Daly might even go to Belfast that night to try to sell the concession—if it should prove worth selling.

They called various people in Northern Ireland to sound out opinion there, but most were away or had not heard the news. The Cardinal asked one man to see what he could discover about the prisoners' reactions.

Then, at four, they left Cardinal Hume's residence to see Atkins. They met him at 4:30.

A lot of time was spent at the beginning of the Atkins meeting explaining minor changes in the prison regime—changes that had already been made. Then a typed document, headed "Final Version," was handed them.

Quickly reading through the earlier sections, they came to paragraph 8, which said that the government had decided to abolish prison uniform and to substitute "civilian-type" clothing.

This looked suspicious. The Cardinal and Bishop Daly questioned Atkins about it; Atkins said that it meant civilian clothing issued by the prison authorities.

The Cardinal felt that he and Bishop Daly had been had. This was not what had been announced on the news bulletins. They'd had nine meetings with Atkins and his people at the NIO during the past seven months, and there had never been any talk of prison-issue civilian clothing. They could never hope to halt the threat of a hunger strike on that basis. Nobody with any integrity would attempt to persuade the prisoners to accept this sham.

The Cardinal told Atkins that the government was in a position where they'd get as much stick from unionists and right-wing Tories for this shabby gesture as they'd get from granting the prisoners their own clothes. There was nothing to gain from this sort of cheap trick. The Cardinal and Bishop Daly went into another room to confer. They agreed that Atkins' "Final Version" was disastrous. When they returned, Atkins offered the Cardinal a drink as if to celebrate. The Cardinal declined. There was nothing to celebrate. Yet Atkins seemed still under the illusion that this concession would avert the hunger strike.

Angry and upset, the Cardinal and Bishop Daly left.

Talking to a reporter later, the Cardinal learned that journalists, too, felt they had been conned. There was some evidence that a decision to let the prisoners have their own clothes—made possibly by a cabinet committee rather than the full cabinet—had been made, then been leaked to the press; and that the leak had stirred a lunchtime reaction from Tory backbenchers or possibly from Thatcher herself, and that the original offer had then been watered down—to this.

The official explanation afterwards was that a garbled leak had caused the confusion. But some of the journalists had asked explicitly, earlier, whether prisoners were to be allowed to wear their own clothes, and had been told, yes, that was what had been decided. A number of commentators had prepared pieces that assumed the prisoners had been conceded their own clothes, and *The Times*, taking this to be the concession, ran a mildly critical editorial.

That night the Cardinal, disgusted with what had happened, flew back to Rome.

On the following Sunday, 26 October, he was invited, together with several Irish and American bishops, to lunch with the Pope, who was to meet Queen Elizabeth.

The Pope asked about the prison situation and the imminent hunger strike—it was scheduled to begin next morning, Monday, 27 October, the day the Pope was meeting the Queen. On Monday the Pope raised the matter with her, and on Monday night he met with Cardinal Ó Fiaich again, privately. The Cardinal gave the Pope a full account of the protest, mentioning especially the humiliations the prisoners had suffered, the deprivations, the criminal uniform issue, and the condition of the cells.

The Pope was very attentive and asked the Cardinal what he could do to help. He could do two things, the Cardinal said: appeal for the release of Pauline McLaughlin, who was very ill in Armagh jail (she *was* released two months later), and appeal to Mrs. Thatcher to take steps to bring the hunger strike to an end. The Pope said that it would help if the Cardinal gave him an *aide memoire* on the matter. So the Cardinal spent the next day drawing up a long account of the protest and its origins. On Wednesday morning he had the material copied. He left it with the Pope's secretary at St. Peter's before rushing to catch a plane home at 1:30 that afternoon.

Seven hunger strikers began their fast on the morning of 27 October; their leader was Brendan Hughes, OC of the Provisional IRA prisoners in Long Kesh. The new commanding officer of IRA prisoners in Long Kesh was Bobby Sands. The National H-Blocks committee began to gear up in support of the hunger strikers.

On 10 November the Cardinal was startled at news of a speech in the British House of Commons by Gerry Fitt, the Catholic MP for West Belfast, in which he not only urged the British government not to give in to the hunger strikers' demand for political status, but criticized the Cardinal and Bishop Daly for seeming to support the hunger strikers and thereby creating polarization between Catholics and Protestants in Northern Ireland. To the Cardinal it was a particularly nasty attack.

In a joint statement with Bishop Daly he replied to Fitt. It was pastoral concern, they said, that motivated their intervention. On Sunday, 27 November, Cardinal Hume of Westminster demanded that the hunger strikers end their fast. Fitt pounced on this as evidence of a split between the Catholic Church in England and that in Ireland. On the same Sunday Garret FitzGerald, leader of the opposition Fine Gael party in the twenty-six county Dáil, echoed Fitt by making a statement in which he urged the British government not to concede political status to the prisoners.

Through that month and the next the seven hunger strikers grew weaker while Thatcher and the NIO, ignoring yet again the Cardinal's appeals to them to settle the matter on the basis of reforms in prison clothing and prison work, kept up their barren insistence that they would never concede political status. At the end of November the NIO announced that they were not going to use any mediators to settle the dispute.

But Charles Haughey, the then Taoiseach, made some helpful statements on the hunger strike, and John Hume, leader of the SDLP, attempted some mediation efforts alc   lines like those the Cardinal and Bishop Daly had been pursuing. On 8 December there was a Thatcher/Haughey summit in Dublin followed by a joint statement announcing study groups to examine new institutional structures and other matters in the context of "the totality of the relationships within these islands." At this juncture there seemed to be a softening in the British government's stance, and on 10 December John Blelloch, one of Atkins' deputies, visited Long Kesh and talked to the hunger strikers about the government's position.

On Friday 12 December six UDA prisoners in Long Kesh went on hunger strike, asking for "political status." The Cardinal had been pressing the Northern Ireland Office to use Canon William Arlow of the Church of Ireland as a mediator in the dispute. Canon Arlow's Feakle talks had set the stage for an extended IRA/British Army truce in 1975. He had maintained contacts with leaders on both sides of the sectarian divide.

At a meeting with Atkins at Stormont on Monday 15 December the Cardinal stressed the fact that UDA men were now also on hunger strike. This presented, the Cardinal thought, a great opportunity for resolving the dispute by making changes in clothing and work that would benefit all prisoners.*

Atkins said that if prisoners were allowed to wear their own clothes that would mean political status. The Cardinal told Atkins he could not agree, pointing out that in his own city of Armagh women prisoners had always been allowed to wear their own clothes. Did Mr. Atkins mean to suggest that the British government recognized the Armagh women as political prisoners? Atkins had a penchant for hemming and hawing, and he had a difficult time dealing with that argument.

Now again he seemed to stall. The Cardinal issued a public warning on the violence that was likely to follow a hunger strike death. And then on 17 December, a week after Blelloch's visit to the prison, the NIO offered a 34-page document, phrased in conciliatory language, which semed to promise major concessions if the prisoners would end their protest. On 18 December, with Seán McKenna near death, the seven hunger strikers, and others who had joined them in Long Kesh and in the women's prison at Armagh, called off their fast.

The Cardinal got busy immediately. He was determined to use the NIO document as a lever to get the protest in the prison ended. The prisoners had fulfilled their part of the bargain by ending their hunger strike. But the NIO seemed all too ready

*As later became clear, the leaders of the loyalist UDA, some of whose members in Long Kesh were suffering much the same treatment as the Catholic prisoners, felt considerable admiration for the Republican hunger strikers, and Andy Tyrie spoke out in favour of British government concessions. There was a certain solidarity across the working-class divide, as there had been in May 1974 when Irish Republicans had privately cheered the loyalist strikers who brought down the British-erected Northern power-sharing Executive.

to leave it at that. The British seemed anxious to give the impression that they had won the day: that the fast had simply collapsed in the face of their principled British refusal of political status.

But what the Cardinal saw was that the document was there; it had been meant to persuade the prisoners to end their strike, implying that substantial changes would be made if they did so. So he tried to float that document, to get the prisoners to end their blanket and dirt protests, saying these had now served their purpose, that the hunger strike had made its point and had brought about a willingness to compromise on both sides.

"I think," he said in a public statement, that "the document [of 17 December] was much fuller, much more detailed . . . much more positive" [than a 4 December statement from the NIO]. The new document "explained what was available in relation to prison work such as vocational courses." The prisoners had found it a sufficiently positive statement, amounting to a substantial granting of what they'd been after, he said.

Yet the Cardinal knew that there was confusion among the prisoners as to what the government was actually going to concede. As December 1980 wore into January 1981, the prisoners waited to see what the British would do about the promises implied in the document and in its positive and conciliatory language.

The prisoners, despite their doubts, tried to cooperate. Still Atkins and his NIO stalled.

There was increasing bitterness among the prisoners because of the lack of real concessions by the NIO. They became angry, and there was talk of a new hunger strike. The NIO had been clawing back on promises they'd made to the prisoners' spokesmen, led now by Bobby Sands. Atkins and his people, as far as the Cardinal could see, were playing games, to see how little they could give in terms of the document. They seemed frightened to death of giving the prisoners concessions that would even remotely suggest Special Category status.

These were the parameters within which the Cardinal was working, at the beginning of 1981, trying to avert a second and possibly far more destructive hunger strike. On Thursday 5

February 1981 the prisoners announced a new series of strikes, to begin on 1 March, the fifth anniversary of the day the British had set as the key date for ending special category status. Through the month it became clear that the prisoners were very determined, and that Atkins and his people were unable or unwilling to act to prevent the hunger strike.

On 18 February the Cardinal met with Atkins and put some proposals to him.

The European Commission on Human Rights had strongly criticized the British government the year before for inflexibility in the prison. It was obvious that the government had been using its talks with the Cardinal and Bishop Daly as evidence of its flexibility. So one of the things the Cardinal sought to do that day was to restate the point about the British government's inflexibility, while diplomatically suggesting that it had shown willingness to make concessions.

Again nothing happened, so on the eve of the second hunger strike the Cardinal put the points he'd made at the meeting in a letter to Atkins:

1. It is essential, before the date fixed for the beginning of the hunger strike, that some opportunity should be given to the prisoners on protest to come together in groups to discuss what are the various courses open to them. The present system of shouting from cell to cell offers no possibility for rational discussion.

2. The prison authorities should depart completely from their attitude in the past that a prisoner must be deprived of all privileges for breaches of the prison rules. This was the inflexible attitude which merited the condemnation of the European Commission for Human Rights last year. There is already a precedent for what I was recommending, in the restoration of a few privileges to non-conforming prisoners in 1980. It is now time to accept that the refusal of the prisoners to wear prison-issue civilian garb for one quarter of every week should not be punished by the refusal of the prison authorities to allow them to wear their own clothes at *all* other periods.

3. If the attitude recommended in (2) were adopted, it would be possible—by allowing protesting prisoners to wear their own clothes for recreation, visits and at weekends and by locking them in their cells during working hours for their refusal to wear prison issue clothes and do prison work—to avert the hunger strike and to bring the "dirt" aspect of the protest to an end almost at once.

4. I pointed out the differences between your statements of 17th December 1980 and 5th February 1981 regarding what would happen if prisoners ended their protests . . . I said that in dealing with people who were already highly suspicious of the authorities, it was disastrous to introduce verbal differences of this kind.

Now on the eve of another hunger strike I think it is deplorable that this area is going to be torn asunder once more for the next few months by a confrontation between a government which had so many opportunities to resolve the prison problem in recent years and did not grasp them, and a paramilitary organization which will only gain new support and recruits out of hunger strike deaths.

It is innocent people who are going to be the main sufferers in such a situation, and I must express, in the name of the Catholic people of the North, our strong objection to being placed in this extremely dangerous position.

The Cardinal felt he could hardly have put the case more urgently, yet it wasn't till *nineteen* days later that Atkins replied with his now customary waffle about principles, and a defensive, self-righteously phrased refusal to concede the substance of the prisoners' demands—which the 17 December document had implied would be granted if the hunger strikers ended their protest.

Allowing the prisoners to gather in groups to discuss the options open to them would only strengthen the hands of the prisoners' leaders, Atkins wrote. Prisoners who had broken prison rules but accepted clean cells and furniture had had some of their privileges restored and got an extra parcel each month, he added, saying that the prisoners had no right to determine what work they should or should not do, and that the British government could not concede anything that would give the prisoners the status or the kind of prison regime they wanted.

Atkins said he wholeheartedly shared the Cardinal's concern for the innocent in the community. But the government, he said, had made great efforts over the past year to cure the situation in this prison, and the great majority of the community knew that it was the prisoners who were at fault. The community expected the government to refuse to yield, on a matter of sound principle, in the face of any form of violence. The Cardinal himself would surely support such a principled stance, Atkins concluded.

How often, over the centuries, had British colonial governors written that sort of rubbish? Yet the Cardinal hadn't entirely given up on Atkins—he couldn't afford to. Atkins was Thatcher's missionary in this part of the world.

But it was evident that Atkins had never got to grips with his job, and that in himself he had no authority. Talking to him was like talking to a suit of clothes. The British were going to have to give way at some point, but Atkins didn't seem to know this. While men lay dying, he had been diddling over matters like extra parcels and visits.

On 1 March Bobby Sands began his fast. The Cardinal was happy to see that at least the dirt strike had been called off for the time being, in order to focus attention on the hunger strike as the prisoners' mode of protest.

Then after a month or so, this far more carefully orchestrated second hunger strike began to have its effect . . .

ALL THROUGH 1980, while the Cardinal had been busy trying to help prevent the hunger strike, and then to get the British to act to end it, he had found his own life quiet enough. Now, as the second hunger strike moved towards its flashpoint, the world seemed to be camping on his doorstep. There were times when his secretary, Father Clyne, was besieged by journalists looking for appointments, and times when his housekeeper, the always cheerful Madge Walsh, was getting phone calls at three and four in the morning. Some of the phone calls were pleading, some hostile, some friendly. All the callers seemed to be asking him: can't you do something to end this terrible situation? There were a lot of calls from England, even from priests there. One priest, who seemed to be a bit daft, used to ring up at half-two or three in the morning.

Finally the Cardinal had an Ansafone installed.

At times the Cardinal felt like a man on the run. He'd look out the window and there'd be a crowd of television people setting up their cameras without so much as an announcement, let alone permission. One Sunday morning, a crowd from London rang up from Portadown, while the Cardinal was saying the ten o'clock Mass at the cathedral next door. They told Madge they were coming to Armagh and wanted to interview him. She asked whether they had an appointment. They said no, but that they were coming down anyway before lunch, and would set up outside the residence. When they arrived the Cardinal was having a bite of breakfast, and Madge told them he wasn't in. It was a mistake, because they wouldn't take that as a signal to go away; they said they'd wait till his return. Since he was in, he couldn't very well go out.

So he did his work and had his lunch. Still they sat waiting. It was a lovely sunny day. And the Cardinal said to himself that he wasn't going to stay in just because of that TV crew camped out there. So he phoned his driver, John Ward, and asked him to get, not the house Peugeot, but another car somewhere in town and come up. There was an entrance towards St. Patrick's college, the secondary school, behind the residence. Wasn't there a hole in the wire, he asked John, opened up by the boys so that they could get into the orchard? John said there was. And so he got a car and came up the back road; the Cardinal got out through the hole in the wire, into the car, and away.

During Bobby Sands' hunger strike the Cardinal met Sands' parents and was very impressed by them, and by their faith. He talked several times on the phone to Bobby's first cousin, Sister Bernadette Sands, a nun then at the Mater Hospital in Belfast. He would always remember the Sandses in his sitting room at Ara Coeli. They represented to him the decency of the families who were losing their sons—largely because of the inflexibilty and incompetence of this British government.

First Sands died, then Francis Hughes from Bellaghy in South Derry. The Cardinal wired Margaret Thatcher as he had done before and would do again, to get her—she had the power—to make the concessions that could end the hunger strike and the protest once and for all:

13TH MAY 1981
RT. HON. MARGARET THATCHER MP,
10 DOWNING STREET, LONDON.

DEAR PRIME MINISTER,

HAVING ALREADY APPEALED TO THE HUNGER-STRIKERS ON SEVERAL OCCASIONS TO GIVE UP THEIR FAST I NOW REPEAT MY EARNEST REQUEST TO YOU AND THE CABINET TO ABANDON THE INFLEXIBLE POLICY IN NORTHERN IRELAND REGARDING PRISON DRESS AND THE FRATERNIZATION OF PRISONERS AT WORK OR RECREATION. NORTHERN IRELAND, WITH A FIVEFOLD INCREASE IN PRISON POPULATION, REQUIRES A DIFFERENT APPROACH FROM OTHER AREAS, FOR THE VAST MAJORITY OF ITS PRISONERS (1) ARE VERY YOUNG; (2) COME FROM LAW-ABIDING FAMILIES; (3) HAVE BEEN SENTENCED TO VERY LONG TERMS; (4) DO NOT SHARE THE RELIGION OR NATIONAL IDENTITY OF THEIR JAILERS.

YESTERDAY'S DEATH OF FRANCIS HUGHES IS A FURTHER BLOW TO THE EFFORTS OF ALL TRUE CHRISTIANS HERE TO UPHOLD LOVE OF NEIGHBOUR AS THE SUPREME LAW AND ONLY ADDS FUEL TO THE FIRES OF HATRED AND VIOLENCE. IN GOD'S NAME, DON'T ALLOW ANOTHER DEATH. I BESEECH YOU TO MAKE THE FIRST MOVE IMMEDIATELY BY MAKING PRISON DRESS AND WORK OPTIONAL FOR ALL PRISONERS IN NORTHERN IRELAND--PRISON DRESS [WAS] ABANDONED HERE IN ARMAGH PRISON NEARLY A DECADE AGO. SUCH CHANGES WOULD BE WELCOMED BY PRISONERS OF ALL DENOMINATIONS. PLEASE SEND A REPRESENTATIVE TO TALK TO THE PRISONERS' SPOKESMEN, AS WAS DONE DURING THE LAST HUNGER-STRIKE, AND THE DANGER OF FURTHER DEATHS CAN BE REMOVED.

CARDINAL TOMÁS Ó FIAICH

Obviously she had given Atkins no power to act on his own. Just as obviously she had the power to finish this thing at a stroke, and ease the pressure that was claiming the lives of the hunger strikers and so many other lives besides. But her reply was full of cant, reiterating the tiresome line the NIO had been rehearsing during the past year and a half:

31614 CAPO EI
27582 CABOFF G

FROM: THE PRIME MINISTER, 10 DOWNING ST., LONDON.

TO: THE MOST REVEREND TOMAS O FIAICH, ARCHBISHOP OF ARMAGH.

THANK YOU FOR YOUR TELEGRAM OF 13 MAY ABOUT THE HUNGER STRIKE AT THE MAZE PRISON. I UNDERSTAND YOUR CONCERN. I FULLY SHARE IT.

THE GOVERNMENT HAVE REPEATEDLY MADE CLEAR HOW MUCH THEY REGRET THE LOSS OF LIFE THROUGH ALL FORMS OF VIOLENCE IN NORTHERN IRELAND. THE GOVERNMENT IS NOT THE INFLEXIBLE PARTY IN THIS ISSUE. THE PROVISIONAL IRA, AT WHOSE BEHEST THE HUNGER STRIKE IS TAKING PLACE, HAVE STATED AND RESTATED FROM THE BEGINNING THAT THEY WOULD CALL OFF THE STRIKE ONLY IF THE GOVERNMENT WERE TO CONCEDE ALL FIVE OF THEIR DEMANDS. WHAT THEY WANT IS NOT PRISON REFORMS, BUT A SPECIAL DIFFERENT STATUS FOR SOME PRISONERS. THIS THE GOVERNMENT CANNOT CONCEDE, SINCE IT WOULD ENCOURAGE FURTHER BLACKMAIL AND SUPPORT FOR TERRORISM. WE CANNOT TREAT PERSONS CONVICTED OF CRIMINAL OFFENCES AS PRISONERS OF WAR, WHICH IS WHAT THEY WANT.

IN CONTRAST, THE GOVERNMENT HAD DEMONSTRATED FLEXIBILITY IN A NUMBER OF WAYS. WE INTRODUCED IMPORTANT AND HUMANE CHANGES IN THE PRISON REGIME LAST YEAR. WE TOOK THE INITIATIVE TO DE-ESCALATE THE DIRTY PROTEST IN JANUARY, AND RESPONDED PROMPTLY TO THE ENDING OF THE DIRTY PROTEST IN MARCH, CUTTING THE RATE OF LOSS OF REMISSION BY HALF. WE ALLOWED THE THREE DUBLIN TDs, THE ECHR REPRESENTATIVES AND THE POPE'S REPRESENTATIVE TO VISIT THE MAZE IN THE HOPE THAT THEY COULD FIND SOME WAY TO PERSUADE MR. SANDS AND THE OTHER HUNGER STRIKERS TO CEASE THEIR ACTION. I HOPE THE REMAINING HUNGER STRIKERS WILL EVEN NOW RESPOND TO THE POPE'S MESSAGE.

YOU MAKE A NUMBER OF POINTS ABOUT THE PRISON POPULATION IN NORTHERN IRELAND. I AM VERY AWARE OF THEM, AS IS THE SECRETARY OF STATE FOR NORTHERN IRELAND. WE ARE COMMITTED TO MAINTAINING AN ENLIGHTENED AND HUMANITARIAN PRISON REGIME, AND I BELIEVE WE DO SO. WE ARE READY TO LISTEN TO REPRESENTATIONS FROM RESPONSIBLE QUARTERS--INCLUDING FOR EXAMPLE THE EUROPEAN COMMISSION ON HUMAN RIGHTS--ON ALL ASPECTS OF THE

ENVIRONMENT FOR ALL CONFORMING PRISONERS: BUT WE CANNOT YIELD
ON THE ISSUE OF POLITICAL JUSTIFICATION FOR MURDER AND VIOLENCE
AND OF PRISONER OF WAR STATUS FOR THOSE WHO COMMIT SUCH
CRIMES.

LIKE YOU, I AM ANXIOUS TO AVOID ALL FURTHER NEEDLESS DEATHS IN
NORTHERN IRELAND FROM WHATEVER PART OF THE COMMUNITY. YOU IN
PARTICULAR WILL I AM SURE APPRECIATE THE HEAVY LOAD MY
COLLEAGUES AND I BEAR IN DISCHARGING OUR RESPONSIBILITIES. BUT
THE SOLUTION DOES NOT LIE IN OUR HANDS. IT LIES WITH THE HUNGER
STRIKERS THEMSELVES, THEIR FAMILIES AND ADVISERS. MORE
DIRECTLY, IT LIES WITH THE LEADERS OF THE PROVISIONAL IRA, WHO
HAVE TAKEN A COLD-BLOODED DECISION THAT THE UNFORTUNATE MEN
NOW FASTING IN PRISON ARE OF MORE USE TO THEM DEAD THAN ALIVE.
THIS SEEMS TO ME THE MOST IMMORAL AND INFLEXIBLE DECISION
ANYONE COULD TAKE.

SINCE YOU RELEASED YOUR TELEGRAM TO THE PRESS, I AM SURE YOU
WILL NOT MIND MY PUBLISHING THIS REPLY.

NNNN

Then came Father Brian McCreesh with news of that sordid
business involving his dying brother Raymond and the prison
medical staff. The Cardinal had invited Father Brian to lunch,
and afterwards they went together to the oratory in the house
and prayed together, which Brian said consoled him a great deal.
That night the Cardinal went into seclusion for his annual
retreat.

Four days later Raymond McCreesh died in the prison
hospital, and the Cardinal issued the statement that would later
be used in the smear campaign against him. He wrote the statement out by hand, while on retreat, knowing something would
be needed and should be ready.

In editing the statement, he'd made a change that he afterwards felt he shouldn't have made. It was a paragraph on the
consideration that more than half a million Catholics were being denied their rights as free Irishmen in a British-ruled part
of Ireland, and that only when one understood this did one
understand the background to the troubles.

When he'd drafted the statement, he thought it too long, and took out a paragraph here and there; this, unfortunately, was one of the paragraphs he'd decided to delete.

As the hunger strike wore on he found himself under attack not only by the British media but by the Provos and the Republican movement generally. He could never understand why they spent time attacking him rather than concentrating their fire on Thatcher & Company. He had tried to do all he could; he was not in a position of real power.

At that stage he was often tempted to say to his Republican critics: "What the hell are you talking about? These poor lads in the prison would not have been heard of if I hadn't blown the whistle on the prison regime back in July 1978." Then hardly anyone knew what the prisoners were suffering, and the Republican movement was doing almost nothing to help them. He recalled the rather anemic statement Provisional Sinn Féin had issued at the time:

> The Archbishop's clear condemnation of the Northern Ireland Office's handling of the prison situation must be a clear pointer to all those who, up to now, have failed to make a clear stand on the question of political status · · ·

The blanket protesters, even after the dirt protest was well under way, had got little attention from Republicans outside. Until the hunger strikes they'd been treating the prisoners' protests as a troublesome distraction.

Now the IRA kept doing things that had the effect of lessening the public sympathy the dying men so desperately needed. The IRA and INLA should have stopped the violence and the killing, if only to let the deep emotion aroused by the men's suffering have its maximum effect.

On Thursday 21 May, the Cardinal looked out an upstairs window at the morning sky above the Protestant cathedral on St. Patrick's hill across the way. The sun was coming up, and a few birds stirred against the dawn. He had just got word that

341

Raymond McCreesh, a polite and decent lad, the brother of a priest of the diocese of Armagh, was dead.

The Cardinal put his head in his hands and wept.

Had he done all he could? It had not been enough. Surely he could have done more. But he was powerless, ultimately, to bring reason to bear on a situation in which a British government was so firmly resolved to maintain its show of principle. And now young McCreesh was dead, and a fourth man, Patsy O'Hara, was dying: and the legacy of the British in Ireland would continue through more and more violence. And inside and outside the prison more Irish men and women and children would be added to the long roll of the dead.

WHAT COULD HE SAY to this woman?

He stayed that night before the Oliver Plunkett commemoration, the night of 30 June 1981, the night before his meeting with Margaret Thatcher, at Cardinal Hume's residence at Westminster. Hume had done this much: he had told Humphrey Atkins at a meeting in London on 5 June that he was concerned about the prison problem, and that the Catholic hierarchy's antipathy towards violence was misunderstood. Dr. Robert Runcie, the Church of England primate and Archbishop of Canterbury, had asked that the Irish Cardinal stop in to see him while in London. Dr. Runcie had come to Ireland in early June, and had stayed at Armagh. He had said publicly that he'd been praying for the hunger strikers, which the Cardinal found gratifying, but which made some of the Protestant clergy in Ireland furious.

The only time the Cardinal could call on Archbishop Runcie was at breakfast time next morning. So he began his day on Wednesday by taxiing across Lambeth Bridge for a fraternal meal with the Archbishop of Canterbury. After that he came back across the Thames, to visit the convent at Tyburn near where St. Oliver Plunkett had been hanged. The tricentenary commemoration was to be held at Clapham in South London, because the parish priest there, who was devoted to the saint, had an Oliver Plunkett memorial church and parish hall in Clapham where he had organized the whole affair. At the commemoration the Cardinal gave the sermon at an open-air Mass, paying tribute to his twentieth predecessor in the see of Armagh:

> At first sight he seems a remote figure from a distant past, yet my grandfather with whom I played as a child was baptized by an old priest who in turn received the sacrament from another priest who had worked in the diocese with priests ordained by St. Oliver Plunkett . . .

The wounded head of this saintly and lovable Archbishop, he reminded the people, was still preserved in Ireland, at Drogheda. Oliver Plunkett had defied the English crown by providing a splendid band of priests who brought their people safely through the penal times. Golden priests, the saint had called them: "Golden priests with wooden chalices . . ."

After the ceremony there was a gathering, and then he and Bishop Lennon were driven back to Cardinal Hume's residence by a priest from Westminster Cathedral. After a half hour there they took a taxi over to Downing Street, asking the driver to come back in an hour and wait for them.

It was eight o'clock when they entered Number 10, and were ushered into a room off to the right. Their appointment with Margaret Thatcher was for 8:15. She had been to Buckingham palace for her weekly report to the Queen, they were told. Normally she went on a Monday, but she'd been in the Middle East, so she hadn't gone till this evening.

The Cardinal was determined to let Mrs. Thatcher know how he felt about her handling of the hunger strike, and had asked Bishop Lennon to take notes of the meeting.

She arrived at exactly a quarter past eight and ushered them upstairs to a very large sitting room at the top of the staircase—a room of perhaps twenty by forty feet. She offered them a drink. Bishop Lennon was not a drinker, so he had a mineral. She asked the Cardinal what he wanted, and he said he would like a little Irish. But there wasn't a drop of Irish whiskey to be had at Downing Street. So she asked him if he'd take Scotch, and he said he would. They began talking in generalities, she asking him how the ceremony had gone. Then the drinks were produced and they sat down, she at the top of the room, he and Bishop Lennon at her left, and proceeded to their business.

The Cardinal didn't expect to change her attitude, but here at least was an opportunity to let her know how Northern Irish Catholics felt about what was going on, and to make directly some of the points he'd made with Atkins, who was in the room, far down to the right of Thatcher. (Atkins would speak no more than three sentences the entire time; when he'd try to say something she'd chop him down.)

The Cardinal didn't think that he and Bishop Lennon were going to get her to turn a complete somersault and allow them, intermediaries, to make proposals and get the hunger strike ended. That might have been possible after one death or two. But now there were four, and he had no hope that she was going to come forward and announce any concessions now.

Yet there was that chance to fill in the background, if she'd listen, and to get her to see the Irish Catholic point of view.

She began, airy and shrill. She wanted to know what she was to *do*. Would anyone tell her *why* they were doing this? Why these people were doing this to *her*. She talked in a kind of preaching tone, declaiming—at times almost shouting. Were they trying to prove their *virility*? Why were they on hunger strike? She had asked *so* many people, and no one could tell her. That sort of thing.

Bishop Lennon was to take notes. He took about two lines and then put down his pen. So excited and incensed did he become that the rest of the evening he took no notes at all. She was into a kind of sing-song repetition, oblivious of other people. She didn't sound at all as though she wanted to be interrupted. But Bishop Lennon interrupted her. He began talking, very sensitively, about the feeling of the people in the North: about the young people, especially, and how they were alienated from authority by the hunger strike and the refusal of the government to make any concessions. She tried to interrupt, but Bishop Lennon went on. The NIO, he said, had refused to show any real flexibility at all, and kept issuing counterproductive statements. The British government's stubborn inaction was driving the young Irish of the North into the arms of the IRA.

The Bishop explained that he had a lot of nieces and nephews around Armagh, and in recent weeks he'd been up from Drogheda, where he served as the Cardinal's auxiliary bishop, and had spent a great deal of time talking to these young people in Armagh. He'd urged them to have nothing to do with violence, and they'd refused to listen to him. They'd said, well, violence seems to be the only way to deal with this situation, the only way of dealing with the British. Ultimately, the Bishop said, this meant that the Catholic Church and Catholic moderates were not going to be listened to.

Bishop Lennon gestured as he talked. He had an unusual way of emphasizing things he'd say: he put out his right hand, pushing forward two forefingers. When the Cardinal was telling the story of their meeting afterwards, some of the priests who knew Bishop Lennon asked whether the Bishop had given Mrs. Thatcher "the finger treatment." He had.

Margaret Thatcher started in after this, as though what the Bishop said hadn't registered. What she seemed to have had in mind was preaching a sermon. The conversation never came to scorchers, but it did get very sharp. She kept interrupting, and at times they interrupted her. They had to. She was in a mood, apparently, to give them a good dressing down, and seemed to expect that they would listen timidly, like Humphrey Atkins, and say, "Yes, Mrs. Thatcher," and "No, Mrs. Thatcher," and play dumb. It was a very large room, and she would get up from time to time and stride around.

At one stage she said that the Northern Ireland state was set up to save the Catholics from civil war—a strange sort of reworking of history. The Cardinal felt he just couldn't let her go any further.

After giving her a little lesson in Irish history, he told her, frankly, that he felt that there was only one possible way of settling the Irish question, and that that was a thirty-two county Ireland in some form. He said it wouldn't worry him overmuch whether it took the form of a confederation, a federation, or a unitary state. That was an internal affair among the Irish, and the precise arrangements wouldn't cause him any pain or sleeplessness one way or the other. It depended on what the people agreed to.

She wanted to interrupt, but he went on, hoping that in some part of her mind she might be listening. To talk about Northern Ireland, he said, was to talk about something very, very artificial. There was no basis at all for an entity called Northern Ireland.

The problem of nomenclature was the great proof of that. The British, after sixty years, could still not find an appropriate name for the place. Call it "Northern Ireland," and every Irishman laughs, because he knows that the most northerly part of Ireland is County Donegal. He pointed out to her that she'd used the term "southern Ireland" earlier, for a part of the country which included its most northerly county. In recent years the British had begun calling it "Ulster," or "The Province." But the reality was that the old province of Ulster was a nine-county entity, not a six-county slice of it.

Not only had they no name for it that made any sort of historical or geographic sense, he said, but they were talking about an area with no natural divisions to set it off from the rest of Ireland. What they called Northern Ireland in fact cut across the most sacred divisions in Ireland. The parish where he grew up was divided in two by the artifice of the border; the diocese of Armagh was cut in two by it. So was the diocese of Derry, and the diocese of Kilmore, and Clogher. Only two dioceses in the whole of the country lay entirely within what they called Northern Ireland: the diocese of Down and Connor, and the diocese of Dromore. Every other northern diocese straddled the border.

She didn't seem to be listening, but he went on, just in case. The whole idea of Northern Ireland was based on a lie from start to finish, he said. Northern Ireland, he said, was an area separated off from the rest of Ireland by no natural features at all. There was no mountain range dividing it from the rest of Ireland; no river, no ditch, even. There were places where the local people hardly knew where the border was. At one point in the Cardinal's own native area the border swerved along the side of a road. (British soldiers had been blown up driving along that road.)

The origin of this lie, he explained, lay in unionists selecting an area which would contain a sufficiently large majority of their own people to keep them in control for the foreseeable future—large enough to be viable, but not too large, because then it would have been dangerously near fifty per cent Catholic, on an island where Catholics are eighty per cent of the population. So if the state had been enlarged to include all of Ulster, it would have been touch and go; and if it were narrowed to include only the most heavily Protestant counties, Antrim and Down, then it would be so small as to be unviable as a political entity. The original lie had given rise to a range of falsehoods and false behaviour. Fermanagh, for example, with its Catholic majorities all through the years, would unfailingly return, because of the dishonesty of gerrymandering, two unionist representatives and one nationalist. Derry City, in the past three fifths Catholic (four-fifths now), had been manipulated so that it returned twelve Protestant and eight Catholic councillors.

She had to listen to all this. And when the Cardinal finished, and she had talked for awhile, Bishop Lennon would get back in. There was no meeting of minds at all, and no admission on her part that there was any case for the Irish Catholics in the North, nor any acknowledgment that the British were at all to blame for anything that had happened in Ireland. He wondered whether it might be true, what people said of her: that she was not only completely in sympathy with the unionist point of view but anti-Catholic as well?

It seemed clear from the evening that for her Ireland simply didn't count, and the hunger strike was just something passing that she wanted to be rid of. She seemed to be the sort of person, though, who enjoyed leading the British attack against people she thought of as subversive and terrorist. She didn't seem to realize that Irishmen and Irishwomen could have patriotic feelings, too.

At one point she asked how it was that the Irish must always be a problem. So many wars had been fought in the past between the British and the French, and the French and the Germans, and the British and the Germans, and now they were friends, and all together in the EEC. During the First World War the French and British, who had been enemies, became the best of friends. And the British and Germans who had slaughtered each other through two world wars were friendly now. Why should Ireland be the odd man out? Why can't the British and the Irish be friends, she wanted to know. How was it, when they couldn't get on with the Irish, that the British got on so well with the Germans?

"Because, Madam, if you want a simple answer," the Cardinal said, "you're no longer in occupation of the Ruhr." *

The session lasted till about five minutes to ten. She had been so infuriating that the Cardinal and Bishop Lennon were in a real fighting mood by that time. The Cardinal felt they could have gone on till midnight and no problem. But she said she was sorry, that there was a vote coming up in the House of Commons at ten o'clock and she had to be there.

Besides Atkins, she'd had a secretary in the room, busily taking notes during the meeting. As they were coming down the staircase, the Cardinal said to him, "You'll be very late getting home. I'm sorry we kept you so long."

"Well, I'll say this at any rate," the secretary answered. "It was never at any stage boring."

When they got into the waiting taxi, the Cardinal felt a sense of relief that they were finished with this haranguing and barging match. He turned to Bishop Lennon, and thinking of the Thatcher/Haughey statement after their December 1980 summit, said to the Bishop: "And where in the name of God is this "totality of relationships'?"

There was a story, one of the Cardinal's favourites, about St. Patrick and the people of Kerry.

In pre-Norman times in Ireland there had grown up a custom—strange to those used to the Roman system of geographically bounded dioceses—of distant churches aligned with one or other of the Irish saints who founded them. St. Patrick travelled widely in Ireland, and so the Great Church of Armagh, Patrick's church, had been linked in the pre-Norman

*Perhaps the Cardinal meant the Rhineland. It was the French who occupied the Ruhr, from 1923 to 1924.

era with Church foundations all over the island, among them several in County Limerick.

Now the people of County Kerry, adjacent to Limerick, acknowledged that St. Patrick never founded a church in Kerry. But they insisted that the Saint had given them his blessing. St. Patrick, they said, had climbed Ardpatrick, a high hill in Limerick, reached out, and with a waving motion of his hands, made the sign of the cross in the direction of the people of Kerry, saying "I bless you all, away from me!"

There were times when the Cardinal, who believed in brotherly love and ecumenism, would have liked to climb one of the tall steeples of his cathedral on its high hill in Armagh, face the neighbour island to the east and wave a sign of the cross in the direction of the English, saying, "I bless you all, away from here!"

LATER THAT WEEK the smear campaign, in which English Catholics like Lord Rawlinson, Auberon Waugh, Alberic Stacpoole—and Shirley Williams, the politician—had played so large a part, received its sharpest rebuttal in an editorial comment by Alban Weston OP in the June 1981 issue of the review *New Blackfriars*, published by the English Dominican order. After all that had gone on, the Cardinal was heartened to see an English Catholic priest saying:

> What is the difference, morally speaking, between deliberately putting your life in serious jeopardy by going on hunger-strike for a cause you passionately believe in and deliberately putting your life in serious jeopardy in order to save, perhaps even only temporarily, someone else's? What is the moral difference between the actions which led to their deaths, of Bobby Sands and Captain Oates,* or Raymond McCreesh and Maximilian Kolbe?**
> Is there a distinction?

*When food was running out during an Antarctic expedition, he left his share to his fellow explorers and walked off to die.
**Father Kolbe put himself forward as a replacement for a married father of children who had been selected to die by starvation at Auschwitz. He is now a canonized saint of the Catholic Church.

It was, of course, predictable that the British government, aided by most of the media, would with confidence and alacrity answer yes to that last question. Bobby Sands was literally hell-bent on suicide. Captain Oates is a hero to be admired by every English schoolboy.

What . . . has been alarming has been the anxious haste of certain English Catholics (Lord Rawlinson and Shirley Williams among them), to identify all English Catholics and indeed the whole Catholic Church with the view that Bobby Sands, Raymond McCreesh, Francis Hughes and Patsy O'Hara, by going on hunger-strike to achieve political prisoner status and dying in the process, have committed suicide. Their deaths, so this view goes, were their own choice and their own fault, and anyone who suggests that some of the blame lies with the British government or with Mrs. Thatcher's customary chilling ruthlessness and pigheaded inflexibility is either in a moral muddle or a crypto-supporter of the Provisional IRA. Thus Cardinal Ó Fiaich is branded as a provocative nationalist because he has dared to question the role of the British government in the affair and called for compromise and flexibility on both sides, and a priest—from "Eire" of course—in Berkshire is accused of wilfully misusing his priesthood because he held a Requiem Mass for Bobby Sands.

The editorial comment of this journal has never supported or condoned the methods of the Provisional IRA. On the contrary, neither has it supported or condoned the presence of the British in Ulster nor the methods used to maintain that presence and "beat the terrorists." We wonder, however, why certain English Catholics should rush to the support of the government, shouting "suicide" without pausing to reflect that perhaps they may be using "suicide" in an odd sense when they apply it to the hunger strikers. Normally we use it to describe someone who deliberately takes his or her own life either because they find living intolerably painful and dire, or to escape punishment for, or the consequences of, some action of theirs. We wonder too, why certain

English Catholics, in their anxiety to join the "we-tooism" of condemning the IRA, assert that the Catholic Church condemns all violence, when they must know that it does no such thing. The Catholic Church has never held or taught the pacifist position on violence.

Would it be harsh to suggest that it is because they share in a certain brand of English nationalism (of all people we are the most fair, tolerant, compassionate, just and incorrupt, especially our soldiers and police) that certain English Catholics hurry to join in the chorus of moral revulsion at the IRA while ignoring the barbarous behaviour of the English not only in Ireland but in Cyprus, Aden, Malaya and numerous other colonies where "terrorists had to be beaten"?

It has been said often enough by people like John Hume, and others certainly not sympathetic to the IRA, that British rule and the activities of the British Army in Ulster continue to be the most efficient recruiting sergeants for the IRA. The squalid pretence that the problems of Ulster flow from the flaring up of mysterious sectarian differences and not from the misery, anger and frustration produced by the sorry mess of fifty years of British rule, the whitewashing of the massacre of Bloody Sunday of January 1972, the arbitrariness and brutality concomitant on internment without trial, the hypocritical shunning of the Strasbourg report of 1976 which found Britain guilty of the crime of torture and inhuman treatment in Northern Ireland, the methods used in the interrogation centres like Castlereagh to extract "confessions" for the political Diplock trials, the killing of civilians by rubber and plastic bullets and speeding ferret-cars: all these and many more are equally if not more responsible for the deaths of the hunger strikers and all the violence and misery that has followed.

So long as those beams in the English eye remain, so long does the English condemnation of hunger strikers lack moral credibility, even when it is made by those "speaking as English Catholics." We have to pause and

351

reflect on the possibility that Cardinal Ó Fiaich and the other Northern Ireland bishops may be able to see more clearly, and certainly with more compassion, the complexities and the subtleties of the sorry problem.

Quite apart from its references to himself, the Cardinal thought the piece, and its weight, just right.

NOTE: *Basil Hume and his "Suicide" Notion*

WHERE HAD the English smear campaign got its inspiration? What Cardinal Ó Fiaich seems never to have adverted to—or perhaps deliberately avoided adverting to—was that the (surely unwitting) originator of this campaign, directed against him personally, was Cardinal Basil Hume, his English opposite number. Without question the vilification heaped on the Irish Cardinal by English Catholics and the English media was closely tied to Hume's outrageous assessment of the morality of the hunger strike, and his even more outrageous voicing of this assessment.

To observers it seemed that the Irish and English cardinals got on very well together. On several occasions Cardinal Ó Fiaich had been a guest at Hume's house at Westminster, and doubtless the English Cardinal would have an especially warm welcome whenever he might come to stay at Armagh.

The Irish Cardinal had probably read Basil Hume's books on spirituality and seen in Hume, as others did, a great spiritual quality, a quiet—and very English—saintliness.

Fratres in Unum was the Irish Cardinal's own motto. If any were brothers in unity, these two cardinals should have been. So it must have astonished and distressed Cardinal Ó Fiaich when Hume had turned moral theologian a month earlier—putting on a performance as idiosyncratic as it was exorbitant.

It all began with a visit to Derry by Cardinal Hume on Saturday 25 April. He came for an ordination: a seminarian in his diocese, a native of Derry, was to be ordained priest there. The

352

Irish Cardinal got John Ward, his driver, to take him to Derry that day. Clearly he was there to honour the English Cardinal's visit. Derry was a separate diocese, but was in the ecclesiastical province of Armagh, of which the Irish Cardinal was titular head.

The night before the ordination, Bishop Edward Daly of Derry threw a little dinner party for the English Cardinal. On the Thursday night there'd been a lot of rioting in Derry, so the dinner party was set up at a hotel west of the border, in Donegal. They'd no doubt had a pleasant night of it, but there'd been a lot of people there, and it appears that Cardinal Ó Fiaich was unable to have more than a few minutes' chat with Cardinal Hume. It seems that Hume gave him no inkling at all that he intended issuing a statement. Apparently he hadn't mentioned any statement to Bishop Daly, either, at whose residence the English Cardinal stayed overnight.

After the Saturday ordination, Cardinal Hume flew directly back to London, leaving from Aldergrove airport on Saturday evening. Then on Sunday, all unexpectedly, he published an open letter to Bishop Daly, in which he described hunger striking—meaning specifically the Irish hunger strike—as "a form of violence" which "cannot be condoned by the Church as being in accordance with God's will for man."

The Irish Cardinal must have been astonished at this strange deliverance. It flew completely in the face of Irish tradition, which ennobled the hunger strike as sacrifice. The classic case was Terence MacSwiney, Mayor of Cork, whose 73-day hunger strike to the death during the Irish War of Independence evoked for millions the death of Christ on Calvary.

Basil Hume's open letter certainly wasn't calculated to make things any easier for Tomás Ó Fiaich, who'd been walking his tightrope between impassioned appeals to the hunger strikers on the one hand and the British government on the other. And surely Basil Hume should have known that the conditions in the prison were execrable and that the men had been driven to use the hunger strike as a last resort. And didn't Hume see that the British government—despite all the nods and winks at the end of the first hunger strike—had done nothing but stonewall the men who suffered so horribly in that prison? And yet Cardinal Hume was suggesting that the Catholic Church regarded their hunger strike as immoral!

Then—and it must have been worse from Cardinal Ó Fiaich's point of view—on 30 April, when Bobby Sands was five days away from death, Basil Hume spoke at a press conference after a meeting of the English bishops at which the morality of the hunger strike was discussed. At the press conference Hume said that, while it might be difficult to pass judgment on the details of Bobby Sands' case, yet speaking personally "for myself alone," Hume felt that because Bobby Sands intended to die if necessary, his death would be suicide.

Hume was explicit: "There is no doubt that any hunger strike to death that includes within it the intention to die is suicide." The English Catholics, then, and the English papers, had it on record that their own Cardinal, talking about the hunger strike being "a form of violence,"* meant *suicide*, and that Basil Hume was accusing Bobby Sands *by name* of committing suicide!

Basil Hume's addressee, Bishop Daly, objected (mildly) to the English Cardinal's intervention. But the senate of priests of Armagh diocese sent a strong letter of protest. They pointed out what an embarrassment it was to the Irish Cardinal, who was caught up in the middle of all this, for an outsider like Cardinal Hume to have made a pronouncement of that kind. It seemed to them entirely arbitrary.

Had the shoe been on the other foot—had these things been happening in Hume's jurisdiction—Cardinal Ó Fiaich would surely never have intervened. Yet the Cardinal must have felt it would compound the embarrassment were he to speak out himself against Hume. Though he said nothing, he must have felt disappointed and unhappy at the time.

And now, a month later, Basil Hume's intervention was

*Herbert McCabe OP, the Dominican theologian, writing in the July/August issue of *New Blackfriars*, would mention no names but would say that in the entire argument "Perhaps the silliest comment of all was the suggestion that a hunger strike is 'an act of violence.'"

having its effect in this press campaign, with Catholics like Waugh and Hume's fellow Benedictine, Alberic Stacpoole, simply assuming the suicide notion as though it were Holy Writ.

Of the general run of editors of the English popular press, it could be said that their malice towards Ireland was exceeded only by their doglike ignorance of Irish concerns. But Basil Hume had had his effect. After Bobby Sands' death one newspaper spoke of Cardinal Ó Fiaich's "refusing to condemn" the death as suicide, as though the Irish Cardinal were fighting off the urge to proclaim a self-evident truth. Cardinal Hume, however innocently—one wonders, apart from the physical caricature, what the satirical magazine *Private Eye* means by calling him Cardinal Dopey—had slipped a potent poison into the English news stream.

Did Basil Hume actually get his notion about suicide, or the feeling that he must make a public issue of it, from the ex-paratrooper Stacpoole?

Certainly, apart from their both being English Benedictines, they shared an apparently fanatical loyalty to the English crown in its most imperialist definition. Hume would later show this by his rush to justify British aggression in the Falklands War—in a sad if hilarious outpouring reminiscent of the Salic Law theorizing of Shakespeare's gabbling, self-serving English bishops at the beginning of *Henry V*.

Although Cardinal Hume didn't show the contempt for the Irish cause revealed in Stacpoole's articles, he would later try to lecture relatives of the hunger strikers on the selflessness of British soldiers in Ireland!—another Stacpoole theme.

There was of course more at stake here than the question of who was responsible for the smear campaign against the Irish Cardinal. The question could be asked: After Thatcher what English leader was most reponsible *for the deaths of the hunger strikers*? Did not this woman get all the aid and comfort she needed from Basil Hume and the English Catholics who took their lead from him?

Chapter 8

JOE McDONNELL

Then a hunger strike we did commence
For the dignity of man,
But it seemed to me that no one gave a damn.
But now I am a saddened man;
I've watched my comrades die:
If only people cared, or wondered why.
And you dare to call me a terrorist
While you look down your guns—
When I think of all the deeds that you have done!
You have plundered many nations,
Divided many lands;
You have terrorized our people;
You ruled with an iron hand.
And you brought this reign of terror
To my land . . .

The Wolfe Tones

THE LAST TIME Joe McDonnell's sister Eilish Reilly saw Liz O'Hara was at Patsy's funeral—a few days after they'd locked themselves into the poster-covered caravan parked outside Leinster House. They'd started to arrange themselves for a long wait, trying to figure out how they'd manage with no water and no food—not that they were interested in eating anyway. And what, they wondered, would they use for toilets? But then the gardai came and towed them away to a police station.

Liz never thought Patsy was going to have to die. She was sure she'd find some solution. And Eilish had felt the same way about her brother Joe McDonnell. She still did. How could you say to yourself: he's going to die, there's nothing I can do? Instead, you kept doing everything you could.

Eilish was there with Liz next listening to Haughey and his

Attorney General, Anthony Hederman. Eilish felt that what Haughey wanted Liz to do was to go to the prison and tell her brother to come off hunger strike. Then, once he was off, Haughey would be able to do things. He'd already told her that before. But then he'd said to Liz, "Your brother is not going to die." It seemed to Eilish that Haughey might have a hot line to Thatcher or one of her closest aides. As he was talking Eilish thought: we aren't begging for much. There are jails where prisoners simply wear their own clothes, where they can get educational courses, where they can mix freely with one another.

In fact before the troubles the Northern Ireland jails—now overcrowded—were the emptiest in the world. Not one of these boys would have seen the inside of a jail had it not been for the troubles. Even Eilish's own husband, Thomas Reilly, had been interned in Long Kesh for two years. He was released the day internment was ended: 5 September 1975. It was a year later that her brother Joe was arrested—on 14 October—and then her youngest brother Frankie, in December. Frankie was in Long Kesh, in H-6, on the blanket protest. He'd been given five years for membership in the IRA.

Liz left Dublin, and Eilish, there on her own, got the word that Raymond McCreesh had died at night, and Patsy in the morning.

That was towards the end of May.

Now it was July—eight and a half weeks since Joe had gone on hunger strike, and still nothing was resolved.

Meanwhile the families had been out all over the place. And what it seemed to Eilish that they were doing more than anything else was begging, actually begging, for the lives of their brothers, sons, husbands.

Goretti, Joe's wife, had been busy campaigning for him. He had been the prisoner candidate in the Dáil elections for the Sligo/Leitrim constituency. She'd address crowds by introducing herself as "the very, very proud wife of Joe McDonnell." And then she'd go on: "And these are our two children— Bernadette, aged ten, and Joseph, aged nine—and we're here begging for you, the people, to give us your number one vote . . . You could end this hunger strike. So I'm begging you, give us your support! . . . Joe McDonnell, lying up in the H-Blocks, means nothing to anyone; but if he is Joe McDonnell TD, Maggie Thatcher and Charles Haughey will have to stand up and take heed . . ."

Their daughter Bernadette had gone off to the United States, pleading her father's case there. Eilish's sister Maura had also gone to America. And Alice McElwee, Liz O'Hara, Seán Sands and Malachy McCreesh . . .

Eilish was the eldest at 38; she and Tommy had five children—two boys and then three girls. Then came Robert, 36, married with two children; Hugh, 34, married with three children; Patsy, 32, married with two children—and living in Canada since 1969. Then Joseph—right in the middle—and after him were four more (the youngest, Bernadette, had died at three and a half); Maura, 28, and single; Paul, 26, married with two children; and Frankie, 24.

Joseph had been sentenced for co-possession of a gun and taken to Long Kesh. They didn't see him—he wouldn't take a visit. Joe wrote a smuggled letter to Eilish saying it was going to be a long, hard struggle—he didn't know when he'd see her again. But when he did see her, he said, he'd be wearing his own clothes and not "the monkey garb."

Their mother was afraid she'd never see either of her sons. The family asked Frankie to take visits for their mother's sake. So Frankie did.

Eilish had never seen Joe depressed. He was always very jolly. He liked his work—upholstering. Joe had given them their living room suite. Joe was the sort of man who was always trying to make someone else happy. If he saw Eilish down about something, he'd try to get her to see it from another angle, to look at it differently. Or he'd say, "Ah, you'll get over it." He himself always seemed to be on top. When her husband Tommy was interned Joe would come and take her children for outings along with his own, especially during the two summers.

What puzzled Eilish now was that there'd been plenty of time for those in power to do something. There'd been this long lull. But it seemed to her it had been a time of drift. The first weekend in July was gone. Monday was here again; Joe was on his fifty-ninth day. *Only now* , when things were desperate for Joe, was the Irish Commission for Justice and Peace effort in full swing. But were they making progress? Or just making news?

A month before, on 3 June, the Commission had gone public, putting forward a three-part proposal for a solution based on improved prison conditions in areas of clothing, work and association. There had been much to-ing and fro-ing since then. Members of the five-man Commission met the leaders of the three main Irish political parties. They met Michael Alison, the Northern Ireland prisons minister, and eventually the prisoners themselves. When the ICJP went to meet Alison for the second time, on 23 June at Stormont Castle, he told them there was now no problem with the prisoners getting their own clothes.

The Commission, aware of the deterioration in Joe's condition, had finally shifted their negotiations into high gear in an effort to save his life. On Friday, 26 June, they met with Alison a third time, at Hillsborough Castle. Then on Tuesday 30 June, Humphrey Atkins, the Northern Ireland Secretary of State, issued a six-page statement talking about scope for improvements in the prison, but insisting the hunger strike must stop first. The ICJP requested a meeting with Atkins, while the prisoners dismissed his statement as "arrogant and callous." Garret FitzGerald, the new Taoiseach, put the Irish government's plane at the Commission's disposal, so that, should they be able to advance the date of a meeting scheduled for 2 July in Belfast, they could fly to see Atkins in London.

But Atkins never brought the meeting forward. He was busy fiddling with his constitutional conference. This British appointee was not answerable to Irish demands.

Only last Friday Garret FitzGerald had met members of the families and promised them success. He told several of them that their brothers and sons would not die. Up in Hillsborough Castle, the ICJP was meeting with Alison and other NIO officials. In a well-advertised gesture, FitzGerald ordered a fleet of Mercedes to stand ready to take the relatives to Long Kesh to persuade the prisoners to accept the terms of the supposedly imminent settlement. The media conveyed the idea of car engines turning over. The relatives gathered at two-thirty in the afternoon.

Things seemed to be moving.

But the hours dragged by and FitzGerald had to cancel a meeting with the British Ambassador to Ireland, Leonard Figg, as they continued waiting for word from Hillsborough. Meanwhile, the ICJP meeting with Alison went on without so much as a tea break till 10:30 p.m., when it adjourned for the night. Afterwards the Commission members spoke very hopefully to the press.

But FitzGerald's fleet of waiting Mercedes had to be put away for the night.

On Saturday morning 4 July, the Commission met again with Alison, and he did a complete about-face on the clothing issue. In the afternoon of the same day, the prisoners released a 21,000 word statement through the H-Blocks Information centre in Belfast. It spelled out in detail what they were looking for and was widely described as "conciliatory" in tone. An extension of the five demands to all prisoners in all the Northern prisons would be welcome, the statement said. They made no mention of political status. Later that day the ICJP Commission members went to the prison hospital to personally meet with the hunger strikers for the first time. Ominously, the NIO denied a request to have Bic McFarlane, the prisoners' OC, present at the meeting. The Commission members talked to the hunger strikers for nearly two hours that evening. Only later, after he had been briefed by the ICJP, was McFarlane allowed to meet with the prisoners. Then on Sunday, 5 July, there was another meeting between McFarlane and three members of the Commission.

A TALL, SLENDER, POISED, well dressed young woman wearing a heavy raincoat and flat shoes was among the demonstrators gathering on O'Connell Bridge in the centre of the city of Dublin. It was Monday, 6 July, just after five o'clock. It was raining, windy and cold. As she walked up and down, she had difficulty with her placard because of the gusts blowing up from the River Liffey. Finally, she drew it down and held it in front of her against the wind.

Her name was Jean O'Brien, and she'd just finished her day's work in the office of a computer firm.

O'Connell Bridge was jammed with traffic edging its way over the span in the rain—cars, motorbikes, vans and heavy lorries. There were streams of cyclists peddling their way home: well dressed office workers, resentment on the faces of some of them, but proud of their white collars; students finished with their university classes; men in overalls with parcels lashed to the frames of their bicycles. The street was teeming with pedestrians. A couple of nuns walked by, their veils whipping in the wind, on the way to the bus. Itinerant children pursued the passersby, begging for coins.

Traffic feeding in a southerly direction over the bridge poured into D'Olier Street, past the Dublin Gas Company, forking off to the left in the direction of Ringsend or winding round the corner into the Trinity College bottleneck. On the right was the Bank of Ireland, its half-sandblasted splendour hidden by scaffolding. This was the building which in the seventeenth century housed Grattan's Irish parliament. In those days Dublin was the second city of a burgeoning British empire and, some said, the most beautiful city in Europe.

Later on, Jean would board a bus going in this direction. It would take her out to the sedate in-city suburb of Dartry— where she'd lived all twenty-nine years of her life in a quiet cul-de-sac of brick houses and well kept gardens.

She swung around and walked back alongside the northbound traffic, which moved past the statue of The Liberator, Daniel O'Connell, on its heavy monument base. It overlooked the Liffey from the bottom of O'Connell Street—technically the broadest thoroughfare in Europe. Traffic, slow tonight because of the rain, moved on past the British Home Stores, a blatant reminder of Ireland's status as an economic province of Britain, then past the huge GPO—the General Post Office, centre of the Easter 1916 Rising; eight hundred revolutionaries had seized and oc-cupied the building, in front of which Padraig Pearse had pro-

362

claimed a provisional government of the Republic in the name of the Irish people.

Jean was one of the H-Blocks supporters, still trying to stir Irish public concern for the hunger strikers. Under the big pillars in front of the GPO, other supporters could be found walking up and down with their placards and posters as the hurrying crowds moved past them. Across the way was Clery's Department Store. In the centre, up opposite Henry Street, a stone footpath covered the former site of Nelson's Pillar. The statue of the British Lord Nelson, victor at Trafalgar, had been blown up in 1966 by IRA men anxious to commemorate in a special way the fiftieth anniversary of the Easter Rising. Nelson's chipped head lay gathering dust on the floor of the civic museum, blocks away on the other side of the Liffey.

At the top of O'Connell Street, beyond the once posh Gresham Hotel, stood the monument to Charles Stuart Parnell, the Protestant landlord from Wicklow responsible for the passing of the Land Act of 1881—which loosened the legal strictures against Irish Catholics owning Irish land. Parnell was responsible, too, for the widening of the voting franchise. Were it not for his affair with Kitty O'Shea and the Catholic clergy's reaction to it, he might have secured home rule for Ireland well before the turn of the century, radically changing the course of Irish history.

The GPO was the centre of the demonstrators' activities. They used a desk inside for information and messages, and were allowed to leave their stuff there—black flags, placards and posters of the men on hunger strike. The photo-posters of the men still on hunger strike were different from those of the men who had died. Those who had died had their photographs outlined in black. The placards said things like: Break THATCHER! Political Status NOW! Don't Let Them DIE!

There were pickets on different bridges and in different areas of the city that had H-Blocks groups of their own. The O'Connell Bridge picket was attended by people who didn't belong to a local H-Blocks group, or who worked in town—like Jean. It was the nearest post she could reach at the right time.

Today, Joe McDonnell, a Belfast IRA man, was on his fifty-ninth day of hunger strike, and on the verge of death. Last night,

363

Sunday, Joe had been too weak to attend a ten o'clock meeting between the hunger striking prisoners and a five-member committee of the Irish Commission for Justice and Peace. The ICJP was an agency of the Catholic bishops which had been involved spasmodically for a period of two and a half months, and intensively for the past ten days, in an effort to resolve the hunger strike.

The whole of the long, wet, cold, windy month of June had come and gone. The weather itself seemed a symbol of the pall that hung over the land: a dispiriting sense of being overwhelmed by external forces—which like fog obscured the real issues and like driving wind impeded real progress.

Today, as Jean walked back and forth across the bridge, clutching the poster with its big, happy face of Joe McDonnell, he of the plump cheeks and self-assured grin, she remembered reading how his wife, Goretti, had nearly wept when she visited her husband in the prison hospital and saw his emaciated condition as he was putting on his dressing gown.

To Jean, Joe McDonnell was an unusual man to be in this position. Easily the oldest of the hunger strikers, he was a married man from Belfast with two children. As a boon companion, a strong and reliable operator closely associated with Kieran Doherty—one of the great IRA leaders—Joe McDonnell came across to Jean as a debonair fellow, a jokey type, a man who probably liked his pint. He was reportedly what the Irish call "a bit of a lad," mad for the girls; and he'd met and married one of the prettiest in West Belfast.

He and Goretti had both been at the Lenadoon Estate confrontation in the summer of 1972, when the British Army tried to force Catholics out of homes they'd been allocated by the housing authority. But they'd managed to make a home—Jean understood that Goretti had made it quite a charming and perfect home—in Lenadoon, a pleasant hilly area of West Belfast. Now Goretti was out day and night canvassing support for him. Sometimes his two children were out as well. His daughter Bernadette had gone to America and appeared on television in an effort to gain support. Throughout her ordeal, Goretti McDonnell had maintained an admirable dignity. She attracted attention and sympathy out there on the hustings, her calm blonde beauty making its own appeal as she begged help for her husband.

Before his capture, Joe McDonnell, a veteran Provo, had been trying to help Bobby Sands—a novice at the military side of things—to activate a new IRA unit in Dunmurry. Joe had been picked up, along with Bobby and others, after the Balmoral Furniture company had been firebombed in October 1976. No one was injured, but there was a handgun in the car and four of them got fourteen years each for the joint possession of that one gun. He'd gone to prison at age twenty-six, his life with Goretti and his children over.

Now at thirty he was dying on hunger strike. A solicitor, not of the violent Republican faith, had seen Joe in court and been moved by his tenderness towards his little children, Bernadette and young Joseph. Bernadette had been five then and Joseph four. Now they were ten and nine, and knew their father was dying in Long Kesh prison hospital.

There were stories about how much Joe loved his youngest sister, Bernadette. She had a kidney disease, and everyone in the family knew she was going to die. He spent all his time looking after her—every spare minute he had. He'd bring her around with him everywhere. He'd even play marbles carrying his sister on his back.

Joe was evidently a man with a keen sense of humour, always ready to laugh. He could easily see the funny side of things, and could make everyone else laugh too.

Once in 1980 during a wing shift, Joe's cellmate, who hadn't been given a towel when they were being passed out, tried to leave the cell in a blanket. They told him he'd have to go naked. The cellmate balked and refused. Joe was already in the new cell, while his cellmate was struggling noisily up the corridor.

"Up the rebels!" Joe called out, and began giving a running commentary on his progress: "Here he comes, now, folks . . ." *

*A year or so later, in Dublin, Tony O'Hara gave Jean his impressions of Joe, who'd been in a nearby cell on Tony's wing.

With all the degradation, it was humour that gave the prisoners

Father Brian McCreesh was reported to have said that he thought Joe McDonnell must have been the bravest of all of them, because he had replaced Bobby Sands on hunger strike—just after Bobby had died. And of all the relatives, Jean understood, Father Brian felt most sympathy for Joe's wife, Goretti. Jean wondered whether being a wife was closer, though, than being a mother—especially in the North.

THE WHOLE POINT of the ICJP involvement was to save Joe's life.

Until now, Jean had been buying the whole media commotion, the journalists' line that something definite was going to happen, that the ICJP was going to turn the trick. At this stage, as was remarked in the press, the ICJP represented not only the bishops who had set it up, but also the Irish government. Surely the British would have to listen to a voice representing such powerful Irish interests.

Jean knew she should have known better. She knew that journalists were in constant contact with the Commission, with the Irish government, and with the NIO and RUC, their principal sources of information. But they had no contact with either Margaret Thatcher or the men in prison. They seemed to blithely ignore the fact that the prisoners had insisted, weeks before,

---

the life that took them out of themselves. The buildup of tension before the wing shifts was intense. All the anger and bitterness and frustration welled up in them as they'd listen to the yelling of the screws and the shouting of the men being taken from their cells and beaten along to the new cells. Yet despite their helplessness, when they got to the new wing and heard the loud gusty singing of "Say Hello to the Provos"—the refrain punctuated by four rhythmic bashes against the doors—it put them in great heart. Joe McDonnell was often at the centre of these spirited sessions.

One night Tony himself decided to sing some songs—a personal concert that lasted a couple of hours. Tony's voice was good, but not the best. When he was finished Joe called across the corridor.

"That was great! Really great. Oh, uh—Tony: next time, uh, don't call us. We'll call you!"

that the ICJP proposals were so diluted as to be an unacceptable basis for a solution.

Journalists were limited, as they always had been, by the requirements of hackery: the demand that they chase after the latest official movement or announcement or bubble of publicity. Sometimes they would do think-pieces, but even these were dictated by the vagaries of the ongoing situation. Almost never would they take time to look at the key issue: How could the Irish get the British *off the backs of the Irish people*?

The prisoners were preeminently occupied with that issue.

After Patsy O'Hara died, there'd been a long breathing space, with the focus taken off the hunger strike. Take the pressure off and give the politicians a chance, had been the cry during April and early May. There had been less pressure. The hunger strikers' own schedule meant that the pressure had, in fact, been taken off—for a period of nearly six weeks. Yet nothing seemed to happen until this last week or so—when Joe McDonnell was at death's door. Jean wondered why the politicians and the Commission, who'd had plenty of time to work something out since the first four coffins came out of Long Kesh, had not delivered a positive result before Joe McDonnell's life came into such jeopardy.

Jean had heard different stories. By some accounts the bishops' ICJP was a thin enough reed on which to lean.*

*The Dublin bishop, Dermot O'Mahony, who was both Chancellor of the Dublin Archdiocese and chairman of the ICJP, showed himself, in remarks made some time afterwards, to have peculiar views indeed for a man supposed to be leading a mediation team on the prisoners' behalf:

> All along we were against granting political status to the IRA prisoners. To grant political status would help the IRA, and we couldn't do that. What we were looking for was a compromise.
>
> The IRA would have as their goal not only getting the British Army out of Ireland, but undermining the democratic process in the South of Ireland . . .
>
> One can't forget the crimes most of those in prison are guilty of, even though they were tried in special courts: attempted murder, bombing, all kinds of violence . . .

367

The Irish bishops had in fact been working the other side of the street. In June they delivered a statement in which they vividly emphasized the crimes committed by Republicans, and spoke of *the hunger strikers themselves as performing evil actions by persisting in their hunger strike*, and creating as a result an "appalling mass of evil."

> We . . . implore the hunger strikers and those who direct them, to reflect deeply on the evil of their actions and their consequences. The contempt for human life, the incitement to revenge, the exploitation of the hunger strikes to further a campaign of murder, the intimidation of the innocent, the initiation of children into violence, all this constitutes an appalling mass of evil.

The bishops hurriedly passed over the reasons for the existence of the IRA and made no mention of the violent presence of the heavily armed forces of the British crown.

Bishop O'Mahony or Bishop Cathal Daly would have had a lot to do, Jean was told, with that line of moralizing. Jean couldn't see a man like Cardinal O Fiaich standing over an assertion like that—*that the hunger strike itself was morally evil.*

The bishops did not address the larger questions of justice, either, or the question of freedom. If the hunger strikers stopped tomorrow, and if the IRA died away, the nationalist people of Northern Ireland would be back at Square One—back where they were in 1969 and 1972: living under British rule, with all the injustice that followed from this. It didn't matter whether Northern Ireland was ruled by a British propped-up Unionist government or by direct British rule, except that direct rule seemed to be far more violent.

Suppose the Provos died off or suddenly went to sleep, then what would be done? She was certain nothing would be done. There had been no Provos in 1969 when the people of Ireland watched the news unfold: the civil rights marchers being beaten back, RUC men in a drunken night-time assault against Catholic homes; the eight thousand Catholic people fleeing over the border after the RUC and B-Specials had gone in and burned out Catholic homes by the hundreds.

The argument came back to the ordinary people on the streets. There would always be the Irish nationalists on the ground in Northern Ireland, who were not of the IRA, but who still suffered the brunt of an unnatural, unjust and brutal system set up to suppress them.

Jean found it obnoxious, the bishops talking about the prisoners' obligation to "reflect deeply on the evil of their actions" while never offering any plan or programme for the relief of the nationalist population in the North who were not in the IRA, but who objected to the despicable treatment they received, and to a foreign army being brought into their streets to trample them down.

What the bishops were saying was in effect: "We want peace from you, and when we get it we will ignore you as we did before, because when you are peaceable we won't have to bother about you." Meanwhile, the British loved it when the bishops avoided all speech or action for fear that it might be construed as support for the IRA. Humphrey Atkins welcomed their June statement as being "an immense help."

Ireland, Jean often thought, was a nation that had been founded on violence and rebellion, and was run by men who kept saying that violence and rebellion didn't work. Historically, as these men should have been aware, the violence was the only thing that had worked. And the only time people in power reacted to what was happening in the North was when the level of violence increased. Then the world, and the bishops, took notice. It was perhaps a Western trait—it was certainly an Irish one—to feel sorry for the underdog when the underdog was beaten down, but the minute the underdog started barking back, to turn the whip to him. In America there was great sympathy for black people when they were very polite, petitioning mildly for civil rights. But nothing was *done*. Once they started making demands in more definite terms, the sympathy evaporated. And yet it was their aggressively stated demands that won them their civil rights. Western governments seemed to react to injustice only when confronted with violence or aggression.

The bishops' condemnation of the hunger strikers was so virulent that the *Sunday Times* could headline its article on their statement, IRISH CATHOLIC BISHOPS CONDEMN MAZE FAST AS EVIL.

But as in the Pope's statement at Drogheda, which was supposed to have been written by that "moderate" Irish bishop, Cathal Daly, the bishops were very vague about the political meaning of British responsibility. There was nothing virulent in what the bishops, their toes turned in, had to say to the British. They laid no burden of guilt at the doorstep of the British government. Instead, like children faintly breathing against a windowpane, they timidly offered the hint of an appeal for British government "openness" to the ICJP's ideas on clothing, association and work.

Gerry Adams of Provisional Sinn Féin remarked afterwards that the bishops' statement had "failed to mention the presence of a British government and military forces as being in any way instrumental or responsible for the situation here" and that the bishops had failed to examine the moral damage done by the "British-imposed partition of our country."

In Jean's reading of history, the Catholic Church had almost always inveighed against popular violence that threatened the status quo. Rarely had it made statements against the violence of those in power. In this case, in Jean's view, the violence of the weaker side was actually a *lesser* violence, because the IRA men were not in government. Violence emanating from a government was always a worse violence, she felt, because a government was obliged to show responsibility on the moral as well as the physical level. The Church could say terrorists were terrorists, but what did they say when a government was being purposefully violent, when it was doing the terrorizing? The British Army was allowed to murder children like Julie Livingstone and Carol-Ann Kelly with plastic bullets and get away with it. The bishops' voices were muted. There was no outcry: "You are murdering our children in the streets!" They were terrified lest any word of theirs seem to give some solace or comfort to the IRA.

And yet . . . At the moment the Irish bishops' Commission for Justice and Peace was the only game going. Jean, walking back and forth across the bridge and thinking about this, suddenly realized that all that was happening for certain was that the days were passing, and that Joe McDonnell's time was running out.

Or was the breakthrough that the journalists kept predicting really imminent?

Jean had joined the picket demonstrations right after Bobby Sands had gone on hunger strike in early March. She hadn't expected the hunger strike to go on for five months. She thought that it would have the effect of a short, sharp shock, and that if she and the other demonstrators put their whole hearts into it, as the men in prison were doing, then it would quickly be resolved. All through these months Jean had been marching, handing out leaflets, picketing on O'Connell Bridge, at the GPO, or at Leinster House. Every night there was a picket somewhere. Sometimes there was a picket up at the British embassy in Ballsbridge, and sometimes two or three pickets on the same evening.

Jean had come to feel a great tiredness and great disappointment about it all. She was continually upset. She couldn't talk to people at work about what she was doing and they wouldn't talk to her. She began to dislike them, all the people who didn't care about the hunger strikers.

But if the people at the firm she worked for were reacting badly, Jean was sure she was reacting badly to them. She got to the stage where she couldn't imagine how Irish people could digest their dinner while this was going on. In late April, when Bobby Sands was on the fifty-fifth day of his fast, Jean's sister had arranged a women's outing, all of them going off together for a meal. Jean was on a picket that evening. She was quite looking forward to the outing as a bit of light, non-political relief. But when the meal was served, she just couldn't eat it. The food wouldn't go down. The conversation seemed frivolous. She was incapable of dining out while Bobby Sands was dying.

All along she'd known that Bobby was a marked man. All along, after the first week or so, she'd known that he would die.

Jean had never thought of the first hunger strike as a death fast. She knew that the men hadn't affected the British government with their blanket and dirt protest, and that they had become desperate. But she didn't believe that the seven men were going to go through with it. She thought that they were only threatening, and that it was like the hunger strikes in the Curragh, and the Joy—Mountjoy prison in Dublin—which were really forms of demonstration.

Then the first hunger strike wound past the month mark, and it became clear that the men were very determined. Seán McKenna went blind—the young fellow who looked a bit like the Beatle, Paul McCartney, with dark eyes and boyish face and a shock of dark hair—and it began to dawn on Jean that he might actually die. She was horrified. She wondered how many people knew that his father was one of the fourteen "Guinea Pigs" tortured by the British in the early days of internment, and had died at the age of forty-two, just a couple of years after his release? The people who didn't care: if that had been done to their father, or to their brother or sister, how would they have reacted?

Then in December, when the British made conciliatory noises and the other men came off the strike to save Seán McKenna's life, most of the H-Blocks supporters thought, like Jean, that the problem had been solved. But as January and February dragged on, and nothing happened, Bobby Sands, who was the prisoners' OC at the time, announced he was leading a new hunger strike. Jean knew that Bobby would have to die. She supposed that he knew, too. A man couldn't just push the British government around like that. And then he had the audacity to humiliate them by getting elected to their parliament. There was no way Britain would let an Irishman get away with that. So when Bobby died, it didn't come as a shock. Jean had already imagined the black border around that happy, smiling face.

But when Francis Hughes died Jean felt angry. The British had had their pound of flesh, yet they wanted more! They let the Irish soldier die, the man so admired by Republicans, respected as a military man who fought the British hard and clean, wearing his uniform with the word "Ireland" blazoned on his sleeve. Then Raymond McCreesh died, very much a gentle sort of revolutionary. Jean had gone to his funeral and had been touched by the hospitality she received from the people at Camlough. Then came Patsy O'Hara, with his striking face on the posters. She thought he looked like a pirate—tall and swashbuckling, a man with a great and gleeful presence. He died, too. By the end of May there were four posters outlined in black and by then there were already four new men on the death fast, replacing the four who had died: Joe McDonnell for Bobby Sands; Martin Hurson for Francis Hughes; Kieran Doherty for Raymond McCreesh; and Kevin Lynch for Patsy O'Hara.

And where had the ICJP been at the end of May? Now June had come and gone and Joe McDonnell was sinking towards death.

Jean was so exhausted when she got on the bus after picketing that she would sometimes cry. Picketing took an enormous amount of energy. They'd be out on the bridge, closing off the streets every night. The police had obviously been told to give them a free rein. At that stage they were getting away with all sorts of things. People were going in and taking over offices, the British Airways office for one. At Dublin airport they took over a plane for a few minutes. On another occasion they tried to get into the British embassy and take the flag down.

In the beginning, about the time Bobby Sands was dying, the picket was manned mainly by students. In late May the students went away for their summer holidays and it was left to the local people from action groups or political parties, and the few ordinary Dubliners like herself, to maintain the pickets. In the April and May days, when their protest was at its height, they'd blocked the road every night on both sides of the bridge, stopping the flow of traffic for half an hour at the busiest time. There were plenty of demonstrators in those days. The police were very civil; they'd come over and ask them how long they intended to picket, and that was all. There was no problem at that stage, because the police had their softly-softly policy.

O'Connell Bridge was a marvellous place to catch the crowds. Thousands would flock past. Every day somebody was out there photographing the demonstrators—tourists, journalists from various countries. Jean even found an element of fun it it. Then on the way home, she'd think about the man whose face was on her poster. She'd think about his family and his mother, and it would hit her that there was no fun in any of this. She'd feel shame. How easy for people like her who lived in Dublin to just go home and ignore the consequences! But it wasn't possible for somebody living in the ghettos of the North to ignore the consequences. The hunger strike was a terrible blow to the Catholics up there. Jean remembered a Northern man who said that in those days his sister kept unaccountably bursting into tears because of the dying hunger strikers. He said there were many like that.

And now things weren't so friendly at the bridge anymore. The gardai had new orders from above: quit containing the demonstrators and start moving them. She thought that the police idea at first might have been to let the demonstrators burn themselves out. But because the hunger strike went on so long, longer than anyone had expected, all of them—the Irish, their government (a new one now), the gardai and the demonstrators themselves—had to rethink their approach. The British Home Stores started boarding up their windows each night, and all day there'd be a long line of gardai outside the BHS building, protecting it. This was a new thing.

The picket each evening lasted an hour and a half. Then there might be a meeting. Every Tuesday there was a meeting in the National H-Blocks office in Mountjoy Square. There were meetings at Trinity College, with speakers like Seán MacBride and Bernadette McAliskey. On Saturdays there were marches to Leinster House or the British embassy, and after the march was over they'd go back to the GPO and hand out leaflets again.

Jean bought the three Dublin papers each morning, and read every word even remotely connected with the hunger strike. She'd catch the radio news at one on her lunch break and try

374

to get home to see the news on TV in the evening. There was the nine o'clock news on RTE and BBC. Usually, even when she was late, she could catch the ten o'clock news on UTV. She'd watch "Newsnight" on BBC 2. She'd listen every night to "Today in Parliament" on BBC Radio 4, hoping to hear news of the issue being brought up in the House of Commons. All her free time was spent reading, listening to the radio or watching television for news about the hunger strike.

It was difficult for Jean to talk to her friends. After months of involvement Jean realized that she'd become touchy and sensitive—even, in a way, paranoid. She found she couldn't talk easily anymore to friends who weren't involved. Whenever she'd bring up the topic of the hunger strike—her all-consuming interest—friends would shy away. She'd open her mouth and they'd more or less shut her off. It was a bit unfair. Her friends had always known her as an apolitical sort of person. Why didn't they bother questioning *why* she'd become so politically sensitive? Instead there'd be whispers. "Oh, don't talk to Jean," they'd say. "She's involved with the H-Blocks campaign. She's one of *them*."

Jean felt that their attitude was building a wall around her. Here was something that touched her very deeply and they didn't want to know about it. Had she been feeding them a lot of propaganda, their avoiding her would have made sense. But she hadn't been; she was still only learning and reading about the issues, and experimenting with her own responses. She would have liked to share her reactions with people who weren't involved, but these people didn't want to discuss the situation at all. Occasionally one of them would say something really stupid, like "You're in bad humour," and when she'd begin telling them why, they didn't want to know why. She realized that all they wanted to hear was that she had a headache or something: something they could empathize with. Well, if she was in bad humour, she was bloody well going to keep on being in bad humour until this hunger strike ended!

Jean was out on the picket line one evening in June and it started lashing rain. That summer it seemed to rain every evening at five o'clock. She was trying to hold a placard, when what she really wanted to do was to put her hands into her pockets to keep them warm and dry. She used to think that she'd shrink after a while with all the rain; that there'd be a midget walking around with a placard at the finish of it all.

But this evening it was coming down in buckets. Her friend was there with her and she was saying to Jean: "Will we go on? It's raining pretty hard."

A man, a passerby, overheard this. He looked around at the other pickets, as though he thought that she was worried about the rest of the picket trying to intimidate her.

"Don't be afraid of that lot," he said to Jean's friend. "Go in and shelter from the rain."

Jean would have loved to run after him and tell him that her friend was not being intimidated, that she was weighing the soaking she was getting against the prisoners' lives.

That June, the wettest, coldest June in thirty years or so, Jean had to tell herself sometimes that it didn't matter if she froze to death, that she had committed herself to this campaign and that was what counted.

She had arguments with some of her fellow protesters who were beginning to get caught up in red tape and differences within their own little clique. A couple of times she felt she had to speak up.

"It doesn't actually matter," she would say, "whether you agree or not. You agree with the overall principle, trying to end this hunger strike. Now get out there and try to stop it. I don't care if you're offended, if you think this fellow is wrong, or that fellow. You know what we're here for. It's our job to act as a cohesive force. We can have our fights later on when we have leisure for them."

Jean didn't have the herd mentality. But she felt that if they didn't come together like a clenched fist, with singleminded and driving resolve, then nothing would happen.

The one time so far that summer that Jean had had a good social evening was the night of the election count.

Encouraged by Bobby Sands' victory in Fermanagh/South Tyrone, and by the success of candidates in local Council elections in the North in May, the National H-Blocks committee had put up nine prisoners as candidates in the Dáil elections. Among them were four hunger strikers: Joe McDonnell, Martin Hurson, Kevin Lynch and Kieran Doherty. The blanketmen were represented by, among others, Paddy Agnew and Tony O'Hara. O'Hara was run as a candidate in Dublin West, and Jean had worked for awhile in his campaign.

All of the workers were out hoping to have something to celebrate the night of the election count, and Jean realized it was the first time they'd all been together having a good time. Usually the bond was their common desperation. During the run-up to the election, the media were waiting like vultures to pounce on the poor result they'd been forecasting for prisoner candidates. To the press, a good result would be like a slap in the face. Jean herself believed the grim projections: she was afraid the prisoners would be made a holy show of at the ballot box. She didn't feel that the prisoners had a hope in hell of getting a single seat. She remembered her younger sister saying that they'd get a seat or two—there'd be one anyway. She couldn't understand her sister's confidence.

So when the election results began coming in that night, everyone was over the moon. They had hired a room in the back of a bar and were being watched by people from the front, interested and curious, who could see their posters and knew they were hunger-strike campaigners. In a friendly fashion they kept shouting the results back to them: "Kieran Doherty is nearly in!" and so on. The H-Blocks people would go hysterical with delight at the news, and there'd be another round of drinks for everyone. It was wonderful, the euphoria of some kind of triumph after such a succession of terrible defeats.

Paddy Agnew topped the poll in County Louth. On the twenty-first day of his hunger strike Kieran Doherty was elected TD for Cavan/Monaghan. All the prisoner candidates made a respectable showing; Joe McDonnell, Kevin Lynch and Tony O'Hara did especially well. What emerged later, of course, was that the prisoner candidates had upset the electoral applecart in the twenty-six counties. The two prisoner TDs displaced Fianna Fáil candidates and, largely as a consequence, the Fianna Fáil leader Charlie Haughey was replaced as Taoiseach by Garret FitzGerald, leader of the principal opposition party, Fine Gael.

After the election, an old woman came up to Jean on the picket, and started screaming at her. "You've elected the wrong man, you know! You've elected the wrong man. That bastard FitzGerald will let them all die—I know him!" The woman simmered down, and Jean gathered that she felt that Haughey had been *about* to do something. But as far as Jean was concerned, Haughey had four dead men on his hands. He'd had his chance—four chances. Had Haughey pushed, the Irish people would have swung in behind him. *The Irish people were looking for leadership*, particularly from Haughey. People mightn't have agreed with Haughey making a decisive move, but they'd have respected him for it, and supported him. Yet he'd been so quiet and controlled that he'd achieved nothing.

Jean felt that if the British government were to see the whole of Ireland rising up—as some of the H-Blocks supporters thought might happen—if they'd been confronted with an Irish nation shaking its fist at them, with their government in the vanguard, then the British would have had to react. It wasn't going to react to a couple of thousand people, or to twenty thousand, but it would have had to react to a million or three and a half million people.

With Garret FitzGerald now Taoiseach, many of the demonstrators were optimistic. The ICJP had come into play. There was hope that something would happen. There was a lot of noise from FitzGerald at first, suggesting that he was determined to do something to resolve the hunger strike. Jean felt that, from a personal point of view, he would very much like to be the man who ended the hunger strike, but he didn't seem to have the nerve for it. He seemed to have a congenital inability to *do* anything.

IT WAS OTHERWISE with Jean.

More than once she'd been told that she'd make a fine Mother Superior, and sometimes she thought this was true. She was outspoken enough. She realized she'd never been very good at teamwork. Even when she was younger, and an athlete, she'd gone solo. She'd been a good sprinter, running with the Avondale Athletic club in Harold's Cross, and a good swimmer too, until she gave up sports for the pleasures of an active social life. And then, despite her independence of teams and gangs, she discovered she was a gregarious creature who loved not only partying and dancing, but talking, arguing and debating.

Jean also felt she had to at least try and build some integrity into herself. Without that, life would be just an exercise in getting from one day to another, living hand to mouth.

Her weakness was for underdogs and causes, but she had the advantage of being clear-headed. She was always arguing in terms of what was real and there in front of her. Her wishes and her dream world were set safely away on a separate little shelf.

Jean was born on 25 July 1952, the third of a family of six children. She had a younger brother and two younger sisters. When she was fourteen, in 1966, her mother died. And as the eldest child at home—her older sister was away in England, and her older brother was married—she had to take charge of the household just as she was turning fifteen.

The family was not at all Republican. Her father was one of the directors of a large printing firm. His family would have been very much Castle Catholics. His father had actually been a senior civil servant in Dublin Castle, and had begun his service there under the British. Her grandfather must have been, if not wealthy, at least very comfortable. Jean remembered her father telling her of watching Michael Collins' funeral procession as a nine-year old boy from the balcony of the Gresham hotel. She reckoned he must have been pretty well-off to be watching from there. The uncles were chiefly lawyers and civil servants, well in with the Dublin establishment. "You must all be pro-Brit," she kept saying to her father. It turned out that they did have, back in the eighteen hundreds, an O'Brien who was given six months in prison for sedition. He must have been a Republican. Her father denied all knowledge of the man.

Jean's interest in the national issue grew slowly over many years. She'd been thirteen in 1966: the year of the fiftieth anniversary of the Easter Rising. She was an impressionable schoolgirl, and went around with an Irish flag sewn onto the arm of her jacket. It was the year when Nelson's Pillar was blown apart by the IRA.

To her schoolgirl's mind the IRA commemorated in the Easter Rising celebrations was a wonderful organization, its members all heroes. That's the way the government of the day presented them. Commemorative coins and stamps were issued for each of the leaders of the Rising. At Bolands Mills in Dublin there'd been a presentation for tourists in words and pictures, describing the fighting in 1916. Jean went in and studied it. She remembered how excited everyone was about Nelson's Pillar being destroyed.

When she was sixteen or seventeen she became aware of a neighbour, the late Peter Berry, a civil servant deeply involved in the revelations in the 1970 Arms Trial of Irish cabinet ministers accused of supplying guns to the defenceless Catholics of the North. For awhile there were a lot of protesters outside his house calling out, "Hang Peter Berry!" Another neighbour down the road was the High Court judge responsible for jailing Seán MacStiofáin, then head of the Army Council of the Provisional IRA. Jean recalled being amazed that anything connected with the North could be having repercussions in their quiet little Dublin community.

In February 1972, when the British embassy in Merrion Square was burned, Jean was nineteen, and she was there as an onlooker. She'd been working at her first job in a wholesale jewellers, and like thousands of other young people she'd gone to the square, outraged by news about the thirteen boys and men gunned down in cold blood by British paratroopers in Derry on Bloody Sunday. There had already been a lot of flak about the evils of internment, and Bernadette Devlin was the heroine of the day. Jean recalled how interested ordinary Irish people were at the time, with even priests walking around displaying black 13s clipped onto their Roman collars. It was so different from now, from the hunger strike. At that time everyone was asking the question they should be asking now: What the hell is going on up there?

The embassy had been cleared the night before, and the German embassy next door as well. Jean somehow knew in advance that the British one would be burned.

It was strange. It *was* burned, but there were no after-effects. The people released their anger and then forgot about it. The attitude of the gardai at the burning of the embassy was, "Just make sure you don't injure yourself." They cordoned the front of the building so that anything thrown at the embassy wouldn't endanger the crowd, but would hit the building or fall into the empty space in front of it. Nice gardai. They made no attempt to interfere. It was afterwards that Jean heard they had orders not to interfere.

The issue of the British presence in Ireland was a very clear-cut issue then, and the whole of the press in Ireland was mobilized against the injustices being done to Northern nationalist Catholics.

In the North, in 1972, the victims began to hit back. The IRA, which had been in trouble and in the shadows, got back on its feet. Then they got very nasty. The press, taking its cue as usual from the British media, began to swing against the IRA, and public opinion went along. It wasn't just Bloody Friday in Belfast; it was the car bombs in Dublin too. An awful lot of people thought that the car bombs in Dublin, particularly those in 1974, were planted by the IRA. It was strange that people should think that. There'd been an earlier bombing in Nassau Street organized by British Intelligence. The 1974 bombing, in Abbey Street, had been organized by the UDA and UVF. But people blamed the IRA for the bombs. They could hardly remember their thinking of three years or so earlier. By now most people had swallowed the British line: all violence was attributed to the IRA.

For a period in 1974 when she was 21, Jean lived and worked in Manchester, England. Jean was going out with a Mayoman at about the time Michael Gaughan died. She hadn't a notion who Michael Gaughan was until, because of her friend, she came slap up against it. And then Gaughan's death on hunger strike made quite an impact. The Mayoman wasn't at all political, but he had a county patriotism—Mayomen all sticking together—and he was extremely angry over Gaughan's dying on hunger strike. He would curse and shout and roar with anger, because it was a fellow Mayoman who was suffering and dying.

Jean remembered how angry the English were at the time of the Birmingham and Manchester bombings.

"Oh, you bloody Irish," people in the office would say, suggesting that all the Irish were bombers or bad troublemakers. These were people, many of whom knew nothing about Ireland or the Irish, who didn't even know where Dublin was. If Ireland had been involved for five years in a war in another country, Jean would have to know something about it. Yet these people had had soldiers on the roads of Ireland for five years, and for eight hundred years before that, and they didn't even know where the capital was.

But they were convinced now that the Irish were evil. There was terrible rancour in England because of the bombings.

In 1975, she'd been half-arrested in England—taken into custody for a short time. She was over in Manchester on a holiday. She and another girl, a friend of hers, were staying for a couple of weeks with some lads they knew, one of them Jean's Mayoman.

Jean's friend went home after ten days or so—Jean planned to stay on—and the three of them were driving the girl out to the airport. They were late and in a great hurry to get her to the plane. They drove in, and since they had no time to park they chanced leaving the car in a car rental spot. They'd got the girl onto the flight, and a few minutes later the three of them were meandering out.

"Hey, someone's stealing my car!" one of the fellows said.

The car was slowly moving off, and he flew off after it and hammered on the roof. A policeman stepped out. "All of you come with me," he said.

They were brought to a room, a kind of holding centre in the airport. The police were terribly interested in the two lads. At one stage, they left one of them with Jean and took the fellow from Mayo into another room. Jean could hear them shouting and screaming at him. It startled her. Why were they shouting? What did they want to know? She called in to this fellow and said something to the effect that he shouldn't lose his temper—he might hit one of them and be had up for assault.

At another stage Jean was standing alone in the corridor, and asked a policewoman if she could sit down somewhere. The policewoman more or less told Jean to go to hell.

They must have been running a telex on them, because a plainclothesman came up to her.

"I see you drive," he said.

He went through Jean's handbag. There was a letter in the bag from a friend of hers, accompanied by the words of the song "The Men Behind the Wire":

> Armoured cars and tanks and guns
> Came to take away our sons.
> But every man will stand behind
> The men behind the wire . . .

The policeman began reading through all her letters.

"I don't think that's really necessary," Jean said.

"You know you're in the wrong bloody country at the wrong bloody time," said the plainclothesman.

"Well, we don't like you much either where I come from," Jean replied.

Her comment seemed to surprise him. Apparently he thought dislike between the English and the Irish was a one-way affair.

They were held for awhile, and then brought to the fellows' flat. The police, convinced that the two men were IRA or something, were all excited and searched the place from top to bottom. They looked under the carpets, up the chimney, everywhere. When they were going out they turned to the other man—he had a few petty crimes behind him.

"You're bent, mate," one of them said. "But you are not bloody IRA."

Jean was still not remotely interested in politics. But the foundations had been laid. Then in 1977 she began to become interested.

She was talking to a man from the North whom she'd met,

quite by accident, in a Dublin pub. She had a roaring argument with him about the war up there until he finally pointed out to her how absolutely innocent she was of any real knowledge of the North. He'd been very patient with her, really, considering her ignorance of what was going on.

She remembered thinking later about their argument. What the man said about the North was that if she wanted to understand it, she'd have to try living there. That really made her think. She realized that had she been living there, she'd have reacted—against, for example, the imposed poverty. For the first time she learned a simple enough truth: people don't react to what is not on their own doorstep. The man had made her feel guilty. Before that, she hadn't been remotely interested in what was going on in the Northern prisons. She was into dancing and parties and having a good time. But a couple of weeks later she went to her first march.

She saw fifty people walking by, protesting about the prisoners in Long Kesh. She thought to herself: This is what that man from the North was talking about. She just strolled in and tagged on at the end of the procession.

Then there were the two journalists. Jean met them at the same time, when she was working as a secretary in a local radio station. The first journalist was from Dublin, the second from Derry. The Dublin man was not prepared to object to British Army violence in the North. But the Derryman had a deep sense of what was going on. By the time she'd met the Derryman she'd gone on a march or two, and she'd make it clear to anyone who'd listen that she was there, not because she was an IRA supporter—she wasn't—but because of the principles being violated in the way Irishmen were treated in Northern prisons.

Because she wasn't all that knowledgeable Jean worked into the demonstrating slowly. Wanting to understand her own motivation, she began to read books. She felt that she should keep herself a little removed. She hoped she'd learn an awful lot more that way; she'd see what aspects she could support and what aspects she couldn't.

One thing she learned from her independent stance was how

conventional people manufactured blinders for themselves, to deliberately shut out the light. She remembered saying to the Dublin journalist that with all the killing in the North, something had to be radically wrong. He'd answered that wherever there was an army there'd be excesses and that was that. Jean didn't like his making excuses for British violence.

Then she met the Derry journalist and they talked—or rather she talked. He let her talk herself out. He said nothing, just let her run on with her own notions. She wondered at one point whether she was making a fool of herself—perhaps he was a loyalist? She finished, thinking he'd make mincemeat of her, and would argue down her every point. Instead he gave her a broad grin. "Well, I'm glad you think that way, Jean. My brother is in the H-Blocks, on the blanket. You may be politically naive, but your heart's in the right place."

Up till then, Jean had felt that only people who committed crimes were bothered by the police. All she'd done was to go off marching. So her first house call from the gardai was a sort of baptism of the innocent.

They came to her home one day after one of the marches— two Special Branch men, out of uniform. She wasn't in. When she came home and heard they'd been looking for her, she knew it was because she'd been on a march. This was at a stage when things were beginning to heat up, in late 1978.

Archbishop Ó Fiaich had come out, described the H-Blocks, and said he wouldn't keep an animal in such conditions. As a result the media had begun to pay more attention to Long Kesh. Jean was working on the idea then that, because the situation in the prison was wrong, as soon as people became aware of what was happening they would shout stop.

A couple of days later Jean was watching television when she heard footsteps in the back garden. Then there was a lot of running—large, heavy men racing about. Some of them ran around the front of the house, and there was a knock on the door. Someone else answered and said Jean wasn't in—out of fright, she supposed. But she was quite willing to face them. She was highly amused, in fact, at their antics. They called a

385

third time, when she was out shopping. The fourth time, she was in. When she did finally speak, it was to one man. She didn't ask him in, but talked to him at the door. Was she in Sinn Féin? he wanted to know. Was she a member of the Communist Party? Was she in some other left-wing group? She was amused at his equating left-wing groups with trouble. She wanted to ask him what his definition of "left-wing" was. The policeman told her that a lot of kids going on marches didn't realize that they were dealing with very sinister forces. Youngsters could be dragged into all sorts of things, he said. They didn't understand . . .

Most of her family reacted with shocked horror to this invasion by the gendarmes. There'd never been a policeman on their doorstep before. Her father, though, took it with equanimity. All he wanted to know was whether she and her younger sister— who was now going off to marches with Jean—were doing anything illegal. When he learned that they weren't, he had no objections.

But that the police should be interested in interviewing her, surprised Jean. Why would a policeman be asking her questions. She told someone about her astonishment at being given all this attention. "Oh, Jean! Don't you know? You're being harassed! That's what harassment is all about."

Afterwards a couple of the peelers would appear out of nowhere and sidle up to her at a bus stop. She soon began to anticipate the familiar, swift movement of the hand, which meant that the garda identity card was about to be produced. And she'd say to herself: Oh, this oaf, or this crowd, again.

The routine was quite informal.

"Oh, hello, Jean! Are you still living up in Dartry?"

She later learned that whenever new people appeared on the scene they tended to get this treatment, designed to put them off demonstrating. It nearly put her off. She was questioned about where she worked, about where her father worked, and so on. They gave her the impression that her job was under threat. It was her old job, and Jean had a boss there who called her in and suggested that if he saw her again on a march, she wouldn't be working for him for very long.

But threats did not have the intended effect on Jean. She might be frightened at the time, but on consideration would feel that if they were threatening her then they must be worried and frightened themselves.

There were other factors that affected Jean's involvement. She met some Northerners who'd been interned. She met some Protestant Republicans, real, live, young present-day Protestant Republicans. She met Pat McGuigan who'd been interned just for writing "The Men Behind the Wire."

HERE SHE WAS on O'Connell Bridge, walking up and down, watching the faces of the people passing by. She remembered the days when she thought that all that people had to do was know what was going on and they'd put a stop to it. But people were naive about prison life. Unable or unwilling to use their imagination, they never stopped to think about how terrible it would be to lose their liberty. She remembered the ridiculous argument she'd had with one fellow.

"Prisoners these days have central heating, television; they have all kinds of comforts," he said.

Jean leapt back at him.

"The room you're standing in has central heating, television, and comforts. How would you feel if I locked the door and kept you in it for twenty years?" She found herself shouting. "It doesn't matter how many concessions there are. A locked door is a locked door, and means you lose your liberty!"

People in the South had the notion, too, that if someone committed a crime, whatever the nature or seriousness of the crime, then whatever happened to them afterwards was just too bad. They were simply getting what they deserved. It didn't matter that some were in for minor charges, or short sentences.

"Well, they are convicted terrorists, and deserve to be treated roughly," people would say. They didn't seem to understand that prisoners had rights. They seemed in fact offended by the idea that prisoners had any human rights at all.

Every time she heard the argument about terrorists deserving rough treatment, Jean would answer back, "I don't care if they have monkeys in the H-Blocks. They still shouldn't be treated the way they're treated! They shouldn't have to be on the blanket."

Jean felt that the so-called forces of law and order must be required to behave themselves in a lawful way. If they weren't treating the prisoners decently, but instead cruelly punishing them, they became the guilty party. When the authorities started turning things upside down, ignoring the principles on which their own laws were supposedly based, then it was their legitimacy that came into question.

The argument of the authorities in the H-Blocks and Armagh had always been that the reason the prisoners were so cruelly punished was that they had broken prison rules. But Jean couldn't see any justification for this. How could petty rules create such an enormous problem? Prison rules might require punishment for the occasional prisoner who stepped out of line. But when the authorities found hundreds of prisoners out of line for a period of months—for a period of four or five years!—they should have re-thought their bloody rules.

By 1980, in Jean's view, Long Kesh prison had become a hell on earth. By the time in March 1981 when Bobby Sands was leading the prisoners into a second hunger strike, it was clear that desperate measures would be needed to get the British to yield on their criminalization policy. Jean recalled something about Sands himself being worried about the younger men coming into the place. The dirt protest had been on for nearly three years; they mightn't be able to stand it. He felt it was his responsibility to prevent them being condemned to this living hell. It was quite clear to Jean that Bobby Sands had decided to go on hunger strike for practical as well as political reasons.

As far as the five demands were concerned, Jean never saw them as anything other than an attempt to gain the practical equivalent of political status. The men in Long Kesh had the political acumen to see what criminalization and normalization were really aimed at. They had to break the idea that Northern Ireland was a normal sort of political reality. They had to break the British policy aimed at making them appear to be criminals. This is what the men had to fight. Corrupt courts, corrupt judges and a corrupt political system could hardly deliver ordinary prisoners at the end of the conveyor belt. The British couldn't bend the ordinary rules for arrest, trial and conviction without delivering a special prisoner at the other end.

A lot of Dublin people thought that asking for political status meant asking for some form of absolution for their misdeeds. They didn't understand that what prisoners were demanding was a recognition that they had emerged from a political process; that their violent acts were political acts—soldiers' acts, and that their arrests and convictions and maltreatment in the prison were political.

There were people outside who seemed to think that if they won political status then they suddenly wouldn't be prisoners anymore.

Late that Monday evening, 6 July, the ICJP was called in to meet with the NIO to discuss what the press described as a last minute hitch in the promised arrangements. On Tuesday 7 July, as Joe McDonnell slipped into a coma, the ICJP demanded that the NIO do as they had promised, and send in a senior NIO official to describe authoritatively to the prisoners what would be on offer if they went off the hunger strike. Otherwise the ICJP would reveal what had been agreed. To Jean, the Commission's anxiety, inspired by their fears for the life of Joe McDonnell, was coming very late in the game.

But the NIO told them that McDonnell's life was in no immediate danger.

MAURA McDONNELL was with her brother Joe at the last—when he began to sink. She'd never been with anyone who was dying before, and didn't know what the signs were. She'd fallen asleep at his bedside, and woke to find the orderlies moving around Joe. He'd been sick, and when they were trying to make him comfortable, she'd been awakened. She saw they'd put a plastic bowl on one side near his face. Maura reached over to touch him.

"He feels cold," Maura said anxiously.

"We'll get him another blanket," one of them said. Nothing else.

The first time anyone in the family saw Joe was after he had been on hunger strike for five days. He was expecting only Goretti. But Maura walked in with Goretti and his two children, and Joe's mother along with them. Her mother said afterwards that it nearly killed her to see how his eyes filled with tears when he saw them all. Even when he was slapped as a child he'd never cried.

Her mother Eileen told Maura that if she'd had a visit with her son a fortnight before he went on hunger strike, she'd have tortured him into not going on.

Instead their visit was the same day Francis Hughes died. Joe said to them, "Poor Frankie Hughes, he's in a bad way. But—" Joe laughed as he added— "he's still singing. He's on the way out, and singing till the end!" And then Joe said, laughing again, "And what a voice!"

Later his brother Frankie got a visit with Joe, who'd just lost the Sligo-Leitrim seat by only 300 or so votes. "That's it for me," Joe said to Frankie. He was prepared to die. But Kieran Doherty had won. Joe felt Kieran would be saved. "They'll not let a TD die," he said.

Maura recalled how he lay there, talking: "Look after yourselves . . . look after Mammy, and Goretti and the kids." He asked Maura not to forget Bernadette's birthday, which was coming up on 10 July. And Goretti's on the thirteenth.

Maura had been in America for four weeks. An exhausting schedule, but that was the easy part. When she came back she had to face the reality—Joe's decline, and the people at work who knew but didn't want to talk about it.

The other day Maura and her brother Robert had gone in for a visit. The screw said they couldn't stay because the ICJP was coming in. Joe wanted them to stay, but they had to leave. Before they left they were brought into the office to meet the men from the ICJP. Maura started crying. Then Robert started crying and then the others—even the priest, Father Oliver Crilly, and the bishop—were crying.

"Don't worry," they told them, "as soon as this is over, we'll be in touch with you." Maura felt that those three nights were like three weeks to Joe, with all the comings and goings and all the expectation of something about to happen. Even when he was very bad Joe wanted to know everything that was going on. They'd try to give him all the details.

Afterwards Maura reflected on that little scene in which the orderlies simply said they'd fetch another blanket. It seemed to be on a small scale just what the British government was doing on the grand scale: The authorities never came out and said directly that they were going to let the men die. Instead, whenever a critical stage was reached, they would busy themselves with some show of activity.

Then, just after five the next morning, Tuesday 8 July, Joe died.

JEAN O'BRIEN went out that day, in front of the GPO. She was holding a picture of Joe McDonnell framed in black. A woman photographer was darting about, and seemed very anxious to take a photograph of Jean. Jean made it clear she didn't want to be photographed. She was avoiding the photographer because she was trying to get Jean and not the crowd.

A journalist standing nearby saw what was going on. "She's trying to get you alone, Jean, because you're dressed up like a nice little girl."

To try to divert the photographer's attention, Jean handed the poster to the man next to her. The photographer walked from behind a pillar at the GPO and aimed the camera. Jean turned her head. The inconsiderate little wretch got her photo, showing Jean with her head turned aside, published next day under the pseudo by-line Kevin McMahon. Jean was sure it was a girl, not any Kevin McMahon.

Jean really didn't care whether she might lose her job because of a photo in the newspapers. Just recently a branchman had been at her door: "I will go and tell your boss what you are involved in," he'd said.

Jean's boss already knew what she was involved in; but she wondered what version a branchman would give him. She couldn't stop a detective going in and putting ideas into her boss's head, suggesting that she was a Provo or a dangerous subversive. She had known that once she involved herself in marches, she was bound to end up on film sometime. Her face had appeared on television, and more than once in the newspapers. She was prepared to be sacked now, if it came to that. But she was determined to put it off if she could.

Not long ago she'd been back to England, and an English fellow had heard her talking.

"Oh, no," he'd said. "Don't tell me you're one of that crowd who go around hiding their faces behind banners!"

She'd reacted strongly then. "Did you ever see these people? They hold banners, but they're not hiding their faces behind them. They're out there ready to be counted. I haven't seen anyone hiding behind them yet."

Some people paid with their jobs for carrying banners.

That night Jean wondered what was going to happen now that poor Joe McDonnell was dead.

At ten that morning a minor NIO official named Jackson arrived at Long Kesh and went in with the prison governor, Stanley Hilditch, to read out a five-page statement from Atkins which reiterated the stony Thatcher position and ignored the proposals the ICJP had worked out with Michael Alison. That afternoon the ICJP held a press conference, describing the agreed settlement and talking about how the British government had reneged on its agreement. But the Commission was at pains to declare that Alison, who had blamed an earlier turnaround on the "lady behind the veil," had kept faith with them.

Jean reflected on the efforts of the Irish Commission. Obviously, it had been a great deal more than an ego trip for Bishop O'Mahony and the other four men. They'd been caught up in the idea that they were going to save the boys' lives. They made strenuous efforts. In the end, when the British government reneged, they'd had the guts to come out and accuse them of reneging. To Jean it was remarkable that a body of middle-class Catholics would do that. They'd experienced what the demonstrators, the prisoners and the hunger strikers themselves had experienced in their dealings with Thatcher's government: they'd beaten their heads against a wall.

Jean supposed that the ICJP commissioners realized they had been used—meaning abused: that they'd been treated as pawns in the British government's end game with the hunger strikers. But why was it that the commissioners had nothing but praise for the hypocritical Alison and his gentlemanly conduct? How wonderful that they'd found the enemy polite! What, she wondered, did that have to do with politics? The Commission was dealing with mannerisms when it should have been fighting hard for substance.

She feared that people like Bishop O'Mahony were so concerned about appearances that they'd let justice go by the way. All the British had to do was to wave the red herring of a suggestion that they were giving aid or comfort to the IRA—surely the deadly Brits' deadliest enemies in Ireland—and people like O'Mahony would fade from the scene.

Next day Jean read the statement published by the Commission. She found it extremely weak. Bishop O'Mahony had said at the press conference that "there seemed to be a definite clawing-back on the part of the British government." He did point the finger, however tentatively. But the Commission's statement made no attack on Britain's brinkmanship with Joe McDonnell's life. The strongest thing the commissioners could find to say was that they couldn't regard the NIO statement read to the prisoners yesterday morning as "a serious attempt to seek a resolution."

Despite the fact that Alison had broken his promise to them on Monday that he would immediately send a high NIO official in to speak directly with the prisoners—and despite the fact that they were lied to about the condition of Joe McDonnell seven hours before he died—the Commission pussyfooted. In the penultimate paragraph came the customary shivering in the shoes. Heaven forbid that anything they'd said be taken as "an excuse for hatred or violence"!

But what about the hatred and violence that had allowed Joe McDonnell to die?

During the entire conflict, Jean had never seen anyone with the political will to resolve the situation. Political will required honesty, imagination and a sense of a free future. But politicians in Ireland liked to maintain the status quo, not rock the boat—get along in order to get on. The bishops, and O'Mahony's ICJP, were very like politicians in that sense. Cardinal Ó Fiaich, whom Jean often thought excessively moderate, now and again met the honesty requirement. Sometimes he'd seem to say, "To hell with what people think. To hell with who makes propaganda out of this. I'm going to speak the truth." He'd spoken out in 1978 when he'd said he had never seen anything like the H-Blocks since the sewers of Calcutta. He didn't qualify that statement by talking about the Provos' misdeeds. He identified malicious injustice for what it was.

The morning after Jean was photographed at the vigil for Joe McDonnell, she had a phone call from her boss.

"I'm here having my breakfast," he said, "looking at your picture in the paper." He didn't seem at all worried about it. Later at work, someone put the photo up on the notice-board for a joke.

Jean had found a couple of friends who didn't agree with what she was doing, yet understood it. It meant quite a bit to her to have friends like that, because she could talk with them even though they disagreed. She could say to them: "You know, Joe McDonnell has died. I'm very upset . . ." They wouldn't ask her why she was in bad humour. She could tell them what was on her mind and they'd discuss it.

It was Thursday 9 July, and the ICJP was holding a three-hour meeting with Garret FitzGerald. Afterwards they announced that they'd be making fresh efforts to resolve the hunger strike.

Jean reviewed in her mind the mediation efforts. Charlie Haughey had promoted the idea of a mediation by the European Commission on Human Rights. They'd been in and out of the prison. The three TDs and the Pope's secretary had gone in and out. A Red Cross mediation was being mooted. Now the elaborate ICJP mediation, its prospects much discussed in the press, had foundered. As far as Jean could see, the boys in Long Kesh were dying of mediation. Yet the British government kept rigidly refusing to negotiate, and were making their refusal a matter of principle.

Friday 10 July was the day of Joe McDonnell's funeral. Jean

had felt a positive force in this vital thirty-year-old man who had declined to join the first hunger strike, saying that in his wife and children he had too much to live for.

It was a terribly sad funeral, with his young children at the graveside, made sadder still by the fact that the British Army and RUC, trying to go after the colour party, had started shooting at the crowd. She later talked to a man who had been there, who'd been horrified at the armed attack on the funeral.

Jean felt that the explanation lay with the British right wing: that the true-blue Tories, disturbed by all the paramilitary funerals, had demanded that something be done to stop them. So the British government, it seemed, had stupidly decided to make a horror show of this funeral. The troops were sent into the crowd with orders to "get" the IRA firing party at the graveside. The masked party fired off their brief salute. Then the Army and the RUC came on, firing off dozens of rounds of live and plastic bullets. The *Irish Times* account the next day said in part:

> It appears that the firing party was trapped by an Army helicopter carrying telescopic equipment. When the first (Army) shots were fired and people in the funeral procession realized what was happening, youths broke away and bombarded the soldiers with stones. Troops and police reinforcements fired dozens of plastic bullets in return. Some observers believe that they also fired live rounds. The RUC deny this.

Obviously they'd fired live rounds! Gerry Adams' brother Paddy, for example, had taken four rounds in his back. (The RUC said he was in the firing party; but photos showed he wasn't.) The *Irish Times* story continued:

> Women holding young children ran screaming into the nearby church, while others crouched on the footpath and in the doorway of the Busy Bee shopping centre. Troop reinforcements sped in armoured vehicles into the middle of the crowd which scattered into side streets. A local priest, the Reverend Dan O'Rawe, said soldiers and police fired indiscriminately . . .

For some time afterwards the procession was seriously disrupted and took nearly four hours in all to reach Milltown cemetery, where a Provisional Sinn Féin speaker told the crowd that they were there "despite British Army terror, profanity and sacrilege."

Jean's friend told her that he'd seen some women sheltering in a lane. The troops came into it, firing away. As the bullets flew the women threw themselves down on the ground. They were screaming their heads off.

The people rallied somehow, and nobody was killed or seriously injured. But Jean thought it must have been horrific for Goretti, who was out that day to bury her husband, and for his mother Eileen, who'd lost the son she thought she could have saved: the fifth born, Mrs. McDonnell had said, and the fifth hunger striker to die.

The same day, in Dublin, Jean met with some violence herself.

Some of the people watching the picket seemed more than ordinarily aggressive. She'd experienced this before—strangers coming up who frightened her, who'd scream and shout and even spit, something she herself wouldn't dream of doing to anyone. Today she was standing at the GPO with a placard. Journalists and police were nearby when a man came up and spat at her. She wiped the spittle off her face and turned her back. But the man was moving in as though to start kicking her. Jean was frightened.

Then suddenly an American tourist saw what was going on and came over. He was outraged. Dragging the man away from her he shouted at the gardai: "What the hell is going on? Why are you just standing there? Get this freak out of here!"

Jean's impression was that the tourist couldn't understand why she wasn't reacting herself. But she knew that if she did it would be she who'd be arrested and not her assailant. It was the people being abused who would get arrested—not the abusers. Had she been out shopping and been treated so, she'd have had grounds for a court case, but Jean knew that here on the picket she'd have to take it because of the campaign. The police and journalists who stood watching would be only too glad to see trouble. If she so much as lifted her hand, she'd become a terrorist or a troublemaker. She had to remember to remain passive. She couldn't even shout back at anyone. If she did, she'd be regarded as a fanatic.

The week Joe McDonnell died, Michael Alison, on a British government "truth-squad" trip to America, was asked why the British government had been so adamant about refusing to negotiate with the prisoners yet had negotiated with the ICJP. He answered that these were like negotiations with hijackers, stalling men until they could be disarmed. He was asked whether he considered the Commission members to be hijackers. That was what he'd implied.

This was the Alison who had blamed Margaret Thatcher (the "lady behind the veil") for the breakdown in negotiations with the ICJP. Now it was clear that he'd been involved himself in the cynical stalling effort. Jean thought it curious that Alison had been the British interlocutor with the ICJP, rather than Humphrey Atkins.*

Father Oliver Crilly, the South Derry priest** who had been the original moving force behind the ICJP effort, and who was one of the five Commissioners, said in response to news of Alison's statement in America:

> There is now a major question mark on the role of Mr. Alison. We said in our statement earlier this week that he appeared to have acted in good faith, but in the light of statements he has since made in the States, this is now in serious doubt . . .

*Two years later Michael Alison, the NIO negotiator whom Bishop O'Mahony had spoken so well of, resurfaced in London as Parliamentary Private secretary to Margaret Thatcher. When she was away for an eye operation in the summer of 1983, there were complaints that Alison was running the British government in her absence. This was the Alison whom the ICJP thought had kept faith with them.

**Father Crilly was a cousin of Francis Hughes and a closer cousin of Thomas and Benedict McElwee, Jean learned afterwards. Francis had said to his brother Oliver Hughes in April that the men didn't

That weekend Martin Hurson suddenly took a bad turn. The demonstrators were becoming terribly despondent now.

British intransigence had made it too long an effort, just as the British had made it too long a hunger strike, and too long a war. One night a man at work had asked Jean whether she was going to join the others for a drink.

"Oh, no," she said, "I have to go off on a picket."

He seemed to be amazed that Jean was still picketing. Wasn't that something someone would do for a day or a week, and then stop? It suddenly dawned on Jean that, though she'd been out there every night for months on end, the people at the office weren't aware of this at all. Well, she was prepared to march forever if she thought it would help resolve the hunger strike. It was such an easy thing for her to do, just put her feet on the ground, one in front of the other. She'd have walked to China if it would have got the prisoners political status.

Jean had come to feel that the sacrifice of Bobby Sands and Joe McDonnell and the others was too good for the Irish. They'd become a nation of till fumblers, as in Yeats' sarcastic verses:

> What need you, being come to sense,
> But fumble in a greasy till
> And add the halfpence to the pence
> And prayer to shivering prayer, until
> You have dried the marrow from the bone?

---

want to die, that they wanted to negotiate. Oliver Hughes had mentioned this to Father Oliver Crilly, and Father Crilly had taken this up to Dublin where he then lived; he was serving as head of the Irish Bishops' Communications operation which included the publishing house Veritas. When the exceedingly slow wheels of the ICJP finally began to grind into negotiations on the hunger strike issue, Father Crilly agreed to join the five-man committee. (When his and Commission member Hugh Logue's extensive notes of what had been agreed between the ICJP and the British were laid before Michael Alison one evening, Alison did what was later described as "a little war dance" of indignation.)

For men were born to pray and save:
Romantic Ireland's dead and gone,
It's with O'Leary in the grave.

The Irish people had bought the propaganda line that they were
only an economy—and an economic dependency of Britain.
They had so little self-respect. Yeats had seen this in the run-
up to 1916, when the people became angry with the patriots
for disturbing their little lives. Two thousand men went out
to man the GPO and the outposts and the barricades, to the
disgust and outrage of most of the people of Dublin. When the
men of 1916 were being led away after their surrender, some
Dubliners threw rotten vegetables at them.

Bobby Sands and Joe McDonnell had been trying to show
the Irish people that it was the quality and not the quantity
of life that mattered. They and the others wanted to live their
lives with dignity. If they couldn't achieve that then they didn't
want to live at all.

For a nation of till fumblers, however, everything was expedient. These people genuinely couldn't imagine what in life
might be so important to them that they'd be prepared to make
such a sacrifice. Theirs was an "I'm-all-right, Seán," attitude:
"We've got our nice little three-quarters of a nation down here
and a few bob in our pockets. We're doing all right, and we
sure as hell don't need that trouble up North."

And when the violence erupted outside the British embassy
in Dublin ten days later, people were scared. Why couldn't life
go on peacefully, as it had before?

Through the months—and the years since 1977—Jean had
discovered something: now that she'd become politicized, she
could never be unpoliticized. She could never go back. In a way
it was disturbing. What she'd gone through was changing her,
and she knew that in changing her it had cut her off from many
people.

Yet she couldn't un-know her knowledge.

Sometimes, in a selfish way, she wished she'd never known
anything. It would have been so much easier.

Chapter 9

A BOY FROM TYRONE

An outlawed man in a land forlorn,
He scorned to turn and fly,
But kept the cause of freedom safe
Upon the mountains high.

Full often in the dawning hour,
Full often in the twilight brown,
He met the maid in the woodland bow'r,
Where the stream comes foaming down,
For they were faithful in a love
No wars could e'er destroy;
No tyrant's law touched Renardine,
On the mountains of Pomeroy!

George Sigerson
THE MOUNTAINS OF POMEROY

FRANCIE HURSON, his wife Sally and her brother Eugene Hughes, had gone with Gene's wife Anna Marie to an H-Block rally at Bunbeg, County Donegal, at which Francie was to speak. It was Sunday, 12 July 1981. They reached Bunbeg some time after five that evening and began driving around to find out where the rally was being held. They were hungry and had a little time so they decided to go somewhere and have a meal. They drove through Gweedore and stopped at one of the hotels near the end of the town.

Just as they were sitting down to the table a girl from the reception desk came with an urgent message. Francie was to phone the Maze prison.

As he walked towards the phone, Francie met John Hume coming in the door.

"John, Martin must be dead—or nearly dead. I just got

a message to ring the Maze prison. Would you help? Maybe you could phone the prison—"

"Surely I can."

When John Hume rang the Maze they refused to tell him anything and said to ring the Northern Ireland Office.

So Hume rang the Northern Ireland Office. They told him to tell Francie that there was no cause for concern, and that anyway some of the Hurson family were visiting with Martin.

Hume passed this on to Francie, adding that they'd said Francie would be allowed into the prison if he could get there by 8:30 that night.

It was nearly seven o'clock. They'd have had to drive a hundred miles an hour for an hour and a half to make it by 8:30. Even as the crow flies, the prison was more than a hundred miles away. On a Sunday night it would take them the best part of an hour just to negotiate the winding roads back to Letterkenny. From there they would make good headway to Strabane and Omagh, and through the Ballygawley roundabout to Dungannon. Then it would be the M-1 all the way, the best stretch of road in Ireland. But it would take them two and a half hours at least, even if they weren't delayed at checkpoints. There was no way that Francie could do it. He asked John Hume to phone and see whether he'd be able to get him in any later.

Hume rang the NIO again and they told him that the 8:30 time could not be changed.

"But they said there was no cause for concern," John Hume added. "You'll be able to get in tomorrow morning okay."

Why did Francie find himself resenting John Hume? John had just made three calls on his behalf. Francie supposed afterwards that he'd expected John Hume to be able to exert his influence with the British authorities and get him in there, no matter what the hour. He was uneasy about the whole thing. Something was terribly wrong with Martin or Francie wouldn't have got this call.

Since Friday evening they'd been worried about Martin. A priest had visited Martin in the prison, and in the evening he'd called down at the house of Francie's brother, Brendan, in Galbally. Martin was very weak, according to the priest. "He's not the same Martin I visited last weekend," he said. "He hasn't been shaved and he's just lying on the bed. He's not in the same spirit. He didn't seem to have anything to talk about. He seemed extremely weak." The priest thought that the family should get to the prison as soon as possible and see him.

Brendan got in touch with Francie immediately and they went about trying to arrange a visit. They rang from Francie's house (Brendan had no phone) and talked to the prison authorities, trying to make arrangements for Saturday morning. But the prison officials refused. Martin was in good health, they said. There was no cause for concern.

Francie explained to the prison authorities that the priest had told them that Martin was seriously weakened and that it was essential to see him. Still the answer was no. They kept trying that night, and then they phoned all day Saturday until late at night. The answer was still no.

Francie got his friend Francie Martin—he trusted Francie Martin, who was in Hume's SDLP but had nonetheless become very active in the support campaign for the hunger strikers— to ring John Hume. He not only rang Hume; he rang Garret FitzGerald's secretary and the TDs for Longford/Westmeath, where his brother Martin had been run as a candidate for Dáil Éireann. The word came back that FitzGerald couldn't do anything. Then John Hume rang Francie Martin to tell him that the NIO was adamant.

The Hursons rang again all Sunday morning until lunchtime. Brendan told Francie that he had been in touch with Francie Martin of Carrickmore and Francie had relayed word about there being no cause for concern. Brendan Hurson told his brother Francie he wasn't too alarmed, because of all that reassurance.

"Martin must be okay," Brendan had said.

Having run into that stone wall at the NIO, they agreed between them that Francie would go to the Bunbeg rally while Brendan went to another rally nearer home, in Belleeks, in South Armagh, the home town of Paddy Quinn. Paddy was a good friend of Raymond McCreesh, and had gone on hunger strike on 15 June. The Hurson brothers felt that it was important to give the other families all the support possible. Generally

Francie, the middle brother, was the one called upon to speak at rallies; Francie had a phone and Brendan didn't. But the two brothers backed one another up.

Brendan, the eldest brother, might have got word in South Armagh—Francie hoped he had. Perhaps Brendan would be able to get to the prison in time. But Francie was still worried, so he and Sally and the others decided to forget about the rally in Bunbeg. They got into the car and drove southeast.

Francie Hurson—the Hursons had grown up on a hill farm up at Cappagh—had married Sally Hughes of Carrickmore in 1972. Her family was in a sense the obverse of the Hurson family, in which there were six sisters and three brothers. The Hugheses had six boys and three girls. Their father was dead, and their mother, Brigid Hughes, presided over the homestead. The Hughes brothers were involved in an engineering and construction business, putting up farm buildings. Before Francie and Sally, with her brothers' help, built their big bungalow at the top of the hill, they'd lived in a house adjacent to the family homestead down below. They were still close by, in the townland of Altinagh, near Carrickmore.*

Francie Hurson had run into difficulties early on in the troubles. In 1973 he was in England, working in Manchester, when an RUC man was killed by a landmine detonated on a hillside near Cappagh. The RUC were trying to connect a friend of Francie's, a farmer from the district, with the explosion.

At the time Francie was working in Manchester for McAlpine's, the huge construction and property company. He used to drive a friend to work every morning, and if Francie overslept, the friend would come and ring the doorbell to get him up. One morning the bell rang. Francie didn't look at the clock. Thinking he'd overslept, he rushed downstairs and opened the door to let his friend in. But instead of his friend two English

---

*"Carmen" is the way journalists liked to render the local name Termon, which with its soft t (very near an English ch sound) might be roughly pronounced as "Tcharmen"—from the town name Termon McGurk, in Irish *Tearmann Mac Oirc*, which was itself derived from the Latin *terminus*, meaning the monastery boundary. Dean Brian McGurk (or McGuirk), was a vicar general of Armagh diocese at the end of the 17th century.

detectives were standing there, in white raincoats, while another stood across the road with a rifle—pointed straight at Francie. They told him that they'd got orders, from Northern Ireland, to arrest him. Francie said he wasn't going anywhere until he'd washed and had his breakfast, and walked back up the stairs. So they followed him in and waited while he took his time eating. Then they brought him to Manchester barracks. Francie was kept two hours in the barracks before a pair of detectives arrived from Belfast. They'd travelled over specifically to question him about the explosion at Cappagh.

They kept him the whole day in Manchester barracks. Sally rang every hour to find out if he was getting home, but they refused to give her any details. Francie was questioned until eight in the evening. When Sally rang again they told her he was going to be taken back to Ireland. Then they came to the house—five detectives, two of them from Northern Ireland and three from England—and, leaving Francie in the car below, tore the place apart in Sally's presence. They wouldn't tell her what they were after. They tore up floorboards, smashed things, and left the house a complete wreck.

Sally was working as a domestic orderly in a nearby hospital at the time, and the next morning she was picked up for questioning at work. She wasn't happy about either the questioning or the housebreaking. Anyway, they found nothing, and had to let Francie go. That was one of several times during their English sojourn that the police came to the house where Francie and Sally lived with their young children.

Francie's brother Martin wasn't in England at the time. When he did come over, in 1974, he wasn't bothered much, but the RUC did harass Martin when he came back to Northern Ireland. They knew that Martin often set charges at the quarry in Cappagh where he worked. All the men were familiar with the tenchiques. But Martin was particularly adept at handling explosives. Every time they'd find him on the road they'd accuse him of being an IRA man. It was easy for Martin, with his quiet ways, to shrug this off.

When Francie came home to Tyrone, and he and Sally went to live at Altinagh, he was hounded by the RUC. Every time he went out on the road they'd be after him. The police in that area used bullyboy tactics. Francie's brother-in-law, Gene Hughes, used to remark that the RUC were not like the gardai. When the RUC came to your house they'd take over the place: they'd lock everyone into one room, and root and search the place from top to bottom, doing whatever they liked, pawing over personal property, prying into private papers to their heart's content.

The British Army was worse. The soldiers, too, became frequent visitors at Altinagh. It got to the point where Francie and Sally simply didn't allow them in. If soldiers came up the lane while Francie was in the house, they would shout that they wanted to talk to him, and he and Sally would pretend not to hear. They would draw the curtains. The soldiers could keep banging on the windows and shouting till they were blue in the face for all Francie cared. Eventually they would go away.

The UDR didn't turn up very often in the Cappagh/Carrickmore area. Local people regarded the UDR as merely a legal Protestant paramilitary organization. In practice even the British authorities acknowledged the fact that the UDR was unacceptable in such close-knit nationalist neighbourhoods. UDR men were afraid, too, if they were local men, of being identified. Once they became known they'd be picked out by local Republicans and given unwelcome attention.

The problem in Northern Ireland was that there was no civil police force whose prime objective was maintenance of law and order. The RUC and UDR were still, as far as Francie could tell, 98 per cent non-Catholic. What these were were armed police and military forces, selected from one section of the community, used as an instrument for repressing the other section.

An incident in 1979 was typical. A local man had been working all day, and in the course of his work had got a flash from a welder. His eyes were very sore. He felt the soreness acutely while driving home, through Dungannon. Finally he had to pull up. He simply couldn't drive any further. Soon two landrovers appeared.

"What are you doing here?" they asked him.

He told them what he was doing—the problem with his eyes.

They asked for his driver's licence.

One of the UDR men made a grab for him.

"I'm fucking sure there is nothing wrong with your eyes, you Fenian bastard."

The man pulled back.

"Hold on," he said. "I'm talking to this other man."

"And I'm talking to you," the agressive one said, and reached in at and tore his jumper. The man got out, and the UDR man backed off.

"I'm going to report this," the man said, noting the licence plate on the landrover.

"No, you're not," they said.

He got back into his car. They tried to block it, but he got around them and drove off, heading for the police barracks in Dungannon. They followed him. When he reached the barracks and got out, they passed on by. He went in and reported the incident.

Nothing came of it, of course. Like so many other people in the area, the Hursons felt that the only point in reporting such incidents was defensive. If a man got involved in some sort of confrontation, the RUC or UDR might claim anything they chose to afterwards. Making a complaint against them was a form of protection against disorderly behaviour charges—charges difficult to disprove, and the burden was on the accused. After three disorderly behaviour charges a man would be liable to a jail sentence. So they tried to prevent this by lodging complaints. Complaints meant taking excessive trouble, going to the barracks, filling in forms, establishing the cause for complaint. The routine afterwards was always the same. After six months or so there would be a polite letter from the Chief Constable or the Director of Public Prosecutions, saying that they had investigated the matter and were satisfied that there were no grounds for prosecution. It seemed to be a useless exercise, but if a man didn't lodge a complaint, then the UDR or RUC might turn around and charge him with assault. It was simply a case of getting your oar in.

After Martin was arrested in late 1976 the Army and RUC stepped up their harassment. They began stopping Francie and the other local men on the road, hassling them, and continually calling at their houses. It was easier to tolerate in the beginning than it was in 1981, when it had reached the point where the soldiers and police were really annoying the Hursons.

Once this year three local people, two men and a woman, were stopped and held at an Army checkpoint. The soldiers ordered them out of the car, but they refused, demanding that the police be called. So the soldiers dragged one of the men out of the back seat and gave him a kicking, smashing the rear window in the process. A helicopter arrived and they took the man over to it. The other man tried to prevent this, with the result that he and the woman were trailed off to the helicopter, then trailed back to a wall at the side of the road. As the other man was taken off in the copter, the man and woman, fearful now that the soldiers woud kill them, ran to the car and lay down to protect themselves. Francie and Sally drove along, and stopped, just as the soldiers disappeared into the fields. The man and woman were so badly injured that they had to be taken to hospital in an ambulance.

Later the two men were charged with "assaulting" the soldiers. When they went to a lawyer he told them that they were trying to beat the system. They took the matter to court. The soldiers lied and their version was accepted. The local men were fined twenty-five pounds each for assault. Francie had had plenty of evidence besides this to prove that the system just couldn't be beaten in Northern Ireland.

The security forces were constantly harassing nationalist men and women at checkpoints. The idea was to get them to retaliate and thereby get grounds for filing charges. So the people tried to control their anger—however difficult it was to do this, however sick it made them to act with restraint.

FRANCIE ALWAYS FELT that whatever the problems with the police and the Army, the UDR were the most brutal. They seemed to enjoy stamping down Catholics. They would go as far as they could. Then, when a complaint was made, they'd send for the police. The first thing a policeman would do when he came was to get out his book and go around and look at the car; and if there was a disc out of date or a bald tire, or anything wrong with the car, they'd say that that justified the UDR stopping and questioning the driver. RUC men were quite ready to cover up for the UDR.

Francie regarded the regime in Northern Ireland as very different from the South. What was expected in Northern Ireland was that the nationalist people, which meant the Catholic Irish, would knuckle down and act as yes-men. They liked Catholics who conformed, who never insisted on their rights. Catholics who had no principles at all suited them down to the ground.

British soldiers in Ireland always tried, Francie felt, to lord it over the Irish. Even strongly nationalist people had to be prepared to go along at times. Once Gene Hughes's lorry was stopped at a checkpoint. One soldier told him to move the lorry off to the side of the road; another told him to stop where he was; a third told him to angle the lorry so that another car could pass—three different instructions. They liked to search a man's lorry, and break something, so that they could hear him say, "It's okay, boys, I'll fix it myself." They wanted the nationalist people to eat dirt.

The UDR and RUC reserves were in it, Francie thought, as a sectarian thing. They were also in it for the money. It was a job in a time of wholesale unemployment; they got danger money, tax concessions, interest-free mortgages.

But there was another side to this. Until recent times Orange lodges would bend over backwards to help loyalists if they got into financial trouble. Francie remembered that in the days of the Stormont government there would be short-term schemes for money grants. Catholics wouldn't be told about the grants until it was too late. The loyalists did everything they could to keep their own people in control. But now the Orange lodges had lost interest. Part of it had to do with the growth of the banks, and part of it had to do with the fact that they weren't running everything their own way in Northern Ireland anymore. The British direct rulers had clipped the wings of absolute Orange control, and the old system had pretty well fallen apart.

Francie had noticed changes in Orange attitudes. In times past the planters had taken the good land, forcing the Catholics up onto hilly land or out onto the bogs. But now UDR men and RUC reservists who had good farms and good businesses let them run down so they could spend time out on the roads parading their bigotry. They had to hire help they couldn't afford and would get into debt.

Yet it was still an uphill fight for the Catholic Irish. A young lad leaving school might have only a small bit of farmland; or his family would have a few pigs or cows. But he'd work hard, borrowing and gradually building up. He'd take a chance and buy something else. In fifteen or twenty years he'd make enough money so that, with borrowings, he could buy a bigger place. If he was prepared to work he could redeem the outstanding debt, and go on from there. The Catholics in this country learned to work hard that way—adding a pig to a chicken and a cow to a pig. Loyalists had lost the initiative. They manned the security forces and got all the comfortable jobs—office jobs, civil service jobs. They had become, Francie thought, like spoiled children; they had forgotten how to fend for themselves. Catholics were much more ambitious, because they had to be.

Francie had seen the new pattern emerging over the past twenty years or so. Paddy would start out as a farm labourer when he left school. The lad living down the road, Sammy, might join the police and earn four times as much money. But Paddy had the incentive to prove himself, and he'd work twice as hard. At the end of the day he'd buy a business, and start generating income. The other man would have only his paycheck. Sammy had the idea that the troubles were going to last forever and he was getting well paid, with overtime. But when the troubles were over Paddy would have a business and Sammy would have nothing much at all. So the Orangemen were slipping. By the age of forty they'd be finished, while Paddy, even now, might have money to buy a farm of a hundred or a hundred and fifty acres.

A local man was once stopped. The UDR told him to empty his pockets.

"Are you trying to take money off me?"

410

"No. We don't need the money."

"You wouldn't think it, to see you tramping the roads."

British soldiers in 1981 weren't cavorting around in landrovers as much as they'd done in earlier years. They were lying out in fields and ditches where they wouldn't be seen. Fifty per cent of their time was devoted to surveillance. The soldiers had a regular dug-out in front of the Hughes house, watching everything. They'd build up a dossier so that if a Catholic were arrested they could rhyme off the details: where he was on a certain day, what he did, and who he was with. They tried to use this to break him psychologically, to make him think they knew all about him.

The soldiers could be vicious towards people. Sally's uncle, Peter Grogan, came back from England. He'd only been back a short time when soldiers from the Queen's Guards, which had a notorious reputation in the area, came to the house making inquiries about a murder. The Guards were well known for trying to get a man away from a well-lit area to a dimly lit place where there were no witnesses, so that they could beat him up. That night Francie saw them pulling at triggers and releasing the safety catches on their guns. As Francie saw it they were trying to get themselves worked up so that they could shoot someone.

Peter, an old man then, found the strain too much and collapsed. Francie was there at the time. The soldiers were out near the shed in the back, where Gene had his equipment for engineering work. When Francie saw Peter fall to the ground he tried to get near him, and so did Oliver Hughes. But they wouldn't let anyone near him, saying that the old man was only bluffing.

One of the soldiers ordered the others to put Peter in the shed. When they picked him up Oliver could see that the back of his head was bleeding where he'd fallen. The soldiers carried him into the shed and threw him down again on his back.

"The bastard is dead," a soldier said.

So Peter Grogan died that way, at the hands of British soldiers.

411

And during the wake they set up a checkpoint at the end of the lane leading to the Hughes house and stopped and questioned everybody coming in.

SOMETIMES THE PEOPLE were in a position to fight back.

There was the night a man was supposed to have been shot in Ballygawley. The Hughes family had gone to a school concert in Carrickmore but Sally had stayed at home. She'd locked the door of the Hughes house next door and was going across the lane to her own house, when she thought she heard something.

Sally went in and phoned the school.

"I think the place is surrounded," she said.

Francie and Patsy Hughes got home first. When they arrived the police were in the house, and asked about a tax disc that was lying in the cupboard.

"Who owns that disc?" one of them asked.

Francie grabbed it.

"It's nothing to you who owns it."

The RUC had been accused of a lot of things about that time. A priest from Ahoghill had been kidnapped. Women had been raped. The police were supposed to be out looking for whoever murdered the man up near Ballygawley, but they knew that they were under heavy suspicion themselves.

A confrontation seemed to be building, when Sally intervened.

"It isn't my house, but the owner will be back shortly."

The RUC started explaining about the murder—and why they were asking questions.

"What right have you to ask questions?" Francie said. "Isn't it your own people who are being charged with kidnap, murder and rape? Why don't you get out of here?"

Francie reached for a brush and brandished it.

"I'll knock the fucking head off you if you don't get out of here," Francie said. He looked out the window. Patsy Hughes was outside trying to see what the other RUC men were doing. The small shed hadn't been locked and there were a lot of things there that they needed for their building and engineering work.

412

But some of the police were preventing Patsy from going to see what they were up to in the shed.

"If they don't let you through," Francie said, "I'm going through." And he made a break from where he was standing, across the kitchen to the other door. The RUC grabbed the two men and arrested them. They threw Patsy into one of the landrovers, and were taking Francie to the other one down the road when Granny—Brigid Hughes—arrived home. She was with Father Crowley, a local curate, whom she'd taken with her from the concert—for protection. Granny wanted to know what was going on. The inspector told her they'd arrested Francie and Patsy.

"What for?" Granny demanded.

"For being disorderly."

"Disorderly? Where?"

"Here."

"On my own doorstep? In my own house?" She kept on arguing with the inspector about why they were arresting the two men. "Those men are all I have to protect me. You have guns. They have nothing but their bare hands. All I have are my sons to protect my house."

"They've been disorderly—"

"That's a slim excuse," she said. "It's nonsense that they've been disorderly. It would be different if they'd been out trying to start a row with the likes of you on the public road. But being disorderly *in their own house*—?"

The priest chimed in, asking why they were being arrested. The inspector turned around and said something about terrorists.

"Do they look as if they are terrorists?" the priest asked.

"You can't judge anyone by just looking at them," the inspector said. "That's why we're taking them in."

"Well, I want to see them before they go," Granny said.

"No," snapped the inspector. "You don't get to see them. They're going right now."

"I tell you I'm going to see them," Granny said.

The priest said he wanted to see them too. So Granny stomped off and the priest went following along after her. She went over to speak to Patsy first.

"Watch out, Father Crowley," Patsy shouted from the landrover. "There's kidnappers here!" As Granny was going down to speak to Francie in the other landrover the first driver started to drive up towards her.

"Are you taking me with you?" Granny asked.

Just then a policeman shouted out to the driver in Francie's van.

"You can let him go."

The driver turned to Francie: "You can go," he said.

Granny was watching all the while.

"I thought you said you were taking me with you," Francie said.

"Oh, no. You can go," the policeman said.

"Make up your mind."

But Francie knew, and they all knew, that the police didn't have any grounds for arresting them. They'd arrested them all right, but they hadn't figured out what for.

Then they turned and let Patsy out of the other landrover.

"Go on," they said.

It was Granny's quizzing that had freed them. She had stood her ground, and unnerved the RUC.

Father Crowley looked at the retreating police.

"Who was I supposed to come here to protect?" he said.

On another occasion Granny Hughes was getting herself ready to go to see two of her sons, who'd been taken to the barracks and detained for three days. When she was ready, she sat down and waited for her son-in-law Francie Hurson, who was to drive her there.

A neighbour came in, and she and Granny were talking when two landrovers came down the lane to the house.

"Oh, my God!" Granny said. "What are they coming for today? Are they back for the whole lot of them—?"

"Go out and see who they're looking for," the neighbour said.

"I wouldn't be fit to go out," Granny said.

414

Francie came in from the house next door.

"Francie, will you go out?"

"I don't think I will."

"If I go out will you come out after me?"

"I might," said Francie.

So Granny went out, and Francie followed after her. When they got outside, one of the landrovers, which was covered and had doors at the rear, was backing up almost to the doorstep, and the two doors were flung open. Three soldiers came past the side of the house, carrying bags of potato manure. The RUC were there, too.

"Where do you think you're going with those bags?" Granny asked.

"These are explosives," they said. "We're taking the bags with us."

"Oh, no. Those are not explosives. I paid for those bags myself."

"We've proved it—they're explosives."

"No. Those are bags of pirdy manure and you're not taking them with you. I bought them and they're mine. Terry McGarrity sold them to me. You can check with him."

"We're taking them," said the soldier.

Granny got to the landrover, and blocked the flaps at the opening with her two arms, as far as she could reach out. She was a small woman, but she faced up to the policemen. One was in front of her and one on either side of her. A large policeman came up and pulled a gun on her. He grabbed her jumper.

"Don't you lay a hand on me," she said. "I'm under doctor's care." Then she hit him in the chest.

A policewoman came up from the side—a big, stout woman—even stouter than the policeman. She tried to pull Granny's hand away from the side of the landrover opening Granny had been blocking.

"It's in your own home you should be, sweeping your dirty floors," Granny shouted at her. "You're not doing anything to me!" And then she kicked out sharply at the policewoman.

The woman retreated and didn't come near Granny again.

Finally they took the bags, and gave Granny a receipt for them. She said their piece of paper was no good to her.

"I've bought and paid for those bags and I want them back. Terry McGarrity isn't selling explosive manure as far as I know!"

Once the RUC had stopped and were examining a car near the Hughes house. Granny went out and challenged them. Families nearby started to come along to see what was going on. Men, women and children came down the road and across the fields. Suddenly there were stones whizzing through the air.

"Let's get away," one of the RUC men said. "It's not safe here." And they quickly drove off.

There was good fun in recounting incidents like that, after the police or soldiers had gone. But Francie and Sally's little children were always frightened when the soldiers came.

Francie would hear a landrover down the road in the early morning, and he'd get out of bed, knowing he was liable to be arrested. They'd push in past Sally and search the house inside and out. Francie would tell Sally to get the tea made because he knew he was going to be arrested. He could tell from the way they were carrying on. The children would all be crying. Then they'd take Francie for questioning, usually to Omagh.

It really bothered Sally the way the soldiers and police would come to the house with their guns. The children would be frightened half to death thinking that they were going to be shot; or that the soldiers and police were coming to take their daddy away. They'd heard stories of children shot by rubber or plastic bullets. Every time they saw a policeman or soldier, they started screaming. It was fear of the guns they carried.

"Is that what the rubber bullets come out of?" the children would ask.

One time the house was raided at five o'clock in the morning and they trailed Francie out the door, dumping him onto the ground. The children saw it all and they never forgot it. Whenever their father was taken away, they asked questions.

"Will Daddy be in the same place as Uncle Martin?"

They knew Uncle Martin was in Long Kesh because they had gone to visit him. They knew the kind of place a prison was.

NOW FRANCIE WAS DRIVING hard from the forgotten rally at Bunbeg. He and Sally and the others went as far as Sion Mills, south of Strabane. Francie got out and rang the prison again. It was about 8:10 and there were still eighty or ninety miles to drive. He asked whether they'd be able to get in that night.

"No. Eight-thirty is the latest we'll let you in."

Disappointed again, Francie got back in the car and they drove on home. When they arrived it was about 10:15.

Francie decided to try the prison again.

"If you can get here by 10:30, we'll let you in—"

"There is no way I could get there by 10:30," Francie said. "If you'd told me that when I rang from Gweedore or Sion Mills, I could easily have made it."

Francie was really worried now. The families were not allowed to stay overnight until a man was seriously ill. Only a week ago he and Sally had visited Martin. Martin hadn't known they were coming, and when Francie walked into the room, Martin was standing at the sink, washing his face. He had to hold on to it with one hand and wash his face with the other. Francie saw him staggering. If Martin had let go he would have fallen.

When Martin turned around, his eyes were glazed—there was no spark in them. He grabbed the bed and by holding on was able to get back onto it, hand over hand.

He was surprised to see them because he hadn't been expecting anyone in till Tuesday. Francie had actually forced his way in that Monday. It wasn't possible for him and Sally to get there on Tuesday, so he had made a special effort to convince the NIO to let them in. They went through all the procedures on the Saturday before, and finally it was arranged that Francie, Brendan and Sally could see Martin on the Monday.

That was the weekend the negotiations between the ICJP and the British government were supposed to be coming to a head— the weekend when it looked as though the hunger strike might be resolved.

Francie and Brendan had gone in first to see Martin. Sally

had to wait until they came out. Then she went in alone. She could tell by looking at Martin that he was in bad shape.

"If nothing comes of this ICJP thing, Martin, what are you going to do?"

"We'll take the same stand," Martin answered.

"Are you prepared to go the whole way?"

"Unless we get what we want, we're going the whole way."

Martin was terrible looking that day. Sally thought he had the look of death in his eyes.

Sally came out and the men went back in again. When they finally came out, Sally turned to Brendan.

"I'd give him ten days to live."

Brendan thought that Martin might have a month.

"About ten days," Sally insisted.

Francie Hurson and the others stayed on the phone steadily after that until three in the morning. They phoned John Hume in Gweedore. They phoned Garret FitzGerald in Dublin. They phoned Bishop Edward Daly in Derry, and anyone else they thought might help them.

Finally, at about three on Monday morning, John Hume phoned back saying they could all get in at seven-thirty in the morning.

Francie thought that this was reliable. He trusted John Hume because of his friend Francie Martin. Francie Martin was a man of his word.*

*Francie Hurson had the impression that Francie Martin and John Hume were close friends, and that Hume relied on Francie Martin as one of the most principled SDLP men in the area. But Francie Martin had involved himself in the H-Blocks/Armagh campaign. During the hunger strike, since the time Martin had come on, Francie had been with Francie Martin day after day, night after night. They had become close friends. And whenever Francie Martin said that John Hume would be in such and such a place at a given time, John Hume was there.

The problem with John Hume, Francie Hurson felt, was that Hume was the leader of the SDLP, and that when a man was the leader

The last statement from the NIO that night had been that "there was no immediate cause for concern," that Brendan was with Martin, and that Brendan in fact had gone to bed in one of the hospital rooms. So Francie decided that Martin must be okay. He and Sally got in the car and drove—it took about a quarter of an hour—from their home near Carrickmore to Brendan's house in Galbally, to be with Brendan's wife, Sheila. Sheila and Sally sat up making curtains. Francie was exhausted and decided to take a nap. He slept for an hour and a half. When he woke, at about five o'clock, he turned on the radio . . .

BRENDAN HURSON had gone to Camlough in South Armagh that afternoon. Brendan didn't have a car with him, and he'd been given a lift by his friend John Campbell. The march began at Camlough and proceeded to Paddy Quinn's home village of Belleeks nearby. As the line of marchers approached Belleeks, one of the Quinn family came running up to say that there was an urgent message for Brendan. It was waiting for him in the pub in Camlough. Brendan had no way to get back to Camlough, but a man next to him said it was no problem.

"Jump into my car, and I'll take you to get the message."

When he got to the pub, the woman there said a Father McPeake had rung saying that it was urgent that Brendan go to the prison hospital at once, that Martin was seriously ill. It

---

of a party he couldn't say what he felt. It was Francie Hurson's theory that anyone in power was limited: there were things he couldn't say or do if he wanted to maintain his power. His brother Brendan had put it to Francie once: "John Hume is not a man of his word; he is a man of his party." The Hursons knew that Francie Martin had acted as mediator between Gerry Adams and John Hume. They knew, too, that Danny Morrison of Sinn Féin had met Hume several times, although the meetings were kept from public knowledge. John Hume had often told the Hughes brothers what he thought: that the five demands were justified, and that he was disgusted with British intransigence. But he wouldn't say this in public. The Hursons thought that was wrong, but they understood it. If John Hume had spoken out what he felt in his heart, his party might have turned against him.

was seven o'clock. According to the message Brendan was supposed to be at the prison hospital by seven-thirty. He was shocked. It was too far to go in so short a time and the man who had brought him over to get the message had to get the car back urgently. He couldn't take him up to the prison.

"Well," Brendan said, "take me back to Belleeks and I'll see what I can find."

When Brendan returned to Belleeks, he spoke with Bernadette McAliskey. She rang through to the prison governor, but they refused to give her any information and told her to ring the NIO. Bernadette rang the NIO.

"This is Brendan Hurson, a member of the Hurson family—" she said, as she handed the phone to Brendan.

He explained that he had received an urgent message to go to the hospital. He wanted to know how seriously ill his brother was.

"Ring the prison governor," they said.

So Bernadette rang the governor for him again.

"I rang the NIO," Brendan said to the governor," and they told me to get back to you, that you are to give me the information."

"I can give you no information," the governor said. "You have to get back to the NIO. They are the people—"

Brendan just dropped the phone and stood there.

By this time John Campbell had arrived, and said that he'd drive Brendan to the hospital. Bernadette was to do an interview with an American TV crew. Bernadette Donnelly, Martin's fiancée, was also there. As she and Brendan prepared to go with John Campbell, Brendan turned to Bernadette McAliskey.

"Would you like to come with us?" Brendan asked.

"I'd be only too glad to go," Bernadette McAliskey said. So she dropped the interview and went off with them in John Campbell's car. When they arrived at the front gate of the Maze prison, Brendan and Bernadette McAliskey got out to explain who they were. The first prison officer they talked to was unable to tell them anything about Martin. Brendan said he was anxious to get in to see his brother. They told him that other members

420

of the family were in with Martin—his father John, his sister Rosaleen and his brother-in-law Paddy McElvogue.

"That's all right. Can I get in?"

He was taken to another officer.

"I came to see my brother Martin," Brendan said. "And this is Martin's fiancée, Bernadette Donnelly. I would like her to go in with me. And Bernadette McAliskey, if possible."

The officer said that Bernadette Donnelly was not a close relation; it had to be a brother or sister or a parent.

"How come?" Bernadette McAliskey asked. "She's part of the family, too. She's engaged to Martin. She has a right to get in."

But they wouldn't let Bernadette Donnelly in, or Bernadette McAliskey.

IN THE CAR on the way up, Bernadette Donnelly had been worried about the 7:30 deadline. She was afraid they wouldn't be let in.

They'd reached the prison at about ten minutes to eight.

Now Brendan and Bernadette McAliskey were making representations on her behalf, but the warders were saying she couldn't get in because it was after hours. Only the immediate family could come in at night. She was worried about Brendan. Finally, at 8:30, they let him through. The warders knew that Martin was very bad.

After Brendan went in, Bernadette kept trying, with Bernadette McAliskey's help, but to no avail. Then Martin's father came out. That took awhile, with the search procedure and all the rest of it. She heard that they wouldn't let Francie in, if he arrived after 10 o'clock. She didn't know whether Francie knew about Martin's condition and even if he did whether he would make it in time.

Martin was in the hospital: so near to her—just inside the gates.

She and Bernadette McAliskey tried again, but the screws refused. Bernadette felt terrible. Martin was there, and he needed her, and these people would not let her in.

After trying twice more they gave up, and John Campbell drove them home. He dropped Bernadette McAliskey off at her house in Coalisland, and then drove Bernadette to Galbally. Bernadette wanted to go to Brendan's house to tell his wife Sheila that Brendan would be staying the night at Long Kesh. When she arrived, Martin's father and Paddy McElvogue were already there. Bernadette said she hoped to see Martin in the morning.

"He might not last," Paddy McElvogue said.

But Bernadette was hopeful. Martin had been on hunger strike for forty-five days. The other hunger strikers had lasted longer—sixty days or so.

Bernadette Donnelly had met Martin at the wedding, in August 1975, of a cousin of his, Seán Kelly, who'd married her sister Mary Rose Donnelly. Bernadette had grown up near Pomeroy, and was seventeen when her sister was married. Her sisters were all bridesmaids. They'd been matched up according to height, and she'd drawn one of the other young men as her partner. Her sister Eileen had drawn Martin. Bernadette remembered being disappointed. She'd fancied Martin Hurson right away, the moment she saw him.

She'd been going with another boy who was at the wedding, so she didn't expect to hear from Martin. She went to dances at Ardboe; Martin went to dances at the Gap near Carrickmore. But one night she went to the Gap, around Christmas 1975, and met Martin again. He asked her to dance and it started from there. She'd already stopped going with the other boy—he'd gone right out of her head when she'd first seen Martin. So they began dating early in 1976 and went out for eleven months. They'd never go to Mass together, because they didn't want people to know that they were going together. So they'd go to church at Galbally, the boys on one side and the girls on the other, and she would go along with Martin's sisters.

Martin used to drive over to Pomeroy in his orange Avenger to meet her four times a week: Friday, Saturday, Sunday and Wednesday.

Martin was very strong. He was about the same build as

Francie and looked like Brendan, but with a boy's face. Bernadette remembered him as a hard worker, always on the go. During the week he had a job at Powerscreen as a fitter, but he didn't lie around the house on Friday and Saturday. He'd be out working, doing odd jobs, helping his brother Brendan; or he'd help Francie, when Francie was working on cars. He always came to Bernadette on the four nights of the week, and sometimes on a Monday too, if there were a concert on. He was nineteen then, and she'd turned eighteen in March 1976.

Martin liked going to the pub. Sometimes he'd get a bit merry. They used to listen to country and western music—Big Tom, Gene Stewart, the Indians, Philomena Begley, Eileen King. The songs were "Nora," "Daddy Frank," "Rhinestone Cowboy," "The Black Hills of Dakota"—things like that. Bernadette didn't drink alcohol at all. She'd have a ginger ale or usually an orange. They went to the cinema and dances, and often went places with their friends. Martin was gregarious: he liked people a lot. He liked being with them. Occasionally they went with Martin's family for a few days to Donegal.

Once when they were in Bundoran, Francie and Sally and their first two children were all asleep in a caravan. In the morning they woke and found themselves off the caravan site and on the road nearby. During the night Bernadette and Martin had towed them off.

She loved Martin—his thick hair, dark brown, with sideburns. He had light blue eyes, and a very boyish face. His voice was rough and ready but easy to listen to, like Brendan's or Francie's. What she most loved about Martin was the look of his face.

Bernadette knew nothing about his military involvement. She did know he was Republican-minded; not because he talked about it all the time, but because of his reaction to events in the newspapers and on television. She had always felt that the Catholics in the North were badly treated, but she hadn't thought along Republican lines herself—not until Martin was taken from her.

Bernadette was stunned when she heard Martin had been arrested and brought to jail. Then, when she went to visit him, she saw the effect of the terrible beatings. But Martin would never say anything. He was beaten in Omagh barracks and in Crumlin Road jail. Even then she didn't want to ask about his military activities because she knew that if he'd wanted to tell her he would have.

Martin spent part of his remand time in Long Kesh, and the first thing he made there was a jewellery box for her: a wishing-well motif with a little pulley wheel that lifted a bucket up and down into the well, with a toothpaste tube top as the bucket. It was beautifully crafted, a treasure. He signed it: "Bernadette from Martin, Long Kesh, 1976."

During her visits to Martin in Long Kesh, the warders were always leaning over them, making it difficult to carry on any kind of personal conversation. But the period of remand back at Crumlin Road jail wasn't so bad. Martin was there for the best part of a year.

There were lots of fellows with him, including an old man, Felix Meenagh from Carrickmore, who was sixty-seven years old when he went in, and who took a certain pride in being described as "the godfather of the terrorists" which he wasn't at all. Martin met a number of men at Crumlin Road who would be on hunger strike with him several years later.

In November 1977 Martin was tried and convicted, solely on the basis of a signed confession forced out of him by beating and torture in Omagh barracks. When he went into the H-Blocks he was beaten again. In December 1978—he was on the dirt protest then—he got a terrible going-over. The screws came into the cell at five or six in the morning and dragged him out to a big room where they beat him and shaved his head. They stripped him and threw him into a bath, some screws scrubbing him with heavy brushes while others held him down. His kidneys were badly damaged and he was severely kicked in the spine. After the beating one of his toes was broken and his left leg paralyzed. He was so badly bruised and injured that they had to put him into the prison hospital.

Throughout 1978 Martin had refused to put on the uniform to go out for a visit, but Bernadette was allowed in to see him, in the prison hospital, three or four days after he'd had that beating. She was shocked when she saw him lying on the bed.

Even close up she was convinced it wasn't him. But then he began to talk, and she knew it was Martin. She saw some of his bruises. His stomach was badly discoloured and his head was cut from the scrubbing brush. Brendan and Francie were with her—it was the first visit Martin had taken in a year—and they were very angry when they saw what had been done to him. An orderly told them that Martin had looked even worse when he first came to the prison, after his trial. It was then that she really began to feel hatred towards the screws, the Brits, and the whole setup in Northern Ireland. She learned to hate every man she saw in a uniform, and most of all she hated the screws. She'd always connect them with what Martin had suffered.

One day in early 1979, about six weeks before her twenty-first birthday, Bernadette was visiting Martin when he suddenly said: "Why don't we get engaged?" She hadn't been thinking of marriage—not while he was in there—and she wanted to wait until he got out. But she agreed that it would be a good idea to become engaged. He was twenty-two then, and they'd known one another for three years. She went with two of Martin's sisters, Rosie and Annie, and their husbands, to get a ring. They drove to Dundalk, and tried several shops before they found the right one. And then Bernadette and Martin became engaged, in March 1979, over a prison table in the visitors' room in Long Kesh.

The next time she saw Martin he was back in Crumlin Road jail, still on the blanket protest. After his first trial in November 1977, he'd been granted a retrial—set for September 1979, on the grounds that the original judge had not sufficiently considered the medical evidence. Before the retrial he was moved to Crumlin Road. The first time she saw him there she was with Brendan. She much preferred the Crum for visits. The warder would stand eight feet away and they could talk in an ordinary tone of voice. They used to pass notes to one another by kissing, both in Crumlin Road and Long Kesh, and although they were watched closely they were never caught.

After they were engaged Bernadette kept thinking that Martin might be freed in the retrial. She pictured him out of prison wearing the bluey-green corduroy jacket she'd got him in

September 1976, with a shirt and tie that he usually wore underneath. When Martin's retrial came, he stood in the witness box and told the truth about what had happened to him in Omagh. It shocked Bernadette, because of his sincerity, to see policemen get up and tell the judge that they hadn't touched him. The judge accepted their lies as truth and that was the end of the retrial.

Even when the retrial went wrong, Bernadette had hope. He'd originally been sentenced to twenty years. With the remission he wasn't getting because he was on the protest, that would mean ten years. If he served a full sentence, but somehow got the remission, he'd be out when he was thirty years old. She never thought he'd be in prison for ten years. Every year she'd think of it as a period of two or three years to go. She was happy to wait for him.

She remembered how religious Martin was—and that long before he was put in prison. He always said his prayers, and had a special devotion to St. Martin de Porres after whom he'd been named. (Oddly, she'd had her own devotion to St. Martin before she met him.) He'd had the St. Martin magazine mailed to his house every month. When they started to allow books into the prison, the first thing he asked for was St. Martin's magazine.

Bernadette thought about how boyish he'd always looked, how innocent. And he *was* innocent. A lot of people thought he looked like a schoolboy, even when he was on hunger strike. He was twenty-four then, but he still had that boyish look.

And now tonight Bernadette couldn't sleep. She couldn't even go to bed.

BRENDAN, AT THE PRISON GATE, went across with the warders to a wooden hut.

"In there," they said to him. "There'll be someone here shortly to interview you."

Brendan went in. A warder barred the door behind him.

In a few minutes the warder came back and opened the door of the hut.

"You're the brother?" he asked, taking out a paper. He took

down Brendan's name and some other information.

"Are you prepared to stop the night?"

"It depends on how seriously ill Martin is—"

"I can't tell you that. I don't know. I only do the check-in."

It was after eight-thirty now.

"If you're not staying, you must be out by ten," the warder said, "and you won't get in again because the gates close and there's nobody allowed in or out after ten."

"If that's the case," Brendan said, "it's okay: I'll stay."

The warder left the hut, barring the door behind him. Brendan sat alone for a quarter of an hour. Then he heard the sound of a motor outside. The hut door was opened, and Brendan saw a minibus. Sitting in it were his father, John, his youngest sister Rosaleen, and his sister Eilish's husband Paddy McElvogue.

They brought Brendan's father into the wooden hut.

"Do you know this man?" one of the warders asked his father.

"Surely I know him. That's my son Brendan."

"Are you certain you know him?"

"Surely I am."

"That's okay, then."

One of them turned to Brendan.

"You'll be going over to the hospital in the minibus—"

"I'd like to see my family here first, to find out how Martin is."

"You can talk in the minibus."

So Brendan climbed into the bus and closed the door behind him.

"How bad is Martin?" Brendan asked.

"He isn't well at all," said his father. Martin was in bad shape: he'd been screaming a lot.

Brendan told them that he was prepared to stay the night and he wondered whether anybody else wanted to stay with him. His father and Rosaleen said they would prefer not to stay.

Brendan turned to his brother-in-law.

"Will you stay, Paddy?"

"I'll stay with you, surely."

He and Paddy discussed how they'd work out the car arrangements. Then Brendan told the warder that Paddy would be staying with him.

"Oh, no. He's not allowed to stay. He's not a close relative."

Brendan thought that Francie might make it in time.

"Okay, then," Brendan said to Paddy McElvogue. "I'll stay on my own. Maybe Francie'll be along." So Paddy left with the others.

Brendan was driven to the hospital where they questioned him again at the door. A man in a white coat led Brendan down to Martin's hospital cell.

He saw Martin, his face white and shrunken. The first thing he noticed about the bed was that there were rails up all around it. His impression was that Martin was dying.

"How long has he been like this?" Brendan asked the man in the white coat.

"Just today."

"No longer than that?"

"No. Just this evening, in fact."

"Is that so?" said Brendan. "I'd say he's been ill longer than that. Anyway, what are those rails for? Are you trying to cage him in the bed?"

"Oh, no!" The man in the white coat began waving his arms around the bed. "We didn't want him to fall out."

Brendan told him he wanted the rails down.

"I don't see any sense in the rails. Are any of you boys in here with him?"

"We're here all the time. We never leave him."

"Well, when I came through that door there was nobody here with him. Yet you're telling me that there is somebody with him all the time."

Brendan moved over to the bed and looked at Martin. He leaned down and spoke into his ear.

"Martin, do you know me? This is Brendan. Do you know that I am here beside you?"

Martin's head moved slightly. He was biting on his lips and had a very worried look. He was agitated about something.

Brendan had to keep shouting in his ear.

"Martin, Martin, this is Brendan. I'm here beside you."

After a minute or two, Martin seemed to come around. A smile broke across his boyish face. He spoke in a hoarse whisper.

"Hello, Brendan."

That smile gave Brendan heart. Martin still had some strength.

The Hursons had all grown up on the farm, high up on a hill in Aughnaskeagh, a townland near Cappagh in the Dungannon district of East Tyrone. Cappagh was as quiet a country town as could be found in Ireland. The whole area around Cappagh was overwhelmingly nationalist—mostly farmers, about two or three hundred closely-knit families. The land was full of hills, rolling mounds coated in green, with hedgerows and ribbons of tarmacadam marking off the fields below Cappagh Mountain, with the odd newly-built bungalow perched above the road. The Hursons' was an old house, the nub of a farm of thirty acres or so, like most of the farms in the area. The land was good only for raising chickens or pigs or grazing a few cattle.

At times, in that part of the country, the older men closed off streets and played bowls. There were quiet local pubs that were open at odd times, or open when there was a customer.

Catholic farming families like the Hursons had been in this place since before the time of the Ulster plantations. Hurson was a Norman-French name. But some of their forebears must have been in Ireland for thousands of years. They were the people the British had sent settlers to replace, people driven off the good low land and up into the hills. But their feeling for their country was strong. What little they had they held proudly, with affection and tenacity, passing the homesteads down from father to son. They worked on them constantly, pouring in money and care, and in recent years using the

429

improvement and building grants provided by the State when they could get them. People helped one another build their houses, and there had always been a tradition of mutual help in times of crisis.

Brendan himself was trained as a fitter/welder. He was always helping with repairs to machinery, outbuildings, fencing. He lived with his wife Sheila and their children in Galbally, down the south side of the mountain, but he had been making plans to build a new bungalow up at the old homestead at Aughnaskeagh—a new house he'd hoped Martin might come home to.

The families in that part of Tyrone all knew one another and many were closely-knit through marriage. Cousins married distant cousins, brothers or sisters in one family married brothers or sisters in another. Cousins cared for small toddlers. Older sisters tended the baby. They all fitted themselves easily and familiarly into the routine of one another's homes, repairing and washing up as if each place were their own.

Some of the children were brought up almost communally. Their nurture was shared: they'd do their homework, while their mother was away, under the supervision of an aunt who had dropped by; or they'd go off to spend the day at the house of an uncle who had stopped with his truck to pick up some machinery. They took Irish dancing classes, and practiced the tin whistle. When the grown-ups talked they listened in, pretending to be absorbed in colouring books or reading. Their breathing would come slow, their eyes cautiously appraising the bearer of news or tales from a world beyond the hills and valleys they knew.

The men helped with preparing food for the children, listening to homework, settling disputes, stoking the fire, feeding the dog and cat. But the women were the all-purpose helpers, picking up a toddler and carrying it around on the hip, listening to the prattle of an older child, marshalling energies, acting as control centres in their sisters' or cousins' households—helping with christenings, holy communions, weddings and the elaborate and hearty meals provided piping hot at wakes; entertaining visitors, answering the telephone, carrying, collecting and distributing

430

messages, arranging for people to come or be driven here or there, even settling accounts and paying bills.

Edward Martin Hurson, youngest of the three brothers and second youngest in the family of nine, was born into this way of life on 13 September 1956, at the little hill farm at Aughnaskeagh. Eilish was the eldest of the nine; then came Mary and Brendan, followed by Annie, Francie, Carmel and Josephine. Martin and Rosaleen were the youngest. His father, John Hurson, was nearly fifty when Martin was born. Martin's mother was a local girl, the former Mary Anne Gillespie.

Martin went to the Crosscavanagh school in Galbally, and then to St. Patrick's Intermediate school in Dungannon. At home he learned as a boy to drive a tractor, and helped with the farm work, rearing "croppy pigs" and looking after the cattle. He was a very reliable youngster, hardworking and always an early riser.

Brendan, who was about ten years older, looked after Martin almost as an uncle would. From the time he was a boy, Martin was very religious. He had a strong devotion to the Peruvian saint Martin de Porres, a Dominican laybrother who'd tended slaves brought to the New World from Africa—a man of great humility devoted heart and soul to the service of the poor.

Brendan remembered Martin as always saving up his money from the time he was small. He'd give every penny and shilling he got to a neighbour to keep for him. When Christmas came the neighbour would have a full box of money ready. Martin would always send some of the money to the priests of St. Martin and used the rest for presents. The family used to have a St. Martin's candle at Christmastime. When Martin was working in England he had a candle sent, and used to kneel nightly and pray before a tiny statue, an inch and a half high, of St. Martin de Porres. He had a novena to St. Martin going fifty-two weeks of the year, and used to give St. Martin medals to his friends.

Martin had great faith in the saint. Once when he was a boy, their brother-in-law Paddy McElvogue had a calf which was so ill the vet could do nothing with it. Martin, a schoolboy of eleven or twelve at the time with a great interest in all animals, went to see the calf and got down on his knees beside it. Taking out his book of St. Martin de Porres' prayers, he began rubbing his hand over the calf and saying prayers to St. Martin. The next day the calf was up and about again. On another occasion he said prayers over a car that wouldn't start. And next morning, sure enough it started.

Martin's devotion to his saint didn't cover all contingencies, however. He had a terrible scare when he was about ten years old. Their brother Francie used to have a pellet gun to deal with packs of dogs that would come ravaging around the farm from time to time. One Saturday, as Martin watched, Francie got the gun out and scared the dogs away. Afterwards he had some work to do on a car, and when a man came for him he left the gun sitting in his room with a pellet in it. When Francie was away working on the car, he was startled when one of the man's brothers ran up.

"Eilish Hurson's been shot," he said.

Francie immediately thought of the gun.

It turned out that Martin had gone up to the room, taken the gun, and come down into the hallway where Eilish was painting the ceiling. Martin put the gun up to her and not knowing there was anything in it, put a pellet straight through the fleshy part of her nose. When he saw the blood, he ran to a neighbour's house to ring the doctor.

"Eilish is shot!" he cried into the phone.

By the time Francie got out from underneath the car and down the road, the doctor—and a priest—had arrived at the house. But Eilish was not seriously hurt. Francie smiled whenever he remembered how alarmed Martin was at what he had done. ("Eilish is shot!")

When Brendan was about seventeen he had a car—an old banger. One Saturday, he and some friends were driving out to Pomeroy. Martin, who was always with him at that stage, was along for the ride. His friends wanted to go find a rear axle for a Ford. They were driving along the road, coasting around the bends. Out of one of those bends an old Ford appeared.

"There, boys," Brendan said. "There's a car with a good back

432

end. Why don't some of you jump out and ask him if we can have his axle?"

Brendan continued along the road. Suddenly he began to hear chop, chop, chopping sounds, as though feet were coming along the road.

"Stop!" the boys shouted at him. Brendan stopped.

There was Martin with the door of the car open. He'd been running alongside it, hanging on.

"What the blazes took you out of the car?"

"I got out," Martin said, "to ask that man if we could have his axle." Martin was about seven years old at the time.

In 1968, Martin went to a civil rights march in Dungannon where Catholics were batoned by the RUC. It was after this that he began to become interested in political change. Brendan supported the civil rights marches, and whenever there would be a civil rights meeting or demonstration he would be there. But Martin belonged to the new generation coming up to manhood, whose political interest would take a different form.

First a family tragedy intervened.

One Saturday evening in April, 1970, when Martin was thirteen years old, Brendan returned from work. Usually he came straight home, but that evening he had called into a neighbour's house. When he arrived home, his mother was ill. She was bleeding through the nose and it wouldn't stop. There was a terrible pain in her head. His father and Carmel were looking after her. Martin went to a neighbour's house to phone the doctor and priest. That night their mother was taken to Omagh hospital. She recovered a bit by the next morning, but she still wasn't well. So she was taken to the Royal hospital in Belfast.

When his mother had become ill Martin went down to a Father McDonald at the parish house. Father McDonald told him that his mother was going to be all right. Martin visited her nearly every day.

Brendan was preoccupied with his own worries about his mother, and didn't notice what was happening to Martin, though he did notice that the boy was a bit absent-minded. At one stage,

433

Martin, who was usually careful about his appearance, put his good suit on over the top of his old clothes as he was preparing to go to the hospital. Brendan noticed this and decided that he would have to keep an eye on Martin. The family were with him that day in Omagh. When they went shopping, Martin began picking children's toys off a display counter and fooling around with them. It wasn't like him at all. Brendan brought him to a doctor. The doctor said there was nothing wrong, so Brendan and the others were satisfied. He seemed to be okay, though he was still acting oddly.

Their mother died on Thursday, 20 April, of a brain haemorrhage. A few days later Brendan and Martin and their father were out with the tractor. Martin was driving down a lane and their father was standing on the back on two bags of corn. On a steep corner the tractor went out of control and overturned. Mr. Hurson was thrown off. Brendan ran down the lane towards them. He could see that his father was all right but he couldn't see Martin. Just then Martin began running towards him. He'd been caught underneath the tractor, but he'd come up without a scratch. Martin was laughing. Brendan asked him how he'd got out from under the tractor.

"I got out through that wee hole there, just beside the mudguard," Martin said.

Later that day they went down to their sister Eilish's home in Cappagh, where Mary was staying. Mary had come home a week earlier, while their mother was in hospital, and had been with Martin a lot during those days. Martin was sitting in the house when Mary came into the living room. He jumped up.

"In the name of God, Mary, where did you come out of? When did you get home?"

That was the first time they realized that Martin had lost his memory. He'd had amnesia from the night their mother was taken ill till the day the tractor overturned.

After he'd recovered from his amnesia, Martin went down to Fr. McDonald. He was cross with the priest, who had told him that his mother would be all right. Now she was dead.

"I told you she would be all right," the priest answered him, "and she *is* all right. Your mother is in heaven."

Martin seemed content with that.

When Martin left school, he went to work as an apprentice fitter/welder at Johnny McKenna's engineering works. The money wasn't great and he wanted more experience in heavy engineering, So Brendan got him started in Finlay's. He stayed on at Finlay's until he went over to England.

In 1972 Francie married Sally Hughes and went over to work with McAlpine's in Manchester. Martin came to England the next year—he was nearly seventeen—and Francie was able to fix him up with a job at McAlpine's as a fitter/welder. He began making good money and saving it, and in time he became a main fitter/welder with McAlpine's, working from six in the morning till nine at night.

Martin and two friends stayed with Francie and Sally in Crumsill in Manchester. There wasn't much room and the three lads had to sleep in the same bed. Sally would come in from work and there'd be a record player, a radio and a TV going at the same time. They'd listen to a country-and-western program on the radio from 11:45 till 12:15 at night and they'd have the record player and TV going on as well. Martin always wanted to hear the news.

One night, when Francie and Sally were very tired, and wanted a bit of peace and quiet, the boys had all three machines going full blast.

"For God's sake," Sally said, "switch one of those things off!"

"This place," Martin said, "is worse than Long Kesh!"

He was thinking about what he'd heard of the cages. At the time Martin would have known very little about Long Kesh.

In 1974 Francie and Sally returned to Ireland. Martin returned too, at Christmas, when the job he was working on was finished. He'd been in England a year and a half.

When Martin got back to Ireland, he lived with his father and younger sisters at the farmhouse in Cappagh. Brendan got him a job at Powerscreen. It was the last job Martin had.

At night he was often up at "Ruby's"—Francie Boyle's place

up in the village of Cappagh. Francie Boyle was called Ruby because of a fancied resemblance to the Jack Ruby who'd shot Lee Harvey Oswald in Dallas, Texas in 1963. Ruby had a food shop, a petrol pump and a shebeen-like pub in the village. He and his father had carried many families through hard times, and Ruby had given a number of businessmen in the area their start.

Ruby had a story about Martin and a trip to Donegal. He'd gone with Bernadette and a friend in a car he'd bought on hire-purchase; their destination was Bundoran. On the way up Martin's car broke down and none of them had enough money to pay for repairs. A garageman fixed the car and gave them petrol. When they got back, before he went to the Hurson house, Martin came straight to Ruby with his problem: he wouldn't be paid until the following Friday but wanted to settle his account with the garageman right away. Ruby loaned Martin what he needed so that he could post a money order to the man.

"Many's the lad," Ruby told Brendan, "that would have said, 'Oh, to hell,' and either wait until he was paid on the weekend or else forget about it entirely. But Martin was always a man of his word."

NOW BRENDAN was in the hospital trying to talk to Martin. He kept repeating that Da and Rosaleen had been in, along with Paddy McElvogue, and that Francie would be in soon.

Brendan could see that Martin was parched. He turned and addressed the man in the white coat standing behind him.

"What is your profession?"

"I'm a nurse." He told Brendan he'd been attending Martin day and night. "You can call me Gerry," he said. "What's your name?"

Brendan told him.

"Is there any water?" Brendan asked.

"Oh, I've been giving him sips all night."

"Where do you get the water?"

"There's a cup there with a mouthpiece on it."

"Do you get this water from the sink?"

"No, we've been giving him pure spring water."

436

"Where is it? I'll give him a drink."

"It's in the bottle."

Brendan lifted the bottle but there was nothing in it. He turned to the nurse.

"Oh, I'll get a new bottle of water."

He went off and came back with a bottle of water. The label said it was from Scotland.

Brendan opened the bottle and asked him to put water in the cup. Brendan took the cup to the head of the bed. He put his arm around Martin's neck, supporting his head and lifting him up.

"Take this wee sip of water, Martin."

The nurse said that he had tried to give him water but he wouldn't take it. Brendan kept giving Martin sips, but found that he was starting to bring the water up. Brendan eased off, giving him only small sips.

Every so often Martin would swing his arms in the bed. His lips were cut because he'd been chewing them. He kept moving his arms about and sometimes his legs as well. The water seemed to bring him around a bit. He seemed to get just a little more relaxed. Brendan continued to give him tiny sips.

Occasionally the nurse would take out his stethoscope and listen to Martin's chest. To Brendan's mind, this Gerry hadn't a clue what he was doing. Brendan began to suspect that he had in fact no medical experience at all, that he wasn't actually a nurse—

"How long has Martin been like this?" Brendan asked.

"Oh, he was always getting up—until now."

"But it was back on Friday that we got word he wasn't well."

"He was grand on Friday. He got up on Friday morning and shaved himself and all."

"Well, that's very wrong, because the priest was in here and he said Martin wasn't shaved."

"Oh, but he got up that evening and he shaved. He got up on Saturday and shaved. He was grand today; he was doing perfectly well. He just took bad about five o'clock this evening; he suddenly got weak and deteriorated."

"I don't believe you," Brendan said. "Martin's been like this longer than five o'clock this evening. This lad is dying. It's as simple as that. He's dying—he couldn't possibly have been able to get up and shave himself."

Finally Gerry admitted that he'd shaved Martin that day.

"Why did you have to wait for me to accuse you of lying? I want one thing: for you to tell me the truth. My brother's dying, and what you say is not going to make any difference here or there. But I want the truth."

Gerry left the room and Brendan was left alone with Martin.

Then another man in a white coat, called Paul, came in. Brendan asked him the same questions he'd asked Gerry. When had Martin taken ill?

"He got weaker on Friday. I wasn't on then. But when I came in on Saturday he was very ill. He was in a wheelchair all day Saturday."

Paul seemed willing to tell the truth. He said that on Saturday one of the other hunger strikers had wheeled Martin down to the TV room where they could watch television and smoke cigarettes. They didn't have their own cigarettes but had to ask the warders for them. It struck Brendan that some of the nurses or warders would have been sympathetic to the men. Paul seemed to be a qualified nurse. Compared to Gerry at least, he seemed to know what he was doing.

Gerry came back into the room with a cup of tea for Brendan. Then the chief came in—a senior warder—a man dressed in black prison trousers and a white shirt and tie, with shirtsleeves rolled up. It wasn't the blue shirt the warders wore.

"There's a room and a bed available for you here," he said to Brendan. "You can come back after you finish your cup of tea."

Martin was settling down and wasn't so restless now. There wasn't much Brendan could do. So he took the cup of tea and a plate with two cheese sandwiches on it, and followed them to the other room.

"You can shut the door, lie down, have your tea and a smoke—whatever you want."

438

He was grateful for the tea, but then they locked the door and he couldn't get out until they came back to unlock it. He'd been in there ten minutes when he knocked on the door and said he wanted to go back to Martin's room.

As he sat with Martin, Gerry would come in, or Paul. Sometimes the two of them would be there together. The chief also came and went. Through the early part of the night, Brendan continued giving Martin small sips of water. At about half past eleven, the chief came in again.

"Your brother is quiet now. Why don't you go back down to the room and just relax?"

Martin was peaceful at the time. There was a window open and Brendan asked that it be closed. They closed it. Then he went down to the other room as they'd suggested.

He sat for awhile, smoking, and looked at a newspaper that had been left there. About ten minutes to twelve they opened the door and asked if he wanted to come up again. He went back to Martin's room. Martin was very restless now.

"He's just started this up again," one of them said. "We wanted you to see it."

His arms and legs were flailing about. Even his head was going. He seemed to be in the grip of some strong emotion, as though he were struggling against something.

"God," Brendan thought, "he's in awful shape." Martin went on that way for ten minutes. Brendan tried to give him sips of water, but he wouldn't take anything. He kept struggling. As the minutes went by Brendan himself became more and more distressed. He was seeing something he'd never seen before in all his life.

"Is there a priest here? Please ring the priest."

"We've already rung the doctor."

The chief came in. Brendan asked him to ring the priest.

"Oh, there's no trouble about that. He lives just around the corner. All we have to do is ring him and he'll be up in about five minutes."

"Okay then, ring the priest."

"The doctor is already coming—"

"I have no objection to the doctor coming. What I want is the priest."

The chief went out. When he came back he told Brendan the doctor was on his way and the priest was coming as well.

Brendan sat beside Martin, doing his best to help him. A long time passed and neither priest nor doctor came. Brendan took hold of one of Martin's thin arms, not trying to fight against him but just holding him lightly, trying to prevent Martin from hurting himself. As Brendan watched, it seemed to him that the boy's whole effort and his whole expression was saying "You won't put me down. You *won't* put me down." He was fighting against something very terrible—something vicious. It seemed to Brendan that it was the people around him, the prison staff, he was fighting against.

Brendan stayed close to him, trying to read his lips. Martin kept getting worse. He was less and less audible. Still there was no priest—and no doctor.

As Brendan watched his face, now, he thought of the night he and Martin were out watching the helicopters. Had he known, Brendan could have prevented Martin's getting caught the next day.

Brendan had had no idea at all that Martin was involved with the IRA until the time of his arrest. It was only later, after Martin had been picked up, that Brendan started thinking back, looking for hints and clues.

Brendan knew that Martin was not only fearless; he was well-motivated. While still a youngster at secondary school in Dungannon, he'd seen the police and vigilantes assaulting people. That taught him what the RUC was prepared to do to Catholics. Then there was the Army.

When the British troops first came to Northern Ireland, Brendan regarded them as greenhorns—but greenhorns who'd come to save the Catholic population from sectarian savagery. The problem, as Brendan saw it, was that the RUC took virtual control of the British Army almost from the start, thereby maintaining the sectarian position.

Martin, a child of the new generation, would never have seen the British Army, even for a brief time, as a benevolent peacekeeping outfit. By the time he was thirteen the Army had begun to show itself as a violently anti-Irish, anti-Catholic force. He had decided to fight it. Martin had probably been influenced by stories about a man from the district named Dan McAnallen who, though he was blown up in 1973 by his own bomb, was considered a great and courageous Republican leader and had become a folk hero in that part of the country.

Brendan, though he wasn't involved, would give a man who went out to fight credit for his courage. He had long since come to see the war as a just war, and he believed in it, even though he had been raised differently in a different time.

Brendan and Francie had been brought up to tolerate the repression that was part of a Catholic countryman's life in Northern Ireland. There was no political upheaval when Brendan was Martin's age, and the message drummed into him was: "Don't get involved in politics." That would have been their mother's advice. It was strange, but when Brendan was a boy he didn't know what politics was: yet those words were implanted firmly in his head. When he was young there were B-Specials around, but they didn't give the Hursons much trouble. Brendan generally stayed within three or four miles of home. He wasn't constantly travelling over to Dungannon or up to Carrickmore or Omagh, as Martin would when he was a young man. Brendan rarely got further than Galbally, just over the hill.

As a man and a soldier, Martin had a great many things going for him. His manner was a lot like Francie's, gregarious and congenial. And like Francie, behind the genial facade he'd have three levels of thinking going on at the same time. Yet there was nothing of the hard man about Martin. He was not the type to pick a fight. He loved being in the midst of a bit of crack, and he was as good at laughing as he was at working.

Brendan went back over his recollections—what he knew or had heard about Martin's activities in the area.

Martin spent a lot of time at Brendan and Sheila's house on the Cappagh road, and every day Brendan drove Martin to work at Powerscreen. With all the odd jobs and the constant trips to Pomeroy to see Bernadette Donnelly, Brendan wondered where Martin had ever found time for military activity. But when he thought about it, Martin's regular visits to Bernadette in Pomeroy meant that he always had an alibi for being out on the road at night. When he'd be stopped by the security forces he could say in all honesty that he was going to visit his girlfriend, or coming from a visit with her. Yet he could leave at any time in the early evening, saying he was going to see Bernadette, and he might not have to be in Pomeroy until ten or eleven that night. Or if he saw her earlier, he could stay out up to any hour afterwards.

There was a UDR patrol from Pomeroy that used to give Martin a bad time when he was going up and down to visit Bernadette. The road from Cappagh to Pomeroy was quiet and they could give him trouble without anybody knowing. They'd make Martin take off his shoes and socks and stand in the road barefoot. They'd assault him and beat him up. But then it happened that a member of this patrol went to investigate a house in Dungannon. He stepped into a booby-trap and was killed. The IRA issued a statement to the effect that they'd got their man and they'd more to get. The Pomeroy squad never operated near home after that. They worked out some sort of exchange with UDR men from the Moy, south of Dungannon. The men in the squads were known, and it was becoming too dangerous for them to work in their own areas.

Brendan had heard it said that the Cappagh IRA unit was one of the most efficient in the six counties. It had the problem of all units, though, in this kind of war. It was impossible to meet the enemy forces in direct confrontation. They had to work by stealth. It was guerrilla war—hit and run.

Not surprisingly, there was a lot of muddling. Once, so the story went, a directive came from the IRA Army Council: there was to be a concerted effort to blow up telephone exchanges throughout the six counties. So men in the local unit set out to do the exchange down the road.

The exchange was surrounded by a large fence. The men got through that without setting off the alarm. They next had to get into the building. It was strange—they found a window open.

442

They climbed in and were looking for the best place to set the bomb when suddenly they heard an ominous sound. "Tick, tick, tick—" The men scrambled out as fast as they could. No sooner were they clear of the building when, bang! the whole place went up.

Another unit had got there before them.

Martin was like the rest, an ordinary young man, trying to wage war, part-time, in extraordinary circumstances. He was regarded as a simple farmer boy, an easy-going culchie lad—and he knew exactly how to use this reputation. He was very discreet. He was apparently very choosy, too. Though Martin was not a leader—some of the family thought of him as highly suggestible and easily led—Brendan learned later that when he was asked to do anything he would always make careful inquiries about details before agreeing to go ahead. When he was on a job he wasn't happy-go-lucky at all.

Then, Brendan was told, once Martin understood what he was to do and why, and had agreed to it, he'd follow through without hesitation. He was highly intelligent about his work—and very cool: "A manly little buck," one of his leaders had said of him. Even on his own, Martin would do a job others might be afraid to do. And he was determined and tireless: he'd do an operation, lie out in the fields all night, come in in the morning—"with water running out of his ass," as one man put it—shower and go off to work. Nobody ever caught him out. He covered his tracks too well. Because of his easy-going reputation and habits he could make excuses and get away with what he'd done. Most people who knew him refused to believe, even to this day, that Martin was in the IRA. At home they never thought of him as being involved, although there were times, Brendan learned, that Francie had his suspicions.

All three of them were nationalist to the core, and Martin, like Brendan and Francie, believed that the fight to remove British rule from Ireland was legitimate. It was a just war: British soldiers shouldn't be in Ireland, and particularly in such a heavily Irish part of Ireland. And because of their antipathy towards British rule they didn't accept the other crown forces, the RUC or the UDR, either. Martin had been antagonistic towards them since an early age. But Martin was also personally committed, in ways Brendan had never known, to what the IRA was doing.

Martin had been an active IRA man for about eighteen months. This was hard for Brendan to realize. He'd always thought of his brother as a quiet, modest young boy.

In late 1976, there'd been a lot of shootings and bombings in the Cappagh area. On Tuesday 9 November, three local boys were rounded up and arrested under the Emergency Provisions Act. There had been helicopters out that night and all sorts of activity in the area. There'd been a lot of talk around town about the lads who were lifted.

In late 1976, there'd been a lot of shootings and bombings in the Cappagh area. On Tuesday 9 November, three local boys were rounded up and arrested under the Emergency Provisions Act. There had been helicopters out that night and all sorts of activity in the area. There'd been a lot of talk around town about the lads who were lifted.

The next day, Wednesday, Brendan was vaguely aware of searches going on. On Wednesday night Martin was with Brendan when Army helicopters began searching the fields around Cappagh. The house where Brendan lived was down a quarter-mile lane off the Cappagh Road. Brendan and Martin were in one of the outbuildings—a wooden shed with a red corrugated roof. Martin's car had developed a clutch problem and he'd towed it over to Brendan's with a tractor. Brendan had told him to put the car in the shed and they'd take out the clutch and fix it.

That night the helicopters began playing their searchlights over the area. It was a bright starry night and the planes circled around Cappagh, working the whole district well into the night. With Brendan beside him, Martin stood out in the lane, behind some fir trees, looking up at the helicopters. There seemed to be no fear in him. Brendan thought he was merely curious, like himself. Later Brendan realized that they'd probably been looking for Martin's car that night, but hadn't seen it because it was in the shed. Brendan realized, too, that that night the whole search had probably been concentrated on finding Martin.

They'd already picked up the two or three other boys whose capture they would announce next day.

Martin had stayed at Brendan's the two previous nights. Brendan urged Martin to stay that night, too. Thinking about it afterwards, Brendan was glad in one way that he hadn't known Martin was involved. They could have beaten Brendan's head in, yet been unable to make him tell them anything. But he did wish that, when the helicopters were searching the place, Martin would have told him something. He could have saved Martin. Had Martin said to Brendan, "I'm in deep water," Brendan would have known what to do. He could have hidden Martin in the shed or helped him settle down for the night out in the fields. It was a thing that saddened him whenever he thought of it afterwards.

Oddly, Brendan had been unusually persistent in trying to coax Martin to stay. He felt there wasn't any point in Martin's going home. If he did go, he'd have to walk back across the fields in the morning to get a lift from Brendan to work. But although it was already one o'clock Martin was still anxious to get home.

"Stay here," Brendan said. "You stayed last night and the night before—what's the difference?"

"Well, I'd like to get home to see Da. I haven't been home these last couple of nights."

"Stay here tonight. It'll be easier for you to get to work in the morning. How about seeing Da tomorrow evening? It's too late to go home now anyway."

It was strange in retrospect how stubborn Brendan had been, with Martin just as stubbornly refusing the invitation. Brendan realized later that Martin hadn't guessed they'd come for him so quickly. He'd been so discreet he hadn't reckoned on anyone finding out about him.

But someone had talked—under torture.

Martin went home that night, and at six o'clock the next morning he was taken from his bed and arrested. He and the other lads were hauled off to Omagh police barracks and given terrible beatings. Martin heard Jimmy Rafferty shouting and screaming in a nearby cell.*

Martin himself was dealt with viciously. RUC detectives punched him in the stomach, pulled his hair, kicked him in the testicles, banged his head against the wall, and beat him all over his body. Seven doctors examined Martin afterwards and six of them found evidence of serious injury.

Rafferty refused to sign a confession, and he and one of the other seven arrested at the same time were released without charge. Rafferty spent four days in Tyrone County Hospital being treated for the injuries he'd sustained. The other five were all charged and later convicted on the basis of confessions produced by their interrogators.

Martin's signed confession, extracted while he was in Omagh barracks, admitted involvement in various activities. He was then taken to Cookstown barracks, where he filed a complaint against the police at Omagh. They didn't torture him at Cookstown, but they threatened to send him back to Omagh unless he confessed again to the same offences. He was charged with exploding a landmine at Galbally in November 1975, a charge that was later dropped. He was also charged with possession of the Galbally landmine, conspiracy to kill members of the security forces, exploding another landmine beside a passing UDR landrover in February 1976, and with IRA membership. There was no forensic evidence in support of the charges—only Martin's signed statement. At the trial, a year later, in November 1977, Judge Rowland dismissed the extensive doctors' evidence about the seriousness of Martin's injuries, yet admitted Martin's statements, sentencing him to twenty years for possession of landmines and conspiracy, and handing down two concurrent sentences of five and fifteen years on other charges. Rowland was contemptuous of Martin's complaints of maltreatment and torture:

> My conclusion about the medical evidence is that there

*The ordeal of James Joseph Rafferty, who was tortured and then released, became a celebrated case—a classic case of the application of the Roy Mason/Kenneth Newman policy of brutality towards Republican suspects in Northern Ireland.

446

were virtually no objective signs of recent injury to the accused. Having observed the accused in the witness box and in court over a number of days and having heard the way he answered questions, I am in no doubt that the tenderness he complained of was purely subjective, and that apart from fairly insignificant swelling at the back of the head, there was nothing consistent with the severe treatment he described . . . His evidence is not capable of reasonable credence and I reject it . . .

So callous had Rowland been in the handling of medical evidence that a retrial was finally ordered by the Court of Criminal Appeal. It was heard by a Judge Murray in September 1979.

The prosecuting counsel at the second trial was a barrister named John Creaney, a sharp and effective lawyer. Brendan and Francie were very disappointed with Martin's barrister and solicitor. The barrister was slow and ineffective in arguing the case, and he repeated himself over and over again. His attitude put Martin off, and Martin found it impossible to work in tandem with him. Because of the solicitor in the case, Brendan and Francie did not get the lawyer they wanted, a man like Desmond Boal or Tom Cahill, whom they thought the best in the six counties. The solicitor got another man, who on the last day of Martin's trial came out of the court during a recess, rubbing his hands together, and telling Brendan that they were doing very well.

"We have the case ninety-nine per cent won," the man said.

"What do you mean ninety-nine per cent won?" Brendan said. "As far as I can see it's far from won."

The barrister went back into the courtroom and when he came out again he'd lost the case.

"What were you doing, coming out blaring that you had the case ninety-nine per cent won?" Brendan asked him.

Judge Murray had declared the statement taken at Omagh barracks inadmissible. But then he turned around and accepted the Cookstown statement, which had been extracted under threat of returning Martin to Omagh for further torture.

Brendan told the barrister he didn't think he was capable of winning a case. Francie and he had talked afterwards, and Francie agreed with him that the man was useless. Brendan felt that way about most of the lawyers in the country. They were too busy helping each other out—like the solicitor and his friend the barrister in Martin's case—working together, getting themselves rich. Brendan knew about the Diplock bungalows, as they called them—the resort houses Catholic lawyers had built themselves up near the resort of Ballycastle on the Antrim coast. The Hursons wished they had insisted on getting a man who would have fought Martin's case properly. At the very least, Martin should have got political status, since the offences he was alleged to have committed were all pre-March 1, 1976—the criminalization date.

Meanwhile, Jimmy Rafferty had instituted a case against the police at Omagh for torture and ill-treatment. The authorities in Northern Ireland, despite outspoken pressure from Jack Hassard—a Protestant councillor from Dungannon—held up the inquiry into Rafferty's case.* They said that Rafferty's evidence against the police might prejudice Martin's retrial in Martin's favour! So the Rafferty inquiry was postponed until well after Martin's retrial.

After the September 1979 retrial, Martin appealed Judge Murray's verdict. Nine months later, in June 1980, the appeal was disallowed.

Now he was lying in a hospital bed in the prison at Long Kesh on the forty-fifth day of a hunger strike.

One of the things that had worried Brendan about his brother

*Jack Hassard, a man who looked and sounded like a first cousin of Ian Paisley, was anything but a bigot; he was in fact the opposite: a great-hearted, entirely tolerant man, with an extraordinary commitment to justice. A post office labour union leader, he had served on the Northern Ireland Police Authority. Finally, in disgust at the way it connived in the delay of the Rafferty inquiry, he quit the Authority. In the end, the Omagh detectives—who had been administering the beatings to Martin Hurson, Jimmy Rafferty and the others—refused to give evidence at the Rafferty inquiry on the grounds that they might incriminate themselves!

was that he'd become very angry in prison. Martin had always been a calm, easygoing lad. He had a temper, but he kept it well under control and never got into fights. In prison he had become quite different. At the end of a visit the warders would annoy him and he'd tell them to go to hell. He had no respect at all for them and refused to show them any deference. He'd ask them for nothing and he didn't want his visitors to be polite to them either. Once helpful and considerate to people, he'd been turned, by the beatings and maltreatment in prison, into an angry young man.

During the Dáil election campaign, Martin had been run as a candidate in Longford-Westmeath. Brendan and Francie, along with other people in the area—especially their friend Francie Martin—had worked very hard for their brother's candidacy. In the election on 11 June, he won more than four thousand first preference votes and got over a thousand transfers from other candidates. Only at the end of the sixth count was he eliminated from the balloting.

On 24 June, Martin had been moved to the prison hospital. He had evidently slipped much further and faster than Kieran Doherty or Kevin Lynch, who had gone on the hunger strike a week earlier than he.

At the bedside Brendan sat holding Martin's left wrist while Gerry or Paul held the other one. Brendan tried to keep him from scratching or tearing at his face or from hitting himself with his fist. At one point, with his fist clenched, Martin hit Gerry in the face. Although sweat was pouring from him there wasn't a sponge to wipe it. So Brendan got up and went to Martin's cupboard to get a facecloth from his toilet kit. He went to the sink, rinsed the facecloth out in cold water, and then came back to the bed and spread it over Martin's forehead. He did this several times during the hours from twelve to two.

Through most of that time there was a horrible moaning sound from Martin. It was a kind of screaming, without being real screaming, because Martin was too weak to scream out. It was like very loud moaning, a terrible, penetrating sound. Brendan

449

was shattered by the sound from the time it began. He had been prepared to accept that Martin was dying. He knew there was very little he could do. But Martin's screaming, his obvious agony, upset Brendan terribly.

Finally, at a few minutes to two, the doctor arrived and examined Martin. Brendan thought he'd ask the doctor a question.

"Can you guarantee me that if I do something for Martin, he'd come out perfect, that he'd come out of this clear and well?"

"I can't guarantee you anything," the doctor said, "because the boys that died in here—none of them died in the same way. They've all had different deaths. A lad could snap out of it just like that." The doctor clicked his fingers. "But then again, you can't be certain."

"Have you even seen a patient as bad as Martin?"

"Patients can vary—"

"I know that."

It was then that the truth froze Brendan: the cold truth that Martin's death was staring him in the face.

All that Brendan could do now was to try to help him as much as he could during those last hours, giving him sips of water and wiping his face. It was not until two o'clock that the priest came in—Father John Murphy, one of the prison chaplains. Brendan was very relieved to see him—someone there he could trust. The doctor was much too casual about Martin's condition. He wasn't concerned. The male nurses, the chief, the NIO—none of them really cared.

Father Murphy went over to the side of the bed to say some prayers.

"Hallo, Martin, this is Father Murphy, can you hear me?"

Martin gave a light nod, and the priest took out his oils: the last sacraments—

Before the anointing Martin was at his worst—flailing about, sweating heavily, screaming silent, terrible screams. As soon as Father Murphy had anointed and blessed him, Martin suddenly settled down. From then on Brendan was able to relax. Before two o'clock, Martin's eyes were wild; now he was

450

absolutely peaceful and calm. It was as though the priest's hand had a miraculous power.

During the hours that followed, Brendan and the doctor said very little to one another. The doctor came in and out to check a heart monitoring machine he'd set on a bedside table. Brendan talked to Father Murphy. He and the priest went into the room set aside for Brendan and chatted for a little while. Brendan learned that the priest didn't live just around the corner, as the chief had said. He was a curate in a parish out on the airport road. He lived a considerable distance away. And they hadn't notified him until very late. The minute he got word he'd left for the prison.

Brendan shook his head. The authorities here wouldn't tell him the truth, about anything.

He and Father Murphy went back into the room. At one point Martin started to move about in the bed again, very weakly this time. His lips were badly cut where he had buried his teeth into them.

After three o'clock, Brendan noticed Martin's features changing. His forehead started to turn a strange yellowish tint. There was a radical change in his colour, moving down from the top of his face. Brendan, holding his hand, could feel the fingers getting cold. And then the coldness went up the back of Martin's hands. His feet were getting colder. His features seemed to be changing, as though something was passing over them. The changed colour went down to his throat. Father Murphy said nothing. He simply waited. Several times Brendan noticed that the priest was looking at him. Brendan knew he was in a bad state himself, because he knew what was happening, that Martin was dying, and now he was having to struggle to hold back his tears.

Suddenly there was a sound in Martin's throat, as though something were strangling him—his spittle perhaps. The doctor brought up a suction machine. He put a tube into Martin's mouth and cleared the mucus. But Martin's colour had gone completely. He seemed to close up. His head went back and he let out a very deep sigh.

Brendan touched Martin's chest and face; they were starting to become cold and stiff. As he sat there, he could almost feel the whole process in his own body. He was crying. He began shouting at Martin, but knew that Martin could no longer hear him.

Then about four o'clock the cardiograph stopped moving; there was only a straight line. The doctor looked at his watch and said that Martin had died. Brendan thought that the doctor seemed very shocked. Everyone in the room was affected. Clearly the doctor had thought Martin was going to come out of it. He hadn't thought Martin was going to die.

Brendan learned later that all the men went into a kind of trough when they were somewhere past the halfway mark in their hunger strike. Then they'd emerge and get a kind of second wind. Martin never got that second wind. Because of the damage the police beatings had done to his kidneys, he was unable to keep water down. Hunger strikers needed a great deal of water to prevent dehydration, but Martin had become unable to hold water down.

Now, suddenly, the warders left the room. The doctor put the machine under his arm and walked out, too. Only Brendan and Father Murphy were left. They knelt down and began saying the rosary.

Brendan was in the midst of his grief when a warder came in and asked them to leave Martin's room, so they could tidy up. Brendan and Father Murphy went in to the other room. Then the warder returned and said that they could re-enter the room. They came back and continued their prayers. When they were finished, Brendan kissed his brother.

He wanted to ring home. He asked a warder, who said that would be all right, but that Brendan would have to wait. As they were waiting, a policeman came into Martin's room.

"Is this your brother?"

"It is," Brendan said.

The policeman wanted to have a few words with Brendan. So Brendan went along with him into the other room.

The policeman wanted to know his brother's proper name—

452

Edward Martin Hurson. He asked his age. Brendan gave it. Who was the undertaker, the policeman asked. Brendan gave them the name—Massey McAleer. He knew that if he didn't answer, the police might deliver the body to the house or have it dropped off in a field, or on the road somewhere. He remembered how Francis Hughes' coffin had been treated, and he'd heard about the threat to have Patsy O'Hara's body dropped on the O'Haras' doorstep.

"I've only been with him while he was dying," he said. "*You've done the rest.*"

"Oh, I'm sorry to be upsetting you."

"You've been upsetting me longer than one night, you know."

"Thanks very much," the policeman said. "That's all the information I need."

Then, as he went hurrying out, Brendan told him he was trying to make a phone call. The policeman said the chief would see to that.

Brendan was glad that Father Murphy was there. At least he could talk to the priest. There was no point in talking to these other boys. They'd only be laughing up their sleeves at him.

He thought about how all through the night they wouldn't tell him the truth. The doctor was genuinely shocked, though, and Paul, too. As far as the Gerry boy was concerned, it was hard to know. Then the chief came down. He'd probably enjoyed Martin's dying, Brendan thought.

"We don't like to see this happening," the chief said.

Brendan was still waiting to make his phone call. The warder came back, saying that they only had one outside line and the police had it engaged. When the line became available they'd let him use it. Where did Brendan want to phone?

At first Brendan couldn't even think. Then he decided he would ring Father McGuckin at Galbally.

Brendan wasn't given a line until after six o'clock in the morning, more than *two hours* after Martin had died. Every time he asked they told him there was no line available—the police

453

were busy using it. It wasn't until 6:20 a.m. that he got through.

Brendan finally reached Father McGuckin. He gave him the message about Martin's death, and asked him to tell the family.

"How are you getting home, Brendan?"

"I don't know. Someone—"

"I'll come straightaway and pick you up at the prison."

"That'd be too much trouble for you, Father—"

"No, not at all. I'll leave right now."

Brendan told the officials that the priest was coming for him, and went back into the waiting room again.

After the policeman had taken the statement, Brendan had gone back to see Martin, but the body was gone. It was gone by a quarter past four. Brendan asked the police where Martin would be and they said his body was in the morgue.

"It's in the hands of the Northern Ireland Office," a policeman said.

"Where is it being taken?"

"Wherever they decide," the policeman answered. He had no say in the matter, he insisted. Nor had Brendan.

It was ironic, the policeman saying that the body was in the hands of the NIO. Yes, this whole place was in the hands of the NIO—of the British government. It was their beating and torture and their courts that had brought Martin into their prison. It was their attempts to criminalize him that had ended in his death by hunger strike. And it was in their prison hospital that he had died, with their people lying to Brendan. The British government was in charge, all right.

Brendan kept inquiring about where the body might be taken. One of the warders said to him that it would go to the nearest hospital, but he found out later that it hadn't gone to the nearest hospital; it had gone to Omagh.

Finally, at about a quarter past seven, one of the warders came down and told Brendan that his transport was ready. What they didn't tell him was that Francie's wife Sally had been on the phone, and that Sally and Francie were driving down to pick Brendan up. They hadn't even told Sally that Father McGuckin was coming on the same errand. Instead they let Sally and Francie drive all the way to Long Kesh.

Father Murphy stayed with Brendan while he was waiting for Father McGuckin. At last Brendan heard the minibus back up to the hospital door. He said goodbye to Father Murphy, and was taken out to the gate.

Brendan wasn't sure that it would be Father McGuckin in the car. He'd asked Father McGuckin to get down to Galbally and tell the family that Martin was dead. But Father McGuckin had come directly to the prison.

Father McGuckin told him he preferred that Brendan be with him when Sheila was told. He thought there'd be nobody home but Sheila and the children. He didn't realize that Francie and Sally and others would be at the house. On the motorway, as Father McGuckin was driving Brendan back, they must have passed Francie and Sally going to the prison.

FRANCIE HURSON WOKE at five o'clock and turned the radio on. He had a feeling they wouldn't be getting in to see his brother this morning. The news on BBC Radio 2 was that another hunger striker had died, and that his name was Martin Hurson.

Francie went to a neighbour's phone and began ringing people. Among others he rang an independent councillor in the area, Owen Nugent, who lived in Coalisland, and made arrangements to meet him there at the roundabout. He and Sally left Sheila and drove to Coalisland to pick up Owen Nugent. Then they drove to the prison, where they inquired about Brendan. They were told he had already gone home.

Francie asked to see Martin's body.

"No way," they said. His body wasn't even there. The warders at the gate laughed at them. British soldiers cheered.

It was 13 July. That year the Twelfth of July celebrations of the victory at the Battle of the Boyne were held on 13 July, because the Twelfth was a Sunday. It was eight o'clock in the morning and already loyalists had their cars out and were driving around, Union Jacks flying. There were people leaning out of the windows, cheering. "The fuckers all died!" some of them shouted.

Francie thought it was typical of the way things were run in Northern Ireland that they wouldn't even tell them where Martin's body had been taken. So he and Sally and Owen Nugent drove back to Brendan's house.

Brendan had arrived about twenty minutes earlier and Father McGuckin was with him. Francie and Brendan phoned the undertaker from the booth in the road. They asked him to find out where the body was, and to try to get it to the home by two or three that afternoon.

Then Francie and Brendan went up to Francie and Sally's house to receive the messages coming through on the phone. There were about a hundred neighbours who'd stayed up all night and kept vigil around the house in Galbally. Almost as many were waiting up in Carrickmore at Francie and Sally's house. When Francie, Brendan and Sally arrived there, along with Owen Nugent and Francie's friend Cormac McDonnell, the undertaker rang to say that Martin's body was in Omagh. He'd pick him up whenever the Hursons wanted, he said.

Francie sent Brendan off to the back room for a couple of hours' sleep, and he and Sally handled the crowds that came by that morning to pay their respects. At about 11:30 the undertaker phoned again and told them that the RUC had rung and said unless the body was collected by noon it would be dumped at an unspecified location. It was a nasty stipulation. Nobody could get from Carrickmore to a mortuary in Omagh by twelve o'clock. The RUC were also saying that only parents and close relatives would be allowed to accompany the hearse—four cars in all.

So the family, along with relatives and friends, piled into cars, and raced to the mortuary as quickly as they could. Massey McAleer arrived just a few minutes before the first of the family did, at twelve-thirty.

When they got to Omagh, the police and Special Branch were massed in great numbers around the mortuary. The body was still there. But clearly there was going to be another kind of problem.

A police landrover was parked across the entrance to the mortuary grounds. The police said that only four family cars would be allowed to pass in through the gates. Francie saw what they were up to, and knew that there was no way that he would cooperate with them. What they wanted to do was to block the family cars inside and then, after locking the gates, divert the hearse onto a road of their choosing. So Francie parked his car outside on the road and walked up to the mortuary. There a green van was backed up against the door. Meanwhile other members of the family were trying to get through the gates. Friends of the Hursons were there with their cars. RUC men came up to them and said they were blocking the road. One of them said that they were only trying to get into the mortuary.

"You'll have to get your car off the road," a policeman said angrily.

"You can fuck off," the man said.

The policeman looked as though he couldn't believe his ears.

"You'll have to move your car," he said sharply.

"Fuck off!" the man repeated.

He was built like a small bull, and wasn't going to be moved. The Hursons' friend Francie Martin was there. He said that if this boy was going to stand his ground like a man, then he was, too. So he stepped forward, and other neighbours did, too.

Francie Hurson, up at the mortuary, watched them removing Martin's body to the green van. He squeezed between the wall and the van and stopped them. It was then that the rest of the family were finally admitted to the grounds.

Apparently the RUC had been afraid that too many people would move in on them and they'd be outnumbered, and that the people would organize things for themselves and conduct some sort of demonstration at the mortuary or on the way back to Carrickmore. The Twelfth celebrations were taking place all over the country that day, and the funeral was getting in the way; so the police wanted the body and the cortege off the road as soon as possible.

Now they were refusing to let Martin's coffin through the

gate. They were planning, as Francie had guessed, to reroute the cortege along back roads—and in and out of God knows what hostile areas, on a day when loyalist Protestants liked to parade their bigotry towards the Catholic Irish.

The families stood there for an hour arguing with the police, trying to get Martin's body released. Francie refused to budge, saying they wouldn't leave the mortuary grounds until all the people standing outside waiting to accompany Martin's body could get in their cars and follow the hearse home. At the moment Francie didn't give a damn what route they took. A couple of times the RUC set Alsatian dogs on the people. But eventually a plainclothesman took charge and overruled the refusals of his own men. The actions of the police simply swelled Martin's funeral cortege by dozens more cars, with the added complication that the RUC had the Omagh Road blocked from Omagh to Ballygawley.

With all the delays, they didn't get away from Omagh till three o'clock. All the family wanted was to get Martin's body safely home. But the police tried to shake off the parade of following cars. Several times they tried to break up the procession by driving landrovers up to block the cars at the head. Everytime they took a wrong turn or tried anything, Francie, who kept his car immediately behind, swerved out around and stopped the hearse. When he did so, as though at a command, everybody else got out of their cars. Some of the police abused them with violent and vulgar language, and set dogs on them—a neighbour of theirs had his jacket torn off.

Eventually this police circus came to an end when they got back safely to Cappagh with Martin's body.

A thousand people lined the road as the coffin was carried from the tiny village up to the Hurson home at Aughnaskeagh more than a mile away. The procession was led by a lone piper.

> As we marched back home again,
> In the shadow of the evening
> With our banners flying low
> To the memory of our dead.

We returned on to our homes
But without our soldier laddie,
Yet I never will forget the words he said:

I will stand in the van
Like a true Irishman
And we'll go to fight the forces of the crown.
I will march with O'Neill
To an Irish battlefield
For tonight we're going to free old Wexford town.

Among the mourners who came to the wake next day was Cardinal Ó Fiaich—Cappagh was in his diocese. Francie Hurson was proud of Cardinal Ó Fiaich that day. There were cameramen out, standing on the stoop, watching as the Cardinal came up the lane. Probably they'd thought there'd be no clergymen coming to the house. But there had been four priests there, who'd followed Martin's body to the house and said the rosary. The brother who taught Martin at school had arrived at the house that morning. And here was the Cardinal coming.

As the Cardinal walked down the lane he looked sad and solemn, as if he were saying he was sorry that he hadn't been able to do anything about Martin. Tears came to Francie's eyes as he looked at the Cardinal's face. *He didn't do anything to save Martin,* yet he was a sincere man. Francie was very glad to see him come that day.

When the Cardinal came into the room where Martin was laid out, he knelt and prayed and then blessed Martin. For Francie the look on the Cardinal's face as he walked around the coffin honoured Martin.

They gave him a cup of tea and a sandwich and Francie went over and started talking to him.

"Father, you've got the power of the Catholic Church. And right, you didn't do anything to save Martin—"

The Cardinal was nodding his head sympathetically.

"Young men like Martin," Francie said, "are dying on hunger strike, starving themselves to death for their country. They only wanted to be Irishmen, Father. They have proven themselves

459

to be Irishmen. And you couldn't even save their lives."

"Francie, what can I do? I honour Martin. I've come here to the house to be with the Hurson family. But I have no power. England has the power."

Francie admired Cardinal Ó Fiaich, even if he challenged him that day. Where were the politicians who hadn't seen fit to honour Martin? John Hume and all the rest—as far as Francie was concerned they were only looking for glory. Was there no glory here, in the way these men had died? Not that they were looking for glory, Martin and his friends. They wanted an Ireland free of British rule, and had died for that.

There was a large and dignified funeral. It was all that Martin himself could have wished. Some weeks later, Francie went with other hunger strike relatives to London on a trip in support of the men still on the protest. When they got off the plane and went into the airport there was a news conference. One of the reporters asked why it was that these men were dying on hunger strike.

"My brother Martin died on hunger strike," Francie said, "a young man of only twenty-four, because he was an Irishman. Why is the British government murdering young Irishmen? Why do young Irishmen have to die? It's because of British rule in Ireland. How long is Maggie Thatcher going to let them die? Why has she to murder them? It's their own country. Irish they are, and Irish they want to be. And as soon as the Irish people get rid of the British government and British rule, they'll be the merrier."

Chapter 10

KEVIN LYNCH OF DUNGIVEN

Let Erin remember the days of old,
    Ere her faithless sons betray'd her;
When Malachi wore the collar of gold,
    Which he won from her proud invader,
When her kings, with standard of green unfurl'd,
    Led the Red-Branch Knights to danger;
Ere the emerald gem of the western world
    Was set in the crown of a stranger . . .

Thomas Moore

THERE HAD BEEN PRESSURES on other families—more on some than others. Great drama attended the fasting and dying of Bobby Sands, but Bobby himself was so much the central figure that it didn't matter what heavyweight media or political pressure would be brought to bear on his people. His mother Rosaleen stood as a symbol of Irish motherhood; his sister Marcella marched as a symbol of the sorrowing loyalty of young Irish women. But given Bobby's absolute determination to defeat what he called "the monster" of British oppression prowling the corridors of Long Kesh, Rosaleen and Marcella—for all their efforts to win him media and popular support—could only bear witness, as a kind of family pietà, while he embraced death, for the sake of the younger men whom he felt could not endure what he had endured. Bobby controlled the entire scenario, right up to the last.

The Hughes family—though the mother was especially tormented by the prospect of the death of her youngest son— was known to be strongly Republican, and so there was no effort to try to get the Hugheses to hand their soldier Francis over to the doctors as he neared the end. Those watching Peggy O'Hara saw her waver and then find her strength again. Only

461

later was it learned how broken she was at the thought of losing Patsy. Though the prison authorities isolated her from her family, she did not succumb, because when it came down to it, in the lonely night, she wept bitterly but held fast to what Patsy had made clear he wanted ("Please, Mammy, let the fight go on"). The attempt to break Raymond McCreesh or his family was more insidious: the British government and their prison authorities were heavily involved. They lied to Raymond; they lied to the family; they lied to the press. They thought that this visibly Catholic family, with one brother a priest, could be got at—could be softened and made to ask for help. They programmed the family's collapse as artfully as they could, but in the end their varied and shabby deceits became transparent to the family, and through the family to Raymond himself, and he died as, in the circumstances, he felt he had to. Joe McDonnell was an unbreakable Belfastman, and his wife and family were city people who fought for his life but bowed to the inevitability of his death. With Martin Hurson's mother dead, and Francie and Brendan in charge, the British were dealing with men who would not have given way even had the end not come so suddenly. In their callousness the British denied Francie access to his brother the last night. But because of Martin's early death the Hurson family had not come under severe pressure.

That brought the weight of the media to bear—each family having to carry its own cross as its son and brother came to the point of crisis—on the Dohertys and the Lynches. There were no stauncher Republicans in Ireland than the Doherty family, with the agonized honesty and loyalty of Kieran's Protestant-born mother a great focus of attention. Tempered in the cauldron of Belfast, she and the Dohertys—her husband Alfie most vividly—stood foursquare with Kieran and the integrity of his sacrifice. Kieran would not yield unless in his considered judgement the five demands were fully met. His dying was the longest; but there was no chance of the British, or even the priests, breaking the Dohertys.

With Kevin some thought it would be different: not the prison authorities, who had so meanly treated the McCreesh and O'Hara and Hurson families—but the humanitarians outside,

462

and later the priests and the angle-hunting media. Something had to give. The hunger strike couldn't go on forever. The question was asked: was the Lynch family in the same mould as these others?—the Hugheses of Bellaghy, the O'Haras of Derry City, the Hursons of Tyrone; the McDonnells and Dohertys of Belfast who had been toughened by over half a century of grinding sectarianism and a decade of battering by the British Army.

There were journalists who calculated the effect on this family of the new pressures from the clergy; and weighed it against the brutal hardness of Thatcher and the British, and the growing weakness of Garret FitzGerald's initiative, which had ballooned and then popped, leaving by 22 July only a gaseous memory.

The family form chart seemed to promise all that could be wished for in the way of background for the anticipated drama of a major breakdown in the hunger strike.

AT THE FOOT of the Sperrin mountains, far distant from the madding intensity of occupied Belfast, far in spirit from war-ravaged Derry—the corrupt and beautiful city of this latest Irish rebellion—lay the pleasant and predominantly Catholic town of Dungiven (*Dun Gheimhin* in Irish: Given's Fort). In a pleasant setting above the village a substantial two-storey house stood on the main Derry-Belfast Road. This was the home of builder and former publican Paddy Lynch. He and his wife Bridget (née Cassidy) had come originally from Park, a Catholic but not political village eight miles away, where their eight children had been born.

The Dungiven house was very comfortable—the solid sort of house in which a lawyer or businessman in smalltown America would feel happily at home. It had a facing of orange brick and pebbledash, and attached to it was a garage, with doors painted the same bright green as the trim. One of the upstairs windows had a balcony outside it. The large lawn in front was neat and well-cut, with roses growing against a slatted wooden fence. The house had four picture windows facing the road, and below the two on either side of the front door sat a black and white bench. At the entrance were potted plants in white ornate metal stands.

The Lynches had been in the house for six years—since Kevin was seventeen and went to work with his brothers in England. While he'd been in prison (since 1976), his room upstairs had been kept as he·left it.

Kevin was a strong, handsome, good-natured lad with brown eyes. His frame of six feet or so would have filled out as he got older and his thick dark hair thinned, so that he'd look a lot like his brother Pat (often called Patsy). Patsy lived in Park, and at 37 was the second eldest of the eight sons and daughters. Michael was 39, and had lived for a year in Kildare, in the South. He and his wife had moved there so that his family could have easier access to the Irish culture he loved, and could get away from the militarized North. As the eldest, Michael coordinated the family effort of support for Kevin with Pat and Francie, who were closer to home. After Patsy came Jean, 35, who with her husband Brendan McTaggart co-owned and managed the Finvola Hotel down in the village, which had one of the town's two main pubs and provided, upstairs, one of Dungiven's most popular social venues. Next was Francie, 33, who'd been seven years out in Australia where he met and married a Co. Derry girl, with whom he'd returned in the late 70s to Dungiven; then came Mary, 30, who was married and living in Enfield, Co. Meath; young Bridie, 29, who stayed at home and looked after their parents; and Gerard, 27, who was married and working in England. Kevin was 25. The boys were all builders like their father—and like him their specialty was bricklaying.

Kevin, growing up, sometimes got the short end of the stick. But he could adapt; and because of his age and charm he could manipulate not just his mother but his older brothers and sisters if he wanted to. Yet he gave reason even as a youngster to make them proud of him.

Hall (from the Irish Micheál, pronounced Me-hall), was on the way to play a football match one day when he was about twenty-two. It was an important game, with Foreglen. There were no dressing rooms at the field, so they changed in the car on the roadway, while Kevin and other small boys walked on

464

ahead. Someone, idly kicking a ball, put it up into a tree, where it stuck. Kevin, then about eight, clambered up to get the ball. Another boy hurled a stone at the ball but hit Kevin, splitting his forehead open. Kevin managed not to fall. Hall only became aware of what had happened when he saw a big lad, Fonsie O'Kane from Foreglen, carrying Kevin towards the car. Hall drove him to Altnagelvin hospital near Derry city, where he was given five stitches in his forehead. Hall was fourteen years older than Kevin, and when Kevin was brought out afterwards to the waiting room, a nurse said to the boy, "There, Kevin—there's your Daddy over there!"

From boyhood on, Kevin was kind and considerate. Though something of a practical joker, he was as gentle and as popular a lad as could be found in Dungiven. He was also a lively and self-confident competitor. He liked fishing. He was a regular at Gaelic football, often playing on the same teams as his brother Gerard. He did well in his weight as a boxer. But his great sport was hurling. He was captain of the Derry under-16 team that won the All-Ireland cup in 1972, beating Armagh in the finals at Dublin's Croke Park. What he missed most when he went to work in England was the hurling.

The English building trade had been a natural choice for Hall and Patsy. Farming or building—that was the choice for most young men, and building work was scarce enough at times in Ireland. It was Patsy who had first taken permanent work in England. He'd gone in 1967 to work as a bricklayer—the trade their father had taught them all. Then Hall went over in 1973, and Kevin followed the same year. Most of their Irish friends in England were from the South, sympathetic but relatively non-political where the North was concerned.

In the early 70s they were working in and around Bedford, a clean, quaint little town in Bedfordshire in East Anglia, 35 or 40 miles from London. The boys used to work together on the same site—sometimes for an Irish, and sometimes for an English company. When they moved to a new site or company, they moved together. When the two younger boys, Kevin and later Gerard, came over, Hall and Patsy, who were both married and well looked after, used to fry up steaks for the younger boys every morning to make sure the lads would get enough to eat.

Gerard married early, and Kevin—who'd lived for a year with Hall—stayed for a time with Gerry and his English-born wife Noleen. He maintained his interest in sports and played for St. Dymphna's, a Bedfordshire team.

But Kevin kept coming back to Ireland, and Dungiven. Finally after three years he seemed to get fed up with England. In August 1976 he returned home to stay. He was nineteen.

Kevin was hardly home when, as he was returning from a dance one night with nine other young men his own age, he was stopped by British soldiers. The boys were thrown up against a wall and given a very bad kicking and beating. This may have been a factor in Kevin's joining the INLA.

Those who were looking for a break in the hunger strike thought that the Lynches were better fixed than country families trying to eke out a living from, for example, small plots of land in Bellaghy in South Derry. They were aware of a spirited quality in Kevin Lynch's nature. But he was also a gregarious lad, who could look forward to a good life ahead after a relatively short prison sentence. They judged that these were the sort of comfortably-fixed parents who could prevail on this sort of son to abandon the protest. Surely they would not allow their boy to die.

The other Lynch brothers, with their self-sufficient if hard-working ways, were not in the same mould as the deprived unemployed of Belfast and Derry. Snobbish or money-conscious observers focused heavily on the "respectability" of the Lynch family, part of which lay in their being considered non-political. The Lynch boys, it was assumed, might have nationalist thoughts and might sometimes feel stirrings of Republican sympathy, but they were not the sort to go out and plant bombs or shoot soldiers or police.

But among the factors such observers hadn't reckoned with was what it was like for these strong-minded brothers growing up in this atmosphere. Dungiven was an overwhelmingly Catholic town where some of the police at the RUC barracks on the main road were especially sectarian, and often abusive towards the local boys. When Kevin was picked up and taken to Castlereagh, he met more police hostility, except that this time it took the form of a brutal interrogation. Kenneth Newman was RUC Chief Constable; it was the beginning of Roy Mason's tenure at Stormont: the Mason/Newman get-tough policy was underway.

THE INLA had the same problem in North County Derry as it perennially had in Derry City—acquiring weapons. There was some question in the minds of Kevin's family afterwards whether he and his INLA friends did much of anything *but* acquire weapons. The young men would turn up at a home— usually a Catholic one—where the man of the house kept legally-held shotguns. One of the boys would nervously cover the family while the others went off with the man to find the gun and its shells. They seemed to be forever building up their arsenal.

Kevin's most celebrated INLA exploit involved an encounter with the RUC. The story made his parents sometimes wonder afterwards whether all this dangerous activity had meant for Kevin much more than practical joking, if on a rather serious scale.

In the autumn of 1976 Kevin and three other boys were in a car, approaching an RUC checkpoint on the Limavady Road outside Derry City. There were four policemen there. The boys hopped out of the car—they had one shotgun between them— surprised the police, and disarmed them. Afterwards, in Crumlin Road jail, other prisoners would laugh at this story and say,

"But Kevin, why didn't you shoot them?" He would answer that they'd got more mileage out of disarming the police and making a laughing stock of them. And that if they'd shot the policemen they probably would have all been tracked down very quickly and arrested. Their whole unit would have been wiped out. They weren't yet strong enough in manpower or weaponry to have a fully-fledged guerrilla cell. In any case it was one of the INLA's biggest propaganda coups in the organization's early days. And it was said that after five years the RUC still hadn't got their guns back.

For Kevin the road to Long Kesh began when an RUC man was injured in an ambush near Dungiven in November of that year. The police and Army moved quickly against suspected Republican activists in the neighbourhood.

Kevin had been home from England little more than three months when, at 5:40 a.m. in the cold and frosty dark of the morning of 2 December 1976, British Army redcaps—military police—and armed RUC men came barging into the house. Paddy, Kevin's father, counted fifteen of them. Bridie Lynch had known nothing. She'd had no suspicion that Kevin was involved in the INLA. She got the biggest shock of her life that morning. The house was turned upside down. Dragged from his bed, without being allowed even a drink of water let alone a cup of tea, Kevin was bundled off. He was taken to Castlereagh for three days' interrogation, during which he was cruelly beaten and forced to sign a confession.

He was charged, along with Liam McCloskey, at a special court in Limavady on 4 December. Kevin refused to recognize the court. But in their confidence, or eagerness to lock him up, the police had muddled their statements. The judge said he couldn't possibly accept their evidence, and threatened to throw out the charges. Within twenty-four hours the police got their paperwork in order. Kevin was charged with conspiracy to disarm members of the security forces, with taking part in a punishment shooting, and with the taking of legally-held shotguns.

Kevin had been very badly beaten in Castlereagh. On a visit after his court appearance his mother asked him why he couldn't sit down. "Mammy," he said, "it wasn't Butlins." Not only was he unable to sit, he couldn't lift his left arm, either. It was clear to Bridie that he'd gone through a terrible ordeal, but there was no complaint from him—he was never one to complain.

Between the time of the charging in December 1976 and the trial a year later, Kevin was a remand prisoner in Crumlin Road jail. While there he became friends with a Carrickmore man in his mid-sixties named Felix Meenagh, who was there almost by accident. He had been picked up and brought to Omagh Barracks for interrogation in connection with a shooting across the road from where he lived. His interrogators wanted to know about two young men who had arrived at Felix's house asking for a meal, two men whom Felix thought might be on the run.

Felix had fed them. Later he told the police he didn't know anything about them, and he didn't. He was accused of withholding information and sent to Crumlin Road jail for nine months on remand. Despite his obvious innocence but because of his age, Felix was called by one of the warders "the Godfather of the Fenians." Felix and young friends like Kevin got a kick out of this: Felix as Godfather of the Fenians! But the younger men held him in high esteem.

Kevin knew Felix well. He used to walk about with him in the Crum, and his affection for the old countryman was fully reciprocated. Felix would say about Kevin: "It's a sad thing to see fellows like him—so dedicated—and yet the politicians in this country would sell him down the river in the morning." For Felix the Crum was interesting and his time there was an education. But he was saddened to see young men eager for the freedom of their country—really committed lads prepared to live and die for a principle—locked away during the best years of their lives. After nine months on remand Felix was eventually tried and given a two-year suspended sentence.

IT WAS CLEAR TO BRIDIE LYNCH that her son didn't like to see other people suffering. He'd rather suffer himself. She had asked Kevin one day in late 1977, before he was sentenced, not to go on the blanket protest. She was worried at the talk about the torments the blanketmen were going through.

"Please, please," she said. "Don't do it."

"Mammy," he said, "you're thinking of me. But I'll be out in a few years. You're not thinking of the rest, of those poor fellows who are going to be in for twenty-five or thirty years. Mammy, I've got to do it, for their sake. They took everything away from those boys except their principles . . . "

And so Bridie had stopped asking him not to go on the blanket.

In December 1977 Kevin was sentenced to ten years. Had he conformed to the prison regime he would have got five years' remission of sentence and (with the one year he'd already done) been released in December 1981. Instead he immediately joined the blanket protest. He was put in H-3 and soon found himself sharing a cell with his friend Liam McCloskey from Dungiven, who'd been arrested and jailed on much the same charges as Kevin. Liam had spent the same year on remand in Crumlin Road jail. A few days before his trial Liam's father died, yet he was refused compassionate parole. He too was sentenced to ten years. In the H-Blocks the two men underwent several severe beatings at the hands of the warders.

In April 1978, six warders—one carrying a hammer—came in and searched their cell. Kevin, his bare foot slipping on the urine-drenched floor, happened to splash the trouser leg of one of the warders. The screw cursed him, then kicked urine at him. Kevin kicked urine back at the warder. The warder with the hammer swung it at Kevin but missed. Then two warders attacked him, punching and kicking him to the floor, and he was dragged off to the punishment block.

On Friday, 15 September, 1978, Liam McCloskey, then 22, was taken out to the circle in H-Block 3, and was beaten about the head and body by eight warders. His right eardrum was perforated. The following Tuesday, 19 September, he was searched before being moved to another wing of H-3. Totally naked during the search, Liam was thrown down on a table by four screws—each of whom held a leg or an arm—to have his back passage examined. Then a fifth screw caught hold of Liam's head—Liam was lying face down on the table—and smashed his face down onto the tabletop so hard that his nose was broken.

Two of Liam's family were given a visit with him the next Friday, 22 September, but the visit was stopped after seven minutes because a screw took objection to discussion of the attacks on Liam, and to questions being asked about who the attackers were.

Father Michael McEldowney, a curate at Drumsurn chapel in Dungiven parish, had arranged a pastoral visit with Liam at the time. When he went to Long Kesh he was told that Liam was no longer in the prison hospital but had been taken back to his cell. Father McEldowney gave an account of this afterwards.

"I said that I still wanted to see him," the priest said, "but they returned after ten minutes and told me that Liam had refused to undergo a physical search and as a result is not getting a visit. I asked to see the governor but was told that he was

470

busy. I saw the deputy governor but got no information from him except that Liam had been moved back to his cell. I was told nothing about his medical condition and was referred to the NIO."

Kevin's parents could see from published accounts of what had happened to Liam what Kevin must be going through.

Clearly Kevin, their gregarious and easygoing lad, was hardening under the prison system. For the first six months of Kevin's time in the Kesh he refused to wear the prison uniform even to take visits. It was only through Father Denis Faul that the family was able to get any information about his health. Then his mother went off to Lourdes with the particular intention that Kevin would consent to a visit. When she came back Kevin had relented. He agreed to see his parents.

Bridie didn't know what to expect. Her son hadn't been outdoors, and hadn't had any fresh air except what came in the window. They found him pale and wan. But they found more than that. They found him changed. He was not the boy who'd been taken from the house in December 1976. His gaiety had given way to a terrifying seriousness. There was a fierceness in him they'd never seen before. Kevin put on the brightest face he could. Despite what he'd suffered from the searches and the beatings, he made no complaint to them about what was happening to him in Long Kesh.

One incident showed how stoic he'd become. Kevin had developed a serious toothache, and badly needed treatment. But to see the prison dentist he would have to put on the uniform. Kevin endured the pain for fourteen days. Then one day while at Mass he fainted. Father Denis Faul, who was saying the Mass, noticed Kevin standing, leaning, then slowly slipping down onto the floor. But he'd never said anything and Father Faul had no idea what caused him to faint. He spent two more agonizing hours back in his cell; then the abscess burst, and his teeth didn't trouble him anymore.

It wasn't Kevin who told the Lynches, but other boys who'd been there.

In the prison Kevin learned Irish, and spent a lot of time discussing with Liam and the other men what they were doing in prison. Bridie and the family found him very sharp politically. He'd thought through his position—what was going on in Long Kesh. He had the Bible and made full use of that. This was new: Kevin prayed a lot—an awful lot, his mother was told. But what dominated his life was the intense comradeship of the prison, shaping his strong views and that new toughness he had acquired. The prison was competitive: the warders versus the men. And the men were determined not to yield.

Kevin had never lost his buoyant quality; and his old determination showed through in the way he refused to compromise. He wouldn't back down from any challenge. It was a trait that was to worry his mother more and more as talk of a hunger strike grew.

It wasn't so much the talk Bridie heard he used in the prison— about pulling the plug on the British, blowing them away, and so on—but his talk about principle that really worried her. She knew he meant it; he was absolutely sincere. "If they took every thing else away they'd never take my principles," he'd say, striking his chest. "I'd die before they'd take that away from me." She remembered how he'd refused for months to put on the uniform even for a visit—the uniform that was the symbol of everything that was opposed to his and the others' principles: the symbol of submission to criminalization and the British prison system.

Kevin quietly told Hall in August 1980 that he'd volunteered for the hunger strike that was coming in October. He joined with the other men at the end in December, for five days.

Afterwards Bridie was grateful it was over. But Kevin was angry. Someone—not Bridie—had asked him on the day it ended what he thought about the outcome, and all that the British seemed to have promised would happen. His reply was brief and, typically, an INLA man's view of the supposed promises: "I don't know what the fuss is about," he said. "We got nothing."

In the wake of the first hunger strike, when the regime became very nasty, there was a forced wing shift. It was near the end of January 1981, and Kevin, along with Liam McCloskey and Matt Devlin of Ardboe and three others, were the men most brutally victimized by the warders' assaults. The incident was so bad it was reported in the papers. Kevin had often said himself that when the establishment was down on them, there was little they could do; that the establishment was very hard to beat.

The brevity of his first spell on hunger strike had given his mother something to hang onto. He'd been lucky: it was over before it did him any damage. He wouldn't be at risk anymore, she thought. Since he'd already been on, surely he wouldn't have to go on again. It turned out that Kevin saw the same facts she and the family saw—but saw them as a threat. He *worried* that he wouldn't be allowed to go on again.

Then at the beginning of March Bobby Sands, who was on Kevin's wing and was OC of the blocks, went on hunger strike. Even though Bobby was IRA and not INLA, Bobby had become, in a sense, Kevin's personal OC. In tactical disagreements between Bobby Sands and Patsy O'Hara, the OC of the INLA prisoners, Kevin tended to accept Bobby's version. There were communications problems between the INLA men, who were few by comparison with IRA prisoners and widely scattered around the blocks. But Bobby was there on the wing, and Kevin had come to know and trust him absolutely.

Hall used to remark to Bridie how loyal the men were to one another, how close to one another. When Bobby died, in early May, Kevin was disconsolate and bitter. He took Bobby's death, Bridie thought, as hard as a mother would take her own son's death—so deeply did he admire the Belfastman. There was a sense with Kevin that after Bobby's death he didn't care whether he himself lived or died. He could have faced death next day and walked blindly on into it—so terrible did he feel about Bobby's dying. When Bobby died, Kevin was beyond her comforting.

Worse was to come—an agony for Bridie Lynch.

Kevin had been talking principles long before the second hunger strike developed. So when it did, Bridie was troubled.

So was Kevin. As he faced into the likelihood that he'd be allowed to go on, what most troubled him were his worries about his parents. He seemed to think that his brothers would understand, or would not interfere. It was his parents who would have the authority to take him off. He was worried about his father Paddy, and especially about Bridie.

A visit had been arranged, through the Belfast IRSP, so that his parents could see Kevin on Tuesday 19 May. Paddy and Bridie Lynch were to meet a man—a senior member of the IRSP—in the prison car park near the gate. He had the registration number of the family car so that he could identify Paddy and Bridie, and would join them to see Kevin.

Just as Paddy parked the car, a man in a suit, drinking tea from a plastic cup, sauntered up.

"Lynch?" he said, addressing Paddy.

"Who are you?" Paddy asked.

"I'm the one who's going in to visit Kevin with you."

"Get into the car and we'll have a talk," Paddy said.

The man got in.

"Times are bad," Paddy said.

"They are," the man replied. "Patsy O'Hara could be dead tomorrow or the next day—your Kevin is taking his place." All in one breath—

Paddy and Bridie were stunned and shocked by this curt, sudden barrage: the worst news they had ever heard—to them a sentence of execution—coming from a total stranger. The man's manner had been brutal, clinical. It was as though this man saw the hunger strike as nothing more than another kind of conveyor belt, carrying young lives to their doom: *your Kevin next*.

They left the car and went through the humiliating visiting procedures. Eventually they found themselves in a cubicle. Kevin was already there. He smiled as he greeted them. Bridie and Paddy saw immediately that Kevin was under the impression that someone from the IRSP had visited the family at the weekend to cushion the blow about Kevin's decision to join the hunger strike. But Bridie and Paddy had had no such cushion—though they gave no indication of this to Kevin.

Kevin turned to his father.

"I'm sure you're aware I'm going on hunger strike," he said. "I'll need your full support, Daddy."

Bridie knew that her husband Paddy had been through tough situations before. But nothing like this. He tried to reason with Kevin.

"I'll need your support," Kevin said again.

"Well, you'll not have it!" Paddy said. "No way."

Kevin turned to his mother. He clasped his hands over hers and looked into her eyes.

"I need you to stand by me," Kevin said. "Mammy," he said, clasping her hands tighter. "You've never let me down. But I never needed you more than I need you now. Please, Mammy, understand! Please stand by me. You always did. And if it comes to the worst of all, I'll have to count on you. All I'll have is your word."

She was in anguish. She turned to Paddy. Her son was asking her to be some kind of murderer. But Kevin was pleading with her, begging her to understand that this was what he felt he must do, and that he needed to have her accept it. She saw that her and his father's promise was what he most wanted—and was determined to have. She knew that if she refused, or if she would ever go back on her promise, he would never forgive her: he would have a heart of stone for her for the rest of his life.

So she promised. And Paddy was dragged into consenting. The fact that she had promised would keep haunting Bridie. But she was haunted more by what Kevin had said.

"And if it comes to the worst . . . all I'll have is your word."

After the visit Bridie was very, very angry. The news, horrible for her to hear, could not have been presented in a more savage fashion than it had by that man in the car park. From that moment, and for weeks afterwards, Bridie—and the family—wanted nothing to do with the IRSP and the INLA.

Her decision, so bitter for her, was comforting to Kevin, as she learned talking to Liam McCloskey long afterwards.

Going on hunger strike had been no worry to Kevin, Liam said. He had asked repeatedly to be allowed to go forward. He

475

thought he was going to be put off, because he'd been on hunger strike those few days in December. He wanted to be the next to go. He would be happy to go on, he told Liam, for the sake of the other men. What had been bothering him—*all* that had been bothering him, but it had been bothering him terribly—was that she and his father might refuse, or, if worse came to worst, might call for medical aid when he was in a coma. But the day after the visit, Kevin said to Liam, "My trouble is over now. Mammy and Daddy have given me their word. I know in my heart that they'll not wreck it for me."

And then on 23 May Kevin joined the hunger strike.

Micky Devine was OC of the INLA prisoners, but there had been an agreement that Kevin and not Micky would be the one to follow Patsy.

Bridie was heartsick. She felt trapped, because of her promise.

On her next visit she did notice that Kevin was more relaxed. He was no longer bitter. And he didn't seem to think he would really have to die. He thought there would be some break.

When he was two weeks into his hunger strike, though, he shocked Bridie by saying to her that if the strike continued he was prepared to go the whole way. He talked endlessly about the other men—men who were married, many of whom had children as well as a wife to live for, and who faced long prison sentences. He wasn't just thinking about dying for Ireland, but about the effect he might have in breaking the regime under which these men, with their deep personal commitments, were suffering. The prisoners would get their demands, he said.

His closest friend and companion on the hunger strike was Kieran Doherty; but there was Joe McDonnell, too, who had a wife and two children. Then Martin Hurson came on, who had a fiancée, Bernadette Donnelly; and Thomas McElwee, whose fiancée Dolores O'Neill was in Armagh jail . . .

Bridie had resolved, and promised, to stand with Kevin in the end, and she was steadfast on this point from that day in May when she'd given him her word. It was a pledge she insisted Hall and the other boys keep. "If it comes to it, and he's dying,

476

you stand firm," she told Hall and Patsy and Francie. They agreed they would not interfere.

That was her side of the obligation—to stand with Kevin.

Yet the brothers—with her strong encouragement—felt obliged to do all they could against the world outside to change the picture, to alter the rules, to weigh in against the circumstances which threatened their brother's life. If there were the slightest hope of the British government conceding the demands, or of help from the ICJP, or Garret FitzGerald, or the voters of Waterford, or the people at rallies; or if the Catholic Church or Father Faul or the military leadership of the INLA could shift the balance, then Hall and Patsy and the others were going to do their damnedest to make that hope a reality. Not surprisingly Bridie herself believed that the INLA had *ordered* Kevin onto the hunger strike. Sound logic led straight to the idea that they should order him off.

But when Hall and the boys asked Kevin who gave the orders, he laughed and said that it was his decision, and his decision only, to go on. He had never been asked or ordered to join the hunger strike. He had volunteered for the first hunger strike, and then volunteered afresh for the second.

The brothers worked hard along with all the other families involved. They attended all the meetings and rallies: meetings in Dublin, with Charlie Haughey, with Neil Blaney, with Garret FitzGerald and Michael O'Leary, with the ICJP—all the meetings and rallies organized by the H-Blocks hunger strike committee. They went to all the various meetings Father Faul organized . . .

Maybe it was true, as some outsiders said, that it was unfair for the Lynches to be put in this position—like people without any sailing experience set adrift on the ocean, or quiet country folk set down suddenly in the middle of Times Square. But the boys weren't at sea for long. They learned quickly where the sensitive or soft spots were in others' armour. And at one stage their shrewd father Paddy asked Gerry Adams directly: "Well, why don't *you* go on hunger strike?"

Kevin was doing this for the five demands, so the members

of his family determined to do all they could to get those demands met, so that Kevin could come off without abandoning his principles. From Hall's and the brothers' point of view, if the prisoners could get sufficient of the demands—through the ICJP or some other means—that would end it. The hunger strike had to end; men could not go on dying forever. It was Hall's prayer, and Patsy's and the family's—Paddy's and Bridie's above all—that it would end without the sacrifice of this life they held most dear.

Bridie was despondent. Yet her hopes would rise from time to time: maybe the family, by working very hard for the demands, or for a shift in the circumstances, could prevent his death. They were always on the move—back and forth to Dublin, sometimes two or three times a week; over to Belfast, out to rallies all over the North. They would split up and, with the other men's families, try to cover every bit of ground.

During the early days, from the end of May to mid-June, Waterford was an important place on their itinerary. The family—especially Paddy, Hall, young Bridie and Francie—spent a lot of time in Waterford, because Kevin was being run as a prisoner candidate in the Dáil elections. Waterford was at the other end of the island of Ireland, nearly, and the trips were long and wearisome. But there was the hope that Kevin and the other eight men, by running for the Dáil, could stir the consciences of people in the South. And there was the conviction that if some of them were actually elected TDs, then the Southern government would have to come out in full support of the five demands. The more votes Kevin got, the family felt, the greater the chance that his life would be saved.

It was a difficult constituency for a Northern candidate. But in the election Kevin received more than three thousand first preference votes before being eliminated, and he lasted longer than a Labour party and a Fianna Fáil candidate.

Had the election helped? They didn't know. They went on redoubling their efforts in other directions. It wasn't easy.

When Kevin was moved to the prison hospital he tried to give his mother practical reasons why it was better to be a hunger

478

striker than just a prisoner. "Mammy," he said, "it's worth it just to get to smoke a cigarette. We get to watch TV, and to walk around the grounds." He really loved getting outdoors. But Bridie could hardly agree that these things were worth the jeopardy he had put himself in.

In early July they were given 24-hour visiting permission. But it was a bad system. They always thought it odd that there was no opportunity—unless they met outside, leaving Kevin unattended for a longer period—for family members who were leaving to talk to the ones going in. Instead the authorities would lock the incoming visitors in huts and wouldn't let them into the van until the ones coming out had gone their way. Paddy complained about this once, but of course he could get nowhere.

In the hospital cells they had to speak guardedly.

Kevin himself never really bothered much about the warders. One of them would sit at the bottom of the bed, trying to make sure he heard everything that was said to Kevin. They had a book there, and if any of the family left the room the warder put down the time they left and the time they returned again. The warders didn't seem to be writing accounts of what was said. But the family wasn't sure what was being written down, or whether they were being tape-recorded.

One day in July when Bridie and Paddy were in, the warder broke into their conversation.

"Kevin, speak up, I can't hear you."

Kevin turned to him.

"Do you have to hear?" he said. "This is my mother, and my father. Can I not be personal with them?"

"Do you want me to leave the room?" the warder said threateningly. He was challenging Kevin. Kevin didn't speak because if he'd said yes, the visit would be finished then and there.

Otherwise they had little bother from the warders. There was in fact one male nurse or orderly they liked very much. His name was Paul, and he was a benign presence in the room. He was kind and good to the men. When, at a later stage, he'd lift

Kevin up to get a drink, he'd lift the pillow too, so as not to hurt him.

HALL COULD SEE that Kevin, even though he was weakening, was no less determined than before to go through with it if necessary. He constantly insisted that the movement outside could do nothing to get the hunger strikers to come off.

Kevin and Kieran and the others were always passing messages of mutual support. "Tell Kieran to keep his spirits up," Kevin would say.

The men felt they were engaged in a war in the prison.

"I am a soldier," Kevin said to Hall. "We're all soldiers. We're fighting a war—and our war is in here. You probably don't realize that."

After the time in early July when the Irish Commission for Justice and Peace announced that they had been let down by the British, the family became despondent. Despite their hopes, they were all worried that it was just a matter of time. FitzGerald tried, Hall thought, but his hands were tied. And he was a southerner. A southerner's attitude was different. The Republic was a different world. Hall felt that FitzGerald wasn't in a position to do very much anyway. It was Margaret Thatcher who held the key.

Hall felt that both were motivated by extraneous considerations: that the reason FitzGerald tried hard for awhile was because the hunger strike was creating problems in the twenty-six counties; and that Thatcher's intransigence had to do with her close friend Airey Neave. It was the INLA, Kevin's organization, which had claimed responsibility for Neave's death; and this vengeful woman wanted her pound of flesh. She had no concern for the fellows dying. Hall felt that Humphrey Atkins was only a weak sister: Thatcher's messenger boy.

Hall remembered the July night two NIO men came into the prison. The Lynches were in there at the same time as the Doherty family, on a 24-hour watch at their sons' and brothers' bedsides. Francie was with Hall that night, taking turns to go in and see Kevin. Then at two o'clock in the morning, they and the Dohertys were called out to see one of the governors. He wanted to know whether the families would like to meet with two NIO men who were willing to speak to them.

"There's no point in asking us," Hall said to the governor. "It's the boys on hunger strike you'll have to ask."

They were only soft-soaping, Hall thought. They had no intention of *doing* anything. And the hunger strikers would make no decision on their own—it would have to involve all the prisoners, through Bic McFarlane, the prisoners' OC. The two NIO men went around the hunger strikers individually. But the men said they would talk only as a unit, and that McFarlane had to be party to any conversation. These two Tories, Hall thought afterwards, used the prisoners' refusal as an excuse. They were only making a pretence of talking. It was a miserable effort to begin with—their coming in at two o'clock in the morning! Clearly the Dohertys were as disgusted as the Lynches.

There was a great bond among the families. The Lynches got on very well with Alfie and Margaret Doherty and their sons and daughters. They grew close to Eileen McDonnell, Joe's vibrant mother, and they liked his wife Goretti, too. They thought very highly of the Hursons: the Hurson boys, like the Lynches, worked with their hands. They became quite close to the McElwees as well, through the sharing of pain through those terrible hours and days. Bridie was especially fond of Alice McElwee, Thomas's mother.

IT LIFTED BRIDIE'S SPIRITS, even though she was terribly distressed with Kevin dying, when on Friday 31 July she heard that Paddy Quinn was taken off. Paddy's mother was a fine woman in Bridie's eyes, and her son, who was in the hospital cell just next to Kevin's, was screaming in dreadful agony. Bridie was sitting with Kevin at the time, and she was never so glad to hear anything in her life—that Paddy Quinn was getting out and going to a proper hospital for treatment.

What kept Kevin and Kieran alive so long, Bridie felt, was the fact that they were continually with their families. It helped their morale to see them and be with them so much—it kept

481

them going. The usual procedure—this went on over a period of four weeks or so—was that Alfie Doherty and Paddy Lynch and their sons would be in at night; in the daytime the two mothers and daughters would be there, while the men would go home to eat and get some sleep before coming back for the night.

One night when Bridie was leaving—she had to leave so that the boys and his father could get in—Kevin took her hand.

"Mammy," he whispered, "you're not going?"

"Kevin," she said, "I'll stay with you till morning—I'll stay with you as long as you want me to stay. But if I don't go they won't let the others in."

"No, you're not leaving me, Mammy?"

Father Murphy, the chaplain, came in just then.

"Father, what am I going to do?" Bridie asked. "I'll stay, surely, but either his father or somebody else will have to go back home if I'm to stay."

"Bridie," he said, "it would be too much for you to stay the night. I can stay till the others come in—"

Kevin heard this.

"Kevin, will I stay?" she asked.

"It's all right," Kevin said. He'd been worried, apparently, that he'd be left alone. He was afraid of interference from the screws, his father Paddy thought. So Father Murphy stayed with him until the men came in . And then the male nurse Paul came in—a man who couldn't have been more helpful to Kevin.

It seemed to Hall that towards the end Kevin became, if possible, even more determined than he'd been before. He was suspicious of the cardiograph machine attached to him, and kept pulling the wires off. Knowing that Kieran Doherty was dying made him very upset, but he would take nothing to ease his own pain.

Kevin had terrible ulcers in his mouth and throat. But he wouldn't let them give him a mouthwash. Bridie was with Kevin one day. There was a big fellow standing in the corner. He had mouthwash in a jar, and a small brush, and was asking her whether it would be all right to wash out Kevin's mouth. She said she didn't know. Her son Patsy was there, and he didn't know either. Father Murphy came in. He said it would be all right. He had seen Kieran Doherty having this done. So the man went over to put the brush into Kevin's mouth. But Kevin held his lips tight.

"This is only a mouthwash," the man said. "Nothing is going down your throat."

But Kevin shook his head. He wouldn't even let them put vaseline on his lips. Bridie asked him the Thursday before he died about the pain from the ulcers—were they sore? "Mammy," he said—he was barely able to speak—"what do you expect?" But he never said he was in pain.

On Friday morning, 31 July, Bridie heard a news bulletin about Kevin being in a coma. She rushed to the hospital, afraid her son wouldn't know her. Father Murphy, who'd been in and out with Kevin all night, was waiting in the corridor. He told Bridie that Kevin was not in a coma and that he'd been asking for her. She spent the day beside him.

Some of his brothers had been at Kevin's bedside when the story about his being in a coma was broadcast. Kevin, hearing this on the radio, looked around. "More Brit propaganda," he said. And he never went into a coma. To the very last he was aware of what was going on.

Hall and Francie came that Friday evening, at seven. Bridie and Patsy had just come out from their visit so that Hall and Francie could get in. Hall saw her and Patsy only briefly.

"Kevin could be dead when you go up there," Patsy said to Hall outside the prison hospital. "Or he could be living tomorrow morning."

Hall and Francie sat with Kevin that night—they could see he was slipping away. But there was no screaming or groaning. It was not just that he had never complained—the boy who'd played Gaelic football and when he got knocked down got right back up again. He was simply too weak to cry out.

He didn't seem to be in any great pain at the end. Hall felt that Kevin was well-prepared mentally and spiritually for death.

He'd told them he was at peace with himself and with God.

At 1:10 early next morning Kevin died.

NOT ALL WHO GATHERED around Bridie and the family afterwards were prepared to let them bear their grief in peace. Some of the journalists, and some of the clergy, had misread the family's efforts to prevent Kevin's death, and had misinterpreted Bridie's position.

It was true that the Lynches had worked aggressively—and had shown their anxiety at various relatives' meetings convened by Father Denis Faul—to get the hunger strike resolved somehow and thereby save Kevin's life. Hall and Patsy were particularly active. But the outsiders' expectation seemed to be that in this respectable, supposedly middle-class, supposedly non-political family, the mother would break: the mother, in the view of some of them, *ought* to have broken, and taken her son off hunger strike.

But they hadn't known Kevin, and how he'd begged his mother to give him her absolute support: told her in fact, and in no uncertain terms, that he must have her support. They hadn't known that in the end this boy from a comfortable home had turned out to be as iron-willed as any of them.

The outsiders didn't realize that about Kevin, or that he had *compelled* his mother to see herself as the instrument of his iron will. She had kept hoping, of course, that the scenario would change: that in the final days, for example, the INLA or the priests—Denis Faul and Michael McEldowney and the others—would be able somehow to do something to save her son and the others. She was for saving lives. And that's why she'd been overjoyed that Paddy Quinn's mother was able to save Paddy's life. But she had discovered her role before Kevin had even gone on hunger strike: her responsibility was to act as the executor of Kevin's will, against all her mother's instincts, and to make what he wanted her ultimate rule of conduct. She had not been operating on Republican principles. The principle Bridie had worked on was that she had *given her word* to her son that she would not interfere in what he was determined to do.

Hall recognized the roots of the outsiders' misinterpretation: though the family supported Kevin, they did everything they could to save his life. That effort was very visible to the media. Taken as a whole the family was not so obviously Republican.

The parents were not political at all. Their mother never called herself a Republican. And yet, in this crisis, to the consternation of some of the priests and journalists, and to the embarrassment of those who were trying to break the hunger strike, she'd said to Hall and her other sons: "You stand firm."

Her position was misunderstood not only by the media, but by their parish priest as well. Some statements of his compounded the confusion, and handed the media the kind of story it wanted to hear.

Bridie liked Father John Quinn, their parish priest. He was very considerate towards Bridie when Paddy had been in hospital for an operation a while back. She had great regard for him. But he managed, at the time of the funeral, to play the air to which so many of the journalists had their instruments tuned—that this was a woman who until the end resented what had been done to her son by outside forces (which was true enough); and a woman who, given half a chance, would have called in medical help to save her son (which was false); and—Father Quinn's special contribution—that the family resented the paramilitary funeral (also false).

The media was already flogging the story about outside control. It was the British story. It was also the Denis Faul story—that the *prisoners* were being manipulated by outside forces; that the Republican leadership was responsible for Kevin and the others dying on hunger strike, and that Kevin was their victim.

And so along came the parish priest with his story that the *funeral* was being manipulated by outside forces, and that the members of the Lynch family were the victims. Bridie Lynch and her family emphatically did *not* agree with that. But what the priest said fitted very snugly into Faul's and the journalists' preconceptions of what had been going on.

For Father John Quinn, what seems to have most symbolized the baneful influence of the paramilitaries was the illegal volley of shots at Kevin Lynch's funeral. Father Quinn didn't want guns and a volley at a funeral at his church. He said the Lynches didn't want it either and the media picked this up. The headline in *The Irish Times* the day after Kevin's funeral read: LYNCH VOLLEY BROKE AGREEMENT — PRIEST. *The Irish News, The Derry Journal* and other papers took a similar line.

The priest was right, so far as his own feelings were concerned. And *he* did have a broken agreement. But he was utterly wrong about the Lynch family. Not only were they not against it: they were determined to have a volley. To the priest, apparently, the volley symbolized something he hated. And he was adamant about it: the paramilitaries would not take over his churchyard. To priests like Father Faul, and to much of the media, the volley symbolized what Faul and the British propagandists said was going on: the paramilitary organizations outside the prison had taken over the hunger strike.

But to Kevin's family the volley symbolized what Bridie stood for, despite her grief, despite everything: standing firm with Kevin, with what he did and what he wanted, and with his sacrifice. Kevin had belonged to this Republican movement. Under its banner—and under the banner of love of country, and of the Irish freedom Faul and Quinn and the others were so uninterested in, or cynical about—Kevin Lynch had briefly fought, and for nearly five years had suffered, and for seventy-one days had slowly died. The final volley of shots was to be the recognition of that service and suffering, and of the cause for which he sacrificed his life.

The Lynches were well aware of the meaning of the volley.

But there had been conflict, earlier, between Kevin's organization and the family.

When Kevin had been on hunger strike about six weeks, his brother Patsy was approached at a rally at the Guildhall in Derry by an IRSP man. He wanted to talk about arrangements for a military funeral for Kevin, and said that authority for the funeral had been passed from IRSP headquarters in Belfast to the Derry City IRSP. As Kevin was still in good health, this city man's matter-of-fact tone shocked Patsy. He was angry. It was early yet to be talking in such terms. It was as though the man *wanted* this funeral.

The IRSP man inquired if he might come to the Lynch home in Dungiven, with other members of the IRSP, to have discussions with the family. Patsy said that that would be all right.

TERRY ROBSON of Derry and Seamus Ruddy of Newry were the men sent to Dungiven on behalf of the IRSP.

It was a difficult thing for these men to have to do. Kevin was still alive, and might somehow be saved. And Robson, for one, was well aware of the lingering antagonism the Lynches felt towards the organization and anyone connected with it— IRSP or INLA: to the Lynches they were all the one. It was an IRSP representative who'd abruptly said to them that Kevin would be next on hunger strike. And it was the INLA Kevin had been involved with. In the Lynches' view it might have been as a result of a direct order from the INLA that he was now lying in a hospital bed in Long Kesh, slowly dying.

But for a volunteer from a town like Dungiven, funeral arrangements could not be made on the spur of the moment. The likelihood was that Kevin was going to die.

Patsy Lynch represented the family in discussions with Robson and Ruddy. If the IRSP wanted to do something for the family, Patsy said, they should get an order from the INLA to Kevin to come off his hunger strike.

"We can't demand that," Terry said. "The INLA can't order Kevin off hunger strike. The INLA is powerless here. Because going on hunger strike and coming off are matters for the prisoners themselves."

This confirmed what Patsy had heard from Kevin, that the hunger strike was controlled by the prisoners themselves. But, despite Kevin's insistence that this was so, the family still didn't fully believe it.

What Robson and Ruddy knew, but couldn't see how to discuss with the Lynches, was that the INLA Army Council *had already taken a decision* to do precisely what Patsy Lynch had been asking—to order their prisoners off the protest—but had run up against a stone wall.

Like Sinn Féin and the IRA, the IRSP and the INLA had had their problems with the continuing hunger strike. Before the second hunger strike the movement had been *notified* by the prisoners, not asked for its permission. The leaders of the movement had become more and more opposed to the strike, because of the pressures they were under from the families of the men and from their supporters, pressures that were far harder for the INLA, a smaller organization, than for the IRA to cope with. The prisoners were informed that if they wanted to come off they would have the full and unequivocal backing of the movement.

It was after the death of Patsy O'Hara that the INLA developed its strong opposition to the hunger strike, particularly when the leadership realized that the other prisoners were not going to come off. From the movement's point of view the situation couldn't be tolerated. Far too many men would die; Thatcher was not going to give in. What the INLA leadership was especially afraid of was a sudden surge of public reaction—a massive nationalist backlash against the hunger strike and the Republican movement—and its leaders didn't want to find themselves in the position where they'd be suddenly forced to back down and order the men off under that kind of pressure. Moreover, the leadership of the INLA and the IRSP believed that the IRA and Sinn Féin were probably also opposed to the continuation of the hunger strike*

*For a while Terry Robson was unconvinced of the *bona fides* of the Provisionals. He saw it from the view of someone in the competing Republican camp, of course. But he was also prepared to listen to *some* of the people who were saying: "The IRA and Sinn Féin are getting a great deal out of this; they're advancing their cause through

So the INLA had decided to order the men off. But when they conveyed this decision to IRSP people like Ruddy and Seán Flynn who were in contact with the prisoners—and who would therefore be the men to relay the order—word was passed back that if the leaders of the INLA attempted to order the prisoners off, the men would ignore them, and would carry on independently. They simply *would not obey* such a command from the INLA. The prisoners were saying: It's our decision. We're *volunteers*. We're living in this hellhole and we have to continue the war in here, in our own way. You didn't have to live in the filthy conditions we've had to live in, in here, month after month, year after year. *We* made the decision to hunger strike in protest against these conditions; and we will make the decision, not you, as to when to come off.

The danger to the INLA of such a refusal was obvious. From a political point of view, if from no other, they had to rethink their position. So within a couple of days the INLA revoked

---

the hunger strike. So why should they want to stop it?" But as time went on Robson became convinced that the Provos genuinely didn't want the hunger strike to continue.

Much later, when Terry was in prison on remand on an informer's charges (thrown out of court after a year and a half), he had several conversations with Jim Gibney of Sinn Féin, a shrewd political thinker who'd been a major organizer of the H-Blocks campaign. His talks with Gibney confirmed that the Provos had genuinely wanted the hunger strike to end—because it was something over which they could exercise no control whatever and because, despite the advances they had made in the course of the hunger strike, the result could have been total loss of control of the prisoners. So the Provos had faced, too, the dilemma the IRSP and INLA faced—the possibility that they might suddenly, publicly, lose all credibility with their membership and their supporters. Terry found corroboration of this in Sinn Féin's subsequent opposition to suggestions that the prisoners *return* to this kind of protest—for example, when prison conditions worsened in the aftermath of the mass escape from Long Kesh in September 1983. Once the prisoners would take a decision to go on hunger strike, that was the end of either movement's control. No attempt by those outside to exert pressure, moral or organizational, would have any effect.

its decision and rescinded the order. This had occurred only shortly before Robson and Ruddy met Patsy Lynch.

Terry Robson had gone over the ground in his mind often enough.

When the hunger strike began, nobody thought that Bobby Sands would have to actually face death. When not only Bobby but other men began to die, it became that much more difficult to stop the hunger strike. Once the process was underway and the snowball started to roll, it became increasingly hard for those outside to have any effect at all on the protest, because of the bond that had been built up among the prisoners and their sense of loyalty to the men who had gone before. These men, who did not even see their fellow prisoners on a day to day basis, had got to know one another far better than men outside would know close colleagues. It had gone beyond material benefits and reforms and even the crucial issue of criminalization The intense bond of friendship, built up over the years among the men who had lived through the blanket and the no-wash and dirt protests, had now become the decisive factor, giving the protest its continuing momentum.

There was no point Terry could see in trying to tell the Lynches at this stage that a decision had been taken to order the hunger strikers off, but that this had been reversed. And why had it been reversed? the Lynches would have asked. The honest answer was that the INLA would have been severely, and pointlessly, damaged both inside and outside the prison when the prisoners continued on, as they would, despite the INLA's order.

This would have cut no ice with the Lynches, Terry felt. They would have found the INLA's logic bizarre. As far as the family was concerned, the INLA, as an organization with a military structure, could order its volunteers to do anything. If the INLA could order its volunteers to shoot someone, or rob a bank, wouldn't it be a simple task for it to order one of its men off hunger strike?

The Lynches saw it differently. On a nightly basis for a fortnight before Kevin's death, the Derry IRSP contacted the Lynches, inquiring about Kevin and how long he might last on hunger strike.

This really annoyed the family. It was bad enough that Kevin was dying. Instead of talking about a funeral, why couldn't they issue an order to the men? By this time the Lynches had faced the fact that only the prisoners had the power to end the hunger strike. But they wanted to serve notice on the IRSP men that they felt that they and their colleagues in the INLA could take a more active role in solving the problem.

Yet, despite this and despite the past bad feeling towards the IRSP, the family knew that Robson and his colleagues had to discuss procedures with the family and consult with them about what was going to be done. And it didn't need the IRSP men to point out to the family that Kevin wanted recognition of the Republican context in which he had lived and fought and died.

During the final days the family was busily involved with trips to the prison hospital, with meetings and rallies. Yet they were willing to accomodate the IRSP while concentrating on how the life of their son and brother might be saved.

The IRSP men settled down to the problem: how were they going to handle a very large funeral which because of its military aspect would very likely attract great attention from the British forces? Dungiven was an unprotected place where the IRSP had only limited contacts. It was not like Derry City where, as in Patsy O'Hara's case, there were great numbers of local people available at all times to meet the coffin. Because there was nobody from Dungiven itself, all the men who would appear at the funeral in uniform—21 of them—had to be brought from Derry and lodged in Dungiven: for a period, as it turned out, of seven days before Kevin died. The only thing to do was to make contact with individual people in the area who might be willing to help. Contact would have to be made by the INLA itself with people who might provide safe houses for their volunteers, for the storing of uniforms and the dumping of weapons.

Though the family's antagonism towards the IRSP men had changed during the last week to a kind of cordiality, there was

491

one residual problem. The one thing the Lynches wouldn't approve was the presence of INLA volunteers in the house standing guard over the coffin. Robson and Ruddy had to accept that.

Terry Robson knew that the decision not to have INLA volunteers in the house was a family decision. The Lynches thought that the presence of uniformed volunteers might open their house to the kind of assault the army and police had made after Kevin's arrest—turning the place upside down in their search for evidence they could use against Kevin and possibly others. And there were other considerations. The Lynches didn't want their and Kevin's friends and visitors crowded, so that people would have to march in, pay their respects at the coffin and march out again. They wanted an easier atmosphere than they felt would have been possible with the uniformed men there.

Terry Robson found that the Lynches agreed readily to his other suggestions. Traditionally the body had to be met in the town and escorted from the reception point to the home. That was fine with the Lynches. In fact, Terry found that *more* was expected here in the countryside than would have been the case in the city—more fidelity to Republican funeral customs and traditions, and to the proprieties in the way they were carried out.

As it happened, this expectation, too, would focus on the symbol of the volley.

Arrangements were made for houses where men from out of town could stay. It remained for Robson and Ruddy to talk to Father Quinn. It was essential that they see him, and not just about the use of the chapel. In Derry the city cemetery was run by Derry City Council. In Dungiven the cemetery was run by the church—it was on church property.

They talked to Father Quinn the day before the funeral. At first the parish priest said flatly that there would be no military funeral—no flags, no uniformed marchers, no speeches, no guard of honour, no volley. He insisted that this was the family's stipulation as well as his own.

"That's just not true!" Terry said. "The Lynches are quite happy with the final wishes of their son, who wanted the full honours an INLA volunteer would normally have in the circumstances."

The priest would not yield. He based his assessment, he said, not only on personal conversation with the Lynches but also on the fact that the Lynch family would not allow a guard of honour inside the house.

This much Terry knew to be true. But perhaps, Terry thought, the priest had talked to the Lynches ten days ago, when they weren't in a mood to think at all about the funeral. That had changed now.

"The family," Terry said confidently, "wants Kevin to have the funeral of a volunteer. They want to follow Kevin's wishes in the matter."

Still the priest refused to authorize the military funeral.

"We might arrange a compromise," Terry suggested.

"Compromise? What sort of compromise?"

"We could have the uniformed personnel and the flags and the speeches, but not the volley."

He got the priest to reluctantly accept that compromise: no volley on the church grounds. There was a promise there.

Yet it was a promise Terry had absolutely no intention of keeping. He would not make arrangements that ran counter to what Kevin wanted for himself: a full Republican burial.

Various people had the impression that the volley was to be fired on the road outside the house, as the coffin was taken across to the chapel. Some thought that strategically it would be a good place, because the crowd would be there to shield the firing party if necessary.

But Terry thought that, without a large mass of people to protect them—as would have been the case in Derry—the firing party would have been extremely vulnerable in the road. In any case, Terry never intended having the volley anywhere except in the church graveyard. Terry was not going to let this priest's

493

anti-Republican prejudices dictate the form of Kevin's funeral.

On the day the hearse brought Kevin's body to Dungiven, the uniformed men from out of town were there to meet it out on the Limavady Road. They marched through the centre of the town, deliberately stopping for a couple of minutes in front of the police barracks.

Terry was in the house when the coffin was opened. Then as members of the family watched, he laid the flags—the Tricolour and the Starry Plough—over the coffin.

On the day of the funeral itself the uniformed men of the honour guard waited in Dungiven castle for word from the house a quarter of a mile up the main road. The men were apprehensive. They recalled Joe McDonnell's funeral in Belfast, and how the police and the British Army had come out shooting as the procession made its way from the church to the cemetery.

The honour guard should have had transport from the castle to the house and chapel, but now they would have to cover the distance on foot. There was a large police presence in the area, and there was reason to believe that the police might be backed up by soldiers dropped by helicopter and lying in wait in the fields and streets near the road. What would they do if they began marching up the road and the police, supported by soldiers racing out from the streets and fields nearby, came out to stop them?

Then suddenly word came that the coffin had left the house for the short journey—a matter of ninety yards or so—across the road to the chapel. Terry's first thought was that they might have been outfoxed by Father Quinn. But he learned later that the coffin had waited for some time outside the house for the men to arrive. There'd been a breakdown in communication, and the Lynch brothers had been told that the guard of honour was in place and that they could carry the coffin out.

So the guard of honour had to chance it. They marched out, the leader in full dress uniform, the flag bearers of the colour party going before, with Terry hurrying alongside. Very quickly they began to cover the road between the castle and the house.

494

They marched fifty, then a hundred yards. Then two hundred, then four hundred yards . . .

There was no sign of the police, and no sudden appearance of soldiers.

They caught up with the coffin, covered with the Tricolour and Starry Plough, and with the gloves and black beret on it, just as the procession was entering the chapel grounds. The leader, the two flag bearers and the eighteen members of the guard of honour—six of the eighteen were carrying sidearms—formed up in two columns around the coffin and accompanied it to the chapel door.

At the entrance to the chapel the flags and gloves and black beret were removed, and the coffin was taken into the church for the funeral Mass.

Afterwards the guard of honour, waiting outside the church, reformed again. The six men of the firing party, moving ahead of the procession and the main body of the guard of honour, took up positions inside the cemetery gate. The procession edged forward, the family and the priest behind the coffin. Inside the gate, on the way to the graveside, the procession stopped and the coffin was set down on trestles beneath the trees.

Then a command was given in Irish and the six armed volunteers fired three volleys of shots over Kevin's coffin.

There arose cheering and a wave of applause from the crowd. As the procession moved forward again, Terry, who was chairing the proceedings for the IRSP, made his way to the platform.

Father Quinn was furious. He came straight over to Terry.

"You broke your word," he said.

It was true. But it was a question of keeping their word to the priest or keeping faith with Kevin.

"Are you going to say the prayers?" Terry asked. "If not, we have another priest who would be glad to." It was Father Piaras Ó Dúill, chairman of the National H-Blocks/Armagh committee.

Father Quinn didn't answer. He hurried to the graveside, and quickly said the prayers. Then he shook hands with members of the Lynch family and, still angry, left the cemetery.

Five British Army helicopters swooped in and out over the crowd.

During the ceremonies the piper played a lament—"I'll Wear No Convict's Uniform"—the great anthem of the troubles, as many thought it, written for the Relatives' Action committee several years earlier by a Dungiven man, the schoolteacher and songwriter Fràncie Brolly, who had been an internee and who had had a brother on the blanket:

> Does England need a thousand years
> Of protest, riot, death and tears?
> Or will this past decade of fears
> To eighty decades spell
> An end to Ireland's agony,
> New hope for human dignity,
> And will the last obscenity
> Be this grim H-Blocks cell? . . .

The playing of the lament was followed by the Last Post and the presentation of the flags to the Lynch family.

Members of the family, led by Bridie and Paddy, came down to the castle afterwards and thanked all the men of the guard of honour for their service at Kevin's funeral.

Later Father Quinn told the press that the volley had been fired in defiance of his wishes and the wishes of the Lynch family. The papers made much of it, and Bridie had to go to Father Quinn and explain that the family had no objection to the volley. She also tried to put the newspapers straight on the point.

Terry Robson knew something that Father Quinn didn't. A day or so before the funeral, one of the Lynch brothers had spoken to one of the IRSP men.

"Will there be a volley?" he asked.

"There will be."

"Good," he said. "Because if you weren't going to do it, we would."

His brothers, who had worked as hard as they could to save Kevin's life, would have fired a volley, with shotguns, over his grave.

496

Chapter 11

THE INTEGRITY
OF KIERAN DOHERTY

You ask what I have found,
    and far and wide I go:
Nothing but Cromwell's house
    and Cromwell's murderous crew.
The lovers and the dancers
    are beaten into the clay,
And the tall men and the swordsmen
    and the horsemen, where are they?

W. B. Yeats

FINTAN O'RIORDAN was twenty-six years old when he began to take a serious interest in Kieran Doherty. They were both about the same age, both tall (Doherty was 6′4″); both came from working-class families. Like Doherty, Fintan enjoyed a game of hurling. But they had led very different lives.

Fintan* came from Blackrock, at the edge of the sea. The town was a kind of buckle on the South Dublin money belt, where would-be well-heeled executives, professionals, bank managers and grafters of one kind or another, harried by lovely upmarket wives, tried—often with desperation—to maintain the high consumer profiles they thought were expected of them.

Fintan was closer to an older and less demanding tradition of poverty and manual labour. He'd studied with the Christian Brothers, then gone on to get a degree in engineering at Bolton Street College of Technology but dropped out halfway through the course, promising himself he'd have another go sometime

*Not his real name. He was anxious, in recounting his experiences, not to cultivate the attentions of either Special Branch.

497

in the future. After a couple of years in London he returned to Dublin·and moved into a flat on the South Circular Road. Later he got a job in the Guinness brewery in Thomas Street.

Fintan had never been involved in the troubles and his parents had no strong views on politics. The O'Riordans' grandfather had been a travelling salesman for a steamfitters' supplier who had got tired of the road, settled down and set himself up as a handyman. Fintan's father was a self-employed plumber, and Fintan's only brother, Peter, who was three years older, had gone into business with the old man when he left school. Fintan had tried his hand at plumbing over a few summers, but he didn't much like the work, and preferred being independent of his father.

At the age of 26 Fintan wouldn't have called himself a nationalist. He had never had any reason to go up North and his knowledge of the troubles was limited to newspaper headlines. The only march he had ever been on was the march to the British embassy after Bloody Sunday, 30 January 1972. He was sixteen at the time and his friend Dermot had asked him to come with him. Dermot was well versed in Irish language and history and held Republican views. Fintan himself didn't feel that angry about the shooting of unarmed civilians by the British Army. He hadn't thought it through. He just went along to see what was going on.

The people marched behind a lorry, from the GPO in O'Connell Street to Merrion Square, singing rebel songs. There were speeches from the back of the lorry. Then some men with black berets and green army-surplus jackets started throwing petrol bombs at the embassy. The crowd parted, leaving a corridor for them to run through. The gardai stood in front of the building, linking arms, and ducked each time a petrol bomb was lobbed over their heads. There was no attempt to arrest anybody. The police seemed to understand the fury many people felt towards the British that day.

The embassy was shuttered up. Fintan reckoned that the staff had left in a hurry. The Ambassador had probably left as soon as he'd heard the news. After a couple of hours, Fintan and

Dermot decided to leave. They had walked about fifty yards down the road, when suddenly a real bomb went off. Even now he could recall the physical sensation of the ground moving. His reaction to the attack on the embassy was similar to the feelings that welled up inside him at a football match.

Though he hadn't done anything but watch, the next morning at school Fintan was flushed with a sense of achievement.

"I was down at the embassy yesterday, doin' me bit," he was telling his classmates. Then the teacher came in. It was his Irish teacher—a young layman who wore an Aran pullover. He spoke strongly against the burning of the embassy. It was a wasted effort, he said, and hadn't achieved anything. Fintan was quite taken aback. But when he thought about it afterwards, he decided the teacher was right and the demonstration had been stupid. He wouldn't go to another march.

In later years he came to suspect that the authorities had purposely allowed the embassy to be burnt down so that the people's anger could be vented and that would be the end of it.

Fintan's only other personal contact with the troubles was in 1974 when Northern loyalists exploded several car bombs in Dublin, and a number of people were killed and maimed. A friend of Fintan's was driving home from work when one of the bombs exploded. Three passengers in the car were killed outright and his friend suffered multiple and severe injuries. What Fintan felt after visiting him in hospital would determine his attitude for years to come. He was deeply disturbed. Who had done it and why were unimportant. His friend was lying there, and would lie there in bed for another two years—an innocent man who had never harmed anyone, his body and life shattered. Fintan felt no anger or lust for revenge. How could one even contemplate revenge? The result would be someone else's friend lying in another hospital bed.

In the early 1970s, at the peak of internment and the internment protest, the troubles were front-page news and the first item on TV news bulletins. There were intense discussions in the pubs. As the years went by, people in the South got fed up with the troubles—the banality of repetition. Gradually the

North, and its problems, and the violence up there, came to be treated less prominently in the media.

Once, in the mid-70s, Fintan asked someone what they thought about the North. "A load of bollocks," was the reply. By then that epitomized it for Fintan. It was a disturbing and tiresome mess, and one he could do nothing about. By 1980, Fintan was working in the Guinness brewery in Dublin and sharing a flat with two other men. He was a pacifist. He could smile at the definition of a pacifist as "an intelligent coward." When the first hunger strike hit the headlines at the end of the year, he knew exactly where he stood: ninety miles away, in mind as well as body.

There was no excuse for killing people, and killing people was the reason these men were in prison, wasn't it? They shouldn't have special treatment simply because they claimed to have special reasons for killing. Political murder was no more justifiable than common murder. *Every* murder has its motive: someone has a few pints too many, loses his head, and smashes in somebody else's skull. Maybe the killer's victim was driving him round the twist; maybe he was a lunatic. There were reasons for all murders. He didn't see why political murder should be a special case.

But the lads in the flat were close friends of his and they were arguing for the hunger strikers. The arguments became very bitter at times. They felt the hunger strikers deserved political status and their five demands. Fintan just laughed when they said all hell would break loose if any of the hunger strikers died. He knew that all hell would not break loose. His friends' bitterness stemmed from Fintan's attitude that the hunger strikers, and the IRA, were criminals who killed people—heavy criminals. His was a simplistic attitude, his friends said. He said he couldn't see what was simplistic about it: he was only talking sense. They told him he didn't understand what it was like to live up there. He said he had no wish to live up there. He'd learned over the years, he told them, to avoid places he didn't want to be, and news about such places. He wanted to avoid violence and even the thought of violence. If there was news about violence on the radio, he would just spin the dial.

Yet for a dial-spinner Fintan had an odd propensity. He liked to have his assumptions challenged. He had to periodically reassess his opinions, just to assure himself that he was growing.

In 1981, with the advent of the second hunger strike, Fintan decided it was time to see if he'd missed something. For Fintan this meant trying to see another point of view. He recalled the American Indian saying: "Grant that I may not criticize my neighbour until I have walked a mile in his moccasins."

A friend, Colum, started to give him nationalist literature—stuff by Fathers Faul and Murray, by Eamonn McCann and Tim Pat Coogan, and some clips of Bobby Sands' "Marcella" pieces from *An Phoblacht*. Some of this made an impression. Fintan slowly came to the conclusion that people were being trampled underfoot in Northern Ireland, day in and out, year after year. Internment, torture, kangaroo courts, the H-Blocks: how on earth was Britain getting away with this?

Fintan had accepted the idea that the British were using violence in a war against violence, even if he didn't think of it in just those terms. Now he saw that members of the IRA saw themselves as the first recipients of the violence. And he asked himself whether Britain was more justified in using violence than the IRA.

Since for years he had deliberately closed his mind to anything about the North, he knew nothing of the prisoners' lives in the H-Blocks, or the lives of people in the nationalist ghettoes. Sands' pieces especially conveyed a personal point of view. Suspicious as he was of the media, Fintan wondered: had he been thoroughly conned by the writers and broadcasters? He had seen the IRA as dangerous and had no desire to meet any of "the boys." He recalled that day at the embassy, after Bloody Sunday: they were so strange, those young men in the green berets and army jackets. Who were they? They were not the same as the rest of the crowd. They had worn a rudimentary uniform and had brought petrol with them. They were organized.

Reading Sands' meditations from prison, he began to see them in a different light.

In Sands' writings he met a man speaking from his own personal experience. It was the next best thing to talking to someone directly. He became acquainted with the hunger strikers' lives—learned about the Sandses getting dustbins thrown through their windows, forcing them to move house, or learned about Francis Hughes getting his head kicked in after a dance, or about the brutality of the Castlereagh interrogations. Fintan still didn't agree with what these men had done. but he began to understand *why*.

Fintan was impressed with Bobby Sands' will to resist. He began to read closely the reports of maltreatment and torture of prisoners in Faul and Murray's H-Block booklets. How could people do this to one another? The stories were sickening, almost unbearable.

In the long hours and years of their confinement the prisoners had had time to think; there was little else to do. They had found a deepened understanding of the historical context in which they could claim a place. They had drawn strength from their forerunners in Ireland, as well as from freedom fighters (as they called them) around the world.

Running away as quickly as his legs could carry him would always be the preferable tactic for Fintan. If pushed far enough, though, he supposed he would eventually strike back. And so he drew the moral for himself out of all his reading and reflection: How could he pass judgement on men who'd been pushed further than he himself would have been able to endure?

If he had been living up there, he might well have done as these men had, and joined the Provos or the INLA. If his father or older brother or his friends had been interned for months and years, with no trial and no reason given, he would surely have joined. He would have felt like hitting back with whatever he could lay his hands on, including guns and grenades. People had to defend themselves.

For Fintan, it was the hunger strike that uncovered the real issue and brought it all out into the open. This was not only a humanitarian issue; it was also, and primarily, political. There was no doubt that the nationalist population of the North had been discriminated against, no doubt that they had grievances.

502

The question remained: had they any right to use violence in protest against these things?

As far as Fintan was concerned, war was not a legitimate activity for human beings. But if it was—if, for instance, it was legitimate to fight against Hitler's storm troopers in World War II, and most people felt it was—then this war in the North was as legitimate as any. Wasn't it Bernadette Devlin who said, "We were not terrorists. It was the British who taught us to be terrorists"?

It had suited the London and Dublin governments to maintain that, while those who fought the Irish War of Independence and World War II were fine, the IRA and INLA were criminals and psychopaths. The War of Independence had allowed Fintan to enjoy the life he had had. And many of the South Dublin bourgeoisie were thriving. That was the problem. Their comfort had led them to abandon their people in the North. He noticed that the strongest support in Dublin for the hunger strikers came from the less well-off areas of the city, from people who understood about social deprivation, poverty and discrimination. They hadn't forgotten the Northerners, because they were in the same boat.

There was a difference, then, between the hunger strikers and so-called common criminals. These prisoners *were* political prisoners.

And, strangely, these men had passed through a furnace, yet instead of being destroyed they had been transformed. Through their agony they had grown in understanding of what they were doing. No matter how far they'd been pushed and what attempts were made to degrade them, the suffering they'd undergone had made them more and more resolute; instead of shattering them, their pain had ennobled them. There seemed no end to what these men could suffer yet still maintain their dignity and integrity.

Fintan felt that something had to be done for them. Men of that quality could not be allowed to go on dying like that. Something *would* be done.

ON 30 JUNE Dr. Garret FitzGerald was sworn in as Taoiseach

503

in the South. Within two hours of his taking office he had a meeting with the hunger strikers' relatives. At a press conference that evening he said that his first political priority would be the situation in the H-Blocks. Fintan was impressed by this. Now finally there would be action.

He was hopeful, too, about the efforts of the Irish Commission for Justice and Peace. They were sincere, and were supported by the moderate forces in the country who wanted to see the problem resolved. Fintan saw something else he found encouraging. The British were allowing these people to go in and talk with the prisoners; and the British, through the Northern Ireland Office, were *talking* to the ICJP. This meant that the British were themselves sincere about trying to reach a solution. Shuttling back and forth between the prisoners and the NIO, the ICJP mediators seemed on the verge of a settlement.

When the Commission failed, it was a blow. Fintan was dismayed by the ICJP statement that the British had "clawed back" on the settlement terms. The Church, through the ICJP, had done all it could. Now it was up to FitzGerald. He had the power and authority to act for the Irish government and the Irish people.

Fintan's hopes remained high. Help would come from the Dublin government.

Two days after the Commission announced its failure on 8 July, John Kelly, Acting Minister for Foreign Affairs, and Professor Jim Dooge, the Minister-designate, met in London with Ian Gilmour, the British Deputy Foreign Secretary, and Humphrey Atkins, Secretary of State for Northern Ireland. Kelly and Dooge stressed the need for Britain to be both flexible and speedy. Kelly, known in the Dáil as a master of invective, emphasized—in what was described as an "uninterruptible" flow of argument—the destabilizing influence of the hunger strike in the Republic, and the increased tension and polarization in Northern Ireland.

On Monday 13 July, Professor Dooge privately conveyed the same view to Lord Carrington at a meeting in Brussels. Martin Hurson had died suddenly that morning, and the Dublin government stepped up the pressure by asking the British government to enter direct talks with the hunger strikers in the prison.

Two days later, the morning newspapers carried the report that the Irish government had appealed to President Reagan to put pressure on Britain to find a solution.

It seemed to Fintan that FitzGerald was pulling out all the stops . . .

On 21 July, the pressure exerted by Garret FitzGerald and the Dublin government seemed finally to be beginning to pay off. It was important and urgent that the effort succeed. By then Kieran Doherty was far advanced in his fast. He and Kevin Lynch had gone more than sixty days without food.

KIERAN DOHERTY: the little that Fintan knew about him came mostly from accounts in Republican literature.

The Dohertys lived in a red brick semidetached home on a hill in Andersonstown, West Belfast. Kieran had been born on 16 December 1955, the third of six children: Michael and Terence were older; Roisín, Mairead and Brendan younger. His mother Margaret had been converted from Protestantism to Catholicism at the time she married their father, Alfie Doherty, a floor tiler, whose family, from Limavady in Co. Derry, had moved to North Belfast in the 20s. Later, when the North Belfast house they lived in was threatened, the Dohertys had moved to West Belfast. It was like the Sands family's forced house moves. But here the families diverged.

The Sandses, before Bobby, had not been at all Republican. The Dohertys had a tradition going back to Kieran's granduncle, Ned Maguire, who had taken part in a legendary IRA rooftop escape from Crumlin Road jail in 1943. Two of Ned's daughters, Maura Meehan and Dorothy Maguire—Kieran's second cousins—were shot dead by the British Army in 1971. Their brother Ned had been an internee and was now a blanketman. In 1972 Kieran's uncle, Gerry Fox, had played on the football team that escaped en masse from the Crumlin Road by climbing over the wall.

Kieran Doherty was as strong as he was big, with a great interest in Gaelic football and hurling. He was an intense competitor at cycling, and did quite well in school. In the summer of 1971, at the age of fifteen, he began training as an apprentice heating engineer. Laid off when the firm closed down, he worked for a time with his father as a floor tiler. During internment, Kieran's brothers Michael and Terence, then in their late teens, were taken off to prison and held without trial. The British Army was on the streets, and the Doherty house was constantly raided.

Kieran joined Fianna Eireann in late 1971. Ten days before his seventeenth birthday, the British Army came to arrest him in the middle of the night. As the Army took him away, Alfie protested that his son was under age. He woke the sexton at St. Agnes' chapel, got a copy of Kieran's birth certificate and went down and got Kieran released. The British Army returned for him on 16 October 1972, but he had gone south to live with an uncle in Limerick. He stayed in the South until early 1973, then made his way back to Belfast. Within ten days he was arrested, taken to Castlereagh, and interned in the cages at Long Kesh. Among the handicrafts he made there was a wooden plaque in honour of his cousins Maura Meehan and Dorothy Maguire.

Kieran was among the last of the internees to be released, in November 1975.

After his release he served as an IRA volunteer for nearly a year and was very active, with Joe McDonnell and others, in the Andersonstown area.

During one operation in which Kieran was involved, an IRA comrade was shot dead. Kieran, told to lie low, turned up for the man's funeral and appeared in a photograph taken of the mourners. Fintan wondered what was going through Kieran's mind as he stood there watching his friend's body pass by? What would he have felt had that been his own friend Colum's hearse?

A few nights later when the talk turned to his dead friend, Kieran had to get up and leave the company.

Kieran was quiet, shy and reflective. He had once been involved in a public fight—when a man had started hitting the girl with him, and Kieran, turning white, gave the fellow a beating. A man hitting a woman, he said, was the height of cruelty.

Fintan tried to reach through the skeleton of facts and grasp what Kieran Doherty was like. In the cages he was tidy and neat, they said, his shoes always polished. He was intelligent. And there was no doubt that he was powerful. "Big Doc," they called him. He was not a man to shout, but one who radiated contained strength. Fintan studied his photo—the picture of a young man who had suffered. Another photo, of Kieran and John Pickering, reminded him strangely of himself and Colum. He'd had photos like that taken during his own drinking sessions with close friends: young men, out for a few beers, laughing and having a good time.

In August 1976 Kieran was arrested, after a bombing. He was with John Pickering and others in a van which was chased by the RUC near Balmoral Avenue in Belfast. Kieran jumped out of the van and got hold of a car. One of the other men was captured almost immediately. The rest, surrounded in a house they had taken over, gave themselves up. Kieran was picked up, unarmed and on foot, a mile and a half from the scene.

The men were brought to court and charged with possession of firearms and explosives. Forensic tests failed to link Kieran to these charges, yet at his trial the RUC got the judge to accept the lie that Kieran had been found in possession of arms. He was given eighteen years.

In January 1978 he went back to Long Kesh, to the H-Blocks this time. He refused the criminal uniform and joined the blanket protest.

Kieran was one of the most fiercely resistant of all the prisoners. His height made him a special target, and he was often singled out for abuse because of his attitude to the warders. He refused to talk to or answer any warder. He would take no orders from them, would not even look at them. While on remand in Crumlin Road prison, he had often been locked in a punishment cell because of his refusal to acknowledge the warders in any way whatever.

In Long Kesh, except for two weeks in H-6, Kieran spent

all his time in H-4. He became a fluent Irish speaker and, in 1980, an H-Blocks chess champion. Like the McElwees and others he was often assaulted. Once, after he refused a mirror search, they squeezed his testicles until he became unconscious. He was so badly beaten up that he had to be taken to the prison hospital.

One of the worst beatings occurred in late July, 1978, six months after Kieran was brought to Long Kesh. His father gave a statement about it to Father Raymond Murray. On a visit he'd had with Kieran, Alfie said, he was shocked to see his son with a black eye and bruises all over his body. Kieran told him that when he was coming out for an appeal visit on Wednesday 26 July, the screws took him into the search cell. There were eight screws in the room. He was told to lie over a stool so they could probe his back passage.

Kieran refused. So they started kicking and punching him, and knocked him to the floor. He was told to open his mouth. Again he refused. They began punching and kicking him in the stomach, and karate-chopping the back of his neck. Still they couldn't get him to open his mouth. Finally they took him, badly beaten, back to his cell. Later they returned and told him that they would take him to the prison hospital, if he washed. He refused to wash. After a time a prison doctor came to examine him, giving him tablets to kill the pain.

He was put in the punishment block. At about midnight he started to vomit. Again the doctor was called. Kieran was taken to the hospital for observation and kept there the rest of the night. The doctor's guess, Alfie said, was that the tablets must have sickened him.

They charged him with attempting to strike a warder and put him on the boards for three days.

In December 1978 the doctors gave orders for the blanketmen to be forcibly bathed, shaved and have their hair cut. In the accounts of torture and ill-treatment at Long Kesh, Kieran Doherty's name was given as an example of how prisoners were severly injured during this exercise.

But Kieran had survived the blanket, no-wash and dirt protests. After the October-December 1980 hunger strike had ended, and none of the concessions the British had suggested they would make materialized, Kieran was very angry. He was, after all, in the forefront of the fight against this vicious prison regime. "They are really rubbing our noses in it," he told a friend. "By God, they will not rub mine!"

In March 1981, in a letter to the members of St. Teresa's, his GAA club in Belfast, Kieran wrote:

> For some time after the ending of the hunger strike, we prisoners moved a lot in order to avail the British government of the opportunity to end this barbaric situation, but once again were faced with that familiar wall of intransigence.
>
> Because of this inflexibility and unwillingness to settle this issue, we were forced, just as we were forced in October last, to revert to the ultimate form of prison protest—hunger strike.

Through March, April and May, Kieran Doherty followed the progress of the first four hunger strikers, as Bobby Sands, Francis Hughes, Raymond McCreesh and Patsy O'Hara died one after the other. Then, on Friday 22 May, Kieran replaced McCreesh, joining Joe McDonnell (for Sands) and Brendan McLoughlin (for Hughes), on hunger strike. McLoughlin, facing a quick death because of a perforated ulcer, came off five days later. Kieran saw Kevin Lynch join as the INLA replacement for Patsy O'Hara, and Martin Hurson come on as the IRA replacement for Francis Hughes.

After Bobby Sands' April victory in the Westminster by-election in Fermanagh-South Tyrone, there was much talk of prisoner candidates for the Dáil elections to be held in the Republic in early June. On 29 May the National H-Blocks committee announced that Kieran and nine other men (including Joe McDonnell, Martin Hurson, Kevin Lynch and Tony O'Hara) would be put forward for the Dáil.

On Thursday, 11 June, voters elected Kieran TD for Cavan-Monaghan. He had a first preference vote of 9,121, the highest of all the prisoners. Another blanketman, Paddy Agnew, was elected TD for Louth. The nine together had amassed forty thousand first preference votes.

By now Kieran seemed to be the acknowledged leader among the fasting prisoners. The men developed a new policy—of putting a man on hunger strike each week to avoid long gaps and so keep up the pressure on the British. On 8 June Thomas McElwee joined; on 15 June it was Paddy Quinn of Beleeks, Co. Armagh; on 22 June Micky Devine; on 29 June Laurence McKeown of Randalstown, Co. Antrim. Meanwhile the Catholic ICJP's mediation, or lobbying, in which Kieran played a central role on behalf of the other prisoners, was reaching its climax. In early July it reached its denouement when the British reneged on the partial reforms they had conceded to the ICJP lobbyists.

BUT WITH FITZGERALD so active behind the scenes during the three weeks after the general election, Fintan's hopes for Kieran and the other men grew. He was certain that the Dublin government would not permit Kieran, an elected TD, to die. Apart from his symbolic interest as a member of Dáil Éireann, Kieran was now a factor in Southern political calculations.

Even from a cold reckoning of party advantage, it was important to FitzGerald that the Cavan-Monaghan seat be held by Kieran Doherty as an abstentionist TD. If he were to die it would force a by-election, which Fianna Fáil might win, putting FitzGerald's already precarious margin in the Dáil in further jeopardy.

On 14 July Kieran issued a statement through his family, appealing to his fellow Irish TDs to take decisive action on the hunger strike, and asking FitzGerald and Charlie Haughey, now leader of the opposition, to publicly declare their support for the five demands.

Fintan didn't think the declarations would come. But the Dublin government and Cardinal Tomás Ó Fiaich were urging the British government to send officials in to talk directly to the prisoners. Through the Irish Ambassador to the US, Sean Donlon, FitzGerald had sought to convey Dublin's "sense of urgency and sense of alarm" to the American government, and had publicly appealed for President Reagan's help in urging the British to send in an emissary for direct talks with the prisoners.

There was a feeling of hope in the atmosphere. Then at 2 a.m. on 21 July, the NIO representatives went into the prison. Was this finally going to be the breakthrough?

On 17 July Kieran, though lucid, was unable to speak to his family. His leg was numb. He was vomiting, and had severe headaches. On 18 July he was on his fifty-eighth day. Raymond McCreesh, Patsy O'Hara, and Joe McDonnell had all died after sixty-one days. Kieran's parents and family were with him now on a twenty-four hour watch, his mother Margaret and father Alfie alternating days and nights, Kieran's brothers and sisters sharing the vigil with them.

Then, on Saturday 18 July had come the bitter riot near the British embassy, now moved to Ballsbridge on the south side of Dublin. The riot, to Fintan, was an unwelcome distraction. It was likely to draw FitzGerald's attention away from the lives of the hunger strikers. FitzGerald's wife Joan went to Ballsbridge to sympathize with the well-heeled people living near the embassy whose property had been damaged. She and Garret FitzGerald visited the hospitalized gardai who had been injured in the riot.

As a member of the Dáil, Kieran had appealed from his deathbed for a visit from the Taoiseach. Why, Fintan wondered, hadn't FitzGerald responded to the request? It would have done enormous good.

And then, day by day, the truth about what was happening began to become plain to Fintan. First came the hammer blow— Alfie Doherty's account of the visit by NIO officials to the prison on 21 July.

At 11 pm on Monday night 20 July, Alfie and his eldest son Michael had been asked to leave the hospital to see the prison governor and two of his deputies. They told him that a priest had informed them that Kieran and Kevin Lynch wanted someone from the NIO to visit them to explain Humphrey Atkins' offer of prison reform.

511

Alfie checked back with his son. Kieran told him he had made no such request.

At 1:20 am the governor told Alfie that two Northern Ireland Office officials were on their way to the prison. They arrived at 1:40 am and met Alfie and members of the Lynch family. The officials began by claiming that recent accounts of the British clawing back on agreements with the ICJP were false.

They started to explain the British view of association in the prison when Alfie interrupted them, saying that they should be telling this to the hunger strikers and their representative, Brendan McFarlane. The officials said that they would not speak with McFarlane. Alfie told them that Kieran was too weak to be disturbed. The officials left Alfie and the Lynches, and went in and woke the hunger strikers. It was now about 2 a.m. The hunger strikers told the NIO officials that unless Bic McFarlane were present they wouldn't talk. The officials refused to see McFarlane. They left the prison, and no discussions were held.

The NIO said afterwards that the visit was in response to the Irish government appeals for direct talks with the prisoners.

Fintan couldn't believe it! Was this all the British saw fit to do in response to the Irish government's pleas? To have their lackeys come slithering in *at two in the morning* to visit men on their deathbeds, in the advanced stages of hunger strike, and then refuse to allow the presence of McFarlane?

The refusal to include McFarlane was proof of the hypocrisy of the British gesture. Had they been serious in wanting to get a dialogue going, they would have welcomed McFarlane. In fact, it was clear from various accounts that Brendan McFarlane's role as prisoner OC, like that of Bobby Sands in the 1980 strike, had been recognized regularly by the prison and NIO throughout the strike. He had been in constant contact with the men in the hospital, the hunger strikers still in the prison, and outside agents such as the chaplains, the members of the ICJP, delegations from the Pope and the European Commission on Human Rights, and even people from Sinn Féin and the IRSP.

To deny his presence now was not only an insult to the

512

prisoners but—as a journalist commented—the introduction of a new principle into the bargaining: as though the British were trying "to cut off the hunger strikers' escape routes, thereby forcing a cave-in."

The entire manner of the visit was a slap in the face to FitzGerald, a contemptuous response to the Irish government's public demand for direct talks, which had extended even to an appeal to President Reagan to intercede. It was as if Thatcher were saying: "You wanted direct talks with the prisoners? All right, this is what you're getting—this pair creeping in, in the middle of the night, under conditions that will ensure the talks will break down before they start—and make it look like the prisoners' own fault!" It was a transparently cynical move. Surely, Fintan thought, the Irish government should have protested strongly to the British!

Yet in the same paper that carried Alfie's account, the Irish government press secretary, Liam Hourican, was quoted as saying: "The government has to point out that the reaction it required of the British was in fact carried out, and officials did in fact go into the Maze to speak to the hunger strikers. The Taoiseach feels that he has done all he can."

"Did in fact go into 'the Maze'": the language itself was British. And FitzGerald did not deny that his press secretary had said these things.

On 24 July the prisoners released a statement, which crystallized for Fintan Dublin's position vis-a-vis the British government:

> They [the British] are offering us nothing that amounts to an honourable solution—the power to move them lies with the nationalist leaders. Were the Dublin government courageous enough to stand against them, the British would have to reconsider their position . . .

The statement called on FitzGerald to put his government's attitude honestly and in a forthright manner.

It was clear to Fintan that Dublin was where the hunger strikers and their relatives had placed their hopes. Why else would the families do as they were doing—keep making the

513

journey down to Dublin and back again—even after all the heartbreak of seeing their men die while Dublin watched on the sidelines? These were Irishmen dying, and the Irish government was the only power on earth they might count on to be completely sympathetic. It was the only quarter from which they could hope for help.

FitzGerald's government had the power. But what had FitzGerald been doing? He'd been passing the buck to the ICJP. To Dooge and Kelly. To the Americans. Despite the fact that the prisoners and their relatives had repeatedly asked FitzGerald to say exactly where he stood, he refused to. He talked a lot but never said anything. The action of Kelly and Dooge in the middle of July was that of deputies talking to deputies. If there was something to be said to Mrs. Thatcher, why didn't FitzGerald say it himself? His refusal to take a stand galled Fintan. As Taoiseach he should either have publicly supported the five demands or forthrightly said he didn't support them.

Fintan could appreciate Gerry Adams' remark that the clash in Ballsbridge near the British embassy was quite understandable, since the Free State was devoting more energy to protecting British interests than to the hunger strikers.

There was a clue. FitzGerald had shown concern—energetic concern—to end the hunger strike. But perhaps his concern was largely motivated by the increasing instability in the South. Perhaps his wife Joan's visit to the comfortable upper middle class in the neighbourhood where the riot had taken place showed where her husband's real sympathies lay. Perhaps FitzGerald was simply a representative of his own class, whose main goal in life was the maintenance of its comfortable life, a secure future made less secure by all that agitation up North conducted by the men of no property. Perhaps therefore FitzGerald *had* decided, instinctively, which side to throw his lot in with. To maintain the way of life of his class, he would be thinking, he had to row in with Britain, had to keep up friendly relations *at all costs*.

Fintan understood this outlook. He recognized it in himself, except that for him and many others the hunger strike had made a great difference. It had forced them to search their minds and feelings and to decide where they stood.

Fintan's heart went out to the relatives, trudging up and down to Dublin, clutching at the hope that the Dublin government might act to save their loved ones' lives. There was FitzGerald telling them he was doing his best, and doing nothing. Was there any difference between FitzGerald's passing the buck to the ICJP, or to Dooge and Kelly, or to Reagan or to the Red Cross (the latest gambit), and the Thatcher ploy—the creation of an illusion of movement?

FitzGerald's real motive now seemed to be the trouble in his own backyard—the instability of the Irish State shown by the rioting in Ballsbridge, by the two H-Block TDs in a hung Dáil. If Kieran Doherty were to die, FitzGerald's fragile coalition would be reduced to a majority of only one seat.

Was that all FitzGerald wanted—to stay in power? He had created an illusion of activity and movement. Yet all he was doing was prolonging the agony of the men and their families. And now he had gone into hiding.

A week later Margaret Thatcher picked up on the press secretary's statement. She had not gone into hiding. In a letter to American politicians she wrote:

> You will no doubt have seen that a spokesman for the Prime Minister of Ireland said that Dr. FitzGerald believed the British government had met his suggestion that an official should speak to the hunger-strikers, that he deeply regretted the hunger strikers had rejected the offer from officials to clarify what conditions would apply if the strike ended, and that in his view responsibility for finding a solution now rested with the prisoners.

FitzGerald was on to the press immediately—through a "spokesman"—complaining about Thatcher's "serious misrepresentation" of his position on the hunger strike.

Why shouldn't she misrepresent him? Fintan asked himself. All that week there had been no repudiation by FitzGerald of *his* press secretary's statement about the prison visit. He'd left himself wide open to misrepresentation.

After that—silence. No more was heard about FitzGerald's pique. No more was heard of the dramatic appeal to Reagan.

On Sunday 26 July Kieran Doherty, then on his sixty-sixth day, had gone almost completely deaf. His sight was blurred and nearly gone. By next day his mouth was so covered with ulcers that a sip of water was terribly painful. The skin on his arms was blackening. He could barely speak.

Kevin Lynch was rapidly weakening, too.

On 28 July, the same day that FitzGerald complained about Thatcher's "serious misrepresentation" of his views, he gave his approval for the Irish Ambassador in London to attend the English royal wedding on 29 July. With millions of unemployed in Britain, savage rioting that summer in English cities, and Kevin Lynch and Kieran dying in Long Kesh, the British and the Irish people were to be treated to endless TV reportage of this spectacle. A circus for the rabble, Fintan thought. Southern Irish television, which was prevented by law from giving air time to any Irish Republican spokesman, was going to cover it.

The international reaction to the hunger strike had been such that President Mitterand of France sounded out the Dublin government over whether to attend the wedding. The Dublin government encouraged him to go, "for the sake of Anglo-French relations." At the same time the French League for the Rights of Man was attacking Thatcher's government for its "barbarous obstinacy" on the hunger strike.

On 31 July, as Kevin Lynch lay dying, FitzGerald—in a desperate attempt to pass the buck once more, this time to the leaders of the IRA and INLA—released a statement. They could order their men off, he asserted. It was their responsibility to end the hunger strike (and they were obstructing *his* humanitarian efforts):

> It seemed to me to be no accident as the efforts of the Irish government to help solve the crisis became more public, the efforts of the Provisional IRA leadership to obstruct a solution redoubled. The hardening of the IRA line thwarted the efforts of those who had pressed for a humanitarian solution . . .

Fintan was amazed. Could FitzGerald seriously think that the IRA leaders were forcing the men to die by starvation in a British prison? The ICJP themselves had accused Britain of dishonesty and chicanery. Fintan doubted whether FitzGerald had ever been so badly beaten by prison warders that his eardrum was perforated like Liam McCloskey's. Or whether, like Kieran Doherty, he had had his testicles squeezed until he was unconscious. It was clear that FitzGerald was now taking the British side in the war up there.

In response, the IRA itself made an interesting observation: "Mr. Garret FitzGerald's statement that the leadership of the Irish Republican Army can end the hunger-strike is ascribing powers to us which we do not have . . Our imprisoned comrades, furthermore, are superior in motivation and politically sophisticated to a degree that has freed them and us from the oppressive discipline of a regular army. We are, above all else, a volunteer army . . ."

FitzGerald had missed the whole point: the hunger strikers *were* the IRA and INLA. They, if anyone, were its leadership— because the hunger strike was now the rallying point in the common fight against Britain. To suggest that these men were being thwarted by some brutal outside force was to insult the hunger strikers themselves, who were sacrificing their lives to break a brutal and monstrous prison regime. A man's life was his sovereign possession. Nobody could order him to slowly die, or could order him to reverse his own decision while that regime, supported by FitzGerald's power (and weakness), was still intact.

To Fintan, FitzGerald's feeble effort to cast aspersions on the motives of the men was revolting.

As Kevin Lynch died, Paddy Quinn's mother took her son off, and the tall, proud, quiet young Irish TD, Kieran Doherty, began his death agony. He had insisted if he fell into a coma, that his family was not to intervene.

At 7:15 a.m. on Sunday 2 August, Kieran Doherty died—the longest survivor among the hunger strikers.

IN THE CRUCIBLE of the prison, Fintan thought, Kieran Doherty must have grown profoundly in his understanding of himself. Fintan saw in Kieran Doherty what he'd only intermittently glimpsed before: that when a person is stripped of everything—possessions, home, family, freedom—only then does he discover what he is. Kieran had approached the regime with an asceticism of his own: refusing to talk to, refusing even to look at the warders. This must have made life extremely difficult for him. It was on the record that it brought him severe punishments.

But what he had in common with the other men was more important still. Like the other prisoners he had lost everything. He and they had been through years of hideous prison life in Long Kesh, and still they maintained their integrity. They were true to themselves, to the point where they were able to die willingly rather than surrender their dignity.

Perhaps the courage that had crystallized in them had prevented their fully realizing how insensitive and arrogant were the people they were dealing with.

Looking at photographs of Kieran Doherty, Fintan recalled the Irish proverb: A brave man never loses. He thought of the bonds between Kieran and the other brave men in the H-Blocks. With full remission Kevin Lynch, had he not joined the prison protest, could have been released in December. Kevin had told his mother that it was not himself but the other men he was concerned for: those who were married with families or with twenty-five or thirty years to serve. The bond between the prisoners was so intense, their love for each other so strong, that young men like Kieran and Kevin, with everything to live for, were prepared to sacrifice their lives for their friends.

Fintan could not imagine what it would be like to slowly starve to death . . . The contrast between this man's life and his own put him to shame. He felt that his own love would never extend that far. All the accusations about violence and terrorism were somehow nothing in the face of this man's sacrifice. It frightened Fintan, and made him feel humble. In Kieran Doherty there was something uniquely precious.

On the day of his funeral, two—only two—of his fellow TDs came to honour him. At Leinster House, where the Dáil sat in Dublin, they flew the Tricolour at half-mast: the flag of Ireland.

So far as Fintan knew, no other TD had ever died for it.

518

Alfie and Margaret Doherty at Kieran's funeral in Belfast. Margaret holds the Irish flag, beret and gloves, marks of an Irish Republican Army volunteer, taken from atop her son's coffin *(Photo: Derek Speirs/Report)*

Garret Fizgerald, Taoiseach during most of the 1981 hunger strike *(Irish Press photo)*

Margaret Thatcher, British Prime Minister during the first and second hunger strikes *(Irish Press photo)*

The McElwee family at Annie's marriage to Martin Mullan in 1976: From left to right: Benedict, Majella, Jim, Joseph, Mary; Martin and Annie; Enda, Pauline, Nora, Alice, James, Bernadette, Kathleen and Thomas *(Photo courtesy of the McElwee family)*

Women on Falls Road banging dustbin lids in the ritual way, announcing the death of Thomas McElwee *(Photo by Pacemaker)*

Father Seán McManus, head of the Irish National Caucus and one of the leading US supporters of the hunger strikers, helps Benedict McElwee carry his brother's coffin *(Photo by Pacemaker)*

Thomas McElwee's sisters carrying his coffin. Visible in the picture are (left to right) Enda, Kathleen, Nora, Annie, and Majella *(Photo by Pacemaker)*

Teresa Moore being ejected from Leinster House after sit-in following unproductive meeting with the Taoiseach, Dr. Garret FitzGerald, on 6 August 1981
(Irish Times photo)

At Micky Devine's funeral in Derry his sister Margaret McCauley holds hands of Micky's son Michael and daughter Louise. At left is Teresa Moore
(Photo: Derek Speirs/Report)

Fr. Denis Faul *(Photo: Derek Speirs/Report)*

Gerry Adams (now president of Sinn Féin and SF MP for West Belfast), speaking at a march following the end of the hunger strike

(Photo by Pacemaker)

Bernadette McAliskey speaking in front of the GPO, Dublin, in July 1982

(Photo: Derek Speirs/Report)

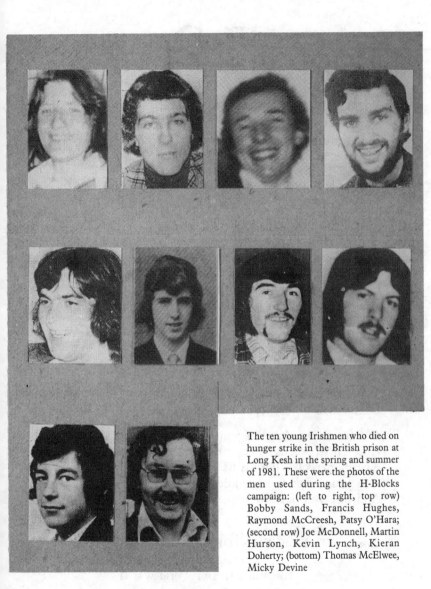

The ten young Irishmen who died on hunger strike in the British prison at Long Kesh in the spring and summer of 1981. These were the photos of the men used during the H-Blocks campaign: (left to right, top row) Bobby Sands, Francis Hughes, Raymond McCreesh, Patsy O'Hara; (second row) Joe McDonnell, Martin Hurson, Kevin Lynch, Kieran Doherty; (bottom) Thomas McElwee, Micky Devine

Chapter 12

THOMAS McELWEE

Sweet brother, if I do not sleep
My eyes are flowers for your tomb;
And if I cannot eat my bread,
My fasts shall live like willows where you died.
If in the heat I find no water for my thirst,
My thirst shall turn to springs
    for you, poor traveller . . .

Come, in my labour find a resting place
And in my sorrows lay your head,
Or rather take my life and blood
And buy yourself a better bed—
Or take my breath and take my death
and buy yourself a better rest.

When all the men of war are shot
And flags have fallen into dust,
Your cross and mine shall tell men still
Christ died on each, for both of us.

For in the wreckage of your April Christ lies slain,
And Christ weeps in the ruins of my spring:
The money of Whose tears shall fall
Into your weak and friendless hand
And buy you back to your own land . . .

Thomas Merton
Poem in THE SEVEN STOREY MOUNTAIN
on his brother,
killed in action in World War II

MARY McELWEE put the small notepad in her purse and followed her sister Nora out the front door of the simple stone bungalow. She felt better now that she'd had it out with her brother Thomas and put the question to him directly last Saturday in the prison hospital: Was it the Republican leaders outside the prison who were forcing the hunger strike? Or were the boys inside doing it on their own—freely? All the talk in the newspapers and on TV had put the doubt in her mind. Some of the other relatives were as disturbed as she was.

"Nobody is putting this on us but ourselves, Mary," Thomas had said with absolute sincerity in his eyes. "Don't listen to propaganda like that." Now she felt she could reassure the other relatives. And today she would have the opportunity to tell it to the Taoiseach.

The girls walked down the footpath in the front yard, and Nora opened the white double gate onto the narrow country road. Across the field was the Hughes house on Scribe Road. Their own little house, St. Anne's, on Tamlaghtduff Road, was banked on either side by ditches and hedges bordering the rolling pastureland and cultivated fields. At Mulholland's corner, at the bottom of Tamlaghtduff townland, the twelve McElwee children—eight girls and four boys—used to catch buses to local schools—along with neighbouring children and their cousins the Hugheses. Tamlaghtduff Road ended on the Mullaghboy Road, which led into the town of Bellaghy itself.

There were more Catholics than Protestants in the district, though on the Derry County council the Catholics were outnumbered three to one. Bellaghy was one of those divided northern towns, with Catholics on one side of the main street and Protestants on the other.

Mary recalled how three months ago, when their cousin Francis Hughes was on hunger strike, they tried to bring an H-Blocks march into Bellaghy. The marchers were halfway down Scribe Road when they were stopped by the police on orders from councilman "Black Bob" Overend. Francis' brother Oliver Hughes spoke to the police, but they refused to let them continue. The road was black with RUC landrovers; and the police were being deliberately provocative.

People left their cars and walked over the fields, coming in from all directions. Mary had never seen so many people. Then some boys started throwing stones. The next thing the police were firing plastic bullets. Mary and her mother Alice tried to catch some of the stone throwers so that the RUC men wouldn't have the excuse to keep firing at them. Eventually the stewards got control of the young lads. Things quieted down and finally the crowd dispersed. But afterwards the youngsters lit pyramids of tyres in the fields as it began to grow dark, and bonfires blazed into the sky. Six or seven boys sat up all night around one of the bonfires. Then at about four in the morning they walked down to the main street of Bellaghy carrying the Tricolour.

Mary, who was particularly close to Thomas, had given up work in Cork to come home when Thomas went on hunger strike in early June. Nora was on holidays from college. So the two girls were free to make the trips to Dublin with other relatives. Their mother Alice, who had gone to America in July—she'd been in Philadelphia when Joe McDonnell died—had no sooner returned than she'd flown off again to London, hoping to get support to save Thomas's life. Kathleen, the eldest, had taken a week off from work to accompany their mother to America. Members of the family went wherever they could—to the torchlight processions, the vigils, the rallies, the marches.

WHEN MARY went to the prison hospital to visit Thomas on Sunday, she met Father Tom O'Neill, a priest of Bethlehem Abbey, the monastery at Portglenone. He'd been in to say Mass and then visit with Thomas. Father Tom had known Thomas as a boy, when he and other lads would go up to pick gooseberries for the monks in the summertime and would stay for ten days or so at the monastery. With the boys away from home, there'd be nocturnal high spirits, which Father Tom would quiet by stomping through the halls and making spooky noises—much to the boys' delight.

"The ghost!" Thomas said, the first time he saw Father Tom again in Long Kesh, when he was a blanket prisoner and Father Tom came to the canteen to say Mass. The priest told the McElwees that the prisoners gabbling just before Mass—it was the one time of the week they'd be out of their cells and together—sounded like the noise of a thousand turkeys. But

Father Tom was very moved when he heard all the men join with him in the words of the consecration. He had a strong perception of their sense of dedication. The thing he would always try to tell them of was Christ's love for each one of them: "You can find Christ now . . . Here in prison . . ."

Father Tom told Mary that after Mass he'd asked Thomas if he'd had a good night's sleep and Thomas said no, that he'd been tossing and turning. He'd been reviewing the situation, thinking it all out again. Then Thomas told him about his conversation with Mary the day before. Father Tom told Mary he felt she'd pressed Thomas too hard. But Mary explained why: she'd had to clear her mind of the suspicions born of rumours about outsiders controlling the hunger strike. Father Tom told her then about his conversation with Thomas the previous Sunday. Thomas had said that if he died he wanted everyone to know that he held no bitterness against anyone.

"All I'm doing," he'd told Father Tom, "is placing my body between the screws and my comrades."

This further eased Mary's mind.

When Mary went in to see Thomas that Sunday she told him she was worried he would be let die. People outside were saying that although the hunger strike was getting some solid support it wasn't getting enough. They'd just be allowed to die, one after the other—

"Mary, if we quit now," Thomas said, "we'd just go back to the same conditions—probably even worse."

Early in his hunger strike Thomas had sent Mary a letter. It was the day that votes were being counted after the Dáil elections:

Hello Mary,

Just a few lines here to let you know that I am well. As I am sure you know, I have joined the hunger strike. This is my fifth day. Time is going on reasonably fast. I thought myself it would drag, but it hasn't. My health as of yet is sound—extremely good according to the doctor. I get a runover from him every morning, weight and all taken. Weight today 64.4 kgm. I started off at 67.35, but on the second day the MO [medical officer] thought that a mistake had been made the first day.

Well, I got your letter a short time back. It was good hearing from you. I was surprised to hear that you were thinking of going back to Canada. I thought you and Séamus would have hit if off. Sure, that's life. My own love life is going a bomb (ha!). I hear from Dolores quite often. I got a letter from her yesterday. She is a good girl, the best (ha!). Like yourself she will be worried at present but praying there is no call. I will be OK. Just place all in the hands of God—that is what I have done—and do all you can down there to let the people understand our plight. We are waiting patiently here for the results of the elections. I am expecting two of our lads in. I'll be disappointed in the people if we fail completely. We had a great boost the other night with the lads escaping from the Crum. It's a great boost to the movement and the people in general.

Well, Mary, as I said this is just a few lines so I must be signing off now. Let any of the locals that you might see know that I was asking, even though they should not be there at this present time. Everyone is well here, morale is high, and I hope will be higher with an election victory. We are determined that our demands are met and please God will cut the loss of more lives. But still we are prepared for the worst. Well, Mary, all the best for now. Hoping all is well with you.

Loving brother,

Tomás   XX
         XX

On the same day he had issued a public statement to their supporters in the area:

To the people of South Derry:

I have been on hunger strike five days now, and a long road stretches ahead of me. Sometimes the thought of the pain and suffering that my comrades Bobby, Francis,

Raymond and Patsy endured scares me. But my determination greatly outweighs and extinguishes any fear that might be there . . .

The British government will only bow to a might more powerful than that of her imperial army. That might is present in our country today. It is that of a risen and united people. With the strength of their unity we will regain the rights of our political prisoners incarcerated behind the barbed wire and steel in these British prison camps. With it also we will march forth to unity and free our long-oppressed nation.

Within every individual Irish person lives the key. I implore you all to use the key.

Mise le meas,

Tomás MacGiolla bhuí

P.O.W.

Éire go Brách

On Mary's first visit to the prison hospital, her brother Thomas, pale and grey, had been lying on the bed. He got up and threw his arms around her. He seemed to be cheerful and in good spirits. He had that great smile. How was everyone at home and what was happening? He was so full of hope. On her second visit he was weaker and had to stay in bed. But he still had that smile.

It was far easier to talk to Thomas in the prison hospital than it had been in the prison itself. He said that he was a Sinn Féin socialist, that he stood for a united socialist Republic of Ireland. He wanted the Protestant and Catholic people to live together as one family, and that British withdrawal was the key. He had nothing against the English, he said, except that they had no right to be in this country. Let them stay in their own, he said.*

*His friend Colm Scullion later wrote about Thomas in the *Republican News*: "He often spoke of the necessity to get amongst the working class people and illustrate why a class system existed, and the need for its removal through force of arms. The construction of local projects demonstrating in the simplest fashion the equality

THOMAS WAS BORN on 30 November 1957. Benedict, his brother who was sent to the H-Blocks at the same time as Thomas, was less than two years younger. They had five older sisters—Kathleen, Mary, Bernadette, Annie and Enda. Then came their brother Joseph, three more sisters, Nora, Pauline and Majella, and then James, the youngest. Mary never knew that either Benedict or Thomas was in the IRA.

Growing up at home Thomas was like a great many other country boys in South Derry: he spent a lot of time outdoors. He was a tall lad, with dark brown hair and the same dark eyes as their mother. He was good-natured and considerate, but quieter and more serious than Benedict.

Thomas always loved motors. From the age of eleven he was interested in machinery. As soon as he was old enough to get a driving licence he bought his own car and spent hours on end tinkering with it. He drove everywhere. For a time he owned his own stock car. Accidents never worried Thomas. He would emerge laughing from a car which had plunged into a ditch.

At school—first at St. Mary's primary school in Bellaghy and then at nearby Clady secondary—his best subjects were English and mathematics, though he liked geography and history, and became something of an expert on local lore.

It was not surprising, since they had plenty of lore within the family.

THEIR GRANDFATHER was Mexican Jim McElwee, a family legend. Among his children were Francis Hughes' mother—their Aunt Maggie—and their father Jim McElwee: brother and sister. Mexican Jim died in 1963 aged 96, when Francis was about seven. Thomas was five at the time and Benedict only three.

Their father had often told the younger McElwees about him. Their grandfather was over six feet tall, weighing sixteen stone (224 lbs.)—but he was agile and quick. Besides being physically

---

and justice of socialism was, Thomas maintained, vital in the unification of the Catholic and Protestant working classes, exposing the evil of imperialism."

powerful, he was shrewd and utterly independent. He had a fierce temper.

Mexican Jim was born in County Derry in 1867, and had left Ireland at the age of seventeen, after a run-in with the RIC, the Royal Irish Constabulary, as the British police in Ireland were then called. The legend was that Jim had killed three RIC men with a spade and had to leave the country. But Thomas and Benedict had got the actual, slightly less dramatic story from their father.

Jim McElwee was no older than 17 when he went out to the New World to try to make his fortune. He spent twenty-six years in Mexico and Arizona, and returned with trunks full of rifles, bayonets, revolvers and other hardware—and half a lifetime's worth of boasts and yarns about how quick he was on the two-gun draw, about his adventures fighting Indians (some of whom, he said, sliced the soles off the feet of their enemies), and about the copper mine he owned half of, and how it failed; and about his experiences working on the railroad.

Soon after his return to Bellaghy he was buying meat from a local butcher when he became suspicious. He accused the man of giving him light weight on the scales. There was an argument, and the butcher called in the police. Six RIC men arrived, and as they came into the shop Jim McElwee clobbered the first pair, then the next three. Only by bludgeoning him from behind was the sixth man able to knock him unconscious. He spent several hours in jail before being released on bail supplied by a local publican.

Shortly after that Mexican Jim bought eighty acres of land in Tamlaghtduff from a Protestant whom he'd tricked into thinking he belonged to an Orange lodge down the road. He clinched the deal in a day, paying two hundred and fifty pounds for Duff Farm. He was almost as quick in acquiring himself a wife. He met their grandmother on a Friday—she came from the area—and he married her the following Tuesday.

The new landowner lost no time establishing his reputation around Bellaghy as a man not to be trifled with. No one would cross him. Apart from his temper, he was also the strongest man about the countryside. Everyone was afraid of him. He

527

wasn't a fighter so much as a wrestler and kicker. If someone tried to do him, he could pop the man's eyes out of their sockets.

Mexican Jim was a bit intimidating to have as a father, but he did have a talent for joking and storytelling. He could make up a yarn on the spur of the moment, like his son-in-law Joe Hughes and his grandson Francis. The grandfather liked dancing, and they often had a céilí in the house. In those days there were few in the neighbourhood who could read or write, so the grandfather, who could do both, would take a newspaper, hold it upside down and pretend to read it. He'd spin out some old yarn and get them to believe he was taking it from the paper.

Once he paid £24 for a cow, but then mislaid the receipt. Later a letter came, asking for payment. He stormed into the house, blaming his wife for not having the receipt. He started throwing things all over the place. Then he slammed the door, went out to a pile of nettles in front of the house, and in his rage rolled around in the nettles. Next he threw himself into the sinkhole. He wasn't drunk, just in a foul temper. At last he got up out of the sinkhole, went indoors, had a bath, shaved, dressed up in his best clothes, and headed down the road, saying he was going off to America again. But he hadn't gone far when he turned and came back.

Soon afterwards he found the receipt in a small purse in his pocket. He wouldn't apologize to his wife or anyone else: he didn't believe in apologizing. Then he got up on his horse and rode down to see the man who had asked payment for the cow. He laid down the receipt, and told the man that, had he been so foolish as to try to take the money twice, he would have killed him. ("Oh!" he used to say, "ye son of a bitch, ye—") Then he got on his horse—he almost always travelled on horseback— and rode away. "And that man," as someone said, "was very glad to see the back of him."

Some of the old grandfather's spirit—above all his refusal to submit himself to his adversaries—must have rubbed off on his grandsons: on Francis and Thomas and Benedict. Sitting on his horse, and just about to ride off, Mexican Jim would give vent to his feelings about the British in the old rhyme: "Ireland was Ireland when England was a pup. Ireland will be Ireland when England's buggered up."

528

After leaving school Thomas went to Magherafelt Technical college for a short time, then switched to Ballymena Training centre to begin an apprenticeship. He wanted to become a motor mechanic. But when he returned home in the evenings he'd often have some story of harassment—his wrenches taken, his screws gone, or threats from loyalists at the centre. Finally, forced to leave, he went to work with a mechanic in the area.

At weekends Thomas used to go to the local dances. He liked music, especially Republican ballads. As the boys grew older they were harassed more and more by the RUC and soldiers. They were stopped along the roads, searched, threatened, and sometimes physically abused. The McElwee house was first raided in 1974. Thomas was arrested for three days and held at Ballykelly. After another house raid Thomas and Benedict were taken to Coleraine for questioning. It was not unusual for South Derry in the mid-seventies.

The last time the family was all together was on the evening of 8 October 1976 at the "Stations" at their home. The custom was that Mass was said in one house in every townland during Lent and in October, the month of the Blessed Mother. That night in Tamlaghtduff it was said in the McElwees' home and a great many neighbours were there with them. After the Mass there was food and music.

The following day, 9 October, was Bernadette's birthday. At 1:30 in the afternoon the phone rang. Kathleen answered, and was told that Thomas and Benedict were in the Waveney hospital in Ballymena. A bomb in a car they were in had exploded prematurely. They were charged the following day. None of the family had known about the boys' involvement in the Republican movement. But Mary always felt they were innocent of the charges on which they were convicted—in a Diplock court. When they were taken in, Thomas was nineteen and Benedict barely seventeen.

During the first year, when Thomas and Benedict were in prison on remand, the family could visit them once a week. But nothing could be discussed, only the case. On one occasion

Thomas asked about a neighbour. A warder overheard them and ended the visit.

Over the years Mary and the others got used to the rigours of the visiting process. On the day of their trip to Long Kesh, which meant an hour and a half's journey each way—they left home at 9 a.m. and arrived at 10:30, if they weren't stopped by one of the three security forces.

Then came the pass—unless they forgot their identification, when it could be refused. Then Mary was searched by three women in a cubicle; one would take her name, another would hand-search her body while a third looked on. After this they went into a room to wait until a van pulled up outside. A screw would unlock the door and call out Thomas's or Benedict's name and number. Then there was a short rough ride in the van. At each of two gates they were stopped and a screw did a head count. They were taken to another waiting room, and sat down until their brother's name was called again.

Then—after a process that might have taken up to an hour and a half—they'd enter the visiting room, two of its sides divided into cubicles containing a table and four chairs, where they sat for a few moments. One of the brothers would come in then, very pale and thin. When the dirt protest was on, he would be dirty, with sticky hair. When Mary asked one of them about himself, he always said he was OK: "dead on." During the visit the screws heard every word of their conversation—and would watch their hands in case they passed something. None of them was ever the better for a visit.

All the time the boys were in prison, Mary and the others kept going to see them, kept thinking about them, kept praying for them. Mary remembered the time she learned that Benedict had been badly bruised and cut. She couldn't understand why they were treated like that. It was this brutality more than anything else, she thought, that led to the hunger strike.

In the autumn of 1980 when Mary heard of the first hunger strike she thought *this is it*: surely the British government will yield. Irish people wouldn't let the lads *die* for these demands. During the first strike Thomas and Benedict were among the later group of hunger strikers who came on in December 1980.

It was a trying time for everyone. But the family put their trust in God that a solution would be found. When the first hunger strike ended, everyone was relieved to think that the lads had essentially got what they'd been looking for. Then, when the families brought them in their own clothes, they were turned away. The British government had gone back on its word.

BENEDICT McELWEE could see seagulls coming down for food. Some of them, flying back up, got caught in the S-wire. They hung there suffering and struggling for days, until they were razored to death.

To Benedict the situation in the blocks was very similar to that outside the prison. If the Irish people tried to resist, or to stand up for their rights, the same systems operated outside as inside to overrule them.

Benedict was sentenced in September 1977, eleven months after he was arrested. He was an SOSP prisoner—his length of time in prison a matter of "the Secretary of State's pleasure." It was a kind of junior form of life sentence. He was kept two months in Crumlin Road while the order was signed by Secretary of State Roy Mason; then he was taken to Long Kesh. On 6 December 1977 he was locked away in H-3.

Benedict got life for being in the car in Ballymena when the bomb went off. The sentence was for murder. In another incident that day a woman was blown up in a boutique. At the first trial the judge convicted them all on charges of murder. Benedict was convicted of eighteen charges connected with the incident.

There were a number of economic targets in Ballymena. But there had been absolutely no intention of killing people. The way the police fixed it, a list of places was found in a green corduroy jacket—which didn't belong to anybody in the car. The boutique where the woman was killed appeared on the list. Thomas took responsibility for the jacket, thinking that otherwise they would tie it to Benedict, who was wearing green cords at the time. So Thomas was saddled with a conspiracy charge and convicted. They built it up so that he was given a life sentence. But on appeal this was reduced to twenty years for manslaughter.

At his appeal Benedict got all convictions dropped except the one for possession of explosives.

The bomb was in a bag sitting in the car. Thomas was driving, and Benedict was sitting in the passenger seat; Seán McPeake and Colm Scullion were in the back. In the explosion Thomas was hurt. His face was badly cut up, his eye damaged and he was in shock. He eventually lost his right eye. Colm Scullion lost several toes and Seán McPeake's leg had to be amputated. Seán wore an artificial leg in Long Kesh. But he did the protest, every bit of it.

First they shared Oliver Kelly as their solicitor, but then two other solicitors were brought in to divide the work. Even though Benedict was in the car, he had a strong case for an acquittal. Kelly suggested Paddy McGrory as the man to take up his case. McGrory was very good; he knew the Diplock system. The case they made was that Benedict had gone to Ballymena for shopping, but was not involved in any bombing plan. Benedict had made no confession under interrogation. The only evidence was the fact that he'd been in the car. According to law he should have got the benefit of the doubt and been acquitted. But this was Northern Ireland, where the prosecution enjoyed the benefit of any doubt.

BENEDICT AND THOMAS shared a cell for about two weeks in H-6, when the prison authorities were trying to isolate the command structure. They were in the same wing as Bobby Sands, Brendan Hughes, Laurence McKeown and some of the other men the screws had identified as leaders. Benedict always wondered why the brothers had been allowed to be together. Had they bugged the cell, hoping that in conversation the two of them would reveal something?

The two boys got on very well. They always had done, since they'd been children in Bellaghy playing about in the fields or in cars. Thomas had a relaxed way about him, but he was serious at the same time. He gave things a lot of consideration. He was forgiving, and unselfish; and he was religious. Thomas had great

532

faith—the faith they'd learned from their parents. But though he had a deep belief in Jesus Christ, Thomas was no bible-thumper, and he saw marked deficiencies in the Catholic Church: he was in fact more radical than the others in the family.

Thomas refused to take any abuse from the screws. When he was coming from chapel one Sunday, screws were standing between the grilles. One of them pushed Thomas. Thomas spun around and began hitting—hard. He managed to get in several good punches, breaking two of the screw's teeth in the process, before he was attacked by five other screws, beaten and dragged off to his cell. They took him out and put him on the boards after that—for two weeks. But no one else in H-3 had broken a screw's teeth.

Benedict didn't see his brother Thomas for over a year before he went on hunger strike. The last opportunity Benedict and Thomas had for a halfway decent conversation was when they'd been in the punishment block at the same time. They were in opposite wings and able to shout across to one another in Irish. The screws would try to keep it down, but couldn't stop them calling out to one another.

Now Thomas had been on hunger strike for nearly two months. Benedict wondered if they'd ever allow him to visit his brother. How long would Thomas last? He was already into his sixtieth day.

BENEDICT'S OWN EXPERIENCES were not all that different from Thomas's. He knew from inside himself much of what his older brother had gone through.

Many of the McElwees' Protestant neighbours were decent people, but Benedict remembered as a boy being unable to understand why some Protestants seemed to be absolutely bitter towards him. He wondered at the bitterness. Benedict hadn't ever done anything to hurt these people. They had no reason for hating or even disliking him. It seemed to be automatic.

In the H-Blocks he began to understand the reasons for this bitterness.

In the blocks Benedict and Thomas, along with the other men, had a chance to ponder over the way the establishment worked—

in Ireland, north and south, in England, America and Europe. The men seized every opportunity they could for discussion. The screws did their damnedest to prevent these discussions, but the men carried on with them anyway, night after night. Through these conversations Benedict came to see class interest and the capitalist ideal as the principal reason for the bitterness he'd experienced in his boyhood: the reason for the situation in the North; and the reason, too, why the Irish in the 26-county Free State were no help at all. He began to see capitalism and class interest as the cause of social hostility in the world.

When he was at Catholic school as a boy he'd never been taught about the damage the system did. In a sense he'd been taught the opposite. After finishing primary school in Bellaghy, Benedict like Thomas had gone to St. Mary's secondary school in Clady. One of his teachers at Clady had developed her own ideas about society and this helped Benedict and his classmates to think for themselves. She had been only mildly critical of capitalism but she had raised questions in his mind.

Apart from that one teacher, his secondary education had been uninteresting. He worked as little as possible and when he was fourteen or fifteen became very restless. He started to play truant, and his truancy helped him to move outside the situation. He felt that had he been diligent at school he might never have gained the insights he had now. The sort of teacher was very rare who could help someone acquire knowledge about life, people, society, history and the basic self-knowledge needed to develop into a good human being.

Long Kesh was a hard school; but in no college could Benedict have learned so much about basics. Benedict had been nine at the time of the 5 October 1968 civil rights march, and had seen the RUC assault on the marchers on television. What had lodged in his mind as he watched the events of the months that followed was the sectarian bitterness of the loyalist police, the B-Specials and the Protestant vigilantes.

Even at that age Benedict knew something of the men who led the Easter Rising. He had been inspired by reading Pearse's

534

proclamation. As a boy he didn't fully understand it, but he knew there was great truth in it. As a schoolboy he'd gone on a trip to Kilmainham jail in Dublin, and learned about James Connolly. Later he read Connolly's writings, and found that he had developed a form of socialism suited to the Irish people. Even at that age he could see in Connolly the clarity and purity of the idealism that had motivated the 1916 Rising.

Benedict remembered wondering as a teenager: Why could the loyalists not put aside their blind bigotry and answer the questions Connolly put to them—questions the whole Republican movement was putting to them: Why should there be sectarianism in Ireland? Why should there be bigotry? There was nothing sectarian about the Easter proclamation.

Benedict decided that the Catholic Church had been too weak in putting forward a larger ideal; but especially weak in dealing with sectarianism. Catholic priests and bishops were constantly giving ground and making allowances for loyalist bigotry. But there was no element of bigotry in true Christianity. Away from the Church, and with people of strong Republican convictions, Benedict found the same idealism he had discovered in Connolly and Pearse.

He had learned early that sectarianism was one of the major problems of Northern Ireland. Wolfe Tone's Republicanism, which looked forward to an Ireland where there was no distinction between Catholic or Protestant or Dissenter, powerfully attracted Benedict. He found it odd, people suggesting that Republicans were polarizing the communities in Northern Ireland. Benedict's experience was that members of the Republican movement had a deep antipathy towards sectarianism and religious polarization, that they fought strongly against any sectarian tendencies in themselves.

The loyalists came from the planter people, whose establishment and ruling elite had joined with the British government in fostering sectarian bigotry, and who had done it to protect their class and economic interest. They whipped up bigotry among ordinary working-class Protestants, cultivating hatred of Catholics as a device to build up and maintain their own wealth and power. This bigotry kept the Protestant and

Catholic working classes divided and maintained the structure which kept them poor and powerless.

As a boy Benedict had seen Catholics attacked to the beat of the Lambeg drum. Fierce hatred of Catholics was fostered in loyalists by their Black and Orange masters, to prevent their rebelling against the system that held them in thrall. Years later, Benedict decided that the sectarian establishment could only be broken by violence. This meant he had to *fight* the evil. Whatever could be done to break its stranglehold had to be done. It was right, it was necessary to use violence to destroy this hideous exploitative power.

Here Benedict was, in Long Kesh, a student at the hardest possible school. Here, as outside the prison but in a more brutal way, the evil power showed its own terrible capacity for violence.

Like his brother Thomas, Benedict often found himself in the punishment block. It was a separate building outside the H-Blocks, in an isolated area; and there was no possibility of contact with another prisoner. What usually got him there was the charge of assaulting a screw. On one occasion he was coming back from a visit and a screw started abusing him, calling him a "murdering fucking bastard."

"Why not step out there on your own without your friends? I'll take you, and no problem," Benedict said to him.

The screw just looked at Benedict and then began walking away.

As a parting shot, Benedict fired the abuse back at him: "You're a dirty bastard, yourself, aren't you? And a yellow one besides."

At that, this screw and another attacked him. Benedict hit out at the screw who'd abused him and got him in the face. They went to the floor, wrestling and punching. Two more screws joined in and the four of them beat Benedict till they were tired of beating him. Then they dragged him off to the punishment block.*

*While working on this material, several months after Benedict's release, the writer spent considerable time with Benedict McElwee. On occasion he gave Benedict a lift in his car. Sometimes there were checkpoints along the road. Faced with a checkpoint, the writer's

536

All this sort of thing Thomas had been enduring, too.

By December 1978, the screws had introduced two innovations into the prison routine: weekly wing shifts and the mirror search. During the shifts, the men were moved from wing to wing while contract cleaners, dressed like spacemen and using compressors and steam hoses, cleaned the blocks in rotation, so that every week each of the blanketmen was moved into a comparatively clean cell. The regularity of the wing shifts meant that they had to undergo the mirror treatment every week, as well as each time they had a visit.

During the mirror search the screws would strip the blanket from a man and put him over a mirror to examine his back passage, then poke at it with their rubber-gloved fingers. The prisoners naturally refused to submit to this degrading treatment. Five or six screws, and at times more, would pull his hair, punch him and kick him, forcing the naked prisoner into position over the mirror. What made it even more objectionable was that there was no point in this sort of search at all. The screws could not see up the back passage with the mirror.

Benedict felt the search was intended simply to intimidate the men and thereby lower the numbers of protesting prisoners; it served also as an excuse to beat them. The messages the screws were supposedly seeking to dig out contained nothing dangerous. They were affectionate greetings to or from anxious relatives or friends, messages about the circumstances they were living in, or parcels of tobacco, flints, cigarette skins wrapped in stretch-and-seal. That's all that was in the little notes or parcels they carried to or from a visit.

One day in late 1978 a large number of screws came on Benedict's wing, D-wing in H-4, and began dragging men off for forced haircuts and forced baths. This was on order from one of the prison doctors, or "quacks," whom the prisoners called "Crocodile Face." Benedict was two days off the

---

instinct was to get through it with as little trouble as possible. Sometimes it seemed that Benedict McElwee's instinct, when confronted by armed police or British soldiers, was to let them know, in no uncertain terms, that they had no business being there.

punishment block at the time, where he'd had a forced bath and been scrubbed and disinfected. The doctor gave the screws authority to take the prisoners to the end of the wing so he could carry out a check on their hair. After his inspection, he insisted that everybody in the wing had bugs and head lice. It was medically impossible for there to be anything in Benedict's hair because a couple of days earlier he had been disinfected. Some of the men were new arrivals at the prison; so it was impossible for them to be infected either. They had been well sheared when they came in. A couple of days after the quack's examination, the screws came back to begin the treatment, starting at the top of the wing.

The prisoners had planned among themselves to resist this. When the screws went into the first cell, the prisoners threw whatever punches they could. They were dragged away, and beaten down the wing. It was dinnertime. Benedict was in Cell 14 at the end of the wing. He had been looking across through the windows into A-wing opposite. Ciarán Nugent was watching—there were no grilles up at the time—to see what was going on.

The screws drew nearer to Benedict's cell—he could hear them coming down the corridor. The butterflies built up. Benedict and his cell-mate, a Derryman named Marcus McChrystal, stood the mattresses up against the wall so that they could manoeuvre around a bit. At least ten screws came piling into the cell. He and McChrystal got in very few punches before the screws kicked over the pots. The two men slipped on the wet floor and went head over heels. The screws took them into separate corners and kicked them senseless.

When Benedict came to he found them trailing him naked down the corridor, one screw holding him by the hair, two holding him by the arms, two hauling on his legs. Other screws were walking alongside, punching and kicking him, and kicking at his genitals, till they got him to the room at the end of D-wing.

The first thing was the haircut. There were three screws standing around the chair, as the others shoved Benedict into it. He tried to get free but they grabbed him, pushing his legs up into his chest. They held him fast while one slashed at his hair with a scissors, making the haircut as ridiculous-looking as he could. Despite his nakedness and their numbers, Benedict struggled. So they stood back, and a big Scottish screw came on—eighteen or twenty stone: up to 280 lbs. Two of them spreadeagled his legs in the chair; another held him by the hair; and two more held his arms down. Though he could hardly move, he tried to resist.

The Scottish screw towered over him.

"I'll make sure you have no other wee Irish bastards!" he said, and came down hard, with all the power he could put in to a punch, onto Benedict's genitals. Benedict's head exploded; he nearly went unconscious.

When they finally finished their obscene haircut they let him up. He was staggering, but he refused to go to the bath. Just as they'd beaten him from Cell 14 down to the haircutting room, they now beat him from D-wing over to the washing facilities in C-wing, throwing him onto a pile of wet towels. Benedict hadn't the strength to lift himself up. One of the worst screws in H-4, a stocky animal no more than 5'4", came over and stood above him.

"Get up and get into the bath," he said.

"No way."

Benedict lay where he was.

"Get into the bath."

Benedict refused.

Then, with the short screw egging them on, they attacked Benedict again. They kicked him, then lifted him and threw him against a partition. A medical officer, who had been supervising the haircutting, was there giving the screws the signal.

"Okay, go ahead," he said to them.

The screws lifted Benedict above the bath full of water and threw him into it. It was scalding, and mixed in the water were strong disinfectants. In their overalls and gloves, some wearing masks, they began scrubbing him, ripping at his skin. They put a strong smelling liquid into his hair and gave him a going-over with heavy deck scrubbing brushes.

After several minutes they dragged him out of the bath and threw him a towel. He could hardly lift his arms to dry himself. His hair felt as though it were coming off his scalp.

Benedict had to endure these brutal bath beatings at least a dozen times during the next year or so. The quack could give any orders he wanted and the screws were more than willing to oblige.

Even the no-wash protest didn't keep the screws off the wing. It actually brought them onto it more often. Benedict thought of them as bloodsuckers. Some were so subhuman that they'd come into the cells, go through the mattresses and then search through the excrement without a second thought. Benedict himself wouldn't touch another mattress that was in a state like his own. Sometimes they came in in their boiler suits and dug with their gloves; sometimes they did it with their bare hands.

The effect on the prisoners was not so much to increase their anger as to make them see the screws as animals. Most of them came from the six counties and a few of them were English. There were some Catholics: one of these used to go out of his way to show his cohorts how cruel he was. Most pretended to be in the game for the money; but they were getting their sadistic extras out of it.

The men on the wing communicated by shouting out the door. Because of the echo a man's voice would carry. To stop him shouting the screws started banging on the doors. If that didn't work, they came down, opened his door and beat him. The minute they were back up the wing, the man would start shouting again. The screws would return and beat him till they got fed up.

The men kept at it. Finally it got to the point where they could shout out the door more or less when they wanted. There was the odd screw who got really annoyed. He'd hear the shouting from the top of the wing, and couldn't be sure who was doing it. So the prisoner would stop for a few minutes, wait until the screw went back up the wing, and then resume. Usually the men in the cells at the top would hear the screw coming and shout a warning: "Bear in the air!" There came a point where the screws just left them alone—a small achievement the men regarded as a considerable victory.*

Probably their greatest success was in organizing discussions after the screws on the wing had settled down for the night.

The screws had done their best to break the command structure. When a directive from the H-Blocks OC reached the wing OC, he would shout the directive out his door. The screws would immediately know that these were army orders, so they would try to listen in. If it was at night they'd put out all the lights and creep down the wing. On a given night they'd conclude that a particular man was the OC. Then they'd find opportunities to put pressure on him. During wing shifts, they'd single him out for the worst beatings. Or they'd make sure to give him very little food. They'd try to turn his cellmate against him by handing in two plates, one heaped high and the other practically empty. The men of course immediately understood, and shared out the food equally. They weren't going to be trapped by such silly machinations. Benedict thought it pathetic the way the screws scraped around for ways to get under the prisoners' skins.

If there was a complaint, there was an interesting procedure in Long Kesh. The prisoner had to ask the screw who assaulted him for permission to see a doctor so that he could lodge his complaint. To see the assistant governor he would have to ask the same screw. It was no use seeing the assistant governor, in any case. The block screws were under his supervision and a prisoner had no chance of getting further than the block governor with a complaint.

The quacks were as bad as the screws. To them the prisoners were "Fenian bastards." They used the same language as the screws, calling the blanketmen "pigs," "tramps," "child killers," "murdering bastards," rhyming off, as Benedict liked to say, all the names of the day.

Benedict felt that neither the screws nor the doctors could

*The warders got used to hearing the men announce, "Bear in the air," or "Bear on the wing." Once when a warder was coming a man shouted, "Screw on the wing!" The warder opened the man's door and shouted in: "I'm not a screw. I'm a bear!"

541

analyze the situation for themselves. They couldn't rise above their prejudice, and ask themselves what force it was that kept the prisoners together. Obviously none of the prisoners was gaining anything personal out of this protest, out of the mental and physical torture he endured.

Here were men who were willing to live on the border of insanity, as was proved by those who did go out of their minds, and willing to accept barbaric treatment rather than wear criminal clothing! Why? This was the sort of question the screws seemed unable to ask themselves. If they were not so blinded by hatred they would have seen that the men were soldiers in a volunteer army, fighting for a cause—and so convinced that the cause was just that they were willing to suffer and if need be die for it.

In seeking to break up the command structure in the blocks the screws were taking their orders, Benedict was certain, from the British government itself: from the NIO. At one point they took 32 men from different blocks, men they had identified as belonging to the command structure or as particularly determined. They isolated them together in a single wing in H-6 for nine months while putting pressure on the remaining blanketmen in H-3, H-5 and particularly H-4, to get them to conform.

Apparently they hoped that by destabilizing the command structure, they could break the will of the other men to continue. "If we take away their command staff," the prison authorities seemed to be saying to themselves, "the men left behind won't know what to do." But the men left behind had no problem. They simply picked new OCs and re-formed the command structure.

Benedict was proud to be among the 32 men moved to H-6, proud that the screws seemed to think he'd been a strong prisoner, or had been in the command structure in H-4, when he hadn't. In H-6 the screws put them into cells that had previously been used by conforming prisoners. The windows were replaced with grilles; they took out everything, all the beds and furniture.

For the men moved to H-6, there were new opportunities

in the rearrangement. For example, the men in H-4 had been teaching themselves Irish before they went to sleep each night and it had given them a deeper realization of themselves as Irishmen. They continued this in H-6, and taught others. They also began to hold night-time discussions along the wing, which later on led to debates on matters of profound personal interest. The leadership qualities represented in the new grouping made for a high level of discussion and debate.

The men began, as many of them had done in other blocks, by talking about books, or by sharing historical or other specialized information any of them might have. Everyone came to know about Bobby Sands shouting the plot line of Leon Uris' *Trinity* down the wing, but there were contributions from other men, too.

They shared background material connected with Irish history. There were the various risings through the centuries, the 1916 Rising, and the War of Independence. They gathered what basic information they could and kept building on it. Most of the men had never had the chance to get themselves a proper education. Here they got their chance, and used it.

As they exhausted their stories and stores of information, they went on to questions of purpose. If they came to a topic on which a number of men had a contribution to make, they arranged to take it up the next night or the night after.

The men agreed that they were on the right track politically, and that the military struggle was necessary. As Irish nationalists, they felt, they were working on the right level. But if they wanted to deepen their grasp of the situation in and outside the prison, they had to face the difficulties and contradictions, and argue them out among themselves. They were as constructive as possible. They often talked about practical matters, about ways of sharpening their protest, about what they could do to gain recognition as political prisoners.

The screws were too blind to realize that the men were carrying on constructive discussion. They didn't have the resources to understand, and didn't want to hear the prisoners taking such liberties in conversation. They saw them only as "Provie murdering bastards." Benedict and the other men understood the screws' mentality, what they were and why they acted the way they did. The screws were so involved in the system, they couldn't recognize their own interest, couldn't see how they were being used by the British authorities.

There was a great deal of discussion of the reasons why the prisoners were refusing to wear the criminal uniform or do criminal work—why, in short, they were fighting against criminalization. They discussed what they owed to the Republican movement outside the prison and what they owed to their own dignity. They realized they must do nothing to discredit the movement.

They asked themselves about the precise content of political status. Their bottom line was not the right to drill, but the right to behave like a military force. The bottom line was recognition of their political motivation. Of course they wanted all the concessions they could get. They wanted absolutely everything! But they would have settled for the dignity of being treated as prisoners of war. As to the protest itself, Benedict's analysis, shared by most of the men, was that it had escalated because of the screws' petty and vindictive harassment.

The British, the men concluded, were trying to create the view outside the prison that everything was normal, that Northern Ireland was normal, that there was absolutely no war situation, no rebellion going on. But people on the unionist side kept making slips—calling it a war. And these *were* the circumstances of war. The slips of the tongue showed the reality.

There was a consensus that in the North they had been brought up under a repressive and sectarian capitalist regime. The question was: What approach could provide, in its place, a just society fit for human beings? They had to go beyond nationalism. Nationalism could not of itself bring complete peace to the country.

Night after night they persisted in discussing the question, often until two or three in the morning. No one was forced to take part. If he didn't want to say anything, a man could stay lying on his mattress. Sometimes Benedict himself would get tired of the discussion. He'd be standing there freezing, pulling his blanket over him, the wind blowing in the window. But for the sake of completeness they tried hard to keep going. They looked in depth at the setup in Ireland, and in the West generally: the dog-eat-dog situation which capitalists thrived on, one man tearing out another man's throat to make himself a little more money. The corporate system was geared to reproduce itself. The legal system went hand in hand with it. Laws facilitated the rich man and the multinationals, supporting the strong against the weak.

The men talked about a free society. But they questioned what freedom might mean in the context of a society controlled by competition, and by a money and success ethic, in which people were caught up like fish in a capitalist financial net. Where was the freedom in this kind of society?

Looking at socialist theory, the men refused to accept anything as dogma. Benedict in particular was unwilling to tie himself down. He came to believe in a kind of evolutionary economics, seeing the human race as going through a continual process of change and development. If the British could be got rid of and the proper foundations laid, people would become competent to determine their own ends and purposes, and move forward towards a society in which human beings were the first priority. To Benedict, any sort of society that exploited people was inhuman and therefore intolerable. Nobody—English or Irish, Protestant or Catholic—should be let use other human beings for his own ends. Benedict didn't want to see English users replaced by Irish users. He kept going back in his reflections to his trip as a child to Kilmainhaim jail, to the Irish socialism of James Connolly, and to the fundamentals of the Easter proclamation:

> We declare the right of the people of Ireland to the ownership of Ireland, and to the unfettered control of Irish destinies, to be sovereign and indefeasible . . .

This was the sort of Ireland for which Thomas was dying.

ALICE McELWEE had gone to America in June.

She was a quiet woman and preferred to stay home and look

after her husband Jim and those of her twelve children who were still in Bellaghy. But she was determined to stand up and be counted when her sons' welfare was at stake. She was proud of her children—her four strong sons; her lovely daughters. Someone told her they were the most beautiful family of girls in Ireland; she'd never say that, but she took great pride in them.

Alice remembered the first time the Relatives' Action committee met, in a small place called Cargin, on the other side of Toomebridge, at the end of December 1976.

Thomas and Benedict had been in Crumlin Road jail for two months at that point; in Long Kesh the blanket protest had just begun.

The idea of the RAC was to contact people of influence. Different relatives went to see the Papal Nuncio—Alice went twice with the RAC to Dublin to see him. The Papal Nuncio listened to them very sympathetically. He said he was keeping the Pope (Paul VI was still alive) in touch with what was going on. Some went to Síle DeValera and Neil Blaney. They tried other politicians, and anybody they could think of who might be able to help. They even got to meet Humphrey Atkins at Stormont when he was Northern Ireland Secretary. He was no use at all, and they said to one another afterwards that they might as well have stayed at home

The mothers and sisters of prisoners kept writing to the clergy as well as the policitians. It went on for years. They wrote to bishops all over Ireland, north and south. One bishop in the south responded by saying that it was Archbishop Ó Fiaich who was supposed to attend to the problem—saying in effect that the prisoners had nothing to do with him. People like him just didn't want to be involved.

Alice remembered the time she went to Knock shrine in County Mayo and spoke to Monsignor James Horan who was in charge there. By then Thomas and Benedict were on the blanket in Long Kesh. She told Monsignor Horan that she wanted the blanketmen prayed for.

"Oh, we can pray for them," he said, "but we can't mention them—that's political."

It was typical enough of the southern attitude. Alice blamed the people of Ireland as much as the English government for the suffering and deaths in the prison. It seemed to her, as it seemed to her daughter Mary, that when FitzGerald said his hands were tied, it showed that the British had as much of a grip on politics in the South as they did in the North.

Alice had gone to the RAC meetings on Tuesday every fortnight since 1976. On Tuesday every week she began going to the Abbey at Portglenone for charismatic prayer meetings. On RAC meeting Tuesdays she'd get a lift to Portglenone where the charismatic meeting started at seven o'clock. When that was over, she'd get a lift back to Bellaghy and go straight to the relatives' meeting which would go on till eleven or sometimes twelve o'clock at night.

Now, with Thomas in the first stages of his hunger strike, the committee, with help from Father Seán MacManus of the Irish National Caucus, put up the funds for Alice to go. She was not allowed to see Thomas, even when he was on hunger strike, except for a brief period once a week. She agreed she might be able to help him more by raising support in America. Alice had been born in America; her brother lived there. She held American citizenship and would be able to travel freely.

And yet all sorts of problems developed when she tried to get a visa. They went to Dublin to arrange an Irish passport but there were difficulties. Alice thought she wouldn't bother to go back again, and would get a visa on a British passport she'd acquired for a trip to Lourdes. She decided the simplest thing to do would be to get a visa at the American consulate in Belfast. They told her to call the next day and it would be ready. Her daughter Kathleen contacted them next day, but they said it wasn't ready. Meantime, the American consulate phoned Alice in Bellaghy to ask her if she were going to America on fund-raising, or to give public speeches. She reassured them as best she could. Arrangements were made for the passport to be sent to her—but it never arrived. Next morning at 5:30 a.m. Alice was driven to Dublin by her son-in-law Martin Mullan. She managed to get an Irish passport there and an American visa.

When Alice was in America she got the US passport her

American birth entitled her to. If she'd known and brought her father's marriage certificate with her to Dublin she could have got it in the American embassy there. So Alice ended up with three passports—Irish, American and British.

Alice was sitting in a newspaper office in Philadelphia when she heard that Joe McDonnell was dead. The ICJP had failed. It was deeply depressing for her, not only because of Joe McDonnell's death after the great hope everyone had that his life would be saved, but also because the failure to save Joe was ominous for Thomas, who by now was a full month on hunger strike.

When she returned home she went to see Thomas. She'd been in Ireland little more than a week when she was off again to England, hoping that publicity generated there where the seat of power was would save her son's life.

Alice's visit to London aroused a lot of interest. The newspapers were outraged that Ken Livingstone, head of the Greater London Council, met with the mother of an IRA hunger striker. One headline read: LEFT WING PLAYS HOST TO TERRORIST'S MOTHER. The *Daily Express* carried a blistering editorial on the "sickening and disgusting spectacle of the majority leader of London giving encouragement and publicity to the enemies of this country." Livingstone spoke at the County Hall and said things that Alice knew would be greatly appreciated by Thomas and the other men on hunger strike:

> I believe that we have in Northern Ireland a colonial war of the sort we have seen in many other British colonies since the end of World War II. I believe that the people who have fought for freedom in all of Ireland have to be viewed in the same way as those who have engaged in national liberation struggles in other countries. The men in the H-Blocks are not criminals. They are people fighting for the freedom of their country.

On the day Prince Charles and Princess Diana were married, as the story was later recounted in the Irish *Sunday Press*:

> Mr. Livingstone virtually declared a day of mourning to

coincide with last Wednesday's Royal Wedding. He allowed hunger strike supporters to stage a token 48 hours' fast on the steps of County Hall. He permitted the release of 500 black balloons in memory of the dead hunger strikers. He hung black flags instead of bunting from the windows of County Hall and he worked at his desk all day instead of joining in the national festivities.

As he explained during the week: "I think it is wrong to pretend everything is wonderful while there is a war going on in Northern Ireland. I think that the young men in the H-Blocks have stirred the conscience of not just many people in this country but people all over the world . . ."

HAD GARRET FITZGERALD'S CONSCIENCE been stirred? A week earlier FitzGerald had personally told Mary McElwee that Thomas would not die. Mary had been to two meetings with FitzGerald. He had avoided other meetings. He would ring up to say he was available, or there would be phone calls about meetings; and then he'd cry off, saying he was sick or giving some excuse. He seemed to be trying to avoid the families.

Before the dramatic meeting with FitzGerald on Thursday 6 August, she was able to comfort the other families with the news from Thomas that the momentum for the hunger strike came entirely from the men inside the blocks. But FitzGerald took no special notice of this information. As a politician he would not make a move he *really didn't want to make*. He wanted to play it safe.

That meeting was oddly like a tea party, with FitzGerald and his ministers busy with their tea and coffee and sandwiches while the distraught family members sat there pleading for the hunger strikers' lives. FitzGerald had asked them to keep him informed, but that seemed in the end to have been mere bluff. Haughey had met Liz O'Hara and promised to save Patsy's life, and that of Raymond McCreesh, but didn't. Goretti McDonnell, who had dealt with both of them, said that, bad as Haughey was,

FitzGerald was a hundred times worse. Mary reckoned that FitzGerald was slyer than Haughey.

The hunger strike relatives had it out with FitzGerald that Thursday 6 August. They told him they wanted a straight answer. They felt they'd been wasting their time going back and forth to Dublin, and had decided that if they didn't get something definite this time, they were going to stage a sit-in, and not move until FitzGerald agreed to *do* something.

He asked them what they thought he could do. They told him he could come out and publicly support the five demands. He could back this up with a threat to remove the troops from the border—a bold move, but he had the power. Oh, no, no, no, he said—he couldn't do that. The hunger strike families said, well, we're not moving from here.

The discussion went round and round. Mary made notes on her writing-pad, jotting down snatches of what was said by this relative, then that, then by FitzGerald:

> *The Irish gov would do anything that wasn't hostile to the gov in the North . . .*
>
> *Irish gov will not publicly support the five demands . . .*
>
> *Reason we are here is because the Taoiseach is the only person the British will listen to . . .*
>
> *Not here because the IRA sent us . . .*
>
> *IRA uses people to win a propaganda war . . . likes to tell the Irish gov what to do . . .*
>
> *What are you going to do to save Thomas's life? (That was Teresa Moore)*
>
> *Will do all they can . . . not go public . . .*
>
> *Gov believes the HS is a propaganda stunt of the IRA . . . impossible for gov to give in to IRA . . .*
>
> *Irish gov do not support five demands—cannot ask British gov to concede the five demands . . .*
>
> *Refuse to act as propaganda agents for IRA . . .*
>
> *Not IRA, they did not put the men on protest . . .*
>
> *They should be able to make suggestions . . .*

> *Negotiating: the IRA—they have it in their power . . .*
> *Appealed to British . . . They are not in business of . .*
> *If we got IRA to stop campaign they would put more*
> *pressure on British . . . ask them to change the prison*
> *regime . . .*

Mary drew three lines across the last page. Beneath them she wrote:

> *Irish gov totally hostile.*

Mary and Nora got upset then when somebody mentioned that Thomas had only a few days to live.

"You promised that Thomas wouldn't die," Mary said to FitzGerald. FitzGerald had nothing to say. Mary decided she couldn't take any more. She couldn't sit there. Leaving Annie's husband Martin Mullan, she and Nora went out into the hall. In the hallway there were some family members who hadn't been able to get in. There were Sinn Féin and H-Blocks people from Dublin. There were gardai at the door and press people—they didn't know what was going on. When Mary and Nora came out in tears they realized that nothing good was happening. After the others had been sitting in for awhile, FitzGerald's secretary came out.

"These people aren't moving," he said.

"Well, there's not much you can do," Mary said, "they're not going to move."

Teresa Moore was inside; and Frank McCauley, Micky Devine's brother-in-law; Francie Hurson was there, and Seán Begley on behalf of his brother-in-law Pat McGeown; there was someone from the Quinn family. FitzGerald had left the room after Mary and Nora.

Then the gardai came in. They carried out the family members—Teresa Moore as well as the men—Mary and Nora walked out beside them. Afterwards—Mary was the spokeswoman—the relatives made a statement to the press. FitzGerald wasn't doing anything for them, she said. He had refused to support the men. It upset them that he had asked the families what he could do. There wasn't anything he *could* do if he was asking them for suggestions and refusing to take any initiative.

That was the third meeting with FitzGerald Mary had attended. Now they were all aware how inept he was.

The statement read:

> We the relatives of the hunger strikers met with Dr. Garret FitzGerald today to ask him to support the following four demands:
>
> 1. Public support for the five just demands of the protesting prisoners.
>
> 2. Recall the Irish Ambassador from England.
>
> 3. Expel the British Ambassador from Ireland.
>
> 4. End collaboration with the British security forces on the border.
>
> After numerous meetings with representatives of the 26 county government, we believe that they are not living up to their responsibilities to pressure the British government. At the last such meeting we warned that we would step up our activities in support of the hunger strikers.
>
> We will not meet with FitzGerald or his representatives again until he will talk constructively with us about a just solution.
>
> Not only has he failed to act over the death of a fellow TD and elected representative of the Irish people; our forcible eviction today further underlines his lack of commitment to finding a just solution.
>
> We publicly call now on the Irish people, particularly the leadership of the Irish working class, to come out in a public and constructive fashion in support of the five just demands before there are even more deaths in the H-Blocks.
>
> We also call on all elected representatives of the Irish people to protest at the rough handling of us today and condemn the murder of fellow Irishmen in the H-Blocks.

The same day the prisoners in Long Kesh issued a statement,

urging the British government to stop refusing "to act sensibly, humanely, realistically, or reasonably," and "to meet us halfway" on terms, "as we have met them." The prisoners were especially concerned with movement on the issues of work and association. As for the demand for their own clothes, this was straightforward: "Prisoner clothes are either abolished or retained."

As far as work was concerned, "We are not going to engage in unrewarding, demeaning work." They were willing to clean prison wings and blocks, to do painting and maintenance and laundry. "But until the government recognizes education as work, it is almost impossible to participate in cultural or academic education during the prison working day. Usually a prisoner has to forfeit his association to attend class."

The prisoners felt that "a substantial degree of compatibility exists on association as well as on work." They saw no reason why the prisoners should not have the freedom of the wing between the hours of unlocking and lockup, and said that Republican and loyalist prisoners should be separated for the sake of harmony in the prison.

Reasonable numbers of visits, letters, and parcels should be a prisoner's right and not be treated as a privilege. The prisoners saw remission of sentences as a byproduct of other problems, and with these resolved there was no reason they could see why full remission could not be restored.

They were not seeking preferential treatment over other prisoners or seeking "to take over the prisons," and so there was no threat to these fundamentals of British policy. The British refusal to settle

> in the face of reason, based on the reality that an obvious and principled solution exists, challenges the authority of every concerned body in Ireland. It is our opinion that every authority has pursued a moderate approach which the British have treated as weakness and dismissed contemptuously.

Many regarded this as a temperate statement. But Mary was afraid that the prisoners' reasonableness would fall on deaf ears. And with FitzGerald now insisting that he was impotent, she had to face the fact that her brother Thomas was almost certainly going to die.

Why did they not let the family stay with him in the prison?

The next day, Friday 7 August, Alice McElwee visited her son and asked for permission to stay with Thomas through the night. She was refused. When she came home they called the Northern Ireland Office to ask again if she and other family members would be allowed to stay. The NIO said that there was no necessity, that there was no immediate cause for concern. The family wanted to put as much pressure as they could on the NIO to get permission for somebody from the family to be with Thomas all the time.

The last of the family to see Thomas—it was that Friday—were their mother and Bernadette and Enda.

Earlier that same day Thomas saw his fiancée, Dolores O'Neill—they'd become engaged while both were in prison. Because the authorities thought seeing her might break his will to continue, Dolores was granted a visit. She'd been brought from Armagh Jail where she was a prisoner. He held her close during the visit.

"God keep me for you," he said.

Father Oliver Crilly had come that day, along with their mother and Bernadette and Enda. Thomas was in surprisingly good spirits. He asked about the prisoners' statement of 6 August and what people thought of it. He had a slight pain in his stomach, he said. And he'd had two bowel movements the same day. (This was the first time any of the family had heard him comment at all on his physical condition.)

On Saturday 8 August, Alice contacted Dr. Hugh Glancy, their family doctor, to get his opinion about the curious fact of Thomas's bowel movements—what did that indicate? Could this get them the 24-hour pass to be with him from now on? Would he push it with the NIO? The doctor said he would call round right away.

Dr. Glancy came over and talked with Jim and Alice. For decades he'd been close to the family. He'd been with Alice in this house the day Thomas was born.

Not more than five minutes after Dr. Glancey arrived, the phone rang. It was Father Tom Toner, one of the prison chaplains.

Afterwards when they discussed it, they thought it strange that Father Toner hadn't asked who was receiving the call.

James, who was only a boy, picked up the phone.

"Thomas has died," the priest said abruptly.

Their mother, Alice, was in the kitchen, separated from the hall, where the phone was, by the sitting room. But she instinctively knew something was wrong. She came out to James. The receiver was down and James was crying. Alice picked up the phone, and the priest told her that Thomas had died. That was all he said.

Mary and most of the girls were out in the kitchen making their breakfast. They couldn't believe it. They were all very upset. Their father Jim was the only one who remained calm. Mary phoned Father Toner back to find what was to be done about Thomas's body. He said that everything was okay.

But everything was *not* okay. None of them had been there with Thomas when he died. Then Father Toner said that Benedict was on his way over to see Thomas.*

This further upset them. Benedict hadn't seen Thomas for a year before that. Mary said to Father Toner that she didn't think it would be good for Benedict to see Thomas. He hadn't seen him for so long: and now to see him dead. But Father Toner said no, that everything was okay, and Benedict was on his way over. He told Mary not to worry, but to get in contact with the RUC and the NIO to find out where to pick up Thomas's body.

When she rang them, the RUC didn't know. They rang back later and told Mary that the body would be taken to Ballymena. The McElwees were worried because Ballymena was a Protestant stronghold. Mary remembered the treatment the

---

*They later learned from Benedict that he'd finally been granted a visit—on the sixty-second day of Thomas's hunger strike. On the way across to the hospital he was told of Thomas's death. They told him to go on over anyway: they needed someone to identify the body.

RUC had given the Hughes family. She asked the police if the body could be brought to Omagh or some Catholic area. The RUC man said she shouldn't worry; he reassured her that everything would be all right. So the family went to get things organized. They got the house ready, and notified Annie and Martin Mullan, and the neighbours.

At the hospital mortuary in Ballymena there were several police landrovers. But there was nobody on the streets except some supporters and friends who had gathered at the mortuary. They went in and stood by the coffin to say the rosary.

Mary thought that Thomas was beautiful in death. "Look at him!" Mary said to the others. "Don't feel unhappy."

The people came in to pay their respects, and then moved on. Finally the coffin was closed and placed in the hearse. There were police in front, then the hearse, then police behind, then the family behind the police landrovers.

The family thought that they'd be taking the route straight through Ballymena and that they'd be home in less than half an hour. But they were taken on a long roundabout way, onto the Ballymena-Randalstown Road, branching off through Portglenone. Then, when they finally came to Mulholland's corner, the road was thick with police, who blocked the road in case they should want to drive through Bellaghy—their own town. In the circumstances the family had no intention of going through Bellaghy.

At Mulholland's corner, where Tamlaghtduff Road began, the hearse pulled up. Everyone got out of their cars, and there was a small scuffle with the police. Then the hearse continued on up the rise, the people following on foot. The hearse stopped, the coffin was taken out, and the Tricolour draped over it. Then they carried it along the road towards the house.

Mary was walking beside Pauline and Majella. Pauline had been to the Doherty funeral, where two of Kieran's sisters had helped carry his coffin. She suggested to Mary that they carry the coffin, and Mary agreed. They all thought it a good idea— to honour their brother in this symbolic way. (They would do this, too, on the day of the funeral.)

So Pauline spoke to one of the undertakers, and the pallbearers handed the coffin to Thomas's eight sisters to carry, through the gate onto the pathway and up to the house.

Then the men brought Thomas's body inside and it was laid out in the little room with a guard of honour. They needed the sitting room for the mourners, who came in a steady stream all that night until seven on Sunday morning.

The road was black with people coming to honour Thomas: there were thousands of them. And they kept coming on Sunday and all through Sunday night.

Chapter 13

MICKY DEVINE

God's curse on you England, you cruel-hearted monster,
Your deeds they would shame all the devils in hell.
There are no flowers blooming,
  but the shamrock is growing
O'er the grave of James Connolly, the Irish Rebel.

Republican ballad

IN HIS SERMON at Thomas McElwee's funeral on Monday 10 August, the Bellaghy parish priest Father Michael Flanagan took advantage of the occasion to demand an end to the hunger strike. This deeply distressed the McElwee family, and it angered Thomas' brother Benedict, who had been released from Long Kesh for the day of the funeral. In protest Bernadette McAliskey and others walked out of the church.

From his prison hospital bed a few days later, Micky Devine listened as Bernadette herself recounted the Father Flanagan episode. If this happened at his funeral, he said, he wanted her to walk out as she had in Bellaghy. But she was to take his coffin with her.

The gesture was not, in the event, necessary. But it underlined something people said about Micky Devine, the frail, 5'4" man with bright red hair and black-rimmed eyeglasses. "He was a radical," they said. "Not so much a volunteer as a political radical."

Many people in Derry could relate some of the basic details of Micky's life. He was in some ways a typical Derry boy, but he had grown up in poverty worse than most. It was a life that didn't hold much promise and gave an air of pathos to the pretend-cynical, politicized little Derryman. The pathos was not, as someone said, to be taken in a "poor little Micky" sense—though Micky was always having problems—so much as in the sense of a man who laughed just to keep from crying.

His was a hard life, and it began on 26 May 1954 in one of those prefabricated and all-too-well-ventilated Nissen huts, left over from a World War II American Army base near Derry called Springtown Camp. Micky's father Patrick, who had served in the British Merchant Navy in the war, was unhappy at having to raise his small family in this slum.

They'd moved from the village of Ardmore in 1948 when the first of their two children, Margaret, was a year old. Patrick Devine was one of the legion of Derry Catholic unemployed—he couldn't even get work as a coalman. During the chill winters, Patrick and his wife Elizabeth and their two children—Margaret, born in 1947, was seven years older than Micky—had to pile blankets and old coats on the beds not just to keep warm but to keep off the rain that leaked through the roof. On sunny summer days the huts weren't too bad, but in the winter they were cold and damp. Springtown was Catholic housing, and the huts were kept in poor repair by the unionist Protestants who ran Derry Corporation. Control of the majority Catholic nationalist city was maintained by the simple expedient of gerrymander.

It wasn't until 1960, when Margaret was 13 and Michael 6, that Patrick Devine was able to get his family moved to a corporation house on the Circular Road in the Creggan estate, a relatively new Catholic ghetto on a hill high above the Bogside on the west bank of the River Foyle. In the sixties, Springtown camp was finally closed. On 6 February 1966 Patrick died of leukemia when Micky was only eleven, and in July that year Margaret married Frank McCauley and settled in her own small house in the Brandywell. Micky was left with his mother and grandmother.

Micky was the caricature of a juvenile academic, very small with freckled face, outsize head, orangey hair and thick eyeglasses. He walked with a kind of duck step, and rolled when he walked. His wit and edge were evident even at the age of eleven. But he was quiet and very serious. Though articulate, he lacked charisma—and the self-confidence that made leaders or heroes. He didn't stand out in a crowd in this way.

From the time he was a boy Micky loved curries and tins of beans. He'd eat them with a big spoon, and he'd always have a glass of milk after his dinner.

He wasn't very enthusiastic about athletics, apart from football. He had a boyhood friend, Noel Moore—one of sixteen children. When they were ten or eleven they played football together. Micky was small and frail, while Noel was big and burly. Once, when they were being beaten 3-1 in a football match, Micky went up to Noel, who was playing goalie.

"You're useless in nets. Give me the jumper."

Noel, who indulged Micky's moods, gave him the goalie's sweater. They ended up losing 8-1.

When a fight threatened, Micky might say to Noel, "Go get him, Noel. Go into him." If Noel was winning, Micky would be on top of him shouting, "Come on, Noel! Let's give it to him, boy!" And if Noel got beaten up, Micky would turn around and say, "Sure I told you, Noel, you shouldn't have gone into him!"

After attending Holy Child Primary school and St. Joseph's Secondary school in Creggan, Micky quit school in 1969 at fifteen and got the first of a series of jobs as shop assistant in the centre of Derry. The city was, then as now, an employment black spot, and for a Catholic boy to get such a job spoke well for his manner and appearance. His shop assistant's career began at Hill's furniture store down in the Strand Road. He climbed, literally and figuratively, in the Derry shop assistants' world, moving on up to Sloan's in Shipquay Street, and ending up on the Diamond working at Austin's, the best furniture store in Derry. (The owner, Campbell Austin, was a liberal unionist who was briefly involved in the civil rights movement in the city.) Well-heeled local Protestants bought their furniture at Austin's from the bright, well-dressed little Catholic boy with glasses, who was slowly moving up in his other career too—as socialist revolutionary.

During the civil rights phase of the conflict, Micky showed an ardent interest in politics, working to help Eamonn McCann and Katherine Harkin of the breakaway Derry branch of the Northern Ireland Labour Party with propaganda, and with the Derry Housing Action committee. Later he joined the Socialist Labour League's youth section—the Young Socialists. The organization was typical of left-wing political efforts—with small, intense discussion groups interested in dialogue and dialectics. Micky was a very enthusiastic member and fitted in well. He sold papers for them regularly, standing under the arches at the corner of William Street, as he would later sell *The United Irishman* for the Officials, and their local paper, *The Starry Plough*. (He would often sell half the copies of *The United Irishman* sold in Derry. He believed in propaganda.)

At the end of 1971 Micky quit the Young Socialists. The parent organization had taken a position strongly opposed to the barricades, arguing that they were a sectarian act because they separated Catholic working class from Protestant working class areas. But Micky's socialism had come to take a much more aggressive and Republican form.

He got to know "Red Mickey" Doherty, leader of the Bogside Officials, whom he would always respect. Later he became "Red Mick" himself for the same reason as Doherty: the colour of his hair. During 1971 Micky became involved in helping to man the "Free Derry" barricades after the internment roundup of 9 August. He began, like other youngsters, manning the barricades with a hurley stick, and like them ended up manning them with a gun.

Micky was not lacking in physical courage. It wasn't hard, of course, for boys in Derry to show physical courage. They weren't isolated and had people cheering them on from the sidelines. In the "Dodge City" days (from 1969 on) it was not unusual to see boys walking openly in the streets with bandoliers and rifles—sometimes masked, sometimes without masks.

Micky had the chance to use guns. There was a sniping place—a hole in the Derry wall above the Brandywell. Boys would take turns on 12-hour shifts patrolling in hijacked cars, doing their tours every day and night around the Bogside. There was a car for boys affiliated with the Provos, and one for those connected with the Official IRA. Their job was to keep the Brits and the police from coming into the area. Sometimes they'd stop and get out of the car to have a go at a British helicopter. Or they'd stop at the hole in the wall, through which they could fire down at The Mex, the army post at the end of the Brandywell, beside a Mex garage.

Eventually the British got wise, and the soldiers mounted a machine gun on a tripod, lining it up with the hole in the wall. The boys were not so venturesome after that.

Micky's brother-in-law Frank McCauley, Margaret's husband, was walking along one time in the no-go days, when he saw American CBS cameramen filming the boys standing with guns in their hands. Frank strolled over to see what was going on. One of the boys was posing with his gun. A TV man, microphone in hand, leaned over to the boy.

"This is CBS," he said. "I'm speaking on behalf of American television. Are you members of the IRA?"

"Aye," said the boy posing with the gun. "We are."

"Does it worry you boys if you shoot a British soldier or a policeman?"

"The only time it worries us," said the boy, "is when we miss them."

One Saturday evening Frank and his daughter Cathy, then six, were walking through town. There was a checkpoint at O'Brien's Pub, where the boys used to stand with their hoods on, brandishing their guns and stopping cars. No one was supposed to address them by name and people were expected to just move on.

Cathy and her father passed by.

"Oh, hello, Michael," Cathy suddenly called over.

Frank took her hand and pulled her after him.

A quarter of an hour later there was a change of guard at the checkpoint, and some of the boys wandered into the Bogside Inn. Micky was standing there with a pint when Frank and Cathy came in.

"How the devil did you know me?" Micky said.

"I knew your feet, Michael," Cathy said. "You were standing

like this"—and she put out her two feet, Charlie-Chaplin style, with heels together and toes splayed out. Micky was not hard to spot—from either end.

Micky's socialism became more Republican and militant. He took great satisfaction in the deaths of British soldiers. Whenever he was sitting in a bar depressed, and there was news that British soldiers had been shot, the depression would suddenly vanish and Micky would sit up and smile.

His humour had an edge and became very black at times. Once a Provo was shot and wounded in Dublin by the gardai, and Micky said, "Ah, that'll stiffen him up." A man was killed in Derry. "That'll stiffen him up," Micky said.

It was after Bloody Sunday that Micky became a member of the Official IRA. As the crowds were running from the paratroops, who were shooting to kill with high-velocity rifles, two lads with Micky, one on either side of him, were shot dead. Micky escaped. Frank and Margaret McCauley were there at the march, which was intended to be a peaceful protest against internment. They watched the paras not aiming but shooting from the hip at people 150 or 200 yards away.

"I told you," the seventeen-year old Micky said to someone that night—"I told you the bastards would start shooting! We can't just sit back and watch while our own Derrymen are shot down like dogs. It's up to us to retaliate."

Afterwards Micky wrote of the coffins lined up in the church: "I will never forget standing in the Creggan chapel staring at the brown wooden boxes. We mourned, and Ireland mourned with us. That sight more than anything convinced me that there will never be peace in Ireland while Britain remains."

Three years after starting work as a shop assistant, Micky gave up his job at Austin's and became a full-time activist, first with the Officials, then with the IRSP, and finally with the INLA.

In some things Micky's aim exceeded his grasp, but he was always shrewd in political matters. His politics never changed. Though temperamental from the time he was a boy, he was considered deep, and his opinion would not change once his mind was made up.

Micky wanted to be a fighter—a soldier. He handled weapons, but he had a liability—extremely bad eyesight. So he was not sent out to shoot soldiers; he handled different operations. Yet he always wanted to do what he could as a volunteer.

One day in July 1972—two months after the Officials had announced their ceasefire—Frank McCauley was sitting in the Bogside Inn when Micky came in.

"Well," Micky said, "are you buying me a pint?"

"Get him a pint," Frank said to the barman.

"I'm waiting on a girl," Micky said.

"Maggie?" Frank asked him—the girl Micky was going out with at the time and would later marry.

"Oh, no," Micky said. "We're going shoplifting."

Frank shrugged. Nothing surprised him in those days.

While Micky was in the gents' a girl came into the bar wheeling a pram. Frank couldn't see the baby.

"Are you with Michael?" Frank asked her. She was, she said. Micky returned.

"I'll be back in about half an hour," he said.

"I'll probably be gone by then," Frank said.

"Be here, and I'll have a few bob on me," Micky said.

Frank waited and half an hour later Micky came back, looking at his watch.

"Are you going somewhere?" Frank asked him.

"No, I'm not going anywhere. I'll buy you a drink."

"Okay. But what's the crack? Where's that bit of skirt you had with you?"

"Oh, she's away on home now." Micky said. He kept looking at his watch.

"What's this about the time?" Frank asked.

Micky said nothing.

Then at three o'clock there was a great bang in the centre of town. Frank jumped.

"Good God," he said. "Would you listen to that!"

It sounded as though the whole city centre had gone up.

"Aye," Micky said. "and it was six seconds fuckin' late."

Frank looked at him.

"That," said Micky, "is the shoplifting I was telling you about. See that pram—the wee child had some wind."

Yet the Officials were no longer supposed to be operating, and anyway they didn't do bombings. But Micky might have been helping some friends in the Provos. Micky may have been ex-Official IRA at the time, and anxious to be somehow involved.

On the first anniversary of internment—9 August, 1972—Micky was one of the volunteers on a 24-hour token hunger strike outside the Bogside Inn. They had a tin hut, with wire around it, to represent the internment camp. There was a bonfire, and they stayed up all night—from 12 p.m. on 8 August to 12 p.m. on 9 August.

Micky was deeply upset late that year when his mother died, in September. Then in April 1973 he married Maggie Walmsley and went to live first in Chamberlain Street, off William Street, and eventually in Rinmore Drive in the Creggan.

Micky's friends in the Officials were surprised when he got married. They didn't think he was the sort who would marry and settle down.

When he was still newly married Micky got into trouble with his landlord. He was living with his wife in a flat in the first house on Chamberlain Street. Micky had trouble paying for things: he always had difficulty finding money. He was like a lot of young husbands in Derry who were struggling, in a way most men living settled lives would find hard to comprehend.

The landlord came one day, demanding that Micky pay his rent. Micky couldn't, and reminded the landlord that he was connected with the Official IRA. So the landlord went to men he knew were leaders in the Officials and said, "Look, I'm being reasonable—very reasonable." The rent was low, but Micky hadn't paid for four or five months.

So two men from the IRA came to see him.

"You're going to have to move out, Micky."

"Just because I've been arguing about a rent which is unreasonable?"

"You used the name of the organization."

The men began to move one of Micky's chairs down the steps.

Micky couldn't understand.

"Look at you!" he said. "And you're supposed to be socialists! Look at this flat!" He took them to the back, opened the wardrobe and showed them some damp. "That's what we're living in. That's why I'm not paying!"

The landlord had to make repairs to the flat. And Micky had to pay up.

Micky was not mean about money, though. He'd borrow it from people who had it—with no particular intention of paying it back—and he'd give it out to people who needed it, keeping some for himself. He might borrow twenty pounds and give five pounds each to two boys he knew were stuck.

DURING LATE 1972 and 1973 the Official IRA men in the city became more and more disenchanted with the organization's ceasefire. In May 1974 Micky, then nearly 20, joined most of the Derrymen who'd been in the Officials, in Seamus Costello's new IRSP. In Belfast and elsewhere the Officials, seeing large numbers of their members going over to the new organization, reacted with a rash of shootings. And the INLA, formed in November-December 1974, used the cover name People's Liberation Army (PLA) when taking defensive and retaliatory action against the Officials.

In Derry the cover name PLA was never really needed. The Derrymen wanted to help their Belfast colleagues and fight the Officials; but there was almost no one for them to fight with, because in Derry something like 95 per cent of the Officials' volunteers had joined the INLA.

The fight with the Officials—the Sticks—eventually worked itself out. Instructions had come from Séamus Costello in Dublin: "Don't escalate the feud with the Officials."

By 1975 the Costello organization had fully secured its

independence and the Irish National Liberation Army had come out into the open.

Micky was one of the INLA's first members in Derry. Although rarely involved in INLA bank and post office raids—mounted to get money for arms—he played other roles.

Micky had problems in areas besides money. He had always been fond of drink, and now his marriage suffered. He and Maggie had two children: Michael, born in August 1973, and an infant daughter Louise, born in April 1976. In 1976 Micky and Maggie decided to separate.

Micky continued as an INLA activist.

One day in September 1976, he and two others went with Patsy O'Hara to raid an arms dealer in Lifford, Co. Donegal. They took nine rifles, three shotguns and eleven hundred rounds of ammunition. Later the British Army and the RUC discovered the haul by accident. They were looking for Provo arms when they stumbled on weapons in a hut in Bishop Street. Micky was arrested. He was trapped into confessing and remanded to Crumlin Road jail.

Frank McCauley had been with Micky before the court appearance. He wanted Micky to make a good impression.

"Why don't you wear my suit?" Frank asked.

"Oh, aye. All right," Micky said.

The next time Frank saw him was in a prison cell.

"That suit of yours didn't do much for me," Micky said.

"I was only trying to help you," Frank said.

"Aye," Micky said. "You helped me all right. Some suit, that."

Micky spent nine months on remand. After sentencing in June 1977, he was transferred to Long Kesh, where he joined the seven months' old blanket protest.

Micky had briefly been education officer in the Bogside unit of the Official IRA. But he'd never held rank in the INLA until Long Kesh. Many of his Derry colleagues were surprised when he took over from Patsy O'Hara at the time Patsy went on hunger strike. But Micky's political self-education had paid off.

Patsy made him OC because Micky was able to articulate the IRSP philosophy. He understood Republican socialism, and could argue his position very effectively. Though in Crumlin Road he was thought of at first as a loner—he often walked the yard by himself, and only rarely with one or two friends—he came into his own in Long Kesh.

INLA prisoners were relatively few in the Kesh, and were scattered through the blocks. But Micky took to organizing quizzes on the wing, recitations, reading, concerts and other activities to help pass the time and keep up morale. He was good at that kind of thing, and became very popular.

Micky took an active interest in the prisoners' letter writing campaign to alert outsiders to conditions in the prison. He became a strong advocate of the hunger strike as a weapon against criminalization, torture and degradation in the prison. "A death of dignity," he wrote in one of his letters, "is infinitely preferable to indefinite torture . . . vicious beatings, starvation diets, deprivation . . . obscene searching . . . twenty-four hours a day every day in cells described by the . . . Cardinal as resembling the sewers of Calcutta."

In 1980 he wrote about the first seven hunger strikers: "They have a courage in their hearts that a tyrant can never understand. They are my friends and comrades, and my heart burns with the knowledge that here in this concrete dungeon I am helpless to save them."

Micky's open letter to the English Cardinal Hume—who had said that hunger striking was a form of violence against one's own body—showed his talent for sarcasm:

> Everyone seems to talk these days about "forms of violence," the most notable of course being you, Cardinal Hume of Westminster. As a blanketman these past three and a half years, I believe I can enlighten Your Eminence on a few forms of violence that you don't know about or have deliberately chosen to ignore.
>
> It would interest me to know what name you would use to describe locking a human being in a prison cell for four

years and never allowing him to see daylight, depriving him of any and every method of easing the days, months and years of loneliness, a loneliness which you, in your mansion in Westminster, could never begin to understand.

Have you ever been dragged from a dirt-infested cell to have your head forcibly shaved? Have you ever been beaten naked over a mirror to have your anal passage examined by a screw with a torch and rubber gloves? It is even less likely that you have had metal tongs inserted into your back passage searching for something which never existed in the first place.

I'm prepared to bet this torn smelly blanket that I'm wearing that you can't remember the last time you were beaten unconscious or the last time you dined on black tea and hard dry bread.

Does Your Eminence know what a Castlereagh interrogation consists of? If you had wanted to know, I'm sure Father Faul would have been only too happy to tell you how the RUC forced their victims to eat their own vomit—the same victims that now fill the H-Blocks.

I can assure Your Eminence that you don't need to lecture the Irish on forms of violence; we have experienced them all from the blatance of bloody Sunday to the subtleness of the Diplock courts.

I would suggest that you investigate the violence of your fellow countrymen who are responsible for driving their victims into near insanity.

The H-Block hunger strike is not a publicity stunt; it is a last desperate cry for help. In the case of Your Eminence, Cardinal Hume, it seems destined to be a cry which will go unanswered.

So much for Christianity.
Michael Devine
H-Block 5

Patsy O'Hara went on hunger strike on 22 March. Even though Micky became OC of the INLA prisoners, it was arranged by

Patsy that Kevin Lynch would replace him as the second INLA hunger striker.

In early June, two weeks before he went on hunger strike, Micky sent word outside that he was going on. Friends told Micky that they thought he was being very foolish.

"I'm going on it," Micky said. "And there's nobody putting me on it."

When Micky had been sent to Long Kesh there were people in the INLA and IRSP who said he wouldn't last a week on the blanket. But then when he went through with the prison protest—the blanket, the no-wash, the dirt protest—they knew that he would, if necessary, carry his hunger strike through to the end.

Shortly after Micky began his fast, his siser Margaret and her husband Frank met Rosaleen Sands, Bobby's mother. Mrs. Sands said that she'd read in the *Irish News* about Micky having no mother or father alive.

"You have an awful lot to take on you," she said to Margaret. "I went through it all. But I had a family to back me up."

It was true, and the IRSP was concerned as well. Frank and Margaret would be going up and down to the prison. There were the public appearances. It was going to go on for weeks and weeks, an exhausting ordeal. The burden would be heavy on Margaret especially. Other hunger strikers had several people at least in the immediate family. Micky had no close family but Margaret and Frank.

The IRSP came up with the idea that a Derrywoman who had known Micky since his days in the Sticks—Teresa Moore—could be represented to the authorities as Micky's aunt.

Teresa was highly regarded in the IRSP and was at the time a member of the *Ard Comhairle*—its national governing body. As an officer of the IRSP, she was in an excellent position to relay messages back and forth.*

*She later went out to America to represent the families, speaking to the hunger strikers' supporters and at rallies. Teresa was honest to a fault, so that when she was in America she hated having to pretend to be a hunger striker's aunt. But she played out the role for the prisoners' sake.

A blonde-haired woman from Beechwood Street in the Bogside, Teresa was the daughter of Paddy and Brigid Sheils. Paddy was a former leader of the Derry IRA, and Brigid was a staunch Republican. Teresa had had nine children, of which seven survived: they were mostly grown up now. She was outgoing and witty, and spoke in sharp, uncompromising tones, with an edged Derry humour Micky liked. As an added bonus, the IRSP had her husband Patsy Moore going in as Micky's uncle. Patsy was a gentle, stocky, good-hearted man who was the organization's Derry area welfare officer. Years before he had been trying to intervene to calm a riot situation when a British soldier shot him with a rubber bullet. He'd been deafened in his left ear and lost the sight of his left eye.

Patsy went to Mass and communion every morning. He used to say he was a Catholic first, a socialist second. Teresa marked his priorities as God, then country, then self.

As Micky's condition worsened, they usually paired off for a round-the-clock vigil at Micky's bedside—Patsy with Frank, and Teresa with Margaret.

TERESA MOORE was involved in the final meeting on 6 August with the Taoiseach Garret FitzGerald, the one that ended with a sit-in in FitzGerald's office. At the meeting the McElwees and Matt Devlin's family were represented. Frankie McCauley and Pat McGeown's brother-in-law Seán Begley were there. Begley was nominated as principal spokesman for the group.

FitzGerald said they were doing all they could but had made no progress. Why, he kept asking them, didn't they tell the IRA to stop the violence?

"How in God's name can we speak for the IRA?" they answered. "No one speaks for those boys. But we'll ask them anyway if it will save lives. If we do ask them to stop, will you come out publicly and say that the five demands should be met?"

He never answered them.

Tea was served. Three waitresses came in with silver platters, bringing tea, coffee, sandwiches and biscuits. It was a big room, with an oblong table, and chairs for over twenty people. FitzGerald sat at the top. The way he and his cohorts ate their food! It seemed to the families, to Teresa in particular, as though they were rubbing salt in a wound. Up there the boys were starving. And here they were eating and clearly relishing the meal, as if to say, "Why don't you go up and tell the boys to come down here and enjoy themselves, the way we're doing?"

If they asked FitzGerald an awkward question he would sit for a minute till he had a note passed to him by one of his secretaries. Then he'd answer the question.

Teresa sat there thinking: How could they bring six families to this table, then sit and eat while men were dying of hunger? There they sat: FitzGerald, and his deputy Michael O'Leary—who seemed to be bored—and James Dooge, the Minister of Foreign Affairs, who was passing messages as well.

"Everytime," the relatives said, "you go to Margaret Thatcher you go with your cap in your hand."

"What do you mean?" he said, munching on a sandwich.

"Well, as far as we can make out, what's happening is that Irishmen are dying in a British prison here on Irish soil. What kind of man are you? Are you going to let them all die?"

He said he was doing everything he could.

"Why don't you bring back your ambassador from England?" they asked him. "And send the English ambassador home?"

"If we did that, we'd be breaking off all links with Britain."

"The British aren't going to help you," they said. "Why are you so anxious to help them? Why not bring the Free State Army off the borders? It's costing you a hundred million pounds a year, which you haven't got."

"I can't do that either," he said. "That's security."

"Security" seemed very important to him.

"Oh," he said about a planned follow-up march to the British embassy, "I'll leave that to my security men."

FitzGerald kept coming back to one point—he would even interrupt a conversation to repeat it.

"I must say this—what's said in this room is confidential. The press are outside and I don't want anything said."

At earlier meetings, Teresa gathered, he'd said the same thing. But the families had other preoccupations: Men were dead, and dying. At every meeting there had been new families coming in as their sons or brothers joined the fast.

Teresa felt that FitzGerald must have thought them very stupid: "I'll keep you in here for awhile," he seemed to be saying, "and I'll give you tea and sandwiches. We'll sit and talk, and the press will be outside saying, 'They're making progress.'"

It was clear to Teresa that through several meetings the families had more or less gone along with this. But it had got to the point where they were desperate, and getting nowhere, so that today they had to speak out.

There was a heated exchange about the fact that eight men were dead, and one, Thomas McElwee, was just about to die.

Mary and Nora McElwee got up to go.

"How long is this going to last?" someone asked. "Are you going to bring your boy back from London? Are you going to chase their boy from here? Are you going to take the troops off the border?"

Mary McElwee left the room.

Teresa Moore addressed FitzGerald.

"Her brother Tom is dying. I'm not asking you. I'm begging you"—Teresa pushed aside her chair and went down on her knees—"to save the life of Tom McElwee."

"There's nothing I can do to save them. It's the organizations that can save them."

Seán Begley spoke.

"We've come to the conclusion that you're never going to do anything. So we're going to have a sit-in."

FitzGerald just got up and walked out. His two secretaries followed him, then came back in again.

"Look," one of them, his press secretary, Liam Hourican, said: "This is getting you nowhere. If you speak to the press he won't see you again."

"We're going to have a protest."

"If the rest of the families want to see him, he's not going to see them."

"FitzGerald's not interested in Matt Devlin or Michael

Devine," Frank McCauley said to Dominic Devlin. "He's going to let them die."

"You're going to spoil it for the rest of the families," Hourican said.

"We know that. But the rest of the families are going to get the same from you—no satisfaction. So that's it. We're staying."

The secretaries went back out again; Liam Hourican came back in and stood there.

"You can leave," Seán Begley said. "We're going to have a meeting here."

"I'm afraid of your locking the door."

"Oh, no," Begley said. "We're not going to lock the door. This is a peaceful protest. As soon as you get the guards you can tell them that. We don't want trouble."

"That's OK." Hourican left and came back again. "The people on the stairs refuse to move, too."

"We know that," someone said. "We had it planned before we came in."

"I see. Well, you aren't getting anywhere this way."

"We're not interested in helping ourselves," Begley said. "It's the men lying in the H-Blocks we're trying to help. So don't worry about us."

Teresa addressed Hourican.

"Excuse me, Liam—"

"What?"

"Any chance of a cup of coffee?"

His look told her what he thought of her request. Still, a silver tray was brought in. But there was no time to drink any coffee.

They heard trouble on the stairs. "Aye," they said to one another. "That's our people getting fired out." Next thing, the door banged open and about forty guards barged in. They lifted up Dominic first, then Seán Begley, then Teresa and Frank and Martin Mullan. It took about five of them to lift big Dominic, who weighed nearly 20 stone. They were carried down the steps and out into the street.

Patsy and Frank were in on a visit on 11 August and Micky

remembered that it was his son Michael's birthday. Micky asked Patsy to send his son a card from him. Patsy bought a card, and Teresa put two pounds in it. Patsy wrote, "Happy birthday! Love, Daddy," and gave it to the boy, saying it was from Micky.

Next day Teresa went in.

"Micky," she said, "You canna' die. You owe me two pound."

"What for?" Micky asked.

"For the two pounds I put inside Michael's birthday card."

Micky was filled with emotion. He squeezed her hand, to thank her.

Teresa would often joke with him.

"Well, Micky. How are you today? Get a good breakfast? What did you have? Scrambled egg and toast?"

There was no use in being morbid, she felt.

And Micky would say he'd been out jogging in the yard and hadn't had time for breakfast.

Right until near the end, when his jaw locked and he could no longer speak, Micky always talked in terms of hope.

In many ways Teresa felt sorry for Micky. Not just because of his suffering there in Long Kesh, but because he'd had a rough, hard life. He was denied the education that could have brought forth his talent for argument and discussion and debate—he could have been a university professor, given the right breaks. He was very much an ordinary Derry boy and he'd suffered from poverty. And so had his marriage. Perhaps nobody put the problem with the marriage better than his father-in-law, Norman Walmsley. Micky had lived in Norman's house for a period before the marriage.

"I would blame the situation," said Maggie's father. "People get married young. A young man gets sentenced. The young woman is left with children. For her it's a long, hard strain. There were dozens of similar cases in Derry alone, and far more in the war zone—the North—as a whole. As a father, I wanted Maggie to stand by Micky when he was in prison. It was difficult, though, for her.

"And it was a personal strain for me—especially because

Micky was a sort of adopted son of mine. Yet Micky's drinking was a factor. I'd be torn, if forced to pass judgement on either of them. The real problem was the situation, British rule in Ireland, and the unemployment—the British never gave a damn about us—and the poverty. That's what created all this havoc among the young."

Teresa learned to love Micky as though he really were one of her own. She often said she couldn't have loved him any more if she'd been his real aunt.

One day, when Margaret and Teresa went to the Kesh, Micky—who was bad then, but was still sitting up—seemed to be bothered by something.

"What's wrong with you, Micky?" they asked.

"Nothing."

"Do you want to come off hunger strike?"

"Oh, no," he said. "The problem is that Maggie is putting pressure on me."

Micky explained that one of the chaplains, Father John Murphy, had been in that day and told him that Micky's wife had been up seeing Bishop Daly in Derry. The Bishop had phoned Father Murphy.

"If you want to see her," Margaret said, "I'll bring her in myself."

"I don't want to see her," Micky said.

So Patsy Moore phoned the Bishop and he agreed to meet them. Margaret and Patsy went to the Bishop's residence behind the cathedral.

"His wife was here to see me," the Bishop explained.

"He doesn't want to meet her," Patsy said. "We'd like you to phone Father Murphy and tell him not to ask Micky again. This has him upset. He's under enough pressure without you putting him under more."

"The INLA put pressure on the girl," the Bishop said.

"The INLA has nothing to do with us," Patsy said.

They all knew why Micky didn't want to see her. They were legally separated, and she'd been living with someone else. Her sister Mary Duddy and her father Norman had visited Micky in Long Kesh. But she'd never visited him during the five years he was in prison, on the blanket and the dirt protest. And she'd been living with someone else.

Then Micky got a solicitor to come to the prison, and draw up a will, declaring Margaret his next of kin. The McCauleys showed Bishop Daly their copy, and he must have phoned Father Murphy, because Micky wasn't bothered about the matter again.

But Micky did very much want to see his children: Michael, who was just eight, and Louise, who was five. Margaret and Teresa brought them in on 15 August. It was painful for the women: the two youngsters seeing their father, who was fully conscious but could hardly speak at all, and couldn't see.

They saw his tears and the way he tried to hold onto the children. He wanted the children to stay close to him, and kept pulling them towards him on the bed.

Finally the visit was over.

When they were in two days later, Micky whispered that he wanted to see the children again.

"Michael," his sister said, "you're not seeing them again."

"Please, Margaret—"

"No," she said. "It was too heartbreaking." He stopped talking then, and looked around. He was blind and couldn't see her, and seemed to be staring past her. He'd said earlier that all he could see was a kind of blur. "Please," he said to her again. "Please."

"All right, then" she said. "We'll bring them up tomorrow—"

He smiled.

"Think what you have to look forward to tomorrow," Teresa said as they left. "The wains will be coming up to see you! It'll be about two o'clock."

"That's great," he whispered.

The children came in with Teresa, Margaret and Patsy.

"Which one is on my right side? Which one is on my left?" Micky whispered.

"Louise is holding your left hand and Michael is holding your right."

But Micky knew which was which when he felt them.

Louise was frightened—a girl of only five—and wanted to leave. But the boy understood. He was big enough to know what was going on. When his father cried, the boy cried and put his arms around him.

Teresa Moore left the room—she couldn't take it—but Patsy stayed. Finally Margaret, fearing that he might try to get out of the bed and would fall, had to take the children out. When she looked back at Micky lying on the bed, he was crying—not the way people usually cry; there was just a trickle of tears. Then the cell door banged shut.

They walked down the corridor, with Patsy holding Michael's hand and Margaret Louise's. Margaret wanted to cry, but she held back because of the children.

Patsy said afterwards that it was the sorriest thing he'd ever seen in his life, knowing it was the last time.

What had Micky's thoughts been, Margaret wondered, when his children were walking down that corridor? He had no one to whisper his feelings to . . .

Now at the time when Micky was in his last weeks, the hunger strike was being broken. Teresa felt that the Catholic Church was acting as an ally of the British government in breaking it. It had to be ended, of course, but this was the wrong way to do it—using the families to thwart the men's own will.

Teresa had heard the story of how Thomas McElwee, on his deathbed, had spoken to Micky about religion. Micky was in a wheelchair and Thomas was in bed. Thomas said to Micky that as a personal favour he'd like him to go back to the sacraments. Micky had never had any time for the Church. He listened and said nothing.

Micky was particularly close to Thomas. The day after Thomas died a priest came to Micky.

"Your friend's gone, Micky," the priest said.

"Aye, he's away."

"He was a good friend of yours?"

"Aye." Micky was in tears.

"Will you and I not say a wee prayer for him?"

"You pray away and I'll listen."

"Micky, it's a bad job if you can't pray for your own friend."

"Well, I don't know—prayers never helped me much in my life."

"That's okay, then."

The priest knelt down and prayed for Thomas. Then, a couple of days afterwards, Father Toner was in.

"I've a bit of news for you," Micky said. "I want you to hear my confession." Father Toner heard his confession, and then—so the story went—headed straight for the phone and rang Father Murphy, the other chaplain.

"I've good news and bad news for you," Father Toner said.

"What's the bad news?"

"You're saying Mass tonight at seven o'clock. And the good news is—I've just heard Micky Devine's confession."

"I'm coming up!" said Father Murphy.

Micky's sister Margaret was as happy as the priests were at hearing the news. It was they who told her first, and then it was in the papers.

A few days before Micky died, Teresa noticed that the warder in the room was constantly trying to get into conversation with them. Micky wasn't talking then; he wasn't really able to talk anymore.

Teresa saw what was going on. She was sitting on one side of the bed and Margaret on the other, and Micky wouldn't let go of their hands. The warder, to pass his time, kept trying to talk to them. This was wearing them out. They weren't getting anything to eat in there, either—just cups of tea.

The doctor came in to examine Micky. Teresa and Margaret went down to the waiting room and had a smoke.

"That screw," Teresa said, "has been constantly trying to

get us to talk to him. Micky can't talk. He can't afford to try, because he'd be using up all his energy, right?"

"Right," Margaret said.

"Now when we go back in there again," Teresa said, "We're not going to get in any solid conversation with Micky—"

Margaret agreed.

"If we go on as we've been doing," Teresa continued, "we'll only be entertaining that screw there. But one thing we can do—we can pray along with Micky."

So they went back in and began saying the rosary and other prayers. Teresa could see that Micky was happy with this. Everytime she would get up, to get a cup of tea or anything, Micky would squeeze her hand—he wanted her to keep on praying.

"Micky, can you hear us?" she'd ask. "Can you understand us?" And he'd squeeze her hand.

So Teresa and Margaret prayed for three full days before Micky died. And Micky was aware of every word that was being said.

Teresa left a message for her husband Patsy with the people they were staying with: "Tell Patsy and Frank when they go in at night to start praying, and that way they'll avoid those silly conversations."

MARGARET REMEMBERED Micky saying he had gained great confidence from Joe McDonnell's sacrifice—Joe was the first to die after Micky went on hunger strike. Micky said that at the back of his mind everyone is afraid of death and the unknown. Margaret was convinced that Joe's example was what Micky most relied on to get through it all. Someone had remarked that Joe McDonnell had the toughest decision, because he knew when he went on that Bobby Sands had died, and that others were likely to die. He was a brave young man. And Micky was, too, because in his last weeks there was a concerted effort to break the hunger strike.

Teresa heard someone say that Micky was the least of them,

but that he may have been the greatest, because he was the last. He'd been loyal to all of them.

Margaret had never seen anyone receiving the last sacraments. But on Tuesday, 18 August, she was sitting at Micky's bedside with Teresa Moore when Father John Murphy came in.

"I'm going to anoint you again, Micky," he said. "It'll strengthen you a wee bit."

First he anointed Micky's head, then his feet and hands. Micky had his hands on top of the bedcovers. The priest put his finger underneath Micky's hand.

"I'm putting my finger here," the priest said. "If you can feel it at all, just nip me."

But there was no response.

The priest started praying. When he got to the Hail Mary, Micky started mumbling. The words couldn't form properly. But he knew what was going on. Hearing was the last sense to go, and Margaret and Teresa knew he could hear everything.

"Isn't that great?" Margaret said. "Look at him praying."

"Great," said the priest. "Now, Micky, come on—out loud."

And he started mumbling louder. Normally they wouldn't have understood him, but they could tell he was saying the Hail Mary. Then the priest took a small box out of his pocket, with the Host in it. He broke off a tiny part and put it inside Micky's cheek. Micky felt the Host and he moved his tongue. They all thought he was going to spit it out.

But Teresa kept saying, "Micky! It's Communion, Micky. We're not giving you somethig to eat. It's Communion." And then he let it sit there and it melted.

During that last period Teresa and Margaret sat with Micky from nine in the morning till six or seven at night, when Frank and Patsy would take over till the next morning.

Micky was lucid all through those final days and nights, though he would sometimes sleep and sometimes go unconscious. He would move his head in response to their questions. His kidneys weren't working, and when he drank water the water, and acid, would run out of his mouth. There

582

were five pillows propped under his head, but he kept sliding down in the bed and would have to be pulled up. His lips were raw from chapping and biting. The bridge in his nose was gone and so he couldn't wear his glasses. He was blind, and couldn't hold his head up. Someone had to put a hand around his chin to lift it.

On Wednesday night, 19 August, Father Toner was in and they said prayers over Micky. Patsy and Frank were sometimes together, and sometimes took turns, at the bedside. At about two on Thursday morning, Frank, in the waiting room having a cigarette, heard Micky suddenly roar out as though in terrible pain. He came racing into the room. Micky quieted down, but he had vomited, and Frank left while the medics cleaned him up.

When he came back he touched Micky's feet. They were freezing. His spindly legs and knees were freezing, too. His forehead and his ears and nose were growing cold. Frank and Patsy stayed and prayed. At about five o'clock, Micky rolled his eyes as though to say something. Then his head slid off the pillows and he went into a coma.

At seven in the morning, Frank was getting a little sleep. Patsy Moore went out to wake him.

"Micky's dying," he said.

Father Toner came in at about 7:10. He'd been sent for by the warders. He anointed Micky again, said the prayers for the dying, and led them in the rosary.

They watched the cardiograph beside Micky's bed. There was a steady pulse—peaks and valleys—then suddenly the graph went flat, and bleeped. It was 7:48 a.m.

Patsy Moore, because they assumed he was a blood relative, was asked to identify Micky's body. He did so, and signed the official form.

They had to go to a mortuary in Coleraine to collect Micky's body. There seemed to be about five hundred police outside, with landrovers, Saracens and trucks. In the cortege there were six landrovers in front of the hearse and three other cars, and six behind.

When they came to Derry and got to the top of the flyover, the police pulled off, and the cars and hearse came down into Lecky Road. There was a great crowd. A guard of honour from the INLA was standing waiting.

They took the coffin out of the hearse and an IRSP man covered it with the Tricolour and the Starry Plough. The coffin was put back in the hearse and carried slowly to Rathlin Gardens at the corner of Rathkeele Way in the Creggan, where the McCauleys lived. From there the coffin was carried by six masked and hooded INLA volunteers to the McCauley house.

Micky's body was laid out in the centre of the sitting room. A guard of honour was set at either side, and maintained for two days.

On Saturday, 22 August, the funeral Mass was said at ten in the morning. Before he'd decided to go back to the sacraments, Micky had told people in the movement that he didn't want any chapel. "And I don't want a right-wing Mass," he said. He'd been very clear about it.

One thing they knew he'd want: that at his funeral the flags would drape the coffin and stay on till he was buried. The priests had always insisted on no flags in church.

During the requiem Mass Micky's body remained in Margaret's sitting room. He was buried at 2:30 from the house. There were muffled drums, and a piper, and a crowd of tens of thousands. The flags didn't come off till Micky went into his grave.

MARGARET McCAULEY was proud of her brother. Micky and the others, she felt, had brought themselves to this extremity because of their commitment. Ten men, and Ireland with a population of only five million. It had never happened anywhere else in the world.

"I know now I'll not be saved," Micky had said to Margaret. "But if I die, sure, it might save Big Laurence"—Laurence McKeown.

Was Ireland worth it? Margaret wondered. And then she turned the question around and said to herself: Well, ten men died, so it must have been worth it.

Chapter 14

THE AFTERMATH

Ourselves alone, their battle cry
And freedom sang at the Easter sky . . .

Tommy Makem
Freedom's Sons

ON FRIDAY 29 AUGUST 1981, Tony O'Hara heard the big gates of Long Kesh close behind him. Only the echoes hung in the air. Tony glanced up at the sky and around at the infinity of freedom that was abruptly his. Teresa Moore was waiting in a car with several friends of his from Derry. Forty people from the IRSP in Belfast were there, too. At home his parents were preparing a party for him.

Next Monday, 1 September—exactly five years after his arrest in 1976—was to have been the day he'd get out. For weeks he had been focussing on that day—imagining it, planning for it. Then this morning he had been taken to the governor's office to be told he was being released two days early. The warders who were to release him would be off that bank holiday weekend.

As he stepped out into the air, what hit him most forcibly was the sensation of a heavy cloud lifting. It was a very physical experience: Something that had been looming over him, pressing down on his head and against his chest, giving him a feeling of tightness around the heart, had suddenly left him.

He could look around and breathe fresh air. No longer would he look around and see walls, locks and barbed wire. No more looking over his shoulder in case a screw was listening. No more the dark, nauseating cell.

Tony could change his clothes—he could *wear* clothes, any clothes he liked. He could feel the rain, he could feel the sun.

n the winter he could laugh at the snow, throw snowballs, make snowmen, ride on a sledge, if he wanted to. He realized he had grown away from these things; but he could *do* them. He could go into a pub and order and drink a pint. He could go home, go to bed when he wanted to. He didn't have to get up at a fixed time. He could cook himself something to eat. He could watch TV at his leisure, he could play a record, play his guitar, read books, read magazines, buy books, spend money.

It would be weeks after he'd returned to Bishop Street—the message WELCOME HOME TONY painted in large white letters on the terrace wall, and the record player playing Francie Brolly's song—till he'd be able to reflect properly on his experience. A person outside could imagine what prison life was like. But he could never fully grasp it. Tony could tell him everything, down to the smallest detail. He still wouldn't understand what it was like to be there.

Worst of all, worse than any other deprivation or suffering, was the confinement: being locked up twenty-four hours a day for years on end. That's what caused the feeling of helplessness. Tony hadn't known how deeply depressed he'd been in there until he got out. He'd been in a state of depression for five years!

TONY HAD MIXED FEELINGS about the role that the clergy—notably Father Denis Faul—were playing in ending the hunger strike. In a statement in an H-Blocks publication, *The Spirit of Freedom*, Tony said that he felt there were sincere clergymen who had dedicated themselves to fight for the prisoners, but who had been isolated and finally subdued by the Church. If the Catholic Church had thrown its weight behind the hunger strikers, Tony felt, probably none of them would have died.

Tony never tried to hide the fact that he was a believing Catholic. And while he respected and admired a leader like Gerry Adams, who did his job in support of the men and what they wanted, Tony felt that Father Faul did the right thing in getting the hunger strike ended. Faul saw two forces in a head-on clash, with neither side willing to give way. The whole British machine was pitted against a few hundred prisoners. There was a stalemate. Then Father Faul slipped in and cut the knot, doing something the British government wouldn't do.

586

Faul was trying to save lives, Tony felt, and had to be given credit for that. It was the way he went about it that Tony found wrong: it was devious. The families had built up an empathy among themselves which Faul set out to shatter.

Tony was present at one Belfast meeting with the families and felt very indignant that this priest, who had once stood up in Long Kesh and said to the men, "We must speak the truth whenever and wherever we can, no matter what the opposition," would use these means to achieve his purposes. This upset and saddened Tony. Yet he maintained respect for Father Faul as a priest, and for other prison chaplains who sometimes worked eighteen hours a day trying to help the prisoners and comfort them.

Tony was aware of course that Faul, along with most journalists, took or accepted the British line, embraced by Garret FitzGerald, that Adams and the Provos were manipulating the prisoners from outside. Their theory was that at some point Adams and Company decided that the protest was gaining them useful attention, and that they eagerly took advantage of that. One journalist was to say when it was over that the British hadn't behaved honourably and the Provos hadn't, either; that the only party to have emerged with honour were the men who died.

Tony agreed with the part about the honour of the men who died: but he didn't agree with the part about the Provos. Adams, after all, had been faithful to the prisoners, and loyal to what they wanted.

At first the Provos thought the hunger strike a bad idea. They were utterly opposed to it. But Tony was there in the prison and he fully supported what the men inside were saying: We don't care; we've had enough. Rather than the men inside being controlled from outside, Tony felt that the Provos and the IRSP didn't fully understand what the men were suffering. They understood in a way, but their understanding was deficient: they weren't in the situation. Of course, when the hunger strike became such a success, it was like offering the Provos a million pounds' worth of publicity—and naturally they took it. It would have been insane of them not to take it. But Tony, who was not a Provo, knew at first hand—no matter what the propagandists and the journalists said—that the Provos were not organizing it from the outside. Naturally the Provos and the IRSP/INLA were with the men once they went on hunger strike—they had to support them. But they also kept sending in word that the men were not going to win. They told the hunger strikers there'd be bonfires lit up and down the Falls Road if they came off. Yet still the men persisted.

As the hunger strike went on, the Provos outside and particularly Gerry Adams—perceived to be the most formidable Republican leader—found themselves on the defensive against accusations that their organization was profiting from the deaths of the men in prison. Yet Adams, who had argued vehemently against the new hunger strike before it began, had written to Bobby Sands and the other hunger strikers three days before Bobby's death, saying that the time to end the hunger strike was then, and that if they persisted the British government was going to let them die.

Adams insisted afterwards that Sinn Féin had regularly put the facts of the case before the men and had continually encouraged them to review their position. Yet the men kept on, and kept dying. Journalists knew that some of the prisoners' statements were drafted not by the prisoners themselves but by Sinn Féin. Adams didn't argue the point, perhaps because the interplay in the drafting and editing of statements was so complex. But he insisted that this made no difference. The men were prepared to die, and the Sinn Féin office tried to help them articulate their position. But it was the prisoners who determined the course of the protest, and decided what response was to be made. If the Republican movement outside had been manipulating the prisoners, and deceiving the public by making decisions against the hunger strikers' interest, Adams suggested, this deceit would have backfired on those outside. Tony agreed with that.

The families who were suffering with their sons and brothers were being stabilized, Adams said, not by Republicans outside the prison but by the men themselves who were fasting and dying.

To those who argued that the hunger strike was being

manipulated by the IRA, Sinn Féin, the INLA and the IRSP, to stiffen and refuel resistance to the British, Adams replied: "The price that is being paid by the men is too high a price simply to refuel resistance to the British presence . . . It didn't need and does not need men to go and lay down their lives in such a fashion for the resistance struggle to be refuelled." Tony felt that was true, too.

The continuing deaths had vividly underlined several things: the decency of the dying men and their families, the falseness of the notion that they were common criminals, the odiousness and general inhumanity of the British in this colonial situation, and the moral evil of British rule in Northern Ireland. For the hunger strikers, the point was to secure recognition of their political motivation, and at the same time get drastic reforms in a prison system that was a living death for them. They were quite ready to give their lives to show the immorality of the British prison system.

Adams and the Provos outside knew well that the men would keep dying, if necessary, to get their point across. There was a measure of internal conflict: In the Irish Republican tradition it was never acceptable to sacrifice volunteers; if volunteers' lives were in danger, a mission would be aborted. Some Provos and IRSP members were angry with their leadership that this was going on and on, with so many good young men being sacrificed . . .

The movement was also confronted with the humanitarian interest the prisoners had generated. Large numbers of people who were involved in working to help the hunger strikers had joined the effort on a humanitarian basis.

FATHER DENIS FAUL was a ruddy-faced Dungannon priest who looked like one of Jimmy Cagney's pug-nosed friends—say, from Father Flanagan's (Spencer Tracy's) Boys' Town—who (after the film ended) had grown up and entered a seminary. Since the troubles began, Father Faul, a teacher at St. Patrick's Academy in Dungannon, had been attacking the British for their inhumanity towards Irish Catholics in the North. His propaganda efforts were based on humanitarian considerations.

Working mainly with Father Raymond Murray of Armagh, Faul had been publishing booklet after booklet on crimes against Irish men and women—particularly prisoners—by the British military and police forces. They worked hard for many years on the theme of torture and degradation and inhuman treatment of prisoners in Northern Ireland under successive British regimes. For the most part Father Faul had written the emotional material, while Father Murray worked up the detailed case histories. A notable book on the "guinea pigs"—the fourteen men tortured at Long Kesh during the early internment period—had helped bring the 1976 condemnation of Britain for torture by the European Commission of Human Rights.

As far as the hunger strike was concerned, Faul had supported its morality without approving of it. He was angry at Cardinal Basil Hume for saying the hunger strike was suicide. It wasn't. It was a legitimate protest against hideous prison conditions.

The men had put their lives at risk in support of their fellow prisoners—to try to change the prison regime. Bobby Sands, who knew Father Faul as visiting assistant chaplain, had called him into the prison to discuss the morality of the hunger strike. While Faul was strongly against the strike—he said it would bring great suffering to the men's relatives and would cause chaos and death in the Northern community—he broadly approved of the morality of what the men were doing, and he certainly didn't suggest it was suicide.

Bobby Sands quoted St. John to him. "Greater love than this hath no man than that he lay down his life for his friends." Bobby had been beaten up. He'd heard young prisoners, beaten and tortured by the warders, screaming in the night. "I will put a stop to this," Bobby had said. He laid down his life for the young prisoners. Father Faul thought Bobby a very noble man, and his sacrifice a very noble sacrifice. The whole world had responded to it.

But more men had died. And then came the events of early July, which brought important new evidence to Father Faul's attention.

In early July Father Faul was given a first-hand account of Cardinal Ó Fiaich's and Bishop Lennon's meeting with Mrs.

Thatcher. It was obvious from the Cardinal's narrative that Mrs. Thatcher was absolutely frozen in her position: that she was as cold and hard-hearted, as ignorant and malicious in private as she was in public. A few days later, on 8 July, came the failure of the Irish Commission for Justice and Peace. The chairman, Bishop Dermot O'Mahony, had accused the British of "clawing back" on agreements they'd made which would have resolved the problem. The clawback led right to Thatcher's door. (Father Faul's friend Father Murray had never had faith in the Commission to begin with; he'd tried to get them to intervene in cases of inhuman treatment of women prisoners in Armagh, and the Commission had done nothing.)

The European Commission on Human Rights, the Red Cross, the SDLP, successive Irish governments—had all proved to be no use. The Church could do nothing further. Thatcher and the British were iron and immovable.

So with the British door bolted tight, Father Faul began to refocus his sense for injustice, and his cultivated taste for inhuman behaviour, on what he perceived to be the Provos' interest.

Unquestionably the hunger strike had turned out to be a good thing for the Provisional IRA and their politicial bedfellows in Provisional Sinn Féin. Recruits of high quality were flocking to their banner. There was a huge increase in donations from Ireland and overseas. The hunger strike had given them a massive boost in prestige. Worldwide it was the IRA and INLA prisoners versus the British government. In the North, polarization between Protestants and Catholics was growing every day, which Faul thought suited the Provos' hardline philosophy.

Cui bono? is what Faul asked himself. Who was getting benefit from this horrible state of affairs, with young men dying one after another, and more men lining up to die, and the inhumane Thatcher reiterating her position of No Surrender? The prisoners weren't harvesting any benefit: they were harvesting death.

It was clear by now—after the earlier deaths—that if the men stopped their hunger strike there would be some substantial

591

easing of the prison regime. Near the end of the first hunger strike the British had indicated by nods and winks that they would give the prisoners enough of what they demanded to satisfy them. Then the British, careful to keep their promises vague, had reneged. Now they were talking about giving the men most of what they wanted—and the prisoners' statement on 4 July had eased the tone in which the hunger strikers' demands were put. There was a chance here for a settlement.

In Faul's view it was the Provos outside the prison who were now standing in the way. Father Faul had inclined more and more to the view, anyway, that after the British and Thatcher it was the Provos who were the guiltiest party in this confrontation. As far as he could see, it was they who were the big winners. And what he saw as their complacency about the continuing deaths made him *sick*.

If the IRA and Sinn Féin had opposed the hunger strike at the beginning, they were now getting too much profit from it to want it to end. Didn't journalists who were watching what was going on keep suggesting manipulation? Didn't they keep pointing out how the Republican movement was flourishing as the men were dying?

In the days following the prisoners' statement and the 18 July riot at the British embassy in Dublin, Faul built up pressure on the families of the hunger strikers—for their own good, as he saw it: to save their boys' lives. It culminated in a meeting at Toomebridge, Co. Antrim, on Tuesday, 28 July, between Father Faul and relatives of the hunger strikers.

Bernadette Devlin McAliskey turned up at the meeting. Faul challenged her. Why was she there? The meeting was for relatives, not for Sinn Féiners or their sympathizers. Bernadette's answer was that she was there as a relative—of Matt Devlin: Matty Ban, her cousin from Ardboe, who was one of those now on hunger strike.

Her presence would mean trouble for Father Faul.

BERNADETTE McALISKEY had done virtually nothing since she'd emerged from hospital—after being almost killed in

January by UDA assassins, with the connivance of the British military— except plan and march and speak on behalf of the hunger strikers. She was a socialist Republican rebel of long standing (she'd been jailed on 22 April 1969, for her part in the Battle of the Bogside, a few months after being elected a member of the Westminster Parliament). She knew exactly why she was supporting the hunger strike.

Bernadette, too, wanted the hunger strike ended.

It was clear to her that they all wanted to end it—Sinn Féin and Gerry Adams, the IRSP leadership, the independent hunger strike supporters like herself: everyone was trying to end it. But she was furious at the way Father Faul was going about it.

Bernadette had the greatest respect for Father Faul's friend, Father Raymond Murray. Father Murray had come to the point where he couldn't involve himself any further in the hunger strike campaign. He had made his case clear to the prisoners: He had done all he could; it had to be ended.

But there was no way that he was going to do what Faul did: essentially to switch sides and then undermine the prisoners. Given Faul's own politics, she thought, he couldn't see that what he was doing was wrong. He saw the necessity of the hunger strike coming to an end—they all did!—but he then proceeded to pursue that objective by totally unacceptable means. Yet Faul was the sort of person who talked about the ends not justifying the means in the hunger strike.

N.B

In Bernadette's view Father Murray did not accept that the ends justified the means. He couldn't find proper means, so like many other people Father Murray said that he'd done as much as he could do, that he thought the strike should be ended, and opted out. But he refused to play any part in undermining the prisoners. Everybody, Bernadette felt, had a right to opt out, a right to say: "I can't go any further down this road; what the rest of you do must be up to yourselves; I cannot in conscience go any further." But what Father Faul said in effect was, "I can't go any further down this road, therefore I'm going to dump the whole load; I'm going to stop everybody else where

I stop and by any means necessary, including distortion of the truth."

It wasn't clear to Bernadette exactly what the purpose was of the gathering on 28 July in the hotel in Toome (the town where Roddy McCorley went to die "on the bridge of Toome today"). Many of the hunger strikers' relatives were there, and a number of interested parties, including two priests from County Derry, Father Michael McEldowney of Drumsurn Chapel in Dungiven parish and a friend of Kevin Lynch's family, and Father Oliver Crilly from Maghera, who was a cousin both of the McElwees and the Hugheses.

To Bernadette's mind Father Faul's behaviour at the meeting was despicable. He manipulated the families' fears. He worked on their emotions. He set one family against another. Faul played on people's faith in the Church and their emotional need for the Church's support in the most dire of circumstances. He threatened the removal of that support, suggesting that while it had not been suicide for Bobby Sands to die, it *would* be suicide if Kieran Doherty died. He created a wholly bogus and fictitious analysis of how a theory of suicide could now suddenly be justified.

The pressure, the manipulation, the twisting of words, and the racking of Gerry Adams that went on later that night shocked Bernadette. She imagined Adams would never have had to suffer in Castlereagh what he suffered in absentia at the hands of the priests at the meeting that night in Toomebridge, and in person later in Belfast.

At Toome Father Faul said from the start that he thought the hunger strike was doomed—a now hopeless gesture. They were morally obliged, he said, to get the men to end their fast. According to Faul, he had learned in a conversation with Bic McFarlane, OC of the IRA prisoners, that the Provo leaders outside the prison were in control, and that "the buck stopped with Gerry Adams"—by which, according to Faul, McFarlane meant that he was the man who had the power to call off the hunger strike. So pressure, argued Father Faul, should be put on Adams.

Bernadette interjected, saying that Faul's statement was

594

preposterous. It was the *prisoners* who controlled the hunger strike. If such charges were being levelled against Adams, she said, then Adams should have a right of reply: he should be invited to the meeting to answer the accusations.

Accordingly a call was put through to Sinn Féin, and arrangements were made on a return call to reconvene the Toomebridge meeting at the Sinn Féin office in Belfast. Father Crilly stopped off on the way to visit his cousin Thomas McElwee in the prison, and then rejoined the meeting in Belfast. After Father Crilly left, Thomas McElwee met with the other hunger strikers to tell them what was going on.

In Belfast, at about midnight, the meeting was reconvened, with Adams, Joe Austin and other Sinn Féin members present. Faul repeated his remarks about what Brendan McFarlane had told him. Adams said that Faul's version of his meeting with McFarlane was inaccurate. Faul insisted it was correct. Adams produced a letter he had received a few days earlier from McFarlane, in which McFarlane said that the remark "the buck stops with Gerry Adams" related exclusively to the conditions Bobby Sands had imposed *three months earlier* on any meeting with the members of the European Commission on Human Rights! Faul was forced to agree that McFarlane's letter contained the true account of what had passed between them. So Faul, as Bernadette had perceived earlier, had not been telling the truth—on a point which was absolutely crucial to his accusation.

The meeting went on for hours. There was a long discussion of whether the IRA should order the men off their hunger strike. Adams explained that this wasn't possible, that the men had embarked on the hunger strike in clear opposition to directives from leaders of the movement outside. He said that the movement had an obligation now to support what the prisoners themselves had insisted on doing; they could not come out and undermine them, especially after all the suffering and deaths.

One of the things that most impressed Bernadette was the single-minded courage of Kieran Doherty's mother Margaret. Her son had gone 70 days and was living on borrowed time. She was hourly waiting for him to die. And here was Faul tightening the screws on her. She never spoke till it came to her turn. Then she got up.

"Father," she said, "my son is dying. And I don't wish to be rude, but if you can be of no support to him I would like to leave the meeting and be with my son when he dies. I've stayed with him this long, and I'm not leaving him now."

There was that great strength in her! She didn't understand whether what Faul was saying was right or wrong, but she was total and single-minded in support for her son. Margaret Doherty left the meeting.

Faul then changed tack, and said that since Adams was so analytical and persuasive, he should go in and persuade the prisoners to come off.

Bernadette knew that Adams had grown up with "Big Doc" Doherty, had been with him in the cages a decade before, and been a friend of his for years. He could not go in now to his friend, who'd been fasting for seventy days—who was dying—and say: "Doc, it's time to quit. We're no longer supporting you."

To Bernadette, what Faul and then Father McEldowney did to Adams was pure emotional torture. They twisted his words, baited him, mocked him. A pictorial image formed in her mind of the passion of Christ. Here were two priests of the Church, and their treatment of Gerry Adams sitting in the chair could be described as a crowning of thorns. And in attacking Adams they were trying to destroy the morale of the families gathered there.

Adams answered, quietly, that he wouldn't go into the prison and ask them to come off. "No," he said, he couldn't do that. Not to Kieran Doherty. "No."

Father McEldowney said to him, "Are you saying that you are not going into that prison tonight?"

"No," Adams repeated.

McEldowney jumped up.

"You've heard it now, ladies and gentlemen," he said. "You've heard it from his own lips. Here is the leader, the man who controls the hunger strike and who has the lives of your sons in his own hands. He has been asked, will he stop this? And you have heard it from his own lips. 'No!' You go out now and you tell the press—''

Bernadette was furious with McEldowney. She was sitting up on a table at the time and she flew off it like a cat.

"You *bastards!*" she said. "You go out and call in the press and I'll be on your tail. I'll recount, honestly, every single word of what has gone on during this so-called meeting, from 7:30 last evening till 3:30 this morning. Not one person in this room will disagree with the truth of it. And we'll see who can stand over what they've done here tonight as either honest or honourable!''

Then Father Faul stepped in and pleaded for quiet. "We'll sit down calmly now," he said. "Don't let anybody get excited."

Adams said that it was not within his power to order Kieran off the hunger strike. Therefore what were they asking him to do? He tried again to explain to them, as calmly and meaningfully as he could, that he had been in prison during the internment period with "Big Doc," that he had grown up with him, that he was a mate. He said to Faul, "What you are actually asking me to do is to go to my lifetime friend on his deathbed and say, 'Die on your own, because I am not with you.'"

Faul said that if Adams would agree to go into the prison that he, Father Faul, could have him at Doherty's bedside in the length of time it took to get to Long Kesh.

To people like Bernadette who were well acquainted with red tape and bureaucracy, that could only mean that *it had already been arranged*: that Father Faul, here pressuring Gerry Adams, had got an assurance from the British government that all he had to do was ring someone and say, "OK, Adams is coming in." It was after three-thirty in the morning. Bernadette herself had been outside the gates of Long Kesh at eight-thirty the night that Martin Hurson was dying, and she couldn't get in, and couldn't get his own fiancée Bernadette Donnelly in. And later on they had denied Martin's brother Francie entry.

597

In short, anybody inside was in for the night, and anybody outside was out for the night.

But now Father Faul was telling them that all Adams had to say was, "All right," and the gates of hell would be opened unto him, and he'd be in there straightaway! Clearance had to have already been arranged, on the understanding that Father Faul was going to work to get Adams in.

It was clear to Bernadette that pressure had been built up through the night. They'd covered the ground over and over, all the relevant questions—of authority, of who motivated the hunger strike, who started it, who controlled it, who could stop it. And this is what it had come down to. Adams had stated his case very clearly: He'd had to deal with Sinn Féin's own dilemma. The Provos had gone over the ground time and again with the hunger strikers and yet the prisoners wouldn't quit. What he was now being asked to do was to betray Kieran Doherty on his deathbed, and there was no way he would do it. Bernadette could see that Faul had created a false and malign scenario, in the hope that the families would march out with him and say, "Gerry Adams—not Mrs. Thatcher—has been killing our sons." That's why Faul's attitude was terrible. It was poisonous.

At the beginning Faul had been supportive of the hunger strikers' "five just demands." What had turned him? Bernadette asked herself. She concluded that it was the Church. Everyone had his own stumbling block, and the Church was Faul's.

Over recent weeks people were becoming more emotional. There had been a meeting of relatives followed by a meeting of the H-Blocks committee. The conclusion from these meetings was that the Catholic Church was dragging its feet. It was their Church and the prisoners were their prisoners. The British could call upon all *their* friends and allies and churchmen to back them up. The people wanted *their* Church—most nationalists were Catholics—to weigh in in support of their prisoners. But the men had got negligible support. The hunger strike had not shaken the British establishment. And because of the Church's ambivalence, the hunger strike—without that being anyone's intention—had come to threaten the power of the Catholic

Church. That was why, in Bernadette's view, Faul had changed sides.

Faul had always worked on a humanitarian basis. But now, as Bernadette saw it, a situation had developed where his humanitarian concerns were no longer the dominant factor in his thinking.

Families of hunger strikers who were not under immediate pressure—whose sons were not yet close to death—had gone to a meeting in Belfast where they unanimously demanded that the bishops issue a pastoral letter from the pulpit, calling for people to support the prisoners, not just pray for them. If the bishops refused, the relatives suggested, then they would consider a number of alternatives: the placing of pickets on the gates of Catholic churches, for instance, with placards saying: "This *Organization* Does Not Support the Prisoners." Not "this fibre of my being" but "this organization"! They'd picketed and placarded shops, factories and political centres, so why not churches? They also contemplated the suggestion that at the part in the Mass where the priest leaves the altar to begin his sermon—that wasn't the sacrifice of the Mass, wasn't effectively, God's business—a prisoner's mother would get to the lectern before the priest did, and deliver a plea on behalf of her son.

These meetings were convened shortly before Denis Faul turned. People were threatening to make the Church their own. Since the clergy refused them support, they were going to demand it. And that, as Bernadette saw it, was quitting time for Faul. He was forced to decide where his ultimate allegiance lay. When the hunger strikers' cause came into conflict with his Church, he was forced to choose sides.

TONY O'HARA LEARNED later that Adams had gone into the prison after all. On 29 July, the day after the Toome/Belfast affair, he met with the hunger strikers. Kieran Doherty was not able to join the prisoners for their hour-long session with the Sinn Féin and IRSP representatives, so Adams saw him in his own cell.

Doherty lay on his pillow, his eyesight blurred but his mind clear. There had been talk from Faul and others of convening the IRA Army Council to order the men to end their fast.

"There is no need for it to go to the AC," Doherty said. "Have we got the five demands?"

"No," Adams said, and then spelled out what Sinn Féin knew the British government was willing to offer: The prisoners would be able to wear their own clothes; they would get remission; and there would be an increase in letters, parcels and visits. Limited association would be allowed within the prison, and prison work would be defined in an ambiguous way. The British would frame these changes in conciliatory language, and a committee of prominent people would be set up to monitor the changes. But first the hunger strike had to end.

"We can't come off the hunger strike," Doherty said, "until we have a basis to settle." He was confident. "We'll get our five demands," he said.

"Even if you do," Adams said, "You'll be dead—"

"The rest of the boys will get them," Doherty said. "Thatcher won't break us . . ."

"Doc," Adams said, "if you want me to, I'll go out now and announce that the hunger strike is ended."

"No," Doherty said. "We knew what was in front of us before we started. I don't want to die, but I'll only end the hunger strike when the Brits give us our five demands. We will go on."

"You'll never see me again," Adams said.

"I know what I'm going to do," Doherty said.

Adams and the two men with him—Owen Carron (who in three weeks would be elected MP in Bobby Sands' place) and Séamus Ruddy of the IRSP—left Doherty and went back out to the other prisoners.

Tony talked afterwards to Séamus Ruddy, who was in the room, and he confirmed the account of the conversation. For Tony, who did not belong to Adams' wing of the movement, Adams' genuineness had proved itself against the false accusations of Faul.

Tony agreed wholeheartedly with Alfie Doherty's remarks in a 1 August statement to the press:

> Myself and my family are extremely angry at the pressure that is being presently put on the families and the prisoners

on hunger strike. Three times this week the families have been summoned to meetings with Fathers Faul and Murray. These meetings discussed not how to pressure the British government, but how to exert pressure on the prisoners and on the leadership of the Republican movement.

My son is not a dupe; he understands clearly what he is doing and the consequences of his actions.

My son was elected as a TD on the basis of the prisoners' five demands. The prisoners' demands are reasonable. Anything short of full public support for the prisoners' demands and public pressure upon the British government to concede them, is a waste of time and is in the interest of the British government, not the prisoners.

My family welcomes any meaningful initiative which is based upon support for the prisoners' position and which is aimed at achieving a principled end to the hunger strike.

Any diversion from this, as we have repeatedly seen since 1 March, causes confusion among the prisoners' supporters and gives valuable time to the British, time which my son and the other prisoners can ill afford.

At 7:15 the next night, 2 August, Kieran Doherty died.

TONY O'HARA saw Father Faul's behaviour in the same light as Bernadette McAliskey and Alfie Doherty had. But he was also inclined to be grateful to Faul, despite what he regarded as Faul's deviousness and treachery, for getting the hunger strike ended.

The protest was still on when Tony left the prison, though fortunately no more men were to die. On the holiday Monday, two days after Tony was released, Gerry Carville began his fast. Then on 4 September, with Matt Devlin in a coma, his mother intervened and took him off after fifty-two days. Two days later, Laurence McKeown's family intervened: he'd been on hunger strike for seventy days. Yet the following day, 7 September, John Pickering joined the hunger strike. A week later, 14

September, Gerard Hodgins joined, and a week after that Jim Devine. The momentum was still there. On 25 September Bernard Fox was taken off hunger strike for medical reasons and on 26 September Liam McCloskey acceded to his mother's five-hour plea that he come off, after fifty-five days. That left six men on hunger strike. It wasn't until a week later that they decided to end the fast.

On 3 October 1981 the 217 day hunger strike was officially ended. A statement was issued that evening on behalf of the Republican prisoners and hunger strikers:

> We, the protesting political prisoners in the H-Blocks and the men on hunger strike, have reluctantly decided in this seventh month of the hunger strike to end our fast.
>
> We have been robbed of the hunger strike as an effective protest weapon principally because of the successful campaign waged against our distressed relatives by the Catholic hierarchy, aided and abetted by the Irish establishment (the SDLP and Free State political parties), which took no effective action against the British government and did everything to encourage feelings of hopelessness among our kith and kin.
>
> The success of this campaign meant that the British government could remain intransigent as the crucial political pressure which flows from the threat of death or actual death of hunger strikers was subsiding, not increasing.
>
> We reaffirm our opposition to the British government's policy of criminalization and recognize that their intransigence and the courageous sacrifices made by Bobby Sands, Francis Hughes, Raymond McCreesh, Patsy O'Hara, Joe McDonnell, Martin Hurson, Kevin Lynch, Kieran Doherty, Tom McElwee and Micky Devine have overturned the objectives of that policy, which was meant to force us into conformity and discredit our cause of Irish freedom through denigrating us as criminals.
>
> Far from discrediting our cause, British intransigence, which created the hunger strike, has given us international political recognition and has made the cause of Irish

freedom an international issue, has increased support at home and abroad for Irish resistance, and has shown that the oppressed national people and the political prisoners are one.

We extend our solidarity to the families of the dead hunger strikers and to all our families and friends. We especially thank the National H-Blocks/Armagh committee and all support groups and urge them to continue with their trojan commitment to the achievement of the five demands by whatever means we believe necessary and expedient.

We rule nothing out.

Under no circumstances are we going to devalue the memory of our dead comrades by submitting ourselves to a dehumanizing and degrading regime.

IN THE MONTHS that followed, Tony assessed what the men had achieved by the hunger strike.

The no-slop-out and no-wash protests had been ended by the decision to concentrate on the hunger strike itself. By December the men were wearing not blankets—and not prison uniforms—but their own clothes. They got fifty per cent of the full remission they'd wanted. Work was confined to about ten things they could agree to do, under orders from their own OC. They had wing association, so that during association periods there would be forty prisoners able to mingle with one another and maybe only five warders present. This meant that the men were less likely to be harassed by the outnumbered screws. The prisoners were allowed out of their cells every night for two hours after tea. And they had an hour's yard exercise during the day.

The men had their command structure on the wings, implicitly recognized by the screws, who were now unable to force their authority on the prisoners. The prisoners went through their OCs whenever they wanted to negotiate, or to ask for certain privileges. If someone wanted a book he would be told he had to ask the governor. But the prisoner would refuse. Instead the wing OC would go to the governor and make the request, which the governor would accede to.

There were hardly any searches on the wings now and no more mirror searches. The screws no longer stood as closely to the people in the visiting boxes. Before and after visits there were only frisk searches of the prisoners' pockets.

The 1981 hunger strike was also influential and decisive in a larger context.*

FATHER DESMOND WILSON of Ballymurphy, who for years had lived and worked among the people of working-class West Belfast, gave this summary of the outcome of the hunger strike in late 1981:

I . . . remember a conversation I had with a very high-

* Among other political events, trends, and perceptions that the hunger strike experience directly or indirectly contributed to were these:

The breakdown of the Anglo-Irish dialogue established in December 1980.

The defeat of Charles Haughey's Fianna Fáil government in the general election of June 1981.

The identification of Garret FitzGerald as an anti-Republican and West-British "nationalist."

The reduction of Margaret Thatcher's approval rating in the polls (post-hunger strike and pre-Falklands) to a level lower than any other British prime minister in modern history.

Charles Haughey's resolute refusal to sanction Thatcher's Falklands aggression.

A worldwide growth in popular sympathy for the cause of Ireland.

The decision of Sinn Féin—emboldened by their success and that of their H-Blocks allies in electing Bobby Sands, Kieran Doherty, Paddy Agnew and Owen Carron, in 1981—to contest the Assembly and Westminster elections in 1983.

The SDLP's decision to contest an Assembly election they were planning to boycott, coupled with their uncharacteristic decision to then abstain from the resultant Assembly.

Sinn Féin's success at the polls, enabling them to gain a sure grip on thirty-

ranking British Army officer in the days when people still thought it a good idea to argue with them.

I said, "You will never help to solve a problem if you do not speak the truth about it. You tell the people that the people who have taken up arms here, the IRA, the UDA, the UVF and others, are nothing but thugs and gangsters. But you know as well as I do that among the military groups there are men and women who are sensitive and highly intelligent political thinkers and strategists. You tell the public lies."

He replied, "But we know this is so."

"Then why do you tell the public that they are only thugs?"

"*We do not tell the public that; the government does. We know differently,*" was his response.

And there was the crux of the matter. A government which was basing its appeal to the public on the assertion that the IRA and the rest were only thugs; and a people slowly awakening to the fact that these young men who

---

five to forty-three per cent of nationalist electors in the North, making them the fourth largest party in that part of the country..

The disintegration of British "law and order," manifest in police, SAS, British Army and UDR shoot-to-kill activities, and in the attempted corruption of nationalist communities by heavy police and judicial use of informers, from 1982 on.

The utter breakdown of British policy in Northern Ireland: their governments, subhuman in practice in the H-Blocks and during the hunger strike, were seen to be increasingly incompetent in Irish affairs, and self-admittedly impotent to resolve differences between people of the Protestant and Catholic traditions.

The convening of the New Ireland Forum, with FitzGerald & Co. forced willy-nilly to back the Forum as a prop for the SDLP, because of the new threat from Bobby Sands' electoral heirs in Sinn Féin.

The underlining of the deplorable weakness of southern governments in dealing with British rule in Northern Ireland.

An increase in the rate of breakdown of the facade of "Northern Ireland," speeding the time when the whole artificial edifice will collapse.

The buildup—inspired by the *scandal* of the hunger strike—of an independent American Irish lobby, determined to *act*, with or without Irish government cooperation, to move forward the day of Irish freedom.

were dying were their neighbours, were dignified in their death, were poets and thinkers too, perhaps. The policy of criminalization was crumbling as the tens of thousands at the funerals and the tens of thousands at the polling booths gave their own answer to it.

Things have certainly changed. They have changed for the pacifist, for example, because . . . the government rendered useless all forms of negotiation, every kind of intervention which anyone might make for the sake of peace. It was as though the Thatcher cabinet was intent on sweeping everyone else away from the scene until it might come face to face with the enemy. Confrontation politics in England means face to face encounter with the trades unions, but in Ireland means face to face encounter with already armed men.

There is no use in our asking people to put their trust in this or that non-armed political movement We know from experience it will get nowhere. We have seen all kinds of people discredited, people whom in Ireland you do not treat in this way, Cardinal Ó Fiaich included.

A hunger strike presupposes that you are dealing with an honourable enemy who follows the same rules as you do. This time the British government has simply moved too far from any of the rules which we recognize; it took their response to the hunger strike to show just how far they had gone.

A lot of people have lost their fear now: their fear of military and police, of preaching men in pulpits and palaces. They have seen too much to be cowed ever again by threats. They will go out on the streets now when they want to . . .

There were people on marches against the government's treatment of the hunger strikers who had never been on a march before . . . Sympathy for the politicians ebbed away and the usual excuses made for the Stormont Castle people that they were ignorant and foolish were voiced less often. Now they were seen not as ignorant but as wicked and vicious. There had not been for many years such determination among the mass of people to have done with Westminster; perhaps indeed the determination was greater than at any time before.

As each death occurred a number of things became possible which had not been possible before. It was now possible to speak respectfully of *members of the IRA* . . .

It was possible to focus attention now on the origins and history of these men who were dying, and to see them not indeed as thugs and criminals but young men who in any normal country would have been happily living in their own homes, doing their own jobs in peace.

It became possible to say: "But I don't know if any one of these men has even committed a parking offence, because the courts through which they were processed convicted them on evidence which proved nothing."

And these things were said, over and over again, and the more the deaths occurred the more often and the more openly they were said.

By its refusal to treat the hunger strike as the unique, symbolic, highly significant and irresistible weapon it really is, the government lost the war.

The trouble with a hunger strike is that so many honourable people in the past have used it and have been praised for it. You cannot now turn around and say a hunger strike is immoral and violent if you have said the opposite in the past. Especially not to people as politically aware as the Catholics of West Belfast. Cardinal Hume made the mistake of condemning the hunger strikers. His being a Cardinal did not save him: he was told in firm words that if he interfered again he would be rebuked in public. He, like many others, went silent on recognizing the depth of the feeling which had been aroused.

In Ireland a hunger strike has a power which governments ignore at their peril. There were some of us in West Belfast who said simply, "If a hunger striker dies, that is the end of British rule in Ireland." I believe that that is so. However long it may be, I believe that historians will, on looking back, point to this hunger strike in which men died as the beginning of the end of the overt political control of Ireland from Westminster.

And in the summer of 1985, Father Wilson added these comments, in an article in *The Irish Nation*, from a perspective of four years' distance:

> What has happened since Bobby Sands and Francis Hughes and their comrades went to their deaths? Already politics has changed in the North of Ireland. And traditional assumptions have been challenged—even traditional theology.
>
> The "criminalization" policy of the British government failed because of the hunger strike. People could not accept that men who were simply criminals would die as these men did. Another result: There grew up a sense of emptiness, perhaps of shame, in the minds of a great many people: they wondered what they could do themselves to rid the country of the cause of so much suffering. For many there was little enough that could be done, except vote, which they did, and stop acceding to the demands of the British government that they condemn that government's most determined opponents. So the increasing vote for Sinn Féin was one of the ways the people replied to the government . . .
>
> The hunger strike, without doubt, had released in people an enormous moral energy, successfully suppressed before. Their consciences had been assaulted by the Thatcher government's violent treatment of the dying men. They were no longer going to be intimidated by government propaganda about the evils of violence . . .
>
> It was in fact the hunger strike, with all its tragedy, which raised the most fundamental questions about freedom and democracy in the Northern state—far more searching questions than the civil rights movement had ever raised. To ask for "one man, one vote" had been to ask for equal participation in a state assumed to be basically democratic—if only "the right people" were in charge. Now it was seen that, no matter who was in charge, the

governing principles under which British politicians and their clones in Ireland (north and south) operated were essentially anti-democratic.

In the light of the obvious immorality of British behaviour during the hunger strike, Thatcher and her government were now finding it necessary to defend themselves in the international arena. What was said at conferences held in France, Italy, the United States and Britain itself showed that more and more people were willing to step forward, whatever the penalties, and say what they believed. What they believed, as was clear in the case of the International Lawyers' meeting in Paris in May 1985, was that the British government should withdraw from Ireland. Thatcher herself was forced to spend valuable minutes while addressing the Congress of the United States, trying to explain—to explain away—British policies in Ireland. In the old days such explanations would have been unthinkable. Now too the Pope was finding it desirable to tell the British that he was anxious to see a settlement, after many years during which the Vatican had remained almost silent.

In a real sense the significance of the hunger strike is that it was a moral watershed. Not that, in what has happened since, Republicans have necessarily given the right answers, but that—stirred by the absolute moral commitment of the ten men—they have forced people to ask the right questions.

IT IS JANUARY 1986, nearly five years since the beginning of the great Irish hunger strike. Things are quiet now in Long Kesh. After the brief return of prison warder violence following the famous escape of 25 September 1983, in which Brendan McFarlane and 37 others broke out through the gates in a blue food truck, Long Kesh settled back into what could be described as prison normality.

What were the latest effects of the 1981 hunger strike?

It was Bobby Sands' victorious run for the Fermanagh/South Tryone seat in the British Parliament, and Kieran Doherty's election to the Dáil (along with blanket prisoner Paddy Agnew), that gave rise to Sinn Féin as an independent political force, especially in Northern Ireland. It was the memory of the ten hunger strikers, and the example of these electoral successes, that inspired subsequent campaigns which delivered up to 43 per cent of the nationalist vote in Northern Ireland to Sinn Féin.

The unsympathetic British attitude to the whole Irish nationalist position—which made it impossible for *any* nationalists to sit in the Stormont Assembly set up in 1982 by British Northern Secretary James Prior—led to the convening of the New Ireland Forum, which provided a role for the "constitutional nationalists" of the faltering Social Democratic and Labour Party—whose first leader, Gerry Fitt, was now, pathetically, a British Lord: a member of that trumpery "nobility" who wait upon the English queen.

Charles Haughey and Fianna Fáil made the Forum a platform for promoting the Republican objective of Irish unity. This objective was formally endorsed by all the parties participating in the New Ireland Forum. But Garret FitzGerald & Company insisted—with John Hume and most of the the SDLP wholeheartedly concurring—that the options also include not just a federal Ireland (which, depending on the content and form of the federation, some Republicans would regard as a tolerable prospect) but joint authority (allowing for continued British rule!), or virtually any other mildly reformist "solution" the British might be persuaded to agree to. There were other serious defects in the Report of this Forum—notably the nonsensical talk of "Unionist" rights in a future Ireland, when what was meant were the cultural and political rights of the Northern Protestant people.

Most important, the Forum excluded Sinn Féin, which along with its military wing, the IRA, would have to be involved in any *real* solution. It invited participation by all sorts of Unionist parties; it took submissions from all manner of people, including even English Tories! But it took no interest in getting the views of members of Sinn Féin. The Forum parties excluded Sinn Féin on the grounds that the Sinn Féiners espoused violence, when of course all the parties invited to the Forum—and

610

notoriously the British government to which its deliberations were addressed—relied on soldiers and police (professional men of violence) to uphold their rule.

The real reason Sinn Féin was excluded, then, was not any unique association with violence on its part, but simply because the Forum could not very well do its work of shoring up the SDLP—yet involve Sinn Féin in its deliberations. This left out a party crucial to an authentic solution to the Northern problem, which could be solved without Fine Gael, probably without the SDLP, and certainly without the Irish Labour Party, but could never be solved without Sinn Féin and the IRA.

But it was not a solution the FitzGerald faction at the Forum was really after, as was proved in the event. They saw the Forum as a matter of Irish constitutional parties rowing in in support of a British constitutional party, as an establishment counterweight to a vigorous and populist Sinn Féin.

Nonetheless the Forum was useful in that it crystallized in contemporary terms many of the issues that would have to be faced by those setting up a future Ireland, and the divergent viewpoints of its participants, who represented electorally most of the Irish people.

Without the hunger strike there would have been no massive vote in the North for Sinn Féin; and without that vote there would have been no Forum. It was far from the hunger strikers' greatest achievement, but it was an achievement—not least because it helped keep the Northern problem, to which the ten hunger strikers had drawn the world's attention, in fairly sharp focus.

The problem was that Garret FitzGerald's version of the Forum Report was the one presented to the British: he was Taoiseach of the day. And what FitzGerald was really enthusiastic about was "joint authority," which had the heavy "security" overtones he liked and would maintain the British presence in the North he seemed to want. The British reaction came in two stages.

The first reaction, at the end of 1984, was one of hooting derision: Margaret Thatcher, who a few months earlier had nearly been killed by an IRA bomb at a hotel in Brighton, left

Garret FitzGerald gabbling embarrassedly as she pronounced her contemptuous verdict on the Forum's proposed solutions: "Out" to a united Ireland, "Out" to a federated Ireland, and "Out" to "joint authority" in the North, which she dismissed as an infringement of sovereignty—as indeed it would be; an infringement of *Irish* sovereignty over a part of Ireland.

Why, in spite of Thatcher's obstinacy, did the FitzGerald crowd keep pursuing the Anglo-Irish talks? The principal motive was the irreducible fact of the hunger-strike borne Northern nationalist support for Sinn Féin, and the alienation from the British "constitutional" police state that this support represented. So, after a year of crafty salesmanship by men like John Hume and FitzGerald's Sean Donlon, the British government's second and more considered reaction came at the end of 1985, when a West British "solution" emerged in the form of the Anglo-Irish Agreement of 15 November.

The Agreement was conditioned by the fact that it had been sponsored, on the Irish side, by two equivocal negotiators: Garret FitzGerald, anxiously presiding over a massively unpopular Dublin government, and the eloquent but disappointing John Hume—a tradeoff man with a great gift for PR who had the makings of an able peacetime parliamentarian, but who seemed, like poor John Redmond early in the century, to have a fatal faith in British constitutional arrangements.

What the Agreement offered was a watery form of joint authority—or rather of Irish responsibility without authority—which was alleged to be a means of ameliorating the nationalist Catholics' lot within the British colony in the North. To get a kind of ombudsman presence in the North, the Irish negotiators had conceded to the Unionists a de jure right to opt out of Ireland! They maintained for the Irish as a whole only the right to an "aspiration" towards (a right to breathe heavily in the direction of?) a united Ireland free of British rule.

Was this what the hunger strikers' sacrifice had eventually come to?

The whole motive for the Agreement, according to Margaret Thatcher and Garret FitzGerald, was to do in the "terrorists" of the IRA—Sinn Féin's military wing—while making the British government's military wing more palatable to Northern

Catholics. But reforms would come, the Agreement's sponsors promised. Reform in the area of increased "security" (meaning increased repression of militant Northern Catholics) was what Margaret Thatcher seemed to have had in mind.

So the Agreement was anomalous in that it promised to make life more humane for people in the North who supported or tolerated the IRA—by cracking down on these very people and punishing them.

There were some sweeteners vaguely on offer: reforms that were supposed to make the British way of life more agreeable for nationalist Catholics. The fact that Thatcher was willing to make any promise of reforms at all was a victory for the hunger strikers' electoral inheritors, testifying to the powerful impact of the men's sacrifice, and to Sinn Féin's resourcefulness in translating this impact into votes.

But it was clear, as the fifth anniversary of the hunger strike approached, that the ten men had left a far greater impact than that. They had moved history a stage forward, and even this meretricious Agreement—perhaps especially *because* it involved a betrayal of all they stood for—could lead to advances.

The memory of what these men suffered would remain as a judgement upon the Agreement, and as a vivid reminder of the evil of British rule in Ireland and its capacity for savagery. So that it was against the ten men's sacrifice, and what that sacrifice said about Irishmen's capacity to refuse British dictation, that the failure of the Anglo-Irish Agreement would be measured. For—as an Agreement mired in contradictions, one that prolonged British colonial rule and was dependent on British goodwill—it was bound to fail. The only questions were how and when.

Yet, though it was ill-conceived, involving a core betrayal of Ireland's inalienable right to freedom and independence and an abrogation of her constitutional claim to the integrity of her national territory, and though it was foredoomed, the Agreement had unexpected good effects. One of these was that it opened the eyes of the world, and even of the English, to the abnormality of the Unionist position.

What the Agreement offered was a kind of Irish charter for

British Unionism for the indefinite future. An Irish government—anxious for Thatcher's approval of something, of *anything?*—had conceded a supposed *right* on the Unionists' part to obstruct Irish freedom and independence as long as they wished. And provision was made for the Irish government to become involved (stupidly—and unnaturally) as co-guarantor with the British of this alleged right.

But the Unionists, with their "Not an Inch" shibboleth and the strange arithmetic that flowed from this, took the Agreement's provision for Irish government consultation as an assault on the closed door of their citadel. They'd been offered a hundred miles of Irish cooperation in repression of their Irish enemies! But the few yards of space required for the ombudsman feature was too much for them to yield.

The deal threatened their hegemony, they said. It was a Trojan horse, which could deliver up a united Ireland, they said. And in an important sense they were right. Fraught with Irish self-betrayal though this Agreement was, anything that took the issue off dead center, where it had lain for so long, was bound to have a chance to lead in natural and useful directions. The Unionists' anger reflected the perils they faced, once dislodged from their fixed position. There was jeopardy in *any* path that led from there. The deal put the Unionists' deep frozen habit of refusal in serious danger of a thaw-out. And that was one good effect of a bad Agreement.

The Agreement delivered something else of great potential value. It brought forward the Protestants' rightful insistence— not as Unionists but as Northern Protestants—on independence of British dictation. They were voicing, however stridently at times, a reasonable and thoroughly defensible demand that they be heard in any negotiation concerning their own affairs. They were quite right to refuse to let a distant regime in London, either alone or in tandem with a Dublin coterie, tell them how to order their lives.

This was the very issue nationalist Catholics had been bitter about during the Unionist years (1921-1972) and had been fighting during more than a dozen direct-rule years since: *the imposition of government without consent.*

The Agreement involved a measure of capitulation by

Thatcher to Irish influences—though of a West British sort. Yet the Agreement provoked among Northern Protestants an insistent demand for democracy, to which—as democracy—they were richly and fully entitled. They had a right not to have Thatcher or FitzGerald or Peter Barry, the Irish Minister for Foreign Affairs, or anyone else not elected by them, tell them how to run their lives. There was a perfectly valid point in Harold McCusker's remark in the House of Commons that he would far prefer to be ruled by a nationalist Catholic from the North than a minister of the Republic from Cork. Or an arrogant grocer's daughter from Grantham, in England?

What had happened over this five-year span? The Northern Catholic hunger strikers had resisted to the death the British government's encroachments on their lives, and they did this for the sake of Irish freedom. Here, at the end of this cycle or sequence of events, most of the leaders of the Protestant people of Northern Ireland were girding themselves to do battle against the same British government for the sake of *their* freedom.

It would take years to gauge the full impact of the hunger strike on Irish history. This much we had already seen.

It was true that Irish prisoners remained locked away in these British prisons, and that an archtypical colonialist, Margaret Thatcher, though perhaps in terminal political decline, remained in power in London. It was true that an Irish government, to its disgrace, had agreed to assist the British in sustaining their wretched colony in Ireland.

But Irish governments would change, and united front efforts to remove the British forever would become possible. It was clear, from the desperation (on both sides) of those trying to explain and implement this pitiful Agreement, as well as from all sorts of other signs—including the rising up now of Northern Irish Protestants, headstrong and proud, under their own banner of democracy and independence—that one way or another British rule in Ireland was all but ended. The occupiers would soon be gone from this country, perhaps much sooner than most people realized.

IN A CEREMONY OF INNOCENCE analogous to that evoked by W. B. Yeats, these ten men laid down their lives for their friends, their companions in suffering, for the Irish people and for the cause of Ireland. They were members of a revolutionary movement whose military record was flawed, as all military records are, by ambiguity and sordid violence. But their heroism identified them as the most honourable contemporary advocates of that ancient cause. Coming forward as they did, one after another, to die broken at the end of painful long weeks of fasting, they gave a certain absolute dignity to a mundane, tiresome, and at times vicious struggle.

These ten men sowed the land of Ireland with the seed of their sacrifice. They left the Irish people the legacy of their honour and valour. And, partly by revealing to the world (once again) the barbarism of which English rule is capable, their sacrifice introduced a kind of surd or irreducible number into the historical equation. As with the failed revolutionaries of 1916, what they worked in Irish history could in the end prove powerful enough to propel the Irish people forward to a new and final Easter of freedom—a freedom more complete for having been postponed until this age.

INDEX

TOM COLLINS, who was born in the United States but now lives permanently in Ireland, holds both Irish and US citizenship. Since 1979 he and his wife Pat have been resident in Dublin with their three children.

Collins is editor of the independent Irish political newsletter THE IRISH NATION. He has been a book editor and publishing consultant since 1963, and as author, agent, editor and publisher has been responsible for some seventy-five books. He wrote *The Search for Jimmy Carter* (1976) and was co-editor of *A People of Compassion* (1972), a book on Ted Kennedy. He also collaborated with Pat on her *Mary: A Mother's Story* (1981) and in 1983-84 published *The Centre Cannot Hold: Britain's Failure in Northern Ireland* (1983), critically acclaimed on RTÉ as 'the best factual account which has appeared of this fifteen years of tragedy: impressive in its objectivity, in the clarity of its analysis of the roots of discontent, as well as the accuracy of the actual reporting of events."

Tim Pat Coogan, who wrote the Foreword, is the Editor of *The Irish Press* and author of *Ireland Since the Rising, The IRA*, and *On the Blanket*.

626